Customer Relationship Management
Emerging Concepts, Tools and Applications

Customer Relationship Management
Emerging Concepts, Tools and Applications

Editors

Jagdish N Sheth
Atul Parvatiyar
G Shainesh

Tata McGraw Hill Education Private Limited

NEW DELHI

McGraw-Hill Offices

New Delhi New York St Louis San Francisco Auckland Bogotá Caracas
Kuala Lumpur Lisbon London Madrid Mexico City Milan Montreal
San Juan Santiago Singapore Sydney Tokyo Toronto

Tata McGraw-Hill

Copyright © 2001, Tata McGraw Hill Education Private Limited.

Fifteenth reprint 2011
RXAYCRDGDXRAQ

ISBN-13: 978-0-07-043504-9
ISBN-10: 0-07-043504-9

Published by Tata McGraw Hill Education Private Limited,
7 West Patel Nagar, New Delhi 110 008, typeset in New Century at
The Composers, 260 C.A. Apt., Paschim Vihar, New Delhi 110 063 and printed at
Sai Printo Pack Pvt. Ltd., New Delhi 110 020

To our wives,

Madhu Sheth, Divya Parvatiyar and Leena Shainesh

Preface

Customer Relationship Management (CRM) is increasingly gaining importance among both academics and business practitioners. As technologies and customer expectations rapidly change, businesses realize the value of having long-term relationship with individual customers and other business partners. They are developing effective and efficient processes of customer relationship management and are focused on enhancing shareholder value by shifting from a 'market share' mindset to obtaining higher 'share of individual customer's business'. The emphasis is on enhancing lifetime value of customers and developing partnering relationship with profitable customers. To be successful in the new millennium, firms will need to extend this practice of developing long-term relationships with all their other stakeholders including suppliers, intermediaries, partners, and employees.

This book is a compendium of the research papers and case studies presented at the first international conference on 'Customer Relationship Management: Emerging Concepts, Tools and Applications' organized jointly by Management Development Institute (MDI), Gurgaon, India and the Institute for Customer Relationship Management (ICRM).

The book has been divided into the following seven main sections:

Section I   - Emerging Concepts in CRM
Section II   - Technological Tools for CRM
Section III - Implementing Customer Relationship Management
Section IV   - Relationship Management in B2B Commerce
Section V   - CRM in Services
Section VI   - CRM in Financial Services
Section VII - Abstracts

The practice of CRM has been greatly enriched by the contribution of researchers and academicians who have developed theories, concepts and frameworks to help us understand and explain various aspects of CRM. The first section focuses on the **'Emerging Concepts in CRM'**. Coverage includes a Conceptual Model of CRM, Knowledge Management for CRM, Implications of Globalisation on CRM, Modeling of Business Relationships, Regain Management, and Research Agenda for CRM.

Rapid advances in technology have created new tools that enable organisations to apply innovative CRM solutions which defy traditional limitations. Technology can help organisations understand individual customer preferences and even predict the next wave of buying patterns. The insights gleaned can be used to tailor solutions to meet individual buyer needs, ultimately increasing sales and promoting sustainable growth. The section on **'Technological Tools for CRM'** includes experiences of organisations like PricewaterhouseCoopers, Infosys, IBM Global Services and Escotel Mobile Communications Ltd. It highlights various technological tools and applications to develop new customer relationships, profitably serve existing customers, and integrate organisational systems with those of their partners, suppliers, and customers.

The benefits of a well-conceived CRM strategy are proven and powerful. Execution of a CRM strategy brings with it the opportunity to realign and reinvent processes that interface the customer in ways more than one. Superior implementations merge the so-called customer-facing front-office and organisation-centric back-office operations. This gives organisations a complete view of their customer relationships, while opening up internal systems so that their customers can service and sell themselves. Managers want to make certain that when implementing such a strategy, they capitalise on CRM's full potential. The section on **'Implementing CRM'**, highlights the steps and actions to be followed to implement CRM successfully. Coverage includes Optimal Allocation Rules for CRM, Measuring the Effectiveness of CRM, Decision Metrices for CRM, Contact Management, and Organizing for CRM. Case studies in this section cover ICICI, Hewlett Packard, Kirloskar Oil Engines Ltd., the cement industry and the pharmaceutical industry.

The emergence of Internet enabled B2B commerce is fundamentally reshaping business relationships, causing dramatic shifts in channel power as information asymmetries disappear. In ways more than one, B2B commerce is presenting customers and suppliers with compelling value propositions to both lower transaction costs and increase the value captured in business relationships. It has now been established that B2B exchanges will be a powerful force in the commerce of the new century. However, B2B commerce presents not only tremendous opportunities but also tremendous risks. Organisations and managers need to deploy B2B strategies in ways that do not disrupt existing successful relationships or that create unnecessary confusion amongst business partners. The section on **'Relationship Management in B2B Commerce'** covers issues like Building Customer Loyalty in B2B Commerce, Cross Border B2B Relationships with Intermediaries, Valuing Information in Transportation Logistics, Value and Stability of Cooperative Buyer-Seller Relationships in Industrial Markets, the Global Account Manager as Political Entrepreneur, and Managing Relationships in Supply Chains of the 21st Century,

Worldwide, marketers in services—like hotels, airlines, etc. have been highly successful pioneers in practicing relationship management through loyalty building programs like frequent flyer programs, memberships, etc. However, now the expectations of customers are greater than ever. Their demand for the "free, perfect and now" experience resonates throughout the business world. Papers in the section on **'CRM in Services'**, cover a wide spectrum of case studies and experiences of practitioners, consultants and researches for CRM implementation in hospitality, healthcare, IT education, retailing and telecom industries.

As financial firms seek to increase market share and revenues in the face of intense global competition, CRM is gaining attention as the number one initiative for most organisations. Companies recognise the need to get closer to the customer and optimise the value of their customers through better more efficient interaction with them. The way to achieve this streamlined interaction is through efficient channels that are most appropriate for a given customer. Consumers are encouraged to move from face-to-face banking to use the ATM, telephone banking and on-line access, each of which has progressively lower transaction costs. Many banks and financial service firms are categorising their customers into best, average and worst, and managing each according to their strategic value (including profitability and growth potential). A better understanding of the customer as a whole and strategic value each customer brings to the organisation will allow the financial industry to deliver the right message to the right customer through the right channel. The section on 'CRM in Financial Services' include a Study of Customer Perceptions in Retail Banking, Winning Strategies for Effective CRM, Introduction of e-CRM in the Indian Insurance Sector, Relationship Building through Call Centres and User Satisfaction of Banking Software Products.

We believe that this book will be of value to practitioners, students, and scholars interested in the concepts and practice of customer relationship management.

We wish to thank all the authors who have contributed their papers. The conference could be organised due to the untiring efforts of lots of individuals. Dr. Devi Singh, Director, MDI deserves special mention for the encouragement and support he provided. Members of the advisory and organising committee went out of their way to support our efforts and we are grateful to every one of them. Prof. Mukesh Chaturvedi and Prof. Amit Mookerjee deserve special mention for their efforts. We take this opportunity to thank Mr. Anil Metre, Editor and Publisher, Spectrum Magazines whose generous support helped us publicise the conference and reach a wide audience. We express our gratitude to all volunteers specially Ramneesh Mohan, Parul Yadav, Rajat Gossain, and Inderdeep Singh whose tireless efforts made the task simple for us. We acknowledge the support of MDI administration specially Mr. Vipin Nagrath, Mr. Bhatia, Ms Saroj Khurana and Mr. Amrish Sharma. We thank Himani Goel, Fred Seifu, Sarat Pathak and Kate Herzeg of ICRM, Atlanta for their help in coordinating with the authors and MDI. Finally it has been the patience and diligence of our publishers, Tata McGraw-Hill, which enabled us present this book to the academic and practitioner communities.

JAGDISH SHETH
ATUL PARVATIYAR
G SHAINESH

Contents

Section III
Implementing CRM

Section IV
Relationship Management in
B2B Commerce

Section V
CRM in Services

Section VI
CRM in Financial Services

Section VII
Abstracts

Section I

Emerging Concepts in CRM

Conceptual Framework of Customer Relationship Management

■ **Atul Parvatiyar and Jagdish N Sheth**

Abstract

Customer relationship management (CRM) has once again gained prominence amongst academics and practitioners. In this paper, the authors explore the conceptual foundations of CRM by examining the literature on relationship marketing and other disciplines that contribute to the knowledge of CRM. A CRM process framework is proposed that builds on other relationship development process models. Research issues as well as CRM implementation challenges are discussed in this paper.

Key Words: *Customer Relationship Management; Relationship Marketing; CRM Process; CRM Definition; CRM Strategy; CRM Programs; CRM Implementation.*

Developing close, cooperative relationship with customers is more important in the current era of intense competition and demanding customers, than it has ever been before. Customer relationship management (CRM) has attracted the expanded attention of scholars and practitioners. Marketing scholars are studying the nature and scope of CRM and developing conceptualizations regarding the value and process of cooperative and collaborative relationship between buyers and sellers. Many scholars with interests in various sub-disciplines of marketing, such as channels, services marketing, business-to-business marketing, advertising, and so forth, are actively engaged in studying and exploring the conceptual foundations of managing relationship with customers. They are interested in strategies and processes for customer classification and selectivity; one-to-one relationships with individual customers; key account management and customer business development processes; frequency marketing, loyalty programs, cross-selling and up-selling opportunities; and various forms of partnering with customers including co-branding, joint-marketing, co-development and other forms of strategic alliances (Sheth and Parvatiyar 2000).

Scholars from other academic disciplines, particularly those interested in the area of information systems and decision technologies, are also exploring new methodologies and techniques that create efficient front-line information systems (FIS) to effectively manage customer relationships. Several software tools and technologies claiming solutions for various aspects CRM have recently been introduced for commercial applications. A majority of these tools promise to individualize and personalize customer relationships by providing vital information at every point of customer interface. Techniques such as collaborative filtering, rules-based expert systems, artificial intelligence and relational databases are increasingly being applied to develop enterprise level solutions for managing information on customer interactions. The purpose of this paper is not to evaluate these application tools and technologies. Those aspects are considered in other chapters in this book as well as by several commercial research organizations, such as Forrester Research and The Gartner Group. Our objective, however is to provide a conceptual foundation for understanding the domain of customer relationship management. To do so, we develop a framework for understanding the various aspects of CRM strategy and implementation. A synthesis of existing knowledge on CRM by integrating diverse explorations forms the basis of our framework. We draw upon the literature on relationship marketing, as CRM and relationship marketing are not distinguished from each other in the marketing literature (Parvatiyar and Sheth 2000).

In the sections that follow, we define what is CRM and what it promises to offer. We also identify the forces impacting the marketing environment in recent years leading to the rapid development of CRM strategies, tools and technologies. A typology of CRM programs is presented to provide a parsimonious view of the various terms and terminologies that are used to refer to different activities. We then describe a process model of CRM to better delineate the challenges of customer relationship formation, its governance, its performance evaluation, and its evolution. Finally, we examine the research issues in CRM.

What is Customer Relationship Management?

Before we begin to examine the conceptual foundations of CRM, it will be useful to define what is CRM. In the marketing literature the terms customer relationship management and relationship marketing as used interchangeably. As Nevin (1995) points out, these terms have been used to reflect a variety of themes and perspectives. Some of these themes offer a narrow functional marketing perspective while others offer a perspective that is broad and somewhat paradigmatic in approach and orientation. A narrow perspective of customer relationship management is database marketing emphasizing the promotional aspects of marketing linked to database efforts (Bickert 1992).

Another narrow, yet relevant, viewpoint is to consider CRM only as customer retention in which a variety of aftermarketing tactics is used for customer bonding or staying in touch after the sale is made (Vavra 1992). A more popular approach with recent application of information technology is to focus on individual or one-to-one relationship with customers that integrate database knowledge with a long-term customer retention and growth strategy (Peppers and Rogers 1993). Thus, Shani and Chalasani (1992) define relationship marketing as "an integrated effort to identify, maintain, and build up a network with individual consumers and to continuously strengthen the network for the mutual benefit of both sides, through interactive, individualized and value-added contacts over a long period of time" (p. 44). Jackson (1985) applies the individual account concept in industrial markets to suggest CRM to mean, "Marketing oriented toward strong, lasting relationships with individual accounts" (p. 2). In other business contexts, Doyle and Roth (1992), O'Neal (1989), Paul (1988), and have proposed similar views of customer relationship management.

McKenna (1991) professes a more strategic view by putting the customer first and shifting the role of marketing from manipulating the customer (telling and selling) to genuine customer involvement (communicating and sharing the knowledge). Berry (1995), in somewhat broader terms, also has a strategic viewpoint about CRM. He stresses that attracting new customers should be viewed only as an intermediate step in the marketing process. Developing closer relationship with these customers and turning them into loyal ones are equally important aspects of marketing. Thus, he proposed relationship marketing as "attracting, maintaining, and – in multi-service organizations – enhancing customer relationships" (p. 25).

Berry's notion of customer relationship management resembles that of other scholars studying services marketing, such as Gronroos (1990), Gummesson (1987), and Levitt (1981). Although each one of them is espousing the value of interactions in marketing and its consequent impact on customer relationships, Gronroos and Gummesson take a broader perspective and advocate that customer relationships ought to be the focus and dominant paradigm of marketing. For example, Gronroos (1990) states: "Marketing is to establish, maintain, and enhance relationships with customers and other partners, at a profit, so that the objectives of the parties involved are met. This is achieved by a mutual exchange and fulfillment of promises" (p. 138). The implication of Gronroos' definition is that customer relationships is the 'raison de etre' of the firm and marketing should be devoted to building and enhancing such relationships. Similarly, Morgan and Hunt (1994), draw upon the distinction made between transactional exchanges and relational exchanges by Dwyer, Schurr, and Oh (1987), to suggest that relationship marketing "refers to all marketing activities directed toward establishing, developing, and maintaining successful relationships."

The core theme of all CRM and relationship marketing perspectives is its focus on cooperative and collaborative relationship between the firm and its customers, and/or other marketing actors. Dwyer, Schurr, and Oh (1987) have characterized such cooperative relationships as being interdependent and long-term orientated rather than being concerned with short-term discrete transactions. The long-term orientation is often emphasized because it is believed that marketing actors will not engage in opportunistic behavior if they have a long-term orientation and that such relationships will be anchored on mutual gains and cooperation (Ganesan 1994).

Another important facet of CRM is "customer selectivity". As several research studies have shown not all customers are equally profitable for an individual company (Storbacka

2000). The company therefore must be selective in tailors its program and marketing efforts by segmenting and selecting appropriate customers for individual marketing programs. In some cases, it could even lead to "outsourcing of some customers" so that a company better utilize its resources on those customers it can serve better and create mutual value. However, the objective of a company is not to really prune its customer base but to identify appropriate programs and methods that would be profitable and create value for the firm and the customer. Hence, we define CRM as:

Customer Relationship Management is a comprehensive strategy and process of acquiring, retaining and partnering with selective customers to create superior value for the company and the customer.

As is implicit in the above definition, the purpose of CRM is to improve marketing productivity. Marketing productivity is achieved by increasing marketing efficiency and by enhancing marketing effectiveness (Sheth and Sisodia 1995). In CRM, marketing efficiency is achieved because cooperative and collaborative processes help in reducing transaction costs and overall development costs for the company. Two important processes of CRM include proactive customer business development and building partnering relationship with most important customers. These lead to superior mutual value creation.

The Emergence of CRM Practice

As observed by Sheth and Parvatiyar (1995b), developing customer relationships has historical antecedents going back into the pre-industrial era. Much of it was due to direct interaction between producers of agricultural products and their consumers. Similarly artisans often developed customized products for each customer. Such direct interaction led to relational bonding between the producer and the consumer. It was only after industrial era's mass production society and the advent of middlemen that there were less frequent interactions between producers and consumers leading to transactions oriented marketing. The production and consumption functions got separated leading to marketing functions being performed by the middlemen. And middlemen are in general oriented towards economic aspects of buying since the largest cost is often the cost of goods sold.

In recent years however, several factors have contributed to the rapid development and evolution of CRM. These include the growing de-intermediation process in many industries due to the advent of sophisticated computer and telecommunication technologies that allow producers to directly interact with end-customers. For example, in many industries such as airlines, banks, insurance, computer program software, or household appliances and even consumables, the de-intermediation process is fast changing the nature of marketing and consequently making relationship marketing more popular. Databases and direct marketing tools give them the means to individualize their marketing efforts. As a result, producers do not need those functions formerly performed by the middlemen. Even consumers are willing to undertake some of the responsibilities of direct ordering, personal merchandising, and product use related services with little help form the producers. The recent success of on-line banking, Charles Schwab and Merryll Lynch's on-line investment programs, direct selling of books, automobiles, insurance, etc., on the Internet all attest to the growing consumer interest in maintaining direct relationship with marketers.

The de-intermediation process and consequent prevalence of CRM is also due to the growth of the service economy. Since services are typically produced and delivered at the same institution, it minimizes the role of the middlemen. A greater emotional bond between the service provider and the service user also develops the need for maintaining and enhancing the relationship. It is therefore not difficult to see that CRM is important for scholars and practitioners of services marketing (Berry and Parsuraman 1991; Bitner 1995; Crosby and Stephens 1987; Crosby, et. al. 1990; Gronroos 1995).

Another force driving the adoption of CRM has been the total quality movement. When companies embraced Total Quality Management (TQM) philosophy to improve quality and reduce costs, it became necessary to involve suppliers and customers in implementing the program at all levels of the value chain. This needed close working relationships with customers, suppliers, and other members of the marketing infrastructure. Thus, several companies, such as Motorola, IBM, General Motors, Xerox, Ford, Toyota, etc., formed partnering relationships with suppliers and customers to practice TQM. Other programs such as Just-in-time (JIT) supply and Material-resource planning (MRP) also made the use of interdependent relationships between suppliers and customers (Frazier, Spekman, and O'Neal 1988).

With the advent of the digital technology and complex products, systems selling approach became common. This approach emphasized the integration of parts, supplies, and the sale of services along with the individual capital equipment. Customers liked the idea of systems integration and sellers were able to sell augmented products and services to customers. The popularity of system integration began to extend to consumer packaged goods, as well as services (Shapiro and Posner 1979). At the same time some companies started to insist upon new purchasing approaches such as national contracts and master purchasing agreements, forcing major vendors to develop key account management programs (Shapiro and Moriarty 1980). These measures created intimacy and cooperation in the buyer-seller relationships. Instead of purchasing a product or service, customers were more interested in buying a relationship with a vendor. The key (or national) account management program designates account managers and account teams that assess the customer's needs and then husband the selling company's resources for the customer's benefit. Such programs have led to the foundation of strategic partnering within the overall domain of customer relationship management (Anderson and Narus 1991; Shapiro 1988).

Similarly, in the current era of hyper-competition, marketers are forced to be more concerned with customer retention and loyalty (Dick and Basu 1994; Reicheld 1996). As several studies have indicated, retaining customers is less expensive and perhaps a more sustainable competitive advantage than acquiring new ones. Marketers are realizing that it costs less to retain customers than to compete for new ones (Rosenberg and Czepiel 1984). On the supply side it pays more to develop closer relationships with a few suppliers than to develop more vendors (Hayes et. al. 1988; Spekman 1988). In addition, several market-ers are also concerned with keeping customers for life, rather than making a one-time sale (Cannie and Caplin 1991). There is greater opportunity for cross-selling and up-selling to a customer who is loyal and committed to the firm and its offerings. In a recent study, Naidu, et. al. (1999) found that relational intensity increased in hospitals facing a higher degree of competitive intensity.

Also, customer expectations have rapidly changed over the last two decades. Fueled by new technology and growing availability of advanced product features and services, cus-tomer expectations are changing almost on a daily basis. Consumers are less willing to make compromises or trade-off in product and service quality. In the world of ever chang-ing customer expectations, cooperative and collaborative relationship with customers seem to be the most prudent way to keep track of their changing expectations and appropriately influencing it (Sheth and Sisodia 1995).

Today, many large internationally oriented companies are trying to become global by integrating their worldwide operations. To achieve this they are seeking cooperative and collaborative solutions for global operations from their vendors instead of merely engaging in transactional activities with them. Such customers needs make it imperative for market-ers interested in the business of companies who are global to adopt CRM programs, par-ticularly global account management programs (Yip and Madsen 1996). Global account management (GAM) is conceptually similar to national account management programs except that they have to be global in scope and thus they are more complex. Managing customer relationships around the world calls for external and internal partnering activi-ties, including partnering across a firm's worldwide organization.

A CRM Process Framework

Several scholars studying buyer-seller relationships have proposed relationship develop-ment process models (Borys and Jemison 1989; Dwyer, Schurr and Oh 1987; Evans and Laskin 1994; Heide 1994; Wilson 1995). Building on that work we develop a four-stage CRM process framework. The broad framework suggests that CRM process comprise of the following four sub-processes: customer relationship formation process; relationship man-agement and governance process; relational performance evaluation process; and CRM evolution or enhancement process. Figure 1 depicts the important components of the process model.

CRM Formation Process

The formation process of CRM refers to decisions regarding initiation of relational activities for a firm with respect to a specific group of customers or with respect to an individual customer with whom the company wishes to engage in a cooperative or collaborative relationship. Hence it is important that a company is able to identify and differentiate individual customers. In the formation process, three important decision areas relate to defining the *purpose* (or objectives) of engaging in CRM; selecting *parties* (or customer

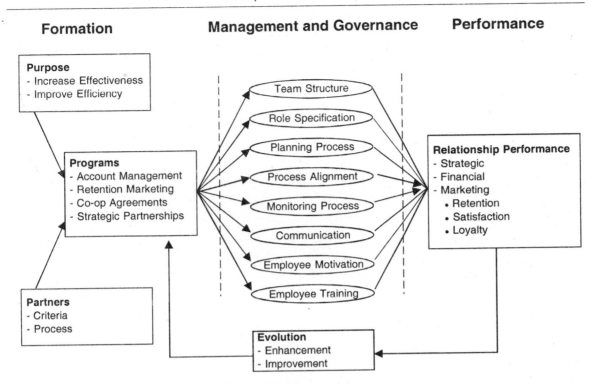

Fig. 1 *CRM Process Framework*

partners) for appropriate CRM programs; and developing *programs* (or relational activity schemes) for relationship engagement with the customer.

CRM Purpose

The overall purpose of CRM is to improve marketing productivity and enhance mutual value for the parties involved in the relationship. CRM has the potential to improve marketing productivity and create mutual values by increasing marketing efficiencies and/or enhancing marketing effectiveness (Sheth and Parvatiyar 1995a; Sheth and Sisodia 1995). By seeking and achieving operational goals, such as lower distribution costs, streamlining order processing and inventory management, reducing the burden of excessive customer acquisition costs, and through customer retention economics, firms could achieve greater marketing efficiencies. They can enhance marketing effectiveness by carefully selecting customers for its various programs, individualizing and personalizing their market offerings to anticipate and serve the emerging needs of individual customer, building customer loyalty and commitment; partnering to enter new markets and develop new products, and redefining the competitive playing field for their company (Sheth and Parvatiyar 1995a). Thus, stating objectives and defining the purpose of CRM in a company helps clarify the nature of CRM programs and activities that ought to be performed by the partners. Defining the purpose would also help in identifying suitable relationship partners who have the necessary expectations and capabilities to fulfill mutual goals. It will further help in evaluating CRM performance by comparing results achieved against objectives. These objectives could be specified as financial goals, marketing goals, strategic goals, operational goals, and general goals.

Similarly, in the mass-market context, consumers' expect to fulfill their goals related to efficiencies and effectiveness in their purchase and consumption behavior. Sheth and Parvatiyar (1995a) contend that consumers are motivated to engage in relational behavior because of the psychological and sociological benefits associated with reduction in choice decisions. In addition, to their natural inclination of reducing choices, consumers are motivated to seek the rewards and associated benefits offered by CRM programs.

Relational Parties

Customer partner selection (or parties with whom to engage in cooperative or collaborative relationships) is another important decision in the relationship formation stage. Even though a company may serve all customer types, few have the necessary resources and commitment to establish CRM programs for all. Therefore, in the initial phase, a company has to decide which customer type and specific customers or customer groups will be the focus of their CRM efforts. Subsequently when the company gains experience and achieve successful results, the scope of CRM activities could be expanded to include other customers into the program or engage in additional programs (Shah 1997).

Although partner selection is an important decision in achieving CRM goals, not all companies have a formalized process of selecting customers. Some follow intuitive judgmental approach of senior managers in selecting customer partners and others partner with those customers who demand so. Yet other companies have formalized processes of selecting relational partners through extensive research and evaluation along chosen criteria. The criteria for partner selection vary according to company goals and policies. These range from a single criterion such as revenue potential of the customer to multiple criteria including several variables such as customer commitment, resourcefulness, management values, etc.

CRM Programs

A careful review of literature and observation of corporate practices suggest that there are three types of CRM programs: continuity marketing; one-to-one marketing; and, partnering programs. These take different forms depending on whether they are meant for end-consumers, distributor customers, or business-to-business customers. Table 1 presents various types of CRM programs commonly developed for different types of customers. Obviously, marketing practitioners in search of new creative ideas develop many variations and combinations of these programs to build closer and mutually beneficial relationship with their customers.

Table 1 *CRM Programs*

Customer Types Program Types	Mass Markets	Distributors	Business to Business Markets

Continuity Marketing	• After-Marketing
	• Loyalty Programs
	• Cross-selling
		• Continuous
		  Replinshment
		• ECR Programs
			• Special Sourcing
			  Arrangements

One-to-One Marketing	• Permission Marketing • Personalization	• Customer Business Development	• Key Account • Global Account Programs
Partnering/Co-Marketing	• Affinity Partnering • Co-Branding	• Logistics Partnering • Joint Marketing	• Strategic Partnering • Co-Design • Co-Development

Continuity Marketing Programs

Given the growing concern to retain customers as well as emerging the knowledge about customer retention economics have led many companies to develop continuity marketing programs that are aimed at both retaining customers and increasing their loyalty (Bhattacharya 1998; Payne 1995). For consumers in mass markets, these programs usually take the shape of membership and loyalty card programs where consumers are often rewarded for their member and loyalty relationships with the marketers (Raphel 1995; Richards 1995). These rewards may range from privileged services to points for upgrades, discounts, and cross-purchased items. For distributor customers, continuity marketing programs are in the form of continuous replenishment programs ranging anywhere from just-in-time inventory management programs to efficient consumer response initiatives that include electronic order processing and material resource planning (Law and Ooten 1993; Persutti 1992). In business-to-business markets these may be in the form of preferred customer programs or in special sourcing arrangements including single sourcing, dual sourcing, and network sourcing, as well as just-in-time sourcing arrangements (Hines 1995; Postula and Little 1992). The basic premise of continuity marketing programs is to retain customers and increase loyalty through long-term special services that has a potential to increase mutual value through learning about each other (Shultz 1995).

One-to-one Marketing

One-to-one or individual marketing approach is based on the concept of account-based marketing. Such a program is aimed at meeting and satisfying each customer's need uniquely and individually (Peppers and Rogers 1995). What was once a concept only prevalent in business-to-business marketing is now implemented in the mass market and distributor customer contexts. In the mass market individualized information on customers is now possible at low costs due to the rapid development in information technology and due to the availability of scalable data warehouses and data mining products. By using on-line information and databases on individual customer interactions, marketers aim to fulfill the unique needs of each mass-market customer. Information on individual customers is utilized to develop frequency marketing, interactive marketing, and aftermarketing programs in order to develop relationship with high yielding customers (File, Mack and Prince 1995; Pruden 1995). For distributor customers these individual marketing programs take the shape of customer business development. For example, Procter and Gamble have established a customer team to analyze and propose ways in which Wal-Mart's business could be developed. Thus, by bringing to bare their domain specific knowledge from across many markets, Procter & Gamble is able to offer expert advice and resources to help build the business of its distributor customer. Such a relationship requires cooperative action and an interest in mutual value creation. In the context of business-to-business markets, individual marketing has been in place for quite sometime. Known as key account management program, here marketers appoint customer teams to husband the company resources according to individual customer needs. Often times such programs require extensive resource allocation and joint planning with customers. Key account programs implemented for multi-location domestic customers usually take the shape of national account management programs, and for customers with global operations it becomes global account management programs.

Partnering Programs

The third type of CRM programs is partnering relationships between customers and marketers to serve end user needs. In the mass markets, two types of partnering programs are most common: co-branding and affinity partnering (Teagno 1995). In co-branding, two marketers combine their resources and skills to offer advanced products and services to mass-market customers (Marx 1994). For example, Delta Airlines and American Express have co-branded the Sky Miles Credit Card for gains to consumers as well as to the partnering organizations. Affinity partnering program is similar to co-branding except that the marketers do not create a new brand rather use endorsement strategies. Usually affinity-partnering programs try to take advantage of customer memberships in one group for cross-selling other products and services. In the case of distributor customers, logistics partnering and cooperative marketing efforts are how partnering programs are implemented. In such partnerships the marketer and the distributor customers cooperate and collaborate to manage inventory and supply logistics and sometimes engage in joint marketing efforts. For business-to-business customers, partnering programs involving co-design, co-development and co-marketing activities are not uncommon today (Young, Gilbert and McIntyre 1996).

CRM Governance Process

Once CRM program is developed and rolled out, the program as well as the individual relationships must be managed and governed. For mass-market customers, the degree to which there is symmetry or asymmetry in the primary responsibility of whether the customer or the program sponsoring company will be managing the relationship varies with the size of the market. However, for programs directed at distributors and business customers the management of the relationship would require the involvement of both parties. The degree to which these governance responsibilities are shared or managed independently will depend on the perception of norms of governance processes among relational partners given the nature of their CRM program and the purpose of engaging in the relationship. Not all relationships are or should be managed alike, however several researches suggest appropriate governance norms for different hybrid relationships (Borys and Jemison 1989; Heide 1994; Sheth and Parvatiyar 1992).

Whether management and governance responsibilities are independently or jointly undertaken by relational partners, several issues must be addressed. These include decisions regarding *role specification, communication, common bonds, planning process, process alignment, employee motivation* and *monitoring procedures.* Role specification relates to determining the role of partners in fulfilling the CRM tasks as well as the role of specific individuals or teams in managing the relationships and related activities (Heide 1994). Greater the scope of the CRM program and associated tasks, and the more complex is the composition of the relationship management team; the more critical is the role specification decision for the partnering firms. Role specification also helps in clarifying the nature of resources and empowerment needed by individuals or teams charged with the responsibility of managing relationship with customers.

Communication with customer partners is a necessary process of relationship marketing. It helps in relationship development, fosters trust, and provides the information and knowledge needed to undertake cooperative and collaborative activities of relationship marketing. In many ways it is the lifeblood of relationship marketing. By establishing proper communication channels for sharing information with customers a company can enhance their relationship with them. In addition to communicating with customers, it is also essential to establish intra-company communication particularly among all concerned individuals and corporate functions that directly play a role in managing the relationship with a specific customer or customer group.

Although communication with customer partners help foster relationship bonds, conscious efforts for creating common bonds will have a more sustaining impact on the relationship. In business-to-business relationships, social bonds are created through interactions, however with mass-market customers frequent face-to-face interactions will be uneconomical. Thus marketers should create common bonds through symbolic relationships, endorsements, affinity groups, and membership benefits or by creating on-line communities. Whatever is the chosen mode, creating value bonding, reputation bonding and structural bondings are useful processes of institutionalizing relationship with customers (Sheth 1994).

Another important aspect of relationship governance is the process of planning and the degree to which customers need to be involved in the planning process. Involving customers in the planning process would ensure their support in plan implementation and achievement of planned goals. All customers are not willing to participate in the planning process nor is it possible to involve all of them for relationship marketing programs for the mass market. However, for managing cooperative and collaborative relationship with large customers, their involvement in the planning process is desirable and sometimes necessary.

Executives are sometimes unaware, or they choose to initially ignore the nature of misalignment in operating processes between their company and customer partners, leading to problems in relationship marketing implementation. Several aspects of the operating processes need to be aligned depending on the nature and scope of the relationship. For example, operating alignment will be needed in order processing, accounting and budgeting processes, information systems, merchandising processes, etc.

Several human resource decisions are also important in creating the right organization and climate for managing relationship marketing. Training employees to interact with customers, to work in teams, and manage relationship expectations are important. So is the issue of creating the right motivation through incentives, rewards, and compensation systems towards building stronger relationship bonds and customer commitment. Although institutionalizing the relationship is desirable for the long-term benefit of the company, personal relationships are nevertheless formed and have an impact on the institutional relationship. Thus proper training and motivation of employees to professionally handle customer relationships are needed.

Finally, proper monitoring processes are needed to safeguard against failure and manage conflicts in relationships. Such monitoring processes include periodic evaluation of goals and results, initiating changes in relationship structure, design or governance process if needed, creating a system for discussing problems and resolving conflicts. Good monitoring procedures help avoid relationship destabilization and creation of power asymmetries. They also help in keeping the CRM program on track by evaluating the proper alignment of goals, results and resources.

Overall, the governance process helps in maintenance, development, and execution aspects of CRM. It also helps in strengthening the relationship among relational partners and if the process is satisfactorily implemented it ensures the continuation and enhancement of relationship with customers. Relationship satisfaction for involved parties would include governance process satisfaction in addition to satisfaction from the results achieved in the relationship (Parvatiyar, Biong and Wathne 1998).

CRM Performance Evaluation Process

Periodic assessment of results in CRM is needed to evaluate if programs are meeting expectations and if they are sustainable in the long run. Performance evaluation also helps in making corrective action in terms of relationship governance or in modifying relationship marketing objectives and program features. Without a proper performance metrics to evaluate CRM efforts, it would be hard to make objective decisions regarding continuation, modification, or termination of CRM programs. Developing a performance metrics is always a challenging activity as most firms are inclined to use existing marketing measures to evaluate CRM. However, many existing marketing measures, such as market share and total volume of sales may not be appropriate in the context of CRM. Even when a more CRM oriented measures are selected, it cannot be applied uniformly across all CRM programs particularly when the purpose of each program is different from one another. For example, if the purpose of a particular CRM effort is to enhance distribution efficiencies by reducing overall distribution cost, measuring the programs impact on revenue growth and share of customer's business may not be appropriate. In this case, the program must be evaluated based on its impact on reducing distribution costs and other metrics that are aligned with those objectives. By harmonizing the objectives and performance measures one would expect to see a more goal directed managerial action by those involved in managing the relationship.

For measuring CRM performance, a *balanced scorecard* that combines a variety of measures based on the defined purpose of each program (or each cooperative/collaborative relationship) is recommended (Kaplan and Norton 1992). In other words, the performance evaluation metrics for each relationship or CRM program should mirror the set of defined objectives for the program. However, certain global measures of the impact of CRM effort of the company are also possible. Srivastava, et. al. (1998) developed a model to suggest the asset value of cooperative relationships of the firm. If cooperative and collaborative relationship with customers is treated as an intangible asset of the firm, its economic value-add can be assessed using discounted future cash flow estimates. In some ways, the value of relationships is similar to the concept of brand equity of the firm and hence many scholars have alluded to the term relationship equity (Bharadwaj 1994; Peterson 1995). Although an well-accepted model for measuring relationship equity is not available in the literature as yet, companies are trying to estimate its value particularly for measuring the intangible assets of the firm.

Another global measure used by firms to monitor CRM performance is the measurement of relationship satisfaction. Similar to the measurement of customer satisfaction, which is now widely applied in many companies, relationship satisfaction measurement would help in knowing to what extent relational partners are satisfied with their current cooperative and collaborative relationships. Unlike customer satisfaction measures that are applied to measure satisfaction on one side of the dyad, relationship satisfaction measures could be applied on both sides of the dyad. Both the customer and the marketing firm have to perform in order to produce the results in a cooperative relationship and hence each party's relationship satisfaction could be measured (Biong, Parvatiyar and Wathne 1996). By measuring relationship satisfaction, one could estimate the propensity of either party's inclination to continue or terminate the relationship. Such propensity could also be indirectly measured by measuring customer loyalty (Reicheld and Sasser 1990). When relationship satisfaction or loyalty measurement scales are designed based on its antecedents, it could provide rich information on their determinants and thereby help companies identify those managerial actions that are likely to improve relationship satisfaction and/or loyalty.

CRM Evolution Process

Individual customer relationships and CRM programs are likely to undergo evolution as they mature. Some evolution paths may be pre-planned, while others would naturally evolve. In any case, several decisions have to be made by the partners involved about the evolution of CRM programs. These include decisions regarding the continuation, termination, enhancement, and modifications of the relationship engagement. Several factors could cause the precipitation of any of these decisions. Amongst them relationship performance and relationship satisfaction (including relationship process satisfaction) are likely to have the greatest impact on the evolution of the CRM programs. When performance is satisfactory, partners would be motivated to continue or enhance their CRM program (Shah 1997; Shamdasani and Sheth 1995). When performance does not meet expectations, partners may consider terminating or modifying the relationship. However, extraneous factors could also impact these decisions. For example, when companies are acquired, merged, or divested many relationships and relationship marketing programs undergo changes. Also, when senior corporate executives and senior leaders in the company move CRM programs undergo changes. Yet, there are many collaborative relationships that are terminated because they had planned endings. For companies that can chart out their relationship evolution cycle and state the contingencies for making evolutionary decisions, CRM programs would be more systematic.

CRM Implementation Issues

One of the most interesting aspects of CRM development is the multitude of customer interfaces that a company has to manage in today's context. Until recently, a company's direct interface with customers, if any, was primarily through sales people or service agents. In today's business environment most companies interface with their customers through a variety of channels including sales people, service personnel, call centers, Internet websites, marketing departments, fulfillment houses, market and business development agents, etc. For large customers, it also includes cross-functional teams that may include personnel from various functional departments. While each of these units could operate independently, they still need to share information about individual customers and their interactions with the company on a real-time basis. For example, a customer who just placed an order on the Internet and subsequently calls the call center for order verification, expects the call center staff to know that details of his or her order history. Similarly, a customer approached by a sales person unaware that she has recently complained about dissatisfactory customer service, is not likely to be treated kindly by the customer. On the other hand if the salesperson were aware of the problem encountered by the customer, her complaint and the action already initiated to resolve the complaint, would place the salesperson in a relatively superior position to handle the situation. Therefore, effective CRM implementation requires a front-line information system that shares relevant customer information across all interface units. Relational databases, data warehousing and data mining tools are thus very valuable for CRM systems and solutions.

However, the challenge is develop an integrated CRM platform that collects relevant data input at each customer interface and simultaneously provides knowledge output about the strategy and tactics suitable to win customer business and loyalty. If call center personnel cannot identify and differentiate a high value customer and do not know what to up-sell or cross-sell to this customer, it could be a tremendous opportunity loss. Although most CRM software solutions based on relational databases are helping share customer information, they still do not provide knowledge output to the front-line personnel. As shown in figure 2, CRM solutions platform needs to be based on interactive technology and processes. It should assist the company in developing and enhancing customer interactions and one-to-one marketing through the application of suitable intelligent agents that help develop front-line relationship with customers. Such a system would identify appropriate data inputs at each customer interaction site and use analytical platforms to generate appropriate knowledge output for front-line staff during customer interactions. In addition, implementation tools to support interactive solutions for customer profitability analysis, customer segmentation, demand generation, account planning, opportunity management, contact management, integrated marketing communications, customer care strategies, customer problem solving, virtual team management of large global accounts, and measuring CRM performance would be the next level of solutions sought by most enterprises.

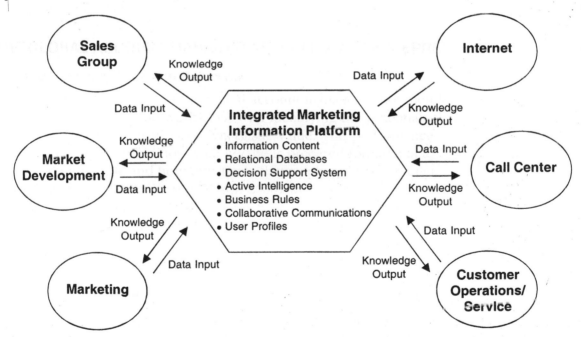

Fig. 2 *Information Platform for CRM*

In the enthusiasm to implement CRM solutions, some companies seem to be overlooking the basic considerations that would make such initiatives successful. Since CRM implementation comprises a significant information technology (IT) component, these companies have handed over the responsibility of CRM implementation to IT Departments. They are focused on simply installing CRM software solutions without a CRM strategy or program in place. This leads to creating an operational tool within the company, but the usability and effectiveness in producing desirable results from such tools is limited. CRM tools would be valuable when they are used to identify and differentiate individual customers and to generate individualized offer and fulfill customized solutions. The lack of a CRM strategy or CRM programs, would leave the front-line people without any knowledge of what they should be doing with additional customer information that they now have access to. For those who apply themselves and develop improvised solutions, it could backfire as ad hoc solutions could cause unintended deterioration in customer relationships. Hence, it is important to consider CRM process framework in totality. CRM tools are meant to supplement a company's strategy for building effective customer relationships. Appropriate strategy and excellent implementation are both needed for obtaining successful results. In the future we expect to see more research on the barriers to implementing successful CRM strategies as well as empirical research on the impact of CRM on company performance.

CRM Research Directions

Wilson (1995) classified relationship marketing research directions into three levels: concept level, model level and process research. At the concept level he indicated the need to improve concept definitions and its operationalization. Concept level research relates to identifying, defining and measuring constructs that are either successful predictors or useful measures of relationship performance. Several scholars and researchers have recently enriched our literature with relevant CRM concepts and constructs. These include such constructs as trust, commitment, interdependence, interactions, shared values, power imbalance, adaptation, mutual satisfaction, etc. (Doney and Cannon 1997; Gundlach and Cadotte 1994; Kumar, Scheer and Steenkamp 1995; Lusch and Brown 1996; Morgan and Hunt 1994; Smith and Barclay 1997).

At the model level, scholars are interested in presenting integrative ideas to explain how relationships are developed. Several integrative models have recently begun to emerge providing us a richer insight into how relationships work and what impacts CRM decisions. The IMP Interaction model (Hakansson 1982) was based upon insights obtained on more than 300 industrial marketing relationships. By identifying the interactions among actors, the IMP model traces the nature and sources of relationship development. The IMP model and its research approach have become a tradition for many scholarly research endeavors in Europe over the past 15 years or more. The network model (Anderson, Johansson and Hakansson 1994; Iacobucci and Hopkins 1992) uses the social network theory to trace how relationships are developed among multiple actors and how relationship ties are strengthened through networks. Bagozzi (1995) makes a case for more conceptual models to understand the nature of group influence on customer relationships.

A more evolutionary approach of integrative models is to look at the process flow of relationship formation and development. Anderson and Narus (1991) and Dwyer, Schurr and Oh (1987) along with numerous other scholars have contributed towards our understanding of the relationship process model. By looking at the stages of the relationship development process, one could identify which constructs would actively impact the outcome considerations at that stage and which of them would have latent influences (Wilson 1995). The process model of relationship formation, relationship governance, relationship performance, and relationship evolution described in the previous section is an attempt to add to this stream of knowledge development on relationship marketing.

For practitioners, process level research could provide useful guidelines in developing and managing successful CRM programs and activities. Some research has now started to appear in the marketing literature on partner selection (Schijns and Schroder 1996; Stump and Heide 1996). Mahajan and Srivastava (1992) recommended the use of conjoint analysis techniques for partner selection decisions in alliance type relationships. Dorsch et. al. (1998) propose a framework of partner selection based on the evaluation of customers' perception relationship quality with their vendors. At the program level, key account management programs and strategic partnering have been examined in several research studies (Aulakh, Kotabe, and Sahay 1997; Nason, Melnyk, Wolter, and Olsen 1997; Wong 1998). Similarly within the context of channel relationships and buyer seller relationships several studies have been conducted on relationship governance process (Biong and Selnes 1995; Heide 1994; Lusch and Brown 1996). Also, research on relationship performance is beginning to appear in the literature. Kalwani and Narayandas (1995) examined the impact of long-term relationships among small firms on their financial performance. Similarly, Naidu et. al. (1999) examine the impact of CRM programs on the performance of hospitals. Srivastava, et. al. (1998) examine the economic value of CRM assets. However, not much research is reported on relationship enhancement processes and relationship evolution. Although, studies relating to the development of CRM objectives are still lacking, the conceptual model on customer expectations presented by Sheth and Mittal (1996) could provide the foundation for research in this area. Overall, we expect future research efforts to be directed towards the process aspects of relationship marketing.

Convergence of CRM and relationship marketing knowledge with some other paradigms in marketing is also taking place. These include database marketing (Shani and Chalasani 1992; Schijns and Schroder 1996), integrated marketing communications (Duncan and Moriarty 1998; Schultz et. al. 1993; Zhinkan, et. al. 1996), logistics, and supply-chain integration (Fawcett, et. al. 1997; Christopher 1994). Some of these are applied as tools and work processes in relationship marketing practice. As more and more companies use these processes and other practical aspects such as total quality management, process reengineering, mass customization, electronic data interchange (EDI), value enhancement, activity based costing, cross-functional teams, etc. we are likely to see more and more convergence of these and related paradigm with CRM.

A number of theoretical perspectives developed in economics, law, and social psychology is being applied in CRM. These include transactions cost analysis (Mudambi and Mudambi 1995; Noordeweir, John and Nevin 1990; Stump and Heide 1996), agency theory (Mishra, Heide and Cort 1998), relational contracting (Dwyer, Schurr and Oh 1987; Lusch and Brown 1996), social exchange theory (Hallen, Johanson and Seyed-Mohamed 1991;

Heide 1994), network theory (Achrol 1997), game theory (Rao and Reddy 1995), interorganizational exchange behavior (Rinehart and Page 1992), power dependency (Gundlach and Cadotte 1994; Kumar, Scheer, and Steenkamp 1995), and interpersonal relations (Iacobucci and Ostrom 1996). More recently resource allocation and resource dependency perspectives (Lohtia 1997; Vardarajan and Cunningham 1995), and classical psychological and consumer behavior theories have been used to explain why companies and consumers engage in relational behavior (Iacobucci and Zerillo 1997; Kahn 1998; Sheth and Parvatiyar 1995b; Simonian and Ruth 1998). Each of these studies has enriched our understanding of customer relationship management. As we move forward, we expect to see more integrative approaches to studying CRM, as well as a greater degree of involvement of scholars from almost all sub-disciplines of marketing into it. Its appeal is global, as marketing scholars from around the world are interested in the study of the phenomenon, particularly in Europe, Australia, and Asia in addition to North America.

☐ CONCLUSION

The domain of customer relationship management extends into many areas of marketing and strategic decisions. Its recent prominence is facilitated by the convergence of several other paradigms of marketing and by corporate initiatives that are developed around the theme of cooperation and collaboration of organizational units and its stakeholders, including customers. CRM refers to a conceptually broad phenomenon of business activity; if the phenomenon of cooperation and collaboration with customers become the dominant paradigm of marketing practice and research, CRM has the potential to emerge as the predominant perspective of marketing. From a corporate implementation point of view, CRM should not be misunderstood to simply mean a software solutions implementation project. Building customer relationship is a fundamental business of every enterprise and it requires a holistic strategy and process to make it successful.

REFERENCES

Achrol, Ravi S. (1997), "Changes in the Theory of Interorganizational Relations in Marketing: Toward a Network Paradigm," *Journal of the Academy of Marketing Science*, 25, (Winter), pp. 56-71.

Anderson, James C. and James A. Narus (1991), "Partnering as a Focused Market Strategy," *California Management Review*, (Spring), pp. 95-113.

Anderson, James C., Hakan Hakansson, and Jan Johanson (1994), "Dyadic Business Relationships within a Business Network Context," *Journal of Marketing*, (October), pp.1-15.

Aulakh, Preet S., Masaaki Kotabe, and Arvind Sahay (1996), "Trust and Performance in Cross-Border Marketing Partnerships: A Behavioral Approach," *Journal of International Business Studies*, 27 (5), pp. 1005-1032.

Bagozzi, Richard P. (1995), "Reflections on Relationship Marketing in Consumer Markets," *Journal of the Academy of Marketing Science*, 23 (Fall), pp. 272-277

Berry, Leonard L. (1995), "Relationship Marketing of Services- Growing Interest, Emerging Perspectives," *Journal of the Academy of Marketing Science*, (Fall), pp. 236-245.

Berry, Leonard L. and A. Parsuraman (1991), *Marketing Services – Competing Through Quality*, New York: Free Press.

Bharadwaj, Sundar G. (1994), "The Value of Intangible Firm Assets: An Empirical Examination," in *Relationship Marketing: Theory, Methods and Applications*, Jagdish N. Sheth and Atul Parvatiyar (eds.), Atlanta: Emory University Center for Relationship Marketing.

Bhattacharya, C. B. (1998), "When Customers are Members: Customer Retention in Paid Membership Contexts," *Journal of the Academy of Marketing Science*, 26, (Winter), pp. 31-44.

Bickert, Jock (1992), "The Database Revolution," *Target Marketing*, (May), pp.14-18.

Biong, Harald and Fred Selnes (1995), "Relational Selling Behavior and Skills in Long-Term Industrial Buyer-Seller Relationships," *International Business Review*, 4 (4), pp. 483-498.

Biong, Harald, Atul Parvatiyar, and Kenneth Wathne (1996), "Are Customer Satisfaction Measures Appropriate to Measure Relationship Satisfaction?" in *Contemporary Knowledge of Relationship Marketing*, Atul Parvatiyar and Jagdish N. Sheth (eds.), Atlanta, GA: Center for Relationship Marketing, Emory University, pp. 258-275.

Bitner, Mary Jo (1995), "Building Service Relationships: It's All About Promises," *Journal of the Academy of Marketing Science*, (Fall), pp. 246-251.

Borys, Bryan and David B. Jemison (1989), "Hybrid Arrangements as Strategic Alliances: Theoretical Issues in Organizational Combinations," Academy of Management Review, (April), pp. 234-249.

Cannie, J K. and D. Caplin (1991), *Keeping Customers for Life*, Chicago: American Marketing Association.

Christopher Martin (1994), "Logistics and Customer Relationships," *Asia-Australia Marketing Journal*, 2 (1), pp. 93-98.

Crosby, Lawrence A. and Nancy Stephens (1987), "Effects of Relationship Marketing and Satisfaction, Retention, and Prices in the Life Insurance Industry," *Journal of Marketing Research*, (November), pp. 404-411.

Crosby, Lawrence A., Kenneth R Evans, and Deborah Cowles (1990)," Relationship Quality in Services Selling — An Interpersonal Influence Perspective," *Journal of Marketing*, 52 (April), pp. 21-34.

Dick, Alan S. and Kunal Basu (1994), "Customer Loyalty: Toward an Integrated Conceptual Framework," *Journal of the Academy of Marketing Science*, 22 (Spring), pp. 99-113.

Doney, Patricia M. and Joseph P. Cannon (1997), "An Examination of the Nature of Trust in Buyer-Seller Relationships," *Journal of Marketing*, 61 (April), pp. 35-51

Dorsch, Michael J., Scott R. Swanson, and Cott W. Kelley (1998), "The Role of Relationship Quality in the Stratification of Vendors as Perceived by Customers," *Journal of the Academy of Marketing Science*, 26 (Spring), pp. 128-142.

Doyle, Stephen X. and Roth George Thomas (1992), "Selling and Sales Management in Action: The Use of Insight Coaching to Improve Relationship Selling," *Journal of Personal Selling & Sales Management*, (Winter), pp. 59-64.

Duncan, Tom and Sandra E. Moriarty (1998), "A Communication-Based Marketing Model for Managing Relationships," *Journal of Marketing*, (April), pp.1-13.

Dwyer, F. Robert, Paul H. Schurr, and Sejo Oh (1987), "Developing Buyer-Seller Relationships," *Journal of Marketing*, 51 (April), pp. 11-27.

Evans, Joel R. and Richard L. Laskin (1994), "The Relationship Marketing Process: A Conceptualization and Application," *Industrial Marketing Management*, 23 (December), pp. 439-452.

Fawcett, Stanley. E., Roger, Calantone, and Sheldon R. Smith, (1997), "Delivery Capability and Firm Performance in International Operations," *International Journal of Production Economics*, 15 (September), pp.191-204.

File, Karen M., Judith L. Mack, and Russ Alan Prince (1995), "The Effect of Interactive Marketing on Commercial Customer Satisfaction in International Financial Markets," *Journal of Business and Industrial Marketing*, 10 (2), pp. 69-75.

Frazier, Gary L., Robert E. Spekman, and Charles O'Neal (1988), "Just-in-Time Exchange Systems and Industrial Marketing," *Journal of Marketing*, 52 (October), pp. 52-67.

Ganesan Shankar (1994), "Determination of Long-Term Orientation in Buyer Seller Relationships," *Journal of Marketing*, 58 (April), pp.1-19.

Gronroos, Christian (1990), "Relationship Approach to Marketing In Service Contexts: The Marketing and Organizational Behavior Interface," *Journal of Business Research*, 20 (January), pp. 3-11.

——(1995), "Relationship Marketing: The Strategy Continuum," *Journal of the Academy of Marketing Science*, Fall, pp. 252-254.

Gundlach, Gregory T. and Ernest R. Cadotte (1994), "Exchange Interdependence and Interfirm Interaction: Research in a Simulated Channel Setting," *Journal of Marketing Research*, 31 (November), pp. 516-532.

Gummesson, Evert (1987), "The New Marketing- A Developing Long-Term Interactive Relationships," *Long Range Planning*, (August), pp. 10-20.

Hakansson, Hakan, ed., (1982), *"International Marketing and Purchasing of Industrial Goods: An Interaction Approach,"* Chichester, UK: John Wiley and Sons, Inc.

Hallen, Lars, Jan Johanson, and Nazeem Seyed-Mohamed (1991), "Interfirm Adaptation in Business Relationships," *Journal of Marketing*, 55 (April), pp. 29-37.

Hayes, Robert H., Steven C. Wheelwright, and Kim B. Clarke (1988), *Dynamic Manufacturing*, New York: The Free Press.

Heide, Jan B., (1994), "Interorganizational Governance in Marketing Channels," *Journal of Marketing*, (January), pp. 71-85.

Hines, Peter (1995), "Network Sourcing: A Hybrid Approach," *International Journal of Purchasing and Materials Management*, 31 (Spring), pp. 18-24.

Iacobucci Dawn and Nigel Hopkins (1992), "Modeling Dyadic Interactions and Networks I Marketing," *Journal of Marketing Research*, (February), pp. 5-17.

Iacobucci, Dawn and Amy Ostrom (1996), "Commercial and Interpersonal Relationships: Using the Structure of Interpersonal Relationships to Understand Individual-to-individual, Individual-to-Firm, and Firm-to-Firm Relationships in Commerce," *International Journal of Research in Marketing*, 13 (February), pp. 53-72.

Iacobucci, Dawn and Philip Zerillo (1997), "The Relationship Life Cycle: 1) A Network-Dyad-Network Dynamic Conceptualization, and 2) The Application of Some Classic Psychological Theories to its Management," *Research in Marketing*, 13, pp. 47-68.

Jackson, Barbara B. (1985), *Winning and Keeping Industrial Customers: The Dynamics of Customer Relationships*, Lexington, MA: D.C. Heath and Company.

Kahn, Barbara E. (1998), "Dynamic Relations with Customers: High-Variety Strategies," *Journal of the Academy of Marketing Science*, 26 (Winter), pp. 45-53.

Kalwani, Manohar and Narakesari Narayandas (1995), "Long-Term Manufacturer- Supplier Relationships: Do They Pay-Off for Supplier Firms?" *Journal of Marketing*, 59 (January), pp. 1-16.

Kaplan, Robert S. and David Norton (1992), "The Balanced Scorecard – Measures that Drive Performance," *Harvard Business Review*, 70, January-February, pp. 71-79.

Kumar, Nirmalya, Lisa K. Sheer, and Jan-Benedict E.M. Steenkamp (1995), "The Effects of Perceived Interdependence on Dealer Attitudes," *Journal of Marketing Research*, 32 (August), pp. 348-356

Law, Wai K. and Homer Ooten (1993), "Material Management Practices and Inventory Productivity," *Hospital Material Management*, 15 (August), pp. 63-74.

Levitt, Theodore (1983), "After the Sale is Over," *Harvard Business Review*, (September-October), pp. 87-93.

Lohtia, Ritu (1997), "A Transaction Cost and Resource-Dependence Based Model of Buyer-Seller Relations," *Research in Marketing*, 13, pp. 109-134.

Lush, Robert F. and James R. Brown (1996), "Interdependency, Contracting, and Relational Behavior in Marketing Channels," *Journal of Marketing*, (October), pp.19-38.

Mahajan, Vijay and Rajendra K. Srivastava (1992), "Partner Selection: A Conjoint Model Application," Paper presented at the First Research Conference on Relationship Marketing, Atlanta, April 1992.

Marx, Wendy (1994), "A Relationship Marketing Primer," *Management Review*, 83 (November), p. 35

McKenna, Regis (1991), *Relationship Marketing: Successful Strategies for the Age of the Customers*, Addison-Wesley Publishing Company.

Mishra, Debi Prasad, Jan B. Heide and Stanton G. Cort (1998), " Information Asymmetry and Levels of Agency Relationships," *Journal of Marketing Research*, 35, pp. 277-295.

Mohr, Jackie and John R. Nevin (1990), " Communication Strategies in Marketing Channels: A Theoretical Perspective," *Journal of Marketing*, 54(4), pp. 36-51.

Morgan, Robert M. and Shelby D. Hunt (1994), "The Commitment-Trust Theory of Relationship Marketing," *Journal of Marketing*, 58(3), pp. 20-38.

Mudambi, Ram and Susan McDowell Mudambi (1995), "From Transaction Cost Economics to Relationship Marketing A Model of Buyer-Supplier Relations," *International Business Review*, 4 (4), pp. 419-434.

Naidu G.M., Atul Parvatiyar, Jagdish N. Sheth and Lori Westgate (1999), "Does Relationship Marketing Pay? An Empirical Investigation of Relationship Marketing Practices in Hospitals," 46 (3), pp. 207-218.

Nason, Robert W, Steven A. Melnyk, James F. Wolter, and Cyrus P. Olsen (1997), "Beyond Strategic Alliances: Fusion Relationships," *Research in Marketing*, 13, pp. 135-156.

Nevin John R. (1995), "Relationship Marketing and Distribution Channels: Exploring Fundamental Issues," *Journal of the Academy Marketing Sciences*, (Fall), pp. 327-334.

Noordeweir, Thomas G., George John and John R. Nevin (1990), "Performance Outcomes for Purchasing Arrangements in Industrial Buyer-Vendor Relationships," *Journal of Marketing*, 54 (Winter), pp. 80-93

O'Neal, Charles R. (1989), "JIT Procurement and Relationship Marketing," *Industrial Marketing Management*, 18 (February), pp. 55-63.

Parvatiyar, Atul and Jagdish N. Sheth (2000), "The Domain and Conceptual Foundations of Relationship Marketing," in *Handbook of Relationship Marketing*, Jagdish N. Sheth and Atul Parvatiyar, Eds., Thousand Oaks, CA: Sage Publications, pp. 3-38.

Parvatiyar, Atul, Harald Biong, and Kenneth Wathne (1998), "A Model of the Determinants of Relationship Satisfaction," paper presented at the Fourth Research Conference on Relationship Marketing, June 16-18, 1998, Atlanta.

Paul, Terry (1988), "Relationship Marketing for Health Care Providers," *Journal of Health Care Marketing*, 8, pp. 20-25.

Payne, Adrian (1995), "Keeping the Faith," *Marketing*, February 2, p.XIII

Peppers, Don and Martha Rogers (1993), *The One to One Future: Building Relationships One Customer at a Time*, New York, NY: Doubleday.

——(1995), "A New Marketing Paradigm: Share of Customer, Not Market Share," *Managing Service Quality*, 5(3), pp. 48-51

Persutti, William D. Jr. (1992), "The Single Source Issue: U.S. and Japanese Sourcing Strategies," *International Journal of Purchasing and Materials Management*, 28 (Winter), pp. 2-9.

Peterson, Robert A. (1995), "Relationship Marketing and the Consumer," *Journal of the Academy of Marketing Science*, (Fall), pp. 278-281.

Postula, Franklin D. and Dwight T. Little (1992), "Dual Sourcing to Reduce Aerospace Hardware Costs," *Cost Engineering*, 34 (May), pp. 7-14

Pruden, Doug R. (1995), "There's a Difference between Frequency Marketing and Relationship Marketing," *Direct Marketing*, 58 (2), pp. 30-31.

Rao, Bharat P. and Srinivas K. Reddy (1995), "A Dynamic Approach to the Analysis of Strategic Alliances," *International Business Review*, 4 (4), pp. 499-518.

Raphel, Murray (1995), "The Art of Direct Marketing: Upgrading Prospects to Advocates," *Direct Marketing*, 58 (June), pp. 34-37

Reicheld Frederick F. (1996), *The Loyalty Effect*, Boston, MA: Harvard Business School Press

Reicheld, Fredrick F. and W. Earl Sasser, Jr. (1990), "Zero Defections: Quality Comes to Services," *Harvard Business Review*, 68 (September-October), 105-111.

Richards, Amanda (1995), CU Pioneers Loyalty Card for Customers," *Marketing*, (March 9), p.1

Rinehart, Lloyd M. and Thomas J. Page, Jr. (1992), "The Development and Test of a Model of Transaction Negotiation," *Journal of Marketing*, 56 (October), pp. 18-32.

Rosenberg, Larry and John Czepiel (1984), "A Marketing Approach to Customer retention," *Journal of Consumer Marketing*, (Spring), pp. 45-51.

Schijns, Joseph M.C. and Gaby J. Schroder (1996), "Segment Selection by Relationship Strength," *Journal of Direct Marketing*, 10 (Summer), pp. 69-79

Schultz, Don (1995), "Understanding the New Research Needs," *Journal of Direct Marketing*, 9 (Summer), pp. 5-7.

Schultz, Don, Stanley Tannenbaum, and Robert Lauterborn (1993), *Integrated Marketing Communications*, Lincolnwood, IL: NTC Business Books.

Schwartz, George (1963), *Development of Marketing Theory*, Cincinnati, OH: Southwestern Publishing Company

Shah, Reshma H. (1997), "All Alliances Are Not Created Equal: A Contingency Model of Successful Partner Selection in Strategic Alliance," *Ph D. Thesis*, University of Pittsburgh, Pittsburgh, PA.

Shamdasani, Prem N. and Jagdish N. Sheth (1995), "An Experimental Approach to Investigating Satisfaction and Continuity in Marketing Alliances" *European Journal of Marketing*, 29(4,) pp. 6-23.

Shani, David and Sujana Chalasani (1992), "Exploiting Niches Using Relationship Marketing," *Journal of Consumer Marketing*, 9(3), pp. 33-42.

Shapiro, Benson P. (1988), " Close Encounters of the Four Kinds: Managing Customers in a Rapidly Changing Environment," HBS Working Paper No. 9-589-015, Harvard Business School, Boston, MA.

Shapiro, Benson P. and Ronald T. Moriarty, Jr. (1980), *National Account Management*, Cambridge, MA: Marketing Science Institute.

Shapiro, B. P. and R. S. Posner (1979), "Making the Major Sale," *Harvard Business Review*, (March-April), pp. 68-79.

Sheth, Jagdish N. (1994), "A Normative Model of Retaining Customer Satisfaction," *Gamma News Journal*, (July-August), pp. 4-7.

Sheth, Jagdish N. and Atul Parvatiyar (1992), "Towards a Theory of Business Alliance Formation," *Scandinavian International Business Review*, 1 (3), pp. 71-7.

Sheth, Jagdish N. and Atul Parvatiyar (1995a), "Relationship Marketing in Consumer Markets: Antecedents and Consequences," *Journal of the Academy of Marketing Science*, (Fall), pp. 255-271.

Sheth, Jagdish N. and Atul Parvatiyar (1995b), "The Evolution of Relationship Marketing," *International Business Review*, 4 (4), pp. 397-418.

Sheth, Jagdish N. and Atul Parvatiyar (2000), *Handbook of Relationship Marketing*, Thousand Oaks, CA: Sage Publications.

Sheth, Jagdish N. and Banwari Mittal (1996), "A Framework for Managing Customer Expectations," *Journal of Market-Focused Management*, 1, pp. 137-158.

Sheth, Jagdish N. and Rajendra S. Sisodia (1995), "Improving Marketing Productivity," in *Encyclopedia of Marketing in the Year 2000*, J. Heilbrunn, Ed., Chicago, IL: American Marketing Association/NTC Publishing.

Simonian, Bernard L. and Julie A. Ruth (1998), "Is a Company Known by the Company It Keeps? Assessing the Spillover Effects of Brand Alliances on Consumer Brand Attitudes," *Journal of Marketing Research*, 35 (February), pp. 30-42

Smith, J. Brock and Donald W. Barclay (1997), "The Effects of Organizational Differences and Trust on the Effectiveness of Selling Partner Relationships," *Journal of Marketing*, 61 (January), pp. 3-21

Spekman, Robert E. (1988), "Strategic Supplier Selection: Understanding Long-Term Buyer Relationships," *Business Horizons*, (July/August), pp. 75-81.

Srivastava, Rajendra K., Tasadduq A. Shervani, and Liam Fahey, (1988), "Market-Based Assets and Shareholder Value: A Framework for Analysis," *Journal of Marketing*, (January), pp.2-18.

Storbacka, Kaj (2000), "Customer Profitability: Analysis and Design Issues," in *Handbook of Relationship Marketing*, Jagdish N. Sheth and Atul Parvatiyar, Eds., Thousand Oaks, CA: Sage Publications, pp. 565-586.

Stump, Rodney C. and Jan B. Heide (1996), "Controlling Supplier Opportunism in Industrial Relationships," *Journal of Marketing Research*, 33 (November), pp. 431-441.

Teagno, Gary (1995), "Gelt by Association," *American Demographics*, (June), pp. 14-19

Vardarajan, P. Rajan and Margaret H. Cunningham (1995), "Strategic Alliances: A Synthesis of Conceptual Foundations," *Journal of the Academy of Marketing Science*, (Fall), pp. 282-292.

Vavra, Terry G. (1992), *Aftermarketing: How to Keep Customers for Life through Relationship Marketing*, Homewood, IL: Business One-Irwin.

Wilson, David T. (1995), "An Integrated Model of Buyer-Seller Relationships," *Journal of the Academy of Marketing Sciences*, (Fall), pp. 335-345.

Wong, Y.H. (1998), "Key to Key Account Management: Relationships (Guanxi) Model," *International Marketing Review*, 15 (3), pp. 215-231.

Young, Joyce A., Faye W. Gilbert, and Faye S. McIntyre (1996), "An Investigation of Relationalism Across a Range of Marketing Relationships and Alliances," *Journal of Business Research*, 35 (February), pp. 139-151.

Yip, George S. and Tammy L. Madsen (1996), "Global Account Management: The New Frontier in Relationship Marketing," *International Marketing Review*, 13 (3), pp. 24-42.

Zinkhan, George M., Charles S. Madden, Rick Watson and David Stewart (1996), "Integrated Marketing Communications and Relationship Marketing: Complementary Metaphors for the Twenty-First Century," in *Contemporary Knowledge of Relationship Marketing*, Atul Parvatiyar and Jagdish N. Sheth (eds.), Atlanta: Emory University Center for Relationship Marketing, pp. 182-184.

CRM: A Research Agenda

■ **D K Shanthakumar and M J Xavier**

Abstract

Customer Relationship Management (CRM), being a relatively new discipline, is replete with opportunities for research studies. Some of the ideas discussed in this article include the development of a scale to measure the depth of relationship, stages of relationship development and also the underlying dimensions of business relationships. Further, research should identify ideal timing (in terms of the stage of relationship and depth of relationship) for cross selling and up-selling of products and services.

Taking the customer lifecycle into account, the article explores research opportunities at different stages, viz., (1) customer need assessment and acquisition, (2) customer development through personalization and customization, (3) customer equity leverage through cross-selling and up-selling and (4) customer retention and referrals for new customers.

Key Words: *Depth of Relationship, Relationship Stages, Types of Relationships, Relationship Dimensions, Psychological Theory of Relationship, Customer Acquisition, Customer Development, Customer Equity, Customer Retention, Cross Selling, Up selling*

❑ INTRODUCTION

"Is there any thing whereof it may be said, this is new? It hath been already of old-time, which was before us." Ecclesiastes 1:10

Relationships are as old as mankind. It has been studied by sociologists, social psychologists, anthropologists, philosophers, theologians and many other people. For that matter even the traders and businessmen of yesteryears relied on relationships for their success. However the modern marketers started taking a fancy to the same only recently.

In the early 90s the concept of relationship marketing was formally introduced into the field of services marketing. Financial service institutions, airlines and other service providers found it profitable to retain and reward the existing customers than running after new customers. It was established that building closer relationship with customers resulted in better returns to companies through the following means (Reichheld, 1993):

- Increased use of company services by loyal customers
- Charging of price premiums for customized services
- Referrals by satisfied customers that brought new customers

The concepts developed for services marketing also found application in the case of industrial as well as consumer products too. This has led to the debate as to whether the whole marketing should be re-written with the new relationship paradigm or should it rest on the traditional 4Ps [Product, Price, Place and Promotion] approach (Gronroos, 1994). However, a whole lot of questions need to be answered before the relationship paradigm is accepted as a foundation on which the entire marketing theory can be built. This paper attempts to throw up a number of research ideas that need to be explored in depth.

□ PSYCHOLOGICAL PERSPECTIVE ON RELATIONSHIPS

There are four theories offered by social psychologists on relationships. They are attraction theory (Aronson, 1980), social penetration theory (Altman and Taylor, 1973), social exchange theory (Thibault and Kelley, 1959) and equity theory (Messick and Cook, 1983). Attraction theory postulates that one is attracted to others on the basis of four major factors: attractiveness (physical appearance and personality), proximity, reinforcement and similarity. Social penetration theory describes relationships in terms of breadth and depth. Breadth refers to number of topics we talk about. Depth refers to the degree of personalness with which we pursue topics. Social exchange theory holds that we develop relationships, which yield the greatest profits. We seek relationships in which rewards exceed costs and are more likely to dissolve relationships when costs exceed rewards. Equity theory claims that we develop and maintain relationships in which rewards are distributed in proportion to costs. When our share of rewards is less than what is demanded by equity, we are likely to experience dissatisfaction and exit the relationship.

□ SCALE TO MEASURE THE DEPTH OF RELATIONSHIP

Similar to the SERVQUAL (Parasuraman, Zeithaml, and Berry, 1988) instrument developed for measuring the quality of service, an instrument to measure the depth of business relationships can be developed. Different dimensions of relationships have been brought out by theoreticians from varied disciplines, such as law, economics, and social scientists. A new holistic approach adopting an eclectic model needs to be developed.

In order to stimulate such a thinking we provide a partial listing of some of the dimensions of relationship.

- Reciprocation
- Mutual benefit
- Trust
- Transparency
- Concern

- Interdependency
- Commitment
- Shared values
- Adaptation

We need to dwell deep into some of the early works on relationship to arrive at the underlying dimensions of any relationship, which in turn can be used to construct a scale to measure the depth of any relationship.

☐ TYPES OF RELATIONSHIP

The nature of relationship varies from situation to situation. Alan Mitchell (1997) has identified the following types of relationship and their relevance for different business situations.

- Parent-child (loan marketer)
- Teacher-student (mass marketer of Internet Software)
- Leader-follower (fashion brand)
- Comrade-at-arms (pressure group)
- Fellow enthusiast (sports car)
- Confidante (financial services advisor)
- Idol to be worshipped (luxury brand)
- Casual friend (beer, crisps)
- Soul mate (special whisky)
- Old flame (brands your mum used)
- A friend whom you seek out to escape from everyday reality (holiday)

A detailed research may be undertaken to classify business relationships into different categories.

☐ STAGES OF RELATIONSHIP

Relationships do not get formed overnight. A typical man-woman relationship goes through stages such as dating, romance, marriage, honeymoon etc. Behavioral scientists commonly use the six stage model, shown in Figure −1, to describe the development of relationships (Devito, 1993). The six stages are contact, involvement, intimacy, deterioration, repair, and dissolution.

A number of studies have looked at relationship between importer and exporter or a company and its vendors. However no significant studies have been carried out to understand the relationship stages in a consumer product situation.

Are there some universal models available that define different stages in a relationship? Can we develop a comprehensive relationship stages model for business relationships too? Depending on the type of relationship (as defined in the earlier section) will the relationship stages differ?

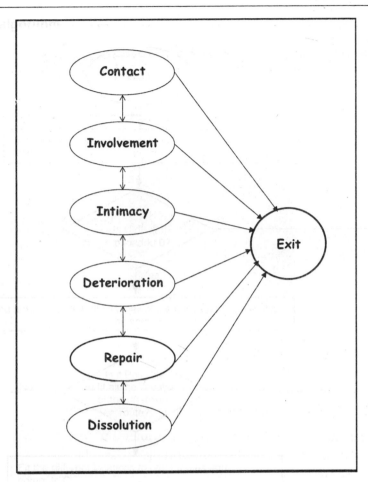

Fig. 1 *Six Stage Model of Relationship*
(Adapted from DeVito, Joseph A. (1993), Messages : Building Interpersonal
Communication Skills, New York, HarperCollins College Publishers. Page 260)

Research needs to be carried out to understand the stage at which cross selling and up-selling should be attempted. Some specific stage may bring better results than others when it comes to seeking referrals from existing customers.

❑ CUSTOMER LIFE CYCLE

Basically CRM revolves around the management of customer life cycle as indicated in Figure–2. We start with customer acquisition either through the traditional advertising or through referrals. Then we move on to customer development through personalization of communication and customization of products and services through a mutual learning process. Then we go on to leverage the customer equity through cross selling and up

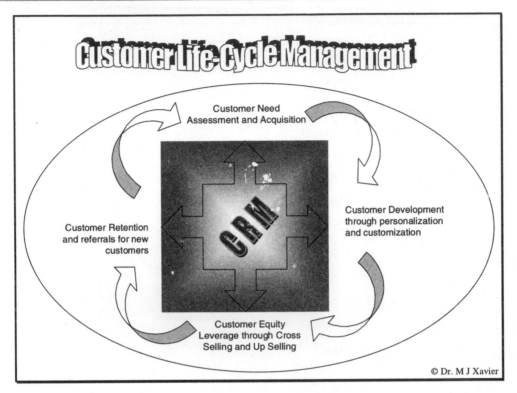

Fig. 2 *Customer Life Cycle Management*

selling. We work for the retention of existing customer and also benefit by the new customers that they get through their personal referrals.

Each stage in the customer life cycle offers immense opportunity for research.

□ CUSTOMER ACQUISITION

Though the CRM literature advocates that customers should be brought in through referrals, we do find that many companies (including dot.com companies) continue to use the traditional mass media advertising to get new customers. Basically we need a critical mass of customers before referrals can bring further customers (or do we?). There is a lot of potential for research as to when and under what conditions do we resort to mass media? How long do we rely on mass media? Under what circumstances, can we do away with mass media advertising?

Personalization and Customization

Though this part has been extensively studied, the question remains as to whether customization is needed in all product categories. Do customers expect customization in commodity type of products?

Cross Selling, Up selling and Referrals

Theoretically cross selling and up selling can meet the customer requirements. However the idea seem to predominately meet with the sellers need to maximize his revenues by exploiting his relationship with the customers. Are there methods to ensure that these CRM techniques result in the enhancement of mutual economic values?

Customer Migration

Whatever be the CRM programs used by companies, there will be a certain amount of customer migration at different stages of the customer life cycle due to various reasons (See Figure – 3). Studies need to be conducted to assess customer attrition at various stages to arrive at recommendations for managers to minimize the same.

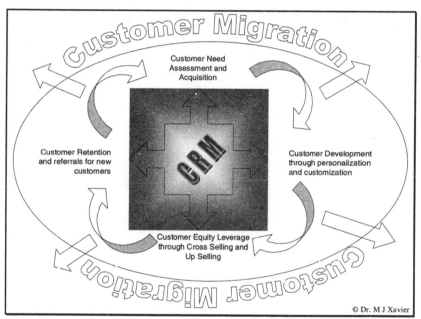

Fig. 3 *Customer Migration*

In sum, the approaches developed so far have only contextual relevance and conse quently they may not be helpful in developing a universal theory of relationship market- ing. Most of the studies conducted in the area of relationship marketing try to look at relationships in a narrow perspective. We need to first of all understand relationships in general and then relate the same to marketing. As relationships are built on the edifice of mutual benefit, the models developed should ensure that they are not exploitative in nature.

REFERENCES

Altman, Steve and Dalmas Taylor (1973), *Social Penetration: The Development of Interpersonal Relationships*, New York: Holt, Rinehart Winston.

Aronson, Elliot (1980), *The Social Animal*, 3rd ed. San Fransisco, CA:W.H. Freeman.

DeVito, Joseph A. (1993), *Messages : Building Interpersonal Communication Skills*, New York, HarperCollins College Publishers.

Messick, R.M. and K.S. Cook, eds. (1983), *Equity Theory: Psychological and Sociological Perspectives*, New York: Praeger

Mitchell, Alan (1997) 'The Secret of a Good Relationship', *Marketing Week*, August 28, p.7

Parasuraman, A., Zeithaml, V. A., and Berry, L.L. (1988) 'SERVQUAL: A Multiple Item Scale for Measuring Consumer Perceptions and Service Quality', *Journal of Retailing*, 64, pp. 12-40.

Reichheld, Christopher J. (1993) 'Loyalty-based Management', *Harvard Business Review*, March-April, p. 71.

Thibaut, J.W. and H.H. Kelley, (1959), *The Social Psychology of Groups*. New York: Wiley

Chapter 3

Implications of Globalization on Customer Relationship Management

■ **Philip J Kitchen, Gurvinder Shergill and Lynne Eagle**

Abstract

This paper focuses on the implications for Customer Relationship Management as a consequence of globalization in the compelling and e-volutionary global marketplace. Managers at all levels of an organization must reach out to and communicate with customers, consumers, and public – each of whom can impact markedly on overall market share and profit performance. Thus the corporation plays a very significant role in brand marketing and strategic business unit management. However, much of the focus to date on globalization research has been on macro issues or on tangible products rather than the rapidly developing services sector. We therefore focus on an often-overlooked aspect of global marketing management – the management of customer relationships across international borders. We see this paper as a prelude paper to a major study, to be carried out in 2000-2001, can rest. For scholars with continued interest in the globalization/globalization debate, we would welcome your comment and involvement.

Key Words: *Globalization, Customer Relationship Management, Marketing Communication*

□ INTRODUCTION

The globalization of markets has been one of the major business developments in the last three decades (Levitt, 1983; Keegan, 1999; Schultz and Kitchen, 2000). Craig and Douglas (1996) contend that choosing not to participate in global markets is no longer optional. The pressure of global competition impacts every domestic market as well as international markets. Marketplaces are transitioning to demand-side approaches with a focus on customer needs and wants. Customer relationship management (CRM) thus should assume a central role in the marketing management of global products and services. The impact of globalization on CRM however represents an under-researched area.

The impact of global marketing is particularly noticeable in New Zealand. In less than ten years, commencing in the mid-1980s, New Zealand moved from being a highly regulated economy to one of the world's least regulated. Lessons taken from the New Zealand market can potentially be compared with, or even implemented in, much larger markets, particularly in countries experiencing deregulation; it may also be of benefit to smaller countries espousing similar intent, and may useful serve as a set of guidelines for both types of economies.

☐ IMPLICATIONS OF GLOBALIZATION ON CUSTOMER RELATIONSHIP MANAGEMENT

Schultz (1998a) suggested that the term "global", though widely used, does not necessarily mean commonality in terms of meaning. A useful starting point in clarifying our meaning her is to Levitt, in Kotabe and Helsen, 1998:

".....the multinational and the global corporation are not the same thing. The multinational corporation operates in a number of countries, and adjusts its products and practices in each—at high relative costs. The global corporation operates with resolute constancy—at low relative cost—as if the entire world (or major regions of it) were a single entity; it sells the same thing in the same way everywhere".

While it would be unwise to follow Levitt's approach in its entirety, it is clear that global marketing presents substantial challenges. Among these are that market segmentation and positioning strategies may need diverge widely to accommodate customer needs and preferences. The structure of competitive environments may also vary widely from country to country, as may product life cycle stage. These factors will inevitably rebound on CRM strategies. It also begs the questions of whether these strategies can be 'globalized' and whether globalized CRM strategies are more or less effective than strategy tailors specifically for local markets.

The merits and demerits of standardization versus localization of product/service offerings and the associated promotional activity are again being debated in the trade and academic literature, admittedly more vociferous in the former than in the latter settings. Some authors suggest that the debate is forcing a false dichotomy and that it should be recognized that different strategies with regard to the degree of standardization or localization should apply. These strategies would be contingent upon the nature of the product or service, and on the market in which it is active (see Schultz and Kitchen, 2000). Millet (1997), for example, contends that, for the service industry at least, decentralized strategies empower those most involved with customers, allowing them to make business decisions, which recognize marketplace variations. Thus marketing itself is now concerned with understanding of target customers and develops the value propositions that customers want and need, and then creating the marketing approach. This does not mean that this approach is followed by international firms, certain other factors, for example corporate edict, may control how country strategic business units approach marketing and marketing communication.

Economies of scale in global marketing are achieved in production costs, manpower and related resources *or* when the same or similar marketing/marketing communication programmes are used across several countries rather than separate programmes being developed and implemented in individual countries. Standardization of marketing communication can also assist in brand image consistency across markets (see, for e.g. Kotabe & Helsen, 1998). However, even when similar marketing strategies are applied across multiple countries, international differences in infrastructure, culture, legal systems and/or regulations across countries means that one or more element of the marketing programme such as product features, promotional appeals or distribution channels must be tailored to local conditions to be effective, or legal (see, e.g. Boyd et al, 1998). The debate then centres on the degree of localization that should be, or is required to be, undertaken.

Market segmentation and positioning strategies may need to reflect wide divergence in consumer needs and preferences. The structure of the competitive environment may also vary widely from country to country, not to mention current product life cycle stage on the temporal dimension. These factors will inevitably impact on marketing communication strategies and techniques, as will other issues outlined below.

Cultural differences may impact on what is or is not acceptable in marketing communication, such as the way women are portrayed and what values, such as individualism versus collectivism are used. Cultural differences may be overstated in the area of technology (e.g. personal computers). Flikkema (1999) cites recent research that suggests that attitudes, motivations and needs for these products transcend national boundaries, with regional differences making no appreciable impact on the purchase process. However, the exclusion of developing countries in the study cited may limit the generalizability of this finding.

Many authors (e.g. Gronholdt et al, 2000) stress the importance of CRM in maintaining and increasing customer satisfaction in order to create greater loyalty and thus enhance business performance for the organization. However, while the importance of CRM is recognized and interest is high, there is also a great deal of confusion regarding how effective strategies can be developed and what operational processes are required to support this at an individual country level, let alone on a global basis (see, for example, Battista & Verhun, 2000). CRM software is increasingly being offered as 'the solution' to many operational problems (see Sowinksi, 2000) but users suggest that simple software 'solutions' may allow technical and organizational challenges to be underestimated. Drucker (2000) suggests that key portions of actual operations can be missed or may be disjointed and that the software is not of itself sufficient to remedy 'system' deficiencies.

The impact of technology on globalization should not be understated. While technology is helping to shrink distances between markets and firms who are able to effectively manage the interaction of technology, knowledge and information management seem to be the most successful (see Craig & Douglas, 1996), technology presents its own problems. For example, while the Internet can help global marketing efforts, it can also create discontent for consumers and distributors in relation to price discrimination across markets and variations in distribution strategies (see Samiee, 1999). This view is supported by Wreden (1998), who warns that companies actively involved in electronic commerce must wrestle not only with all the issues identified by Boyd et al, but also with language barriers which are only now being addressed by Internet-based marketers.

Technology is, however, no panacea for solving one of the major enduring problems being experienced in the global marketplace: cultural arrogance and insensitivity. Champy (1999) notes that while digital marketplaces hold the promise of reaching new markets and travel times between far distant destinations have decreased, there remain vast distances between how business is done from country to country. Champy is particularly critical of the arrogance and lack of cultural sensitivity exhibited by American executives and 'business experts'. The impact of arrogance and insensitivity on the development of customer relationships in both the short and long term is obvious.

□ RESEARCH DESIGN

Given the changeable and changing scenario concerning marketing as a discipline superimposed on the strategic backcloth of an emergent global marketplace suggests there are numerous issues, which need to be tackled from a research perspective. The nature of the research suggested that it would be useful to tackle the problem first from a small country perspective. We chose New Zealand for several reasons. These included:

1. The market is traditional Western in orientation
2. Many multinational subsidiaries or at least marketing activities on behalf of multinational or global companies are located here
3. It is seen as a good training ground for progressing young dynamic international managers
4. Many of the marketing issues, benefits, and pitfalls discussed in the preceding theoretical background are presented starkly in this marketplace.

The research objectives for the initial New Zealand study follow. These will be further refined and developed for a larger study involving a sample with multinational/global corporations in the second half of the year 2000 and early 2001.

□ RESEARCH OBJECTIVES

1. To investigate what significant developments have taken place over the last decade leading to globalization of markets and whether it is perceived as a myth or reality by managers.
2. To study the factors that appears to have influenced or are driving changes in the management of marketing communication.
3. To explore the potential challenges imposed by factors in effective implementation of globalised campaigns to manage customer relationships.

◻ DATA COLLECTION

A pilot study was conducted in early 2000 via a postal questionnaire of 87 major brand marketing organizations in New Zealand (members of the Association of New Zealand Advertisers) and gained a 24% response rate. The focus was issues of globalization and its impact on marketing strategy and management. While this small sample allows little statistical analysis, we believe that these results regarding perceptions of marketing managers are both interesting and should form the basis for a much larger scale study.

◻ RESEARCH FINDINGS

We used factor analysis technique to summarize the responses of managers on a large number of variables. We tested three relationships: factors impacting globalization, forces influencing market communication, and potential challenges to effective implementation of global campaigns for CRM. Results show that in determining the significance of a range of developments impacting on the development of global marketing communications such as worldwide economic trends, technology and global consumerism the barriers to such developments would not appear to be widespread in New Zealand.

In the following sections we will discuss each of the findings in turn by exploring the set objectives. To investigate the first objective, we provided respondents with a list of developments that have occurred over the last decade and were asked to indicate the strength of agreement or disagreement on 5-point scale with each statement in relation to its significance for global marketing communication.

Table 1 shows the factor analysis of 15 variables which were perceived by marketing managers as significant developments that have taken place over the last decade in the global marketing communication field. This factor solution has extracted six factors from a total of 15 variables. Factor 1 loads heavily on first 5 variables, which might be labeled as 'global business environment'. This is because these five variables reveal the perceptions of managers relating to what is happening in the global business environment. This factor alone has explained one–fourth of the total variation in this factor solution. Factor 2 is correlated most highly with variables 6, 7 and 8. It might be termed as 'global business strategies'. This factor indicates that managers think that properly planned business strategies are helpful in globalizing the firm. The third factor can be labeled as 'global consumerism and marketing' because it loads high on variable numbers 9 and 10. The fourth, fifth and sixth factors can be named as 'consolidation and communication', 'organizational structure' and 'communication technology' respectively. These findings indicate that globalization was perceived as a very real and pervasive phenomenon impacting on all areas of business activity both from an internal company perspective and an external market–oriented perspective. The driving forces, according to our respondents, were these 6 factors which are perceived as converging. Thus objective 1, which asked the question as to whether the emergence of a globalization of markets was perceived as a myth or reality,

Table 1 *Rotated Factor Matrix of Factors Affecting Globalization Developments*

Variables		Factors					
		1	2	3	4	5	6
1	Greater focus on brand communication.	.889	.168	−.153	.122	.102	−.178
2	Prevailing competitive environment	.871	.203	−.115	−.009	.171	−.177
3	Worldwide economic trends	.638	.355	.305	−.364	.232	.138
4	Prevailing environmental circumstances	.853	−.005	−.148	.262	.266	.222
5	Channels and distribution	.538	−.1 11	.300	−.358	−.153	.298
6	Global marketing communications	−.001	.862	.168	−.228	.194	.108
7	Integrated business strategies	.206	.846	−.222	.006	.279	−.143
8	Top management objectives	.232	.760	−.297	.222	−.398	−.003
9	Globalization of marketing	−.042	−.050	.943	.099	−.106	.176
10	Global consumerism Integrated commu-	−.090	−.083	.912	.075	−.035	−.026
11	nications	.416	−.001	.304	.746	.106	−.095
12	Consolidation and concentration	−.230	−.042	.051	.841	.234	.225
13	Internal organizational factors	.265	.230	−.161	.067	.872	−.025
14	Business process re-engineering	.235	−.024	−.020	.486	.811	.077
15	Communication technology	−.032	−.002	.096	−.095	.032	.947
	Variation explained by each factor	22.8	15.4	15.0	13.2	13.0	8.3
	Total variation explained by all factors			87.9%			

can be taken to be confirmed in the latter dimension. These findings are also in accord with those from the preceding literature review.

In the above factor analysis, communication technology emerged as a single most important factor explaining 8.3% of the total variations explained by all factors together. Marketing managers perceive this variable to be the most important significant development taken place over the last decade. Communications, in the 21st century, need to be integrated if only because disparate messages underline ambiguity. But while recognizance of the essentiality of integration was pronounced – and driven by customer need and corporate exigency – "saying integration is essential is easy, it's the doing that's causing significant heartburn" (leading board level marketing executive), the ideal of range of customers accessing globally communicated products and services in a global market was applicable only to a tiny minority of customers. Where globally integrated communications was seen to be applicable was in the business-to-business sector. Thus, the drive for globalization insofar as communications was concerned was occasioned more by corporate edict than individual strategic business requirement; but then, of course, corporate headquarters are in a position to gather data globally. However, there is still an underlying perception that strategic business units in a specific area or country invariably *prefer* localized, or adapted, communication strategies as these contribute more effectively to the bottom line.

Objective 2 sought to understand factors that influence upon market communication. The major drivers of any move toward globalization were those occasioned by organizational – not environmental – forces. Often corporate headquarters sought to downsize promotion and communication campaigns, irrespective of whether campaigns were configured for reception in New Zealand markets. The worldwide increase in advertising production and media space costs naturally spells and ostensible advantage in not adapting advertisements.

A 19-item list of factors that appear, from the literature, to have influenced or that are driving change in the management of marketing communication was then tested. Their importance as change factors was tested using a 5 point scale where 1 = disagree strongly and 5 = agree strongly. Also tested was whether these factors are helping drive the move towards the integration of marketing communications. The results are shown in Table 2.

Table 2 **Rotated Factor Matrix Of Factors Influencing Driving Forces in the Management of Marketing Communication**

	Variables	Factors					
		1	2	3	4	5	6
1	Increasing price competition	-.752	.502	-.020	-.056	.234	.177
2	Emergence of global consumer	.922	.123	-.020	-.022	-.173	-.027
3	New markets/global trends	.934	.107	-.125	.058	-.143	-.073
4	Growth of worldwide web	.832	.172	.253	.161	-.162	.132
5	Growth of e-commerce	.721	.064	.007	.227	.271	.388
6	Interactive marketing technology	.869	.068	-.151	.063	.298	-.073
7	Technologically sophisticated consumers	.819	.016	.140	-.381	.132	-.105
8	Growth in database marketing	.066	.830	.199	.129	-.176	-.189
9	Changes in media buying practices	.413	.764	.153	-.151	-.010	.289
10	Specialist direct marketing growth of agencies	-.262	.730	.555	.215	.004	-.106
11	Offering integrated services	.214	.700	.299	.052	-.051	.280
12	Database marketing underpins	-.070	.789	-.020	.396	-.014	-.307
13	Media markets fragmenting	.283	.258	.692	.178	.363	-.197
14	Results required from marcom	-.074	.293	.887	.158	-.088	.017
15	Power shift from manufacturers to retailers	.081	.294	.299	.769	.300	.185
16	Brand management changes	.070	.089	.096	.898	-.201	-.183
17	Saturated mature markets	.043	-.045	.149	.080	.910	.175
18	Short term profits	-.260	-.267	-.201	-.336	667	-.208
19	Increased cost of advertising	-.524	.142	.416	-.212	-.029	.549
	Variation explained by each factor	28.3	17.9	11.0	10.4	9.4	9.3
Total variation explained by all factors together		86.65					

Table 2 shows the factor solution of variables that appear to have influenced or are driving change in the management of marketing communication. This factor solution has extracted 6 factors from the list of 19 variables. Factor 1 loads high on first 7 variables that consists of what is happening in the global markets. This factor can be named as 'global marketing communication environment'. This factor is the most important factor since it alone has explained 1/3 of the total variation explained by the factor solution. Second factor loads high on variables 8 to 12 that can be termed as 'data based and direct marketing'. Factor 3 can be labeled as 'marketing media' whereas factor 4, 5, and 6 can be named as 'changing marketing scenario', 'marketing saturation' and 'advertising cost' respectively. This factor solution suggests that evolution in e-commerce, worldwide web, and database marketing and Internet facilities are impacting marketing communications in a big way. Managers need to incorporate these factors in designing any future or modifying any existing marketing communication systems within their organizations.

Objective 3 sought to examine how global integration of factors such as marketing communications and customer relationship management might be implemented. As already indicated previously, the term 'globally integrated' is associated with corporate edict and corporate will, which to a marked degree here, is not dependent on designing marketing communications from an outside-in (consumer oriented) approach. The benefits of integrated communication are focused on the old-style boxes and arrows inside-out approach. In fact, strategic business unit executives are unable to adopt a more global perspective for brands, as they are driven by corporate edict (i.e. what 'works' elsewhere). Nonetheless, the Internet was perceived to be well suited for international brand building and this was being used wherever possible. Thus, marketing communications could on the one hand be seen as globally integrated, but not necessarily focused on the valuation of customers and prospects at the level of individual countries or for that matter customer. Thus relating communications to the underlying customer database and hence developing sustainable brand relationships may be far more difficult in say New Zealand than it would be in a major marketplace scenario.

Table 3 *Rotated Factor Matrix of Factors Responsible for Potential Challenges to Effective Implementation of Global Campaigns to Manage Customer Relationships*

Variables	Factors			
	1	2	3	4
1 Resource allocation within countries	.717	.043	.081	-.051
2 Different market/competitive structure across countries	-.854	.182	-.294	-.086
3 Senior management myopia	.747	.026	-.376	-.014
4 Cultural differences between countries	-.456	.570	.372	-.107
5 Lack of global database	.021	.716	.231	-.251
6 Communication channels between countries	-.136	.938	-.053	.145
7 Inter-country market research standardization	.463	.698	-.391	.210
8 Vertical co-ordination within countries	.118	.064	.889	-.051
9 Horizontal co-ordination between countries	.075	-.110	-.209	.856
10 Forcing country specific campaigns on other countries	-.325	.187	.427	.647
Variation explained by each factor	23.6	22.8	15.9	13.6
Total variation explained by all factors	76.18			

Table 3 reports the results of factor analysis of variables responsible for potential challenges to effective implementation of global campaigns to manage customer relationships. We asked respondents to indicate agreement/disagreement across 5-point scale on 10 items identified from the literature as potential challenges to effective implementation of globalized campaigns for customer relationship management. This factor solution has extracted 4 factors from a list of 10 variables. Factor 1 loads high on first three variables and can be labeled as 'countrywide resource allocation and marketing structure ' which shows that managers perceive that to manage customer relationship globally within country resource allocation and marketing structure will play an important role. Factor 2 can be named as 'inter-country cultural and marketing differences' which stresses the importance of these factors that are important to manage customer relationships. Factor 3 is 'vertical co-ordination' whereas factor 4 is termed as 'across country co-ordination and campaigns'. This factor solution has stresses the importance of these four factors to manage the global customer relationships. Different markets/competitive structures across countries, resource allocation within countries, and senior management myopia were seen as the major challenges. Lack of global database, communication channels and inter-country marketing research were perceived as equally important factors since these variables explained almost the same variation comparable to the first factor. Vertical co-ordinations in terms of promotional disciplines within countries emerged as a single most important variable loading high on factor 3. Horizontal co-ordination and country specific campaigns were perceived as lesser challenges.

☐ DISCUSSION AND CONCLUSION

In determining the significance of a range of developments impacting on the development of global marketing communications and CRM such as worldwide economic trends, technology and global consumerism the barriers to such developments would not appear to be widespread in New Zealand.

- the major challenge to global campaigns, which presumably have significant resonance and meaning for customers and consumers, are global corporations themselves.
- If we follow the argument that different markets usually equate to cultural, economic, and competitive structure differentials, then when these differentials are evident, there is an expectation that adaptation of promotion would be entertained. In New Zealand, however (and we cannot speculate as to how widespread this may be in other advanced economies around the world) there is clear evidence that other country-specific campaigns are forced upon strategic business units, on the grounds of economy and evidence of success elsewhere. Plainly, this flies in the face of the worldwide trend toward integrated CRM orientated approaches that seeks to develop and sustain two-way, interactive, mutually reinforcing relationships.

- The visible drive for globalization and CRM is simply driven here by the time-honored yardstick of countrywide resource allocation and market structure across countries. Perhaps, of course, in a small economy, this would be acceptable.

There are therefore—at least insofar as this small scale study had shown—few barriers to adopting a globalization communication strategy. There would appear to be many barriers to communications that are effectively focused on CRM needs. The importance of the study shows instead, admittedly among a small group of respondents, a global communications strategy that is driven by corporate edict than strategic business unit management.

One potential way to test this dichotomy is to carry out a study on a wider basis. In Fall 2000, a sample frame mechanism of the top 200 advertisers in the USA will be built using multiple data sources. These sources will include key journals such as Brandweek, Advertising Age and the Wall Street Journal. Each corporation will be contacted by telephone, fax, or email to pre-identify and qualify appropriate respondents and to ascertain willingness to participate. In late 2000, the developed questionnaire will be mailed or emailed to executive respondents around the world. Findings will be available by early 2001 for dissemination

It is hoped to replicate this study in other major markets in 2000/2001, and to thus provide the foundations for a multi-country comparison of the impact of globalization. By extending the geographic parameters of the study, we can gain a wider international perspective on the challenges the globalize marketplace of the 21st century present for marketing communication.

In order to protect and nurture the basketful of brands within their portfolio, corporations (*inter alia* - multinational and global firms) need not only build global brands at the individual level, but also build and protect the corporate entity in its own right. A globalised communication strategy has to be strategically integrated at the corporate and strategic business unit level. To the authors of this piece, communications is the lifeblood of the brand, both at corporate and at the strategic business unit level. More, not less, attention needs to be paid to the parameters of marketing communications that are clearly focused on the needs to customers in specific markets for communication is marketing and marketing is communication. As stated in the preamble, we would welcome comments from interested parties as the [proposed] research passes through its various phases.

REFERENCES

Battista, P. & Verhun, D. (2000) 'Customer Relationship Management: The Promise and the Reality', *CRM Management*, May, pp. 34 – 37.

Boyd, H.W. Jnr, walker, O.C. Jnr & Larreche, J-C, (1998*). Marketing Management: A Strategic Approach with a Global Orientation*. McGraw Hill, London.

Champy, J. (2000) 'The Ugly American Lives On', *Sales and Marketing Management,* Vol. 151, pp. 22 – 25.

Craig, C.S. & Douglas, S.P. (1996) 'Responding to the challenges of global markets: Change, Complexity, Competition and Conscience', *The Columbia Journal of World Business*, Winter, pp. 6 - 18.

Drucker, D. (2000), 'Online Customer Support Doesn't Come in A Wrapper', *Internetweek*, June 5, pp. 14 – 15.

Flikkema, L. (1998). 'Global marketing's myth: differences don't matter'. *Marketing News,* July 20, 1998, p. 4.

Gronholdt, L. Martensen, A & Kristensen, K (2000) 'The Relationship Between Customer Satisfaction and Loyalty: Cross-industry Differences', *Total Quality Management*, Vol. 11 (4-6), pp. S509 – 514.

Keegan, W.J. (1999) *Global Marketing Management*, Prentice Hall, New Jersey, pp7-14.

Kotabe, M. & Helsen, K. (1998). *Global Marketing Management*. John Wiley & Son, New York.

Levitt, T. (1983) 'The Globalisation of Markets' *Harvard Business Review*,

Millet, G. (1997). 'Global marketing and regionalization - worlds apart?' *Pharmaceutical Executive*, 17 (8), August, pp. 78- 81.

Samiee, S. (1998). 'The Internet and International Marketing :Is there a fit?' *Journal of Interactive Marketing*, Vol 12 (4), Autumn 1998, pp. 5 - 21.

Schultz, D. E. (1998). 'Align Marketing Goals with Management Goals'. *Marketing News*, Vol 32 (15), July 20, p. 7 -6.

Schultz, D.E. and Kitchen, P.J. (2000*) Global Communications: An Integrated Marketing Approach*, Macmillan Business, 2000.

Sowinksi, L.L. (2000) 'Customer Relationship Management Software: Feeling Warm and Happy in the Dark Dreary Digital Age', *World Trade*, June, pp. 70 – 71.

Wreden, N. (1998). 'Internet opens market abroad'. *Informationweek*, Nov 16, 1998, pp. 2SS - 4SS.

Chapter 4

Effective Customer Relation Management through Customer Knowledge Management

■ **Bhuvan Sharma, Deepali Singh and Rajiv Ranjan**

Abstract

Faced with extremely tough competition and flat sales growth, companies are finding it hard to secure customer loyalty. Research has consistently shown that it costs four to five times more to acquire a new customer compared to retaining an existing one.

CRM provides seamless integration of every area of business that touches a customer-namely marketing, sales, customer support. It does this through integration of various processes, procedures, technologies, taking advantage of revolutionary impact of internet (i.e. to take help of internet in the integration of e-CRM).

To effectively implement a Customer Relation Management Solution it is very important to identify real knowledge about different types of customers. (Viz. Most valued customers, Most growable customers, Below zero customers) from plethora of internal and external data, figures, surveys. A straightaway technique is to create a data warehouse, thereafter information which is required to effectively implement principles of CRM, could be mined out of this data warehouse.

It is essential to build knowledge architecture instead of just accumulating the plethora of data and figures taken from different places. Knowledge Management, has the potential to give an organization a strategic advantage in design and implementation of a CRM solution. Organizations should look for differentiating knowledge from data and information while creating a knowledge base of customers for CRM.

Once good performance based knowledge architecture is built for CRM, the rest is merely technology and sweat. It provides for a standard for how documents, databases, websites are labeled, organized and populated. It will also provide for keyword adoption that allows marketing professionals to select what they need rather than search for it. The knowledge architecture for CRM will reduce the risk element involved in taking strategic decisions to retain customer loyalty. The strategic decisions of market man will be more judicious, based on past knowledge, which was earlier hidden, and unorganized. Thus decisions making *process will be more agile and effective. The knowledge architecture for Customer Relation Management will embrace a diversity of knowledge sources from databases, websites, employees, customers, partners and cultivate that knowledge where it resides, while capturing its context and giving it greater meaning through its relation to other information in the company.*

This paper tries to synergise the concepts of CRM and Knowledge Management to give an organization a strategic advantage in design and implementation of a CRM solution.

❑ INTRODUCTION

Customer relationship management starts with in depth knowledge of customers, their habits, desires, and their needs, by analyzing their cognitive, effective behavior and attributes. CRM applies this knowledge to develop and design marketing strategies, to develop and cultivate, long lasting mutually beneficial interaction and relationship with the customer. Customer knowledge and customer interaction on the basis of this knowledge are the two pillars on which any CRM design and its successful implementation rests.

Dynamic changes in the form of evolution of marketing environment and development of web as marketing medium and its global acceptance have forced organizations to change the way in which business is conducted, Thus E-business has evolved and is expected that with in few years it will become so mature that it will be the sole survivor in terms of way of conducting business. Supply chain management systems and customer relation management systems are integrated to the existing ERP systems of the organizations to deliver value to the customers. The issue here is about the front end of the value chain namely CRM, which is about integrating marketing, sales and customer service / support. Thus strategic advantage gained through implementing CRM solutions can be most effective when its design is simple, implementation cycle is small and performance is reliable. Best way by which these three factors can be achieved is to use concepts of knowledge management in designing CRM solution, architecture of CRM should take heavy inputs from knowledge management architecture.

❑ KNOWLEDGE MANAGEMENT WITH FOCUS ON CRM

As markets and product change with accelerating pace marketing and sales people, product/service design people must assimilate and apply vast amount of current information about their markets, their competition and the solution they can offer to the customers. Marketing, sales, after-sales people would be the knowledge workers. Forward-looking companies have realized that their front office work force could be substantially more productive if they could utilize customer knowledge. Successful companies not only possess customer knowledge but are also able to harness it to make critical business decisions.

❑ WHAT IS KNOWLEDGE MANAGEMENT?

Core of any knowledge management implementation is to abstract vital and meaningful knowledge from the voluminous amount of data available from variety of internal and external sources and ensure its practical use. Organizations earlier used data processing technologies to assimilate information and effectively disseminate the same among its employees. KM is a management discipline that treats intellectual capital as managed asset, it is not about creating a central database that is a complete replica of all that is known by employees or that is embedded in the system they use, KM is about embracing a diversity of knowledge sources, like legacy systems, existing data-warehouses, portals, websites, customers, suppliers, partners, external marketing research agencies and cultivating this knowledge where it resides. Understanding data in terms of its context and inter-relationship give information, understanding principles of knowledge gives wisdom to satisfy complete needs of customer. This has the potential of developing customers even before product or service is developed.

The rapid advances in the field of information technology enhanced the knowledge creation and knowledge management process and played a key role in collecting transforming and communicating data, information, and knowledge. Knowledge management helps an organization to gain insight and understanding from its own experience. KM implementation also protects intellectual assets from decay, adds to firm intelligence and provides increased flexibility. There are three guiding issues in the concept of KM, People, Processes and Technology.

❑ KNOWLEDGE MANAGEMENT: A CONCEPTUAL FRAME

Understanding of organizational needs, its vision and mission, should determine development of KM system. A KM architecture could be developed more effectively if we know following:

Organizational structure, Information flow, Information usage & storage, any proposed business process reengineering, existing automation levels, existing data warehouse solutions, existing messaging systems and internet applications, any other legacy systems. A phased approach may be adopted in KM implementation may be the four phases:

1. Evaluation
2. System analysis, design & development
3. Deployment
4. System Evaluation.

Evaluation involves leveraging and building KM architecture upon existing databases, data mining and data warehousing systems, project management and decision support system tools. Designing a strategy to integrate existing Intranets, extranets, and group ware into the proposed KM system. Evaluation should always try to align knowledge management and business strategy. It involves a delicate mix of raising of KM system design to the level of business strategy and bringing strategy down to the level of systems design.

Second phase involves a design of knowledge architecture in which we [ ] what internal and external sources to be integrated. Identification of da[ ] retrieval system, platforms, clients, servers and gateways. What components [ ] for searching, indexing and retrieval? Any KM project always begins with w[ ] organization already knows for this knowledge audits and analysis, identifying K-spot is required. A well-structured KM implementation team prepares a blueprint of KM organization. There are layers of KM system namely, Presentation, Security, Intelligence, Application, Transport, Middle ware, Data storage / repositories. Each layer performs a well defined function. Presentation layer has the user interface, the success of any KM system depends on this layer. The functions of each of these layers are derived from the concepts of effective networking.

Deployment phase could be a pilot one which is also known as result driven incremental technique. Availability of chief knowledge officer is vital for KM success. System evaluation phase tries to evaluate actual benefit accrued by an organization as a result of KM implementation. Metrics, ROI, Balance scorecard method, benchmarking are some of the common technique of KM system evaluation.

☐ THE CRM VALUE CHAIN

Customer Data ⟶ Customer Information ⟶ Customer Knowledge ⟶ Wisdom to Completely satisfy Customers

Foundation of customer knowledge rests on variety of data sources, data could be numerical, textual, organized in tables, discrete and so on. Key to leverage this data is to organize it so that it becomes knowledge on the basis of which informed business decisions could be taken. Industry analysts estimate that data that has no external structure (internally there are sentences, paragraphs, words) represents 80 % of the enterprise information compared to 20 % of structured data. It's a proven fact that 80 % of an organization revenues come from 20 % of its customers, it becomes imperative to design CRM solutions keeping in mind these most valuable customers and to leverage 80 % non structured data of about 20 % of these most valuable customers. Thus if CRM architecture could take care of this simple but important fact, CRM implementation will become less cumbersome and would start giving fruitful results very quickly. Only way to leverage this 80 % of unstructured but most useful data is to use KM architecture as discussed earlier very briefly.

As Peter Drucker defined "Information is data endowed with relevance and purpose". Textual data is usually richer than numeric data because in text we rarely deal with individual words but with complete text documents that have a well defined meaning. Hence to access structured data we talk about customer data access, while to access a text document we talk about customer information retrieval. Well managed customer information that is properly catalogued and structured, available and accessible to the right people at the right time becomes customer knowledge. Just as more tangible corporate assets like computer systems have a finite shell life, so too does knowledge, it must be available at the right time to be able to act upon it. It is not only important to capture customer knowledge from the existing structured and unstructured, internal and external sources but to be able to cultivate this knowledge so as to be able to gain a strategic advantage even in future. CRM system should be able to classify, store, retrieve when require this dynamic information which is created every moment.

There are many kind of tacit knowledge, for example troubleshooting a of very complex control system which is used by every valuable customer of an capital equipment manufacturer. A service man when goes to a customer site does number of hit and trial checks on the basis of his experience and thus able to transform system to a healthy state. Since the system is so complex that every visit of service man is a new exercise, in which he uses to past knowledge to solve complex problem. This kind of tacit product knowledge is derived from experiences, data and documents. This is hard to define and can only be shared through consultation, mentoring and giving examples. Retaining tacit knowledge means retaining the individual, which is invariably not possible. It is possible to generate explicit knowledge from tacit knowledge, but it's a complex exercise. The key ingredient of this exchange is face to face sharing of knowledge or using virtual environmental tools like Lotus Notes, which can facilitate tacit knowledge exchange. Hence for tacit knowledge exchange text mining is very useful and important. There are ways to do text mining, like search engines, web solutions, text analysis tools. The key to successful customer knowledge management is personalization, i.e. how to extract the knowledge that is pertinent to the user and translate it into a format that is easily understood. It is important from the point of navigation through various data sources, information and knowledge. A customer knowledge catalogue should be created, in which a categorized collection of company's intellectual assets will exist. It should be built on a database platform that enables enterprise wide scaling, protects and maintains the knowledge content, and allows for consistent fast access to enterprise wide customer knowledge resources.

❏ PROPOSED CUSTOMER KNOWLEDGE MANAGEMENT FOR EFFECTIVE CRM

Phases for proposed customer knowledge management for effective CRM is shown on the next page, As stated earlier like any KM implementation, Customer knowledge management should have four phases as shown on next page. The CKM architecture should have a layered approach. Existing systems should be seamlessly linked with the proposed layer. The choice for a CKM system could be Web (Enterprise information portal) or a packaged solution such as Lotus Notes, Microsoft solution. Some important points concerning CKM architecture are:

1. Integration of internal and external customer knowledge sources.
2. Identification of IT components of knowledge creation, collaboration and application.
3. Identification of existing and required data mining and knowledge discovery techniques including artificial intelligence, genetic algorithms, neural networks expert and decision support system, reasoning tools.

4. Identify push and pull based mechanism for knowledge sharing and delivery.
5. Identification of right mix of searching, indexing and retrieval.
6. Tagging existing knowledge bases depending on attributes domain, form, type, product/service, time, location.
7. Identify platform and elements of the interface layer like clients, servers, and gateways.
8. Identification of components of knowledge architecture.

PHASES OF IMPLEMENTATION OF CUSTOMER KNOWLEDGE MANAGEMENT

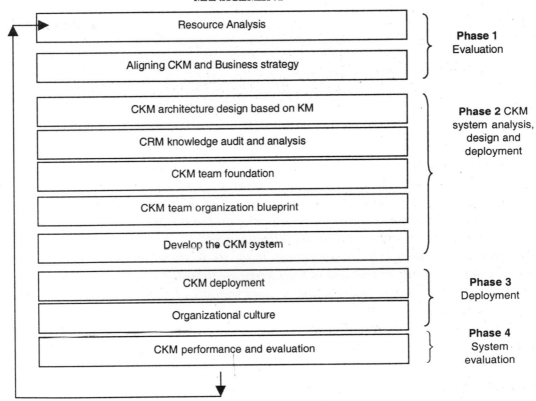

REFERENCES

Bruce Caldwell, (1999) 'Instant marketing', *Information Week*, August.

Bob Evans, (1999) 'Stick with fundamentals', Section on CRM, *Information Week*, February.

C C Shilalakes, J Tylman, (1998), ' EIP', Merrill Lynch, November.

Devenport Thomas, (2000) '*Working Knowledge*', Harvard Business Review, May.

John Foley, (1998) 'Holding the Customer', *Information Week*, March.

Michael McGann, (1997) 'Chase harness data with Lotus Notes', *Bank Systems and Technology*, May

Nonaka & Takeuchi, (1997) *The Knowledge Creating Company*

Tiwana Amnt, (1999) *KM Tool Kit*, Prentice Hall.

Tom Mcmillan, ' Managing content', *Electronic Publishing*, May 1997.

'Impact of market knowledge competence on new products advantage', *Journal of Marketing*, Oct 1998.

Chapter 5

A Generalized Model for the Structure of Business Relationships:

A Meta-analysis of Relationship Literature[1]

■ **Randhir Mishra**

Abstract

The relevance of relationship has been claimed to be universal within the business schema. Business markets demonstrates a network of relationships between firms. The single most significant aspect of a relationship is the continuity of the exchanges within the relationships. The likelihood of continuity of a relationship in the business market dictates the partner's behavior and hence the relationship effectiveness.

In this paper I enumerate the developments in the understanding of relationship structure linking the developments in the field to the idea of relationship continuity. I develop a Relationship Continuity Model (RCM) using a combination of meta-analysis and structural equation modeling procedures.

For the final model, generalizability of the findings and the implications for the management of relationships are discussed. Some of the key issues that emerge from this research provide a rich source for future development in the area of relationship management.

Key Words: *Business Markets, Business Relationship, Relationship Continuity, SEM, meta-analysis.*

❑ INTRODUCTION

The importance of relationships in the business markets have now come to be accepted and established fact. One of the key factors—the likelihood of continuity of a relationship

[1] Author acknowledges the support received from P D Agarwal Foundation (Jaipur), Institute for the Study of Business Markets (Pennstate University), and Clarient Inc. for the conduct of the research.

in the business market dictates the partner's behavior and hence the relationship effectiveness. Once a firm favors entering into relationship with other firms, the next step is to design the structure of the relationship so that it optimizes the returns for the two partners, thus ensuring continuity. The researchers in the area of relationships have developed models that try to explain the dynamics of relationship structure. There have been increasing calls for channeling efforts towards attaining generalizability in the relationship research. Researchers have used multiple factor models to understand the relationship structure and its consequence. The rich source of research in the area of relationship provides the ideal setting to conduct a meta-analytical research in an attempt to generalize the developments so far.

In this paper I look at the empirical relationship research published in refereed journals to isolate the consistent factors and linkages between the factors to develop a generalized model for understanding relationship structure. I use the meta-analytical process to converge the findings from earlier study into a correlation table. I then use this correlation table to test the hypothesized linkages between the factors and evolve the relationship continuity model (RCM). The RCM is a causal model which I develop using LISREL 8.3 package.

Exploring the Relationship Structure

The structure of the relationship has been researched as a combination of the factors that define the underlying dynamics of the relationship. The basic premise that this paper works on is that the successful relationships are continuous by nature. The identity of a relationship structure is held in the intensity of behavioral factors that form the relationship. To extend the understanding of relationship structure I use the developments in the relationship research to isolate the factors that have been identified as the determinants of the relationship dynamics.

Ongoing nature of a relationship has been a common feature that has been dealt in the relationship research literature. Some authors choose to look at it directly as 'relationship continuity' while others have used some surrogate or made implicit reference to the idea. For example, McNeil (1974) look at the 'behavioral concepts' of 'contractual relations' which are the foundations of exchange relationships. He extends the idea further in his subsequent paper McNeil (1980) and contends with an emphasis on contractual exchange behavior that '... (these) contracts are about exchange because contracts capture the relations among the parties, and these relations project the exchange into the future' (Nevin 1995, p 329).

The underlying factors that emerge in the relationship research literature is that relationship continuity is an inherent and desired outcome of the relationship structure design to achieve the benefits, relational approach is expected to yield. The continuity of the relationships is contingent on a score of behavioral factors, which forms the tools and control variables within the relationship structure design.

Likelihood of Relationship Continuity: Relationship Structure Outcome

The idea of continuity is not new to relationship literature. Marketing itself has been seen as having a process (continuous) nature (Grönroos 1993). Thibaut and Kelly (1959) had outlined the essence of continuity in relationships by noting that 'two individuals may be said to have formed a relationship when on *repeated* occasions they are observed to interact' (italics added). Company interaction too has been seen as a continuous complex exchange process (Ford *et al* 1985; Spekman and Johnston 1986). Evans and Laskin (1994) see relationship marketing as a continuous process involving inputs, outcomes and continuous assessment. Available definitions of relationship marketing incorporate the maintenance of relationship as an inherent characteristic (Morgan and Hunt 1994, Grönroos 1993). Literature in services marketing, in particular, has explored the idea of propensity to repeat purchase (for e.g. see Grönroos 1980, Parasuraman, Berry and Zeithaml 1984) based on 'service experience'. Crosby *et al* (1990) argue that successful exchange episodes lead to an enduring buyer-seller relationship in services selling. Similar support can also be found in Anderson and Weitz (1989), Dwyer *et al* (1987), Crosby *et al* (1990)

I use the common theme underlying the concept of relationship continuity to operationalize the dependent variable – *likelihood of the relationship to continue* (LRC). I define LRC as the perception that the relationship would endure the pressures of time (for example dynamics of changing capabilities, the changing business scenarios, industry structure, etc). Having outlined the dependent construct of the RCM, I now go onto the predictors or the relationship structure variables that influence LRC.

Relationship Structure Design Variables

The idea of building and maintaining relationship evolves around the analysis of factors that capture the relationship process. Wilson (1995) identified a set of 13 relationship factors that have both theoretical and empirical support in the relationship structure research. Iaccobucci and Hibbard (1999) took the route of looking at the linkages between variables that have been supported by two or more authors. I qualify a set of variables their operationalization using similar criteria. I also attempt to isolate the factors to minimize the overlap within them by combining some of the factors that have been researched independently. These variables their sources and the operational definitions are given in Exhibit 1.

The Relationship Structure: Mapping the RCM

The recurrent research objective, as mentioned above, has been exploring the constructs and variables relevant to a relationship structure. I present here a map of factors in a relationship that leads to successes or failures of the relationship objectives.

One of the maiden attempts to generalize the relationship map can be found in Iacobucci (1998). The criterion used for including these linkages was—those links that have been supported by more than two published articles. However, the linkages have been generalized only for the direction (causal map). I undertake a similar exercise too start the RCM design.

Exhibit 1 *RCM Constructs, Operationalization and Support*

Construct	Operatonalization	Literature Support
Likelihood of the relationship to continue LRC	Operationalized as anticipation or probability that a relationship would endure in time.	Buchanan and Gillies 1990; Crosby Et Al 1990; Griffin 1995; Grönroos 1980, Narayandas 1995; Brown and Peterson 1993, Gruen 1995; Ganesan 1994; Kalwani and Narayandas 1995; Ford 1980; Dwyer *et al* 1987
Adaptations	Tailoring the resources to dealing with a specific buyer or seller	Ford 1980; Wilson 1995; Han and Wilson 1993; Hallén et al 1991)
Trust	The extent to which a firm believes that its exchange partner is honest and/or benevolent	Wilson et al 1995, Han et al 1993, Morgan and Hunt 1994, Anderson and Narus 1990, Geyskens et al 1998
Commitment	Commitment as a multidimensional construct involving dimensions of continuance, normative component and affective component	Dwyer, Schurr, and Oh 1987; Morgan and Hunt 1994; Ford 1980; Gundlach et al 1995; Geyskens et al 1996, Gruen 1997
Communication	Extent of sharing of information/knowledge	Dwyer et al 1987, Anderson and Narus 1990, Morgan and Hunt 1994, Mudambi and Mudambi 1995
Co-operation	Coordinated action and sharing with expected reciprocation over time	Narus 1990; Heide 1994; Bello and Gilliard 1997; Morgan and Hunt 1994; Han and Wilson 1993
Conflict/Conflict Resolution	The overall disagreements and manner in which past disagreements are resolved (adversarial or collaborative way)	Gaski 1984; Ganesan 1994; Anderson and Narus 1990; Morgan and Hunt 1994; Mohr Fisher, and Nevin 1996
Citizenship Behavior	The sense of belongingness to the whole partnership	Gruen 1995, 1997; Morgan and Hunt 1994
Interdependence	Scale and extent of dependence on the partner	Seth and Parvatiyar 1995, Biong and Selnes 1995, Venkatraman and Bensaou 1995, Wilson 1995, Gruen 1998
Past Satisfaction	Satisfaction level on the basic elements of business elements in the past	Ganesan 1994; Anderson and Narus 1990; Ford 1980
Power Equation	The ability of one partner to evoke a change in other partner (Partner influence)	Anderson and Narus 1990; Gaski 1984

I select a set of studies based on some of the following criteria to set up the RCM. I include empirical research looking at the factors that determine the process of relationship design in terms of physical, psychographic and behavioral components of relationship with an aim to predict the outcome of relationship.

Further qualification of the studies is undertaken using the criterions such as publications, reporting, data quality, context of study etc. Within the selected studies, the constructs and their interlinkages are qualified based on the frequency of reported linkages across studies. I use a minimum frequency of two independent empirical studies reporting the linkages between the two constructs confirmed the significance of the relationship to include the constructs in the meta-analysis.

Selected Empirical Studies: Descriptive Statistics

I identify empirical studies appearing in the marketing or management literature and reporting one or more relationships between any pair of constructs specified in Exhibit 1. I develop a primary list of such studies by means of a computer bibliographic search.

The meta-analysis was carried out based on 31 papers. Some of the studies used more than one independent sample; the samples were treated as independent studies (Rosenthal 1991; Geyskens et. al. 1999). Among the 10 constructs identified for the RCM in the previous chapter, one of the constructs (Adaptations) had to be dropped due to lack of studies giving pair wise relationship between it and other RCM constructs. Thus, 41 samples reporting effect sizes among nine constructs were included. Details of the studies with respect to the sampling plan (number of samples, context of study, and the treatment of the relationship dyad etc) of these empirical studies are presented in exhibit 2.

Exhibit 2 *Legend and support*

Hypothesis. No.	Hypothesis Antecedent	Consequence	Sources
H1a	Overall satisfaction	LRC	Ganesan 1994; Anderson and Narus 1990; Kumar, Scheer and Steenkamp 1995; Bolton 1998
H1b	Trust	LRC	Bucklin, Ramaswamy and Majumdar 1996, Anderson and Weitz 1989, Doney and Canon 1997, Morgan and Hunt 1994; Andaleeb 1995
H1c	Power equation	LRC	Anderson and Weitz 1989; Dwyer, Schurr and Oh 1987; Anderson and Narus 1990; Lusch and Brown 1996; Mohr, Fisher and Nevin 1996
H1d	Interdependence	LRC	Ganesan 1990, Andaleeb 1995, Lusch and Brown; Kumar, Scheer and Steenkamp 1995; 1998
H1e	Conflict resolution	LRC	Bucklin and Sengupta 1993; Mohr, Fisher and Nevin 1996
H1f	Communication	LRC	Morgan and Hunt 1994; Mohr, Fisher and Nevin 1996
H2a	Interdependence	overall satisfaction	Lusch and Brown 1996; Buchanan 1992
H2b	Adaptation	overall satisfaction	Ganesan 1993; Churchill and Surprenant 1982
H2c	Commitment	overall satisfaction	Smith and Barclay 1997; Siguaw, Simpson and Baker 1998; Mohr, Fischer and Nevin 1996
H2d	Conflict resolution	overall satisfaction	Anderson and Narus 1990; Gaski 1984; Mohr, Fischer and Nevin 1996; Bucklin and Sengupta 1993; Brown, Johnson and Koenig 1995
H3a	Communication	Trust	Anderson and Narus 19986; 1990; Anderson, Lodish and Weitz 1987; Morgan and Hunt 1994
H3b	Power equation	Trust	Moorman, Deshpandé and Zaltman 1993; Frost, Stimpson and Maughan 1978; Doney and Cannon 1997

(Contd.)

Exhibit 2 (*Contd.***)**

Hypothesis. No.	Hypothesis		Sources
	Antecedent	*Consequence*	
H4a	Trust	Commitment	Morgan and Hunt 1994; Sharma and Patterson 1999; Geyskens, Steenkamp and Kumar 1999; Grayson and Ambler 1999
H4b	Interdependence	Commitment	Geyskens and Steenkamp 1995; Kumar, Scheer and Steenkamp 1995
H4c	Conflict resolution	Commitment	Anderson and Weitz 1992; Mohr, Fischer and Nevin 1996
H4d	Power equation	Commitment	Anderson and Weitz 1989, Morgan and Hunt 1994, Kumar, Scheer and Steenkamp 1995; Mohr, Fisher and Nevin 1996
H4e	Communication	Commitment	Sharma and Patterson 1999; Mohr, Fisher and Nevin 1996
H5a	Trust	Conflict resolution	Morgan and Hunt 1994; Bucklin, Ramaswamy and Majumdar 1996
H5b	Co-operation	Conflict resolution	Dahlstorm and Nygaard 1999; John 1984
H5c	Power equation	Conflict resolution	Gaski 1984; Moorman, Deshpandé and Zaltman 1993; Anderson and Narus 1990; Morgan and Hunt 1994
H6	Interdependence	Communication	Anderson and Narus 1994; Lusch and Brown 1996
H7	Interdependence	Power equation	Andersen and Narus 1990; Buchanan 1992; Rinehart and Page 1992; Gundlach and Cadotte 1994
H8	Interdependence	Adaptation	Hallén, Johanson and Seyed-Mohamed 1991; Heide 1994; Lusch and Brown 1996
H9a	Commitment	Co-operation	Mohr, Fischer and Nevin 1996; Anderson and Weitz 1992; Morgan and Hunt 1994
H9b	Trust	Co-operation	Morgan and Hunt 1994; Heide and John 1990
H9c	Communication	Co-operation	Morgan and Hunt 1994; Andaleeb 1995

❏ THE RCM DESIGN: LINKAGES AND HYPOTHESES

As mentioned above, I derive the linkages from the review of linkages explored in the literature. The criteria for inclusion or omission of the constructs and linkages are that: (1) two or more independent research findings support them; (2) they have been treated as a direct effect; and (3) the linkage was found statistically significant. Based on these criterions, I develop a model looking at the likelihood of relationships to continue as the dependent variable how it is influenced by other relationship structure variables. Exhibit 3 elaborates the causal antecedents and the path linkages between the relationship level variables, the hypotheses developed, the sources that supports the hypotheses.

❏ RCM ESTIMATION AND TESTING

With the goal as a possible generalization of the relationship level factors from the existing literature, in this section, I conduct the meta-analysis and integrate the findings into the relationship evaluation framework.

Exhibit 3 *Linkages and Hypotheses*

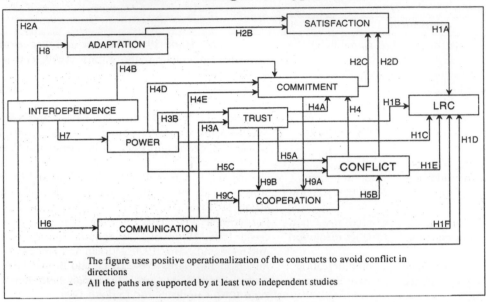

- The figure uses positive operationalization of the constructs to avoid conflict in directions
- All the paths are supported by at least two independent studies

The aim of the meta-analysis is to test the RCM by including the quantitative aspects of the relationship factorial interlinkages as reported in the existing literature. The studies report the quantitative results between the relationship constructs in form of the effect sizes such as correlations, covariances, t and F statistics. The effect sizes are assimilated to develop a correlation table. The correlation table is then used as the basic input in the LISREL 8.3 program of the form 'observed variable path analysis' (Kelloway 1998) to identify the structures.

Meta-analysis Process

The procedure for the construction of that was followed has been outlined briefly in this section. Meta-analysis procedure given by Rosenthal (1991, p72) for comparing and combining the effect sizes of any number of independent studies was followed. Geyskens et al (1999) have also adopted similar procedure in the only other meta-analytical study of market relationships.

A series of conversions were undertaken to ensure that a statistically valid correlation table is prepared and also that the process of combining the correlations confirm to the acceptable practice. These conversions are:

1. For combining the size effects the r-values are converted to the z_r (Fishers z transform).
2. To calculate the pooled correlation for every pair of constructs in the RCM I use the procedure suggested by Rosenthal (1991).
3. Finally, The pooled z-transformed study effects then were reconverted to correlation coefficients using the conversion formula:

The final correlation table is given in exhibit 4.

Exhibit 4   *Meta-Analytical Correlation Table*

	LRC	Satisf-a-ction	Trust	Comm-itment	Conflict Resolution	Commu-nication	Power Equation	Coope-ration	Interep-endence
LRC	1.00								
Satisfaction	0.548 6 1237	1.00							
Trust	0.521 7 1949	0.643 4 937	1.00						
Commitment	0.117 3 915	0.362 4 715	0.488 6 2122	1.00					
Conflict Resolution	0.232 3 737	0.457 5 757	0.585 5 1372	0.236 4 1085	1.00				
Communication	0.370 4 1010	0.356 4 548	0.551 5 1557	0.579 5 1286	0.462 3 666	1.00			
Power Equation	0.285 2 1943	0.098 3 383	0.167 5 1910	0.170 2 760	0.107 3 562	0.178 3 1152	1.00		
Cooperation	0.378 3 1049	0.409 4 818	0.627 7 1596	0.445 4 1067	0.457 5 970	0.255 3 1152	0.269 2 462	1.00	
Interdependence	0.244 5 1493	0.153 4 562	0.164 7 1480	0.347 2 172	0.249 3 731	0.568 4 1356	0.178 3 1152	0.246 4 654	1.00

The table gives the pooled correlations r, number of studies k, and the total sample size N.

RCM Estimation: Model Analysis and Respecification

The correlation table is used as the input matrix for LISREL program. I use the procedure suggested as 'path analysis of observed variable' Jöreskog and Sörbom (1999). For this purpose I treat all the variables except interdependence as endogenous variables. The median cumulated sample size for individual pairs in the contributing studies (N=1030) is used for the SEM. I specify maximum likelihood estimation method with correlation matrix as the input data and the correlation matrix as the matrix to be analyzed.

❑ FINDINGS

The original design of RCM had 10 constructs. However, one of the constructs (adaptations) had to be dropped because of lack of empirical studies looking at adaptation and its effects on the other constructs of RCM. Therefore, out of the original 25 hypotheses, two hypotheses (H2d and H8) could not be tested. A summary of the findings from the LISEL estimation is presented in the exhibit 5.

Exhibit 5 *Theoretical RCM: Summary Findings*

Construct	Antecedents	Effect			Result
		β	T value	P	
LRC	Overall satisfaction	0.36	12.31	<0.01	H1a accepted
	Trust	0.28	8.05	<0.01	H1b accepted
	Power equation	0.02	0.58	>0.10	H1c rejected
	Interdependence	(γ)0.15	5.63	<0.01	H1d accepted
	Conflict resolution	0.03	1.03	>0.10	H1e rejected
	Communication	-0.05	-1.52	>0.10	H1f rejected
Overall Satisfaction	Interdependence	(γ)-0.04	-1.55	>0.10	H2a rejected
	Adaptation				H2b not tested
	Commitment	0.29	9.96	<0.01	H2c accepted
	Conflict resolution	0.40	14.95	<0.01	H2d accepted
Trust	Communication	0.54	20.73	<0.01	H3a accepted
	Power equation	0.07	2.80	<0.01	H3b accepted
Commitment	Trust	0.34	10.69	<0.01	H4a accepted
	Interdependence	(γ) 0.23	9.66	<0.01	H4b accepted
	Conflict resolution	-0.23	-8.14	<0.01	H4c partially accepted (direction accepted, effect rejected)
	Power equation	0.02	0.75	>0.10	H4d rejected
	Communication	0.43	7.23	<0.01	H4e accepted
Positive functionality	Trust	0.47	14.56	<0.01	H5a accepted
in Conflict Resolution	Co-operation	0.18	5.39	<0.01	H5b accepted
	Power equation	-0.02	0.75	>0.10	H5c rejected
Communication	Interdependence	(γ) 0.25	8.44	<0.01	H6 accepted
Balanced Power	Interdependence	(γ) 0.18	5.80	<0.01	H7 accepted
Equation					
Adaptation	Interdependence				H8 not tested
Co-operation	Commitment	0.10	3.38	<0.01	H9a accepted
	Trust	0.42	15.19	<0.01	H9b accepted
	Communication	0.28	8.96	<0.01	H9c accepted

I use the criteria suggested by Jöreskog and Sörbom (1999) for evaluating the adequacy of the assumed model. The overall goodness-of-fit measures suggest a significant χ^2, good GFI (.93), poor AGFI (0.73), and poor NFI and NNFI (0.89 and 0.70). Though the significant χ^2 could be argued to be an imperfect measure of the goodness-of-fit as the sample size is considerably large N = 1030, Kelloway (1998), large χ^2/df (> 25) parameter supports the possibility of bad fit. Moreover difference between GFI and AGFI, poor NFI and NNFI suggests inclusion of insignificant parameters in the model (which is again supported by the standard error criterion) and low improvement of the model fit over the base line independence (or null) model. The residuals RMR and RMSEA again lie outside the acceptable range.

The modification indices given suggest that a linkage between trust and satisfaction (trust leading to satisfaction) could improve the model considerably. Also a link between power and cooperation is a source to improve the model.

Model Respecification

As the model fit parameters for the theoretical model suggested an average fit in the model. I use the modifications to respecify the model in an attempt to arrive at a better model specification.

Following changes is made in the respecified model:

1. $\beta_{15}, \beta_{16}, \beta_{17}, \beta_{47}, \beta_{57}$, and γ_{21} are dropped
2. Constructs 'power equation' and 'communication' are changed from endogenous constructs (which also meant that γ_{61} and γ_{71} are dropped)
3. Linkage between trust-commitment (β_{23}) and power-cooperation (γ_{61}) are added.

This model and the LISREL estimates are represented in the exhibit 6.

Exhibit 6   ***Best-fit RCM: Paths, Coefficients and Fit Parameters***

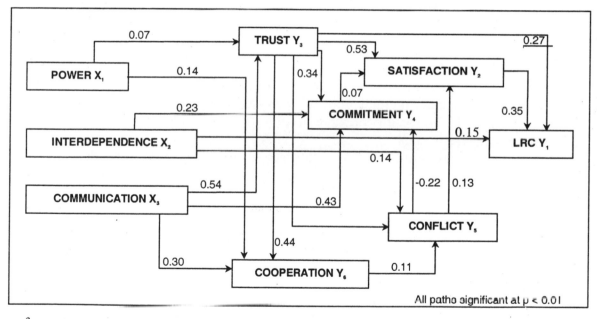

$\chi^2_{df=21} = 63.23$, RMSEA = 0.044, GFI = 0.99, AGFI = 0.97, NFI = 0.98

The respecified model is estimated using similar procedure discussed in previous section. The criteria for evaluating the model fit reveals a definite improvement from the initial model. The overall goodness-of-fit measures suggest a significant χ^2, excellent GFI (.99), AGFI (0.97), NFI (0.98), and NNFI (0.70). Though the χ^2 is still significant same logic as above could be given, however χ^2/df parameter (3.1) supports good fit. Low difference between GFI and AGFI (0.02), high NFI and NNFI suggests no insignificant parameters in the model (which is again supported by the standard error criterion) and significant improvement of the model fit over the base line independence (or null) model. PNFI and PGFI (0.57 and 0.46) shows considerable improve over the theoretical model value (0.32 and 0.27)

The residuals RMR and RMSEA lie within the acceptable range (significantly less than 0.05). The modification indices given by the program suggests no further possible improvement in the model.

Keeping these factors in mind, the respecified model is accepted as the best-fit model for relationship continuity (RCM).

□ DISCUSSION

The fit of data matrix to the specified model suggests that the use of LRC as a dependent variable to understand the structure of relationships is justified. While most of the significant results confirm to the hypothesized paths there are some findings worth highlighting here.

- It may be noted that the rejected hypotheses within the current study should not be seen as a result confounding the original study. It is merely a representation of the generalizability of the path across the study. One could possible explore the factors that lead to the rejection of the hypothesized paths. As I had noted earlier, some of the correlations that emerged from the meta-analysis were weak (but significant). Also there could be some contextual variables that could be introduced to improve the meta-analysis results.
- The best-fit model shows that only satisfaction, trust, and interdependence have a significant direct effect on LRC. This finding brings the key mediating variable for the understanding of relationship continuity and hence the relationship structure.
- The linkage between commitment and conflict (hypothesis H4C) comes out to be negative. It may be recalled that the functionality of conflict resolution was designed as positive. One could conclude that irrespective of the way a conflict is resolved, it would always have an adverse impact on the partners commitment to the relationship, and hence to the relationship continuity.
- Some of the smallest (but significant) coefficients that emerge from the estimation are power and commitment. This however does not mean that they are insignificant parameters.
- Power, Interdependence and Communication emerge as exogenous factors. This has important implications for the relationship management. They are the factors that could be controlled independently in the relationship. Since the effect of these factors on other relationship factors is positive, increasing the positive functionality of these constructs could lead to an improvement of relationship continuity

- Link between satisfaction and continuity emerges as significant and have high value. The linkage between satisfaction and continuity has been reported as ambiguous in the CS/D research. However, the linkage for relationship continuity and satisfaction could be taken as more definite for the business markets.
- The link between trust and satisfaction was not hypothesized in the initial model. Which means that this linkage was not studied in the context of business relationships. However, LISREL analysis clearly showed a strong linkage between the two.

Keeping in mind that this study started with an aim to isolate the generalizible component of the relationship research so far, conceptual contribution to the subject is significant. The clear linkages between satisfaction and trust, satisfaction and relationship continuity, and the isolation of exogenous variable would take the understanding of relationship structure and could initiate new research in the area.

For the managers, the RCM could prove as a starting point to look into the design and management of business relationships objectively. Besides, the identification of some independent variables that could help improving the continuity likelihood the relationships gives managers a freehand to manage relationships. Also it may be noted that the factors used in the RCM are all well accepted, developed, and tested psychometric scales. The managers could thus apply the model directly to real life relationships for better understanding and control of relationships.

I have been working on the model to take it further into being a part of a framework that could help evaluating business relationships. I am currently involved with some ongoing research that looks to dismantle the relationship into smaller units that could help understand the micro-dynamics of the relationships. I am looking to develop some integrating factors to take the understanding of relationships into the realm of business networks. Linking LRC to some objective performance measures like ROI, profitability, growth rate etc is the next step I have planned for the current research. Besides, the current meta-analysis at best can be seen as first attempt to generalize the current understanding of relationship structure. I would hope that this would initiate a rich debate and further understanding of the intriguing, exciting and crucial part of the business markets – relationships.

REFERENCES

Andersen, Erin and Barton Weitz (1989), 'Determinants of Continuity in Conventional Industrial Channel Dyads,' *Marketing Science*, Vol. 8, (Fall), 310-323.

Anderson, James C., (1995), ' Relationships in Business Markets: Exchange Episodes, Value Creation, and their Empirical Assessment', *Journal of the Academy of Marketing Science*, 23 (4), 346-350.

Brass, Daniel J., Kenneth D. Butterfield and Bruce C. Skaggs (1998), *Academy of Management Review*, Vol. 23, No. 1, 14-31.

Brown, Steven P. and Robert A. Peterson (1993), 'Antecedents and Consequences of Salesperson Job Satisfaction: Meta-Analysis and Assessment of Causal Effects,' *Journal of Marketing Research*, Vol. 30 (February), 63-77.

Celly, Kirti Sawhney and Gary L. Frazier (1996), 'Outcome-Based and Behavior-Based Coordination Efforts in Channel Relationships', *Journal of Marketing Research*, Vol. 33 (May), 200-210.

Crosby, Lawrence A., Kenneth R. Evans, and Deborah Cowles (1990), 'Relationship Quality in Services Selling: An Interpersonal Influence Perspective,' *Journal of Marketing*, 54 (July), 68-81.

Dwyer, Robert F., Paul H. Schurr, and Sejo Oh (1987), ' Developing Buyer-Seller Relationships', *Journal of Marketing*, 51, April, 11-27.

Evans Joel R., and Richard L. Laskin, (1994), 'The Relationship Marketing Process: A Conceptualization and Application', *Industrial Marketing Management*, 23, 439-452.

Ford, D., (1980), The development of Buyer-seller relationships in Industrial Markets', *European Journal of Marketing*, 14, 339-353.

_____, Håkan Håkansson and Jan Johanson (1985), 'How Do Companies Interact,' Industrial Marketing and Purchasing, 1, 1, 26-41.

Gassenheimer, Jule B., Franklin S Houston, and J Charles Davis (1998), 'The Role of Economic Value, Social Value, and Perceptions of Fairness in Interorganizational Relationships Retention Decisions', *Journal of the Academy of Marketing Science*, Vol. 26, Issue 4, 322-337.

Geyskens, Inge, Jan-Benedict E.M. Steenkamp, and Nirmalya Kumar (1999), A Meta-Analysis of Satisfaction in Marketing Channel Relationships', *Journal of Marketing Research*, Vol. 36 (May), 223-238.

Grönroos, C. (1989), 'Defining Marketing: A market-oriented Approach', *European Journal of Marketing*, Vol. 23, No. 1, 52-60

_____, (1995), 'Relationship Marketing: The Strategy Continuum', *Journal of the Academy of Marketing Science*, 23 (4), 252-254.

Morgan, Robert and Shelby Hunt (1994), 'The Commitment-Trust Theory of Relationship Marketing', *Journal of Marketing*, 58 (July), 20-38.

Noordewier, Thomas G., George John, and John R. Nevin (1990), 'Performance Outcomes of Purchasing Arrangements in Industrial Buyer-Vendor Relationships', *Journal of Marketing*, Vol. 54 (October), 80-93.

Parasuraman, A., Leonard Berry, and Valarie Zeithaml (1985), 'A Model of Service Quality and its Implications for Future Research,' *Journal of Marketing*, Fall, 41-50.

Seth, Jagdish N. and Atul Parvatiyar (1995a), 'Relationship Marketing in Consumer Markets: Antecedents and Consequences,' *Journal of the Academy of Marketing Science*, 23 (4), 255-271.

_____ and Atul Parvatiyar (1995b), 'The Evolution of Relationship Marketing,' *International Business Review*, 397-418.

Siguaw, Judy A., Penny M. Simpson, and Thomas L. Baker (1998), 'Effects of Supplier Market Orientation on Distributor Market Orientation and the Channel Relationship: The Distributor Perspective,' *Journal of Marketing*, Vol. 62 (July), 99-111.

Smith, J. Brock and Donald W. Barclay (1997), 'The Effectiveness of Organizational Differences and Trust on the Effectiveness of Selling Partner Relationships', *Journal of Marketing*, Vol. 61 (January), 3-21.

Thibaut, John W. and Harold H. Kelly (1959), The Social Psychology of Groups, John Wiley and Sons.

Wilson, David T. (1995), 'An Integrated Model of Buyer-Seller Relationships', *Journal of the Academy of Marketing Science*, 23 (4), 335-345.

Regain Management: Issues and Strategies

■ **Kallol Bose and Harvir S Bansal**

Abstract

Marketers know that retaining customers, not merely acquiring is crucial for service firms. Customer research shows that service quality, relationship building, and overall service satisfaction can improve business relation with consumers. As competition is fierce in the services sector customer satisfaction is becoming increasingly important. Organizations have to develop innovative measures to address their present customers, acquire new ones and at the same time initiate procedures to win back lost customers. Regain management is aimed at winning back customers who have either given notice to terminate the relationship or whose relationship has already ended. This paper focuses on issues and strategies concerning an organization for profitable acquisition of their lost customer segments. For the purposes of this study, we analyze services that are provided at an arm's length as well as those where exists a personal interaction between the service provider and the customer.

Key Words: Service Quality, Relationship Building, Regain Management

□ INTRODUCTION

Service markets are faced with increasing competition and at the same time decreasing customer loyalty. To succeed in these markets, service providers have to address not only prospective and existing customers but also lost customers as a distinct target group for their customer management efforts. This regaining strategy—which so far has been neglected almost completely—is a specific area of customer management and is distinct from retention management (Stauss and Friege, 1999.)

In order to deal effectively with their existing customer base, many organizations have embraced retention management. These programs are primarily aimed at stemming the erosion of their existing customer base. On the other hand, regain management addresses the issues and strategies that an organization should entail in order to attract lost customers.

□ BACKGROUND

Service marketers know that "having customers, not merely acquiring customers, is crucial for service firms" (Berry, 1980). In terms of having customers, research shows that service quality (Bitner 1990; Boulding et al., 1993), relationship quality (Crosby, Evans, and Cowles, 1990; Crosby and Stephens, 1987), and overall service satisfaction (Cronin and Taylor, 1992) can improve customers' intentions to stay with a firm. But what can be done to avoid losing customers? What actions of service firms, or their employees, cause customers to switch from one service provider to another.

The answers to these questions are important to both executives of service firms and service marketing scholars. Service firm executives are concerned about the negative effects of customer switching on market share and profitability (Rust and Zahorik, 1993). In the simplest sense switching, costs a service firm the customers' future revenue stream. First, because continuing customers increase their spending at an increasing rate, purchase at full margin rather than at discount prices, and create operating efficiencies for service firms (Reicheld and Sasser, 1990), the loss of continuing service customers is a loss from the high margin sector of the customer base. Second, the costs associated with acquiring new customers are incurred: New account setup, credit searches, and advertising and promotional expenses can add up to five times the costs of efforts that might have enabled the firm to retain a customer (Peters, 1988). According to Brown, Churchill, and Peter (1985), "The cost of acquiring a new customer is 9 to 12 times that of holding on to an existing customer."

In order to address the switching behaviors companies have started to use what is known as relationship marketing to curb customer dissatisfaction and increase consumer loyalty. The term "relationship marketing" has become a popular concept among the practitioners of marketing as well as academics during the past few years and is becoming more important in today's customer driven market place.

In developing, implementing and evaluating relationship-marketing programs, marketers have to know the nature and strength of their relations with consumers in order to improve the strength of those relationships. By analyzing relationships, it is possible to distinguish several components, which build a relationship. "Relationship marketing (RM) is marketing seen as relationships, networks and interaction" (Gummesson, 1995.)

The concept of relationship implies at least two essential conditions. First, a relationship is a mutually rewarding connection between the provider and the customer, which is to say that both parties expect to obtain benefits from the contact. Second, the parties have some sort of commitment to the relationship over time, and they are therefore willing to make adaptations in the routines with which the exchange situations deal (Ford, 1980.)

□ REGAIN MANAGEMENT

With increasing competitiveness and at the same time decreasing customer loyalty in the service markets, service providers have to address not only prospective and existing customers but also lost customers as a third distinct target group for their customer management initiatives. "Regain Management" is aimed at winning back customers who have either given notice to terminate the business relationship or whose relationship has already ended. Regain management offers service providers a profitable customer market by adopting a specific management process consisting of analysis, actions, and controlling.

Although achievable in theory, retention management will in reality never economically avoid all customer defection. Therefore, it seems reasonable to complete this management approach with a customer-regaining strategy that aim at rebuilding the relationship with customers' who have explicitly quit the business relationship. This regaining strategy, which so far has been neglected, is a specific area of customer management and can clearly be differentiated from traditional recruitment and retention management (Stauss, and Friege, 1999). Whereas traditional recruitment is directed towards prospects who lack experience with the service offered and whose purchasing behavior is relatively unknown, regain management aims at former customers who have experience with the service and a purchasing history with the service provider. Thus in traditional recruiting, segmentation is solely based on external data and communication is directed mainly one way toward the prospect. With regain management, marketing can rely on a proprietary database for segmentation and communication, more often initiated by the expired customer.

☐ CONSUMER LIFE TIME VALUE

Quantifying the "value" of customers is absolutely essential in regain management. Without knowing the value of the customer, it is difficult to know how much the company should spend in order to reacquire the client. This is true whether ones sales are through the mail order channel, the retail channel or through a sales force. Calculating LifeTime Value (LTV) assists a company in a variety of applications for product development, media selection and more.

Essentially, LTV is the difference between "customer marketing" (relational marketing) and "product marketing". It is based on an inflexible rule that achieved general recognition and acceptance among those who embraced the direct marketing concepts years ago. By logical extension, therefore, the more sales a company makes to its original customers, the higher would be the profit margins from those individual sales. In fact, the percentage of profit a company makes from its continued sales to its own customer base is consistently higher than the profit made on the original sale. Each of the customers then delivers an income stream and the stream of profit far exceeds the value of the original purchase. Income streams contribute cash flows in terms of years for any single product.

For example, in the insurance industry, rates and acquisition allowances are normally determined by examining assumptions about income and expenses including the impact of persistency over a relatively long period of time (10 to 20) years. But the product acquisition allowance is assigned to an agent when he/she goes to market, for that one product. The product acquisition allowance is treated as if it is the only product the agent would sell to the policyholder. A policy owner's LifeTime Value is defined as the present value of projected contributions expected from the policyholder during the coming years towards the net income of the organization. The company's profitability, in the long term, would be the result of two factors, the difference between the acquisition allowance developed using policy owner LifeTime Value, and policy owner acquisition cost. Secondly, the number of policy owners that can be acquired at an acceptable investment cost, determined by their LifeTime Value, expands the company's policy owner base.

Thus we find that it is of utmost importance that organizations use appropriate measures to assess their customers' value. It is a general approximation that the top 20 per cent customers produce 80 per cent of the sales in an organization. Therefore it becomes evident that specific customers need to be identified and regaining techniques should be focussed towards them.

□ CLASSIFICATION OF SERVICES

The diversity of the service sector makes it difficult to come up with managerial useful generalizations concerning marketing practices in service organizations. The paper tries to establish a tangible relationship between the practices prevalent pertaining to regain management varying across different service classifications.

A service has been described as a "deed, act or performance" (Berry, 1980.) Two fundamental issues are at whom (or what) is the act directed, and how is it directed. For the purpose of this study we would look into service classifications whereby the customer and service provider deals at an arms' length and where there is a physical interaction between the two in regards to the delivery of the service. We suggest a synthesis between the two matrices with the extent of customer contact required during service delivery, (Chase, 1978) and the service delivery process advocated by Lovelock (1980.) The paper will try to identify the different strategies that a service provider would have for implementing regain management. The study would cross-tabulate services and competition across the different nature of the service provider, those services provided at an arm length, and those where there is physical interaction between the customer and the service provider.

In addition to the above classification, this study also looks at the reasons for customer defections. We label them "push" and "pull" factors depending on whether the customer left the service provider as a result of a core service failure, or as a result of some competitive activity. Hence, a 2X2 framework is used to identify various regain strategies.

□ REGAIN STRATEGIES

This paper will point out three relevant strategies that a service provider could look into in order to regain lost customers; customization, differentiation, and "wow" strategy.

Customization

Once the customer has been lost the company should try to re-establish contact. Since the company believes that it would be advantageous to regain the customer and would go through the process of getting back this customer, hence he/she lies within the 20:80 rule. With advent of technology and information the company has already the requisite information to develop an appropriate profile of the customer. This profile would help the organization with information pertaining to the client's purchasing patterns and usage of the service, which in turn help the organization to design more suitable and customized service bundles to offer. The company could then go forward and make a proposal to its former customer to reconsider their offer. The customization strategy would be operational for both the "push" and "pull" factors.

In today's world of customer orientation, the company realizes the bargaining power of the consumer. Customization is an extension of one-to-one marketing where customers are treated as individuals and not as account numbers. Customization would provide the latitude that the customer would enjoy and therefore feel empowered to choose and customize its options. It could be advocated that such a strategy would have a larger bearing on services operated at an arm's length. Services provided at arm's length are usually an add-on to the convenience aspect. The value added is the operational ease between the organization and its customer. Thus additional customization would be an extension of the convenience aspect. The latitude would provide the customer with a sense of empowerment and he/she would feel associated with the delivery of the ultimate service. Moreover, the actions would prove that the organization recognizes its top customers and is ready to alter its offerings to facilitate its valuable clients.

Differentiation Strategy

Differentiation is the ability to provide unique and superior value to the consumer in terms of service quality, special features, or after-sales services. Differentiation allows a firm to command a premium price or premium market position, which leads to higher profitability. As customers are segmented, hence it is of utmost important that different segments should be addressed and dealt with accordingly. For the purposes of this paper we would only focus on those customers who have a high LTV value i.e. 20:80 rule. A firm creates value for its consumers if it lowers its buyers' cost or raises the buyer's performance in ways that the buyer cannot match by purchasing from a competitor. We would like to stretch this phenomenon a little further by stating that the company can use differentiation in order to attract back the lost customers.

The lost customer would be segmented differently from the existing customer base and the company could provide additional features and benefits to win them back. It would be an act of recognizing the fact that these customers were invited back and hence rendered special privileges. Such a strategy could be exclusively useful when the consumer switches due to the "push" syndrome.

Furthermore, we could expand the differentiation strategy and use gastronomy and formula strategy (Horovitz, 1990) to address the different customer segments depending on the nature of the industry and the services they provide. Differentiation would act as the base strategy and gastronomy and formula strategy would be used as effective tools to bring out the differentiation phenomenon.

Gastronomy strategy (Horovitz, 1990) targets customers who seek highly personalized service a great deal of interaction, and long contact. Such a strategy would be focused at high-end services and at a limited audience. It would mainly dwell in the service classification where the customers are in close contact with their service providers. For example in the airline industry different classes of travelers are treated according to their ticket status. In close contact services, it is visibly possible to differentiate services and address the particular attributes that the consumers are seeking. Similarly as seen in customization strategy the consumers would be segregated and dealt with personally. Intuitively, it may not seem to be a profitable mode of approach but we should remember that the target audience is the top 20 % of the customer base, which usually accounts for 80% of the total sales. Pampering such a strata of consumer segment would be worthwhile in the future. It should be noted that information plays a huge role in deciding what sort to strategy to be used while reaching a lost customer. The consumer profile generated would help the organization to correctly analyze what are the attributes that the customer wishes to be addressed. Since these customers have already defected, hence the company may also have sufficient leads about the cause of defection.

Formula strategy (Horovitz, 1990) refers to targeting a larger market than gastronomy strategy while still offering personalized services. Customers in this quadrant values quality service at reasonable prices. Hence industries operating in this domain should try to marry service customization with appropriate pricing. The strategies used would depend on the consumer's perception towards the service. As different consumers value different attributes, the strategies should be in line with their preferences. The point of focus should be that the organization accepts the value of the lost customer and has developed means to regain them. And so the strategies are altered according to the industry classification and customer perception.

"WoW" Syndrome

When a customer orders something and it is delivered incorrectly, the correct response when confronted is not an excuse. The correct response would be an apology, followed by what would be done and when, as well as a bonus. For example, a client checks into a hotel and his/her room isn't ready. The clerk could respond by "You're in luck! Your room isn't ready. That means you get to eat breakfast "on us" and use our business center for free!" The company should try to provide a little more, in excess to what the customer may have initially expected. The element of surprise is to shock the customer in a pleasant way.

One benefit of the use of this particular plus is the difference between a satisfied and a loyal customer (Gitomer, 1998). Not only is the customer satisfied, s/he is more likely to be loyal under the "wow" syndrome. Another benefit is the difference between a positive and a negative story retold. It is suggested that a higher incidence of positive world of mouth is likely to emanate as a result of this particular approach.

□ ADDITIONAL FACTORS INFLUENCING CUSTOMER REGAIN

Factors such as consistency of the services, employee empowerment in decision-making, along with service guarantees, will further strengthen the implementation of the above strategies. Though it will depend largely on the nature of the reasons influencing the switching behavior, it is felt that the application of all of the above criteria can only enhance the level of customer satisfaction.

An overview of the proposed strategies can be found in Figure 1.

	Regaining Strategies for Service at Arm's Length	Regaining Strategies for Service with Physical Interaction

Switching influenced by core service failure	• Customization of services.
	• Differentiation
	  ■ Formula strategy
	• Consistency.
	• "Wow" syndrome.
	• Employee empowerment
		• Differentiation.
		  ■ Gastronomy strategy.
		  ■ Formula strategy.
		• Consistency. "Wow" syndrome.
		• Employee empowerment

Switching influenced by the competition	• Customization of services.
	• Differentiation.
	  ■ Formula strategy
	• Consistency.
	• "Wow" syndrome.
	• Guaranteed selling
		• Differentiation.
		  ■ Gastronomy strategy.
		  ■ Formula strategy.
		• Consistency.
		• "Wow" syndrome.
		• Guaranteed selling.

Fig. 1 *An Overview of Regaining Strategies*

The preceding diagram encompasses the different relevant strategies for the two types of service classifications in relation to the switching behaviors of the consumer. We find that there is some uniformity of the service strategies among the four quadrants, such as the formula strategy, "wow" syndrome, and consistency of the service provided. However certain strategies are more in-tuned with relevant service classifications when observed in reference to the "push" or "pull" syndrome.

As we run across services at arm's length, we find that customization of services is the most important factor across the two switching determinants. Similarly we see that across services requiring personal contact gastronomy takes on more relevance. Then as we consider switching behaviors, we find that if the customer has switched due to a core service failure, employee empowerment is the more relevant among the various criteria. However when switching is influenced by the competitor, guaranteed selling becomes the dominant factor.

□ CONCLUSION

The paper so far has taken a generic approach to address issues and strategies in regain management. We feel that there is scope for further research in what is a relatively new area of service marketing. The following are the areas where more industry specific research can reap great benefits.

- Primary data collection to study switching behaviors among customers.
- Examination of other classifications of services offered.
- Evaluation of the reactions of lost customers to various ways of communications and various regain offers.

REFERENCES

Berry, L. L., (1980), 'Services Marketing is Different', *Business* Vol. 30, pp. 25.

Bitner, M. J., (1990), 'Evaluating Service Encounters The Effects of Physical Surroundings and Employee Responses', Journal *of Marketing*, Vol. 54, pp. 69-82.

Boulding, W., Kalra, A., Staelin, R., Zeithaml, V. A., (1993), 'A Dynamic Process Model of Service Quality; From Expectations to Behavioral Intentions', *Journal of Marketing Research*, Vol. 30, pp. 7-27.

Brown, T. J., Churchill, G. A., Peter, P., (1993), 'Improving the Measurement of Service Quality', *Journal of Retailing*, Vol. 69, pp. 127-139.

Chase, R. B., (1978), 'Where does the Customer Fit in a Service Operation?', *Harvard Business Review*. Vol. 56, pp. 37-42.

Cronin, J. J., Jr., Taylor, S. A., (1992), 'Measuring Service Quality: A Reexamination and Extension', *Journal of Marketing*, Vol. 56, pp. 55-68.

Crosby, L. A., Evans, K. R., Cowles, D., (1990), 'Relationship Quality in Services Selling; An Interpersonal Influence Perspective', *Journal of Marketing*, Vol. 54, pp. 68-81.

Ford, (1980), 'The Development of Buyer-Seller Relationships in Industrial Markets', *European Journal of Marketing*, Vol. 23, No. 1, pp. 52-60.

Gitomer, J., (1998), 'Sales Secrets: Made a Mistake? How to Win Back Your Customers', *http://www.bizjournals.com/atlanta/stories/1998/09/28/smallb4.html*

Gummesson, E., (1995), *Relationsmarknadsforing: Frn4p till 30R (Relationship Marketing: From 4Ps to 30Rs.)* Liber Hermods, Malmo.

Horovitz, J., (1990), *Winning Ways- Achieving Zero Defect Service,* Portland, Productivity Press.

Lovelock, C., (1980), 'Towards a Classification of Services', *American Marketing Association*, pp. 72-76.

Reicheld, F. F., and Sasser, W. E., Jr., (1990), 'Zero Defection: Quality Comes to Services', *Harvard Business Review,* Vol. 68, pp. 105-111.

Rust, R. T., and Zahorik, A. J., (1993), 'Customer Satisfaction, Customer Retention, and Market Share', *Journal of Retailing*, Vol. 69, pp. 193-215.

Stauss, B., and Friege, C., (1999), 'Regaining Service Customers', *Journal of Service Research*, Vol. 1, No. 4, pp. 347.

Stephens, N., (1987), 'Effects of Relationship Marketing on Satisfaction, Retention, and Prices in the Life Insurance Industry', *Journal of Marketing Research,* Vol. 24, pp. 404-411.

Chapter 7

Winning Markets through Effective Customer Relationship Management

■ **B M GHODESWAR**

Abstract

Information technology and internet are rapidly changing the face of what is possible in customer contact, care, and insight. Moreover, customer expectations for quality, service, and value are rising continually. Keeping this in mind, successful companies are now gearing to organize their businesses around the types of customers they serve rather than organizing their businesses along the product lines or geographic business units. Today, with ever-increasing focus on customers, companies are taking a process-oriented approach to customer relationship management. This paper focusses on a framework in designing a strategy for effective customer relationship management and highlights the important elements viz. Developing Customer Insight, Use of Technology in CRM, Customer Contact, Personalizing Customer Interaction, and Achieving Superior Customer Experience.

Key Words: *Customer Contact, Insight, Customer Interaction, Customer Experience.*

◻ INTRODUCTION

In today's competitive world, achieving total customer satisfaction/delighting the customer is a key element in setting the business goals and objectives of the corporate. Improving performance in service delivery and responsiveness to the customers has become a source of competitive advantage in many industry and service sectors. Customer Relationship Management is being increasingly used to identify, attract, and retain most valuable customers that help businesses to sustain profitable growth. Successful companies are achieving long term performance in customer relationship management by gaining deep insights about their customers which helps them design product/service offerings that match or exceed the customer expectations which in turn help in building customer trust and gain loyalty.

The rapid growth of internet based technologies is making a major impact on managing customer relationships where companies are establishing one-to-one customer relationships online. Internet is getting increasingly used by companies as electronic channel to market, for selling, and for servicing the customers, either directly or in combination with traditional channel intermediaries. It also helps businesses to offer personalized solutions. Besides, it is serving as a catalyst in raising expectations about the customer experience.

☐ LITERATURE REVIEW

In today's new world, imagination, experimentation, and agility are the essential catalysts for wealth creation. In concept and in reality, resource attraction is well tuned to the new world of self-organisation, spontaneity, and speed (Hamel, 1999). In this high-tech, rapidly changing world, people have become accustomed to the "next generation" of products. It is not only anticipated, but also expected. Rather than try to be better, companies need to try to be next (Trout and Rivkin, 2000).

Companies have now to focus more on offering customized solutions, tailored customer experiences across the range of new as well as traditional channels including web, the internet, advanced telephone systems, handheld digital appliances, interactive TVs, self-service kiosks, smart cards, fax, e-mail, etc. and a whole host of emerging technologies. All of these customer-facing technologies are supported, behind the scenes, by integrated customer databases, call centers, streamlined work flows, and secure transactional systems. A successful strategy involves building and sustaining business relationships with customers electronically (Seybold, 1998). Digital Technology allows companies to market products and services more effectively. A company can serve the needs of its customers better by using a database to track their preferences and buying patterns; communicate with customers around the world much faster and more easily using e-mail; and develop sales leads more effectively (Bishop, 1998).

Driven by short cycle times, increased pressure to cut costs and to increase efficiency and customer orientation, today's organizations are organized around business processes to a greater extent than ever before. Companies are focussing themselves more and more on their activities where they can differentiate themselves in the market. (Hiles and Barnes, 1999). It is offerings, not firms, which fit into customers' value creation and compete with each other for their money (Norman and Ramirez, 1998).

A study conducted by Andersen Consulting in conjunction with the EIU found that businesses are intensifying their focus on customers and are taking a more process-oriented approach to customer relationship management. Key findings of the study are:
(a) the number of businesses citing customer retention as a critically important measure in the next five years has jumped to nearly 60%, as companies shift their focus from attracting new customers to retaining their more profitable ones;
(b) by 2002, 83% of companies expect to have customer data warehouses, up from about 40% today; and

(c) companies predict their use of the Internet to collect customer data will surge 430% by 2002.

□ METHODOLOGY

This paper presents a conceptual framework based on the new paradigm by which Customer Relationship Management research and applications might be expanded to provide better and more useful information in effectively managing customer relationships. This framework has been developed on the basis of the work of various researchers and practitioners in the field of customer relationship management and other related areas of marketing and business operations, and author's conceptualization. Key variables were identified from the existing literature and on the basis of informal interaction with executives.

□ CUSTOMER RELATIONSHIP MANAGEMENT—A FRAMEWORK

Customer relationship management (CRM) is comprehensive sales and marketing approach to building long term customer relationships and improving business performance.

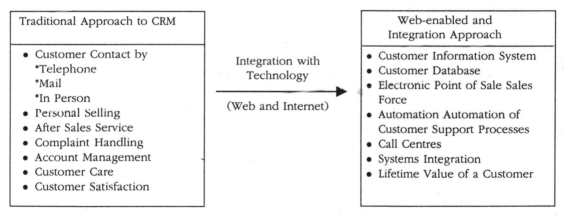

Fig. 1 *Customer Relationship—A Technology Driven Approach*

A framework in designing a strategy for effective customer relationship management is discussed below and highlights the important elements viz. Developing Customer Insight, Use of Technology in CRM, Customer Contact, Personalizing Customer Interaction, and Achieving Superior Customer Experience.

□ DEVELOPING CUSTOMER INSIGHT

Companies gather information from all points of interactions with the customers and make available to everyone within the organisation. This function is facilitated by the customer database.

Customer Database

A good customer information system should consists of a regular flow of information, systematic collection of information that is properly evaluated and compared against different points in time, and it has sufficient depth to understand the customers and accurately anticipate their behavioral patterns in future. The customer database helps the company to plan, implement, and monitor customer contact. Customer relationships are increasingly sustained by information systems. Companies are increasingly adding data from a variety of sources to their databases. Customer data strategy should focus on processes to manage customer acquisition, retention, and development.

Current spread of information in the company over many different databases is often incompatible and therefore has to focus on data warehousing to integrate them into one analyzable data set. Few businesses have the luxury of defining their customer data requirements from the beginning. As customers' needs and behaviour change and marketing strategies respond, new datasets are required. Each dataset collected will therefore need to be developed dynamically. Some data will cease to be relevant, other data will need to be added (Gamble, Stone and Woodcock, 1999).

◻ **USE OF TECHNOLOGY IN CRM**

The application of technology is the most exciting, fastest growing, and changing the way customers get information about products and services. Technology includes all of the equipment, software, and communication links that organizations use to enable or improve their processes, including everything from simple overhead transparency projectors to laptop computers, from fax machines to e-mail, from audiocassette and videocassette players to cellular phones and voice mail (Stowell, 1997). The most widely used tools are explained below.

Electronic Point of Sale (EPOS)

The main benefit of EPOS and retail scanner systems is the amount of timely and accurate information they deliver. Advances in the technology have significantly aided the scope for data analysis. In addition to the original scanner-related data on sales rate, stock levels, stock turn, price and margin, retailers now have information about the demographics, socio-economic and lifestyle characteristics of consumers. They can, in addition, assess the impact of a whole host of variables – price, promotion, advertising, position in store, shelf position, number of facings, and so on. This information drives their choice of product mix, allocation of shelf space and promotional tactics. EPOS has certainly changed the relationship between buyer and seller (Shipley and Palmer, 1997).

Sales Force Automation

These systems help in automating and optimizing sales processes to shorten the sales cycle and increase sales productivity. They enable the company to track and manage all qualified leads, contacts, and opportunities throughout the sales cycle including customer support. They improve the effectiveness of marketing communications programmes for generating quality leads as well as greater accuracy in sales forecasting. The Internet can be used by the company in imparting proper training to its sales force. In-depth product information, specialized databases of solutions, sales force support queries, and a set of internal information on the Internet can improve the productivity of the sales force.

Customer Service Helpdesk

These applications help the company in automating the customer support processes, which enable it to deliver high quality service to their customers. Such software helps in logging the information about customer problems, enquiries, and suggestions, etc. It also helps in directing these queries to appropriate employees within the company. It maintains information regarding status of customer enquiries and stores all support calls and related communications to final resolution, continually updating the database accordingly. With an automated customer service, a company can reduce the costs of maintaining its customer service department while at the same time improving the level and quality of customer service. Customer service using the web provides more information and tools in the hands of customers, which enhances customer benefits by allowing them to learn more about the product and improving their skills in using the product.

Call Centres

Call Centre helps in automating the operations of inbound and outbound calls generated between company and its customers. These solutions integrate the voice switch of automated telephone systems (e.g. EPABX) with an agent host software allowing for automatic call routing to agents, auto display of relevant customer data, predictive dialing, self service Interactive Voice Response systems, etc. These systems are useful in high volume segments like banking, telecom and hospitality. Today, more innovative channels of interacting with customers are emerging as a result of new technology, such as global telephone based call centers and the internet. Companies are now focussing to offer solutions that leverage the internet in building comprehensive CRM systems allowing them to handle customer interactions in all forms.

Systems Integration

While CRM solutions are front-office automation solutions, ERP is back-office automation solution. An ERP helps in automating business functions of production, finance, inventory, order fulfillment and human resource giving an integrated view of business, where as CRM automates the relationship with a customer covering contact and opportunity management, marketing and product knowledge, sales force management, sales forecasting, customer order processing and fulfillment, delivery, installation, pre-sale and post-sale services and complaint handling by providing an integrated view of the customer. It is necessary that the two systems integrate with each other and complement information as well as business workflow. Therefore, CRM and ERP are complementary. This integration of CRM with ERP will help companies to provide faster customer service through an enabled network, which can direct all customer queries and issues through appropriate channels to the right place for speedy resolution. This will help the company in tracking and correcting the product problems reported by customers by feeding this information into the R&D operations via ERP.

"Choiceboards" are interactive, on-line systems that allow individual customers to design their own products by choosing from a menu of attributes, components, prices, and delivery options. The customers' selections send signals to the supplier's manufacturing system that set in motion the wheels of procurement, assembly, and delivery. The role of the customer in this system shifts from passive recipient to active designer (Slywotzky, 2000). Every business, no matter how much it relies on indirect sales channels, now has the opportunity to begin electronically linking its channel partners with its end customers and participating in the dialogue between them (Seybold, 1998).

❏ CUSTOMER CONTACT

Internet is helping companies in improving communication with consumers. Consumers have been increasingly engaging themselves in an active and explicit dialogue with manufacturers of products and services. Individual consumers can address and learn about businesses either on their own or through the collective knowledge of other customers (Prahalad and Ramaswamy, 2000).

Usenet groups and chat discussions allow feedback and targeted e-mail surveys can pinpoint problem areas and options that will have high benefits from improvement. Collaborative design with suppliers allows a much faster turnaround of new designs. This causes the earlier introduction of products, generating much higher satisfaction and feelings of getting state-of-the art products. The connecting of supplier–manufacturer Intranets into functioning extranets has been notably successful (Hanson, 2000).

❏ PERSONALISING CUSTOMER INTERACTION

The modern devices and technology tools are designed to help consumers make informed purchasing decisions.

Customer Communities

Customers in the new economy are finding it easier to form, on their own, self-selecting virtual communities. On-line customer communities can be quite tightly knit. Internet chat rooms are easy to start up, join, and participate in. Chat rooms accommodate a wide range of personalities—many of them assumed ones. Customer communities can exercise a powerful influence on the market. The power of such communities derives in large measure from the speed with which they can be mobilized. Word spreads so fast on the internet that people now refer to word of mouth as "virtual marketing" (Prahalad and Ramaswamy, 2000).

Personalization

Personalization is a special form of product differentiation. It transforms a standard product or service into a specialized solution for an individual. It changes product design from an inherent compromise to a process of deciding what features would benefit a specific individual. Combined with innovative distribution, it can do a better job of matching consumer tastes without the waste of current approach. Online choice assistance takes a set of products, tries to determine an individual's tastes and needs, and makes a recommendation. If this recommendation is accurate and trusted, it creates value and loyalty (Hanson, 2000). In other words, personalization helps the customers in becoming the co-creators of the content of their experiences.

◻ ACHIEVING SUPERIOR CUSTOMER EXPERIENCE

Customer relationship management is about managing customer life cycle through all points of customer contacts ensuring that every interaction leads to a value addition in relationship. This is made possible through each contact point being empowered with the knowledge, capable of being responsive to customer needs, and to offer superior experience to the customer.

Experiences occur as a result of encountering, undergoing, or living through situations. They are triggered stimulations to the senses, the heart, and the mind. Experiences also connect the company and the brand to the customer's lifestyle and place individual customer actions and the purchase occasion in a broader social context. In sum, experiences provide sensory, emotional, cognitive, behavioural, and relational values that replace functional values (Schmitt, 1999). A good customer experience delivers service, product—and peace of mind. Website applications help customers to check the status of their orders. Customers like to be able to check on the status of orders placed, service requests submitted, payments sent, and billing adjustments made. Sometimes they want to check on the availability of items in inventory (Seybold, 1998). Consumers' experiences of a buying and using a product or service depend on their perceptions about actual performance of that product or service.

◻ CONCLUSION

Customer relationship management is a comprehensive sales and marketing approach to building long term customer relationship and improving business performance. Gathering all the information about customers helps the company to develop customer insight and enhance customer interaction. Technology tools and systems such as customer database, electronic point of sale, sales force automation, customer service helpdesk, call center, etc. help in establishing customer relationship. Also, integration of these CRM systems with back-end systems such as ERP helps in offering solutions to the customers' problems with improved speed of response and quality of service. Effective implementation and monitoring of these approaches result in providing superior experience to the customers and help gain their loyalty in long term.

REFERENCES

Bishop, Bill (1998), *Strategic Marketing for the Digital Age*, American Marketing Association, NTC Business Books.

Gamble, Paul R., Stone, Merlin, and Woodcock, Neil (1999), *Up Close and Personal*, Kogan Page.

Hamel, Gary (1999) 'Bringing Silicon Valley Inside', *Harvard Business Review*, September-October 1999, p.83.

Hanson, Ward (2000), *Principles of Internet Marketing*, South-Western College.

Hiles, Andrew and Barnes, Peter (1999), *The Definitive Handbook of Business Continuity Management*, John Wiley & Sons.

Norman, Richard and Ramirez, Rafael (1998), *Designing Interactive Strategy from Value Chain to Value Constellations*, John Wiley & Sons, p. 74.

Prahalad, C. K. and Ramaswamy, Venkatram (2000), 'Co-opting Customer Competence', *Harvard Business Review*, January-February 2000, pp. 79-87.

Schmitt, Bernd, H (1999), *Experiential Marketing*, The Free Press, p. 25.

Seybold, Patricia, B (1998), *Customers Com: How to Create a Profitable Business Strategy for the Internet and Beyond*, New York Times Business.

Shipley, David and Palmer, Roger (1997), Selling to and Managing Key Accounts, *The CIM Handbook of Selling and Sales Strategy*, ed. By David Jobber, Butterworth- Heinemann, p.111.

Slywotzky, Adrian J. (2000), The Age of the Choiceboard, *Harvard Business Review*, January-February 2000, p.40.

Stowell, Daniel M. (1997), *Sales and Marketing, and Continuous Improvement*, Jossey-Bass Publishers, San Francisco, p.214.

Trout, Jack and Rivkin, Steve (2000), *Differentiate or Die*, John Wiley & Sons, p. 155.

Section II

Technological Tools for CRM

Chapter 8

Data Mining for CRM: Some Relevant Issues

■ **Rajesh Natarajan and B Shekar**

Abstract

Data mining, the process of discovering implicit and hidden patterns in data, is one of the most important back end processes. It provides relevant intelligence to the CRM initiative. Depending on the level at which we are mining, we divide data mining operations into two categories: The aggregate or the macro level, wherein, without looking at any customer in particular, we try to find general customer behaviour, trends and preferences from a large database such as market basket purchases from a retail store. The second is the individual or the micro level wherein we attempt tracking a particular customer and try to further the relationship by acting in a timely way to his/her choice and preferences. We identify relevant issues for each category. Next, we discuss the basic tasks relevant to CRM such as segmentation, classification, regression, deviation detection and link analysis. We then discuss some data mining tools that undertake the above operations. Data mining comes out as an important CRM enabler.

Key Words: *Data mining, Aggregate level, Individual level, Data Mining Tasks, Data Mining tools*

□ INTRODUCTION

Advances in information technology, networking, and manufacturing technologies have helped companies to quickly match competition. As a result, product quality and cost are no longer significant competitive advantages. Therefore, today, firms are adopting a more customer-centric approach to leverage on their real competitive advantage i.e. their customers. Customer Relationship Management (CRM) is a process that aims at maximizing customer satisfaction by building mutually beneficial long-term relationships with customers. It may employ technology to share relevant information about a customer's interaction throughout the firm. This enables all employees to work like teams while dealing with their customers. Knowledge discovery in databases or data mining as it is more popularly known is "the discovery and presentation of *non-trivial, novel, interesting and ultimately potentially useful* information from very large databases" (Fayyad et al, 1996). Advances in data storage and processing technologies have made it possible today to store very large amounts of data in what are called data warehouses and then use data mining tools to extract relevant information. Data mining helps in the process of understanding a customer by providing the necessary information and facilitates informed decision-making.

Studies in marketing have brought out the importance of leveraging customer relationships (Day, 2000). CRM has today been enabled by advances in networks, databases and communications technology (Buttle, 2000; Berson et al., 1999). Although, data mining methods have formed the back end of many CRM solutions the relationship between CRM and data mining have been explored by very few researchers. Most of the literature is found in white papers of companies providing data mining solutions or in popular press. In this paper, we wish to bring out the importance of data mining in the process of CRM. The next section discusses CRM, the main ideas behind it, and how data mining fits in the process of CRM. Subsequently, we look at information requirements of an effective CRM solution. We then divide data mining operations into the aggregate or macro level and individual or the micro level, depending on the focus and granularity of our information extraction efforts. The next section deals with data mining tasks relevant to CRM. Then we briefly touch upon data mining tools that enable the above operations and conclude the paper in the last section.

❏ CUSTOMER RELATIONSHIP MANAGEMENT AND DATA MINING

Customer Relationship Management (CRM) is a technology initiative that aims to strengthen the front-end operations and build a mutually valuable long-term relationship with the customers. A firm might enjoy competitive advantage of its customers for a long time by building mutually beneficial relationships that increase switching costs and thus cannot be easily replicated. Studies have also shown that it costs as much as five times to acquire a new customer than to retain one (Source: Magic Software Enterprises White Paper, 2000). All customers do not contribute equally to a firm's profitability – some positively while others contribute negatively to the firm's bottom line. It is the endeavour of a firm to nurture these profitable customers. CRM integrates all front-end operations of the firm so that a customer is presented with a single point of contact that remembers all the past customer interactions.

A typical CRM cycle consists of front-end operations that interact with the customer (like call centres, target marketing initiatives etc.) and obtain data about him/her. This is typically consolidated from various contact points and fed into a data warehouse. The data warehouse consolidates not only transaction data but also data obtained from outside sources like census data and provides a fertile ground for analysis. Data analysis is done by data mining methods. The output is interpreted and new knowledge is transferred to a central customer repository where all employees of the firm might access it. This helps them to customise responses. Thus, data mining provides the intelligence behind the CRM initiative.

One can also view the same CRM task from a technology point of view. "The Meta Group views the CRM process framework as having three primary components operational or process management technologies, analytical or performance management technologies and collaborative or business collaboration management technologies - all of which are required to achieve a balanced CRM approach."(Source: SAS white paper). Operational CRM solutions involve integration of business processes involving customer touch points. Collaborative CRM involves the facilitation of collaborative services (such as e-mail) to facilitate interactions between customers and employees. All this effort produces rich data that feeds the Analytical CRM technologies. It analyses the data using data mining and other technologies and in turn feeds the result (i.e. knowledge gained) back to the operational and collaborative CRM technologies. It is to be noted that there is a very big overlap in the above description and there is feedback between efforts. (Fig. 1)

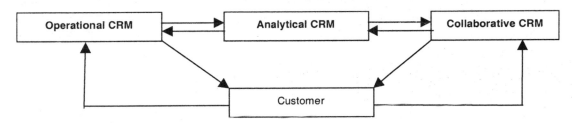

Fig. 1 *Interactions between CRM Technologies*

As can be seen from the discussion above data mining is an activity that provides intelligence to the CRM initiative. Data mining is not just execution of exotic data extraction algorithms but a process (Brachman and Anand, 1996) that enables informed decisions to be taken by the employees at the customer contact point.

☐ INFORMATION REQUIREMENTS OF AN EFFECTIVE CRM SOLUTION

The employees of a firm employing CRM would require rich information about their firm and customer base including the following:

- Information about the market.
- Information about the firm.
- The current customer segment:
- Demographic distribution (by age, sex, education, income, marital status etc.)
- The firm's best customers and the segment they belong to, products they buy, preferences, habits and tastes of each segment.
- Individual level information consisting of:
- Customer personal details such as name, address, family details, education etc.
- The customer group/segment to which the individual belongs.

- History of present and past behaviour.
- Likes, dislikes, habits and preferences.
- Events coming up in their personal life etc.

☐ LEVEL OF DATA MINING OPERATIONS

We propose to look at a large chain of retail stores. Each retail store stocks thousands of products under various product categories and sub-categories. They might typically include grocery and stationery items, household articles, apparels, food items etc. The manager of such a store has to deal with issues of inventory (which items to stock and how much), display and related marketing issues (discounts to be given to each customer) and so on. Suppose the store has a 'store card' scheme, for regular customers where in customers are rewarded for regular purchases. In addition, it helps the store to track customer behaviour. We shall be using the above example throughout to explain data mining operations relevant to CRM. We consider two cases. In the first case, we look at the aggregate customer data either because of lack of information or because of the questions asked. The second case is when we have detailed information about the customer with whom we are having our interaction.

The Aggregate or the Macro level

We mine at the macro level when we do not have specific individual data. While dealing with issues pertaining to a customer segment, we have to look at the broad picture of our audience. Mining at the macro level gives us a broad overview of the data e.g. when customers of the retail store are segmented by profitability criteria, we obtain clusters who are profitable to various extent. Further mining operations identify the characteristics of each of these segments. The natural segments might change if we change the focus of our exercise. Segmentation by demographics rather than profitability would give completely new clusters. Other useful operations at this level include classification, regression and link analysis. Knowledge obtained by mining at the macro level is useful when dealing with situations where:

- We are dealing with a customer about whom we do not have individual information. Hence, we need to extrapolate the characteristics of the group to which he/she might belong. In our retail store example, the store has already segmented its customer base into segments based on age and their characteristics have been extracted. When a new customer enters the store, the salesman could use his intuition in arriving at the customer's age and recover the characteristics of that age group such as the frequently bought products, colour preferences etc.
- Targeting new set of customers. If the retail chain has opened a new store, it can use data from the most similar current store to predict the behaviour of the new prospects.
- We are dealing with aspects of the service, which influence a majority of the customers and therefore cannot be customized to suit individual tastes, example being the design of the physical layout of a retail store.

- Predicting the possibility of an action that the customer has never undertaken. A customer might not have tried out a new product because he/she was not aware of it. A salesman can encourage him/her to try out the product if his/her profile matches that of the current product users.

The Individual or Micro level

As interactions of the individual with the firm increases, the firm obtains more data about him/her. Relationship with the individual customer can be strengthened by offering individualized value adding propositions. For this, we need to track the customer and mine at the individual or micro level. Some important features to note about mining at this level are:

- Micro-level mining provides specific information about a particular customer. For example, the retail store can go to the extent of finding out the preferred colours of his shirt.
- A firm takes up micro-level mining to build a detailed customer profile of a regular customer.
- Data mining at this level might be expensive if the data-mining tool has to cull out individual information from a large database. Having a separate database for profitable customers will be helpful.
- Knowledge obtained at the individual level is useful in dealing with situations where:
  - The firm wants to customise its offering to the customer based on the customer's tastes and preferences e.g. the retail store can offer discounts on the purchase of a bundle of products that the customer prefers buying together.
  - The firm wants to assist the purchase of a new product based on information it has on the last purchase. For example if a customer has bought a suit in his last visit, then the store might offer a discount on the purchase of a tie of matching colour.
  - The firm wants to take advantage of personal events in a customer's life (e.g. birthdays, anniversaries, birth of a child etc.) to further cement the precious relationship.
  - Current patterns that go against usually observed customer behaviour point to interesting phenomenon. If the retail customer suddenly switches brand then he/she might not be satisfied with the last purchase.

Link analysis, regression and deviation detection are the most common operations used at this level.

❏ DATA MINING TASKS (OPERATIONS) RELEVANT TO CRM

Data mining tasks produce knowledge that tend to be either predictive or descriptive (Fayyad, 1996; Simoudis, 1996). Predictive operations assigns value to some variables based on other related ones. Description focuses on describing essential features or characteristics of the data. CRM uses both predictive and descriptive power of data mining tasks to try to understand the customer better.

Classification

Classification is a process that maps a given data item into one of the several predefined classes (Weiss and Kulikowski, 1991; Fayyad,1996; Yoon,1999). CRM uses classification for a variety of purposes like behaviour prediction, product and customer categorization. Suppose the retail store allows customers to buy products on credit and repay in installments. It would like to extend this facility to only those customers who are not likely to default. New customers can be classified into two classes: those likely and those not likely to default based on characteristics of past defaulters and regular re-payers. The classification then guides the staff to allow customers buy on credit. Classification would not be meaningful if we have no pre-defined categories e.g. If our retail outlet is exclusive to a particular class of customers then it would not be meaningful to classify the customers.

Regression

Regression is the operation of learning a function that predicts the value of a real valued dependant variable based on values of other independent variables (Fayyad et al., 1996). Regression finds application in a CRM environment where prediction needs to be made about the behaviour involving real valued variables. Suppose the retail store collects data on the monthly visits of customers viz. frequency, time spent on each visit and purchases made during each visit. If the manager has a strong intuition that the value of the total purchases made during a month is related to the frequency of visits and the amount of time spent in the store, then, this situation can be modelled by regression. This model can then be used to predict future purchases of a customer. Regression needs sufficient amount of data to be reliable and valid. If the store does not have enough data then regression is not the technique to be employed.

Link Analysis

Link analysis seeks to establish relationship between items or variables in a database record to expose patterns and trends (Simoudis, 1996; Yoon, 1999). Link analysis can also trace connections between items of records over time. The most important link analysis application in CRM, called market basket analysis, is an operation that seeks relationships between product items characterizing product affinities or buyer preferences. The retail store collects thousands of transactions daily. A link analysis task performed on this data will point to items that are bought together e.g. bread and butter are bought together rather bread and orange juice. Such information can be used to design store layouts, design coupons etc. Link analysis might sometimes give relations that appear to hold true, but are of random occurrence. Links between items must be properly examined or further tests must be conducted before inference is made.

Segmentation

Segmentation aims to identify a finite set of naturally occurring clusters or categories to describe data (Anderberg, 1973). Segmentation is done in such a way that cases belonging to a segment or cluster are more similar with respect to the clustering criterion while they differ significantly from the cases belonging to other segments. For example, the retailer can segment his customers based on buying habits. He might find two distinct clusters: the first cluster consisting of customers who tend to spend less time in the store and buy less expensive items while members of the second cluster spend more time in the store and tend to buy expensive items. Segmentation of customers based on profitability would help the retailer to concentrate on the appropriate segment. In CRM, segmentation would not be useful if there are no underlying groups. Data on the customers of a section of the retail store, which stores identical products, might not show any naturally occurring segments.

Deviation Detection

Deviation detection (DD) focuses on discovering the most significant changes in the data from previously measured, expected or normative values. Most CRM solutions have a DD task running in parallel on a regular basis. Suppose a retailer finds that sales from a particular section of the store have been much less than expected. This deviation on further analysis points to non-stocking of a popular brand. Deviations sometimes might be a result of a random occurrence while at other times as a result of true change in fundamentals.

It must be noted that most data mining tasks are exploratory in nature. They do not ascertain the reason for the occurrence of the detected pattern. A further point to note is that the use of a data-mining task is dictated by questions that have been raised. Two or more data mining tasks used in proper conjunction would give a manager rich insight into the phenomenon taking place and probably ferret out hidden relationships otherwise impossible to recover.

□ DATA MINING TOOLS AND TECHNIQUES

A variety of data mining tools, techniques and algorithms are available to support the five data mining tasks (operations) described earlier. They differ from each other in type of data handled, assumptions about the data, scope and interpretations of the output.

Decision Trees

Decision trees are classification tools that classify examples into finite number of classes considering one variable at a time and dividing the entire data set based on it (Westphal, 1998;Chou, 1999; Yoon, 1999). Decision trees can be used for inducing rules for classification and segmentation. Segmentation is possible because at each node the decision tree splits the database into segments based on the value of the variable considered. The retailer can classify customers into classes using the decision tree learning algorithm. A new product can be classified into a category by a decision tree by its price, quality and durability. If a decision tree were constructed using very few training cases (over fitting) then it would not give a proper classification.

Rule Induction

In plain terms, rule induction is the process of inducing general rules from a database of specific examples. We will be considering here only association rules. *Association rules* (Agrawal, 1993) are implication rules of the form A=>B, which imply a relationship between A and B, where A and B can be a single items or sets of items. These rules do not give us the exact nature of the relationship but only point towards a general interaction between the two items. They are exploratory in nature, but are versatile enough to handle data mining tasks like segmentation, classification and link analysis. Negative associations and sequence discoveries can be handled easily by association rule algorithms. The retail store can obtain insights on which products sell together by running an association rule algorithm. Customers can be pre-empted into buying related goods by suitably modifying store layout or bundling products.

Case-based Reasoning

Case based reasoning (CBR) methods (Yoon, 1999) try to simulate how a human being thinks. Typically, when an example is presented to a CBR solution it tries to match the current example with other examples that it has in its repository and retrieves the case that is most similar to the current case. Decision is then taken based on extrapolation its power depends largely on the indexing method used to store cases and the matching method used to retrieve relevant cases. The retail store can use CBR techniques to classify items or assign a customer to a class. However, if a database of typical cases is not available then this method will not produce a good classification scheme.

Visualization Techniques

Visualization techniques allow the user to view data from various angles using graphic display techniques like charts, diagrams, displays for multidimensional data etc. Used in conjunction with other data mining techniques, visualization techniques are ideal when users do not know what and where to look for to discover new knowledge. It is very easy to understand data using visualization techniques particularly when the data set is small. They also help in interpretation and evaluation of information extracted by other data mining techniques and tasks. Most data-mining suite of tools includes at least one visualization tool (Westphal, 1998). The store manager can obtain different views of product sales by considering overall sales, sales by territory, products and so on.

Nearest Neighbour Techniques

Nearest neighbor techniques (Yoon, 1999) use a set of examples to approximate a classification model. A similarity measure is used to find the closest example in terms of certain parameters and then it assigns this new case to the class that has the maximum representation amongst its neighbors. In CRM, it is primarily used for classification such as assigning a class to the retail store that has been recently set up.

Clustering Algorithms

Clustering algorithms segment the database into clusters such that intra-cluster similarity is maximized and the inter-cluster similarity is minimized. (Anderberg, 1973; Jain et al., 1999). There are many approaches for clustering each having its own advantages and disadvantages. Recent studies have looked at clustering very large data sets (Jain, A.K. et al.; 1999). Most data mining that support CRM include clustering algorithms (Westphal, C et al.; 1998).

Neural networks, genetic algorithms, inductive logic programming and statistical methods are other popular techniques used in data mining for segmentation, classification and deviation detection (For more details refer to Westphal et al., 1998; Fayyad et al., 1996; and Berson et al., 1997). While Neural Networks make predictions in CRM, they are hampered due to difficulty in understanding them. Statistical methods are used for hypothesis testing in CRM: testing whether two groups are significantly different or not. Genetic algorithms might be used for optimizing the results of segmentation.

Choice of a data-mining tool depends not only on the capabilities of the tool but also on the question we seek to answer. Multiple tools might answer the same questions but to different degrees of satisfaction and completeness. As transactions with the customers are constantly taking place, new data comes into the data warehouse updating old data. Data mining solution for a particular CRM application must be capable of catering to such kind of dynamism. Running the same algorithm over the entire database repeatedly is an expensive proposition in terms of both time and resources. Tools with incremental knowledge updation capabilities can help in dealing with such situations. Finally, tight integration between the front end CRM solution and the back end data mining solution helps to ensure consistency and timely information dissemination throughout the firm – an important requirement of any CRM initiative.

☐ CONCLUSIONS

We have seen that firms are changing their product and process focus and aligning their operations to cater to the needs of the customer. Becoming more customer-centric, they aim at building long term and profitable relationships with customers. CRM is a technology-driven initiative that helps to realize this goal. CRM requires timely and relevant intelligence about the customer. We have explored the interrelationship between the needs of CRM and the output provided by data mining operations. Data mining tasks (operations) extract information that can provide the main intelligence for the CRM initiative. However, data mining is just a tool. In the end it is the way the information is used that makes all the difference. Tight integration between data mining tools and the CRM solution can provide accurate, relevant and timely knowledge at the front end to make informed decisions. Having a central repository that handles all relevant customer data and discovered knowledge and aligning all the processes to reflect the customer-centric approach are also important. If used in an appropriate manner, data mining can be the backbone of the CRM solutions that would help to build and maintain long-term, healthy, and profitable customer relationships.

REFERENCES

Agrawal, R., Imielinski, T., and Swami, A. (1993), "Mining Association Rules between Sets of Items in Large Databases", In Proceedings, *ACM SIGMOD Conference on Management of Data*, pp 207-216, Washington.

Anderberg, M. R., (1973), *Cluster Analysis for Applications*, Academic Press.

Berson, A. and Smith, S. J., (1997), *Data Warehousing, Data Mining and OLAP*, New York: McGraw Hill.

Berson, A., Smith, S., Thearling K., (1999), *Building Data Mining Applications for CRM*, McGraw Hill.

Brachman R. J. and Anand T. (1996) 'The Process of Knowledge Discovery in Data Bases', in *Advances in Knowledge Discovery and Data Mining*, editors Fayyad U., Piatetsky-Shapiro G., Smyth P. and Uthurusamy R., Cambridge, Massachusetts: AAAI Press/ The MIT Press.

Buttle, F., (2000), '*The CRM Value Chain'*, A CRM-Forum Academic Paper, www.crm-forum.com

Chou, C.D. and Chou, A. Y., (1999), "A Manager's Guide to Data Mining", *Information Systems Management*, Fall, 1999, pp.33-41.

Day, S. G.; (2000) 'Managing Market Relationships', *Journal of the Academy of Marketing Science*, Vol. 28, No. 1, pp 24-30.

Fayyad, U.M., Piatetsky-Shapiro, G. and Smyth P. (1996) 'From Data Mining to Knowledge Discovery: An Overview', in *Advances in Knowledge Discovery and Data Mining*, Editors Fayyad U., Piatetsky-Shapiro G., Smyth P. and Uthurusamy R., Cambridge, Massachusetts: AAAI Press/ The MIT Press.

Jain, A.K., Murthy, M.N. and Flynn P.J. (1999), 'Data Clustering: A Review', *ACM computing surveys*, Vol. 31 Issue 3, September, 1999, pp 264-323.

Magic Software Enterprises White Paper, (2000), "*The CRM Phenomenon*", www.magic-sw.com

SAS White Paper, '*The Role of e-Intelligence in Customer Relationship Management (CRM)*', www.sas.com

Simoudis, E., (1996), 'Reality Check for Data Mining', *IEEE Expert*, October 1996, pp 26-33.

Weiss, S. I. and Kulikowski, C., (1991), *Computer Systems that Learn: Classification and Prediction Models from Statistics, Neural Networks, Machine Learning, and Expert Systems*, San Fransisco, Calif.: Morgan Kaufmann.

Westphal, C. and Blaxton T., (1998), *Data Mining Solutions: Methods and Tools for Solving Real-World Problems*, New York: Wiley Computer Publishing, John Wiley and Sons.

Yoon, Y., (1999), "Discovering Knowledge in Corporate Databases", *Information Systems Management*, Spring, 1999, pp. 64-71.

Chapter 9

Changing Patterns of e-CRM Solutions in the Future

■ **Vijay Ahooja**

Abstract

Over the years, there has been a visible change in customer expectations due to rapid changes in technology and development of new economy. Organizations globally are gearing up to meet the challenges offered by the new wave of business patterns.

The lifestyles of individuals have undergone major changes with mobility, Internet, and technology playing a very major role in individuals behavioral patterns.

Customers have become more demanding, and to retain the customers organizations are confronted with improving their pre and post sales service offerings.

"Changing patterns of e-CRM solutions" is a thought paper, which tries to, addresses some of the gaps that have emerged in conventional CRM solutions and the needs of the present times. It also addresses how technology is going assist in bridging these gaps.

The paper is a visioning exercise that is widening the very scope of CRM solutions to cross-functional and service offerings as well as collaborative approach to CRM.

Key Words : *Customer Expectation, e-CRM, Cross-Functional, Service Offerings.*

□ INTRODUCTION

Customer Relationship Management has been the cornerstone of most organizations as they realise the cost of acquiring new customers is far higher than cost of retaining existing customers. Besides there are other added advantages such as referral sales and customer loyalty.

Because reducing customer defection (by as little as 5%) will result in increase in profits (by 25% to 85 % depending from industry to industry).

And the potential loss of a customer over a period of lifetime is huge. Typically in travel loss of a customer over the lifetime may mean a huge loss (As per PricewaterhouseCoopers internal study loss could be of the order of USD $100,000 in travel and in Automobile sector it may mean loss of USD 220,000).

Naturally, organizations are investing heavily to build long term relationships with their customers so that they can continue to enjoy brand loyalty. With new economy emerging and impacting the lifestyles of people across globe, organizations are confronted with a challenge to maintain and nurture the customer relationships to their advantage.

❑ WHAT IS CRM?

CRM in effect implies building long-term relationship with your customers and understanding their needs and responding through multiple products and services through multiple channels.

CRM should finally enable "a targeted mutually beneficial profitable relationship with individuals and groups".

Key CRM Principles: A good CRM solution should allow for:
- Differentiate Customers—All customers are not equal; Recognize and reward best customers disproportionately
- Differentiate Offerings—Customers appreciate customized offerings
- Keep Existing Customers—It's 5 to 10 times cheaper to retain current customers than acquire new ones
- Maximize Lifetime Value—Exploit up-selling and cross-selling potential
- Increase Loyalty—Loyal customers are more profitable

Differentiating Customers

Most CRM systems allow for very little freedom to customize to specific industry verticals. Since the customer needs emerge from the products and offering of the industry, CRM system should respond to the customer needs.

Understanding each customer becomes particularly important. And the same customers' reaction to a cellular company operator may be quite different as compared to a car dealer. Besides for the same product or a service not all customers can be treated alike and CRM need to differentiate between a high value customer and a low value customer.

What CRM need to understand while differentiating customers is:
- Sensitivities, Tastes, Preferences and Personalities
- Lifestyle and age
- Culture background and education
- Physical and psychological characteristics

Differentiating Offerings

A CRM solution needs to differentiate between a low value customer and a high value customer.
- Low value customer requiring high value customer offerings

- Low value customer with potential to become high value in near future
- High value customer requiring high value service
- High value customer requiring low value service

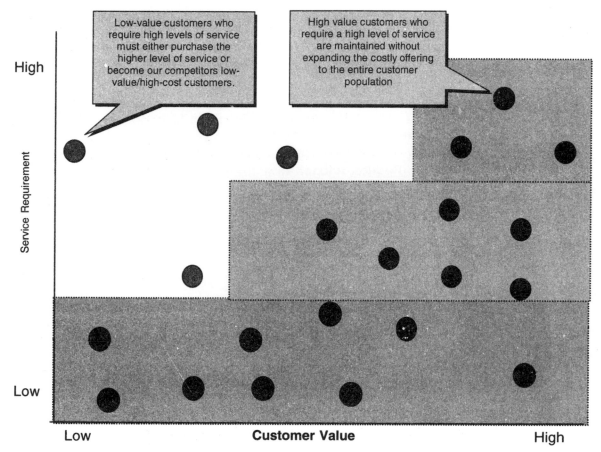

Fig. 1 *Customer Value - Service Matrix*

Keeping existing customers

Grading customers from very satisfied to very disappointed shall help the organization in always improving its customer satisfaction levels and scores.

As the satisfaction level for each customer improves so shall the customer retention with the organization.

Maximizing life time value

By identifying lifestage and life-event trigger points by customer, marketers can maximize share of the purchase potential.

Thus the single adults shall require a new car stereo and as he grows into a married couple his needs grow into appliances.

Increase Loyalty

It is an endeavor of any corporate to see that its customers are advocate for the company and its products. Any company will like its mindshare status to improve from being a suspect to being an advocate.

Suspect → prospect → customer client → supporter → advocate.

Company has to invest in terms of its product and service offerings to its customers. It has to innovate and meet the very needs of its clients/ customers so that they remain as advocates on the loyalty curve.

Referral sales invariably are low cost high margin sales. It has also the implication of being not "one time sale". Besides, referral sales are likely to induce more satisfaction.

Summarizing CRM Activities

The CRM cycle can be briefly described as follows:
1. Learning from customers and prospects
2. Creating value for customers and prospects
3. Creating loyalty
4. Acquiring new customers
5. Creating profits
6. Acquiring new customers

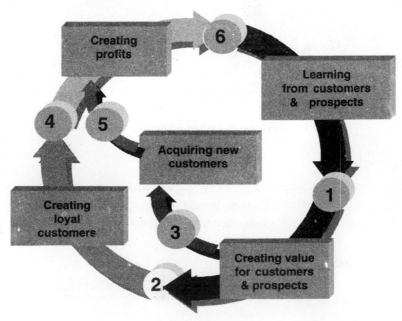

Fig. 2

☐ IMPACT OF TECHNOLOGY

With technology touching the way we live our lives, expectations of individuals is fast changing. Like the television and the PCs revolutionized our lives in the twentieth century so is wireless communication, Internet and pervasive computing going to affect our daily pattern of lives.

Some clear trends that can be seen are:
- More and more individuals will like to be treated as one single person rather than as one among the masses.
- People wish products and services round the clock
- With abundance of product and service offerings, consumers' loyalty can only be commanded by providing better portfolio of services
- Speed of response and understanding each individual one of the major key issues

CRM has become the central focus area around which the entire gamut of organizational activities has to revolve around.

☐ THE EXISTING CRM SOLUTIONS

Strangely enough the corporations today inspite of the fact they are globally competitive do not bring out quarterly CRM balance reports.

Delivering the '360 view' requires automation to bring together all the data concerning a customer. This implies that organizations have to change from :

Mass marketing	➜>	Product focus
Product focus	➜>	Customer focus
Economies of time	➜>	Economies of time
1 way communication	➜>	Interactive
Response time	➜>	Real time

Present CRM Alternatives

Present CRM solutions are offered by host of vendors that are to a great extent not industry specific. While there are some vendors, who have come up with industry specific solutions, the broad model around which the CRM solutions are built remain the same.

Adopting a similar or a look alike solution across industries is what causes major strain in servicing a consumer.

Typical offerings of the current CRM solutions (such as Siebel, Oracle Apps or MySAP.com etc.) vary from solution to solution. However typical CRM Solution offerings comprise of:

Customer development	Field Sales, Tele Sales, Internet Sales
Service center	(Call Centers) Field Service
Sale Mgmt & Support	Internet customer Service
Market Analysis	Service Interaction Center (Call Centers)
Internet, Tele marketing	Business Partner Collaboration
Product & Brand management	

Service center in a very simplistic model may resemble the process described in figure 3.

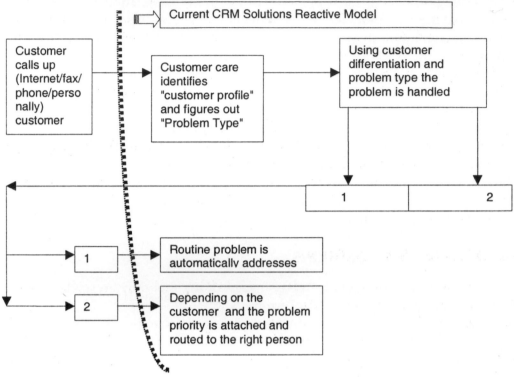

Fig. 3 *Typical Service Model*

❑ EMERGING IMPACT OF E-COMMERCE ON CRM

In a fast changing Internet world there are very clear trends that are emerging:

- *Speed* : People expect service at Internet speed
- *Increase of Globe Market Space* : More and more people, communities across the globe are able to build relationships
- *Around the Clock Availability* : Internet offers round the clock availability of goods and services 24X7
- *Expansion of Partners* : Internet offers exponential ability for the organization and people alike to partner with suppliers and customers alike across the globe.
- *Disappearance of Time Zones* : The only time zone that is applicable is Internet time zone

Similarly the new economy has opened up all together different ways of conducting business as has never been witnessed ever since the industrial revolution.

In a global market place the channels of marketing are already causing an impact on the buying behaviour of individuals as well as organizations alike. Some of the emerging trends are :

1. VERTICAL E-MARKET PLACE: Industry specific market places such as being formed by Auto giants where organized buyers and sellers can meet, list, negotiate, order and track delivery.

2. BUY SITE AND SELL SITES: Where consumers or organizations alike can buy and sell online through online shopping mart concept.

3. HORIZONTAL MARKET PLACE: Services that run across different vertical e_market places or Business to Customer (B2C) Buy and sell sites. Such sites could be delivery sites, insurance etc.

4. USE OF INTERNET TO OPTIMIZE "SUPPLY CHAIN MANAGEMENT (SCM) ": While earlier organizations use to use EDI "rather an expensive preposition" for limited number of partners organizations, organizations are in a position to use internet to optimize their SCM across partners.

□ GAPS WITH EXISTING CRM SOLUTIONS

Corporations are presently applying the same norms of CRM across industry while the consumer behavior is surprisingly different for different products and services. The result is disastrous, as the individual needs are never fully addressed. Thus the same individuals' expectations from a cellular phone operator may be grossly different from that of a car manufacturer.

This is being explained through a series of examples that will be further expanded to show the roadmap for future CRM solutions.

Illustration 1: Finding a missing friend

While travelling a frequent traveller may soon realize that the phone number or an e-mail address that he had fed in his "palm top" may no longer be valid. And he wished if there was some way of automatically updating his "palm top" regularly with all the phone numbers that may have changed.

Illustration 2: Car owners' expectations—Missing service option

For instance a new car buyer will like to be reminded on the due date of mileage automatically that his car is in need of a service.

If the recommended change for new tyres is at 30,000 running miles and for some necessity, one of the tyres of a new car had to be changed at 5000 miles, it is consumers expectations that he be reminded when which tyre needs to be changed when. Thus consumer will like to be reminded at the end of 30,000 running miles that three of his tyres need to be changed while one of the early burst replaced tyres need to be changed at 35,000 miles.

Illustration 3: Cellular phone owners' expectations—Missing service offering

However, the same consumer when confronted with his cellular company may wish to restrain his cellular bill within certain budget. For instance, he will like to be reminded at

80 %(or a predefined limit) of his budget limit that he is about to exceed the budget so that he is little bit more discrete in its usage for the balance of the month.

While on the other hand, a consumer with a different profile might find reminders rather a nuisance.

Illustration 4: Case of riding on consumer loyalty

Ford Company will like its user to always use Ford brand even while user may be posted anywhere round the globe (from US to Japan) and even while Ford may not enjoy a major market share at the place of posting.

The above four illustrations shall be used to explain how organizations are going to technology to improve their customer relationship management.

☐ PROACTIVE VS REACTIVE CRM MODEL

Presently there is an immense focus on how to build customer relationship management from the organizations view point. The entire process begins with customer approaching the organization with a need (It could be a simple query, or a post sale complain). In the figure 3, we see that the trigger point for CRM is "customer meeting the organization say customer desk". That is to say CRM solutions are reactive in nature as the same respond only if customer provides inputs (from the right side of the dotted line in figure 3). This is what we can term as a reactive model.

However, in a proactive CRM model, through the use of technology such as Pervasive computing, Datawarhousing, much before the customer realises the problem exists the same has been addressed.

☐ FUTURE CRM SOLUTIONS

Unlike in the past future CRM solutions will be heavily characterized by:
1. Proactive rather than reactive
2. Personalized care to each individual
3. Heavily technology driven
4. Product and service specific rater than a generic CRM solution across products and ser vices
5. Shall work on extension of product and service offerings beyond the primary product/service sold
6. CRM solutions shall work on collaborative arrangement among different service offerings so as to cater to the complex needs of individuals.

While some of the aspects such as personalized care have been touched above, other concepts have been explained below. For this, wherever applicable, illustrations described above have been used to explain the future trend of CRM solutions.

CRM Based on Proactive Rather than Reactive Model

Presently, for any routine queries that have been addressed earlier CRM solutions, without human intervention, try and resolve the same. User nevertheless still has to be in queue to log in a routine complain for the same to be addressed.

In a proactive model, for whole range of routine issues/queries and complains, user will no longer have the trouble of going to the customer care desk. Technology shall take care of routine tasks/issues/queries and shall be able to approach the customer care much before the problem becomes acute or has actually occurred. Some of the technological factors other than Artificial Intelligence (AI) have been explained below:

Pervasive computing shall ensure that devices talk intelligently to each other as well as are connected through a network to databases (May be without wires).

Exactly in a similar fashion as organizations with their learning curve try and address routine problems, users will be approached with solutions without their intervention much before the problem has occurred.

Datawarehousing/Datamining technology shall help in fairly high accuracy levels of predicting consumer buying behavior, trends and relationships. Datawarehousing and Datamining help in establishing trends that would otherwise not be feasible.

Intelligent Networks

Intelligent networks will be able to recognise the user and based on his needs will immediately link him to the right database catering to his requirements.

Typical examples will be

Device failure (Example of pervasive computing, Intelligent networks and Datawarehousing): Through pervasive computing or remote diagnostics, it is automatically reported to the customer care unit of the device. Customer care then either rectifies the device remotely or personally service the device.

Customer requirements (Example of Datawarehousing): Datawarehousing applications will be able to figure out travel patterns of individuals and approach individuals right at the decision points to convert their leisure travel plans.

We have for the first time witnessed integration at a large scale with ERP systems falling in place across industry. It has helped provide consistent integrated information that may not be necessarily customer centric.

Internet on the other hand provides the end user with enormous power to choose from the product offerings, vendors and maximize value for money.

The next decade provides the challenge to the organizations to fine-tune their systems to become customer centric. Winning organizations are the ones who will be able to integrate all their functions around customer.

Let us revisit the cases above and take a hard looks how organizations shall be addressing customer requirements at various stages:

Illustration 1 Revisit: Finding a missing friend

In a CRM solution of next decade focus will be collaborative databases. Databases across organizations shall start taking to each other exchanging valuable information that may not be really present. For instance, organizations such as Car manufacturers on one-hand and palm tops manufacturers' shall start exchanging information on unparalleled scale.

The future e-CRM will work on collaborative model as needs of individuals shall become increasingly cross functional.

Telephone Company AT&T could collaborate with US Postal department and across the globe with Australian Telecommunication Company. The figure below explains how this will work and benefit the telecommunication customer.

In the above example one would have come to know about ones' colleague any time during the life time about his successive movements around the world by just asking AT&T.

Going a step further, customers' palm top or PC database once hooked to AT&T Database will get automatically updated with the successive changes in addresses, emails, or geographic locations of any of customers colleagues, business partners or community colleagues.

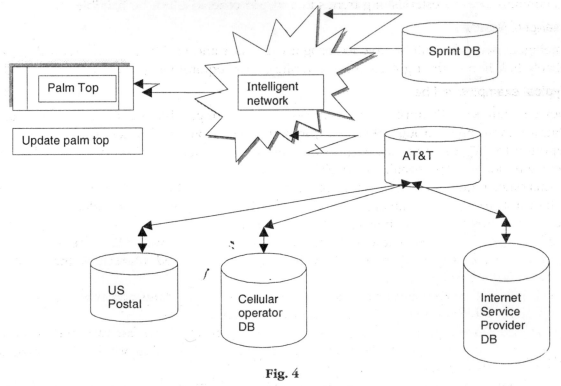

Fig. 4

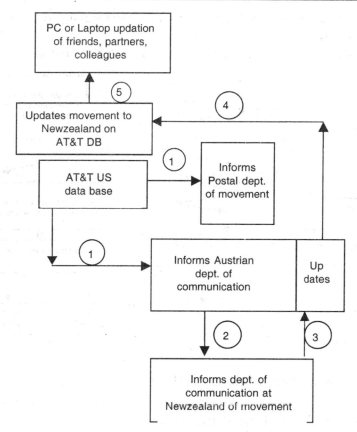

Fig. 5 *Extension of Illustratiion 1*

In this situation, whenever there is a change in address or a phone of a friend, end user will be able to update his database by simply hooking on to AT&T Database. AT & T Database may in turn collaborate with Postal authorities, cellular phone operators as well as Internet service providers. Thus any one by simply hooking on to the network to AT&T will be to update ones local database on the palm top.

Illustration 2 Revisit: Car Owners' Expectations: Missing Service Option

The centralized system in the car will keep communicating with the Database of authorized dealer of car manufacturer or main service Database being maintained by the manufacturer himself.

Car Manufacturer himself may in turn corroborate with the tyre manufacturer who shall keep a track on the mileage run by each car. Using datamining techniques, tyre manufacturers will know when the tyres are due for replacement, service dealer will know when the car is due for servicing and a car dealer may know when the car is likely for sale again. Through pervasive computing cars' internal devices through pervasive computing and datawarehousing will be able to communicate to car dealer about cars' health. The car dealer in turn will know the health of the car and customers buying pattern for a new car preposition to the same customer.

With this information, each of the agencies will approach the customer accordingly.

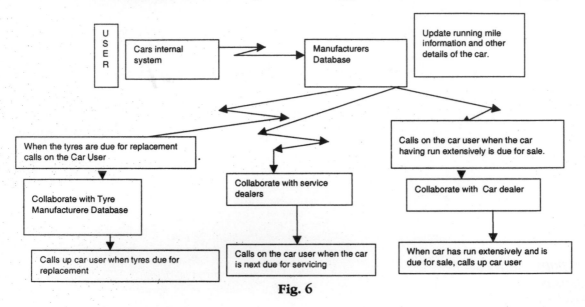

Fig. 6

Illustration 4 Revisit: Case of riding on consumer loyalty

Like in many other areas, Databases across the world will start collaborating to maintain and mange the needs and expectations of the customers.

Typically, as an extension of the illustration 1 of "finding missing a friend", a car manufacturer may be able to track you to Australia though AT&T Database and hold on to the same car model that you were holding in USA. Thus if you were a Ford Loyalist, Ford may still track you to Australia and still sell you the same car.

Figure 7 explains how such a collaborative approach shall work and help in CRM solutions.

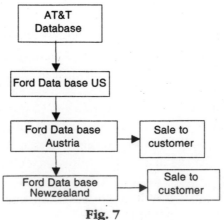

Fig. 7

Chapter 10

How to Structure a Customer Focussed IT Organisation to Support CRM

■ **Arvind Agrawal**

Abstract

The paper addresses the issues faced by senior management in implementing technology-intensive projects with specific focus on CRM. The tussle between implementing the "Best-in-class" technology vs one that is most suitable to the companies' requirement needs to be handled appropriately to ensure ROI results from such investments. The paper identifies these issues, and suggests a solution for the senior management to answer them.

The software vendors are today selling CRM and thus the decision making process focuses on procuring the right technology alone. Experience with NIIT, American Express, GE Capital in implementing CRM has been that the existing infrastructure is inadequate to bring out the best from such forays. CRM is Marketing led activity using IT to support the massive amount of information that one needs to work with. What could really make the difference is the people resources, a properly articulated plan and appropriate product structuring to sell on relationships.

Key Words: *IT Organisation, CRM, Marketing, Organisation Structure, Customer Focus*

❑ INTRODUCTION

In my 17 years as a Sales & Marketing man, driving the new age technology to support the much desired differentiation of products and services, I have seen technology always come out smiling over the ROI forecasts that were the basis for the investments. I am sure a lot of you CEOs and those of you from the Marketing side have also gone through this painful realisation of a similar nature. Some of the reported implementations of ERP and their results are a case in point.

This paper addresses this issue of how to find the best fit between technology and the new age companies that thrive on competencies enabled by technology. And how do we, as decision-makers, need to deploy IT to maximize advantages emerging from the world of computing today.

But before we launch on finding a solution and not live with a placebo, lets understand where the differences stem from.

□ THE IT VS MARKETING "PERSONALITIES"

The IT Mindset

Traditionally organisations have grown by deploying IT to transfer physical processes onto digital medium to enhance productivity and response times. IT has been one of the key enablers in creating easily available, accessible and suitably queriable systems that consolidate information which otherwise would have been buried in reams of paper. Over the years IT has been trained to work with defined "processes" and to find ways of reducing the variations so as to develop efficient systems. The illustrations below will demonstrate the mindset IT has developed over the last so many decades. In fact phrases like "Process Improvement", "Process Re-engineering" are very commonly used in any IT presentation.

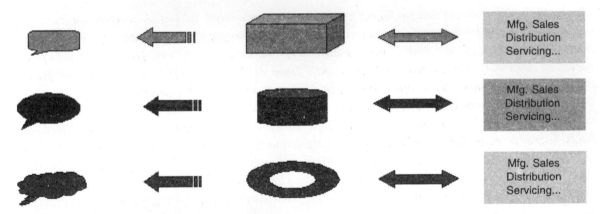

Fig. 1 *How Companies have been Structured Traditionally?*

How have companies been structured Traditionally

Each product line has been invested in separately, with infrastructure dedicated for each.

Wave – 1 of Cost Management

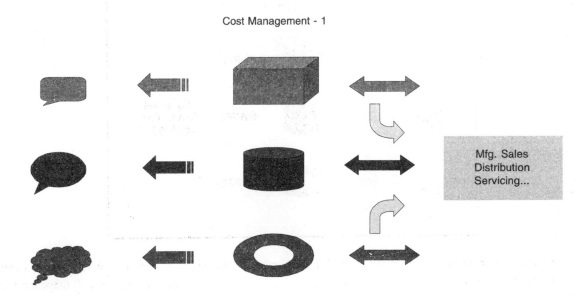

Cost Management - 1

The axe fell on the back-room in the first wave of Cost Management. This was quite effective in terms of both implementation ability and its impact on savings. IT played a crucial role in converging & speeding-up processes.

Wave – 2 of Cost Management

A feeble attempt was made at integrating the "Sales" organization to target common customers. IT attempt at supporting this re-organisation met with little success.

You will notice that the key benefit being targetted above is "Cost Management". Thus ROIs became the benchmarks for budgeting investments. ROIs were also very easily calculated since a clear cost structure of the existing system was available and the same system was being automated. Since majority of systems developed came out of the "Operations" organisation, in most of the companies IT grew as part of the "Operations" group. Even after becoming an independent group, it continued to be aligned to "Operations".

Attempts at creating DSS or MIS systems most of the time extracted information from the existing legacy systems reporting summary information across fast expanding and geographically widespread organisations. The benchmark here being "Control". In fact Artificial Intelligence that supported DSS applications in a big way, fell by the wayside with prefabricated & standard reports ruling the roost of most DSS & MIS applications.

Even the systems developed always had usage restrictions - access to only authorized users, as another key dimension to them. Users could do their part of the job well, but could not "explore" other areas of the system or information.

Thus "Cost Management" and "Control" became the key parameters synonymous to efficient systems in the minds of IT professionals to evaluate any automation effort.

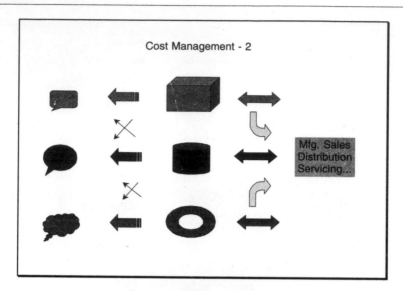

Traditional systems also have very limited alphabetic data to churn. While managing name/address, complaints and requests and such alphabetic data is of critical importance in the new economy, consumer focussed organisations. Most of the time such alphabetical data was relegated to a "Remarks" column, which could not be analyzed.

The Marketing Mindset

Marketing on the other hand was struggling to maintain market supremacy of its products and generate revenue for the company by:

- Providing least cost products
- Creating niche and more targetted products that offered unique need gratification features for ever smaller segments of population
- Enveloping physical products with services and thus offer product plus over competition
- Building strong brand names that stuck into consumer minds as benchmarks representing their emotional and physical needs

All the time Marketing focussed on :

- Being Unique and Different
- Being Path-breaking & New
- Always on the lookout for New Ideas – "Exploring", " Curiosity"

One needs to look at this comparison of competencies before embarking on the new role that IT is desired to play in the New Economy.

☐ MARKETING AUTOMATION

With competition intensifying, the focus has shifted to providing products & services that serve each unique consumer in a personalized fashion. This desire spawned several new IT streams like ERP, Data Warehousing and now Internet marketing / e-commerce. If we take Internet as an example, the initial valuations and their recent downturn is a classic representation of this expectation syndrome. While theoretically it is possible to deliver Brand Value and Emotive Appeal via IT, in reality ample justice does not happen during implementation. Any guesses why?

The Marketing wish-list

It is a classic conflict in our minds as decision makers where we approve Advertising budget knowing fully well that it is tough to draw a direct correlation to profitability and ROI, while no IT investment proposal can ever be approved unless it provides a clear cost-benefit justification. Advertising in fact is evaluated as a percentage of sales. In times of intense competition, organisations are known to use massive ad budgets as a strategic tool to out-shout competition, investing completely out of proportion to their norms. Such risk taking is commonplace in Marketing:

- New Product Launches
- Revamping Old Products (New Coca Cola)
- Advertising Campaigns in Mass Media
- Product Positioning into Niche Segments

	The Direct-to-Customer Business Model	**The Benefit**
✓ Drive down Marketing costs	■ en-cash customer lifetime value & thus generate continuing business ■ reduce dependence on sales channel ■ use Internet, email, local cable channel, partnership programs	
✓ Raise the entry barrier for competition	■ build relationships ■ provide high quality service by niche selling to segments and need-based selling to end users ■ reduced time to market ■ technology to evolve a more value-based front end	
✓ Drive-up profitability	■ envelope the customer by extending services beyond core business ■ channel for others to market their products ■ identify price-elasticity of demand by segments ■ unearth end-user served and un-served markets	
✓ Unearth new revenue lines within the core brand proposition	■ be a reliable and dependable source of information and charge for it ■ market lists and profiles ■ product introduction service for partners - revenue share with them ■ structure new product bundles to meet customer needs	

Fig. 5 *The Marketing Wish-list*

In this new environment of getting closer to the customer, the support role that marketing used to play earlier has changed to marketing being the face of the organisation to the customer.

All the interactions with the customer thus now need to be via the Marketing organisation, which means an operational role now Vs just a planning role earlier.

□ THE 4-COMPONENTS OF AN EMPOWERED CRM

The figure below identifies the 4 segments in which we need to focus to deliver appropriate "Relationship" dimension to our customers.

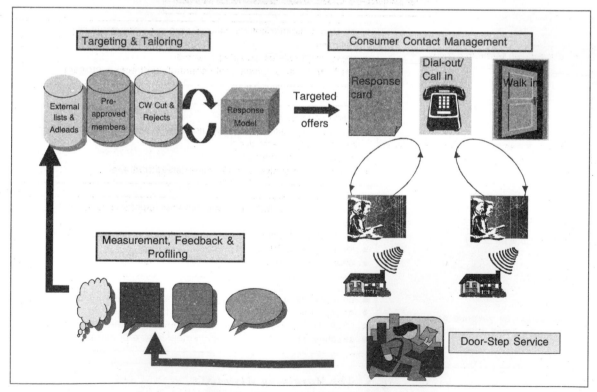

Fig. 6 *The CRM Components*

Notice the infrastructure that's required to support fulfillment in each of the 4 quadrants relies completely on IT support. In fact the ability to process ever increasing information and to be able to pin-point the right one that can be acted upon by the front office has become a vital support that Marketing relies for on IT. This includes information management and retrieval (database management), customer contact infrastructure (telecommunications) and customer services (front-office contact management).

◻ HOW THEN CAN WE STRUCTURE A WINNING STRATEGY ?

Knowing the "process" driven, pre-defined and very cost & control conscious mindset that IT has, we need to identify a completely different set of capabilities that will then define the IT mindset for marketing needs.

(a) Create a separate "IT for Marketing" division, from IT being a single service division in the organisation.

(b) The KPPs (key performance parameters) must be defined for Marketing IT depending on the role it is required to play (or even each role in Marketing IT can have different KPPs) :

S No	Role	KPP
1.	Acquisition	Numbers, Cost per acquisition
2.	Retention	Attrition rates
3.	Relationship selling	Lifetime value share, repeat purchases, % of products subscribed to
4.	Brand salience	Rating, recommendation
5.	Research	% customers for whom profile data is collected, Customer response to targetted offers, Feedback collection points

(c) Hire people with Marketing/Sales aptitude to run the Marketing IT function.

(d) Marketing and Sales people must get rotated into IT function.

(e) Fulfillment services (like e-commerce) must form a part of Operations just like Customer Services today is part of operations. This is again because this is more process driven rather than based on an idea.

◻ THE CUSTOMER FOCUSSED ORGANISATION

The idea here is to develop systems that allow flexibility, work on not completely pre-defined processes so as to enable front office to be proactive to each customer need.

The Mindset impact on CRM

A typical Data Warehouse will have the following components:
While developing a Data Warehouse generally one takes into account all the legacy and operation systems. But typically sales team could be managing leads on an excel worksheet. Sometimes I have noticed that some critical DSS input like "Profitability Analysis" itself may reside on a worksheet. Thus a Data Warehouse solution must be able to

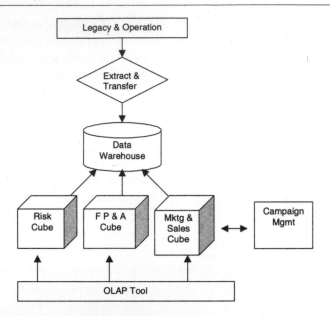

accept information from such "unstructured" sources as well as budget for an open architecture to enable plug-in for systems to be developed in the future.

(a) Generally the existing information is mapped onto a data warehouse. Since a customer centric info-base is being developed, it is critical that extensive customer research is done to identify their information needs and thus what profile data of them will be relevant for us. Thus any data-warehousing project needs to work very closely with the research team.

(b) After extracting the data from various systems, we need to :
   - Scrub & Clean the data
   - Deduplicate

(c) Even though we may find 80% of the names in a database of a million customers using combinations of lets say a 1000 first and last names, to take into account all possible combinations we may actually need a database of 10,000 first & last names. Even then we may not be able to comprehensively cover all possible future combinations. Now, the system must expect this kind of input on a regular basis rather than it happening by exception as is the case with updating "masters" in a traditional system.

(d) Ad-hoc querying is a tool that is most often used in such applications. Unfortunately not enough effort is made to make this tool "end-user" friendly so that even a layman could run his/her own reports. Typically a data warehouse and data minning person is placed in IT to manage all queries. With the advent of tools like Metadata repository, drill-down OLAP tools and Palm Pilots it is now possible for hardcore Marketing & Sales types to directly access and run their queries. In fact we need to budget for training the Marketing and Sales staff to use the data warehouse themselves.

(e) The real power of a CRM system is its ability to provide a rich, value added experience to our customers at all touch points – call centres, kiosks, retail outlets, mobile devices, internet and branches. Integration and information dissemination must happen at all these points. Thus the CRM specialist in Marketing must be well-versed with all these tools and techniques.

□ CONCLUSION

The back-office discipline must not be exported to the front-office. Companies cannot change their front-office to suit the software. In fact the systems have to be flexible enough to support the marketing mindset. Only then we will find the true soul of a data warehousing and CRM system. Most of the large corporates, the so called "old economy" companies, handling businesses in the traditional fashion, need to assimilate these new techniques to remain viable and so that they can retain their share of the customer. They will need to realign the IT function in an appropriate manner so that the capabilities desired of a CRM system become fully available to them. Or else we will have another great concept which will be remembered in the future management annals as one that theoretically was a good idea. Much similar to how ERP is being viewed today with skepticism.

Or else, please make way for the new age organisations.

Framework for Deploying Customer Relationship in Organisation

■ **Alok Kumar**

Abstract

In the deployment of Customer Relationship system in organisations a business case development is critical and crucial in order to garner adequate resources and management alignment. There is a paucity of research and case studies to guide practising Customer Relationship managers within organisations. Since relationship management is a strong emerging discipline of entire Customer Care management system there is a definite need to evolve the conceptual framework around which deployment takes place.

This paper attempts to explain the imperatives that must drive the business decisions around. Customer Relationships and looks at live case example to explain the concepts evolved and implemented in **Escotel Mobile Communication Ltd** *- a leading cellular operator in state of Haryana/Kerala & telecom circle of U.P. (West) with a subscriber base of 2,50,000 and operating from 70 offices and covering 144 towns.*

Key Words: *Customer Relationship Systems, Resource, Management Alignment*

❑ INTRODUCTION

Customer relationship deployment barriers

Marketing concepts and framework around acquiring new customers have been fairly well evolved over the years. Cost of Acquisition are spelt out, marketing plans and selling machinery put in place and customers are brought in through various selling routes – direct sale, multilevel selling, distribution sale, customer get customer schemes, etc......

Having got the customer, the role devolves on customer relationship wing of the organisation to take care of the customer to either

- Maximise revenue opportunities from contracts, consumables, upselling or cross selling

- Remove any irritants during customer interactions
- Prevent customer defection
- Enhance 'Moment of Truth' experience to build loyalty
- Manage and run loyalty programmes

There are organisational constraints encountered in execution of these. Mainly they are as follows:

- A mismatch between resource allocated and service levels desired for building customer relationship
- Absence of financial business case and ROI for investments in Customer Relationship
- Horizontal non alignment of organisations to customers line of sight
- Balance to be achieved between maximisation of revenue and customer satisfaction

☐ DEVELOPMENT OF FINANCIAL IMPERATIVES TO CRM DEPLOYMENT

Referral marketing to reduce selling costs/increase salesman productivity

Customers come through direct efforts of the selling machinery or through referrals (in referrals the selling machinery can facilitates their entry). Customers largely make referral purchase decisions for those products that have greater than normal impact on their budgets/or life. For consumer products referral can be replaced with loyalty schemes/buying inducements (eg. Tazo's with Ruffles Chips)

Direct selling machinery would have costs that are significantly higher than referral sale – hence the need to invest in customer Relationships with an eye on acceleration of referrals so as bring down costs or increase productivity of sales (higher cold call to order ratio)

Figure 1 illustrates the phenomenon that organisations can drive referral sale line in a manner that can reduce time T1 and with that in figure 1(a) the overall unit selling cost (average of direct sale cost + referral sale cost) can be reduced with higher sales productivity.

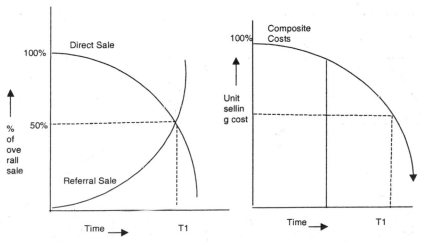

Fig. 1 *'Torpedo' Graph*   **Fig. 1(a)   Sale Cost Line**

Figure 2 illustrates that with a given investment in direct sale channel the productivity can at best be only a slightly increasing line, while a referral line will be an exponentially increasing trend line with growing subscriber numbers. This creates a multiplier effect that quickly overtakes the direct sale numbers. Organisation dependency on direct sale can gradually be reduced since they stand to account for reduced numbers in the overall sums.

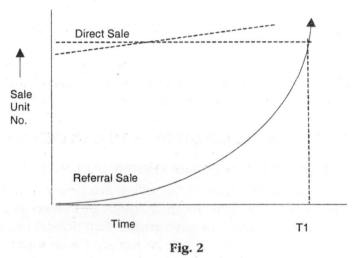

Fig. 2

Organisational measure of referral propensity can be taken through customer feedback on their willingness to recommend the product to their friends and acquaintances. Figures for actual referral sale happening can come from information from increasing sales (if coming direct)/or a response coupon mailback.

Data of **Likelihood to Recommend** from Kerala market of **Escotel** subscriber is illustrated below. This is based on face to face survey conducted through independent market research agency on a sample base with >95% confidence level. Company commissioning the survey was identified to the respondents.

1997	1998	1999	2000
71%	78%	86%	86%

Impact of referrals was measured as a part of 6 Sigma improvement team working on **Sales productivity improvement.** Order conversion rates from various sources of lead generation was taken and the results are as follows

Method of Lead Generation	Sample Size	Conversion rate
Cold Calling	2210	3%
Database	1674	1%
Referrals	352	29%

Organisation/selling channels have to individually draw the sale cost line for their products. This will determine saving rate impact through referrals and can serve as a decision point for how much investment should be made for tracking & accelerating referrals.

□ BUILDING LOYALTY TO INCREASE CUSTOMER LIFE TIME VALUE

The ability to increase customer stickiness to the product or services offered has huge upside in terms of capturing customer life time value through upselling and cross-selling (apart from referral payoffs) explained in part (1)

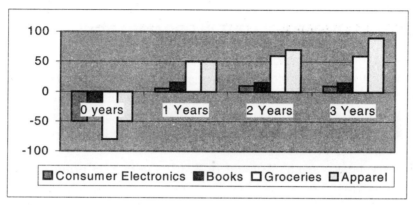

Source: HBR (Economic Times 8/8/2000)

Fig. 3

The impact of Loyalty is measured from the impact on customer defection rate
In **Escotel** a concept of **CORA** —Cost of Retaining Acquisition has been introduced. This alike to **Cost of Customer Acquisition** budgets earmarks a part of the organisation budget to various loyalty programmes/schemes & events aimed at increasing customers affiliation to the organisation.

The impact of this was measured on the target segment where CORA was spent- 2189 customers in Kerala.

Defection rate in the non targetted segment : 2.7%
Defection rate in target segment where defined
Loyalty programmes & ownership programmes are run: 0.38%

With these the spend in CORA is recovered in 43 days and the monthly revenue upside is 26% due to the prevention of defection.

Using similar templates Customer Relationship Managers will require to work out appropriate allocation of resources for CORA in their organisations & use these to make the spends that need to go in building loyalty—superior service, loyalty schemes, ownership programmes for relevant customers base, etc.

□ SUPPORTING FINANCIAL INDICATORS

Research by Strategic Planning Institute, Cambridge working with data from 3000 companies show that

- Service leaders on an average change 9-10% more for their basic products and services

- Grow twice as fast as their low service competition.
- Improve market share by an average of 6% / year
- Organisations rated superior on services have a return of 12% compared to 1% for bottom feeders

(Source: The Service Edge—Ron Zemke)

□ CUSTOMER RELATIONSHIP ROLLOUT IN ORGANISATIONS

Having established the financial imperatives of building relationships for referrals to increase sales & loyalty to prevent defections – organisations will need to position Customer Relationship management appropriately within the management structure to ensure the role is not plainly that of a delivery function but also of strategic in nature.

Each part of service delivery each aspect of the following needs a proper implementation:
- Technology utilisation in service delivery
- Process enhancement at each 'Moment of Truth' interaction point of the customer.
- Customer contact manpower resource Development/Reward & Recognition system, etc.

eCRM: Deriving Value of Customer Relationship

■ **Kapil Chaturvedi and Anil B Bhatia**

Abstract

Companies agree that eCRM (eCustomer relationship management) is critical to their businesses, but unfortunately few understand exactly what it is, what is the difference between traditional CRM and eCRM , how to evolve from their existing marketing practices to an eCRM solution ,what kind of technical architecture should be employed and what are the technical and business issues involved .This paper attempts to address some of these areas .It starts with definition of what is eCRM all about ,goes on to present the alternative viewpoints about eCRM ,elicits the fundamental differences between CRM and eCRM solutions and describes the features of of an eCRM solution .It attempts to evolve a broad framework for assessment of the current situation (eCRM Capability Index calculation) and strategy alignment .At last it suggests a broad technical architecture for a comprehensive eCRM solution.

Key Words: *eCRM, Database Marketing, eCRM Capability Index, Strategy Alignment , Technical Architecture*

❏ INTRODUCTION

Customer Relationship Management

Customer Relationship Management (CRM) embeds the view of the customer in all aspects of how an enterprise conducts business. All processes and actions are conditioned by how the customer views and is viewed by the organization, in order to attract and retain a customer base that optimizes profitability and competitive advantage.

In other words, it is all about bringing the customer to the center of activities in an organization, rather than treating him as an outside entity.

The challenges

In today's competitive arena the market dynamics which companies must address in order to survive and prosper are numerous, some of these are

- Newly empowered customers who choose how to communicate with the companies
- Consumers who expect a high degree of personalization
- Emerging real time, interactive channels including e-mail, web, ATMs and call center that must be synchronized with a customer's non-electronic activity. The speed of business change, requiring flexibility and rapid adoption to technologies.

Seemingly overnight, Vendors from all corners have rushed to introduce CRM solutions. Viewing CRM as the next business frontier. Yet many CRM offerings offer at best only tactical improvements –for example some of them automate fulfillment of web leads, other CRM offerings might patch together sales force automation and customer support, producing a fraction of what is required. Among 175 companies surveyed by Information Week Research (Jeff Sweat, Sept 2000) in US that have deployed CRM or will do so within 12 months, 81% are doing client support and services, and 59% sales and fulfillment. Among all companies contacted, just 28% are tackling online sales and fulfillment, and only 20% are creating customized messaging for their customers This indicates that the majority of the companies which are implementing CRM are yet to realize the full benefits

□ WHAT IS eCRM?

In simplest terms eCRM provides companies with a means to conduct interactive, personalized and relevant communications with customers across both electronic and traditional channels. It utilizes a complete view of the customer to make decisions about messaging, offers and channel delivery. It synchronizes communications across otherwise disjoint customer-facing systems. It adheres to permission-based practices, respecting individuals' preferences regarding how and whether they wish to communicate with you and it focuses on understanding how the economics of customer relationships affect the business.

While the definition above is simple, achieving eCRM itself is hard. For business organizations, evolving to eCRM requires process and organizational changes, a suite of integrated applications, and a non-trivial technical architecture to support both the eCRM process and the enterprise applications that automate the process.

□ eCRM VS. CRM

CRM is essentially a business strategy for acquiring and maintaining the "right" customers over the long-term. Within this framework, a number of channels exist for interacting with customers. One of these channels is "electronic" – and has been labeled "e-commerce" or "e-business." This electronic channel does not replace the sales force, the call center, or even the fax. It is simply another extension, albeit a powerful new one, to the customer.

The thrust of eCRM is not what an organization is "doing on the Web" but how fully an organization ties its on-line channel back to its traditional channels, or customer touch-points.

☐ WHY EMPLOY eCRM?

Companies need to take firm initiatives on the eCRM frontier to
- Optimize the value of interactive relationships.
- Enable the business to extend its personalized reach.
- Co-ordinate marketing initiatives across all the customer channels.
- Leverage customer information for more effective e marketing and e business.
- Focus the business on improving customer relationships and earning a greater share of each customer's business through consistent measurement, assessment and "actionable" customer strategies

☐ THE SIX "E'S" OF eCRM

The "e" in eCRM not only stands for "electronic" but also can be perceived to have many other connotations. Though the core of eCRM remains to be cross channel integration and optimization; the six "e" in eCRM can be used to frame *alternative definitions* of eCRM based upon the channels which eCRM utilizes, the issues which it impacts and other factors; the six 'e's of eCRM are briefly explained as follows.

1. **Electronic channels**: New electronic channels such as the web and personalized e-Messaging have become the medium for fast, interactive and economic communication, challenging companies to keep pace with this increased velocity. eCRM thrives on these electronic channels.

2. **Enterprise:** Through eCRM a company gains the means to touch and shape a customers experience through sales, services and corner offices-whose occupants need to understand and assess customer behavior.

3. **Empowerment:** eCRM strategies must be structured to accommodate consumers who now have the power to decide when and how to communicate with the company-Through, which channel, at what frequency. An eCRM solution must be structured to deliver timely pertinent, valuable information that a consumer accepts in exchange for his or her attention.

4. **Economics:** An eCRM strategy ideally should concentrate on customer economics, which drives smart asset-allocation decisions, directing efforts at individuals likely to provide the greatest return on customer-communication initiatives.

5. **Evaluation:** Understanding customer economics relies on a company's ability to attribute customer behavior to market programs, evaluate customer interactions along various customer touch point channel, and compare anticipated ROI against actual returns through customer analytic reporting.

6. **External information**: The eCRM solution should be able to gain and leverage information from such sources as third party information networks and web page profiler application.

eCRM must address customer optimization along three dimensions

- Acquisition (increasing the number of customers)
- Expansion (increasing portability by encouraging customer to purchase more products and service)
- Retention (increasing the amount of time that customer stays customers) An eCRM strategy must be able to identify the expansion potential for each customer. A Company should be able to identify the opportunities to cross sell and up sell to the same set of customers.

An eCRM solution should also establish a central mechanism to determine which customer should receive which investment at the relationship level.

◻ KEY eCRM FEATURES

Regardless of a companies objectives an eCRM solution must posses certain key characteristics .It must be

- Driven by a data warehouse.
- Focused on consistent metrics to assess customer actions across channels.
- Built to accommodate the new market dynamics that place the customer in control.
- Structured to identify a customer's profitability or profit potential, and to determine effective investment allocation decisions accordingly, so that most profitable customers could be identified and retained and the resources could be invested in relationships, which are most profitable.
- The loopholes in traditional CRM packages can be outlined as follows
- The CRM offering remains channel- centric, not customer centric.
- Customer centric metrics is non-existence- Most CRM offerings have weak metrics and measurement capabilities
- Contemporary customer facing system such as sales force automation and customer care have there own IT set up., these systems rarely interact with each other.

◻ EVOLVING TO eCRM

How does a company go about building an eCRM solution? Traditional brick and mortar companies usually start their direct-marketing efforts through simple list pulls and " one shot campaign", and then gravitate to a data warehouse and software for executing multiple, targeted campaigns that run simultaneously and utilize sophisticated capabilities. The diagram depicts the path that typical brick and mortar companies usually follow toward eCRM, along with the characteristics that mark each stage.

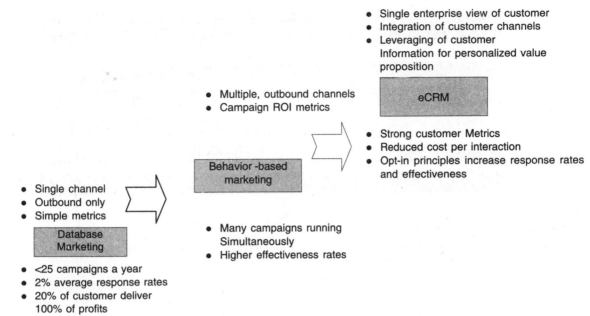

(*Source:* Andy Frawley; Evolving to eCRM: How to Optimize Interactive Relationships with your Customers

Fig. 1 *Various Stages in Evolution to eCRM*

In a nutshell a company evolving to eCRM should:

- Define its business objective; this would be specific and different for different businesses.
- Assess its current position with respect to the environment and determine its current level of "sophistication" along the eCRM continuum (*eCRM Assessment*)
- Define new business processes and align its existing strategy and existing processes in line with the new realities. (*eCRM Strategy Alignment)*
- Define a technical architecture and the criteria's associated with this architecture and the important criteria associated with this architecture. (*eCRM Architecture)*

eCRM Assessment

Before the implementation of a particular strategy in any business scenario, it is worthwhile to know the current state of the business with respect to the prevailing competition. It is very important to devise a numerical measure of how a company measures up in the eyes of the customers with respect to its competitors. In this particular case of eCRM, an eCRM Capability Index could be devised, which provides a benchmark for cross-company comparison. Based on these results, a company identifies quick hits based upon eCRM gap which can be immediately implemented to improve business processes, impact the bottom line and further enhance its understanding of its customers' view of the company. It can also plot the current state of affairs relative to stage, which it wants to attain in the eCRM continuum. eCRM assessment stage would be a diagnostic stage ,followed by eCRM strategy alignment and eCRM architecture stage.

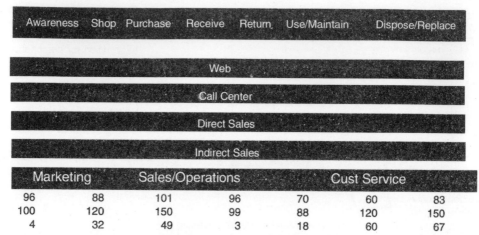

	Marketing		Sales/Operations		Cust Service	
Client Score	96	88	101	96	70	60	83
Peer Score	100	120	150	99	88	120	150
eCRM Gap	4	32	49	3	18	60	67

Fig. 2   *Sample Calculation of the eCRM Capability Index*

Pleasant Transactor	Loyalty Builder (Satisfaction)	Customer Centric	World Class
Levi's	Staples	American Express	????
AT&T	Lexus	Charles schwab	
Cisco	1-800-Flowers		
America Online			
— Efficient operations — Ease of doing business — Lack of specific knowledge of customers — Undifferentiated offering — Volume based — Product based — Emphasis on Revenue — Minimal — Segmentation	— Satisfaction focused — Company "knows you" — Service differentiation based on economic potential — Retention focused — Brand based — Service/event reminders	— Proactive in product/ service development around high value segments — Voice of customer — Active collaboration — Learning organization — Organized (virtually) around customers — Decision making segment driven — Actively grow value of customer portfolio.	— Total experience management — Real-time Information Management — Precision in investments — Coordinated front office/back office — Customer investment focus — Investments based on comprehensive understanding of customer economics — Systematically defined business rules
Price/Volume	Brand	Customer	Value

Fig. 3   *eCRM Continuum on which the Current Position of the Company can be Plotted*

eCRM Strategy Alignment

Every company moving into Customer Relationship Management must make key decisions on a number of significant customer-related factors. Each company must identify, measures, and align to the gaps that exist between customer expectations already measured in the eCRM assessment stage and the internal capabilities that serve these customer expectations.

Stakeholders should be aligned or agree to disagree regarding the following topics

- Common definition of eCRM within the organization
- Where do we fit today in the eCRM continuum?
- How far do we want to/can we go on the continuum
- Segmentation strategy (Tier 1,2,3)
- eCRM scope (sales, marketing, service, fulfillment)
- What channels (direct, agency, dealers, retail)
- What access methods (call center, web, email, kiosk)
- High level routing business rules (customer, event, product)

- Key internal processes (mapped to customer experience)
- Context scoping diagram
- Key knowledge objects (customer profile, product, price, case, etc.)
- Organizational considerations (work group, universal agent, etc.)
- How measured/what measures
- High level technical architecture/interfaces
- 12-18 month plan in 6 month segments
- High level business case
- Quick hits

Fig. 4 *Issues on which Consensus should be built between stakeholders while Implementing eCRM*

Ideally in this module a company should try to build up consensus across functions in the areas shown in the figure on the key decisions, which the company needs to take to satisfy the customers expectations.

The output of these sessions combined with initial eCRM Assessment form a knowledge-book that includes the agreed-upon strategy and alignment areas, a phased transformation approach and supporting high-level business cases.

eCRM Architecture

The primary inputs to this module are mainly from the eCRM Assessment and strategy alignment modules. During this stage the company will try and develop a Connected Enterprise Architecture (CEA) within the context of the company's own Customer Relationship Management strategy. The following is a set of technical eCRM capabilities and applications that collectively and ideally comprise a full eCRM solution:

- *Customer analytic software* predicts, measures, and interprets customer behaviors, allowing companies to understand the effectiveness of eCRM efforts across both inbound outbound channels. Most importantly, customer analytic should integrate with customer-communications software to enable companies to transform customer findings into ROI-producing initiatives.
- *Data mining software* builds predictive models to identify customers most likely to perform a particular behavior such as purchase an upgrade or churn from the company. Modeling must be tightly integrated with campaign management software to keep pace with multiple campaigns running daily or weekly.

- ***Campaign management software*** leverages the data warehouse to plan and execute multiple, highly targeted campaigns overtime, using triggers that respond timed events and customer behavior. Campaign management software tests various offers against control groups, capture promotion history for each customer and prospect, and produces output for virtually any online or offline customer touch point channel.
- ***Business simulation*** used in conjunction with campaign management software optimizes offer; messaging and channel delivery prior to the execution of campaigns, and compares planned costs and ROI projections with actual results.
- *A* **real time decision engine** coordinates and synchronizes communications across disparate customer touch point systems .It contains business intelligence to determine and communicate the most appropriate message, offer, and channel delivery in real time, and support two-way dialogue with the customer.

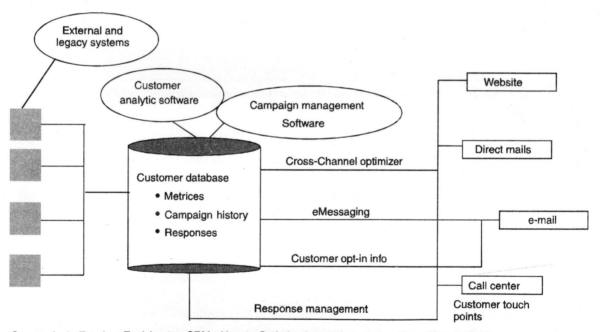

Source: Andy Frawley; Evolving to eCRM : How to Optimize interactive relationships with your Customers

Fig. 6 *Basic Components and Architecture of an eCRM Solution*

☐ TECHNOLOGICAL AND BUSINESS ISSUES INVOLVED

- **Switching costs** involved in shifting to the new system
- **Scalability and Reliability:** Whether the system would be able to adopt to new levels of Usage and functionality
- **Security:** The information risks arising because of the threats to data integrity, violations of confidentiality and data integrity should be taken care of.

◻ CONCLUSION

Regardless of the type of the business a company is into, the companies following the basic eCRM tenets —cross channel coordination, warehouse-centric customer profiling, personalization, permission marketing, and consistent and continuous measurement and assessment-can achieve considerably higher response rates and ROI on marketing programs. These companies will have far easier time attracting, retaining, and expanding profitable relationship with the customer.

REFERENCES

Andy frawley, Chairman and CEO Xchange Inc, *'Evolving to eCRM: How to optimize interactive relationships with your customer'* ,an eCRM white paper

Patricia.B.Sybold and Ronni.T.Marshak, *'Customers.com Hand book, Patricia Seybold Group INC'*, November 1998

Jeff Sweat, *'CRM Comes under Scrutiny'*, Sept 26(Source www.crm-forum.com)

www.xchange.com

Chapter 13

Review and Comparative Assessment of CRM Solutions for Key Verticals

■ **Sanjaya S Gaur**

Abstract

The CRM application market is besieged with products from different vendors, all promising to provide deep and compelling functionality. The functionality needed for a CRM does not come in a neatly packaged suite. Instead application suites are available from multiple vendors, and those applications might not work well together. The objective of this paper is to identify the key requirements both functional and technical for CRM solution and discuss the functional components of CRM solution. An attempt also has been made to discuss the CRM application requirements very specific to some of the verticals viz. Banking, Consumer Goods, Pharmaceutical & Healthcare and Telecom Services and match the requirements of these verticals with some of the solutions available. A comparative assessment of the CRM solutions available from the vendors viz. Seibel, Clarify, Oracle and Vantive has also been done for the four verticals. Finally, recommendations have been made for a suitable solution for a vertical.

Key Words: *Functionality, CRM Solutions, Application Requirements, Verticals, Comparative Assessment*

❑ INTRODUCTION

Customer Relationship Management (CRM) represents the culmination of a long-term, evolutionary shift in the traditional thinking of business. Until the past few decades, the business of the global economy was, essentially, manufacturing. The focus on goods rather than services led to a product-focused, mass-market marketing strategy in which businesses tried to sell the same product to as many people as possible. The result was a high cost of acquiring new customers, and a low cost for customers switching to other brands. When all the value is in the product— rather than in the relationship with the vendor—there's little reason for customer loyalty if a better price or new feature pops up somewhere else. To counter the negative aspects of this situation and to increase customer loyalty, companies are moving toward a more customer-centric perspective and this has been enabled by CRM solutions. CRM takes a customer-centric view of the entire customer life cycle, which means that CRM applications place the customer at the center of the organization's universe. CRM applications facilitate the coordination of multiple business functions (sales, marketing, service, and support) and focus them on satisfying the needs of the customer. CRM applications also coordinate multiple channels of communication with the customer — face-to-face, call center, and the Web — so that organizations can accommodate their customers' preferred channels of interaction.

CRM is both a discipline and a set of discrete software and technologies whose goal is to reduce sales cycles and selling costs, increase revenue, identify new markets and channels for expansion, and improve customer value, satisfaction, profitability, and retention. CRM software applications embody best practices and employ advanced technologies to help organizations achieve these goals. This paper reviews few leading CRM solutions and attempts to match them with the requirements of the key verticals.

□ METHODOLOGY ADOPTED

Methodology adopted includes extensive literature survey to glean information available on the subject. The identification of technical and functional requirements for CRM solution has been done by gathering all the information available on the subject from the Internet sites and from the publications by the CRM vendors. The CRM application requirements for specific verticals have been identified by interactions with the domain experts for the verticals. At least three experts for each vertical were interviewed. The matching of the requirements of the verticals with the solutions available and comparative assessment of the solutions has been done primarily by gathering secondary information on the solutions from the product brochures and from the User Guides of the solutions. Of course the methodology adopted had its own limitations. The information collected from the product brochures and the user guides may have the bias of the product vendor.

Categories of CRM Solutions

Any enterprise, which wants to implement CRM solutions, can choose from four categories of solutions.
- Integrated Application Suite
- Interfaced Application Bundle
- Interfaced Best-of-breed solution
- Best of cluster

Selecting an interfaced best of breed approach for pure functionality or a front-office application suite solely for integration limits enterprise choices. Enterprises need to start with a clear picture of the basic truths of integration, interfacing and functionality. An integrated application suite is a set of applications that employ a common architecture, referencing a common logical database with a single schema. Some suites are more of an interfaced application bundle, i.e. a set of interfaced applications from a single vendor containing more than one technical architecture, or more than one logical database - frequently assembled by the vendor through the process of acquisition or partnership.

An alternative approach to suites is an interfaced best-of-breed solution- an approach whereby an enterprise selects from multiple vendors a set of applications that must be interfaced to work together, either by the enterprise, one of the selected vendors or a third-party integrator. The individual applications are not the best in any objective sense. Rather, some enterprises select the applications because they best meet the particular needs. The challenge with this approach is that, in some cases, the enterprise fails to complete the necessary interfaces to get the individual applications working together; consequently, the applications remain stovepipes. Best-of-cluster is similar to best of breed, except that here best is chosen from the cluster and they are interfaced.

☐ KEY REQUIREMENTS FOR CRM SOLUTION

Some of the functional and technical requirements for CRM solutions are as listed below:
- Business Intelligence and Analytical Capabilities
- Unified Channels of Customer Interaction
- Support for Web-Based Functionality
- Centralized Repository for Customer Information
- Integrated Workflow
- Integration with ERP Applications

☐ FUNCTIONAL COMPONENTS OF CRM SOLUTION

CRM applications are a convergence of functional components, advanced technologies, and channels. Functional components and channels are described below.

Sales Applications

The thrust of Sales force Automation (SFA) is automating the fundamental activities of sales professionals, both in the field and internally. Common applications include calendar and scheduling; contact and account management; compensation; opportunity and pipeline management; sales forecasting; proposal generation and management; pricing; territory assignment and management; and expense reporting. Hand-in-hand with SFA applications is the sales configuration application, which allows application users (either a customer or sales representative) to assemble product components into finished goods. Depending on the level of technical abstraction, users typically do not need to know how the components fit together or even that they can fit together. Rules are programmed into the configuration application and are abstracted from the user. Sales configurators are particularly suitable for the Web because users do not need a technical background to assemble complex products. An example is Dell Computer, which allows its customers to configure and order personalized PCs via the Web. Unassisted web sales capabilities, which enable customers to select and purchase products or services via the Web, round out the sales portion of a CRM solution.

Marketing Applications

The newest breed of application in the CRM space is the marketing automation solution. Marketing automation applications, which complement SFA applications, provide certain capabilities that are unique to marketing. These include web-based and traditional marketing campaign planning, execution, and analysis; list generation and management; budgeting and forecasting; collateral generation and marketing materials management; a "marketing encyclopedia," which is typically a repository of product, pricing, and competitive information; and lead tracking, distribution, and management. Marketing automation applications differ from SFA applications in the services they provide and the targets of those services.

Customer Service and Support Applications

Rounding out the functional components of a CRM solution are customer service and support (CSS) applications. These applications, which are typically deployed through a call center environment or over the Web for self-service, allow organizations to support the unique requirements of their customers with greater speed, accuracy, and efficiency. Typical CSS applications include customer care; incident, defect, and order tracking; field service; problem and solution database; repair scheduling and dispatching; service agreements and contracts; and service request management.

☐ VERTICAL SPECIFIC CRM APPLICATION REQUIREMENTS

Industry verticals especially financial services, high technology, telecommunications and utilities industries need to adopt CRM strategies the fastest as these are the verticals, which sit upon huge amount of customer data because of high amount of interactions with the customer. Any CRM solution cannot isolate itself from the functionalities specific to industry verticals, as each vertical has it's own set of requirements. The functionality set pertinent for certain verticals, viz. consumer goods, Communication, Commercial Banking, and pharmaceutical & healthcare are detailed below:

- Consumer Goods:
    1. Category Management
    2. Promotion Management
    3. Demand Planning
    4. Interactive Selling
- Telecom Service Providers:
    1. Blended sales and service contact center
    2. Competitive Pricing Analysis

3. Integration with Billing System
4. Churn Management
- Commercial Banking:
  1. Contact Center
  2. Profitability Analysis
  3. Integrated Targeted Marketing
  4. Data Mining
- Pharmaceuticals & Healthcare:
  1. Contract Management
  2. Marketing Analysis
  3. Disease Education Systems
  4. Knowledge Management Systems

A serious look into what the CRM applications market talks of vertical functionality clearly shows that most of the front office suites lack vertical functionality.

Given below is a brief review of what some of the known vendors in this area have in their applications for these verticals. The Table-1 at the end gives comparative assessment of the products discussed below for the above verticals.

□ SIEBEL

It continues to outmarket and outsell the competition. It is one of the few front office suite vendors having vertical specific functions. Its functionality is compelling. It can be integrated with most of the back office solutions like SAP and Oracle. It has solutions for automotive, public sector (US), communications, consumer goods, apparel & footwear, energy, finance, insurance, healthcare, life sciences and high technology industry sectors. The solutions for the verticals described above are discussed below:

- *For Consumer goods:* Siebel eConsumer Goods offers eBusiness solution spanning the entire demand chain from the end consumer, through the retailer and the wholesaler, to the manufacturer. It has robust trade promotions planning functionality allowing users to manage customer promotion plans and the funds to support them, while comprehensive route planning functionality enables integrated account targeting. Using Siebel eConsumer Goods, organizations can also identify customer-buying behaviors and translate this understanding into new trade promotions and product offerings.
- *For Financial Services:* Siebel eFinance enables banking, brokerage, insurance, and capital markets organizations to establish and maintain long-term profitable relationships with consumers, small businesses, and corporate customers. The organizations can capitalize on information captured during each customer interaction to more effectively cross-sell and up-sell additional products and services. Additionally, Siebel eFinance provides a comprehensive view of the entire customer relationship across multiple product lines, enabling financial service organizations to provide a personalized experience across all channels.

- *For Healthcare:* Siebel eHealthcare gives organizations the ability to streamline and improve sales, member services, medical management, and network management services. By using multiple distribution channels, including the Internet, field, call centers, home office staff, and independent brokers, Siebel eHealthcare provides organizations with a single view of their customers, thereby ensuring better service and improved quality of care.

- *For Telecom service Providers:* Siebel eCommunications helps wireless, cable, and Internet service providers to target and win the right customers, accelerate service delivery, and provide service across all touchpoints. Siebel eCommunications embodies the industry's best practices for generating accurate service orders, managing billing inquiries and adjustments, and up-selling and cross-selling additional services. By using Siebel eCommunications' integration technology, service representatives and salespeople can instantly access information such as billing, order management, and network management from Operations Support Systems (OSS), to deliver highly responsive customer support and significantly increase sales.

☐ CLARIFY

It offers customer service & support and field service suite; however its sales functionality is immature. As far as verticals are concerned it has separate solutions for some of the verticals such as chemicals, automotive, public sector (US), communications, energy, finance, insurance, healthcare, pharmaceutical, high technology, retail and travel sectors. It can be integrated with most of back office solutions.

- *For Healthcare:* Clarify eFrontOffice integrates how enterprises manage customer and partner relationships while helping them extend their sales and service channels to the web. Clarify's product suite includes logistics capabilities tailored to drug development and testing. On the retail side, Clarify eFrontOffice helps pharmaceutical companies heighten brand value and recognition and increase customer loyalty. Sales force automation capabilities facilitate product promotion for pharmaceutical companies with large mobile sales organizations that need to visit hospitals, doctors, and other influences.

- *For Telecom service Providers:* Clarify eFrontOffice seamlessly integrates customer management and partner relationships while helping them extend their sales and service channels to the web. Clarify's market-leading solution for the communications industry, Clarify CommCenter, integrates the efforts of all customer-facing organizations with applications for customer care and service delivery, service assurance and trouble ticketing, sales force automation, workforce automation, and help desks. In addition to uniquely linking the sales and service side of the communications business, Clarify CommCenter works seamlessly with existing back-office applications to unite the enterprise around the customer.

- *For Financial Services:* The financial service CRM solution of choice is Clarify eFrontOffice. Clarify helps all types of financial services companies to integrate and manage multiple delivery channels for customer access. Clarify also allows them to define products and service delivery quickly, even as business models evolve and market conditions change. Clarify eFrontOffice uniquely addresses workflow processes; key contact points, and integration of each function within the business. Information from each customer interaction is fed into an integrated data model, promoting both detailed analysis and strategic planning—a must for highly competitive, rapidly changing business environment.

❏ ORACLE

Oracle is betting everything on its thin, Web Based, centralized computing model. The internet computing architecture is compelling for connected, non mobile users, Oracle is rebuilding functionality on the new platform and integrates its various acquired products. It offers a broad set of functionality across e-commerce, front office and business intelligence applications. However, functionality in some areas is rich but not integrated within the bundle, while the other modules are too integrated and cannot be easily unbundled from Oracle back office applications. Still other components are light in functionality and immature. As far as solution for the verticals are concerned, though it talks of having a separate solution for each vertical but the functionalities provided for each sector appear to be very superficial. Moreover, it talks of having some modules in the integrated application suite that is suitable for a specific vertical. The verticals are chemicals, automotive, public sector (US), communications, aerospace & defense, consumer products, finance, education, healthcare, pharmaceutical, high technology and retail sectors. It has yet to deliver deep, multi-channel vertical functionality as far as CRM is concerned.

❏ VANTIVE

Vantive offers a compelling customer service and support and field service suite. The rest of its front office functionality makes it suite more of a bundle, since it is based on recently announced partnerships of original equipment manufacturer agreements with complementary providers. Vantive was one of the first suite vendors to offer a solution for managing selling partners, however production sites are still limited. Vantive offers a broad breadth of horizontal functionality that should be further integrated and tested in production environments. The solution is integrated with People Soft at the back office which provides vertical specific functionality for utilities, automotive, public sector (US), service industries, transportation, finance, insurance, healthcare, pharmaceutical, retail and travel sectors The separate solution for each vertical is again missing from the suite as far as front office is concerned.

Table 1 *Comparative Assessment of CRM Products for Vertical Specific Requirements*

Verticals Specific CRM Application Requirements	Siebel	Clarify	Oracle	Vantive
Consumer Products				
Category Management	Available	Available	Available	Available
Promotion Management	Available	Available	Available	Available
Demand Planning	Available	N.A.	Available	N.A.
Interactive Selling	Available	Available	Available	Available
Telecom Service Providers				
Blended sales and service contact center	Available	Available	Available	Available
Competitive Pricing Analysis	N.A.	N.A.	N.A.	N.A.
Integration with Billing System	Available	Available	Available	N.A.
Churn Management	Available	Available	Available	N.A.
Commercial Banking				
Contact Center	Available	Available	Available	Available
Profitability Analysis	Available	Available	Available	Available
Integrated Targeted	N.A.	N.A.	Available	N.A.
Marketing Datamining	N.A.	N.A.	Available	N.A.
Pharmaceutical & Healthcare				
Contract Management	Available	N.A.	Available	N.A.
Marketing Analysis	N.A.	Available	N.A.	N.A.
Disease Education System	Available	N.A.	N.A.	N.A.
Knowledge Management System	Available	Available	N.A.	Available

N.A. = Not Available

P.S.: Apart from the above solutions, there also exist few vendors specific to particula industry that may provide deep, multi-channel vertical functionality but have yet to delive functionality in more than one area of CRM.

◻ CONCLUSION

After looking at the vertical functionality provided by each of the solutions, it can be inferred that still much functionality is desirable from these solutions. But amongst the four Siebel clearly stands apart when talking of vertical specific functionality. A look into the respective strengths of each of the solutions shows that in the verticals where call center is important, like financial services and telecom service providers, solution from Clarify would suit the best needs of the industry but in Consumer Goods and Pharmaceutical sector, Siebel appears to be the best option.

From the above discussions, it clearly emerges that CRM solutions are an intertwined combination of technology and business processes. In order to be effective, CRM service providers will need a balanced understanding of both products and services. Technologists and strategists alike should have their sights focused on the CRM "whole" and not just its "parts". At the same time, it is vital to have deep expertise in not only CRM technology but also customer service processes. Expertise in particular vertical industries will further strengthen the competitiveness of CRM solution vendors. The next step for the CRM solution vendors will be to concentrate on the verticals and develop solution that addresses the issues pertaining to the requirements of the verticals. This will lead to emergence of new kind of vendors who may specialize in solutions for particular industry verticals.

REFERENCES

Following Secondary Sources of information have been extensively referred for the preparation of this paper. Author also thankfully acknowledges all the help received from his ex student Mr. Kunal who is now with Satyam Enterprise Solutions Limited and Mr. Kunal's Colleague at SESL Mr. S. Om Prakash.

'CRM Lifecycle', Report by *Hyperion Solutions*, Feb 1999

'CRM Phenomena', White Paper by *Magic Solutions*, www.magic-5w.com

'Oracle CRM: enabling e-business through unified channels, customer intelligence, and the internet', Report by *Oracle Corp*, May 1999

Bill Schmarzo and David Harper, 'Making Every Relationship Count' Report from *Sequent Systems*, June 1999

'CRM Services Market', *International Data Corp Report*, 1999

David Puckey, 'Modeling Customer Relationships', www.crm-forum.com

Francis Buttle, 'CRM Value Chain', www.crm-forum.com

Frank Teklitz and Robert L. McCarthy, 'Analytic CRM', www.sybase.com

Garrett Brooks, Todd Wadhams, and Brian Siefering, 'Oracle CRM Integration to the back office—Approaching the one stop solution', *Andersen Consulting Report*, 1999

J Golterman, 'Gartner Group's Symposium Conference, CRM Scenario', SYM9CRMScen1099

Lawrence M. Fisher, 'Front Office Solutions', Excerpt from his writings in New York Times

M J Xavier, 'Marketing in Ecommerce Era', www.crm-forum.com

Merlin Stone (1999) 'Paradigms in customer management', *IBM Report*

Michael Meltzer, 'Integrating Call Center with Customer Information', www.crm-forum.com, Oracle Crop Presentation on CRM

Peter Child, Robert J. Dennis, Timothy C. Gokey, Tim I. McGuire, Mike Sherman, Marc Singer, 'Can Marketing Regain Personal Touch', www.mckinseyquarterly.com

Richard Heygate, 'Customer Analysis', *Sophron Partner Report*, 1999

Website: www.clarify.com, www.oracle.com, www.siebel.com, www.vantive.com,

The Evolution of Relationships
in e-Marketing

■ **Stewart Adam, Rajendra Mulye and Kenneth R Deans**

Abstract

Since 1994, Australian and New Zealand business has used the graphical face of the Internet, the World Wide Web (Web), for a number of market-related purposes. Adam and Deans (2000) postulated that these uses depend on the time that businesses, in particular, have used the Web. They postulated that initial business use of the Web involved marketing communication and that over time, business use has extended to use for marketing channel transactions, and from this use to relationship development an enhancement.

The initial study—the WebQUAL Audit—involved an online email and Web form probabilistic study of Australian and New Zealand domain names followed by content analysis by a single researcher of respondent Websites, and personal interviews with a number of respondent sites (Deans and Adam 1999; Adam and Deans 2000).

This paper further analyses WebQUAL Audit data to test the main proposition in the earlier-mentioned paper, which was refuted at that time on an initial analysis (Adam & Deans 2000)

Key Words: *Customer Relationship Management, eMarketing, eCommerce.*

☐ INTRODUCTION

The importance of customer relationships in marketing, particularly the business-to-business (B2B) sector, is well-documented (Gronroos, 1994; Gummesson, 1997; Mattsson, 1997; Palmer, 1997; Payne, 1997; Ravald and Groonroos, 1996; Selnes, 1995). Against a backdrop involving a change in emphasis within marketing science and practice from a prescriptive use of what are termed marketing mix elements to a relationship perspective, the Internet (Net) and its graphical face the World Wide Web (Web) are now causing a further paradigm shift. Since the beginning of commercial use of the Web in 1994, the science and practice of marketing has shown it is no less immune to the advance of this disruptive technology than any other aspect of commerce and government (Downs and Mui 1998; Pattinson and Brown 1996; Slywotzky 1996).

☐ LITERATURE REVIEW

In this section we review the literature relevant to the topic at hand. Firstly, commentary on the movement of customers from being unaware of category needs through to brand loyalty is provided, before examining this in the online context. A review of aspects of eMarketing is also provided.

Marketing and Customer Relationship Management

In concise terms, marketing scientists and practitioners tend to use marketing communications to make customers aware of product category needs and branded solutions, persuade them to consider and buy brands, and then to remind them of their category wants and brand demands. This communication is increasingly targeted, preferably on a one-to-one basis. Moreover, there has been a rise in expenditure on targeted as well as direct and online marketing over mass media communication. In the process, such notions as market share have given way to newer perspectives such as 'share of wallet', among other changes, as business strives to maintain a bridge to loyal and more profitable customers (Peppers and Rogers, 1995; Peters, 1998).

Whether one considers physical goods or products further along the spectrum towards 'almost pure services', there must be effective and efficient fulfilment through management of traditional and digital marketing logistics networks (nee supply chain) as well as upstream marketing channels (Kotler, Brown, Adam and Armstrong 2001). It is after customers have purchased, or products are delivered, that thoughts turn to maintaining and enhancing relationships and attempting to ensure that loyal and profitable customers do not defect (Jones and Sasser 1995). Reichheld illustrated how important customer retention is to profitability when he stated that "At MBNA (US credit card business), a 5 percent increase in retention grows the company's profits by 60 percent by the fifth year" (1993, p.65). Jones and Sasser (1995) examined Xerox customer information and found that its totally satisfied customers were six times more likely to repurchase over the next 18 months than satisfied customers, an outcome they verified across other industries.

e-Marketing

The Gartner Group (1999) describes eBusiness as incorporating: eCommerce transactions, customer relationship management, supply chain management, market intelligence, knowledge management, and collaboration technologies. At no point does the Gartner Group definition acknowledge marketing communication. Adam and Deans (2000) remedy this by referring to three main roles for the Web in their discussion of eMarketing: marketing communication, marketing channel (transactions and fulfillment), and customer relationship management. They acknowledge that government is also using the Web, although differently to business eMarketers.

Until recently, there has been little analysis of how business and government use the Web in the already described processes. There have been published studies and commentaries on aspects of marketing communication such as banner advertising and embryonic perspectives on *interactivity* (Hoffman and Novak 1995; O'Keefe, O'Connor, and Hsiang-Jui 1998; Hofacker and Murphy 1998; Sutherland 1999; Hingston and Adam 2000). The matter of online fulfillment using secure transaction Websites has received much attention by information system professionals in particular (Turban, Lee, King and Chung 2000). How the Web is used in relationship development, maintenance and enhancement has only recently become less of a mystery. On one hand, there are commentaries on vertical and horizontal exchanges, or trade hubs, in the B2B sector (Fitzgerald and Adam 2000). In the B2C realm, Reichheld and Schefter (2000) report that the Web is quite a *sticky* place for U.S. businesses. Stickiness is a term used to describe both how long a guest stays at an individual Website as well as how often she/he returns. These authors point out that at the beginning of a relationship, the outlays needed to acquire a customer are considerably higher in eCommerce than in traditional retail channels. They also point out that in three categories examined most customers defect before the online business reaches break-even point. There are however success stories where relationships develop and customers remain loyal. Reichheld and Schefter (2000) cite the case of eBay.com where the cost of acquiring a new customer is as little as US$10 and referral customers cost even less, with existing customers even helping to maintain the relationship by acting as a helpdesk, for example.

In this paper we endeavour to increase managerial understanding of the use of the Web in relationship-focused marketing science and practice. In doing so, we report on more detailed analysis of data gathered during the survey phase of the WebQUAL Audit in Australia and New Zealand.

◻ WEBQUAL AUDIT IN REVIEW

The WebQUAL Audit methodology has been reported on extensively elsewhere (Deans and Adam 1999; Adam and Deans 2000), and will only receive brief commentary in this paper. The first phase of the study used online techniques (email and Web form) in reaching a probabilistic sample of businesses and government. The first phase involved an email and Web form survey of a probabilistic sample of the 81,563 Australian registered and 17,888 New Zealand registered domain names as at January 1999. An overall response rate of 17% (500/2,976) was achieved taking into account follow-ups. A usable response of 399 (13%) of all domain names in the sampling frame was achieved when taking into account complete responses. A response was received from 319 (13%) of 2,522 Websites forming the business sampling frame and analysed in this paper. The study also employed content analysis and interviews in later phases, however this data is not reported on here.

Adam and Deans (2000) comment on the fact that business lies on a continuum from 'pure bricks and mortar' through 'clicks and bricks' and on to the 'pure dot com' organisation. It follows that these businesses behave differently and have spent differing amounts of time online. Like KPMG (1999), Adam and Deans (2000) observed that most firms—regardless of where the firm lies on the earlier mentioned spectrum—use the Net for marketing communications. They suggest that Australian and New Zealand business is more reticent in its use of the Net as a marketing channel and equally so in use of the Net in customer relationship management. In this paper we use this data from the WebQUAL Audit to analyse the situation further and confirm or refute their proposition in this regard. In particular it seemed that analysis by business type (ANZSIC classification) would present a more meaningful picture concerning Web usage.

Methodology

In this section we examine the data from the WebQual audit to answer the two main propositions raised in this paper.

Proposition 1

The first proposition is that the extent and use of the Web is not uniform across all industries and is likely to vary with key factors related to an organisation's demographics. The demographics examined in this study include the size of the organisation, length of time the company has maintained a publicly accessible Website, the amount budgeted to maintain the company Website in the year surveyed and the company's expected return on investment from expenditure on its Website. This proposition is consistent with Adam and Deans (2000) observation that "business lies on a continuum from 'pure bricks and mortar' through 'clicks and bricks' and on to the 'pure dot com' organisation" and that further analysis of industry groupings would bring forth different results. We identified five industry clusters from our WebQual data based on their similarity of use of the Internet – (1) Manufacturing; Transport and Storage (MTS); (2) Construction; Finance and Insurance; Property and Business Services (CFIS) ; (3) Retail and Wholesale trade (RWT); (4) Accommodation, Cafes and Restaurants; Cultural Services; Personal and Other Services (AFOS); (5) Communication Services (CS). This classification constitutes factor 1 in our two-way ANOVA model discussed later in the section.

Proposition 2

The second proposition relates to the concept of evolution of the functionality of the Internet over time from use solely as a tool for one-way marketing communication to serving a marketing channel role (transactions) and finally to maintaining or enhancing customer relationships. Adam and Deans (2000) observed that most firms, regardless of where the firm lay on the earlier mentioned spectrum, use the Net for marketing communications. They proposed that business was more reticent in its use of the Net as a marketing channel and equally so in use of the Net in customer relationship management.

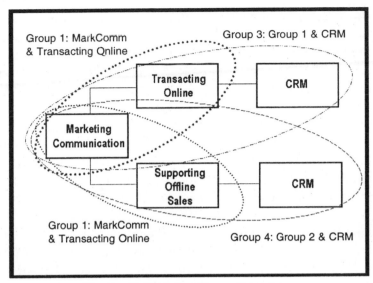

Fig. 1 *Online Business Groups*

To verify this proposition we classified the companies from the WebQual survey into four groups (see Figure 1). The respondent companies were grouped on the basis of whether or not the business is transacting online (eCommerce as earlier defined) or supporting offline sales. In each case, we also examined these groups based on their use of the Net for customer relationship management. This resulted in analysis using the four groups shown in Figure 1. Groups 1 and 2 are mutually exclusive and constitute factor two in our two-way ANOVA model. Groups 3 and 4 are also mutually exclusive and are examined separately; also as factor 2.

The data was submitted to two-way analysis of variance with the two factors described above – industry type and Internet functionality. The five organisational demographic factors (a) Length of time a Website accessible via the public Internet has been maintained; (b) Turnover; (c) Employee numbers; (d) Amount budgeted to maintain the company Website in the year surveyed; and (e) Return on Website investment expectations, were used as the dependent variables.

❏ FINDINGS

The two way ANOVA results for the main effects were found to be statistically significant at the .05 level for three of the five organisational demographic factors – amount budgeted to maintain the Website, turnover, and employee numbers. The results of a post hoc contrast test conducted to find out which particular pairs of industry or functionality were statistically different on the organisational demographic factors are given below.

With respect to amount spent on Website maintenance, the CFIS industry group spent more on Website maintenance followed by the CS group. In terms of Internet functionality, companies using the Web for online transactions spent more on Website maintenance than those using the technology to support off line sales. There is however a significant crossover interaction between the two factors (industry group and Internet functionality). This interaction manifests itself most in the CFIS industry grouping which demonstrates significantly higher amounts spent on Website maintenance in the case of those transacting online as opposed to those supporting offline sales.

The CFIS industry group reports significantly lower turnover than the AFOS and CS industry groupings. Moreover, online transacting companies also reports significantly lower turnover than companies using the Web to support offline sales. Again, interaction between factors is significant and is most pronounced in the case of the CFIS industry group. This industry group also spent significantly more on their Websites where they transact online.

Employee numbers, which is an indicator of company size, is significantly higher for the CFIS industry group. This is particularly so where companies in this industry group are transacting online. There is some interaction between the factors however, the most pronounced interaction, as with the other two variables, relates to the CFIS industry group. The online transacting companies in this sector are significantly larger (higher employee numbers) than those using the Web to merely support offline sales.

When the preceding analysis was repeated for Groups 3 and 4 from Figure 1—using the Web for Marketing communication, marketing channel and CRM—the pattern of results is identical to the pattern already described for Groups 1 and 2.

□ SUMMARY

The first proposition is partly supported in that the industry groups are not uniform in their use of the Web on the basis of three of the five demographic variables examined. They do not differ in their use in terms of the duration of Web usage, nor on the basis of their expected return on their annual Website maintenance budget. They do however, differ in terms of their size as indicated by employee numbers and turnover. Moreover they differ in the amount they spend on their Websites. This is perhaps to be expected given that the CFIS group, particularly the finance and insurance companies, which are 'almost pure dot.coms' (to the extent that they are more information based than groups other than CS) are also large and transacting online.

The second proposition is not supported even though Group 1 differs from Group 2, and Group 3 differs from Group 4, based on the three demographic variables. It can be said however, that there are differences between those companies using the Web for online transactions versus those using the Web to support offline sales. Furthermore, the differences are related to the type of industry involved. While the transition that we suggested is not observed from the current analysis, further investigation at the company level may well show this progression.

REFERENCES

Adam, S. and Deans, K.R. (2000), 'Online Business in Australia and New Zealand: Crossing a Chasm', Full refereed paper, *AUSWEB2K Conference Proceedings*, Southern Cross University, Cairns, (12-17 June): pp. 9-34.

Deans, K.R. and Adam, S. (1999), 'Internet Survey Data Collection: The Case of WebQUAL', Refereed paper, *ANZMAC Conference Proceedings*, University of New South Wales, Sydney, (29 November - 1 December):CD-ROM.

Downes, L. and Mui, C. (1998), *'Unleashing The Killer App'*. Harvard Business School Press, Boston.

Fitzgerald, D. and Adam, S. (2000), 'The Case for Online B2B Trade Hubs', Refereed paper, *AUSWEB2K Conference Proceedings*, Southern Cross University, Cairns, (12-17 June): 81-94.

Gartner Group (1999), *Enterprise Management Alert: Five e-Business Myths that can destroy a Business*, US.

Gummesson, E. (1997), 'Relationship marketing as a paradigm shift: some conclusions from the 30R approach,' *Management Decision*, 35 (4): 267-272.

Gronroos, C. (1994), 'From marketing mix to relationship marketing—towards a paradigm shift in marketing,' *Management Decision*, 32 (2): 4-20.

Hoffman, D.L. and Novak, T.P. (1996), 'Marketing in Hypermedia Computer-Mediated Environments: Conceptual Foundations,' *Journal of Marketing*, 60: 50-68.

Hofacker, C.F. and Murphy, J. (1998), 'World Wide Web banner advertisement copy testing', *European Journal of Marketing*, Vol. 32 (7/8): 703-712.

Hingston, T. and Adam, S. (2000), 'Click-Through Banner Advertising: A Technical Review', Refereed paper, *AUSWEB2K Conference Proceedings*, Southern Cross University, Cairns, (12-17 June): 148-156.

Jones, T.O. and Sasser, W.E. (1995), 'Why Satisfied Customers Defect', *Harvard Business Review*, (November-December): 88-99.

Kotler, P. Brown, L. Adam, S. and Armstrong, G. (2001), *Marketing*. 5th Ed. Pearson Education Australia, Sydney.

KPMG, (1999) *Electronic Commerce: The future is here!* Melbourne.

O'Keefe, R.M. O'Connor, G. and Hsiang-Jui Kung (1998), 'Early Adopters Of The Web As A Retail Medium: Small Company Winners And Losers', *European Journal of Marketing*, Vol. 32 No. (7/8): 629-643).

Mattsson, J. (1997), 'Beyond Service Quality In Search Of Relationship Values,' *Management Decision*, 35 (4): 302-303.

Pattinson, H. & Brown, L. (1996), 'Chameleons in Marketspace', *Journal of Marketing Practice: Applied Marketing Science*, (2/1): 7-21.

Payne, A. (1997), 'Relationship Marketing: The U.K. Perspective,' Keynote address, *Australian and New Zealand Marketing Educators' Conference Proceedings*, Monash University, Melbourne, (December): 1-3.

Pattinson, H. & Brown, L. (1996), 'Chameleons in Marketspace', *Journal of Marketing Practice: Applied Marketing Science*, (2/1): 7-21.

Peppers, D. and Rogers, M. (1995), 'A New Marketing Paradigm: Share Of Customer, Not Market Share, *Managing Service Quality*, 5 (3): 48-51.

Peters, L. (1998), 'The New Interactive Media: One-To-One, But Who To Whom?' *Marketing Intelligence & Planning*, (16/1), pp.22-30.

Ravald, A. and Gronroos, C. (1996), 'The Value Concept And Relationship Marketing,' *European Journal of Marketing*, 30 (2): 19-30.

Reichheld, F.E. (1993), 'Loyalty-based Management', *Harvard Business Review*, Vol. 71 (March-April): pp.64-73.

Reichheld, F.E.& Schefter, P. (2000), 'e-Loyalty: Your Secret Weapon On The Web', *Harvard Business Review*, (July-August): 105-113.

Selnes, F. (1995), 'Antecedents And Consequences Of Trust And Satisfaction In Buyer-Seller Relationships', *European Journal of Marketing*, Vol.32 (3/4): 305-322.

Slywotzky, A. (1996), Value *Migration,*.Harvard Business School Press, Boston.

Sutherland, M. (1999), 'Putting 'Click-Through' In Perspective', *Professional Marketing*, (December, 1999-January 2000): 38-39.

Turban, E. Lee, J. King, D. and Chung, H.M. (2000), *Electronic Commerce: A Managerial Perspective*. Prentice Hall, Inc, Upper Saddle River, New Jersey.

Chapter 15

Implementing a Technology Based CRM Solution

■ **Saket Verma**

Abstract

Evolution in technology and revolution in managerial thought feed on each other. Various 'in-vogue' solutions like Customer Relationship Management (CRM), Supply Chain Management (SCM) etc are a consequence of extant technology supporting academic concepts. CRM as a concept has long been practiced in the industry. However, the increase in transactions, process orientation, decrease in customer loyalty and above all technology advancements have given it a new meaning.

CRM solutions stand on large databases containing customer/transaction data and use it to focus on and acquire/develop profitable customer segments. Processes, people and technology are the cornerstones of CRM. Industry nuances are to be kept in mind while designing a CRM solution for a particular Organization. The CRM market is still evolving. The ERP majors are adding the CRM functionalities to their product suites while other best-of-breed solution vendors are promising the world to their customers.

Key Words: *Technology, Customer Segments, Customer Loyalty, Databases and Functionalities*

□ INTRODUCTION

The romance between business and information technology has frequently resulted in celebrated love childs. The last three decades are witness to the sequential rise of MRP, MRPII, ERP and presently Supply Chain Concept/Customer relationship management. The success of these seemingly simple academic concepts into mega industry trends was enabled and powered by the simultaneous advancements in computing power/technologies. Greater processing power eased the transition from MRP to MRPII and the client server architecture proved to be the mid wife for ERP! With the required data available through the enterprise wide applications, companies have started to think in terms of 'optimising' on the supply chain side and 'connecting' to the *individual* customer on the sales and service side....World wide web and voice-data *technologies* are the moving force behind these advancements!

Yet it is worth remembering that most of the disconnects/disruptions in history were not caused by (though triggered by) a single factor . It is when a number of forces e.g. political, social and technological converge at around a certain point in history that a breakthrough occurs. Seen in this context the emergence of CRM can be attributed to the growing scale and scope of competition, technology enablement, increasing consumer expectations and decreasing customer loyalty.

☐ MANAGEMENT CONCEPT: CRM

Traditionally, the marketing function of any organization has tried to answer the following question:

What needs of *which* customers (to serve) in what *way*?

- *Needs* entails products, services and all the offerings (at a price) that a company makes to its prospective customers. Needs drive the concept of *value*. Simply put, *Value* is the set of benefits a customer is ready to pay a price for......and as a consequence, is *defined* by customer. Any product or service must be designed in such a way so as to deliver maximum value to the target customers. Theodore Levitt in his landmark work " The Marketing Myopia" has elaborated on the issue of defining the industry while keeping the broader consumer needs in mind. Top Information Technology companies has matured from (or is trying to!) product/service organisations into *solution providers*. The jargon has not caught up without reason. The old hat at "Big Iron" hardware i.e. IBM is a case in point. Its metamorphosis from a mainframe vendor to a platform and services company has a lot to do with its financial turnaround. Any CRM initiative must first comprehensively address the customer value management aspect.
- *Customers* covers the concept of segmentation , profiling and profitability et al. Peter Drucker has declared that the aim of any organization is the "creation of customers". The choice of selecting the customer segments and servicing them lies with the company. At the root lies the concept of customer profitability and the strategic fit between the organisation's strengths and it's future vision. Historically, focussed market surveys were the most popular way to gain customer knowledge although people like A.Morita and Sabeer Bhatia might suspect their effectiveness.
- Lastly, *Way* identifies with the channels, distribution strategy, logistics, campaign management etc. The traditional distribution model was based on the chain analogy where inventory stocks were not only the 'links', which kept the chain intact but even defined it. Today more and more organisations are replacing inventory with information and consequently making their supply chains leaner. The customer facing organs of the enterprise have changed dramatically as online web catalogues compete with street corner billboards.

Organisations exercise their choice in selecting particular strategies and structures to fulfill this quest for market leadership. The issue being faced today by corporations is how to identify, select, acquire, develop and retain their customers. For life. The answer to their quest is named as Customer Relationship Management (CRM). CRM addresses all the issues related to *needs, customers and ways* discussed above. In CRM initiatives customer value management is the driving force and business intelligence tools act as enablers.

The cornerstones of CRM are process, technology and people.

- What processes to put in place for managing the customer 24 × 7 × 365?
- What are the mind set, skill and empowerment issues involved?
- Which technologies to leverage/select keeping in mind industry nuances?

It should be clear that the concept of CRM not only encompasses the four P's (Product, Price, Place and Promotion) of marketing but considers the long-term customer retention issue in totality.

The packaged CRM applications try to model the concepts outlined previously on user-friendly technology solutions. These solutions run across a wide spectrum of technology components. Further the three cornerstones of CRM mentioned previously can be mapped on these technology components as explained in the proceeding section.

☐ CRM : APPLICATION AND TECHNOLOGY SOLUTIONS

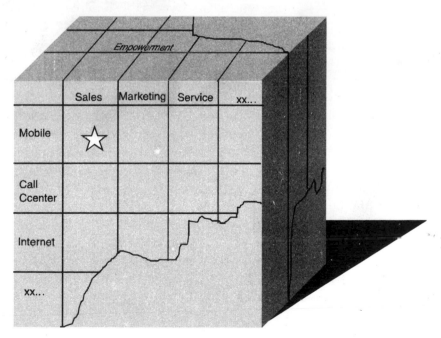

To do the mapping, various scenarios can be formulated by mixing and matching *Processes, Technology components* and *People issues.* These scenarios can then be analyzed and their applicability studies for different business environments. As an illustration, the gridcell for *service* and *mobile devices* has been recently filled up in the banking sector as one can access the account details (for certain) banks on the cellular phone ! As this article goes to the press I am sure more banks will be finalising their plans of filling this gridcell!

Additionally, we can take the scenario (marked *) of a sales man (employed in a FMCG or a white goods company) going to the dealer for a routine call. He can process the customer order by checking his credit limit, finished goods stocks at various company warehouses and the amount outstanding against the dealer plus his past payment behavior. All this and much more if he has the required devices (say a Laptop in this case) along with the appropriate decision making authority! Similarly we can draw up different scenarios for each of the grid-cells. Each will be of significant value for different industries.

The criticality of CRM tools varies as per the industry nuances. Traditionally banking, insurance and brokerage firms etc. are the ones to benefit most from these tools. The reason being that:

- These are *transaction-based businesses,* where capturing each transaction gives you incremental information about the customer. Number of transactions is also high.
- Service is delivered mainly through transactions
- Effect of customer retention on the profits is higher than other industries. The ROI (on technology infrastructure investment) in these industries is highly sensitive to incremental customer increase as these are fixed cost driven businesses where once the fixed costs (technology *and* traditional establishment cost) are covered, contribution goes straight to the bottomline profits.

On the product side, companies involving after sales service leverage the CRM power more than the rest. The key to manufacturing today is to reduce the *production lot size* to ONE unit. CRM tries to do just that for the *customer segment.* Reduce it to ONE unit. Together the two help the company respond quickly to specific customer needs by doing mass customization. Thus the whole order fulfillment cycle time is reduced. More the value of the product and more the product differentiation, higher is the applicability of CRM tools (Mercedes Benz, Three-door refrigerators, Earth-moving equipment etc).

Advancements in analytical databases i.e. warehousing, mining, use of data marts coupled with new channels of reaching the consumers (e-mails, cellular phones, websites etc) will result in CRM taking the shape of a strong revenue driver. The potential use of CRM lies in it being a *leading indicator* of future revenue than just being used as a customer facing transaction processing tool or as a *lagging indicator* communicating past consumer grievances.

The complete concept of CRM can be mapped on a technology solution as per the following blueprint. The databases feed the technology infrastructure which links up with the customer touch points.

Thus we have four components of a CRM initiative roll-out:

- Customer value management strategy
- CRM roadmap keeping in mind the industry nuances

- Database solutions
- Customer access channels

Above all, the IT security issues will have to be addressed as we are discussing large customer databases/ customer knowledge, which are the key to competitive edge.

The following figure should be seen in light of the marketing philosophy explained previously. The strategy and vision aspect refers to the 'needs' perspective. The Customer contact management relates to the 'ways' we discussed. The Customer Intelligence management is the soul of the CRM philosophy as it contains the 'customers' information elaborated in the framework.

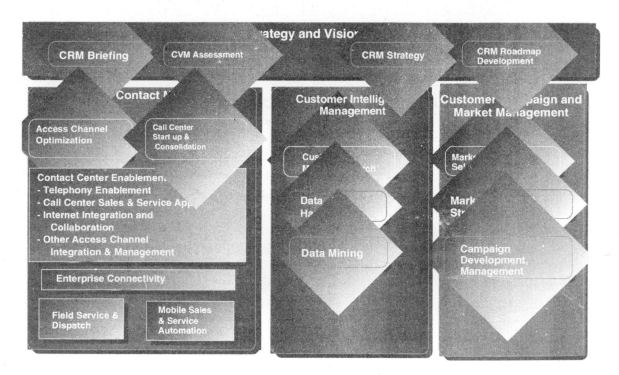

Any implementation services vendor has to address all these factors in the right perspective to ensure a successful project. The key issue is to select a service partner offering the complete suite of CRM initiative requirements as that would not only minimise the project risk but also positively impact the total cost.

☐ CRM: ORGANIZATIONAL VIEW

The CRM initiatives must be viewed from a company wide perspective rather than a 'call center' approach. Any organization is as customer centric as its people. The key to success of an Interactive Voice Response (IVR) or a Computer Telephony Integration (CTI) solution is certainly not the technology working at the back-end but the people using this

Business Value

Business Strategy + Process

e-commerce Applications

Knowledge Management

SUPPLIERS

CUSTOMERS

Supply Chain Management

ERP

Customer Relationship Management

Supplier Facing

Business Operations

Customer Facing

Business Intelligence

Enablement Tools and Services

Web + IT Integration

Technology Value

technology. Organization's policies and procedures should be aligned to the CRM initiatives. Empowerment and training is essential to make the most of the investment. It is only when the employee is able to get the 360-degree view of the customer the moment he/she calls that he will be able to serve the customer better and identify future business prospects. Companies in India have taken the lead in this regard and are gradually maturing in their line of business.

In today's wired world it is important to examine the place of CRM in the organization form the enterprise solutions perspective. The following map clearly explains the face of the technology-fed enterprise!

It is to be appreciated that organizations can harvest a great deal of profits by smartly leveraging one solution over the other. CRM or SCM would perhaps be more beneficial if the organization has already matured by undertaking the ERP initiative and stabilizing on it.

Indeed technology (applications?) breeds technology!

☐ THE WAY AHEAD....

The concept of CRM has been mapped on technology solutions and is evolving at a rapid pace. Most of the of the enterprise solution vendors have added the CRM component to their offerings and the rest are in the process of doing so. Erstwhile ERP vendors are now hawking the 'complete suite' with ERP (Transaction processing), CRM (Customer facing solutions) and SCM (Efficiency focussed optimizing tools) as their Unique Selling Propositions.

The future lies in an integrated enterprise-wide business planning and transaction system that will enmesh technology, business processes and people in a manner, which can deliver value to all stakeholders and provide sustainable competitive advantage to the enterprise.

But will one integrated package (ERP, SCM & CRM) win the battle or many best-of -the-breed solutions will keep mushrooming? The jury is still out on this issue!

Section III

Implementing CRM

Chapter 16

Optimal Allocation Rules for Customer Relationship Management

■ **Kalyan Raman and Madhukar G Angur**

Abstract

Customer Relationship Management (CRM) is a complex process because it raises a host of challenging business issues that lie at the interface of both Marketing and Finance. Our goal is to mathematically model an important subset of those issues, empirically validate our model and develop decision rules for dynamically optimal allocation of the total marketing resources between an existing customer segment and a new segment. The forces that determine the optimal balance are interconnected because the development of each segment requires resource allocation that comes at the expense of the other segment. The two segments differ in terms of the risk-reward structure because the existing segment is less risky and has a predictable growth pattern whereas the new segment is unknown and will typically have greater uncertainty regarding its future prospects. On the other hand, in keeping with traditional financial wisdom, the new segment will also offer higher rewards compared to the existing market, and indeed it is the possibility of greater rewards that creates an incentive to develop the new segment. Furthermore, payoffs received in the future are worth less than payoffs received today because of the time value of money. On the other hand, salespeople with a strategic perspective may be willing to wait longer to receive payoffs compared to a short-term or myopic optimizer. Since salespeople vary in their degree of risk tolerance, it is clear that the optimal allocation of resources between the two customer segments will depend upon all the following factors: (1) the growth rates of the two segments, (2) the riskiness of the two segments, as measured by variability in growth, (3) the discount factor reflecting the time value of money, (4) the risk tolerance, as measured for instance through conjoint analysis or through self-elicitation, and (5) the extent to which the salesperson is strategic or myopic as measured by the length of the time horizon considered for these activities. From this problem description, it is evident that the formulation of this problem requires a methodology that is capable of modeling dynamic growth, uncertainty in growth and optimizing dynamically under these conditions. We accomplish these tasks by drawing upon the machinery of stochastic optimal control. Our analytical results give clear and unambiguous guidance for the optimal allocation of resources between the two important activities of servicing an existing segment and development of new segment that are central to CRM in all firms.

☐ INTRODUCTION

Customer Relationship Management (CRM) is a complex process because it raises a host of challenging business issues that lie at the interface of both Marketing and Finance. Relationship marketing is a company's effort to develop and sustain a long-range, cost-effective, link with individual customers for mutual benefit. CRM has the potential to improve productivity through enhanced marketing activity under highly competitive environments (Sheth and Parvatiyar, 1995). Although database marketing is significantly better than the traditional market segmentation strategy, it still is far less superior to relationship marketing. In today's world of efficient and effective use of information technology, companies can systematically move from the traditional segmentation approach to the one-to-one personalized mode of relationship marketing (Rogers and Peppers, 1997). Successfully implementing CRM requires a strategic assessment of multiple aspects including organizational learning, employee empowerment, technology solutions, and the creation and effective retrieval of longitudinal customer knowledge base (Shainesh and Ramneesh, 2000).

Our goal is to mathematically model an important subset of those issues, empirically validate our model and develop decision rules for dynamically optimal allocation of the total marketing resources between an existing customer segment and a new segment. The forces that determine the optimal balance are interconnected because the development of each segment requires resource allocation that comes at the expense of the other segment. The two segments differ in terms of the risk-reward structure because the existing segment is less risky and has a predictable growth pattern whereas the new segment is unknown and will typically have greater uncertainty regarding its future prospects. On the other hand, in keeping with traditional financial wisdom, the new segment will also offer higher rewards compared to the existing market, and indeed it is the possibility of greater rewards that creates an incentive to develop the new segment.

It is evident that the formulation of this problem requires a methodology that is capable of modeling dynamic growth, uncertainty in growth and optimizing dynamically under these conditions. We accomplish these tasks by drawing upon the machinery of stochastic optimal control. Our analytical results give clear guidance for the optimal allocation of resources between the two important activities of servicing an existing segment and development of new segment that are central to CRM in all firms.

☐ THE CRM OPTIMAL ALLOCATION PROBLEM

Consider two customer segments: a current segment growing predictably and a new segment growing uncertainly over time. The growth of the existing segment can be modeled deterministically, reflecting the lower uncertainty and higher quality of information about the firm's current market. The growth of the new segment must necessarily be modeled stochastically, reflecting the higher level of uncertainty about the firm's new market segment. The firm's objective is to maximize the utility of expected return from the resources that are allocated between the new segment and existing segment. What is the best allocation between the segments to maximize the expected utility?

Such a problem cannot be characterized as lying exclusively within the domain of either marketing or finance. It has elements of both marketing and finance in that every business faces the problem of deciding how much growth to seek in each of its market segments, and the risk-reward relationship varies between segments in the manner that is typical of financial assets. It is a dynamic problem because the markets are growing over time and it is simultaneously a stochastic problem because the new segment growth rate is uncertain, making it a riskier prospect than the current segment. Given these considerations, it is natural that the development of our optimization methodology is influenced by the literature on optimal asset allocation models and market response functions.

□ THE CRM OPTIMAL ALLOCATION MODEL

Assumptions

(A1) An investment in the current segment enjoys a deterministic rate of return m_C over time, while an investment in the new segment grows with uncertainty at the *average* rate m_N over time. Thus, the *actual* rate of return from the new segment at any given time fluctuates randomly around m_N. Note that these rates of return apply to the entire industry represented by each segment.

(A2) The firm invests a total marketing effort of \$ B in the two segments. The firm faces the twin problems of determining the optimal budget B and its optimal allocation between the two segments.

(A3) We will assume that the product is sold at the price \$p in both segments. The firm's marketing effort is represented by its expenditures on advertising and promotions. Thus, the budget \$B represents the total dollar amount allocated to advertising in all media, sales promotions and personal selling. The firm knows its response functions with respect to marketing effort.

(A4) The firm (or decision maker) is risk averse, and is characterized by a utility function $U(y)$, with $U_y > 0$ and $U_{yy} < 0$.

(A5) The firm seeks to maximize the expected utility of the total return generated by its investment in marketing effort for the two segments, by finding the optimal budget B and its optimal allocation between the two segments.

Optimization Strategy (Stage 1)

In the first stage, the firm decides what proportion of any arbitrary amount B to allocate optimally between the two segments, so that it maximizes the expected utility of the total return across its entire market. In the next stage, it determines the total investment B to maximize its total expected profit from the entire market, given response functions for its marketing effort in each market segment.

The Mathematical Framework (Stage 1)

The above assumptions can be captured in a mathematical framework as follows. Suppose the total market size at time "t" is $Y(t)$. Define the following quantities.

Y_0 = Total marketing investment at the start of the planning period

$Y_N(t)$ = Investment in marketing effort for the new segment

$Y_C(t)$ = Investment in marketing effort for the current segment

$u(t, y)$ = Proportion of total marketing effort allocated to the new segment at time "t."
Clearly, $u(t, y)$ must satisfy $0 \leq u(t, y) \leq 1$; $Y_N(t) = uY(t)$ and $Y_C(t) = (1 - u)Y(t)$ $u(t, y)$ is the firm's control variable, the notation indicating that the firm chooses its investment in the new segment as a function of the current time «t» and current value of its total investment $Y(t) = y$.

μ_C = rate of return from the current customer segment

μ_N = rate of return from the new customer segment

The mathematical model representing the rate of return from the current customer segment growing deterministically at the rate μ_C is an ordinary differential equation (ODE) formulated as follows. The instantaneous rate of return at any time "t" is given by $\dfrac{dY_C}{Y_C}$, which is equal to m_C dt by assumption, and therefore, we obtain the ODE:

$$\frac{dY_C}{dt} = \mu_C Y_C$$

The mathematical model representing the rate of return from the new segment is a stochastic differential equation (SDE) because that rate fluctuates randomly. Hence, in this segment, the rate of return at any given time "t," is a random variable $\tilde{\mu}_N(t)$, where $\tilde{\mu}_N(t)$ = $\mu_N + \varepsilon(t)$, where $\varepsilon(t)$ is continuous-time white noise with zero mean. It follows that the rate of return $\dfrac{dY_N}{Y_N}$ at time "t" satisfies the following equation driven by white noise:

$$\frac{dY_N}{Y_N} = \tilde{\mu}_N(t)dt = (\mu_N + \varepsilon(t))dt = \mu_N dt + \varepsilon(t)dt$$

But White Noise in continuous time is related to Brownian Motion through the well-known relation $W(t) = \int_0^t \varepsilon(s)ds \Rightarrow dW(t) = \varepsilon(t)dW$, whence it follows that $Y_N(t)$ satisfies the SDE:

$$dY_N = \mu_N Y_N(t)dt + \sigma Y_N(t)dW$$

It can be shown that the solution $Y_N(t)$ to the above SDE will be a lognormal process. As $Y_C(t)$ and $Y_N(t)$ grow, the total value of the firm's investment $Y(t)$ grows. The value of the total market investment $Y(t)$ at time "t" is $Y(t) = Y_C(t) + Y_N(t)$.

Objective Function (Stage 1)

Given a planning horizon of length T, the firm wishes to allocate resources between its new and existing segments to maximize the utility of the accumulated value of its total investment in the market over the entire horizon.

$$\underset{u}{\text{Max}}\left[E\{U(Y(T))\}\right]$$

The investment value $Y(t)$ fluctuates randomly over time because the new segment's rate of return is randomly distributed over time. The random evolution of Y(t) may be described by the following stochastic differential equation (SDE).

Stochastic Growth of The Total Market Investment

What proportion of its total growth should the firm seek in each of its market segments? Clearly, greater dependence on the new segment exposes the firm to higher risk but also offers the potential for higher reward. Let dY denote the change in the total value $Y(t)$ over $[t, t + dt]$. Then dY is influenced by two sources: growth from the new segment, given by $u(t, y)Y(t)$, at time "t," and growth resulting from the current segment, given by $(1 - u(t, y))Y(t)$. Consequently, given $dY = d[Y_N + Y_c]$, the dynamics of the processes $\{Y_N(t)\}$ and $\{Y_c(t)\}$, and that a proportion $u(t, y)$ of $Y(t)$ is allocated to the new segment, we obtain: This may be rewritten as follows:

$$dY = u(t, y)\{\mu_N Y(t)dt + \sigma Y(t)dW\} + (1 - u(t, y)) \mu_c Y(t)dt$$

This may be rewritten as follows:

$$dY = \{u(t, y)(\mu_N - \mu_c) + \mu_c\}Y(t)dt + \sigma u(t, y) \ YdW$$

Optimization Solution For Stage 1 (*Optimal Allocation Rule, Given Total Budget*)

Starting at an arbitrary level $Y(t) = y$ at time "t," we wish to maximize the expected utility of the total accumulated value $U(Y(T))$ at the end of a planning horizon of length "T," where $U(.)$ is a given utility function. Let $J(t, y)$ denote the maximum utility attainable by using a dynamically optimal allocation rule $u(t, y)$ over the *remaining* time horizon $[t, T]$, when starting from the value $Y(t) = y$ at time "t." Then $J(t, y)$ satisfies the Hamilton-Jacobi-Bellman (HJB) partial differential equation of stochastic dynamic programming.

$$\frac{\partial J}{\partial t} + \underset{u}{\text{Max}}\left[\{u\mu_N + (1 - u)\mu_c\}\frac{\partial J}{\partial y} + \frac{\sigma^2 u^2 y^2}{2}\frac{\partial^2 J}{\partial y^2}\right] = 0$$

If $J_y > 0$ and $J_{yy} < 0$, where $J_y = \dfrac{\partial J}{\partial y}$ and $J_{yy} = \dfrac{\partial^2 J}{\partial y^2}$ then the optimal solution for $u(t, y)$ in terms of the unknown function $J(t, y)$ is:

$$u(t, y) = \frac{(\mu_N - \mu_c)J_y}{y\sigma^2 J_{yy}}$$

Substituting this into the HJB equation, we get a nonlinear boundary value problem:

$$\frac{\partial J}{\partial t} + \mu_C\, y \frac{\partial t}{\partial y} - \frac{(\mu_N - \mu_C)^2}{2\sigma^2} \frac{J_y^2}{J_{yy}^2} = 0$$

subject to the boundary conditions: $J(T, y) = U(y)$ for any y, and $J(t, 0) = U(0) = 0$ for any t.

A flexible class of utility functions permitting convex as well as concave and linear functions is provided by the specification $U(y) = y^\theta$, where $\theta > 0$. Risk aversion corresponds to a choice of θ such that $0 < \theta < 1$, while risk seeking behavior corresponds to a choice of q such that $\theta > 1$. Finally, a risk neutral decision maker would correspond to the choice q = 1. Assuming risk aversion, we require the condition $0 < \theta < 1$. With this choice of utility function, we can obtain the explicit optimal allocation rule by solving the HJB equation in closed-form. The optimal control is given by:

$$u(t, y) = \frac{(\mu_N - \mu_C)}{\sigma^2(1 - \theta)}$$

The following points about the optimal allocation rule are noteworthy.
(1) It is a time-invariant rule and therefore easy to implement.
(2) It is optimal to allocate a *greater* proportion of the marketing investment to the new segment as its rate of return increases relative to the growth rate of the existing segment.
(3) It is optimal to allocate a *lower* proportion of the marketing investment to the new segment as its variability σ^2 increases.
(4) It is optimal to allocate a *lower* proportion of the marketing investment to the new segment as risk aversion increases (i.e., as θ decreases).

Finally, solving the ODE for the function $J(t)$ yields the following solution for $J(t, y)$:

$$J(t, y) = e^{\lambda(T - t)}\, y^\theta, \text{ where } \lambda = \mu_C\theta + \frac{(\mu_N - \mu_C)^2 \theta}{2\sigma^2(1 - \theta)}$$

Taking logarithms on each side, we obtain:

$\text{Ln}\{J(t, y)\} = \lambda(T - t) + \theta\, \text{Ln}(y)$

$\text{Ln}\{J(0, y)\} = \lambda\, T + \theta\, \text{Ln}(y)$

$\text{Ln}\{J(0, Y_0)\} = \lambda T + \theta\, \text{Ln}(Y_0)$, where

Since $J(0, Y_0)$ is the optimal performance obtainable by following the optimal allocation rule throughout the planning horizon $[0, T]$ starting from the given initial condition $Y(0) = Y_0$, it represents the maximum expected utility obtainable under the given conditions. Thus, given that any *arbitrary* initial marketing investment of $Y_0 = B$ is available for market growth, the firm can maximize the value of its marketing investment by allocating B optimally between the two segments according to our decision rule, and this maximum value $V(B)$ is then given by:

$$\text{Ln}\{V(B)\} = \left\{ \mu_C \theta + \frac{(\mu_N - \mu_C)^2 \theta}{2\sigma^2 (1 - \theta)} \right\} T + \theta \text{Ln}(B)$$

Since the logarithm is a monotonically increasing function, maximization of the value $V(B)$ of any given budget B is equivalent to maximization of the logarithm of $V(B)$. The firm would want to find the budget B in such a way that its expected profit is maximized.

Optimization Strategy (Stage 2)

In the next stage, we determine the arbitrary B in an optimal fashion to maximize expected profit, given market response functions that relate marketing effort to sales in each segment.

The Mathematical Framework (Stage 2)

The firm invests an amount A_C (A_N respectively) in the current (new respectively) market segment, and the total marketing communications expenditure $B = A_C + A_N$. This amount B is allocated optimally between the two segments according to our optimal allocation rule developed in Stage 1. Thus, $A_C = (1 - u)B$ and $A_C = uB$. The response functions relate sales (in units) to the communications expenditure within each segment. The response functions are stochastic and include error terms to capture the effect of other omitted mix variables that may potentially influence market response.

Q_C = Market Response Function for the current segment = $f_C(A_C, \varepsilon_C)$
  with the error term satisfying $E\{\varepsilon_C\} = 0$
Q_N = Market Response Function for the new segment = $f_N(A_N, \varepsilon_N)$
  with the error term satisfying $E\{\varepsilon_N\} = 0$

Objective Function (Stage 2)

Combining the response functions, we derive the total revenues from the current and new markets, subtract advertising costs and find the total expected profit as a function of the total budget.

Thus, the complete budgeting and resource allocation solution for the firm optimally marketing to a current and new segment are given by spending a total marketing investment given by the above expression for B_{OPT}, of which the firm should allocate the amount uB_{OPT} to the new segment and the amount $(1 - u)B_{OPT}$ to the current segment, where the

optimal u is given by the formula $u = \dfrac{(\mu_N - \mu_C)}{\sigma^2 (1 - \theta)}$. Under this optimal behavior, its maximum expected profit is given by the expression for π_{OPT} shown above.

A Numerical Example To Show How The Model Works

Consider the following scenario.
  Selling price p = $10
  New Market Return Rate μ_N = 20%

Current Market Return Rate μ_C = 10%
Standard Deviation of New Market Return σ = 1
Risk Aversion Parameter θ = 0.5
Market Response Function Parameters
$\quad \alpha_N$ = 10, $\quad \beta_N$ = 1.5 in New Market
$\quad \alpha_C$ = 20, $\quad \beta_C$ = 1.0 in Current Market

A graphical representation of our optimality analysis shows the expected profit as a function of the total budget (which has been optimally allocated between the two markets), displayed below.

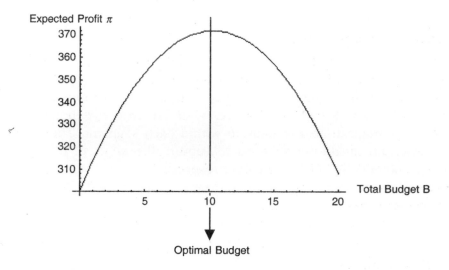

Optimal Budget

The exact solutions (optimal allocation, total budget and maximum expected profit) output by our formulas are shown below.

$$u = 0.2, \qquad B_{OPT} = 10.29, \qquad \pi_{OPT} = 372$$

Thus the firm spends $10.29 units, of which it allocates 20% to the new market and the remaining 80% to its current market and realizes a total expected profit of $372.

□ CONCLUSIONS

In sharp contrast to the flat maxima that have been consistently noted in studies of advertising response, note that the expected profit function in the context of budgeting and allocation is quite steep. Consequently, a firm that determines its budget and budget allocation between market segments on the basis of sub-optimal rules will suffer considerable losses. The steepness of the expected profit function shows that sub-optimal budgeting and allocation imposes heavy penalties on the firm. Our decision technology makes these losses unnecessary. Indeed, by implementing our optimal budgeting and allocation technology, the firm can realize considerable gains from optimal budgeting and allocation.

We have developed a scientific and widely applicable method for optimally making marketing budgeting decisions and for allocating the budget optimally across various market segments. The method takes into account the rates of return from each market segment, variability of return, risk aversion and market response characteristics in a dynamic and stochastic way. Decision makers need not rely on rules-of-thumb and seat- of-the-pants decision-making. By using our model, they can maximize profitability and the productivity of their marketing investments.

REFERENCES

Rogers, M., and Peppers, D. (1997), 'Making the Transition to One-to-One Marketing', *Inc.*, January, pp.63-65.

Shainesh, G., and Ramneesh, M., (2000), 'Status of Customer Relationship Management in India - A Survey of Service Firms', Hosted on the Academic Papers Section of the *CRM Forum Website*, http://www.crm-forum.com/academy

Sheth, J. N. and Parvatiyar, A. (1995) 'Relationship Marketing in Consumer Markets: Antecedents and Consequences', *Journal of the Academy of Marketing Science*, Vol. 23, No. 4, pp. 255-271.

Chapter 17

Measuring the Effectiveness of Relationship Marketing

■ **A Lindgreen**

Abstract

Despite a large relationship marketing literature, there is no consensus as to what it constitutes. Relationship marketing is often described with respect to its purposes as opposed to its instruments or defining characteristics. This being the case, it follows that there are related gaps in our knowledge with regard to how to develop effective relationship marketing programmes and how to measure the level of effectiveness of such programmes. This paper reports on a three-year research programme that involves twenty-four case studies theoretically sampled from the Danish food sector and the New Zealand wine sector. Most of the data stems from in-depth, face-to-face interviews with marketing directors and other people in senior positions. The paper then reports on first the loyalty accounting matrix that is being used by a food catering company in its successful relationship marketing programme and then on the relationship quality between exporters and importers. The paper finally proposes that relationship quality translates into first customer retention and then shareholder value creation and outlines how to test this proposition further.

Key Words: *Relationship Marketing, Loyalty Accounting Matrix, Relationship Quality, Customer Retention, Food Sector, Wine Sector*

□ INTRODUCTION AND LITERATURE REVIEW

Relationship marketing has emerged as one of the major marketing issues in the 1980s and 1990s. Many marketers have considered relationship marketing as a necessary and effective way of achieving competitive advantage - through the creation of relationships, networks and interactions that are long term. Relationship marketing has also constituted a major focus of academic research within different disciplines, including marketing and management (Buttle, 1996; Collins, 1999; De Jong *et al.*, 1998; Möller and Halinen-Kaila, 1998; Rexha, 1998).

Despite the fact that the term 'relationship marketing' was introduced by Berry (1983) more than fifteen years ago, there is still a lot of debate about what is meant by relationship marketing. For example, Brodie *et al.* (1997), Cooper *et al.* (1997), Eiriz and Wilson (1999), Gummesson (1994), Harker (1999), Lindgreen and Crawford (1999), Palmer (1998) and Stone and Woodcock (1995) have noted that relationship marketing means different things to different researchers. As a result, even though a number of approaches to designing, implementing, monitoring and measuring a relationship marketing programme have been suggested in the literature, there is no consistent story of how relationship marketing fits into the greater marketing landscape.

Perhaps the greatest challenge to the theoretical development of relationship marketing has been the lack of empirical investigations that aim at describing and exploring relationship marketing programmes implemented in real-life settings (e.g., Buttle, 1996; Collins, 1999; Lindgreen and Crawford, 2000; Snehota and Söderlund, 1998). To advance our knowledge of relationship marketing, this research, therefore, seeks to describe and explore particular aspects of relationship marketing. That is, measuring the effectiveness of relationship marketing: In what way(s), if at all, might returns on relationship marketing be measured?

❏ RESEARCH METHODOLOGY

The case study method was suitable because relationship marketing programmes are complex, dynamic and not well understood at this time. The research involved twenty-four case studies that were theoretically sampled from the Danish food catering sector, the Danish dairy sector, the Danish bacon sector and the New Zealand wine sector. Each case was embedded, and the unit of analysis was the marketing programme of the winery. Theory was developed using the eight-step procedure that Eisenhardt (1989) has suggested. Most of the data stems from in-depth, face-to-face interviews with marketing directors and other people in senior positions. The use of qualitative in-depth interviews is, by and large, considered to be the most valuable source of information when investigating the underlying meaning of complex phenomena and processes (Dey, 1993; Easton, 1995; Lincoln and Guba, 1985; Miles and Huberman, 1994; Patton, 1990; Perry, 1998).

The analysis of the case study data was carried out in two steps: a within-case analysis and a cross-case analysis (Miles and Huberman, 1994). Each case was evaluated by means of construct validity, internal validity, external validity and reliability (Table 1).

❏ PRELIMINARY FINDINGS

At this stage, only two research findings are discussed briefly: (1) the loyalty accounting matrix and (2) the relationship quality – customer retention theory of creating shareholder value.

Table 1. *Design Tests and Case Study Tactics*

Design test	Theoretical explanation of the construct	Case study tactics
Construct validity	Construct validity is to secure that correct operational measures have been established for the concepts that are being studied (Yin 1994)	• Multiple sources of evidence • Chain of evidence • Interview respondents reviewing the draft of each case study report
Internal validity	Internal validity is to make sure that a causal relationship – certain conditions lead to other conditions – has been established. Internal validity is a concern for explanatory or causal case studies but not for exploratory or descriptive case studies, which do not attempt to make causal statements (Yin 1994)	• Pattern matching • Rival explanation as patterns • Explanation building • Time series analysis
External validity	External validity is to prove that the domain to which a case study's findings belong can be generalised (Yin 1994)	• Specification of the population of interest • Replication logic in multiple case studies
Reliability	Reliability involves demonstrating that the findings from a case study can be repeated if the case study procedures are followed (Yin 1994).	• Interview protocol • Clearly conceptualised constructs • Multiple indicators • Execution of pilot tests • Case study data base

The Loyalty Accounting Matrix

In the Danish food catering sector, customer loyalty is measured by employing a loyalty accounting matrix that follows a customer's relative attraction to, and satisfaction with, the company. Every customer is categorised according to a colour scheme: green, yellow or red customer (Figure 1).

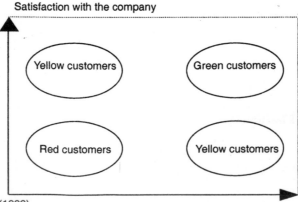

Source: Lindgreen and Crawford (1999)

Fig. 1 *Customer Loyalty: Relative Attraction to and Satisfaction with the Company*

In contrast to 'yellow customers' and 'red customers', 'green customers' are generally more attracted to, and satisfied with, the company than competing businesses. Although 'red customers' and 'yellow customers' have the potential of turning green, experience has taught the companies that 'red customers' are strongly deal-oriented and will usually move their business around to suppliers of lower priced products. With that knowledge, the companies concentrated its efforts on the 'green customers' and 'yellow customers'. In one case, customer records show that in 1996, 14 per cent of the customers were 'green' but already a year after the implementation of a relationship marketing programme, the number had risen to 20 per cent. Indeed, following the two-year programme, 43 per cent of the customers believed that the company had become a better supplier with only 3 per cent having the opposite view.

☐ THE RELATIONSHIP QUALITY—CUSTOMER RETENTION THEORY OF CREATING SHAREHOLDER VALUE

The quality of the relationship between an exporter and his importer was found to be key. Overall, the research explored what constitutes relationship quality and found strong anecdotal evidence that it is made up by six key constructs that have been suggested theoretically by Roberts (1998). That is trust in credibility, trust in benevolence, affective commitment, affective conflict, satisfaction and social bonding. The research also gives evidence that relationship quality translates into first customer retention and then shareholder value creation (Figure 2).

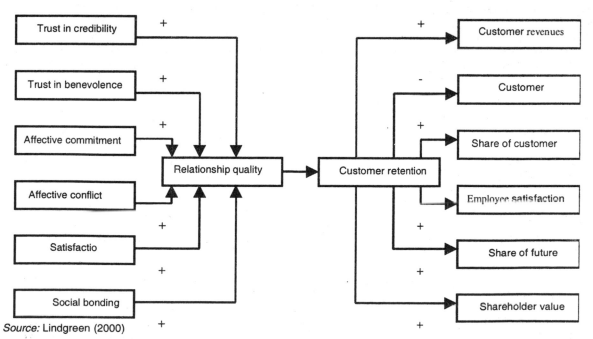

Source: Lindgreen (2000)

Fig. 2 *The relationship quality – customer retention theory of shareholder value creation in relationship marketing*

There is a positive relationship between all of the antecedents and relationship quality and there is a positive relationship between customer satisfaction and all of the consequences (except for customer costs). The measures of relationship quality and customer retention (the focal construct) and the antecedents and consequences of relationship quality and customer retention must capture the importance of a particular construct in a relationship to the respondents. Different items from the literature could be adapted to measure relationship quality and customer retention and also the antecedents and consequences of relationship quality and customer retention. Means, standard deviations, intercorrelations, variances and co-variances for the summates of all research variables could provide an initial test of the hypotheses. For a much stronger test of hypotheses, the model could be tested using LISREL (Bagozzi, 1994; Page and Meyer, 2000).

REFERENCES

Bagozzi, R. P. (Ed.) (1994), *Advanced Methods of Marketing Research*, Malden, Massachusetts: Blackwell Publishers.

Berry, L. L. (1983), 'Relationship Marketing', in Berry, L. L., Shostack, G. L. and Upah, G. D. (Eds.), *Emerging Perspectives on Services Marketing*, Chicago, Illinois: American Marketing Association, pp. 25-28.

Brodie, R. J., Coviello, N. E., Brookes, R. W. and Little, V. (1997), 'Towards a Paradigm Shift in Marketing? An Examination of Current Marketing Practices', *Journal of Marketing Management*, Vol. 13, No. 5, pp. 383-406.

Buttle, F. (1996), 'Relationship Marketing', in Buttle, F. (Ed.), *Relationship Marketing: Theory and Practice*, London: Paul Chapman Publishing, pp. 1-16.

Collins, B. A. (1999), 'Pairing Relationship Value and Marketing', *Australasian Marketing Journal*, Vol. 7, No. 1, pp. 63-71.

Cooper, M. C., Gardner, J. T. and Pullins, E. B. (1997), 'A Benchmark Bibliometric Approach to Identifying the State of Theory Development in Relationship Marketing', in Meenaghan, T. (Ed.) (1997), *Proceedings of the AMA Relationship Marketing Conference,* June, Dublin: University College Dublin and American Marketing Association, pp. 187-203.

De Jong, G., Nooteboom, B., Helper, S. and Sako, M. (1998), 'The Nature of Long-Term Supply Relationships', in Gray, B. J. and Deans, K. R. (Eds.), *Marketing Connections: Proceedings of the Annual Conference of the Australia and New Zealand Marketing Academy*, Dunedin: University of Otago.

Dey, I. (1993), *Qualitative Data Analysis: A User-friendly Guide for Social Scientists*, London: Routledge.

Easton, G. (1995), 'Methodology and Industrial Networks', in Möller, K. and Wilson, D. (Eds.), *Business Marketing: An Interaction and Network Perspective*, Boston, Massachusetts: Kluwer Academic Publishers, pp. 411-492.

Eiriz, V. and Wilson, D. (1999), 'Theoretical Foundations and Research Priorities in Relationship Marketing', in Hildebrandt, L., Annacker, D. and Klapper, D. (Eds.), *Marketing and Competition in the Information Age: Proceedings of the 28th EMAC Conference*, 11-14 May, Berlin: Humboldt University Berlin.

Eisenhardt, K. M. (1989), 'Building Theories from Case Study Research' *Academy of Management Review*, Vol. 14, No. 4, pp. 532-550.

Gummesson, E. (1994), 'Making Relationship Marketing Operational', *International Journal of Service Management*, Vol. 5, No. 5, pp. 5-20.

Harker, M. J. (1999), 'Relationship Marketing Defined? An Examination of Current Relationship Marketing Definitions', *Marketing Intelligence & Planning*, Vol. 17, No. 1, pp. 13-20.

Lincoln, Y. S. and Guba, E. (1985), *Naturalistic Inquiry*, Beverly Hills, California: Sage Publications.

Lindgreen, A. (2000), 'The Relationship Quality – Customer Satisfaction Theory of Shareholder Value Creation in Relationship Marketing', in Trienekens, J. H. and Zuurbier, P. J. P. (Eds.), *Proceedings of the International Conference on Chain Management in Agribusiness and the Food Industry*, 25-26 May, Wageningen: Wageningen Agricultural University & The Foundation for Agri-Chain Competence, pp. 313-322.

Lindgreen, A. and Crawford, I. (1999), 'Implementing, Monitoring and Measuring a Programme of Relationship Marketing', *Marketing Intelligence & Planning*, Vol. 17, No. 5, pp. 231-239.

Lindgreen, A. and Crawford, I. (2000), 'A Multiple, Embedded Case Study of Contemporary Practices of Relationship Marketing in the Danish-British and New Zealand-British Food Supply Chains: Research Issues', *Cranfield School of Management Working Papers Series SWP 5/00*, Cranfield.

Miles, B. and Huberman, A. M. (1994), *Qualitative Data Analysis: An Expanded Sourcebook*, 2nd ed., Thousand Oaks, California: Sage Publications.

Möller, K. and Halinen-Kaila, A. (1998), 'Relationship Marketing: Its Disciplinary Roots and Future Directions', in Andersson, P. (Ed.), *Proceedings of the 27th Annual Conference of the European Marketing Academy*, Stockholm: Elanders Gotab, Vol. 1, pp. 289-310.

Page, C. and Meyer, D. (2000), *Applied Research Design for Business and Management*, New York: McGraw-Hill.

Palmer, A. (1998), *Principles of Services Marketing*, 2nd ed., London: McGraw-Hill.

Patton, M. Q. (1990), *Qualitative Evaluation and Research Methods*, Newbury Park, California: Sage Publications.

Perry, C. (1998), 'Processes of a Case Study Methodology for Postgraduate Research in Marketing', *The European Journal of Marketing*, Vol. 32, No. 9/10, pp. 785-802.

Rexha, N. (1998), 'An Integrated Model that Facilitates the Supplier in Developing Relationships with Focal Customers', in Gray, B. J. and Deans, K. R. (Eds.), *Marketing Connections: Proceedings of the Annual Conference of the Australia and New Zealand Marketing Academy*, Dunedin: University of Otago.

Roberts, K. T. (1998), *Assessing the Value of Relationship Quality in Comparison with SERVQUAL: A Scale Development and Evaluation*, Auckland: Auckland University, unpublished MA thesis.

Snehota, I. and Söderlund, M. (1998), 'Relationship Marketing - What does it Promise and What does it Deliver? An empirical examination of repeat purchase customers', in Andersson, P. (Ed.), *Proceedings of the 27th Annual Conference of the European Marketing Academy*, Stockholm: Elanders Gotab, Vol. 1, pp. 311-330.

Stone, M. and Woodcock, N. (1995), *Relationship Marketing*, Kogan Page, London.

Yin, R. K. (1994), *Case Study Research: Design and Methods*, 2nd ed., Thousand Oaks, California: Sage Publications.

The Past, Present and Future of CRM

■ **Graham Hoskins**

Abstract

CRM has become a globally recognised business practice and yet it is still loosely defined and rarely well executed. This paper provides some reference point in the search to understand CRM better by looking at its forebears and history. It examines current thinking and challenges many views and perceptions about what CRM is and what it is likely to become. It uses real examples to support the view that CRM is not about technology, databases or the market of one. It is about providing choices for customers, enabling them to manage their relationships with us. It is about changing the way we do business and valuing those people who manage our customer interactions. It accepts the role of technology and customer information, but only as enablers.

Key Words: *CRM, Service, Customers, Retention, Business, Technology Enabled, ROI*

□ INTRODUCTION

CRM means many different things to different people. It is possible to develop a greater understanding of it by looking at its origins and the principles that drove its development. By then examining the present day definitions of what it means and examples of who does it well, it is possible to understand more clearly how it could be applied to our own businesses. By looking at the future of CRM, we more clearly see where the benefits may be derived and where we should see CRM developing over the next few years.

□ THE PAST

Looking back at a snapshot history of marketing, we can see the following clear developments and progression over the last four decades:

- **1960's**—the era of Mass Marketing, when Gibbs SR toothpaste began the first marketing of this kind with its black and white TV campaign

- **1970's**—saw the beginning of segmentation, direct mail campaigns and early telemarketing (such as publishing
- **1980's**—where Niche Marketing made millionaires of those who were best at it. You only need to think of Sock Shop, Tie Rack and Anita Roddick of the Body Shop.
- **1990's**—Relationship Marketing. The explosion of telemarketing and call centres, all set up to develop relationships with customers. The recognition of the true value of retention and the use of Lifetime Value as a business case.

In addition to this, a number of key marketing concepts can also be used to see where CRM has developed from:

- Satisfying Needs, Customer Orientation
- The organisation needs to be arranged so that all functions contribute
- Profit must be the consequence of delighting customers (Kotler, 1988)

It is possible to draw further information from the definitions of marketing and direct marketing:

Marketing

"Determining the needs and wants of target markets and delivering the desired satisfactions more efficiently and effectively than the competition"(Philip Kotler, Marketing Management, 1988)

Direct Marketing

"The planned recording, analysis and tracking of customers direct response behaviour over time.... In order to develop future marketing strategies for long term customer loyalty and to ensure continued business growth"

If you now take the key concepts from those drivers and definitions, you can see how they develop into a definition for CRM:

Marketing krywords	CRM
• Understanding target markets • Analysis of response behaviour • Developing loyalty strategies • Ensuring business growth	"... a means of engendering customer loyalty in order to increase revenue and deliver business benefit by focussing on the delivery of customer service throughout an organisation"

☐ THE PRESENT

The key differences between the concepts of marketing and direct marketing is that CRM is about change throughout the whole organization (focused around the customer) and that technology developments are enabling the concept.

What we are finding is that organisations are now moving through several stages of CRM:

STAGE	STATE	CULTURE
SATISFACTION BASED	RE-ACTIVE	Meet costomer needs Respond to complaints Mininal evaluation of customer service levels
PERFORMANCE BASED	PRO-ACTIVE	Evaluate customer preception Identity customer retention factors
COMMITMENT BASED	VERY PRO-ACTIVE	Evaluate miltiple customer needs Continuous inbound/outbound flow and feedback Continuous improvement

Fig. 1 *The Key Stages of CRM*

Source: Customer Service Centres in European Retail, *Datamonitor*, July 1998

Leading them to understand that CRM is about developing organisational change. To be completely successful it must work across all elements of a business from contact centre to web to sales, marketing, logistics, fulfilment and finance. An end-to-end view of process must be taken.

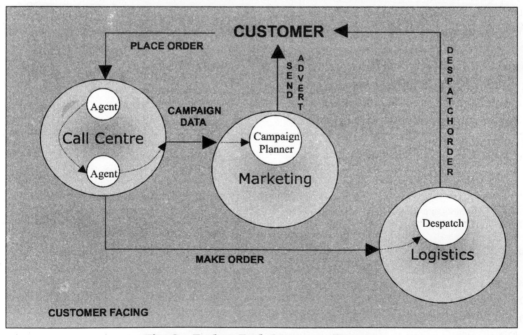

Fig. 2 *End to End Customer Process*

Many practitioners in the CRM marketplace understand the key concepts outlined above. However, the feedback that we get from clients and what we see in the marketplace paints a slightly different picture.

- Business issues remain the same: differentiation; loyalty; profit margin; segmentation; channel
- Until recently, service has progressed nowhere near as fast as it should have or as fast as we would have liked to think it had
- Almost everyone talks about the importance of people – but we rarely see anyone 'walking the talk'
- Whilst business visions are still important, long term (5 year) business plans cannot work—but they still exist.
- The vision 15 months ago that IT and the Internet would replace people in managing relationships, will not happen in the foreseeable future
- Business modelling, forecasting and planning still takes place in isolation and normally at the financial operational level.
- Addressing the balance between user (customer and supplier) frustration with IT solutions and the cost and challenge of integration
- The view that CRM has to be a single system vision is a fallacy. It is a way of conducting business which can – in some instances – be facilitated by single systems
- More and more questions are being asked about the ROI of implementing CRM – particularly by large retailers with multiple access channels

Interestingly, Eastman Software conducted a study recently of the UK's top 1000 companies asking what they saw as the most important elements in successful CRM. The results were:

- Proactive customer management
- Product quality
- A single telephone number
- Web address for all enquiries

In many respects these results are not surprising. There is no mention of end to end process or organisational change. It is still viewed by many to be just about access and the web.

So there are a number of key CRM misconceptions, particularly about technology:

- "New customer-available technology will lead to less service needs and therefore less people".
- "New technology is all about WAP phones, e-mail and Internet via PC's".
- "I need to throw all my systems away and start again in the brave new e-world"
- "The market of one exists"

A recent study by the CRM specialists, Round UK, found the following Top 10 CRM organisations.

1. Direct line
2. Amazon.com
3. Dell
4. HSBC
5. Hewlett Packard

6. BBC
7. Kwik Fit Insurance
8. John Lewis
9. First Direct
10. British Airways *(Round UK, 2000)*

If you were to take Amazon.com as an example, their site is easy to navigate. Their database remembers your previous sales choices and will move you towards appropriately related material. It also remembers your credit card number. Such small details are what make the relationship they develop with you so different.

However, there are still many flaws in the CRM that these businesses provide. There is still a long way to go.

But, it can work. Although we have yet to see any businesses that can prove categorically that the whole CRM strategy creates ROI across every function and at every level, smaller and more easily defined pieces are proven. Providing phone access from the web has doubled one major IT hardware supplier's conversion rate. Giving the customer access choice improved their propensity to buy.

Look at Tesco in the UK. They did not go CRM across the whole organisation in one go. Many retailers cannot because of the implications for legacy systems. However Tesco did embrace the principles of CRM and took more easily digestible chunks and developed new customer propositions that linked together. And it has worked.

□ THE FUTURE

So what does the future hold? The astronomic development rates of technology are what many people see as the key driver. However, they need to look beyond this to the changes in customer expectations (some of which have been increased by what technology enables them to do):

Changing Customer Expectations	*Developing Technology*
• A direct service is no longer enough (19% of customer are unhappy with am/pm delivery) • Speed, ease of access, cheaper transactions • Many customer's still like the personal interaction and 2two way service • There is a choice of communications medium and the customer will choose their access route for acquisition and retention • Automation is becoming less acceptable	• Reduced cost of surfing (AltaVista, NTL) • Web TVs (Alba/Bush) or set top boxes • Web enabled mobile phones • Convergence of data and telephony

Business operations will also need to develop:

- Sales, marketing and service delivery will need to become one, or at the very least, act like one
- Future customer contact models will be based heavily around access

So there is a balancing act between what the customer expects, what the technology enables and how far businesses are willing to go in allowing the customer to manage the relationship.

However, we must bring ourselves back to the principles of CRM. It is not about developing a web portal. It is not about automating contact centre services. It is about enabling customer access, providing choice and allowing the customer to manage the relationship. It is also about centralising and creating easy access to customer information so that the relationships can be better understood, managed and maximised. This will not be easy for some organisations. Generally speaking, the bigger an organisation and the older its legacy systems, the harder it is develop an effective CRM strategy. The newer more flexible businesses that can develop new systems and processes rather than adapt old ones have an advantage.

In terms of what the future holds, here is a summary:
- Customer will play a significant role in managing relationships
- Service models will continue to change (skills, remuneration, volumes transaction types)
- The web will create globalisation but will replace the need for people, at least not for the foreseeable future
- Technology will consolidate (fixed and mobile telephone, email/web/ecommerce)
- WAP and VOIP—wait and see. It has not been the great explosion that was expected

And what do you need to do to get there?
- Develop end to end customer processes
- Make the best possible use of customer knowledge – particularly when you are transacting with them
- Be interactive
- Provide seamless and integrated choice for customers
- Use your people
- Recognise customer individuality
- Rethink telephone automation

CRM can and does work. Move quickly but be nimble and adaptable.

REFERENCES

Kotler, Philip (1988), *Marketing Management*, Prentice Hall, Engelwood Cliffs, New Jersey.

Chapter 19

Implementing a Technology Based CRM Solution

The ICICI Experience

■ **Avijit Chaudhuri and G Shainesh**

Abstract

ICICI has transformed itself into a technology intensive financial services group in the last decade. To achieve its long term goal of being in a position to practice 1to1 marketing, ICICI has taken a series of initiatives. As part of the plans, it is implementing various projects to establish world-class CRM practices, which would provide an integrated view of its customers to everyone in the organization The paper discusses some of the lessons learnt while implementing these projects.

Key Words: *CRM Roadmap, Business Transformation, CRM Business Cycle*

□ INTRODUCTION

ICICI, set up as a Development Bank over four decades ago to provide products and services for the corporate segment, diversified into the retail segment of the financial markets in the early 1990s. In the last decade it has transformed itself to a technology intensive financial services group.

The first such move came in the mid-nineties when ICICI raised debt from the retail market. Since then, ICICI has been increasing its reach to this segment in terms of resources mobilization, and by offering quality investor service through ICICI Infotech Services, its subsidiary. In 1994, it established ICICI Bank as a commercial bank that is flexible, innovative and prompt in meeting customer requirements.

In addition to the bank, the retail initiatives include—

- Prudential ICICI AMC—a tie up with the Prudential Group of UK for its foray into the mutual funds business,
- ICICI Personal Financial Services (PFS)—to offer retail asset products like home finance, automobile finance, durables finance, etc

- ICICI Capital Services—to service retail liability products like bonds and deposits
- ICICI Web trade—to facilitate end-to-end integrated web based trading service through the web site www.icicidirect.com
- Prudential ICICI Life Insurance—to offer life insurance services, and
- ICICI Lombard General Insurance—the latest venture to offer non-life insurance services,

This apart the retail initiatives of ICICI also include a plethora of web-based businesses including city portals and various other utility sites such as billjunction.com, icicimoneymanager.com, magiccart.com, among others.

All these group companies are jointly spearheading ICICI Group's foray into the retail market.

□ THE RETAIL STRATEGY

ICICI has ambitious plans for its retail business initiatives. The retail strategy revolves around intensive deployment of technology. Information technology will help reduce cost of service, increase customer retention, help in cross-selling and up-selling while improving process efficiencies. Electronic channels including internet, ATMs, call centers, contact centers, desktops, kiosks, mobiles and other hand held devices will perform financial activities while ensuring that customer has multiple options for access and transactions

The group has adopted a 'click and brick' strategy to leverage the power of electronic channels and physical presence to ensure rapid product delivery, fulfillment of financial deals and documentation.

As part of the plans, it is implementing various projects to establish world-class CRM practices, which would provide an integrated view of its customers to everyone in the organization. CRM at ICICI involves increased communication between the virtual universal bank and its customers and prospects, as well as within the group itself. The underlying idea is to enhance every instance of contact with the customer. ICICI believes that a true customer-centric relationship can only be accomplished by considering the unique perspectives of every single customer of the organization. Hence the pressing need to put in place a technology enabled CRM solution.

□ THE CRM ROADMAP

CRM, at ICICI, is viewed as a discipline as well as a set of discrete software technologies, which will focus on automating and improving the business processes associated with managing customer relationships in the areas of sales, marketing, customer service and support. The organization aims to achieve the end goal of one-to-one marketing.

The CRM software applications will not only facilitate the coordination of multiple business functions but also coordinate multiple channels of communication with the customer —face to face, call centre, ATM, web, telephone, kiosk, bank, branch, sales associates, etc.—so as to enable ICICI carry out cradle-to-grave customer management more efficiently. It should allow ICICI to engage in one-to-one marketing by tracking complete customer life-cycle history. To begin with, it will automate process-flow tracking in the product sales process, and be able to generate customized reports and promote cross selling. It will also enable efficient campaign management by providing a software interface for definition, tracking, execution and analysis of campaigns.

From an architecture perspective, the enterprise-wide CRM solution should seamlessly integrate non-transactional related customer information housed in the Front-Office with the transactional information housed in the Back Office. Creating the enterprise CRM strategies required the combination of nine distinct steps as shown below.

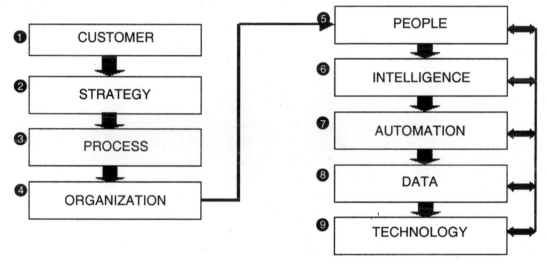

Source: "Creating the Enterprise CRM Strategy" by Aslam Handy, Chief Technology Officer, DiaLogos

By combining these nine steps can one really start listening to the customers, and understand what they are saying, maybe even in real time. Once that is achieved, profits begin to follow as optimization techniques are applied. Only then will the two crucial goals for a successful business-case driven project be achieved, viz.:

1. Effective change management
2. Technology-enabled evolution

CRM will essentially focus on providing optimal value to customers—through the way we communicate with them, how we sell to them, and how we service them—as well as through the traditional means of product, price, promotion and place of distribution. ICICI recognizes that customers make buying decisions based on more than just price...more than just product. *Customers make buying decisions based on their overarching experience that includes product and price,—and sales, service, recognition and support.* If ICICI can get all of those factors right—consistently—we will be rewarded with ongoing customer loyalty and value.

▢ IMPLEMENTING CRM

A very detailed and comprehensive CRM Action Plan was developed based on the understanding that CRM will require an enterprise wide transformation.

The CRM Business Transformation Map below shows the various aspects of that change. There are five inter-related areas. These include:

1. Business Focus 2. Organizational Structure 3. Business Metrics 4. Marketing Focus 5. Technology

Five Core Areas of Business Transformation

BUSINESS FOCUS					
Product	Sales	Channel	Marketing	Service	Customer

ORGANIZATIONAL STRUCTURE					
Product Management	Place Management	Promotion Management	Channel Management	Contact Management	Customer Management

BUSINESS METRICS					
Product Performance	Place Performance	Program Performance	Customer Revenues	Customer Patterns & Profitability	Customer Lifetime Value and Loyalty

MARKETING FOCUS					
Mass Advertising	Sales Promotion	Marketing Campaigns	Integrated Marketing Communications	Segment Specific Marketing	Customer Relationship Management

TECHNOLOGY					
Transaction Processing	Data Maintenance	Data Access	Data Warehouse	Data Marts	Customer Touchpoint Systems

Source: "How To Get There From Here" by Melinda Nykamp, President, Nykamp Consulting Group

The key to building the CRM action plan was in understanding where the organization stood relative to each of the five aspects of change. Interviews with key individuals throughout the organization helped identify different initiatives that have been launched, all focused on CRM. While all of these initiatives may have merit, failure to address the total business transformation requirements can lead to very short-lived success.

The next step in the planning process was a Gap Analysis. This analysis essentially compared current stage against optimal relative to the five aspects of business, to identify and specifically describe the gaps. In addition to the more obvious gaps, this analysis helped identify the CRM organizational holes:

1. Marketing, sales and service practices
2. Collection, capture, processing and deployment of customer information
3. Distribution and operations effectiveness at customer touch points

Another key factor in identifying gaps is to understand how the organization functions relative to the CRM Business Cycle. There is a universal, underlying cycle of activity that should drive all CRM initiatives and infrastructure development. All initiatives and infrastructure development should somehow be tied to this core cycle of activity. Careful evaluation of the organization's ability to execute this cycle will pinpoint and qualify additional organizational gaps.

☐ THE CRM BUSINESS CYCLE

As shown in the diagram, for any organization, business starts with the acquisition of customers. However, any successful CRM initiative is highly dependent on a sound understanding of customers.

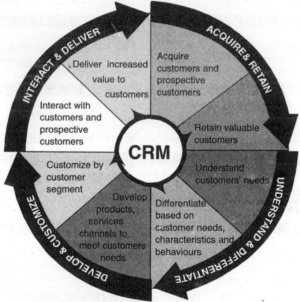

Source: "How To Get There From Here" by Melinda Nykamp, President, Nykamp Consulting Group

☐ UNDERSTAND AND DIFFERENTIATE

Organizations cannot have a relationship with customers unless they understand them... what they value, what types of service are important to them, how and when they like to interact, and what they want to buy. True understanding is based on a combination of detailed analysis and interaction. Several activities are important:

- Profiling to understand demographics, purchase patterns and channel preference.
- Segmentation to identify logical unique groups of customers that tend to look alike and behave in a similar fashion. While the promise of "one-to-one" marketing sounds

good, we have not seen many organizations that have mastered the art of treating each customer uniquely. Identification of actionable segments is a practical place to start.

- Primary research to capture needs and attitudes.
- Customer valuation to understand profitability, as well as lifetime value or long term potential. Value may also be based on the customer's ability or inclination to refer other profitable customers.

Analysis and research alone, however, are insufficient. To create and foster a relationship, organizations have to act on what they learn about customers. ICICI Group's customers need to see that the company is differentiating service and communications based both on what they've learned independently and on what the customer has told them. At the same time, differentiation should be based on the value customers are expected to deliver.

❑ DEVELOP & CUSTOMIZE

In the product-oriented world of yesterday, companies developed products and services and expected customers to buy them. In a customer-focused world, product and channel development has to follow the customer's lead. Organizations are increasingly developing products and services, and even new channels based on customer needs and service expectations.

Most organizations today are not able to cost-effectively customize products for individual customers. However, products, services, channels and media can be customized based on the needs of quantitative customer segments. ICICI believes that the extent of customization should be based on the potential value delivered by the customer segment.

❑ INTERACT & DELIVER

Interaction is also a critical component of a successful CRM initiative. It is important to remember that interaction doesn't just occur through marketing and sales channels and media; customers interact in many different ways with many different areas of the organization, including distribution and shipping, customer service and online.

To foster relationships, organizations need to insure that:

- All areas of the organization have easy access to relevant, actionable customer information.
- All areas are trained how to use customer information to tailor interactions based on both customer needs potential customer value

With access to information and appropriate training, organizations will be prepared to steadily increase the value they deliver to customers. Delivering value is a cornerstone of the relationship. ICICI is strongly of the opinion that value is not just based on the price of the product or the discounts offered. In fact, customer perceptions of value are based on a number of factors including the quality of products and services, convenience, speed, ease of use, responsiveness, and service excellence.

□ ACQUIRE & RETAIN

The more ICICI learns about customers, the easier it is to pinpoint those that are producing the greatest value for the organization. Those are the customers and customer segments a company will want to clone in its prospecting and acquisition efforts. And, because they will continue to learn about what is valuable to each segment, they will be much more likely to score a "win" with the right channel, right media, right product, right offer, right timing and the most relevant message.

Successful customer retention basically involves getting it "right" on an ongoing basis. And that is exactly what ICICI Group aims to achieve out of its CRM initiatives.

Successful customer retention is based very simply on the organization's ability to constantly deliver on three principles:

- Maintain interaction; never stop listening.
- Continue to deliver on the customer's definition of value.
- Remember that customers change as they move through differing lifestages; be alert for the changes and be prepared to modify the service and value proposition as they change.

And so the cycle continues... As a cycle, the stages are interdependent and continuous. As one moves from one stage to the next, ICICI Group hopes to gains insight and understanding that enhance the subsequent efforts. The organization shall become increasingly sophisticated in the implementation of CRM processes, and over time shall become increasingly profitable by doing so.

□ PRIORITIZING THE CHANGES

Because there might be many gaps, and therefore many changes that an organization will need to make, prioritization was critical. The evaluation of each of the strategies identified to resolve the gaps at ICICI were based on:

- Cost to implement—including initial one-time costs, as well as anticipated ongoing expenses.
- Overall benefit—some changes may have larger impacts on the organization's ability to increase customer value and loyalty.
- Feasibility—based on organization readiness, data and systems support, resource skill-sets and a number of other factors.
- Time required—including the time necessary for training and addressing "cultural" change management issues related to a specific strategy.

□ CREATING AN ACTION PLAN

The next step in the planning process was the development of a very detailed action plan. While the complete plan might span three or more years, it was based on three-month phases with clear deliverables that will demonstrate both progress and quick hits or measures of success. The plan identified interdependent activities and should comprehensively detail the time and resources required for each activity.

Another key factor for the planning process was the Leadership Action Plan. Advancing on the CRM Transformation Map required significant organization change. This part of the action plan helped assess the drivers and restraints of this change and the organization's readiness to embrace the change. It created additional strategies by identifying specific leadership actions necessary to lead the organizational change. As a result, executives were able to identify their roles and responsibilities, and the actions necessary to eliminate barriers and to nurture change.

☐ SELECTING AND IMPLEMENTING A TECHNOLOGY BASED SOLUTION

Technology

The success of the CRM initiatives were contingent on various decisions pertaining to technology. Some of the key issues were:

(a) Make or Buy—The decision to buy was based on an evaluation of an identified set of criteria. The criteria set included the following :

- Functionality
- Flexibility in incorporating changes
- Scalability—with growth
- Fit with existing architecture (legacy systems)
- Fit with global best practices
- Upgradability—which basically means that if the technology that enables CRM advances tomorrow, the installed system should be able to take into its fold the increased functionalities
- Commercial impact—evaluated in terms of the life time of the solution

Taking into account all the above factors, it was decided to purchase an off-the-shelf CRM solution and customize it to suit ICICI's requirements.

(b) From whom to buy – Once the decision to buy was made, the next step was to identify the product seller and the system integrator.

The global CRM product market space was scanned to shortlist about 15 large players from a very fragmented market comprising of over 150 players claiming to have some sort of CRM capability. Based on discussions with a global technological analysis group, another set of criteria was drawn to shortlist the prospective product providers. This included:

- CRM expertise
- Retail finance expertise
- Implementation worldwide specially in Asia Pacific
- Company focus on CRM (specially important in the context of many large ERP providers having moved into the CRM space in recent times)

- Credentials including financials, client list, life history, etc
- Understanding of ICICI's pain points to gauge how well they have been able to comprehend ICICI's pressing needs and their views on whether the product concerned could provide a long-term solution
- Preferred implementation partners

A detailed Request for Information (RFIs) was sent to each of the shortlisted companies. After receiving the RFIs, another round of evaluation was done on the basis of

- CRM solution implementation experience
- Clientele (specially in Asia Pacific), scope and scale of implementation
- Understanding of ICICI's experience
- Suggested solution including implementation timeline
- Technical handholding expected
- Training and maintenance

A similar process was followed to shortlist the system integrators. Some of the criteria included

- CRM expertise & Retail finance expertise
- Focus on CRM
- Project team specifics including indicative CVs of project team
- Product preferences

After shortlisting two product vendors and system integrators, reference calls were made to several of the past clients of all the shortlisted companies. The reference calls followed a specific pattern, and were qualitatively adjudged. Some of the parameters included strengths and weaknesses of the vendor/system integrator, timeliness, cost and time overruns, commitment, training, quality control of customization and post-implementation support.

Processes

All processes were mapped on to product by understanding the details. During the course of the process mapping, several opportunities for improvement were identified and implemented. To illustrate, the buying process of a loan product involves the following steps –

(a) Prospect contacts the call center and leaves details
(b) Call center personnel passes on this lead to the DMA responsible for the area from where the lead has come in
(c) The DMA contacts the prospect and collects documents. The DMA also fires a Field Investigation (FI) request from a FI agency. The FI agency is external to ICICI, and checks on the basic veracity of the statements submitted by the prospect (e.g. that he has his own house in New Delhi etc.)
(d) The documents collected by them are filed and forwarded to the Credit Processing Agency (CPA). The CPA also receives the FI report.
(e) The CPA checks for completion of the file, generates a credit scorecard, and passes on the document to the Credit Buyer.

(f) The Credit Buyer (CB) is an ICICI personnel, and takes the final call on the loan sanctioning. He in turn passes on the documents to the central operations team for processing. The central operations team is also internal to ICICI.

The Sales Process—Pre CRM and Post Implementation of CRM

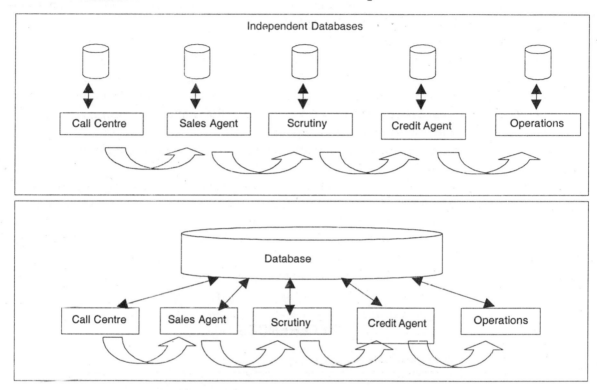

Similarly, even the customer service and support function also has well-defined processes depending on the nature and type of query/complaint.

□ LESSONS SO FAR FROM THE ICICI EXPERIENCE

If CRM involves optimizing product, price, place of distribution, promotion, sales and service, why are so many companies struggling? Hasn't anyone really mastered the art and science of CRM, and if not, why is it so difficult?

CRM is difficult because *it is an enterprise-wide initiative.*

- CRM is not a technology initiative. Many have confused CRM as a technology initiative, and assigned the CRM implementation project to their information system or IT group. CRM conferences often equate to technology exhibits and demonstrations. Technology is needed in order to implement CRM—particularly the customization part—but technology is not the driver of CRM, or the solution to successful CRM implementation.

- CRM is not exclusively a marketing initiative. Many organizations have merely equated CRM with customer-focused marketing, or data-driven/database marketing. CRM results in more effective, data-driven marketing efforts; CRM requires marketing expertise. But CRM is not strictly a marketing initiative.
- CRM is not exclusively a sales initiative. Similar to marketing, CRM is often lodged within the sales department. The sales-force, after all, is extremely close to their customers...understanding their needs and wants, and trying to fulfill them. Sales, however, is just one functional area that can benefit from CRM, and that is necessary for effective CRM.
- CRM is not exclusively a service initiative. As with sales and marketing, customer service is one functional aspect of successful CRM implementation. But customer service is not the sole driver of the process.

CRM involves marketing, sales, service and technology, as well as the other inner-workings of an organization.

Thus, it is properly described as an enterprise-wide initiative. It involves all areas of the organization and all functions of the organization, and it requires all areas of the organization to be working together in harmony. CRM requires all areas of the organization to not only exist in harmony, but to be working toward the common goal of stronger customer relationships.

Having even one "broken spoke in the wheel"...one area of the organization that is less than committed to CRM...can make the difference between success and failure.

REFERENCES

Handy, A, 'Creating the Enterprise CRM Strategy'

Nykamp, M.,'How To Get There From Here', www.crmittoolbox.com/peer/docs/crm_howto.asp

Peppers, D. and Rogers, M. (1993), 'The One to One Future: Building Relationships One Customer at a Time', Doubleday; New York.

Peppers, D. and Rogers, M. (1998), 'Enterprise One to One: Tools for Competing in the Interactive Age',

Vertical Applications: CIOs Are Facing Tough Decisions: 16 June, 1999 (Inside Gartner Group)

Chapter 20

Decision Metrics for CRM Solutions

■ **Sandip Mukhopadhyay and Prithwiraj Nath**

Abstract

The role of Customer Relationship Management (CRM) has gained tremendous significance in the world of e-business solution providers. This paper deals with the basic issues that determines the selection for a particular CRM vendor or solution. In the first phase, it analyses the importance of customer perceived attributes in selecting CRM solution providers and the impact of different information channels on the selection procedure. The research shows that eleven attributes can be represented through four factors: pricing innovation, technical superiority, understanding and commitment, customer interaction effectiveness. Among the different information channels considered, direct interface and consultant are most critical. The management can use it as a guideline, while selecting a particular consultant or implementation partner. In the second phase, a model has been formulated to find out the efficiency of a CRM solution, which can be used by the management to improve their performance on the different parameters and use it for proper resource allocation.

Key Words: *CRM, e-business, Vendor Selection, Efficiency, DEA*

□ INTRODUCTION

CRM combines business process and technology that seeks to understand a company's customers from multifaceted perspective. As most companies are becoming more and more customer-centric, venturing into new CRM territory is no longer an option but a necessity. The core process competencies in CRM are cross-selling, upselling, customer service and support, storefront and field service and retention management. In the present day context, customer relationship management solutions go beyond automating just the interaction processes to automating the data warehousing, processes of data integration, data analysis and customer interaction personalization.

Implementing CRM is not a technical issue. The business processes also need to be redefined to accommodate the challenges of acquiring, servicing, and managing a new breed of on-line customers and other internal web-based applications. It is very important to select the right solution and implementation methodology to get the maximum benefit.

Like other parts of the world, the corporates in eastern region are becoming increasingly aware of a long-term relationship with their customers. The relationship is shifting from commerce to collaboration. Networked customer is advantageous for a company to innovate and compete successfully. Corporate strategy is formulated around maintaining the highest level of customer satisfaction. CRM implementation also involves significant commitment (financial and time) from top management, change in organization behaviour and inter-departmental collaboration.

Our study will be done in two phases. In the first phase, we would find out most important issues and attributes that the CIOs think when determining the selection of a particular type of CRM solutions. The management can use it as a guideline, while selecting a particular consultant or implementation partner. In the second phase, we would build up an efficiency measurement model of CRM solution providers, which can be used by the management to improve their performance on the different parameters and use it for proper resource allocation.

☐ OBJECTIVE OF STUDY

We broadly start with three research questions in the first phase of our study:
1. What are the criteria that drive customer's preference from one solution provider to another?
2. What is the relative importance of each of the attributes that drives the customer's choice or preference?
3. What are the likely information channels that influence the CIO's decision and their relative importance?

In the second phase, we wanted to device a benchmarking scale to measure the effectiveness of CRM solution providers where we want to rate the companies according to their efficiency in providing their customers a better solution. The method which we are going to introduce is a non-parametric efficiency measurement technique which has been widely used in measuring productive efficiency of homogeneous units and thus develop a benchmarking scale for an industry. This method is called Data Envelopment Analysis (Charnes et al, 1978).

☐ METHODOLOGY

From secondary research and in-depth interviews of few CIO's, we identified 11 attributes (refer to Fig. 1) that influence decision making in terms of selecting CRM solution providers. Primary research on the perceived relative importance of these attributes among the CIOs of eastern region, mostly in Calcutta and Jamshedpur representing IT, manufacturing, FMCG, consulting and engineering (total 30) were conducted. For primary data collection purpose, a written questionnaire in two parts was designed. The first part of the questionnaire was designed to get the importance of the 11 attributes in a scale of 0 (of no importance) to 3 (extremely important). The second part asks about the influence of different information channels in selection procedure.

□ ANALYSIS

Factor analysis was carried out on the data obtained on 11 variables used with Cronbach's alpha for reliability check for the factors obtained. It was done to examine the "strength" of the overall association of the variables in terms of a smaller set of linear composites of the original variables that preserve most of the information in the full data set. In the course of computing the various factor scores and factor loadings, a specific approach to factor analysis, called principal components was used along with Varimax rotation. On the basis of 0.5 cutoff for the factor loadings, four factors were identified explaining 73.16% of the cumulative variance.

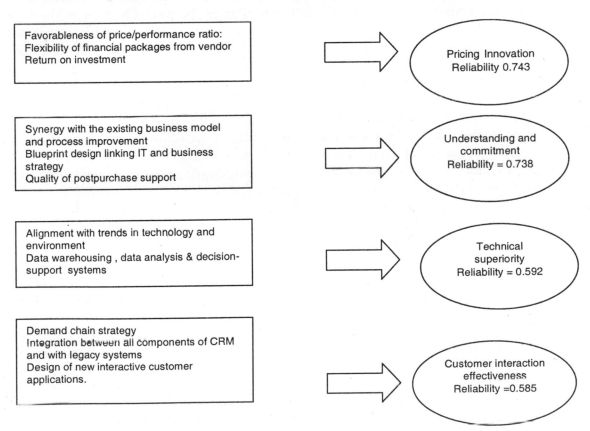

Fig. 1   *Factor Solution Obtained with the Attributes and Cronbach's Alpha*

The factors obtained were:

(1) *Pricing innovation*: This factor indicates the real cost of the implementation of CRM application for the companies. Indian market, particularly East Indian market is extremely cost -sensitive. So, companies favour cost-effective yet efficient solution, instead of hottest technology. Vendors can reduce the perceived cost by deferred payment, and other innovative financing like risk/reward sharing, equity participation. Also higher return on investments (by process improvement, getting newer customers, retention of existing customers and increasing the revenues from existing customers) reduces the total cost-to-use of their systems.

(2) *Understanding and commitment*: Vendors should have good understanding of the particular business of the client and be in a position (geographically and technically) to provide continuous and high quality support. CRM is a nothing but a business strategy for selecting and managing customer relationships to optimize profit over the long term. So, any enterprise implementing CRM does so within the context of an established business protocol. Understanding the established business practices for an industry is particularly critical for B2B effort, since the model influences the type and frequency of information exchange. The solution-provider should have competence with the intricacies of the industry's business requirement. Companies are looking for integrated customer-centric models that are capable of supporting complex business designs. But it has been seen that a vast majority of technology infrastructure investments fail to deliver expected returns because they are poorly linked to organizational plans, the strategies and tactics are flawed, the plan was not properly executed. In most cases, the failures are management problem and not a technological issue. The tough task for vendor is to align business strategies, processes and applications fast and right. The vendor should also have commitment to provide adequate system support. The sales team should get a fast and easy way to get answers of system related questions. Also in an online processing environment, the cost of downtime is very high—so the vendor should provide system with some amount of redundancy.

(3) *Technical Superiority*: This factor indicates strong technological competencies and understanding of future trends in technologies. In continuously changing environment, identifying new trends in technology can help to identify new opportunities and to eliminate uncertainty. Smart solution-providers should be not only well versed in IT but should have a knack for anticipating the future of environment surrounding itself. The vendor should provide strong customer data management and analysis expertise. This helps to turn information into insight companies can use to serve your customers better CRM-centric data warehousing, data mining and other related technologies is an integral part of the overall IT solution for the closed-loop CRM system.

(4) *Customer interaction effectiveness*: The vendors should have solution to knit together all the interactions of the customers and provide him interactive and superior experience. Customer should get interactive user experience, reach content and seamless interactivity. To meet this need, service providers, in addition to cutting-edge

technology skills, must also be able to offer behavioral and usability expertise. This skill set will allow them to assess why users visit, stay, and purchase online—and why they don't. CRM solution has to provide a seamless, real-time integration between the distribution center and customer response process to eliminate costly back orders. Complete integration will allow real-time tracking of merchandise as it moves through the pipeline, allowing for a smoother supply chain as well as up-to-date information for online customers. CRM vendor should be able to determine the best communication methods with customers to increase efficiencies, such as real-time chat, e-mail, Web forms, and self-help solutions for a particular business.

We considered six information channels and their relative influence on selection procedure for the vendor. It shows, direct interface and consultant's advice, recommendation plays a crucial role in selecting a solution. The vendors having no direct presence in the market should tie-up with the existing IT companies and consultants active in the eastern-region market (PWC, COMPAQ, HCL, and NIIT). The vendors should share information with the consultants and other decision-makers to get an early foothold in the market.

Table 1 *Different Information Channels and Their Importance Score (where 4 is very important and 0 is not at all important).*

1. Media/advertisement	2.4	
2. Consultant /expert	2.95	Critically influence selection.
3. Direct interface	3.3	It has maximum influence.
4. Prior experience	2.9	
5. Word of mouth	2.4	
6. seminar/tradeshow	2.65	

□ EFFICIENCY MEASUREMENT

From the first part of our study, we found four factors, which mostly affect vendor selections to be pricing, understanding needs of the consumers, technical expertise of the solution provider and its customer friendliness. In this part of the study, we developed a model, which can measure the efficiency of the solution providers. A customer's choice is determined by the value he gets on each of these parameters from the different solution providers. We define efficiency of a solution provider as the amount of input it is giving in terms of these four factors to the customer which we can consider its resources and the outputs which a solution provider is getting in terms of its financial performance and customer satisfaction figures. The method which we are going to introduce is a non-parametric efficiency measurement technique which has been widely used in measuring productive efficiency of homogeneous units and is called Data Envelopment Analysis (Charnes et al, 1978). This is a linear programming technique where the set of best practice units are those for which no other decision making units or linear combination of units has as much or more of every output (given inputs) or little or less of every input (given outputs). The basic DEA formulation has the following form:

Maximize

$$E_b = \frac{\left(\displaystyle\sum_{r=1}^{R} u_{rb}\, y_{rb} \right)}{\left(\displaystyle\sum_{i=1}^{I} v_{ib}\, x_{ib} \right)} \tag{1a}$$

subject to

$$\left(\sum_{r=1}^{R} u_{rb}\, y_{rj} \right) \Big/ \left(\sum_{i=1}^{I} v_{ib}\, x_{ij} \right) \leq 1 \quad \text{for all } j \tag{1b}$$

$$u_{rb},\, v_{ib} \geq \varepsilon \,\ldots\, \text{for all } r,\, i \tag{1c}$$

where y_{rj}: observed quantity of output r produced by unit $j = 1,2\ldots N$

x_{ij}: observed quantity of input i used by unit $j = 1,2,\ldots\ldots N$

u_{rb}: the weight (to be determined) given to output r by base unit b

v_{ib}: the weight (to be determined) given to input i by base unit b

ε: a very small positive number (non-Archimedean infinitesimal)

If we consider figure2, a solution provider is using the four factors found from the earlier part of our study as its resources to satisfy its customer requirements and in return generate performance for itself. The resources can be measured from a solution provider's customer responses and the financial performance figures can be obtained from the solution provider's balance sheet whereas the other outcome of customer satisfaction again has to be measured from their customer response. Thus, how efficient each CRM solution provider is can be calculated by using eq. 1 and a proper benchmarking scale can be developed. The objective of this model building exercise would be to develop a ranking scale for the CRM solution providers so that we can identify who are the better performers in this trade. A solution provider can find out its position in the industry and benchmark itself to the best performer (efficiency = 1).

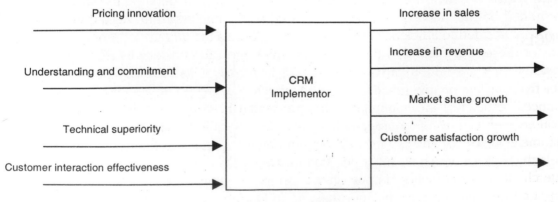

Fig. 2 *Efficiency Model*

For inefficient organizations (efficiency < 1), their slack can be calculated on each performance parameters and thus a strategic guideline on a macro scale can be provided. Slack is defined to be how much improvement that a solution provider can make on each of its performance parameter if it can become efficient. Thus, by calculating each of them and by comparing with an efficient unit, we can find the relative efficiency on the performance parameters for each of these CRM solution providers.

To compare efficiency with profitability, we can draw the efficiency-profitability matrix (Boussofiane, 1991). Units in the star quadrants are the flagship units and should become the benchmark for other solution providers. Units coming under sleeper are profitable but inefficient. Thus, they may be working under favourable conditions rather than having good management practices. Units in the question mark can improve both their profitability as well as their efficiency. Units in the dog quadrant are efficient still having less profit. This signifies that they are working under unfavourable condition. So, in extreme case, it may be sensible to divest or do resource allocations.

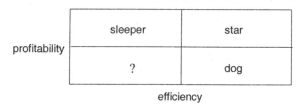

Fig. 3   *Efficiency/Profitability Matrix*

Thus, using the non-parametric method of DEA, we can not only determine the relative efficiencies of the CRM solution providers, calculate their slacks on their performance parameters and also help in understanding what is the impact of environmental variables on the performance of the solution providers. Resource allocation decision can be made using the efficiency-profitability matrix and thus help in management of performance.

In the second part of the study, we have tried to develop a model to measure the efficiency of CRM solution providers. This model can be tested empirically by taking the necessary data and the analysis explained can be carried out using DEA.

◻ CONCLUSION

In this study, we have tried to answer questions like what are the attributes that a customer look for from a CRM solution provider and how is decision is influenced by their relative importance. We found that factors like pricing, understanding customer's requirements, technical expertise and customer interactions are the most important factors as perceived by customers. We also tried to find out what are the relative importance of information channels that affect a CIO's decision and found that direct interface which a provider has with the client is the most effective mode of influencing decisions. Moreover, we tried to develop a model to measure the efficiency of a solution provider, which can be validated empirically in future studies.

REFERENCES

Boussofiane, A., Dyson, R.G., and Thanassoulis, E., 1991. 'Applied Data Envelopment Analysis', *European Journal of Operational Research*. Vol. 85, pp. 700-710.

Charnes, A., Cooper W.W., Lewin A.Y., and Seiford, L.M, 1994. *Data Envelopment Analysis-Theory, Methodology and Applications*, Kluwer Academic Publisher, pp. 24-61.

Charnes, A., Cooper, W.W. and Rhodes, E., 1978. "Measuring Efficiency of Decision Making Units', *European Journal of Operational Research,* Vol. 2, pp. 429-444.

Clemons, E. K. (1991). 'Evaluation of Strategic Investments in Information Technology', *Communications of ACM*, Vol. 34, No. 1, January, pp. 24-36.

Coelli, T., Prasada Rao, D.S. and Battese, G.E, 1998. *An Introduction to Efficiency and Productivity Analysis*, Kluwer Academic Publisher, pp. 133-180.

Fried, H.O., Lovell, C.A. and Schmidt, S.S. 1993. *The Measurement of Productive Efficiency*, Oxford University Press, pp. 120-159.

Gurbaxani, V. and Whang, S. (1991) 'The Impact of Information Systems on Organizations and markets', *Communications of ACM*, Vol. 34, No. 1, January, pp. 59-73.

Kaufman, R. J., Ghosh, A., and Bansal, A. (1989) 'Parameter Non-Stationary in a Model which Estimates the Business Value of Information Technology' Working Paper No. 197, *Center for Research on Information Systems*, New York University, January, 12 pp.

Mahmood, M.A. and Mann, G.J. (1991) 'Measuring the Impact of Information Technology on Organizational Strategic Performance: A Key Ratios Approach" in the Proceedings of the twenty-fourth Hawaii International Conference on System Sciences, Vol. 4, 1991, pp. 251-258.

McLean, E. R. (1990) 'Measuring MIS 'Goodness", *Information Week*, September 10, pp. 120.

Peter, G. (1990) 'Beyond Strategy—Benefits Identification and Management of Specific for Investments' *Journal of Information Technology*, Vol. 5, pp. 205-214.

Silk, D. J. (1990)' Managing IS Benefits for the 1990s' *Journal of Information Technology,* Vol. 5, pp. 185-193.

Ward, J.M. (1990) 'A Portfolio Approach to Evaluating Information Systems Investments and Setting Priorities' *Journal of Information Technology*, Vol. 5, pp. 222-231.

Chapter 21

Characteristics of a Good Customer Satisfaction Survey

■ **John Coldwell**

Abstract

The basic concept of business-to-business CRM is often described as allowing the larger business be as responsive to the needs of its customer as a small business. In the early days of CRM this became translated from "responsive" to "reactive". Successful larger businesses recognise that they need to be pro-active in finding the views, concerns, needs and levels of satisfaction from their customers. Paper-based surveys, such as those left in hotel bedrooms, tend to have a low response rate and are usually completed by customers who have a grievance. Telephone-based interviews are often influenced by the Cassandra phenomenon. Face-to-face interviews are expensive and can be led by the interviewer.

Key Words: *Customer, Satisfaction, and Surveys.*

□ INTRODUCTION

CRM is based on the premise that, by having a better understanding of the customers' needs and desires we can keep them longer and sell more to them.

Growth Strategies International (GSI) performed a statistical analysis of Customer Satisfaction data encompassing the findings of over 20,000 customer surveys conducted in 40 countries by InfoQuest.

The conclusions of the study were:

- A Totally Satisfied Customer contributes 2.6 times as much revenue to a company as a Somewhat Satisfied Customer.
- A Totally Satisfied Customer contributes 17 times as much revenue as a Somewhat Dissatisfied Customer.
- A Totally Dissatisfied Customer decreases revenue at a rate equal to 1.8 times what a Totally Satisfied Customer contributes to a business.

Consider the following situations...

A large, international hotel chain wanted to attract more business travellers. They decided to conduct a customer satisfaction survey to find out what they needed to improve their services for this type of guest. A written survey was placed in each room and guests were asked to fill it out. However, when the survey period was complete, the hotel found that the only people who had filled in the surveys were children and their grandparents!

Why?

Business travellers don't have the time or the interest in participating in this kind of survey!

A large manufacturing company conducted the first year of what was designed to be an annual customer satisfaction survey. The first year, the satisfaction score was 94%. The second year, with the same basic survey topics, but using another survey vendor, the satisfaction score dropped to 64%. Ironically, at the same time, their overall revenues doubled!

Why?

- The questions were simpler and phrased differently.
- The order of the questions was different.
- The format of the survey was different.
- The targeted respondents were at a different management level.
- The Overall Satisfaction question was placed at the end of the survey.

Although all customer satisfaction surveys are used for gathering peoples' opinions, survey designs vary dramatically in length, content and format. Analysis techniques may utilize a wide variety of charts, graphs and narrative interpretations. Companies often use a survey to test their business strategies, and many base their entire business plan upon their survey's results. BUT...troubling questions often emerge.

Are the results always accurate?

...sometimes accurate?

...at all accurate?

Are there "hidden pockets of customer discontent" that a survey overlooks?

Can the survey information be trusted enough to take major action with confidence?

As the examples above show, different survey designs, methodologies and population characteristics will dramatically alter the results of a survey. Therefore, it behoves a company to make absolutely certain that their survey process is accurate enough to generate a true representation of their customers' opinions. Failing to do so, there is no way the company can use the results for precise action planning.

The characteristics of a survey's design, and the data collection methodologies employed to conduct the survey, require careful forethought to ensure comprehensive, accurate, and correct results. The discussion on the next page summarizes several key "rules of thumb" that must be adhered to if a survey is to become a company's most valued strategic business tool.

□ QUESTION TYPES

Survey questions should be categorized into three types:
1. Overall Satisfaction question—"How satisfied are you overall with XYZ Company?"
2. Key Attributes—satisfaction with key areas of business, e.g. Sales, Marketing, Operations, etc.
3. Drill Down—satisfaction with issues that are unique to each attribute, and upon which action may be taken to directly remedy that Key Attribute's issues.

The Overall Satisfaction question is placed at the <u>end</u> of the survey so that its answer will be affected by a more in depth thinking, allowing respondents to have first considered answers to other questions.

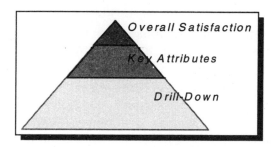

Fig. 1 *Pyramid Structure of Overall Satisfaction question*

□ QUESTION DESIGN

A survey, if constructed properly, will yield a wealth of information. The following design elements should be taken into account:

First, the survey must be kept to a reasonable length. Over 60 questions in a written survey will become tiring. Anything over 8-12 questions begins taxing the patience of participants in a phone survey.

Second, the questions should utilize simple sentences with short words.

Third, questions should ask for an opinion on only one topic at a time. For example, the question, "how satisfied are you with our products and services?" cannot be effectively answered because a respondent may have conflicting opinions on products versus services.

Fourth, superlatives such as "excellent" or "very" should not be used in questions. Such words tend to lead a respondent toward an opinion.

Fifth, "feel good" questions yield subjective answers on which little specific action can be taken. For example, the question "how do you feel about XYZ company's industry position?" produces responses that are of no practical value in terms of improving an operation.

☐ THE PERILS OF PAPER

Though the fill-in-the-dots format is one of the most common types of survey, there are significant flaws, which can discredit the results. For example, all prior answers are visible, which leads to comparisons with current questions, undermining candour. Second, respondents subconsciously tend to look for symmetry in their responses and become

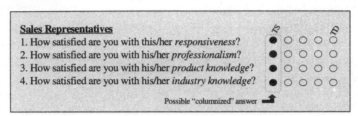

guided by the pattern of their responses, not their true feelings. Third, because paper surveys are typically categorized into topic sections, a respondent is more apt to fill down a column of dots within a category while giving little consideration to each question. Some INTERNET surveys constructed in the same "dots" format, often lead to the same tendencies, particularly if inconvenient sideways scrolling is necessary to answer a question.

In a survey conducted by Xerox Corporation, over one third of all responses were discarded because the participants had clearly run down the columns in each category rather than carefully considering each question.

☐ TELEPHONE SURVEYS

Though a telephone survey yields a more accurate response than a paper survey, they may also have inherent flaws that impede quality results, such as:

First, when a respondent's identity is clearly known, concern over the possibility of being challenged or confronted with negative responses at a later date produces a strong positive bias in their replies (the so-called "Cassandra Phenomenon".)

Second, studies have shown that people become friendlier as a conversation grows longer, thus influencing question responses.

Third, human nature says that people like to be liked. Therefore, gender biases, accents, perceived intelligence, or compassion all influence responses. Similarly, senior management egos often emerge when trying to convey their wisdom.

Fourth, telephone surveys are intrusive on a senior manager's time. An unannounced phone call may create an initial negative impression of the survey. Many respondents may be partially focused on the clock instead of the questions. Optimum responses are dependent upon a respondents' clear mind and free time, two things that senior management often lacks. In a recent multi-national survey where targeted respondents were offered the choice of a phone or other methods, ALL chose the other methods.

Taking precautionary steps, such as keeping the survey brief and using only highly trained callers who minimize idle conversation, will help minimize the aforementioned issues, but will not eliminate them.

☐ THE NEED FOR A HIGH RESPONSE RATE

The objective of a survey is to capture a representative cross-section of opinions throughout a group of people. Unfortunately, unless a majority of the people participate, two factors will influence the results:

First, negative people tend to answer a survey more often than positive because human nature encourages "venting" negative emotions. A low response rate will generally produce more negative results (see drawing).

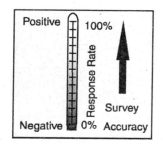

Second, a smaller percentage of a population is less representative of the whole. For example, if 12 people are asked to take a survey and 25% respond, then the opinions of the other nine people are unknown and may be entirely different. However, if 75% respond, then only three opinions are unknown. The other nine will be more likely to represent the opinions of the whole group. One can assume that the higher the response rate, the more accurate the snapshot of opinions.

☐ THE ACCURACY OF TERMS

Totally Satisfied vs. Very Satisfied.....Debates have raged over the scales used to depict levels of customer satisfaction. In recent years, however, studies have definitively proven that a "totally satisfied" customer is between 3 and 10 times more likely to initiate a repurchase, and that measuring this "top-box" category is significantly more precise than any other means. Moreover, surveys which measure percentages of "totally satisfied" customers instead of the traditional sum of "very satisfied" and "somewhat satisfied," provide a much more accurate indicator of business growth.

Other Scale issues...There are other rules of thumb that may be used to ensure more valuable results:

Many surveys offer a "neutral" choice on a five-point scale for those who might not want to answer a question, or for those who are unable to make a decision. This "bail-out" option decreases the quantity of opinions, thus diminishing the survey's validity. Surveys that use "insufficient information," as a more definitive middle-box choice persuade a respondent to make a decision, unless they simply have too little knowledge to answer the question.

Scales of 1-10 (or 1-100%) are perceived differently between age groups. Individuals who were schooled using a percentage grading system often consider a 59% to be "flunking." These deep-rooted tendencies often skew different peoples' perceptions of survey results.

The scale to the right is an effective way to illustrate percentages of totally satisfied customers and also indicates the relative urgency of satisfaction issues. Depending upon the industry, the 30% to 45% Totally Satisfied range may be considered as holding market share.

◻ SOME ADDITIONAL THOUGHTS

There are a few additional details that can enhance the overall polish of a survey. While a survey should be an exercise in communications excellence, the experience of taking a survey should also be positive for the respondent, as well as valuable for the survey sponsor.

First, People—Those responsible for acting upon issues revealed in the survey should be fully engaged in the survey development process. A "team leader" should be responsible for ensuring that all pertinent business categories are included (up to 10 is ideal), and that designated individuals take responsibility for responding to the results for each Key Attribute.

Second, Respondent Validation—Once the names of potential survey respondents have been selected, they are individually called and "invited" to participate. This step ensures the person is willing to take the survey, and elicits an agreement to do so, thus enhancing the response rate. It also ensures the person's name, title, and address is correct, areas in which inaccuracies are commonplace.

Third, Questions—Open-ended questions are generally best avoided in favour of simple, concise, one-subject questions. The questions should also be randomised, mixing up the topics, forcing the respondent to be continually thinking about a different subject, and not building upon an answer from the previous question. Finally, questions should be presented in positive tones, which not only helps maintain an objective and uniform attitude while answering the survey questions, but allows for uniform interpretation of the results.

Fourth, Results—Each respondent receives a synopsis of the survey results, either in writing or - preferably—in person. By offering at the outset to share the results of the survey with each respondent, interest is generated in the process, the response rate increases, and the company is left with a standing invitation to come back to the customer later and close the communication loop. Not only does that provide a means of dealing and exploring identified issues on a personal level, but it often increases an individual's willingness to participate in later surveys.

◻ ... AND FINALLY

A well-structured customer satisfaction survey can provide a wealth of invaluable market intelligence that human nature will not otherwise allow access to. Properly done, it can be a means of establishing performance benchmarks, measuring improvement over time, building individual customer relationships, identifying customers at risk of loss, and improving overall customer satisfaction, loyalty and revenues. If a company is not careful, however, it can become a source of misguided direction, wrong decisions and wasted money.

Contact Management: Give 'em What They Want
How to Make the Most of your Customer Relationships with a Campaign Management Solution

■ **Michael Emerson**

Abstract

The Internet offers businesses the potential to develop personal relationships with individual customers through a direct channel of communication. Mike Emerson, Senior VP of Marketing at Recognition Systems, discusses how companies can gain a competitive advantage through the implementation and execution of a successful campaign management solution. He looks at targeting appropriate customers effectively and managing these customer contacts profitably.

Emerson explores how to extract maximum value from each customer interaction step by step, focusing on the principal elements required to achieve a comprehensive customer management solution, including: Reaching the right customer, knowing what your company needs, defining explicit priorities and rules, finding the "Next Best Contact", touch point strategies, technology requirements.

Emerson explores how complex management rules can provide an organisation with a strategic method to divide up resources and ensure an extra level of productivity.

Key Words: *Campaign Management, Personal Relationships, Direct Channel, Competitive Advantage*

❑ WHAT IS CONTACT MANAGEMENT?

Contact Management has traditionally been used to describe an approach taken by a sales manager to plan for specific actions of sales personnel in interacting with their prospects. Today, marketers of all types are using these techniques on a much wider scale to maximize the effectiveness of their enterprise marketing efforts. Any company that is considering the implementation of a CRM solution should view Contact Management as one of the parts of the overall puzzle.

What Is Campaign Management?

A Campaign Management solution allows a business to grasp the significance of *all* its marketing programs currently in place. Details could include: who is being targeted, what offers are they receiving, how often should they be targeted or who is a likely candidate for additional offers. Campaign management ensures that the same set of customers will not be targeted too frequently, and that interested customers will not be ignored. It also allows the company to customer database.

❑ CONTACT MANAGEMENT HISTORY

In the past, marketing campaigns have generally been a stand-alone process, with companies sorting through massive amounts of customer data on large-scale mainframe computers to discover the results from different programs. Little thought was given as to how all these individual campaigns should fit together to interact with the customer in the most positive manner.

In a lot of big companies, every product manager would launch their own campaigns — and every business unit would also launch their own campaigns. Many businesses soon found out that their very best customers were being contacted repeatedly—to the point of being offensive. They also discovered that many customers weren't being contacted at all. Oftentimes, conflicting marketing programs were being sent to customers, since no one had an overall sense of what the company was doing. For example, a major provider of business services was selling a $500 software package to a set of customers. The company realized it had a problem with managing campaigns when it discovered that another business unit was making hundreds of thousands of dollars annually on user fees for the same service offered in the software package.

This is a prime example of where the contacts and campaigns weren't really thought about—should the company be trying to sell a software package that made $500 for one business unit, but cost the corporation hundreds of thousands of dollars in lost revenue each time they sold it?

Targeting appropriate customers and effectively managing customer contacts were not addressed very well in the past. Today, companies such as Recognition Systems are providing solutions that deal with the challenge of contact management and actually turn this into a major competitive advantage for the companies that deploy them.

❑ LET CUSTOMERS DEFINE THE RULES

In today's business environment, developing and maintaining an ongoing relationship with the customer is more important than the success of any one product or service. It's a higher-level purpose that everything has to fit under.

Keeping this thought in mind, contact management needs to start with the customer. Companies need to respect their wishes on how often and in what manner they would like to be contacted. For years, direct marketers have understood the importance of using a marketing database to track those customers who do not want to be contacted by marketing messages. Processes such as the Direct Marketer's Association (DMA) "Do Not Pander" file must form the starting point for all contact management processes.

Leading edge marketers should also provide their customers with ample opportunity to specify preferences about frequency and preferred channel of contact.

Macromedia, a leader in the e-commerce space that uses Recognition Systems' Protagona software, has a 100% opt-in policy. They allow their customers to define specific subject areas that they want to receive communications about. Customers will receive product information based solely on this explicit opt-in request, as opposed to anything else. Campaigns are then delivered that selectively include content only within those categories of interest to each individual customer.

☐ REACHING THE RIGHT CUSTOMER

Managing the frequency and content of interactions with end customers is one of the primary reasons companies install a campaign management system. As customers become more bombarded with marketing messages, it is critical to get the maximum value from each customer interaction. Marketers must look at inefficient marketing from both an ROI perspective, as well as a lost opportunity to use a contact for a business advantage.
While heeding customer desires has largely been seen as a defensive approach, investors in campaign management systems should see this as a competitive advantage. Leveraging the capability to respect the individual needs of each customer puts a business in a position of competitive advantage.

Once a campaign management system is in place, marketers should use every opportunity to collect information about interest areas, preferred channel, and appropriate frequency of contact.

Added Sophistication

When companies select a campaign management solution, the rules for delivering marketing messages to customers can become more sophisticated.

For example, a company could establish a policy such as 'no customer should be contacted more than four times per month' or 'customers should be contacted two times for this product and two times for that product'.

Even more sophisticated rules would rank the order and relevance of contacts. Complex campaign management rules become a very strategic method to divide up your resources. Think of it as spending account—but with customer contacts, instead of dollars. If you only have a certain amount of money to spend, what is the best way to use each dollar? If a customer can only be contacted once or twice, what is your best product or service to offer that customer in that context?

☐ KNOW WHAT YOUR COMPANY NEEDS

Once the customer's needs and wants are taken care of, the next contact management issue relates to the needs of the enterprise. Most businesses have many different departments that have an interest in communicating with customers.

Typically, these include product and market managers, as well as diverse business units that all stand to gain from selling their wares to the customers contained in the enterprise customer database. The installation of a Campaign Management (CM) system to manage this effort oftentimes exposes the conflicting nature of these various factions, such as the earlier example of the company losing money every time it sold a $500 software package. Define Explicit Priorities and Rules

Business should define explicit priorities for access to the customer database based on the enterprise benefits of each customer contact. The primary consideration will be the net impact on the customer lifetime value. Preference should always be given to those customer contacts that will benefit over the lifetime of a customer (frequently computed as the net present value of profit — projected for 3 to 5 years). However, special considerations are often required to accommodate business requirements, such as new product rollouts.

Enterprise rules should be agreed upon and built into the campaign management system. Once all stakeholders have agreed upon the contact priorities, the CM process should ensure that all users of the system follow these priorities. Some rules can be defined by query definitions, such as frequency and recency of contact.

Other types of rules may require pre-defined pools of customers that are reserved for use by a specific stakeholder. This approach recognizes that contact management is more than "first come, first served" and may require that certain customer segments be set aside for use by a high priority user.

Establish a Marketing Council

In addition to rules and structure defined within the CM system itself, business processes must be established that support the established contact rules. A marketing council with representatives from various product and market groups can meet at regular intervals to set priorities and make adjustments to the contact rules contained in the CM system. This council can also make decisions on conflicts between various users of the database.

☐ FINDING THE "NEXT BEST CONTACT"

First generation database marketing efforts focused on the concept of "next best product" to sell to a customer. While this remains the ultimate goal of most marketing efforts, there are many considerations that have to be taken into account prior to defining a comprehensive marketing strategy.

Recognition Systems calls this paradigm *customer experience management*, because it looks at a much broader view of what should be marketed to a customer. The tactical consideration becomes the delivery of the "next best contact"—which will eventually create an experience that will result in the sale of the next best product.

Touch Point Strategies

A touch point strategy is a systematic look at how you can take advantage of *every* contact you have with a customer. For example, in a customer service center, the obvious reason for a 'touch point' is for someone to call in if they have a problem or concern. However, you need to examine that touch point as an opportunity to also improve the relationship, or to sell or market additional goods and services.

One major decision that a business must make is: what functions will be focused–on at each of the touch points you have established in your enterprise rules and priorities. However, not all touch points are created equal and each has different characteristics in terms of cost of transaction, available functionality, and customer reach.

With a touch point strategy defined, the CM system becomes the primary tool for providing customer experiences that move customers from one point to the next. Campaigns should be designed to explicitly support the overall touch point strategy by moving customers toward those touch points where business transactions are most likely to occur.

Two broad strategies are possible: focusing on breadth, and focusing on one primary touch point.

Focus on Breadth

Airlines are excellent examples of businesses that are setting up many different ways to transact with their customers. Customers can come to their web site, visit an independent travel agent, call an 800 #, or go to a retail site to transact business. The business strategy is to deliver consistent messages across these touch points and be ready to interact with the customer in whatever medium they have selected.

Focus on One Primary Touch Point

Focus on a primary touch point—e-tailers such as Amazon.com and emerging ones, such as Macromedia also touch customers through different touch points. However, the primary focus of the end transaction is the Web.

Using this strategy, customers are marketed through several different channels (catalogs, e-mails, Web pages, and advertising) with the end goal of pushing the customer toward the Web, where the business has prepared a site that completes the cycle.

Another example of this type of touch point strategy is the traditional insurance company that sells through an independent agent network. Customers are marketed through a variety of mediums, all with the end result of pushing them toward an agent who can complete the transaction.

☐ TECHNOLOGY REQUIREMENTS

Business users who are looking to implement an enterprise contact management strategy need to consider several requirements:

- The ability to enforce contacts based on frequency and how recently the last contact was made. A communications log must be maintained that records every marketing contact with a customer. This log must be updated quickly enough so that campaigns that are executed consecutively will be able to include the information entered from a campaign that just completed.

- The ability to implement campaigns in an automated fashion. Routine contact management rules must be executable under "lights out" production controls. Increasingly, campaigns are setup to run on an on-going basis. To support this production paradigm, contact management processes must be run and updated in a mode where no user intervention is required.

- The ability to accommodate exceptions. The axiom "rules are meant to be broken" holds true for contact management strategies. Enterprises will find many situations that require that any or all enterprise-defined rules be suspended for the needs of specific campaigns. Specifically, schedule queues must be flexible enough for an *ad hoc* campaign to be entered as a part of a sequence of campaigns to be run in one large batch.

◻ CAMPAIGN MANAGEMENT SUCCESS STORIES

Acxiom

Acxiom provides a wide spectrum of data products, data integration services, mailing list services, modeling and analysis, and information technology outsourcing services to major U.S. and international firms. In the last 12 months, Acxiom has recorded more than $900 million in revenue.

Acxiom has partnered with Recognition Systems to build multiple-contact campaigns for the insurance industry on a more rapid basis. At the same time, all of this will be accomplished while respecting the customer's privacy.

With this partnership, insurance organizations, and other companies who want to sell insurance, will be able to move into a more multi-channel marketing approach versus a single-channel initiative.

Macromedia

In late 1997, Macromedia hit an air pocket on its way to rapid growth and market success. In response to this business challenge, Macromedia made a commitment to reinvent itself as a totally Web-focused company. At the core of this strategy was the development of a membership repository that stored information on the millions of software developers who regularly used their products.

Macromedia installed the Protagona product as the application that managed all marketing interactions with their customers. As contacts were made with the customer, they were recorded to the repository and used to control the next contact with the customer. The result is that all marketing activities are directly driven by customer preferences. The business results have been dramatic, as they have successfully reduced cost while maintaining a high rate of revenue and profitability growth.

□ SUMMARY

Contact management can move from a purely defensive tactic to a powerful strategy to build customer relationships. By using a campaign management system to implement a marketing strategy, businesses can deliver influential messages and consistent customer experiences that will deliver a high rate of financial return and increased customer loyalty.

For an effective campaign, marketers should remember to:

- Let the customers decide how often and in what manner they wish to be contacted
- Use every opportunity to collect information about potential and current customers
- Define explicit priorities within the company for access to the customer database

Building Relationships with Doctors for Effective Marketing
The Case of the Pharmaceutical Industry

■ **Sameer Lal**

Abstract

The Indian Pharmaceutical market is a very fragmented market and does not recognise product patent. Hence brand differentiation is very difficult in a market where there are over 50 brands for every molecule. Thus the relationship between the Medical Representative (the main medium of promotion) and the doctor is the key driver for sales. A detailed step by step process is given to start a CRM initiative based on the IDIC model suggested by Peppers and Rogers. An example of a loyalty programme for the key doctors is suggested along with a possible measurement system to gauge the impact of the programme. The paper also highlights the use of direct marketing initiatives as well as call centres by companies to build relationships with doctors.

Key Words: *Pharmaceutical Industry, Loyalty Programme, Direct Marketing, Call Centre, Customization*

"In an industry where each of the top competition already has a quality product the competitor who can create the highest quality relationship with its own individual customers will win those customer's loyalty."

Perhaps this has been written keeping the Indian pharmaceutical industry in mind.

□ INTRODUCTION

The Indian Pharmaceutical market is worth approx. Rs. 140,000 million growing at a healthy 10%. There are around 16,000 players both in the organised and the unorganised market vying for a piece of this pie. It is a very fragmented market with the number one player, GlaxoWellcome, having a market share of 5.8%. In fact the combined market share of the top five companies does not exceed 20%.

Branded Generics Market

The Indian Pharmaceutical market is among the few markets in the world that recognises process patents and not product patents.

As a result India is a branded generic market where there are at least 50 brands for every molecule, making it a total of more than 30,000 brands in the country[3]. In such a situation brand differentiation is very difficult. Earlier M.N.C.'s used to sell on the quality plank but today quality is a table stake condition where even the smallest player is able to meet the highest quality norms.

Doctor Population

There are approximately 500,000 doctors in India who are registered with the Indian Medical Association.[4] The largest of the Pharmaceutical companies cannot meet more than 125,000 of this doctor population. As a result most of the doctors are being met by at least 60-100 companies.

Out of the total doctor population as much as 60–65% are General Practitioners with the basic MBBS degree. The higher specialities constitute the remaining 35–40%. Physicians, Gynaecologists and Paediatricians form the bulk of the specialists.

In chronic therapies like hypertension once a patient starts on a particular medication he is expected to continue the medication for life. Thus the lifetime value of a single patient of these ailments is very high. Thus specialist doctors like a Cardiologist are a very important segment.

Promotion

In an ethical market product promotion is directed solely to the qualified doctors. No advertising mentioning brand names is allowed in the lay press. The Medical Representative (M.R.) is the major means of promotion though other media like direct mail, journal advertising, conferences also play a role albeit a limited one.

☐ STARTING A CRM INITIATIVE

Having understood the major characteristics of the industry, the Identification, Differentiation, Interaction and Customisation (IDIC) Model as suggested by Don Peppers and Martha Rogers would be used to understand the steps to a CRM initiative.

Identification

The first step towards any CRM initiative is identification of your customers. Each Medical Representative maintains a list of doctors of his area. This list is generated through interviews with the stockists, retailers well as his peers from other companies. The list called the MSL (Must See List), MVL (Must Visit List), Customer List etc. typically lists the name, address, telephone phone number, speciality, qualification, visit timings and other basic data of the doctor. The key driver for a CRM programme is integration of this data from all the M.R.s to a central database.

The next step is to add to this data by collecting details from other sources like

- Membership directories of associations: Almost all cities have their branches of the Indian Medical associations (IMA). These have a directory of all their members listing their contact details and some personal information. These are a good source to begin with but most are updated at very long intervals hence the veracity of the data has to be checked. Similarly, there are individual associations for almost all the specialties whose membership directories are also easily available.
- List of conference participants: Each specialty of doctor organises a national level conference every year where members from all over the country attend. Details can be collected through sponsorship of the front desk, organising contests or distributing give aways in exchange for information.
- Doctor referral: Another route would be akin to a member get member scheme wherein doctors would be encouraged to refer fellow practitioners.

Thus a semblance of a database would take shape. The term is a misnomer since at best it is a customer list, as it contains nothing more than contact information along with some basic information. But nevertheless it is a starting point.

The 'database' (for want of a better word) at no stage can be termed as 'final' as collection of doctor details is an ongoing process. Continuous additions, updations and deletions are always taking place.

The list can be mined for details of speciality wise break up, geographical coverage etc. to serve as a tool for the marketing decision making process.

Differentiation

The success of any loyalty programme lies in differentiating the key customers. Typically a MSR would classify his doctors using the ABC method as Core, Important and Others based on the amount of business he gets (or expects to get) from them. The number of subclasses would vary but the principle would be the same. In a typical pyramidal fashion the top rung doctors who are the least in number would be commercially most important and the importance would linearly decrease as one goes down the pyramid. The numbers would proportionately increase as per the Pareto principle.

The point to be borne in mind is that the whole basis of differentiation is been done on very subjective terms of the perception of the local M.R. unlike other industries viz. Airlines who would classify frequent fliers based on data collected from reservation. Since there is no formal mechanism of capturing data about the revenue generated from a doctor, the Medical representative is the sole and final judge.

Thus the database formed is step one can now be subclassified into the important doctors and the not so important ones.

Interaction

Now comes the stage of building on the database collected and refined in the above two stages. The basic idea now is to build on the data collected in the first stage. The idea is get to know the doctor intimately. His hobbies, likes, dislikes, family details etc. The fundamental premise being that the doctor is as human as anybody else is and hence we should recognise his individuality. It is of utmost importance that it is decided beforehand what kind of information would be collected and much more importantly **how it will be used**. Interaction can be done at two levels

- Firstly, personally at the MR level: The most productive would be using human intervention. The MR can easily collect most of the information from his day to day interactions with his customer. Alternatively a formal structured questionnaire can also be administered.

The biggest hurdle to this approach is not surprisingly enough the MR. A level of conviction has to be brought into him that the data he would collect would actually be used and more importantly will help him do his job better. Numerous instances abound of companies who have gone about collecting loads of information on their doctors through their M.R.s and finally not using them at all.

- Secondly, direct at the corporate level: The structured questionnaires requesting further details can also be mailed to doctors with each response entitled to a token gift etc. This approach typically would yield a lower rate of return but the quality of information would be superior to the first approach as it is coming directly from the doctor.

The information collected is then incorporated to the basic database earlier formed. Just to give an idea of the type of information collected by companies consider the following

- Personal information: Date of birth, marriage anniversary, details of children, qualification and experience
- Hobbies and interests: activities during spare time, TV channels watched, general interest magazines read, favourite vacation destinations
- Professional interests: Type and names of medical journals read, professional membership of association(s), attendance at national conferences
- Ownership details: Household durables owned, vehicle ownership

Companies have been able to collect enormous amount of such data through either of the means enumerated earlier. What is important to note that they have been able to demonstrate their sincerity in actually using this data.

Customisation

This is the time to start using the data. The easiest and the most preliminary step is to start greeting the doctor on his birthday and marriage anniversary. From a simple card personally signed to a personal phone call from the head office anywhere in the country to a birthday cake being actually presented are some of the ideas. Even bouquets can be delivered at the doorstep. A company even arranges for the doctor to have dinner with spouse on their marriage anniversary, with the tab taken care of course!

But more important is to customise the interaction with the doctor based on the data we have on him. Gifts based on the interests and hobbies can be presented. If a doctor has expressed interest in national conferences of his speciality the same can be arranged.

The success of the whole programme hinges on how well can the companies pass on the data of the doctor to their field force and train them on how to use this data. He is actually the man of the moment. It is necessary that information received on an interaction be fed back into the system so that it can be used for the next interaction. A sort of a 'master database' can be generated which would record every contact with a doctor through the field, mail, telephone, web etc. This master database would be the key driver to foster a learning relationship.

□ LOYALTY PROGRAMME

The next obvious step is to have a loyalty programme as a frequency marketing initiative. An ideal loyalty programme would be able to identify its key accounts, reward them for their custom and encourage them to increase their spend.

This concept in the context of the pharmaceutical industry has a twist since the customer (the doctor) is not the actual consumer (the patient) of the product. Thus there are ethical issues involved in rewarding points in return for prescriptions. One cannot have a reward programme based on redemption of these points.

One approach would be to set the whole programme based on the classification into which the doctor falls. Thus the lowest rung would be restricted to the basic of activities. The number and level of activities would increase as the importance of the doctor grows. A branded programme can be started for the most important doctors. It is important that it is clearly defined at the onset what will be the objective of the programme and more importantly conveys the exclusivity of the programme. The doctor has to be made to realise that he is the 'chosen one'. All activities and inputs should only reinforce this communication.

The success of such a programme hinges on making the doctor covet membership to the programme. Thus a continuous monitoring is required of the returns generated from the doctor. If they fall below a predefined limit then the doctor can be downgraded and his privileges reduced.

□ DIRECT MARKETING

It is a valuable tool for effective CRM. Since a captive database has been put into place it can easily lend itself to direct marketing initiatives. As the primary fields captured are the contact addresses a programme through mail is the easiest to accomplish. Brand awareness mailers, new launches, contests all can be conducted by mail. It has several advantages

- It is very cost effective: A large audience can be touched at a relatively cheaper cost as compared to personal selling
- It can be targeted and specific to the right target audience in term of specialisation or geographical location

- It is measurable with the use of reply devices one can immediately gauge the efficacy of a campaign. In fact since the target audience for a brand is usually sharply defined in terms of their specialisation e.g. An allergy product to ENTs, Dermatologists and GPs, the response received is usually much higher then that accepted as a norm in other industries. A response of 15 – 20 % can be easily achieved through such communications.

Most of the pharmaceutical companies have realised the advantages of this mode of communication. The primary rationale is to save the time of the field by promoting the low involvement (for the doctor) products, promote brand recall for a new product, exploit alternative avenues for brand promotion etc.

Apart from mail other DM media like telemarketing and the web have also been tried. While telemarketing has been tried for promoting new launches to get instant feedback the web has still to achieve its potential. The PC penetration in India is still very low which handicaps growth of this mode. Using the e-mail to correspond and interact with doctors is being tried. It is especially useful for targeting higher specialities, which is more tech savvy and also information hungry.

□ CALL CENTRE

In case of chronic therapies like hypertension, serious conditions like AIDS and in hitherto unknown conditions (atleast in India) like erectile dysfunction the call centre provides the answer.

The medium lends an ear to three types of customers
- Doctors who would like to know more about the drug profile, discuss a specific case, ask for a reference on use in a specific condition
- Patients who seek counseling, the nearest physician or chemist shop. The telephone provides anonymity to the caller especially when discussing taboo subjects
- Retailers asking for pricing details, product availability

With the advent of paging companies who can provide a single number nationwide, facility of leased lines from DOT and the toll free 1600 numbers in select metros this medium is set for take off.

There are certain factors to be borne in mind whilst setting up a call centre. The sheer diversity of the country means that callers would speak different languages and may not be comfortable with English. This is especially relevant if the centre would cater to calls from patients. Also doctors would not prefer their queries being answered by a lay person without any medical background. Thus most medical queries have to be escalated to a qualified physician who responds to a doctors queries within a set time limit.

These limitations notwithstanding, the call centre is an excellent medium to come closer to the customer and the pharmaceutical industry is realising the potential.

□ MEASUREMENT SYSTEMS

No programme can be without a formal measurement system to gauge its effectiveness as well as the impact. As discussed earlier the peculiar industry dynamics where the customer is just an influencer and not the final consumer tend to complicate the establishment of a formal measurement system.

One method has been tried and has provided some direction though doubts may remain of its effectiveness. But in the absence of any other alternative it can be taken to be as the most relevant.

The measurement system would require studying the prescription profile of the doctors who are being exposed to the CRM programme vis a vis a control sample who are met by the field force but not exposed to the CRM activities. The prescription given by the doctors can be studied over a particular time frame and the amount of prescriptions before exposure to the programme and after can be measured. The idea is to check if the prescription levels have increased after the doctor has been made the member of the loyalty programme. There are specialised Market Research agencies that undertake prescription research and can provide turnkey solutions for such questions.

This method at best would provide a qualitative idea but would nevertheless give an idea of the success or otherwise of the programme.

□ CONCLUSION

The paper cannot be concluded without a mention of the importance of internally marketing the CRM programme. The success of the whole programme hinges on the support of the top management who can act as a mentor. The programme takes time to take off and much more time to actually show results.

The conviction for the importance of the programme has to be sold to the lowest level of the organisation especially to the field force who are the ultimate beneficiaries. Their role assumes significance all the more since most of activities are dependent on them for implementation.

REFERENCES

Don Peppers and Martha Rogers (1993), *'The One to One Future'*, Currency Doubleday, New York

ORG - MARG Retail Audit, 'Retail Market for Pharmaceutical Product in India July 2000', Operations Research Group, Baroda, India

Business Times Bureau, 'Healthcare Is The New Healthline Of Ad Agencies', *The Times of India*, 19 August 2000. pp. 15

Vijay Jung Thapa and Subhadra Menon, 'Growing Distrust – Doctor Versus Patient', *India Today*, 25 September 2000, pp. 38-48.

Chapter 24

Process Reengineering to Enhance Customer Relationships

A Case Study of Kirloskar Oil Engines Limited

■ **R Nargundkar and Chetan Bajaj**

Abstract

An Indian company which has always held customers in high esteem is Kirloskar Oil Engines Ltd. (KOEL). In spite of its regard for customers, KOEL found it had to work harder to retain them with increasing levels of global competition. The company decided to aggressively pursue a reengineering exercise with customer relationship management as its major focus. This paper provides a glimpse of the three-year long and ongoing efforts of the company to enhance its relationships with its existing customers, and the process which was followed while attempting the change. Based mainly on the authors' own findings during their involvement as consultants during the project, it is supplemented by findings from discussions with selected top managers of KOEL. Findings indicate that customers have benefited significantly in terms of reduced transaction and delivery times, error-free order registrations and in general, better service. The ambitious exercise was backed by an ERP package implementation, and satisfaction measurement systems to measure gains made.

Key Words: _Reengineering, Customer Relationship Management, Order Registration, Satisfaction, ERP_

□ INTRODUCTION

Competition in this age of Information Technology (IT) has assumed new dimensions. Customers have become very demanding. They now demand fast and frequent deliveries in small lot sizes. They are no longer satisfied with standard products but want a wide variety. Quality is assumed and defects are no longer tolerated.

KOEL, a leading manufacturer of diesel engines, had always enjoyed a high reputation in the market because of good and consistent quality. However, in the mid 1990s with the onset of economic liberalization, many foreign companies were eyeing the growing Indian market and competition had heated up. Customers were not satisfied with KOEL's delivery time and had become very demanding.

KOEL's diesel engines are sold to three distinct market segments:

1. Industrial buyers—who use it as a prime mover for various industrial applications,
2. Dealers -who couple them with an alternators and sell them as Power Generation sets (PG) to agricultural and small industries sector, and
3. A major automobile OEM (Auto)- which manufactures tractors.

Before 1997, the delivery time for all the three segments was two months. This meant that the customer had to place his order two months in advance. The inventory was very high total inventory including raw materials, work in progress and finished goods was about 35 days.

Five major components/assemblies of a diesel engine were being machined by KOEL namely—crankcase, crankshaft, camshaft, con-rod and gear- casing. All other components and parts were out-sourced in finished form. These five major components were procured in raw form from suppliers .The final assembly was done in KOEL's plant. An analysis revealed that these components spent only 25-30 hours on the company's shop floor. This included time for all processing and machining operations, which numbered 26, as also assembly, testing, painting and packaging. The long lead-time was largely due to time lags in registration of orders, receipt of materials from suppliers and material waiting in stores.

The break-down of the total lead-time, in percentage terms, was as follows:

- Order registration and acceptance: 20%
- Communication of purchase orders to vendors   12%
- Receiving of components from vendors and sub vendors   40%
- Material reaching shop   12%
- Processing, assembly, packing   4%
- Despatch   12%

  TOTAL   100%

This suggested that faster order registration and speedier receipt of materials could reduce delivery time from suppliers. This could be achieved by fast information flow across the supply chain and streamling the manufacturing activities to enable quick movement of parts/components and the final product pulled as per the requirement of the customer.

The company did not have adequate information about the operations of its vendors and the reason for long lead-times in receiving supplies. But this was largely due to delay in communication of information and due to manufacturing, machining and assembly operations in big batches by a large number of vendors.

☐ INITIATING THE CHANGE PROCESS

The dissatisfaction about long lead times voiced by the customers in satisfaction surveys was used, along with increasing technological sophistication of competitors, to push for a range of initiatives. Primary among these was the decision to go for an Information Technology backbone in the form of a company-wide ERP implementation. It was expected to counter any technical advantage that future MNC competitors may have, by enabling a relationship-oriented strategy for KOEL with its customers. Simultaneously, a Business Process Reengineering exercise was undertaken to reinvent some of the obsolete marketing processes which had become hurdles in the delivery of superior customer value.

The reengineering exercise was spearheaded by one vice president in the company with enough authority to involve SBU (Strategic Business Unit) heads of the three major SBUs of the company, and recruit members into change teams with their concurrence. Change teams consisted of 6-8 bright employees, and each change team member had to be on the BPR exercise for about 4 hours a day for as long as needed. The vice-president who was overall in charge as the BPR Project Coordinator, had two young assistants to do the coordination and assist with the documentation. These young assistants attended all meetings and presentations made by the change teams to the steering committee consisting of the Project Coordinator, the concerned SBU head, the Information Technology Department head and external consultants, in this case the authors. Changes ratified by the Steering Committee were cleared for implementation.

□ BREAKTHROUGH IMPROVEMENTS

KOEL achieved major improvements in delivery lead time, inventory levels, rejection levels, wastages etc. between April 1997 and October 1999. These improvements are summarised below.

The lead time for the delivery of oil engines which was two months for all segments earlier was reduced for different market segments as follows:

Standard engines produced in small quantities for PG segment	One /two days
Standard engines mass-produced for automobile OEM	Just In Time (Against Production schedule)
Custom- built engines	Ten days.

Improvements in other parameters were as under:

Parameter	Before 1997	After 1999
Inventory (total)	35 days	7 days
Wastages in material	2 lakhs/month	Negligible
Rejections on KOEL assembly line	1.5%	0.2%
Rejection on customer's assembly line	9%	1%

These improvements were achieved by introducing the following techniques/initiatives:
1. E-commerce for instantaneous order registration
2. Market segmentation and customer focus.
3. Dedicated and flexible manufacturing systems
4. Vendor development and rationalization
5. Supply chain integration through IT networking and organisational focus

We discuss in detail how KOEL conceptualized and implemented some of the above initiatives. Our first example is the reengineering of the Order Registration Process.

□ REENGINEERING THE ORDER REGISTRATION PROCESS

KOEL had a very extensive and dispersed marketing operation spread across the country with over 1200 distributors, who booked orders: 12 warehouses and 19 sales offices. The order registration was a complex long-winding process with distributors placing orders with local sales offices, which routed them to regional sales offices, which in turn routed them to the head office, all through couriers. The order was keyed at multiple locations. The whole process took on an average about 10 days, and involved 8 persons and processing of 6 documents. Very often errors crept up leading to customer complaints. A diagrammatic representation of this process is shown in Fig. 1.

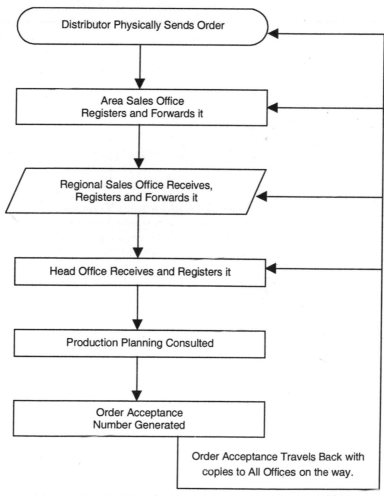

Fig. 1 *The Old Order Registration Process at KOEL*

The redesigned order registration process, shown in Fig. 2, enables instantaneous order registration through a software module-Web Customer, which connects KOEL with all its customers and distributors through the World Wide Web (www). A KOEL dealer now E-mails order requirement directly to the head office. An automatic translator interfaces the E-mail data packet with KOEL's Oracle-based ERP. The Oracle system automatically registers all standard orders and electronically sends an order acceptance note to the dealer/customer. It simultaneously updates all other modules and triggers the workflow. In exceptional situations when the order does not follow standard specifications, a sales executive authorises the order registration. The improvements resulting from introduction of electronic order registration were as under:

Order Registration parameters	Prior to networking	After networking
Average cycle time	10 days	Instantaneous
Number of persons involved	8	0/1 (special cases)
Number of documents involved	6	None

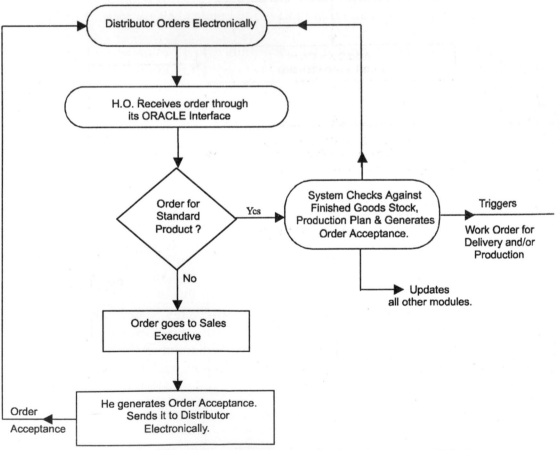

Fig. 2 *The Reengineered Order Acceptance Process at KOEL*

☐ KOEL'S WEBSITE FACILITIES

KOEL established a website to facilitate E-commerce This dynamic web site offers the following facilities to KOEL's customers:

1. Displays product catalogues
2. Displays customer-specific pricing and discounts
3. Permits order entry for multiple receiving locations
4. Submits customer orders to Oracle's order entry module and provides on-line confirmation.
5. Enables viewing of order status, invoices, debit/ credit balances etc.

KOEL is also soon introducing payments and collections over the electronic network. This will proceed as follows: On receipt of an invoice from a web based supplier KOEL will authorize its bank to debit KOEL's account and to direct the suppliers bank to correspondingly credit supplier's account. All these transactions will be on the net. Similarly KOEL will receive collections from its customers (including dealers) electronically.

KOEL is also planning to develop its brand image further with its dealers and end users of its product which include industrial customers and farmers -who purchase diesel engine-fitted gensets and pumpsets by initiating an interactive dialogue on the net. Its website will soon offer advisory, educational and entertainment services including those on:

1. Proper use and maintenance of agricultural equipment.
2. Latest irrigation practices and farm productivity
3. Advice on selection of farm tools and equipment including tractors, tillers, gensets etc.
4. Mechanical design and repair of farm equipment

☐ MARKET SEGMENTATION AND CUSTOMER FOCUS

The three market segments served by KOEL namely automotive OEM, power generation set manufacturers and industrial users had distinct requirements, which were as follows:

1. The OEM-Auto segment required a standard diesel engine model in large volume. It needs an efficient and highly reliable supply chain, which ensures that there are frequent supplies and that there are no disruptions in supply to enable introduction of JIT at its plant.
2. The dealers of PG equipment required a larger variety of standard models. They need an efficient supply chain, which delivers a variety of standard models frequently and consistently. The more frequent the delivery, the lower is the inventory with dealers.
3. The industrial segment requires one off or a few custom built models for various industrial applications. This segment needs to be serviced by a fast responsive supply chain, which delivers customized models at short notice.

The supply chains for the three segments had to be correspondingly distinct. KOEL has accordingly developed separate supply chains with a different vendor and distributor base as far as possible for the three segments. It has developed efficient supply chains for automotive and PG segments to minimise cost and ensure frequent delivery and a highly responsive supply chain for industrial product manufacturers to deliver customized models. We discuss below in greater detail the requirements of the three segments and how each supply chain has been organised to meet these requirements.

Automobile OEM

The automobile OEM -Auto- located about 2000 kms from KOEL's plant was concerned about committing production schedules two months in advance. Like other automobile companies Auto was looking forward to implementing Just -In -Time (JIT) production system at its plant. This required daily delivery of all parts/components. KOEL was one of the major suppliers of Auto and its support was essential in implementing JIT at Auto.

To implement JIT a steady production schedule was worked out which meant fixing up the numbers of tractors to be produced per day based on average market lifting. KOEL committed to delivering the fixed number of diesel engines every day based on this production schedule to facilitate introduction of JIT at Auto. KOEL is now electronically networked with Auto and all changes in production schedules at Auto are communicated instantaneously to KOEL. A major change in lifting pattern can be accommodated within a week.

To enable JIT deliveries one production-cum-assembly line at KOEL was dedicated exclusively to manufacture engines for Auto. Seven workstations were set up along this line and the daily target was divided amongst them. Thus a steady and fixed production volume was achieved. The exact number of components/ parts down to nuts and bolts needed for the determined production level was fixed and communicated to suppliers. The exact volume of components are now received at the beginning of each shift.

The assembly of whole diesel engine at a workstation is given to one operator/one team creating a feeling of ownership and making it possible to trace back a defect to a workstation and operator. Higher motivation and accountability resulted in increase in percentage of first pass at Auto's plant from 90% to 99%. There was also reduction in wastages of about Rs. two lakhs per month at KOEL's plant. The greatest benefit however was increased customer satisfaction as KOEL worked on a pre-determined production plan set by the customer instead of a two-month lead-time, thereby facilitating introduction of JIT at Auto's plant.

Power Generation Segment

The diesel engines are coupled with alternators for use as gen-sets. A large number of models are being marketed to this segment through a dealer network across the country. The two-month lead-time made it necessary for the dealers to stock a large volume of inventory. Though the dealers received daily supplies from KOEL's plant they received only one model on a day depending on which model was under production at KOEL's plant. Hence, distributors were not sure which model would be received when. Consequently, as per KOEL's requirement they had to forecast sales two months in advance and place an order accordingly. Accuracy of forecasts is dependent on the time period for which forecasts are made - the longer the period the greater the uncertainty. The results of a wrong forecast in this case were lost sales due to under-estimated demand, or excess inventory.

The dealers wanted KOEL to supply all models more frequently and if possible on a daily basis in proportion to daily market demand. This would help dealers to reduce stocks at their end very drastically. It would also reduce errors in forecasting sales as orders can be modified on a daily basis. Besides, as dealers pointed out fluctuations in sales were often due to uncertainty in supply. If steady daily supply of all models is achieved the demand fluctuations would reduce. This would help KOEL in planning production and delivery better.

To improve the responsiveness of this supply chain KOEL agreed to supply all models on a daily basis to its major dealers based on market lifting. The volume of daily supply was fixed and the dealer had to communicate only if there was a significant change in lifting pattern.

This required manufacture of all the 40 models on a daily basis in proportion to market requirement. To achieve this KOEL introduced short runs in both manufacturing and assembly operations. Six workstations /cells were organised to which all the models were allocated so as to achieve balanced production. Each cell had to assemble six to eight models every day.

With this restructuring of assembly operations a balanced production of all models on a daily basis has been achieved. This makes it possible to supply all models on a daily basis to distributors. The distributors can now place orders on a daily basis instead of placing them two months ahead. Since the demand does not fluctuate on a daily basis a consistent ordering pattern has been established which facilitates smoothening of production operations.

Industrial Applications

Oil engines are also used by industrial customers as prime movers of industrial plant/ machinery etc. These oil engines are custom built and the demand for such applications does not follow any consistent pattern like the other two segments. As such the production cannot be pre-planned .For diesel engine models used by this segment KOEL is developing a quick response supply chain. It now commits delivery in ten days instead of two months. This is being made possible by instantaneous order registration and on- line communication of all orders to the company's plant and all its vendors involved in manufacturing critical components. Besides, vendors of critical components/ parts are being geared to make dedicated facilities available for meeting rush orders.

Most of the companies the world over are developing customized products built on standard platforms and differentiation is done only towards the end of the assembly process. This is also largely true of diesel engines where only a few components/parts are differentiated.

KOEL has developed an assembly line with three workstations dedicated to assembling customized diesel engines to ensure speedy response. This line has some dedicated vendors with committed production capacity largely for making highly customized and low volume components/parts.

Besides helping in achieving faster deliveries small batch production also helped reduce defects on the KOEL assembly line. The defects for five major components at assembly came down from 1.5% to just 0.2%. This is because small batch production helps identify defects quickly and helps take corrective action at an early stage.

The inventory has come down very significantly from 35 days to just one week.

☐ INTEGRATING SUPPLY CHAINS

Electronic transfer of information, shared databases, joint organisational task forces and integration of business processes of customer, distributors, company and suppliers is enabling the functioning of the entire supply chain as a seamless whole. Information on orders accepted, manufacturing and delivery plans, the current manufacturing status etc. is communicated on-line to all participants. This enables joint planning, dovetailing and execution of all manufacturing and delivery operations as per customer requirements. Customer orders trigger manufacturing along the critical paths with minimum manual intervention. The computer system rather than the manual purchase order suggests manufacturing plans to vendors. Task forces have been formed with participants from all constituents to work on common problems/ projects. KOEL has re-engineered its two main business processes namely- order registration and order execution and integrated them with key suppliers and distributors.

☐ PHASED IMPLEMENTATION PROGRAMME

A large number of components and parts go into the manufacture of diesel engines. These get assembled into five major parts/assemblies. The delivery time of the engine is however dependent on the critical path or the longest path. KOEL first concentrated its resources on reducing delivery time along this path by developing vendors on this path on a priority basis. Later on improvements were focussed on other paths on the basis of criticality. KOEL plans a small inventory just before bottleneck vendors or bottleneck operations on the critical path. This follows principles of synchronous manufacturing prescribed by Goldratt (1993) in his cult book—The Goal (1). According to Goldratt, inventory has to be concentrated just before the bottleneck operation to ensure that the bottleneck operation is not starved of raw materials. In any given operation there are only one or a few bottleneck operations. Improving the efficiency/speed of the bottleneck vendor or operation improves the speed of the entire chain.

Many problems were faced. The vendors and distributors had to be educated and convinced about the merits of the changes and motivated to invest in computers and networking technology. Attitudes and mindset had to change. Resistance to change had to be overcome. Some hard decisions had to be made while reducing suppliers from 500 to just around 100. The whole exercise has been on for three years and will be an ongoing process. Educating every one about the need for change and often forcing the pace has been necessary.

Authors' Note: Some numbers have been disguised for protecting confidential data.

REFERENCES

1. Goldratt E. and Cox J (1993), *The Goal*, Chennai : Productivity Press
2. Womack J. and Jones D (1996), *'Lean Thinking'*, New York : Simon & Schuster

Customer Relationship Management in Cement Industry

A Marketing Strategy Perspective

■ **Pramod Paliwal**

Abstract

Indian Cement Industry, which benchmarks its business processes with the best in the world, is a truly global Industry today. The developments in the last 10 years have made the nature of cement Industry extremely competitive. Earlier the demand – supply equilibrium was in favour of the manufacturers. Cement as a product used to be just another commodity product with almost negligible differentiation properties and hence there was no scope (and need) for the marketer to think much in terms of competitive marketing of cement. But the times have changed now.

Cement as a product undergoes value addition at each stage of usage. And at every stage different intermediaries deal with Cement who directly play a role in proper and quality usage of this unique product which still has no substitute. Cement marketers have to deal with a unique set of customers who are all of different nature. Any customer ranging from the owner to Civil Engineer, Architect, Contractor or even a mason can be crucial by virtue of their expert advice. And at every stage of its usage cement has to come up to the expectations of its user (i.e. the customer of that stage) in terms of quality, efficiency and economy. Each customer is unique in its own way and has a distinct set of parameters of customer satisfaction and expectations The issue that is constantly challenging the cement marketers is that of customer integration and loyalty and to use this as a tool to gain competitive advantage.

☐ INTRODUCTION

Customer Relationship Management has a great significance for the cement industry in order to satisfy and retain customers and thus gain a long-term equity. It involves establishing long run sustainable relationships with the customers (which are of different types and at different levels). This sustained relationship between the cement marketers and the customers will be based on the credibility of the seller and his sensitivity and promptness in meeting changing customer needs.

The cement marketer has to take care of three important set of customers (influencer, buyer and end user) and an attempt must be made to build long term productive relationship in distinct ways and manage them to its optimum advantage.

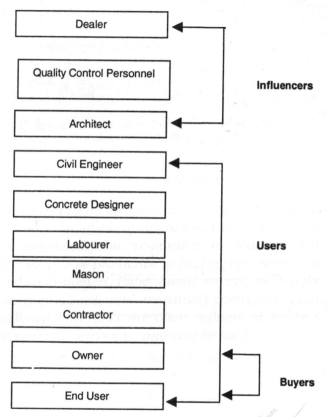

Fig. 1 *Stakeholders in the Cement Buying Process*

□ BUILDING EQUITY IN CEMENT MARKETING THROUGH CRM

In cement marketing, pluralistic buying behaviour, technology and applications play a major role in acting as key buying influences apart from several other variables which may vary from one buying situation to another. There seems to be a good scope to build up this credibility factor through Customer Relationship Management in the present day context, if a company is able to identify specific areas/customer groups where it could be done. As cement has a derived demand and thus is used in manufacturing of mortar, concrete and final structures, the credibility factor built up in the marketer-customer chain of interaction will enhance the satisfaction level of the ultimate customer (user group).

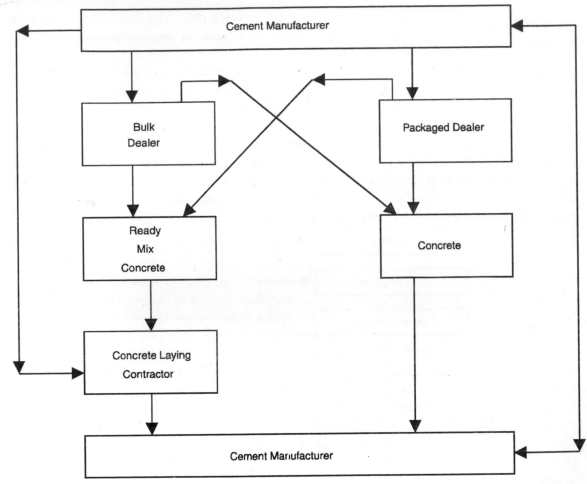

Fig. 2

As the figure indicates, cement primarily reaches the end user via a network of interme-diaries, which make it very difficult for a cement company to monitor the market and stay ahead of the development of the market/ customer requirements. But once the network is understood clearly, it becomes relatively easier to focus on each customer group and build credibility using CRM as a strategic tool.

This credibility chain is distinct from the marketer-customer chain. The basic aspect in the credibility chain is the possibility of reaching those influences which are beyond the traditional seller-buyer interactions (dyadic relationships) If differentiation is to be brought in through the credibility factor, a marketer has to identify several stages and relationships in the credibility chain and analyze a host of factors (ranging from pre sales service and advisory aspects to after sales services) as well as analyze the possibility of addressing these factors.

Customer Relationship Management is a vital tool to address these issues because a warm and fruitful relationship with customers forms the bedrock of any successful business.

CRM as a strategy in cement marketing-which may involve additional costs and efforts in terms of manpower, information system, diversity of needs from various customer segments etc-should be considered as an investment in serving two distinct purposes:

1. In the short run it could be an immediate distinguishing factor to position the company/product among competition.
2. In the long run the credibility factor itself develops the equity of the company in a rational manner.

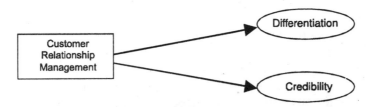

Cement marketers can hardly afford to ignore this vital purpose for the simple reason that a product like cement does not gives the cement manufacturers/marketers for differentiation and distinct positioning as there are incidentally a few characteristics to distinguish one produce from the other. In most situations these characteristics are governed by official standards and for a product the market may not value being better than the standard as there may not be much of a need for better performance.

Hence one of the basic issues in cement marketing is the limited scope of differentiation of product often resulting in confused marketing.

Therefore strategic marketing tools like CRM could be an "immediate" distinguishing factor to position the company/brand among competition. This immediate factor can be further leveraged to enable the company to gain sustainable competitive advantage.

Cement manufacturers must segment the customers so that they may be served as per their specialised needs. Giving strategically important customers such attention builds customer loyalty.

Different CRM strategies are to be deployed at various stages in usage of cement thus focusing on specific customer influences.

Stages in usage of cement	*Specific Customer Influences*	*CRM Strategies*
Primary (Decision making to buy certain brand) Buying Cement	Owner of structure/ end user/ architect / civil engineer / distribution channel Distribution channel/ quality control personnel/ contractor	Relationship through offering Total Solutions proposition Relationship to be established by creating confidence about service orientation and training users.
Using Cement in making concrete	Concrete designer/ mason/ labour/ contractor	--Do--
Laying of concrete Finished structure	Mason / labour /civil engineer Owner / end user / quality control personnel	--Do-- After sale service, exploring enhanced needs related to original offering, probing areas of dissatisfaction or usage problems.

□ CASE STUDIES OF RELATIONSHIP BUILDING IN CEMENT MARKETING

The Case of Indian Rayon

Indian Rayon an Aditya Birla Group company, was one of the first cement companies which felt the need to gain this immediate distinguishing factor and further long run equity by using CRM as a strategy.

The company wanted to bring about a transformation in the way in which it interacted with its customers. Dealers being the interface with the customers were identified as one of the major areas in this direction.

The company consciously worked on the aspect of maintaining long term productive relationships with its set of customers and came out with the conclusion that if the user-customers can build long term relationships with the distribution channel (and thus the company) of Indian Rayon Cement Products, this will be a major gain in the overall strategic marketing objectives of the company and also it will provide the company a distinct positioning.

Indian Rayon decided to upgrade select dealers to become Birla Super Shoppes. The intention was also to make the retailer go beyond being a mere sales channel. The Birla Shoppes were geared to become centers for what the company prefers to call "techno-marketing service" and relationship outlets focused at maintaining long term relationships with its customers, which no other competitor can offer.

The idea of building relationships with the customers through this unique route came after studying the buying behaviours of customers more closely. For one, the customers base was not homogenous- there were different categories of cement buyers in the market: the mason, the civil engineer, the architect ,the contractor and the institutional or large scale buyer along with the end user.

While each of these customers had some degree of knowledge and practical experience of the product's qualities and usage, there was a latent need for technical information and advice before purchase. In most cases though this need was never addressed simply because the dealer himself did not know much. At the same time most dealers tended to stock multiple brands were more concerned with pushing their stocks than spending time explaining the exact details of any brand.

In order to tackle this issue Indian Rayon consciously chose service as the cutting edge to maintain relationships with its customers. Therefore each of these shoppes had a qualified civil engineer who offered free technical consultation to every customer. Customers were provided with comprehensive information right from manufacturing of cement to its applications in various end purposes. Based on the type of construction, the right type of cement is recommended along with the free advice on the usage of cement and other additives & building materials. To further consolidate customer relationships each shoppe organizes a regular "mason meet" where the actual users are invited and given technical and practical knowledge and solutions. Besides, the shoppe owners of a particular area also get together, once a week on an average for market and technical information sharing.

Here the differences are ironed out and collective strategies shaped. The company's involvement manifests through the regular seminars and training programmes that are organized for the shoppe personnel.

Indian rayon has been successful in achieving results on twin fronts of CRM:

(a) Consolidating relationships with customers through the unique distribution channel route.

(b) The company has also been able to strengthen bonds with its distribution channel (who is also amongst the company's customer groups)

Thus by using CRM as a strategic tool companies like Indian Rayon are trying to achieve the long-term credibility factor which will help the company develop its equity in a rational manner.

☐ IMPORTANT INFLUENCER IN THE CEMENT BUYING PROCESS: SOME MORE CASES

Architect

JK Cement which has strong presence in Rajasthan, Delhi and Northern India clearly understands the distinct role of Architects as one of the important customers by virtue of their being expert influences in the cement buying process. JK Cement has constituted "Architect of The Year Award" and the decision to confer this prestigious award vests in a panel comprising eminent Architects and other construction Industry professionals. This strategy of JK Cement goes a long way in cementing the bonds with Architects as customers and other things follow in natural succession.

Masons

ACC Limited, India's premier cement company organizes a well-structured training programme for the masons, which covers all the major aspects of efficient usage of Cement and storage. This training is provided by the technical experts drawn from the company's Research & Consultancy Directorate- one of the largest R&D facilities in Asia. The masons at the conclusion of these programmes are a confident lot and derive a sense of dignity and affiliation provided to them by none other than one of the largest cement companies of India. The certificates of "ACC Trained & Certified Mason" again inspires a sense of achievement, which helps them render better services to their respective clients and in turn their bonds with the company are strengthened.

There are other Cement companies who offer yet another innovative tool like Cement Credit Cards for select masons. Masons can use these credit cards in times of their need of cement in small quantities. The modus operandi is such that the masons derive a great sense of dignity and respect in the eyes of the company and in turn they can use it to build a respectable image in the eyes of their own clients.

Dealer clubs

Cement companies like ACC Ltd. And L&T have formed unique clubs of their important dealers who are entitled to enjoy certain special privileges like distinct stationary, Holiday Home facilities, Medical facilities, preference to become dealers in the businesses of other group companies and above all to attend company sponsored conferences with family. Such measures where the dealers being on the 3rd and 4th level of Maslow's Need Hierarchy theory, develop an even more close affinity with the Cement company.

Indian Rayon and ACC appoint Reference Concrete Designers, Civil Engineers and Quality Control Personnel at various locations. These professionals are not on the formal rolls of the company but instead are prominent professionals and influencers in their areas who enjoy privileges like attending professional seminars etc. organized by the company and enriching their professional knowledge by free subscriptions of technical journals etc. The results of such CRM efforts are not difficult to understand.

□ CULTIVATING RELATIONSHIPS WITH THE END USERS/BUYERS:

Cement Companies have been trying their best to develop CRM strategies for this hitherto scattered customer segment. Large buyers are often taken care of by the Cement marketers in the ways described above. But even small buyers, which are large in numbers, are taken in the cement marketers' CRM ambit through the channels of distribution. Frequent buyer benefits and other service aspects are extended to them by the Channels of Distribution (which are initiated by the company through the dealers). As discussed in the case of Birla Super Shoppe, this helps consolidate the customer relationship bonds.

□ CONCLUSION

To conclude, CRM in cement Industry although in a very nascent stage has strong strategic connotations. CRM is a strategy towards the marketers' objective of providing value to its customers. This value when translated is able to provide a distinct equity to the Cement marketers to stand apart & gain an edge in the clutter of intense competition, and relatively undifferentiated products-which is peculiar to the cement Industry.

REFERENCES

Cravens, David W (1991), Strategic *Marketing* : Irwin

Duggal, Sanjeev (2000), 'Face to Face With Your Customer', *Economic Times.*

Kerin, Roger A & Peterson. Robret A (1998), *Strategic Marketing Problems-Text & Cases,: Allyn* & Baron,Inc.

Majumdar, Nanda (1995), 'All Products are Services' *The Strategist Quarterly*, pp 63-67

Miller, Alex & Dess, Gregory G (1996), *Strategic Management:* McGraw Hill

Rameshkumar, S (1998), *Marketing Nuggets,: Vikas* Publishing, New Delhi.

Chapter 26

Probing Demand Forecasting in Indian Firms

■ **Rakesh Singh**

Abstract

Fully understanding firms' demand, i.e. what drives and what makes it change, is the only effective way to synchronize your organization to quickly and consistently drive out costs and increase customer satisfaction. Achieving accurate forecast is critical to achieving these goals. But despite substantial commitment to forecasting many companies do not feel they are getting their money's worth. In order to understand the practice of forecasting in Indian firms, we conducted an exploratory survey. We looked into the use of forecasting techniques, use of forecasting techniques, and the practice of demand planning in Indian firms. Results indicate that the demand forecasting practices are still dependent on time series methods or rule of the thumb. Demand has become dynamic but the organization forecasting techniques have remained same. The organizational design does hinder the process of forecasting demand.

Key Words: *Demand Management, Forecasting, ERP, Organisational Design*

□ INTRODUCTION

Fully understanding firms demand i.e. what drives and what makes it change, is the only way to effectively synchronize your organization to quickly and consistently drive out costs and increase customer satisfaction. Achieving an accurate demand forecast is critical to achieving these goals. The objective of any supply chain initiative is to bring the penetration point (a point on the time axis where demand side information meets supply related information flow) as closer to the supply as possible. Since supply chains today rarely operate in the make to order mode, predicting or forecasting demand is the key driver on which all supply decisions will depend.

Forecasting is an activity, which is no longer associated with the logistics function. Nonetheless, a well-designed forecasting system can contribute significantly to the firms' performance. It can help to both lower inventory cost and improve customer service.

But despite substantial commitment to forecasting and availability of wide range of techniques, many companies do not feel that they are getting their money worth. There is no dearth of forecasting techniques. Due to the volatility in the demand patterns even time horizons are being compressed further. Companies are now scanning an ever-increasing set of variables that could affect demand.

This has brought out fresh challenges for firms to not only understand demand, but also to build up the right kind of organizational design to facilitate forecasting. By organizational design we mean the cross-functional teams and cross-organizational teams as well as distribution channel design. A number of studies have found that in the absence of these essential organizational flexibility firms cannot optimize on their investment in information technology and end up with problems.

In this research project we make an attempt to understand the overall process of demand planning in Indian firms. The objectives of this study are:

1. To understand the role of demand planning in effective supply chain management.
2. To understand the practice of demand forecasting in Indian firms i.e. commitment to forecasting and uses of existing techniques. The problem of prepares and users of demand forecast. What horizons and time periods are considered? How are statistical and judgmental consideration combined.
3. To understand the role of right kind of organizational design, which enhances the use of demand planning in creating value for the firm.

☐ METHODOLOGY AND RESEARCH DESIGN

We will use the survey method to understand the difference in the practice of demand planning in agrochemical firms in India. We will also use other exploratory methods to gather the right kind of information from our sample firms. Our sample consists of around 25 Indian firms in pharmaceutical, agrochemical and industrial product companies.

The extensive questionnaire was sent to assess the status of forecasting of our major companies. Two copies of the questionnaire were sent to each Company - one for the user and other for the preparer of the forecast. Recipients were instructed to fill out one copy and give the other to the most knowledgeable counterpart.

The data analysis involved a number of tests, using the matched pair's responses in some instances and all responses in other instances where there was no significant difference between the matched and the unmatched responses. Only results that were significant from a statistical point of view and meaningful from a management point of view have been included here.

☐ LITERATURE REVIEW

The changing business environment have reinforced the need to forecast demand. A number of companies have hired professional statisticians, operation researchers and management scientist to serve as forecasters. Also, an extensive literature on forecasting has begun to appear, and a major concern corporate executive now, has, as a consequence of, is trying to find out how they can more effectively use forecast.

There's growing and pervasive evidence that understanding and managing demand is a central determinant of business success.

Analyzing the true demand for the product, both current and future new product is essential. True demand analysis help build capability portfolio of the company. Dynamically, assessing the various portfolio options using both intuitive and analytical tool such as market intelligence and computer simulation is necessary to select the markets with highest economic liability.

In the more dynamic environment, the old view of the Demand Forecasting and management is changing fast. The old view is also referred to as the tactical view of Demand. Demand is formally expressed as a functional equation in simple terms, such as—D = f (HS, L)

where D is the demand that is both the function of historical sales (HS) and a lift factor (L).

One problem with this definition, however, is that in most competitive and changing environments, the past is not a reasonable guide to the future. Further, at a strategic level, there is a need to demand should not only be used to capture a forecast but also to create collective and highly probable scenarios for the future.

These emerging requirements mean that in addition to re-defining demand, companies need to define a set of goals that distinguish the uses and value of strategic demand management. Langeer II (2000) has defined strategic demand function as follows:

$$D = f(C, D^1, D^2, P, CB, S, E, B)$$

where demand is a function of competition (C), organizational direction (D1), portfolio differentiation D2, price elasticity, consumer buying behaviors (CB, e.g. trends, fads, tastes, regional differences), seasonality (S), exogenous influences and endogenous influences and casual factors (E), and brand equity (B). Demand forecasting and management, according to this view is both exogenous and endogenous variables. Managing demand and forecasting demand has become a challenging task. Companies, who recognize this change, will be able to add more value to themselves and their consumers.

In this study, we are concerned with status of demand forecasting in Indian industry. This study will help us to understand the overall practice of Demand Planning in Indian industry.

In general term, forecasting is interpreted as being a scientific process of estimating a future event by casting forward past data. The past data are initially analyzed to establish the underlying trends and which characterize the data and this information is then used in a pre-determined way to obtain an estimate of the future. Prediction, however, is then used in a pre-determined way to obtain an estimate of the future. Prediction, however, is generally interpreted as a process of estimating a future event based on subjective considerations. However, a scientifically produced forecast is established on the assumption that characteristics trends identified in past data will continue into the future (Lewis 1997).

Though managers make forecasts everyday, these forecasts turn out to be totally subjective to rigidly scientific. A subjective 'seat of the pant' approach could be that of a group of experienced sales executive who meet to offer their estimates of next year's volume. The Sales Vice-President gathers a consensus from their collective judgement and combines it with his own to arrive at a forecast. Although such unscientific forecast turn out to be inaccurate, many seasoned managers continue to use them because they are unable to identify or explain the exact relationships of the external factors which they believe influence their operations, even if they can identify the factors themselves. In the absence of systematic definition and testing, they substitute conjecture to real analysis (Parker and Segma 1971). Another frequently used method involving less guesswork is simple extrapolation. In this case, the manager merely attempts, through visual inspection or fitting a curve by manual means, to identify a pattern. He is not trying to understand the basis of these trends or the subtleties; instead he is presuming that future results will move along the same path as past results.

Such methods, no matter how unscientific, often suffice for the user. Indeed, a recent study indicates that simple extrapolation of trends in sales and earnings have been fairly adequate as a predictor in stable and less volatile situations. With the changing business environment and an ever-demanding customer, the demand for more precise forecasting techniques has increased, resulting in a wider use of regression analysis (Singh 2000).

As the uncertainty in business environment increases due to (1) increasing global competition (2) rapid technological evolution leading to reduced product life cycles (3) convergence of product differentiation (i.e. products now are easily emulated, copied, matched and outdone). A firm faces multiple level of challenges. It has not only to understand the size of the market but will also have to now take care of how well can it retain customer (Wheeler and Hirsh 1999).

As product differentiation declines, service differentiation is becoming even more important. For this, the firm has to develop deep knowledge about its customer, manage new channel selling opportunities, enhance customer support, speed field service delivery and provide customer with quality self service for fulfilling these services, it is but imperative for the firms to invest in information technology, logistics to deliver product and services to the end consumer, and provide value-added services to augment the product or the service (Caruso 2000).

In sum, firm has to plan its demand. Forecasting demand is the first part of the forecasting value chain. Firms have to forecast demand at various time intervals, i.e. the firm has to use 48 various forecasting methods on the basis of the time period associated with the demand data (Lewis 1997)

As discussed above, in order to plans demand and manage it, firm has to use scientific statistical method for forecasting and understanding the size of the market. Use of regression and neural networks are becoming necessary to understand the right level of future demand.

But this is not enough, as firms move towards being responsive to sensitive customer intermediate and short-term demand forecast becomes necessary to be a customer responsive organization. Enterprise resource planning (ERP) which form a subset of TEI (or Total Enterprise Integration) is a means of collecting, organizing, processing and maintaining data to understand the changing consumer behaviour and his expectation for value-added services.

Though many firms do understand that it is necessary to forecast demand using scientific methods, in practice the story is different. Lot many Indian firms who thought that the investment in ERP would take care of their problems, are now finding it difficult to justify their investment in ERP. In the next sections, we probe into these issues in detail and try to answer why?

□ FINDINGS OF THE SURVEY

What is the status of corporate forecasting in the Indian industries? What accounts for that status? What can be done to make effective use of forecasting resources? Based on a study done by Steven C Whee Wright and Darral G Clarke (1976), we tried to answer the above raised questions as far as Indian industries are concerned.

Table 1 *Accepted and Use of Alternative Forecasting Methods*

Method	Use of the method by those familiar with it	Those unfamiliar with the method
Jury of executive opinion	84	7%
Regression analysis	55	25%
Time series smoothing	80	15%
Sales force composite	74	05%
Index numbers	45	20%
Econometric numbers	56	25%
Customer expectations	75%	25%
Box-Jenkins	25%	55%
Neutral Networks	20%	80%

(Based on preparer's responses)

What is the status of forecasting in Indian industries today? What accounts for that status? What can be done to make more effective use of forecasting resources? The past decade has witnessed a tremendous increase in corporate and management.

Respondents were asked questions regarding nine different methods of forecasting demand in their company. Majority of the respondents said that they use jury of executive opinion, Time series smoothing as technique of forecasting demand. This is basically the so-called "rule of the thumb" method. Where past data are extrapolated to the tune of 15% to 20% and the targets are fixed. There is a large scale misunderstanding among these companies regarding targets and forecasting. These methods worked very well in the pharmaceutical companies, as the demand is very stable. Few of the fast-moving consumer goods have moved a little ahead and majority of them was of the opinion that forecasting based on customer expectation is gaining ground. The cement and tractor companies used Regression Methods to forecast their future demand. But the use of scientific methods likes Regression, Box-Jenkins and Neutral Network and relatively lows. Around 25% of the respondents were unfamiliar with regression analysis method and customer expectation method. Around 55% did not know about Box-Jenkins Method. 80% were not aware of Neutral Networks.

Table 2 *Criteria for Selecting a Forecasting Method*

Factor 1 : user's technical ability
Level of forecasting sophistication
Understanding of the method
Formal training in forecasting

Factor 2 : cost
User's time
Preparer's time
Computer time
Data collection

Factor 3 : problem-specific characteristics
Time horizon to be forecast
Length of each time period
Functional area involved
Degree of top management support
User-preparer relationship

Factor 4 : method characteristics desired
Accuracy
Statistics available

While each industry tends go have its own approach to forecasting, we tried to identify a number of common criteria which companies try to use for selecting a forecasting method. We found that the four factors, which were responsible for selecting a forecasting method, were User's technical ability, cost of forecasting, problem specific characteristics, and methods characteristics desired. Most firms did not have the requisite technical ability to apply scientific forecasting methods like Box-Jenkins Regression and Neutral Networks. Cost was another factor, which deterred from going for forecasting methods. Forecasting expenditure was assumed to be a cost rather than investment. Most respondents who used a basket of these forecasting methods, did so because of the need to forecast demand at different time horizons. Even the statistics available and belief in forecasting were other factors, which influenced selection of a forecasting method.

To assess how individual companies are doing in their use of forecasting, we asked the following questions: What is your company's current status in forecasting compared to similar companies in your industry, in regard to forecasting method applied, management's use of forecast and accuracy of forecasts? The response of this question is summarized in Table 3.

Table 3 *Users' and Preparers' Perceptions of Company's Forecasting Status*

	Behind industry	Average
Method applied		
Preparers	16.1%	30.5
Users	20.4	38.5
Management's use of forecasts		
Preparers	18.1	39.2
Users	18.4	42.0
Accuracy of forecasts		
Preparers	11.5	40.0
Users	20.5	45.0

Most of the companies feel that they are ahead of their industry on all three dimensions, viz. methods applied management's rise of forecasts and accuracy of forecasts. Clearly, the preparers see the companies as substantially more advanced than the users do.

As a first step in identifying the factors that may explain the status attributed to forecasting, we asked users and preparers to rate themselves and their counterparts in their company on several dimensions.

Table 4 *Differences in Ratings of Users and Preparers*

Preparer's ability to :	
Understand sophisticated mathematical forecasting techniques	+ 2
Provide forecasts in ongoing situations	− 15
Understand management problems	− 25
Identify important issues in forecasting situations	− 30
Provide cost effective forecasts	− 34
Provide results in time frames required	− 28
Provide forecasts in new situations	− 39
Identify best techniques for given situations	− 60
User's technical ability to:	
Understand essentials of forecasting techniques	+ 28
Evaluate appropriateness of forecasting techniques	+ 22
Understand sophisticated mathematical forecasting techniques	+ 10
Identify new applications for forecasting	+ 5
Effectively use formal forecasts	− 6
User–preparer interaction skills, ability to :	
Work within organization in getting forecasts (users)	+ 2
Communicate with preparers of forecasts (users)	− 3
Understand management problems (users)	− 4
Work within organization (preparers)	− 8
Understand management problems (preparers)	− 18
User's management ability to :	
Work within organization in getting forecasts	+ 3
Make decisions required for job	− 3
Effectively use formal forecasts	− 6
Describe important issues in forecasting situations	− 8

Note: Each figure is the percentage of users rating good or excellent minus percentage of preparers rating good or excellent divided by percentage of preparers rating good or excellent.

The first grouping is the preparer's ability, which includes providing forecasts for different situations in the time required and best techniques for the given situation. Preparers rated their own ability much more highly than the users rated them. As to the user's technical ability to understand, evaluate, understand, identify and effectively use formal forecasts, just the opposite was the case. Users rated them more highly than the preparers rated them, in regard to their ability to understand forecasting techniques and to evaluate the appropriateness of a given technique.

It is quite true that each user as well as preparers rated themselves as better than the others as far as interaction skills and ability to work within organization, communicate with each other and understand management problems (users) were concerned. In another question where we inquired about the functional areas involved in forecasting, we found that only 3 out of a sample of 25 firms were having cross-functional teams. Hence, despite forecasting department consisting of atleast one persona dn. at the most three persons existed, the forecasting was hijacked by the marketing department. "The rule of the thumb" was the only reliable and accepted forecasting techniques. The difference in these perceptions are noteworthy because they signal what, in many instances we refer it as communication problem.

Table 5 *Elements of Effective Forecasting*

Function	Percentage of companies in which neither user nor preparer is rated better than adequate
Understanding the management problem	15%
Identifying the important issues in a forecasting situation	30%
Choosing the best forecasting technique	52.1%
Identifying new forecasting situations	55.3%

Another element in effective forecasting is making sure that a minimum set of skills is available in the company. We found that 15% of our respondents (including both users and preparers) did not rate themselves better than adequate in understanding the management problems. Around 30% did not understand and were not able to identify the important issues in a forecasting situation. 52.1% did not know how to choose the best techniques for the given situation. And 55.3% were inadequately trained to identify new forecasting situations. Most organizations (50%) were unable to provide forecasts in an ongoing situation, chose the forecasting technique, identify new forecasting situation, choose the best forecasting techniques, identify new forecasting applications and understand forecasting methods. Thus, inspite of commitment to forecasting, the skills that are essential to make it effective, are apparently not necessarily present.

In a question on use of ERP to capture customer-related variables, both quantitative and qualitative, around 30% of the firms believed the investment in IT is a huge cost and there is no commensurate return in it. As said earlier, customer expectation as a source of forecasting is reported to be practiced by around 75% of the firms studied, but what is surprising is that most of these firms are today not even convinced about their ERP investments. The ERP as a tool in gathering information, has failed measurably.

As seen in the Table 6, it was found that the major reason for the failure of ERP and hence forecasts have been due to various factors. 69% of the respondents in these firms said that they do not have cross-functional teams. Most of the firms we found were unable to move from the functional mode into a process mode. The structures were not laid down and linkages too, were undefined. Most of these (51%) did not link demand and customer management to their business strategy. Around (53%) had not even made an attempt to create an appropriate alliance with their channel partners. Technological incompatibility was another factor (20%) which inhibited the effective information flow from the customer-end

Table 6   *Reasons for Failure of ERP-Based Forecasting*

Absence of cross-functional teams	69%
Demand management/forecasting not linked to the business strategy	51%
Absence of appropriate alliance with the channel partners	53%
Technological incompatibility in the organizations	20%

(Multiple responses)

❏ HOW TO IMPROVE FORECASTING?

While many companies in the survey are involved in forecasting the feeling all across the board is that full promise of time and money invested in forecasting has not been realized. The stumbling blocks of successful applications of forecasting identified by the respondents fall into the following categories :

1. Lack of effective communication between users and preparers.
2. Lack of understanding of business and marketing environment among the preparers.
3. Disparity in user-preparers perception about the company's forecasting status and needs.
4. Failure to plan a progressive set of actions to realize the company's full potential for forecasting.

The next question is what needs to be done to improve forecasting as well as use of forecasting in Indian firms? First of all, Indian firms which work under function silos needs to move towards cross-function and cross-enterprise teams. For information to reach the user of this information this shift in the organizational design is essential. We found that their were conflicting view about the status of forecasting in the organization. For forecasting to become a strategic tool to enhance value, there is a need to make it the basis of demand management. And this demand management needs to be linked to the overall business strategy of the firms. Secondly, organization should use more scientific method. Regression Method and Neutral Network if adopted properly, can minimize the forecast error. In many cases, we had a feeling that firms were letting finances drive the forecasts.

Demand forecasting must be viewed as an investment rather than a cost. Firms must track and measure forecast errors. A good forecasting software package and analytical tool set is critical for good results. Finally, some companies must understand that to make forecasting a strategic tool, they need a formal forecasting process and a specified forecasting owner.

As companies begin to use demand management more strategically, the demand chain will continue its evolution. As the demand chains evolve, organizations will focus more on integrating valuable business excellence—including internet agents, market research and other demand signals - to address the strategic decision facing them more effectively. The enabling technology will continue to move away from simple spreadsheets and supply chain planning systems and towards enterprise decision support systems, such as customer-relationship management, strategic planning, business intelligence applications, external industry databases and Internet websites.

REFERENCES

A, Caruso, 'CRM in the Digital Age', *Supply Chain Management Review,* March - April, 2000.

Colin, D. Lewis, *Demand Forecasting and Inventory Control,* John Wiley and Sons Inc., Toronto.

George, G.C. Parker and Edilberto, L. Segura, 'How to Get a Better Forecast', *HBR,* March - April, 1971.

Jim, R. Langabeer II (2000), 'Aligning Demand Management with Business Strategy', *Supply Chain Management Review.*

Rakesh, Singh, 'Is Demand Enigma?', *Pharmavision,* July 2000.

Steven, Wheeler and Evan, Hirsch, *'Channel Champions',* Jossey-Bass Publishers, San Francisco, 1999.

Steven, (C) Whee. Wright and Darral, G. Clarke, 'Probing Opinions', *HBR,* November - December, 1976.

William, C. Copacino, *'Supply Chain Management',* The St. Luis Press/APICS Series on Resource Management, Boca Raton . 19.

Chapter 27

Organising for Customer Relationship Management

■ **Rosalind Hopewell**

Abstract

The whole concept of customer relationship is to ensure from day one the customer feels part of the customer base they have joined, more importantly they do not feel just sold to and then left to get on with it. A customer, no matter what they have been sold, has just used up resource and therefore should be seen as part of an ongoing long-term relationship for any business. The suppliers of customer management software/services also have the business of managing 'their' customer relationships. Customer Relationship Management is about 'caring' about the customer, not only doing business with them, it includes understanding their business and customers. It is only by understanding who the customer is and where the customer is going, that any company becomes able to manage the relationship and ongoing business. Customers are a business's 'unique asset' and make a difference, when, managed effectively. Always remember when a customer no longer wants a supplier, they are firing everyone from the Chairman down.

Key Words: *Customer, Business, Retention, Caring, Unique Asset, Manage.*

◻ INTRODUCTION

Most companies today are reviewing all areas of customer management, most are beginning to realise that a differentiator for them is the service and support they provide to their customers. Management of information from this vital source of business is becoming increasingly important to the business that wants to stay ahead of the competition. Captured customer information not only gives trends in sales activity but vital history on a customer relationship with a business. This data when analysed can be used to encourage the new customer as well as keeping the existing ones. Understanding customer requirements needs companies to review as an ongoing project the trends and activities of the existing customer, and also sharing this information with the customer. Customers like to know you have recognised them and identify with their requirements, albeit not all, but at least meeting those that the business can supply.

The following are the 5 questions any business should ask itself when Organising for Customer Relationship Management, (CRM):

☐ WHAT IS CRM, WHAT DOES IT MEAN TO YOUR CUSTOMERS, YOUR BUSINESS AND YOUR STAFF?

CRM has become a very 'hot' three letter acronym (TLA) and every business who has a customer is being courted by the suppliers of such applications to install their technology to enable this business process.

If a business does not ask itself the above question then they will never achieve CRM. It is not the technology that makes the installation of a Customer Relationship Management programme work, it is the people and the ownership a business takes to ensure such a project really works.

A complete view of Customer Relationship Management must be taken from the very top of the business, the boardroom, and include all areas of where there is human contact. This must be viewed from the internal customer, staff, and the external paying customer who keep the business alive financially.

Effective CRM involves 2 key aspects of Customer Value:

- The value a customer delivers to the organisation.
- The value the organisation delivers to the customer.

Look at the business and ask the question what would 5% improvement in customer retention mean to the bottom line on increase in profit?

Can you replicate the mind of the customer?

☐ HOW DO YOU KNOW YOUR BUSINESS REQUIRES CRM?

It is very easy for a business to get caught in the latest 'customer trap' when it is being driven by the Information Technology (IT) market. Every business does require CRM; the question is to what level?

Trends

Many businesses are pushed by the current trend to change their business strategy, especially around CRM.

There are basically 3 Trends that affect a business:

Consumer

The customer is an ever-changing image, to be really successful with CRM you must recognise the consumer trends that are effecting the business. If a business does not understand a customer profile and the changes that have occurred then it is not possible to provide true Customer Relationship Management.

Products

It is the business providing the products that meet the changing customer trends. Products need to be reviewed constantly, perhaps enhanced, or even removed. Supermarkets are a perfect profile to look at for viewing 'product trends', they constantly add and remove products, and they constantly view customer buying profiles and set out the pattern of the store to meet the strongest buying trend. This may not always be by using the latest 'technology', it could be by just reviewing the empty shelves at the end of the day, but the supermarket is at a minimum watching for the 2 basic trends in Customer Relationship Management.

Technology

Ensure that the business is ready to install new technologies, is the Customer Data up to it, or is it time to start again? Do you need to review every technology being used or just one area. Will it assist the business, is it going to grow with the business requirements, or is the technology just another 'trend'? Relationship management should not be an alternative to existing functions/technology; it should be a logical extension to enhance those in existence, though it could, radically change some of the operational processes.

☐ IS YOUR BUSINESS READY? ARE YOUR CUSTOMERS READY?

Whatever degree of CRM a business is considering installing, introducing or even enhancing existing procedures/processes, they need to take a detailed view of the existing business. This must include asking the customer, they are the very people CRM is targeting, and often are the last to get asked for an opinion.

In a recent study measuring the response times of Fortune 100 companies to a simple e-mail enquiry, the following results show insight into how not to treat customers:
- 13% replied within 3 hours
- 18% replied within 3 days
- 7% took more than 3 days
- 62% did not reply at all

(Survey conducted by NewGate Internet, December 1999)

It is vital that the whole business is ready when a CRM project is introduced, this means from the Cleaner to the Chief Executive, you never know who is going to answer a phone when the office is closed!

Prepare the business to give the 'perfect customer experience', and decide whether to be selective or universal.

What are the costs, monetary, time, people and long term issues?

When any business is viewing its processes and procedures regarding the management of Customers, it has to look at the monetary involvement. All businesses require profit to exist and if the installation of a CRM project is to work, it has to bring a business profit. The view needs to include the cost of time, people and what will the long-term business benefit be?

Then there is the obvious actual real financial cost, money, this has to be budgeted for and a cost/benefit for the business recognised.

Points for Consideration

- Training—budget for the people costs.
- Technology—budget for the cost of all areas of implementation, not just the solution.
- ROI—identify what the real Return of Investment will be for the business.
- Future—can the business afford to sustain the ongoing cost of CRM?

CRM is not easy; it needs careful planning and execution. There are no quick fixes, it takes time and the very core of the process needs to be built into the organisations' infrastructure.

There has to be a process underlying all of the CRM project which is the CRM Results Improvement Process, therefore ensuring constant review of results, Return of Investment etc. and allows for ongoing improvement or change.

☐ DOES CRM REALLY MATTER?

What ever the business activity is all companies have to ask themselves is CRM a real factor for their company to succeed. Some customers do not need long term relationships with their suppliers; therefore only minimal information is required from that customer. That however is still a form of CRM. Other companies have high quality and high value customers that they need to know information about, they need to provide exceptional service, the 'pedigree' of CRM.

What ever the business is, if it has customers it has to ask, does Customer Relationship Management matter? What does it mean to them in business terms? At what cost? What is the overall loss if not adhered to?

☐ THE KEY ELEMENTS OF CRM

- Business Vision—view the whole business and where it is going.
- Competitive Characteristics—what can you add as a unique.
- Increase Shareholder Value—remember the shareholder.
- The Right Sort of Customers—what measure of CRM to what customer.
- Segment Customers—what potential value do they give the business.

No matter how well a business grasps customers' desires and needs, the way its people produce, create, offer and deliver products and services, add probably more value to the total customer experience.

Satisfied versus very satisfied customers

The difference between a satisfied customer and a very satisfied customer in terms of their willingness to buy again is SIX TIMES. (*Source:* Xerox Research).

How an organisation is structured and processes organised to meet customer requirements and expectations will dramatically effect a business's ability to manage customer relationships profitably over a minimum of the coming 5 years. (*Source:* General Market Research, Hopewell, R.).

CRM: Yes it does really matter!—the Strategy needs to last, be constantly reviewed and can evolve over time.

Employee and Customer Management Processes for Profitability
The Case of Hewlett-Packard India

■ **Vinnie Jauhari**

Abstract

This paper attempts to give an insight into the customer relationship management processes at Hewlett Packard India (HP). The company strongly believes that there is a strong relationship between employee satisfaction, customer satisfaction and market share. This paper attempts to study the employee management processes at HP. It also tries to map the customer management processes at HP. The employee satisfaction processes include the HR initiatives taken within the organization, measures taken by the top management to sustain a suitable climate within which innovation thrives and concern for employee welfare and development becomes extremely important. The customer management processes include creation of databases, managing the call centre, ensuring skill and knowledge upgradation by the engineers and service providers in touch with the end consumer. The organizations should focus on customer loyalty rather than just attempting to achieve customer satisfaction. Customer loyalty in the long run acts as a source of profitability for the firm.

Key Words: *Customer Relationship, Employee Satisfaction, Customer Satisfaction, Customer Loyalty*

□ INTRODUCTION

This paper attempts to map the customer relationship management processes at Hewlett-Packard India. Customer relationship management refers to those processes which aim to build a life long relationship with customers. It is a long term approach concerned with long term profitability. The case study of Hewlett-Packard (HP) has revealed that customer relationship management has number of dimensions rather than just customer satisfaction. This study particularly focuses on the employee satisfaction and customer satisfaction processes initiated at Hewlett-Packard India. The study was conducted by carrying out indepth interviews with the senior managers at Hewlett-Packard including their ex CEO Suresh Rajpal.

Hewlett-Packard's operations in India include Delhi based HP India (sales, support & PC configuration), HP India Software Operation and Verifone which has a software R&D lab. HP India employs 240 employees. The software operation employs 1000 employees and Verifone employs 210 employees. The head office of HP is located in New Delhi. The sales and support is offered at Delhi, Bangalore, Hyderabad, Chennai, Mumbai and Calcutta.

In 1994, HP India had achieved sales to the tune of $75.4 million. In 1999, the sales had increased to $231.5 million It won CII Exim Award for Business excellence (the first company in India to receive the award since its institution). In 1997-98, in ISCW User Opinion Poll HP India was declared the no. 1 IT company in India as per the Information Systems Computer World User Opinion Poll. According to the Dataquest it was declared the top multinational vendor for the year 1997-98 and the top printer vendor in 1997-98. According to the PC Quest it was the winner of User's Choice 2000 for best inkjet and laser printers, scanners and workstations. It was rated at No. 5 in the A&M Marg Poll in the year 1997-98.

☐ RELATIONSHIP BETWEEN EMPLOYEE SATISFACTION, CUSTOMER SATISFACTION & MARKET SHARE

HP's operations in India started in the year 1988 under the leadership of Suresh Rajpal. According to Suresh Rajpal, the making of an excellent organisation consists of two very important aspects—employee satisfaction and customer satisfaction. Traditionally the literature has pointed out very strongly towards customer satisfaction. However in HP it has been a belief that customer satisfaction is not possible without employee satisfaction. The following paradigm is proposed for a growth in the market share.

For an employee to be satisfied, job satisfaction is extremely important. To achieve job satisfaction one must have the right skills and the other factor that becomes important is

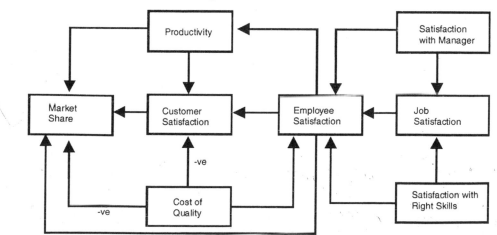

Fig 1. *Relationship between Employee Satisfaction, Customer Satisfaction and Market Share*

the satisfaction with the job. If the score on satisfaction with the job and satisfaction with the right skills is high, then it would contribute to an enhanced employee satisfaction. When employee satisfaction is high, the productivity is high and the cost of quality is low. When the satisfaction level is high, it would lead to an enhanced market share which further reinforces employee satisfaction.

The figure 2 indicates the trend in the growth of the market shares, employee satisfaction and the customer satisfaction over the five years in Hewlett Packard. The graph indicates a similar trend in all the three cases. The data taken for this graph is only for the medical equipment division.

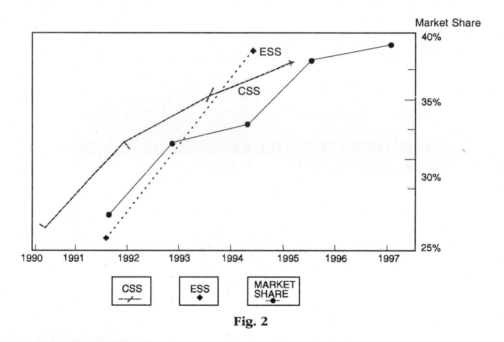

Fig. 2

☐ INITIATIVES FOR EMPLOYEE SATISFACTION

To satisfy employees, HP has taken a number of steps. There is a proactive HR Department, which treats all the other departments as its internal customers. The HR division has identified for itself a mission statement that it would promote innovation and a feeling of competitiveness in its employees to enhance their performance while contributing to organization goals. There are five values, which are considered to be sacrosanct. These are trust, teamwork, integrity, innovation and high achievement. The objectives that are desirable to be attained are profitability, employee care and customer care. Not only are these values treasured but the element of institutionalisation is very high through the deployment of different strategies in different areas. This is achieved through the communication of these values to the employees and demonstration of these values in the day to day behaviour of the employees. When the new CEO Carly Fiorina took charge of HP in July 1999, she drove the new HP Invent global campaign. This consists of a charter called, "The Rules of The Garage" which has been circulated to every employee and is before his eyes all the time so that there is a constant drive towards achievement and a culture of entrepreneurship is created in an organization. The behavior is reinforced by linking the performance of an individual to his growth in the organization. Every employee has to demonstrate these key values and the performance measurement system does track down all these aspects. The culture in the organization is very open. The communication systems are open. The sitting spaces are open and there are glass panels and there are instances when call escalations could reach the CEO Carly herself. That is the extent of reach to the top.

Whenever a new employee joins the organization, the values are communicated to him at the time of induction within the organization. The HR manager views each of the business areas as an Account. He maintains an ongoing dialogue with the different accounts and identifies their needs and reverts back to them after getting the expert's advice. The vision of the HR department is to achieve a higher level of employee satisfaction, higher level of satisfaction with the HR department and decline in the attrition rate of the organization.

A demotivated, unenthusiastic and unhappy employee will never care for the customers. Also organizations willing to spend money when they are doing well should spend on employees more rather than less when things get bad. An employee satisfaction survey is carried out regularly on an ongoing basis. In the employee satisfaction survey, input on number of parameters is taken such as management, supervision, communication job, recognition, pay, and worklife among other factors. Out of a number of issues, the top three/five issues are identified which are critical and also the three least scoring areas. The least scoring areas are then assessed for their criticality. Then those critical areas after being identified are then passed on the owners of the problem. They then prepare a HOSHIN Plan for that particular area which consists of objectives, precise goals, and strategy and performance measures. So each of the critical area is addressed in all the areas - be it HR, finance, production, Sales support. Hoshin Plans are made so that the performance improves considerably. After the implementation, again when the survey is carried out, it can be seen whether there is an improvement in the score on a particular parameter.

For every employee training needs are continuously assessed. Assessment is made on which training programs are essential to do the current job well, which programs are essential to grow to the next level and what are the unique strength of an individual which could be deployed usefully by the organisation. Every six months the employee survey is conducted which is kept confidential. The questionnaires are filled and sent to the corporate HQ directly. The feedback is also given regularly to the employees about the steps, which are being taken to check the discrepancies if there are any.

Some of the initiatives taken by the top management are:

Right Genetic Code

It is an organization whose genetic code is right. This means that the value system is in place and there is a shared vision. Even the mail room boy knows about his operational objectives. Every employee's performance is measured and is synchronized with the organization's performance. The yardstick for performance measurement is absolutely fixed and one knows at the end of the year how ones performance is going to be measured at the end of the year. Every individual within the organization knows about his growth path at a particular level. He is even aware of skills and knowledge base required to move at the next level.

Balance between work and private life

The workplace has to be a funplace. One would enjoy work only if there is an element of fun. Drawing an analogy of a three-legged stool, he says that one leg should reflect excellence in the current job, the next leg should be the continuous learning and the third should be having lot of fun. All the three components need to be balanced to be a successful person. The CEO practices the concept of Management by Walking Around. Everyday in HP, Suresh Rajpal would spend 40–45 minutes walking around the office, calling people by first names and exchanging greetings. The end result was amazing. In an industry characterized by an attrition rate of 25% , HP had an attrition rate of about 3.8%. HP even has a programme by the name of Alumini targeted at people who have left for greener pastures. They are invited over at HP parties and are told about the current achievements of HP. Eighty percent of people want to come back. They are still considered to be a part of HP family.

Doing the right things

One should know what to speak at an appropriate time. One should not tell people to do right things but to find people doing the right things, thank them and congratulate them. The bottleneck in the most organizations is not people but the leadership.

Making the workplace a funplace

One needs to reinvent things to make the workplace a fun place. One way of getting lot of ideas is to reward people who generate these ideas. HP capitalises on these ideas and rewards employees who make these useful contributions.

Creating positive surprises for the customers

To create special surprises for the employees, every engineer, manager and functional manager is given a certain amount every month to surprise others. For instance Suresh Rajpal volunteered to surprise his employees by booking the entire theatre screening Titanic for the weekend and handing out four tickets to each employee. The result was that every one in the HP Family was overwhelmed by the gesture and the CEO was flooded.by thankyou mails and with compliments that the family was proud of the fact that someone in their family was working for HP.

Life made easy

Another aspect that is very unique is learning from ones mistakes and not looking at the things in a conventional manner. One should not just be satisfied with one best answer but one must continue with the quest for the next best answer. Most people stop thinking when they arrive at the first best answer. There is a flexibility given to the employees so that they could work at the hours of their choice but put in requisite number of hours at the workplace. Productivity is not measured by the number of hours that one puts in the workplace but by the actual contributions made by the employee. To ensure that the employee does not feel harassed to pay off the bills or go in for pollution checks the organization has arranged for all these services by charging nominal amount of money. All the bills can be paid, repairs can be got done, food could be ordered, clothes could be laundered by just picking a phone and assigning the responsibility to an individual.

CII Excellence Award

HP India got the CII Business Excellence Award for the year 1997. The employee satisfaction in HP was 82% whereas the norm in Asia was 50%. The award is given after tracking the performance of the organization for five years on different parameters each of which carries certain number of points. These parameters are divided into Enablers & Results
Enablers comprise of

- Leadership
- People Policy Deployment
- Resources & Partnership
- Processes

The results include parameters such as

- Employee satisfaction
- Customer satisfaction
- Society
- Business Results

☐ CUSTOMER MANAGEMENT PROCESSES

The customer care model has witnessed a lot of changes over the years, moving from a negligible part of after-sales to special service packages developed to meet the specific needs of the customer. A call center is one such model that has been developed to handle customer query instantly. It is fast emerging as a front end for many customer-care and service centers set up by the companies.

☐ INTERACTIONS WITH THE CUSTOMER

The customer life cycle with HP typically follows the following cycle (Figure 3) :

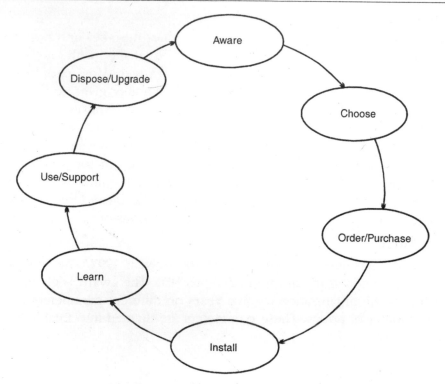

Fig. 3   *Customer Life Cycle with HP*

Evolving business paradigm at HP

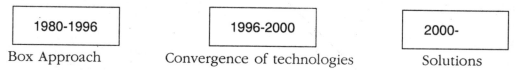

1980-1996	1996-2000	2000-
Box Approach	Convergence of technologies	Solutions

The solution oriented approach & value for money would be the key drivers of success for the organisation.

There is a rolling survey, which is carried out for resellers and customers. The customer loyalty index is tracked. The customer loyalty index tracks the existing customer on various parameters and puts them into four categories:

- At risk
- Vulnerable
- Favorable
- Loyal

HP sells its products through its channels. Whenever the customer purchases a product, and there is an issue to be resolved, the point of contact is the Front Line Team. It handles the usage-related issues. The application related, the real product related and the backend team handles upgradation issues. The partners provide the hardware support. The sales and services are provided by DPSP's and the ASP's are only authorised to provide service. Typically in a month, the total number of customer calls logged in at HP are 21,000 out of which 4600 are through web support, 1270 emails and 15,000 telephone calls. They use automated call distribution software, which also enables to track history of a particular customer. The service providers are assessed continuously. It is a challenge to motivate engineers who are the employees of the service providers and are not HP employees. The engineers/service providers' performance is monitored on

- Turnaround time
- Number of parts requested per call
  (Multiple part consumption)
- Closing the call
- Customer satisfaction
- Repair rate
- Effective handling of customer escalations

HP has allocated points for each of these parameters for partner performance measurement. In case the partner performance falls below the desired level of points, then there would be deduction in the reimbursements of that reseller. However if he exceeds the given point scale then he qualifies for additional reimbursements which are offered as rewards. The organisation is very careful about choosing it resellers. They have to undergo an accreditation process and have to meet certain standards such as amount of office space, level of investments, qualifications and level of training required. Each partner is made to undergo training in both technical skills and soft skills like customer handling, customer intimacy, customer orientation - resolving difficult problems and so on. The reseller is then made to undergo a test and has to qualify it before being certified. The reseller has to constantly upgrade his skills so that at all points of time there is resonance with the HP values and the objective of customer relationship is achieved. The quality of repair is also monitored through India Rolling survey. In this a mailer is sent to each and every customer who has contacted HP through its service network for repair.

All the customers, who are not happy with the service, are then contacted by HP and through the partners it is attempted that certain steps are taken so that the customer is happy. The training programme for partner is also regularly revived. The partners are given lot of technical and training support. The documents are regularly updated and pocket references are regularly circulated. There is a magazine, which is brought out for partners and every quarter about 500 copies of that are circulated which contain regular updates on technologies and new policies. The engineers working with the partners are expected to keep themselves updated on all these developments. To ensure compliance every engineer has to answer a quiz based on the magazine and has to send it back to the support department. If the score is low and one does not respond, it leads to the loss of bonus points which reflects a loss in profitability in terms and reimbursement to these service providers. So linking the knowledge update with performance of a reseller ensures that there is no complacency at their end.

There is also a Reward 1000 plus program where there are points awarded. There are points for various aspects such as training, quiz bulletin, customer feedback, customer service, re-repair rate. The top contributors among the resellers are identified and are sent for training or entertainment apart from monetary incentives.

Customer Orientation is primarily achieved by

1. Managing the customer contact
2. Management of the resellers
   - Training
   - Management of Processes
   - Linking Rewards with Productivity
3. Making use of customer histories to bring about improvements in the product. Attempts are being made to prepare record of every customer who buys a HP product.

So at HP, there is a synchronisation of the employee satisfaction and customer satisfaction process to ensure a higher market share.

Chapter 29

Critical Factors of Corporate Choice of Non-Profit Organisation for Social Contribution

❑ **Sangeeta Mansur and R Srinivasan**

Abstract

The study makes a basic contribution to CRM in the context of relationship between NPO sector (Non Profit Organisations) and corporate sector by providing the former with currently non-existing customer knowledge in terms of basic customer expectations from NPOs. Apart from borrowing SERVQUAL dimensions, the study explores additional dimensions from the field and arrives at a set of underlying, critical factors that could act as a basic framework for NPOs in their self evaluations, measurement of customer satisfaction and strategies for promotion, image analysis, long term customer relationship, enhancement of service quality experience etc. The NPO sector in India suffers from severe lack of funds but is not equipped with much needed marketing guidelines or even customer knowledge or database to tap the huge potential of the corporate sector for fund generation and relationship building. This paper provides a starting point for NPOs to move in this direction.

Key Words: _Non-Profit Organisations, Customer Expectations, Business-NPO Relationships, Social Marketing, Corporate Philanthropy._

❑ INTRODUCTION

The objective is to find a set of critical factors corporate philanthropists look for in an NPO for making a social contribution through it. The purpose is to provide the NPOs with basic customer expectations, which act as a framework for further strategy formulations.

❑ BACKGROUND

NPO sector in India represents a potentially effective social change agent but suffers from perennial funds crunch. This is a highly fragmented, nondocumented sector (Sen 1999,

Norton 1996) that varies in its estimates on the number of NPOs and also lacks database. (Norton 1996, Mohanty and Singh 1996).

The governmental funds are characterised by bureaucratic hassles (Sen 1999), misuse of funds and constraints on capacity building(AWARD 1991). Foreign funding on the other hand is connoted with separatist and fundamentalist influences leading to scepticism about the funds and is also perceived to make the sector over reliant and less self-sufficient (Sen 1999). In this context the corporate sector provides an effective alternative for fund genera-tion. This is a segment inadequately tapped and 60% of the business sector is estimated to be consisting of potential donors (Norton 1996). Very few companies prefer the NPO-mode to social contribution (16% according to Action-Aid-IMRB study, 1997). This makes a clear case for marketing principles and CRM methodologies to be applied in the sector in order to enable it to move towards the stage of ' third generation strategy' (Korten, 1987), to develop, maintain and sustain customers with long term perspective of relational mar-keting rather than transactional marketing.

Relationship marketing is about ' attracting, maintaining and enhancing customer rela-tions' (Berry, 1983, p. 25), about 'establishing, developing and maintaining successful rela-tional exchanges' (Morgan and Hunt 1994), about 360 degree view of the customer. At the heart of CRM is the customer database, customer knowledge in terms of customer needs and expectations. Service quality literature recognises the importance of Expectations as a precursor to Satisfaction. Satisfaction is related to repeat purchase (Zeithaml, Valarie and Berry, 1996). Since the NPOs lack basic inputs of customer expectations, this paper at-tempts to explore the relevant dimensions of customer expectations to facilitate further strategies on CRM.

☐ METHODOLOGY

Qualitative study

The study borrows five original dimensions of SERVQUAL, viz., Reliability, Tangibility, Responsiveness, Communication and Sensitivity used by Parasuraman, Zeithaml and Berry. It was necessary to elicit other relevant variables from the field before the front-end instru-mentation began. A qualitative study was conducted for this purpose (Miles and Huberman, 1985; Patton, 1984) and depth interviews were conducted with respect to key expectations and parameters of NPO selection. Data triangulation was used and the sam-ple was divided between NPOs and companies to ensure data heterogeneity and better construct validity (Denzin, 1978, p. 28; Patton 1984, p. 109). The field data was subject to content analysis with procedures like Contact Summary Sheet, Coding, Pattern Coding, Code-frequencies and the final data display produced five additional variables, viz., Capa-bility of NPO, Experience with NPO, Channel used for reference, Preference of CEO of company and Credibility of NPO.

Questionnaire

All the ten variables were itemised on Likert scale, keeping the number of items to a minimum in line with principle of parsimony (Gujrathi, 1995, p. 40) and for better response rate. Items were not borrowed from SERVQUAL but emerged from variable definitions and field inputs. 26 items emerged and nine additional questions were added for the profile of the companies and to screen responses. Face validity checks were done with eight colleagues and pretesting with debriefing technique was done with five respondents. Reliability was tested with Internal Consistency method and the pilot study on 53 respondents from 30 companies yielded a Cronbach alpha of 0.8812, standardised alpha being 0.8896, indicating good overall reliability of the measure. 24 items had item-total correlation above 0.30 and two items, which had 0.28, and 0.279 were retained on a subjective judgement after noticing that their deletion did not change alpha even marginally.

Final Data Collection

House-lists of donors from different NPOs were pooled and the compiled list, after screening for exclusion of overlaps, public sector companies, small companies, yielded a list of 156 private sector, middle and large size, donor companies, all of which were targeted. Personal interviews and mail survey were both used and yielded 190 responses from 95 companies, which led to 178 complete responses from 89 companies after deleting incomplete responses and responses from companies that did not qualify for philanthropic contribution exactly.

Data Analysis

Factor analysis of the responses by Principal Component method and Varimax rotation with criterion of eigen value more than 1.00 produced eight internally consistent and meaningfully interpretable factors that explained 76% of the total variance. The factors were ranked based on factor means. Table 1 shows the factor structure and the factors ranked on factor means.

The results showed that Experience with NPO & Reliability combined under the first factor. It was named 'Confidence'. Communication and Sensitivity combined under the second factor, called ' Communication'. The rest of the six dimensions emerged as six distinct factors as conceptualised earlier.-viz., Credibility, Responsiveness, Capability, Tangibility, Channel and Top Management.

When ranked on factor means the order (column 1) showed Responsiveness ranking highest, followed by Credibility, Capability, Confidence, Communication, Channel, Tangibility and Top Management. Top management is at 2.64, indicating its relative non-importance. Tangibility touches 3.00- the least important of all dimensions in the context. The most important factor is a service quality parameter-Responsiveness.

Further, three types of segmentations were examined with respect to these eight factors and z tests (2-tailed) for significant difference between means were done for each type. For each segmentation, the factors, which differed significantly, were noted down as factors of interest and further, one-tailed tests were done to know the direction of difference. The Table 2 shows the factors where significant differences were found (column 1), t values (column 2), level of significance for 2-tailed test (column 3) and results of one tailed test for the segments (columns 4 and 5).

Table 1   *Factor Structure*

Rank	Factor	Items
1.	**Responsiveness**	❖ Prompt Service ❖ Readiness to serve clients
2.	**Credibility**	❖ Transparency in transactions ❖ Regular feedback to donors ❖ Accountability to donors ❖ Company's trust in NPO ❖ Reputation of NPO
3.	**Capability**	❖ Efficiency of service delivery system ❖ Productive use of funds ❖ Specialisation in a particular cause ❖ Track record of good work
4.	**Confidence**	❖ Long term relationship ❖ Past satisfaction ❖ Consistency in service to donors ❖ Consistency in service to beneficiaries
5.	**Communication**	❖ Assurance of good quality work ❖ Clarity in communication ❖ Convincing communication ❖ Effective follow up ❖ Understanding of donor's objectives, needs ❖ and convenience ❖ Courteousness of personnel
6.	**Channel**	❖ References from others ❖ Image depicted by the media
7.	**Tangibility**	❖ Visual appeal of office, premise ❖ Professional look of the personnel
8.	**Top Management**	❖ CEO's personal preference

Table 2   *Segment Comparisons on Critical Factors*

Sig. Factor	T	Sig. (2tailed)	1 tailed Result	1 tailed Result
			Consumer Companies	**Industrial Companies**
Channel	2.317	.022	Higher	
Communication	3.115	.002	Higher	
Confidence	3.291	.001	Higher	
Responsiveness	4.308	.000	Higher	
Tangibility	4.402	.000	Higher	
			Indian Companies	**MNC Companies**
Channel	-4.461	.000		Higher
Tangibility	-3.312	.001		Higher
			Direct Contributor	**Through NPO**
Capability	4.631	.000		Higher
Channel	2.646	.009		Higher
Tangibility	2.693	.008	Higher	

□ CONCLUSIONS AND RECOMMENDATIONS

General Recommendations

Table 1 presents a basic framework of dimensions for NPOs for different strategic purposes.

1. **Measurement of customer satisfaction**: The study does not measure satisfaction with respect to any particular NPO but presents basic dimensions to NPOs for the exercise. An NPO can apply the framework on its customers to know current problems, gaps to fill, to help service recovery, to prevent defections, to help loyalty etc.

2. **Segmentation**: An NPO marketer can use these factors themselves to segment his market, in line with the more recent perception that the other traditional criteria (e.g. demographics) could be inadequate and the consequent attempts at segmentation on expectations (Martin, Iglesias, Vazquez and Ruiz 2000, Webster, 1989, Thompson & Kaminski, 1993) .

3. **Self-Evaluation**: The factors can serve as basis for setting performance standards for NPOs on which they can do self-appraisals on a periodic basis.

4. **Comparative Image Analysis**: Images of different NPOs can be obtained using the factors as the attributes, perceptual mapping can be done and the exercise can guide further strategic interventions, e.g. Image-building, Positioning, Repositioning etc.

Specific Recommendations

Table 1, column 1, showing the ranking of the factors can help NPOs in the following way.

5. **Promotion Thrusts —short term**: The promotional planning, in terms of its thrusts, can follow the order of Responsiveness, Credibility, Capability, Confidence (Experience and Reliability), Communication (and Sensitivity), Channel, Tangibility and Top Management. Tangibility does not seem to be highly important as in other service contexts and an NPO could be better off reducing investments on building CEO's personal preferences. The present trend in NPO strategy focuses a lot on CEOs of companies but the results of the study suggest a re-look at this practice. While CEO's involvement is high for basic decision of philanthropy itself, his personal preferences may not be very important when it comes to choosing the NPO.

6. **Promotion thrusts-long term**: The same order of importance may not hold good in the long term and hence NPOs should track the shifts in the rankings on the factors longitudinally and adapt their promotion thrusts accordingly.

7. **Adapting service delivery system:** The results suggest aligning the service system to the key expectations.

   a. The most crucial point is to build high responsiveness across the NPO by institutionalising willingness to serve clients and prompt service. The importance of responsiveness of service personnel has been recognised as a key factor in service recovery literature and the results of the study confirm the importance of the factor in the NPO context as well.

b. Next is the factor of Credibility. The results confirm the importance of trust in relationship marketing. The task entails ensuring regular feedback to donors, keeping all transactions and work transparent, involving clients wherever possible, creating interfaces between clients and beneficiaries-all of which contribute to credibility which can not be built by the media alone.

Conscious steps to build credibility can go a long way in dispensing the criticism and scepticism NPOs face in India.

c. The issue of Capability entails steps to enhance efficiency of funds donated, specialisation and developing competence in defined areas and effective work towards beneficiaries.

d. Confidence as a combination of Experience and Reliability requires consistency in service with good service recovery systems to be built in. Employee empowerment could be a worthwhile idea to implement.

e. Communication should be kept simple, clear, convincing, sensitive to the clients needs, expectations and to the objectives of their philanthropy and should be courteous. These principles should be followed as basic guidelines for communication in all areas- advertising, direct marketing as well as staff—interaction with clients.

These should not be looked upon as mere quickfixes for a short term gain but as key measures to be implemented and institutionalised across the organisation- far enough to be a part of the value system.

Specific Recommendations for some segments

1. **Consumer/Industrial Segments**: Factors of interest are Channel, Communication, Confidence, Responsiveness and Tangibility. As the one-tailed tests imply, the task is to capitalise on Consumer companies' higher emphasis on Channel reference and Communication, to sustain their Confidence and perception of Responsiveness. For the industrial segment the task is to build on the above factors.

2. **Indian/MNC Segments**: Factors of particular interest are Channel and Tangibility. As per one-tailed tests, both are more important to MNCs. NPOs can focus better on channel references and tangibility proofs for MNC companies

3. **Direct Contributors/ Through-NPO Contributors**: Capability, Channel and Tangibility are the factors of interest here. Companies adopting the NPO mode to philanthropy could respond better to a sustained focus on the first two factors whereas direct contributors may need tangibility proofs.

Future Work Guidelines

The framework presented in the paper could act as a starting point for further work. NPO sector in India lacks studies of even basic insights into its markets and extensions of the study could be a worthwhile contribution in the area. Segmentation of corporate donors on the critical factors of customer expectations could be an interesting exercise. Actual measurement of customer satisfaction on these eight dimensions for one or several NPOs could be beneficial for NPOs. Perceptual mapping, Image analysis could be attempted. This paper studies private companies. A similar exercise applied on public sector companies could result in an interesting set of factors with possible deviations from the results of this paper.

REFERENCES

Alperson, Myra (1995) 'Corporate Giving Strategies that add Business Value: A Research Report', *The Conference Board Report* No. 1126-95-RR.

AVARD (1991), '*Role of NGOs in development: A Study of the Situation in India (Final Country Report)*', Association of Voluntary Agencies for Rural Development Publication, New Delhi.

Berry, Leonard, L.(1983) ' Relationship Marketing', in *Emerging Perspectives on Services Marketing*, Leonard L. Berry, Lynn Showstack and Gregory Upah, Eds. Chicago: American Marketing Association, pp. 25-28

Culshaw, Murray (1999), '*Building Credibility*', draft of study by Culshaw Advisory Services, Bangalore, Unpublished Document.

David Clutterbuck & Dez Dearlove (1996), *The Charity as a Business*, Directory of Social Change Publication, UK.

Denzin, Norman K. (1978), 'The logic of Naturalistic Inquiry' in N.K. Denzin (Ed.), *Sociological Methods: A Sourcebook*, New York, McGraw-Hill.

Gujrathi, Damodar (1995), *Basic Econometrics*, 3 Ed, Mc-Graw Hill, Singapore.

Jaishankar Ganesh, Mark Arnold and Reynolds Kristy (2000), 'Understanding the Customer Base of Service Providers; an Examination of the Differences between Switchers and Stayers', *Journal of Marketing*, Vol. 64., July, pp. 65-87.

IMRB-Action Aid (1997) 'A Survey on Corporate Philanthropy', conducted by IMRB and Action Aid, Unpublished Company document.

Korten David C., (1987), 'Third Generation NGO Strategies: a Key to People-centred Development', *World Development*, 15, Supplement, pp. 145-160.

Martin-Diaz, Ana, M., Iglesias, Victor, Vazquez, Rodolf and Ruiz, Agustin V. (2000), 'The Use of Quality Expectations to Segment a Service market', *Journal of Services Marketing*, Vol. 14, No. 2, pp. 132-144.

Michael Norton (1996), *The Non-Profit sector in India*, Charities Aid Foundation (CAF) Publication, UK.

Miles, Mathew and Huberman, Michael A. (1985), *Qualitative Data Analysis*, Sage Publications, London, New Delhi.

Mohanty, Manoranjan and Singh, Anil K. (1996), *Foreign Aid and NGOs*, Voluntary Action Network India Publication, New Delhi.

Morgan, Robert M. and Hunt, Shelby, D. (1994), 'The Commitment-Trust Theory of Relationship Marketing', *Journal of Marketing*, Vol. 58, July, pp. 20-38.

Parasuraman, A., Zeithaml, V. and Berry, L. (1994) 'Reassessment of Expectations as a Comparison Standard in Measuring Service Quality: Implications for Further Research', *Journal of Marketing*, 58, January, pp. 111-124.

Parasuraman, A., Zeithaml, V. and Berry, L. (1991) 'Refinement and Reassessment of the SERVQUAL Scale', *Journal of Retailing*, Vol. 67, No. 4, pp. 420-450.

Parasuraman, A., Zeithaml, V. and Berry, L. (1985 fall) 'A Conceptual Model of Service Quality and its Implications for Future Research', *Journal of Marketing*, pp. 41-50.

Patton, Michael, Quin (1984), *Qualitative Evaluation Methods*, Sage Publication, London.

Siddhartha Sen (1999) ' The Non Profit Sector in India', in *Building Civil society*, Conference Proceedings, 11th Annual John Hopkins International Fellows Conference, Bangalore, pp. 198-293.

Schultz, Don E. and Scott, Bailey (2000) ' Customer/Brand Loyalty in an Interactive Market Place', *Journal of Advertising Research*, May-June, pp. 41-52.

Thompson, A.M. and Kaminski, P.F. (1993) ' Psychogarphic and Lifestyle Antecedents of Service Quality Expectations. A Segmentation Approach', *The Journal of Services Marketing*, Vol. 7, No. 4, pp. 53-61.

Webster, C. (1989) ' Can Consumers be segmented on the basis of their service quality Expectations?', *The Journal of Services Marketing*, Vol. 3, No. 2, Spring, pp. 35-53.

Zeithaml, Valarie A., Berry Leonard L. (1996) ' The Behavioural Consequences of Service Quality', *Journal of Marketing*, Vol. 60 , April, pp. 31-46.

Zeithaml, Valarie A., Berry Leonard L. and Parasuraman, A. (1996) ' The Behavioural Consequences of Service Quality', *Journal of Marketing*, 60, April, pp. 31-46.

e-CRM: "Lies, Damn Lies and Statistics"

❏ **Don M Darragh**

Abstract

Peter Drucker says, " The ultimate purpose of business is to create and keep profitable customers". eCRM has emerged in the last few years as a powerful ally in this quest. This paper offers a contrarian view of fundamental assumptions in eCRM about trust, loyalty, relationship management and client control. Implications regarding electronic commerce's impact upon these concepts are discussed along with the importance of process over tools and people over technology. The changing role of statistics and the appearance of new technologies in putting a human face on ecommerce are presented. And a new concept, Sm@rketingÒ, is introduced.

Key Words: *Trust, Loyalty, Relationship Management, Client Control, Sm@rketingÒ, Statistics.*

❏ INTRODUCTION

The truth shall set you free. But first...., It makes you miserable. This concept, CRM, is not new. In fact, it's as old as man's first gathering to form a market place. With the advent of the Information age, dramatic changes are occurring in commerce, giving rise to ecommerce, the electronic, virtual market place. As far back as 1990, a visionary, Don Peppers, saw the paradigm shift occurring in commerce, mass marketing and advertising And in a speech before the Advertising Club of Toledo, Ohio, USA first presented the fundamental principles that essentially created the entire CRM industry.

This paper sets forth perspective on what I believe are several **myths underlying the most basic assumptions about CRM.** Trust, loyalty, relationship management and client control. It doesn't refute the success of the $3.3 billion CRM industry or even disparage it. Although a recent Cutter Consortium survey (1999) reveals that, "dissatisfied CRM customers outnumber satisfied ones by 2 to 1". CRM and its electronic counterpart, eCRM for ecommerce, are tools, but still only tools. Tools requiring significant human involvement. Or as my grandfather once said, "No one goes to the hardware store because they want a drill. They go because they need a hole". So, eCRM is about trust, not technology; about people and process, not tool. Just as it was thousands of years ago, in that very first market place.

What eCRM does; however, is automate the tedium of memory and history. Like an elephant that never forgets, allowing us to remember all our previous interactions with customers and therefore present one, personal face to them. But elephants are intended to be our servants, not our masters. What eCRM doesn't do is provide an understanding of the process or the will and desire to use it properly, thus creating a rogue elephant run amok, wreaking terror and havoc in its' wake. Current research findings as well as extant books, articles and papers are used in highlighting and interpreting eCRM concepts. Preliminary thoughts are also offered on; where locus of control in ecommerce actually lays, the changing nature of sales, marketing and statistics caused by the impact of the Internet and how technology can improve customer interaction. And finally, a profound business truth,

"Don't be too proud of this technological terror you've constructed. The ability to destroy a planet is insignificant, compared to the power of the force." (Darth Vader, CRM Consultant Star Wars, Episode Four)

Trust

That peculiar quality most commonly held by those about to be betrayed. It's a roaring mouse that can render our eCRM elephant powerless. Trust is hard to earn, dynamic and easily lost. Based upon reciprocal experience between individuals over extended periods of time. Trust comprises three elements. 1. Doing what we say we'll do. 2. Not doing what we say we won't do. And 3, Telling in advance what we will or won't do. These three provide reliability in predicting behavior and establishing trust. "If". If; that is, we practice them.

So, how are we doing on the trust issue? According to Dr. Jacob Neilsen, PhD, in his Alertbox of March 7,1999 at http://www.zdnet.com/devhead/alertbox/990307.html, "The current climate on the web is one of disregard for customers who are traded like sheep." Also, the United States Federal Trade Commission (FTC) determined that only 20% of sites with 39,000 or more unique visitors a month protect consumers' privacy. Not so good. In fact, the very tools we're using to improve customer relations have unintended consequences. Are being misused creating suspicion, doubt and fear. Double Click and Real Player with their recent privacy violations and attendant customer trust woes are notorious examples.

The key point here is that we trust each other, not companies or products. We may depend upon a product, service or organization to perform as stated, but ultimately we trust each other to back up those claims.

Because technology removes human interaction clues, those subtle verbal and non-verbal markers present in open, honest dialogue needed for establishing and keeping trust; extraordinary effort is required. And if the effort is not made, trust and collaboration are replaced by adversarial commerce denoted by transaction; i.e., price and volume, and legal contract. Perhaps this is why Shop.org, http://www.shop.org/, in it's analysis (The State of Online Retailing 3.0, 2000) found that, *"the average industry-wide conversion rate— the ratio of buyers to unique visitors—is only 1.8%"*. No bricks and mortar business can survive with that kind of ratio. And the recent collapse of numerous dot.com businesses show that electronic commerce can't either.

Customers experience trust when they receive what we promise. And the proper use of technology as an ally in gaining and keeping trust is to make sure our electronic interfaces improve personal interactions and communication. How do we do that? By asking our customers, of course. And by employing web site usability testing, like that available from Dr. Neilsen at; http://www.useit.com. Maybe "customers' experience of our employees' ability to meet their needs in a caring manner while protecting their interests" is a more descriptive, although cumbersome term.

Loyalty

Religion, nation and family deserve loyalty. Loyalty implies sacrifice and occurs in an atmosphere of high ideals and shared experience of threat. Thus I'll make the ultimate sacrifice if need be, to die for my God, country or family. Do we really believe that our customers will sacrifice to use our products or services? With so many alternatives a mouse click away? Certainly, eCRM intends to have customers invest sufficient time, effort and money making it painful for them to switch by having to teach competitors what we already know. But what do we offer in exchange? And are we "loyal" to our clients? Or do we abandon them at every turn, using planned obsolescence and technological advances as excuse to wring ever more money from them? Eventually, these same tools we use to remember our customers' unique needs, wants, and preferences will ultimately be available for their use. Then, what will we do? "Customer retention" or "customer repeat business" seem far more accurate terms to me.

Commerce is unworthy of loyalty and always will be. Maybe this is why consumer loyalty initiatives as a whole are counter productive, because loyalty cannot be bought. Don't think there's only one person to blame for this, someone else.

Commerce may be worthy of repeat business; however. So don't place responsibility for declining margins on disloyal customers or even competition. Instead, remember this, "the greater the mystery, the greater the margin". And the greatest mystery of all has nothing to do with technology; ephemeral at best, or tools or products, or even manufacturing or marketing processes. The greatest mystery is this; how to create long-term, profitable customer relationships. We can start by looking closer to home. By asking our customers:

How trustworthy am I?
How easy is it to do business with my company?
How friendly, helpful, pleasant and entertaining are my employees?
How valuable are my offerings for your effort, in time and money, to buy from me?

But don't expect loyalty; you don't deserve it.

Relationship Management

Yes, I know, eCRM is supposed to mean the tools we use to automate and manage our internal customer facing processes. **Yet, more often than not, it seems what we're actually referring to is managing the customers themselves.** Price Pritchett's book, Service Excellence (1989), http://www.pritchettnet.com/ disagrees, stating, *"There's only one way you can effectively manage the behavior of your clients and customers. You do it by managing your own behavior."* This is process, not tool; people not technology. It's the extraordinary effort on the part of people, your employees, to serve your customers using "satisfying customer experience" attitudes and behaviors.

Look at your own spouses, children, family and friends. Who among you is so bold as to say, I "manage" those relationships? Processes and things might be managed, but relationships? With some thought, I think you'll agree that personal relations are interactive and always changing, never managed. As Gerry McGovern says in, The Caring Economy, http://www.thecaringeconomy.com/about/chapters/chapter1/index1.shtml *".... human relationships cannot be automated, cannot be commoditised."*

Would you not feel a deep sense of resentment if you determined that your spouse, children, friends or family; or worse, a stranger were managing you? In some way determining and controlling your actions.

What customers really want are convenience and a satisfying experience. And the best way to provide that is through the recognition, protection of, and catering to each person's unique individuality. This is where the technologies behind eCRM excel. Don Peppers and Martha Rogers, PhD, in their book, *The One to One Future* (1993), http://www.1to1.com/, state, "Technology has brought us back to an old-fashioned way of doing business by making it possible to remember relationships with individual customers – sometimes millions of them—one at a time, just as shop owners and craftspeople did with their few hundred customers 150 years ago". Customers want involvement with your firm and more crucially each other. They want participation in the development of your products and services; their delivery, advertising, pricing, and most importantly, servicing. By partnering with your organization, seeing your solutions as synonymous with their needs, your customers not only buy from you, but also buy more profitably, more frequently. And far more significantly, enlist others in their desire to help you succeed, thereby dramatically lowering your cost of customer acquisition & retention. Industry studies on the effectiveness of properly deployed eCRM initiatives reveal that lowering customer defections by as little as 5% per year can increase bottom line profits as much as 25%. In the case of ecommerce, that's an estimated, "customer experience fund" amounting to an astounding $19 Billion annually, as determined by Creative Good, Inc., http://www.creativegood.com/ in its *Dot Com Survival Guide* (2000).

Perhaps "Relationship Learning" or eCRL is more descriptive. I learn about your needs, wants and preferences. But I don't manage that process. I learn from it, modifying behavior accordingly, thereby providing greater value and making it easier for you to do business with me. Pritchett's Managing Sideways (1999) confirms this, saying "It's reported that customers are five times more likely to leave because our business processes are poor than because we have poor products." For decades, product total quality management, or TQM, was the mantra. What's needed now is "customer relationship" TQM, judging everything we do from our customers' perspective.

Client Control

Closely allied with the lie of customer relationship management is the damn lie of client control. If your client grants you power of attorney and authorizes your signing their payments for your products on their behalf, then and only then will you have client control.

People become clients, first because they trust, then because it's easy, and finally because they receive value, real or perceived. And that decision as to where and how trust is given and value obtained rests solely with the customer. Don't think so? A Forrester Research Inc. survey (1999) determined that 90% of consumers want to control how their information is used. And a Business Week/Harris poll (2000) found that 56% would opt out of any personal information collection scheme, if given the choice. This signifies that we are failing to acknowledge, let alone implement the reality of customers being in control and failing to fulfill all four parts of the U.S. FTC Fair Information Practice Principles.

According to FTC statistics, only 20% of all companies—or 42% of the 100 most-trafficked Web sites—are following these guidelines:

Notice—Clear and conspicuous statement, in plain language, of what information is collected and how it will be used.

Choice—Letting consumers choose whether their information can be used for any purpose besides fulfilling the transaction.

Reasonable access—Giving consumers access to the information collected on them and reasonable opportunity to correct any errors or delete the data.

Adequate security—proper handling of consumer information to prevent unauthorized access or identity theft.

How do we reconcile our need for better customer information with our customer's conflicting desire for convenience and their need for privacy? By practicing these principles and utilizing products like those available from Youpowered.com's Orby Privacy Plusä, http://www.youpowered.com/home.html and ZerÆKnowledge's FreedÆm, http://www.zero-knowledge.com/privacy/default.asp you'll be giving customers the control they demand over use of their personal information. In exchange, they'll be willing to give you more and better information, i.e.; trust.

Locus of control

The primary connection among these myths is the perception that companies somehow have the power and control. That our technology and tools in some way grant us the all knowing, all seeing ability to peer inside our customer's psyche. Nothing could be further from the truth.

The Internet not only collapses time, space and hierarchies, it also collapses myths. People are networking worldwide as never before. News about your product, company or service travels at the speed of light. In reality, your market, the people buying and using your product, knows more about it than you do. If you don't believe this, visit Epinions.com, http://www.epinions.com/, a web site where customers post their user experiences on any product or service available today. Also, study the Internet hoax played upon Nike. Upset with Nike manufacturing and marketing practices, disgruntled customers perpetuated a massive retaliation against the company. How? Via an email campaign stating that Nike would exchange any pair of worn out athletic shoes with their latest version for free. Nike began receiving 4,000 pairs of stinking, torn, dilapidated shoes a day, every day! Completely overwhelming the company and rendering it virtually powerless to continue its normal business operations.

For additional perspective on locus of control, see "Personalization Bill of Rights" posted at; http://www.crm-forum.com/crm_forum_white_papers/ÒSm@rtketingÒ

As obvious as it might seem on the surface, **the Internet is not TV or radio, not the movies, not newspaper or even magazine.** Yet many companies act as if it were merely another, similar distribution channel. That the same marketing strategies and sales tactics working for mass media work for the Internet.

What's ignored is the fact that the Internet is cold, cognitive and interactive; i.e., customer controlled. While mass media is warm, emotional and passive, controlled by corporations. Digital Entertainment Network, now bankrupt after burning through $65 million dollars in two years, is only one of the more recent and highly visible testaments to this mistaken identity. Boo.com's mistake vaporized $135 million dollars within a year! Largely due to a fatal usability flaw in their web site.

As stated in the 74th thesis of Cluetrain Manifesto (1999), http://www.cluetrain.com/index.html by Levine, Searls, Locke and Weinberger, "We are immune to advertising. Just forget it." Industrialized countries are creating the most prosperous citizens in history. Thus commerce, the act of buying and selling goods and services, is trickling down to ever-younger consumers. And shopping is a learned skill, both social and practical, taught as a way to maximize our experience of satisfaction.

In watching my own children, nieces and nephews learn this skill as young as age 13, or even younger, it never ceases to amaze me how quickly they become immunized to advertising hype and manipulation. Sure, Pokemon and other youth fads are raging successes. Yet, these very successes inoculate against the same tired, worn-out techniques to attract more business and profits. Creating "exponential expectations" in customers and making yesterday's strategic masterstroke today's clumsy miscalculation. The best advertising is "word of mouth", decidedly low tech, which works because of the "built-in" trust factor. Your friendly recommender has no hidden agenda, just open, honest sharing of what delights them. The problem is, you can't control word of mouth. Although, Seth Godin in The Ideavirus (2000), http://www.ideavirus.com/ shows how facilitating word of mouth through viral marketing increases sales.

Sales tactics are usually considered a subset of marketing strategy. With the Internet and savvier consumers; however, I submit that this distinction is also collapsing. Strategy and tactics on the web are inextricably intertwined with each other and must be deployed simultaneously, creating what I call Sm@rtketingÒ. A real-time, interactive, self-learning, permission-based feedback loop for a satisfying customer experience as provided by YellowBrick Solutions Visitantä platform, http://www.yellowbricksolutions.com/

Properly understood and employed this provides value to company and customer and more closely approximates our normal human experience of collaboration.

Statistics

Instead of relying solely on statistical analysis for data mining of confiscated, static demographic information such as name, address, gender, education, age, income, etc., I believe greater reliance on real-time, consensual databases and e-analytics is occurring. Rather than ivory tower, forced segmentation, I see customers "self-segmenting" through their online actions. Instead of blind differentiation, I see companies "auto-differentiating" by responding to their customers instantly and interactively. Like living organisms, company and customer embrace in mutually beneficial relationships where both party's actions significantly and lastingly impact each other's experience.

The tools are all ready here. Using associative memory (there's that elephant again) and artificial intelligence as applied to neurocomputing, we are creating intelligent agent technology that mimics how we relate and interact with each other, similar to Saffron Technology, Inc.'s Saffron One™, http://saffrontech.com/index.html. Coupled with computer animation based upon biomedical engineering and speech to text for creating digital people, like that from Life F/X, http://www.lifefx.com/, we are putting a human face on electronic commerce. Bringing us back again to Gerry McGovern's statement about..."technology becoming transparent and people becoming paramount."

Does this mean that we should throw away our eCRM tools? No, it merely means that we who serve customers must realize our symbiotic learning relationship with them, eCRM. Realize that learning cannot take place where there is no trust and no remembrance of past interactions.

And just as critically, realize that non-adversarial customer relationships can't occur where:

- Technology is considered more important than those for and by whom it's created.
- We try to manage relationships, control clients and demand loyalty.

Highlighting, I believe, the truth that the most advanced eCRM technologies, sophisticated statistical algorithms or accurate data, are useless if we fail to learn how to earn & keep our customer's trust.

Patricia Seybold in her book, Customers.com (1998), **http://www.psgroup.com/index.asp** provides clues in her five step guide for creating a profitable and successful electronic business strategy;

Step 1: Make it easy for your customers to do business with you.

Step 2: Focus on the end customer for your products and services.

Step 3: Redesign customer facing business processes from the end customer's point of view.

Step 4: Design a comprehensive, evolving electronic business architecture.

Step 5: Foster Customer loyalty. (While I disagree with the word, I agree with the process).

☐ SUMMARY

Finally, the most meaningful summary I can give is from my friend and associate, Tom Bajzek, (http://www.bajzek.com), Carnegie Mellon University MISM professor, telecommunications, industry consultant and founder of Pennsylvania's Internet; "I think we do better using our technology tools to improve the quality of interactions with our customers rather than the quality of our information about them."

Section IV

Relationship Management in B2B Commerce

Chapter 31

Building Customer Loyalty Business-to-Business Commerce

■ **Sharat Bansal and Gagan Gupta**

Abstract

Rapid changes in the business-to-business commerce landscape are driving the need for vendors to identify & retain their best customers. Building customer loyalty has become the only way for vendors to build sustainable competitive advantage. PwC's vision of a Market Intelligent Enterprise helps vendors in addressing the key strategic imperatives for building customer loyalty.

PwC defines a Market Intelligent Enterprise as one which "institutionalizes the capacity to acquire and apply market information quickly across and effectively manage customer relationships with your best customers and best prospects".

This paper describes how the vision of "Market Intelligent Enterprise" can be realised by companies (vendors) who have businesses as their customers, i.e. in a business-to-business (B2B) setting. The concepts are equally applicable, whether the vendor has a brick and mortar business model, or is a new economy enterprise. The paper explains how realisation of this vision helps the vendor in enhancing customer loyalty through achieving excellence in following key areas:

    i. Collecting customer information as a strategic asset
    ii. Identifying customer expectation
    iii. Aligning strategies and processes with customer value and expectation
    iv. Managing customer experience
    v. Managing customer relationships on basis of ongoing customer value
    vi. Embracing Market Intelligent technologies

Each of the above areas is explained in detail in the paper, along-with illustrations and examples from PwC's own CRM experience.

❑ NEED FOR BUILDING CUSTOMER LOYALTY IN BUSINESS-TO-BUSINESS COMMERCE

"Customers have come to accept that we do things their way rather than they do things our way." —Michael Hammer

The business-to-business commerce landscape is rapidly changing due to evolving customer needs. The evolving end-consumer expectations have driven vendors to be more responsive and provide a better value-proposition to their customers in terms of quality, convenience and variety. This has translated into customers demanding greater responsiveness, reliability and quality-consciousness from their vendors.

The rapid rise of e-commerce and electronic marketplaces has resulted in better visibility of demand and supply and lower switching costs. The new technologies have also enabled closer collaboration between businesses and their vendors. Customers are increasingly adopting differential buying approaches: open market purchase for commodity items and closer collaboration with vendors offering monopolistic/proprietary/value-added services. Customers now use vendor management as a key tool to raise market responsiveness cut costs and enhance product quality. This has resulted in a trend towards more careful selection of vendors and closer collaboration with key vendors.

Business customers now typically demand from their vendors greater value addition, tighter integration with their processes and systems and lower total cost of ownership. As customers consolidate their vendor base and work more closely with select vendors, they are increasingly demanding higher service levels, bundled products and services, greater responsiveness and more cost-effective solutions.

Fierce competition for the top customers, rising customer acquisition costs and maturing markets have forced vendors to focus on building loyalty with their customers, rather than seeking a rapid expansion of customer base. Added to this is the rapid commoditization of many products & services through E-commerce. This is especially true of market leaders in mature industries, who must continually defend their customer base as challengers close performance gaps and replicate marketing innovations. The best-in-class companies in many industries have taken the lead in implementing CRM concepts & enabling technologies, resulting in greater competitive pressure on the followers.

❑ STRATEGIC IMPERATIVES FOR BUILDING CUSTOMER LOYALTY

"Companies have to find ways of growing and building advantages rather than eliminating disadvantages" —Michael Porter

Building customer loyalty is not a choice any longer with businesses: it's the only way of building a sustainable competitive advantage. Building loyalty with key customers has become a core marketing objective shared by key players in all industries catering to business customers. The strategic imperatives for building a loyal customer base are as follows:

- Focus on key customers
- Proactively generate high level of customer satisfaction with every interaction
- Anticipate customer needs and respond to them before the competition does
- Build closer ties with customers
- Create a value perception

This paper describes the PwC vision of a Market Intelligent Enterprise and describes how the realization of this vision helps in building customer loyalty by addressing the strategic imperatives listed above.

◻ PWC'S VISION OF A MARKET INTELLIGENT ENTERPRISE

PwC defines a Market Intelligent Enterprise (MIE) as:

"An enterprise that institutionalizes the capacity to acquire and apply market information quickly across and effectively manage customer relationships with your best customers and best prospects"

The Market Intelligent Enterprise achieves excellence in six key areas, as depicted in Figure 1.

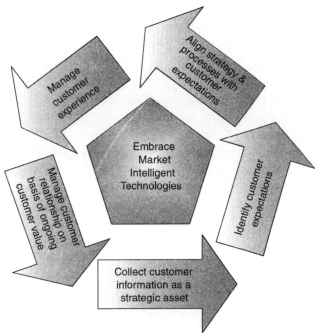

Fig. 1 *The Market Intelligent Enterprise Framework*

◻ COLLECTING CUSTOMER INFORMATION AS A STRATEGIC ASSET

A Market Intelligent Enterprise derives its strategic advantage from its ability to collect, assimilate and act on customer information swiftly and in the right manner. Customer information serves as the foundation of the strategy & processes of the MIE, and is key to the MIE managing its customer experiences and relationships. An MIE collects information not only on its current customers, but also its prospective/target customers. Customer information needs to be captured at all the customer touch-points, including marketing & sales, customer support and billing and payment.

Collecting customer information is frequently simpler in a B2B situation than in B2C, simply because the customer are typically fewer, interactions more frequent and relationships with the top customers better established. However, the challenges are in collecting the right information, integrating the various sources of information, and making the integrated information available at all the customer touch-points.

The advent of e-commerce and eCRM has greatly facilitated capturing customer information from these diverse sources. Data mining technology offers the possibility of integrating information from various sources, and drawing meaningful conclusions from it. CRM tools like Siebel make it possible for a company to institutionalize the ability to act swiftly on multiple fronts, on basis of customer information.

A rich source of information in a B2B situation is the field force, including field sales and technical/post-sales support team. It is important to educate them on the value & methodology of collecting the required information, and make this an integral part of their performance evaluation. It is also essential to invest in the enabling technology, infrastructure and resources, so that the information can be captured & collated easily.

For a CRM client, PwC identified the vital information to be captured on the client's industrial/business customers, and designed a market intelligence process to collect & assimilate this information. Close links were also established between the market intelligence and planning processes. The main challenge here was to integrate the information being captured by field sales, technical support and logistics. It also became very important to demonstrate the utility of collecting this information to the field force, to obtain their commitment. The recommendations were developed with an acute awareness of the reality that the extent & accuracy of information collected depend to a large extent on the motivation and skill-set of the field force. The ambiguity was minimized by clearly defining what information was to be collected, the frequency of collection, the reporting formats and the impact of adherence on the performance evaluation of the field force. Measures were also taken to drive home the utility of the information to the field force.

❑ IDENTIFYING CUSTOMER EXPECTATIONS

The truly successful business positions itself for fully satisfying both current and future customer needs. The foundation of such a positioning is a precise understanding of customer expectations and a clear perspective on the evolutionary path of these expectations. In a B2B setting, the customer expectation can be typically mapped on the following dimensions:

    i. Supply reliability & flexibility

   ii. Supply lead time

   iii. Quality

   iv. Price

   v. Technical support

   vi. Integration with customer's processes & systems

Most industrial customers have a well-defined vendor evaluation methodology that is used for selecting vendors and allocating them share of business. In such cases, it becomes easier to understand & quantify the expectation of the customer. However, the Market Intelligent Enterprise must validate such an understanding with other information on the customer and the market. Also, certain expectations (such as supply preference, value engineering etc.) may not be expressed at all in the vendor rating, but are discovered when an ongoing relationship is built up with the customer.

The customer expectation could be driven by the realities of the customer's markets (and therefore uniform across customers in an industry) or the specific competitive position of the customer. It is necessary for the MIE to identify the drivers for customer expectation, to be able to anticipate shifts in expectation.

PwC has a Voice of Customer (VoC) methodology, to map customer expectation through direct interviews with customers and internal stakeholders. In this methodology, a representative cross-section of customers is scientifically chosen, and detailed interviews are conducted with specific questions, to elicit customer expectation and current performance of the client against this expectation. This exercise forms an integral part of PwC's CRM engagements, and provides very valuable inputs that serve as a starting point for diagnostics of performance gaps & discovery of opportunity areas.

A mapping of customer expectation should lead to identification of discrete customer segments that buy similar products & services, and demand similar service levels. This segmentation should then serve as a basis for setting differential strategies for delivery of products & services to the customers. Understanding the demand drivers in a customer segment enables a vendor to anticipate trends in his markets, by analyzing the purchase behavior of the end-consumer, i.e. the customer of his customer, in most cases.

❐ ALIGNING STRATEGIES & PROCESSES WITH CUSTOMER VALUE AND EXPECTATION

"Companies will have a golden opportunity to build a more comprehensive offer around any product they sell." —Philip Kotler

A determining factor in customer loyalty is the customer's perception of the indispensability of the vendor. An Enterprise can assume a high level of strategic importance for its customers by becoming a partner to the customer's growth and an indispensable part of the customer's supply chain.

The Market Intelligent Enterprise uses structured customer information to find answers to the three key questions:

i. Where to compete
ii. How to compete
iii. When to compete

As the B2B environment becomes more dynamic, the MIE will gain a competitive edge by its ability to ask these questions more often, find more accurate answers and monitor transition more closely.

A key part of formulating the business strategy is examining the offerings and value proposition to the customer. Business customers are increasingly seeking greater value-addition from their vendors. This has resulted in vendors offering comprehensive solutions for customer needs rather than selling a stand-alone product. Offering a comprehensive solution has increasingly become a pre-requisite to retaining the best business customers. Often, it is possible to build exit barriers by leveraging current skills to offer a value-added product/service to the customer. This may be in form of vendor-managed inventory, value engineering, collaboration for new product development, management of a support process (e.g. maintenance) of the customer, etc. etc. A well-designed value-added offering helps the customer focus on his core competence, reduce his costs and improve his delivery capability.

An MIE will need to mix & match product delivery systems and channels to deliver the appropriate service standards to different sets of customers. This may need close participation with channel members and outsourcing technology-intensive services like call center, web-support etc. For example, a PwC client making capital equipment uses a mix of direct selling and channel sales to match the different purchase behaviors of its customers. Long-term customers and government agencies are approached directly, while channel members help get sales for new customers are acquired primarily through channel members associated with project consultants and having expertise in project execution. This company has also out-sourced its call center, and is thus able to provide a 24x7 helpline to its customers, without diverting management attention to resolving the complex human-related and technological issues arising out of running a call-center.

The MIE should align its business processes closely with the customer expectation. This can be done by identifying key process metrics and setting targets on these metrics in a manner that enables full delivery against customer expectations. For example, if the target market segment wants quick deliveries for highly customized products, an MIE could identify delivery lead-time as a key process metric and set a target of 5 days for full delivery of any product to the farthest customer, from the date of placing the order. This would then need to be further broken down into targets for procurement lead-time, manufacturing cycle time and distribution lead-time. The MIE could then set corresponding targets for cycle times & lead times of individual sub-processes, to accomplish the overall target. It would then need to measure the current cycle-times & lead-times, and take steps to reduce them by process re-engineering.

For a specialty chemical manufacturer, PwC helped identify the service expectations of different customer segments, and redesign the supply chain to deliver on these expectations. Two distinct sets of expectations were identified with respect to delivery capability: one set of customers operating in dynamic markets wanted low response time, and another set operating in mature industries wanted delivery reliability. The demands of the first set of customers necessitated a responsive supply chain, whereas rigorous planning & execution was needed for the second set. PwC designed differential supply chain strategies & processes to deliver on these expectations.

☐ MANAGING CUSTOMER EXPERIENCE

Every interaction with a customer is an opportunity to delight the customer. In B2B relationships, the major customer touch-points are:
- Marketing & sales
- Customer support
- Billing & payment
- Dispute resolution
- Product development & testing

Each of these interactions offers the Enterprise an opportunity to demonstrate its commitment to total customer satisfaction.

A typical Enterprise has a broad spectrum of customers, right from "Terrorists" (extremely dissatisfied/alienated customers who actively erode the brand equity of the Enterprise) to "Advocates" (delighted customers who actively work to strengthen the market presence of the Enterprise). One of the objectives of managing customer experience for an Enterprise is to convert key customers to Advocates and address the issues of the "Terrorists" & "Rejecters" to minimize the negative impact on brand equity.

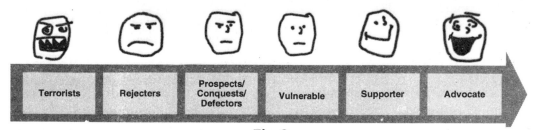

| Terrorists | Rejecters | Prospects/ Conquests/ Defectors | Vulnerable | Supporter | Advocate |

Fig. 2

Building loyalty starts with taking the right marketing approach. Relationship marketing is a very effective approach in a B2B setting, where the focus is on building & reinforcing a long-term relationship with the customer with every interaction. The philosophy here is that the relationship starts when a prospective customer is approached. Availability of the right information on the customer and ability to offer the right value proposition are key to continuance of the relationship.

Many business/industrial customers demand a high level of customer support as a prerequisite for offering a significant proportion of their business to a vendor / service provider. This necessitates a large investment in people, infrastructure and enabling technology. The Market Intelligent Enterprise is able to leverage this investment to proactively offer support to other, lesser demanding customers. Moreover, offering active customer support enables the MIE to develop a closer relationship with the customer, discover new business opportunities, receive early warning of performance gaps and better anticipate shifts in customer expectation.

Billing and payment could be quite complex in a B2B scenario, with the customer needing to keep track of consumption of the product/service, returns, commercial terms and credit periods. The Market Intelligent Enterprise leverages its understanding of customer needs and its systems to make it easier for the customer to keep track of its payables & make them when due. The MIE also integrates with the procurement & payment systems of its key customers, to lower transaction cost & complexity, and make the relevant billing information readily available to the customer.

PwC recently consulted a leading telecom services company on developing its Customer Relationship Marketing infrastructure. This telco was operating in an environment of swift technological changes, rising competitive intensity and falling margins. Consequentially, there was heavy pressure on retention of the top business customers of the telco, who were also its most profitable customers.

For this client, PwC designed and implemented a closed-loop relationship-marketing infrastructure including campaign management, mining and modeling environments. It also developed a comprehensive marketing database consisting of both internal customer information and external prospect data. An end-to-end marketing process was also developed & implemented, to enable targeted customer relationship marketing. To enable the new marketing approach, Marketing was reorganized into a matrix organization aligned with target segments. All this has enabled the telco in retaining a large proportion of its existing high-value customers and aggressively targeting the large-business segment.

□ MANAGING CUSTOMER RELATIONSHIPS ON THE BASIS OF ONGOING CUSTOMER VALUE

Typically, a small proportion of the customer base - about 20% or less- accounts for a disproportionately high proportion - about 70-80%- of its revenues and profits. The first step in managing customer relationships is identification of these key customers. This should be done on basis of two factors:

i. Lifetime value, i.e. what the customer contributes to the Enterprise over his lifetime, and

ii. Strategic importance, i.e. how much the customer contributes to maintaining the competitive edge of the Enterprise

Customer Lifetime Value is defined as the value today of a customer based on the future profits over its life expectancy. The steps to estimating customer lifetime value are:

i. Estimate the annual revenues that customers generate each year

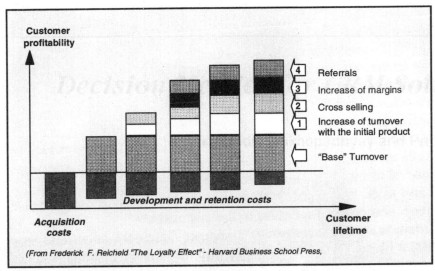

Fig. 3

ii. Estimate the cost of acquisition

iii. Estimate the cost of retention

iv. Estimate how many years customers are likely to stay with the firm

v. Know how to discount future earnings due to customers to their present value

Determining customer lifetime value in a B2B scenario can be difficult, if the market offerings/customer needs/profit margins are changing rapidly. Moreover, it may not be easy to determine the probability of losing the customer, especially if the customer is quite price-sensitive or the market is very competitive, with a high churn rate. However, this tool still retains its utility if educated assumptions are made uniformly and business judgement is applied in the final customer categorization.

Strategic importance of a business customer can be determined by asking a few simple questions:

i. How important is the customer, to achievement of the mission of the Enterprise?

ii. What will be the overall impact on the customer base of the Enterprise, of loss of the customer?

iii. Does the Enterprise gain substantial technical know-how, skill-set or market intelligence from the customer?

iv. Is the customer key to maintaining/enhancing presence in a focus market segment?

A strategically important customer may have a comparatively low lifetime value. For example, one of PwC's CRM clients is a lubricant major for whom power utilities constitute a focus segment, with the lubricant being a mission- critical consumable in the turbines. The customers in this segment have a high inclination to continue with the lubricant vendor who supplies to the turbine OEM for initial fill. This makes the turbine OEMs strategically very important, although their purchase volumes are comparatively low.

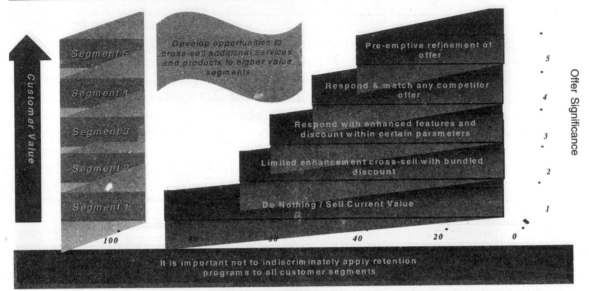

Fig. 4

Moreover, the contribution to net earnings from these OEMs is still lower, because the OEMs leverage their strategic importance to negotiate a discounted price. The second step to managing customer relationships is to create a tiered retention strategy that directly ties retention effect to the lifetime value and strategic importance of the customer.

An MIE also uses its analysis of customer lifetime value and its understanding of customer segments to better target its marketing efforts. It discovers significant cross-selling opportunities to existing customers, e.g. an industrial equipment manufacturer offering maintenance/remote monitoring services to a customer with high installation base. It also identifies prospects more accurately, lowering marketing costs and raising the effectiveness of sales force. For example, Fedex built a new campaign management program for its business customers, on basis of a detailed analysis of its base of customers & prospects. This program helped Fedex compress its marketing campaign from 26 to 8 weeks, enabling it to execute six marketing campaigns a year, instead of two earlier. This approach yielded an 800% RoI (return on investments) for Fedex and dramatically raised the productivity of its sales & marketing teams.

☐ EMBRACING MARKET INTELLIGENT TECHNOLOGIES

"Disruptive technologies bring to a market a very different value proposition than had been available previously." - Clayton Christensen

The value proposition offered by current technologies to CRM truly makes these technologies "disruptive". Figure 5 depicts the Technology Template for a Market Intelligent Enterprise. Each of the modules depicted in Figure 5 contributes to the goal of acquiring & applying market information swiftly to effectively manage customer relationships.

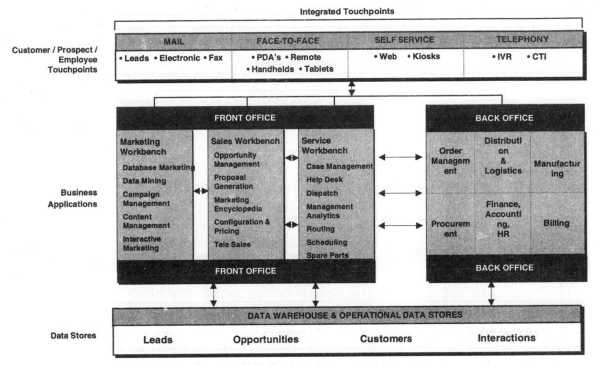

Fig. 5 *MIE Technology Template*

Technology and connectivity will remain the two great enablers for a Market Intelligent Enterprise: together they determine the velocity and quality of information flow. Extensive capturing of customer information, its collation & analysis and swift responding to the identified customer needs is possible only through enablers like E-commerce, CRM packages, data mining solutions etc.

Technology plays a vital role in building relationships, by facilitating information flow across the value chain. Business customers are increasingly investing in technology to collaborate more closely with their vendors. A key promise of technology is the visibility of demand across the extended supply chain: this enables vendors to be more responsive to their customers while shedding excess inventory and minimizing the risk of stock obsolescence. The better inflow of customer data also helps vendors analyze the purchase behavior of their customers more closely and take proactive measures to build brand equity with customers.

However, seamless integration of disparate technologies could be a major challenge. A recent PwC survey discovered that businesses experience a 70% success rate at implementing one eCRM technology (for example, internet or Call Center), but the success rate drops quickly when several eCRM technologies have to be integrated, especially when more than three technologies are involved. The survey discovered that the success rate was less than

40%. Companies that have created pockets of excellence by implementing disparate CRM systems, may need to invest substantially in system integration, to realize the true benefits of CRM.

The benefits from a successful CRM implementation can be truly dramatic. A case in point is Pitney Bowes, a manufacturer of postage meters and related office equipment. The company has reportedly achieved a 45% reduction in delivery lead-time and 27% reduction in cancellation due to wrong orders, through its CRM initiative. The productivity of the sales persons also rose considerably, with five times more sales proposals being generated, leading to a 7% rise in sales.

PwC implemented Siebel system for a major telecommunications services provider, with the objective of enhancing the responsiveness of the client to customer needs. This has enabled the client to:

i. Tailor marketing approaches to specific large-value business customers
ii. Conduct in-depth analysis of customer interaction data to identify cross-selling opportunities, and offer tailor-made services to different business units of their customers
iii. Offer the sales-force and customer support team an overview of all the interactions between the company and its business customers

◻ CONCLUSION

"Catching up to where others have been is necessary to stay in the game, but the winners will be those companies who have the ability to invent fundamentally new games." - Gary Hamel

The vision of Market Intelligent Enterprise is a key tool for businesses to fundamentally re-invent themselves for remaining competitive an operating environment that has evolved considerably in the last few years. Realization of this vision has now become a strategic imperative for businesses seeking to survive & prosper in this environment of fluid customer expectation and disruptive technology.

Businesses that take the lead in realizing the MIE vision will have the opportunity to invent "fundamentally new games". The rewards for this can be very substantial, especially if these businesses are able to put together a substantially better value proposition to the top customers in their markets. Dell Computers is a famous example here: its web-based sales model enabled IT managers to devolve purchasing power to the end-users, while ensuring consistency of specifications.

On the other hand, companies that lag behind in realizing the MIE vision could be risking a large proportion of their customer base & profitability. The B2B markets are typically concentrated, with a few large buyers accounting for a large proportion of the market size. A Company that is not ahead of its competitors in terms of responsiveness to customer needs could face an exodus of its top customers to a nimbler, more responsive MIE.

The vision of Market Intelligent Enterprise has been formulated to address the core strategic imperatives in the B2B market-space. Each of the areas addressed by MIE has the potential to yield substantial benefits to an Enterprise in terms of enhanced customer value, higher market share and better earnings.

Chapter 32

Cross-border B2B Relationships with Intermediaries: Between New and Old

■ **Sudhi Seshadri**

Abstract

New interfaces in cross-border B2B transactions bring into question the relevance of a broad range of contractual relationships. One question that arises in this new environment is what marketing behaviors and perceptions in the "new economy" distribution channels will carry over from cross-border transactions between manufacturers and their channel intermediaries in the "old economy"? A preliminary step in answering this question is taken in this paper. We develop a framework from the Transaction Cost Economics (TCE) perspective. Based on our field research we propose a conceptual model of cross-border marketing with distributors in "new economy" B2B markets. We then test our conceptual model, and hypotheses with an "old economy" survey research data set. Using path analysis, we show where older practices support our "new economy" conceptual model. The results indicate what aspects of our model for the rapidly evolving international B2B marketplace carry over to the older bricks and mortar export marketing company.

Key Words: *B2B, International, TCE, Path Analysis, Contracts, Relationship Marketing.*

❑ INTRODUCTION

In the new economy, global transactions in B2B markets often occur in the absence of cross-border market entry or vertical integration. Increasingly, manufacturers are able to provide information and establish contact with geographically distant business purchasers through electronic media, or the internet. Some challenges have been raised to the traditional models of business marketing, chiefly questioning the premise of bilateral relationships in the new paradigm. The vastly greater reach and interactivity achieved by new economy electronic commerce between businesses is thought to pose a market alternative to the closeness and continuity of business relationships.

In particular, the pundits predicted disintermediation, or the withering away of intermediaries in the distribution chain. Often, however, channel intermediaries in the host country still offer value by aggregating demand and providing a variety of local services. Traditional marketing agreements with intermediaries were often contractual in nature, and cover quantity discounts, royalties, profit sharing, and the like. In the new economy paradigm there have been shifts in the revenue model to syndication, usage-based royalties and fees, access fees, maintenance revenues and a variety of other instruments. The role of an intermediary is to validate the contractual agreements between the actually transacting parties.

The conceptual framework for our investigation is drawn from transaction cost economics (TCE). The literature on TCE is extensive (for instance Williamson 1986), and will not be reviewed here. Key TCE concepts include (a) opportunism and its impact on transaction costs; (b) transaction-specific investments in human and physical capital within a business relationship; (c) costs and efficiencies in processing information, and the attendant information structures; and (d) institutional mechanisms and structures that allow comparative assessment of transaction costs. TCE has been successfully applied in marketing to explaining the degree of vertical integration in international distribution channels (Klien et al 1990). The main theoretical prediction of TCE relevant to our concern here can be summed up succinctly. In his article, "Transaction Cost Economics: The governance of contractual relations," Oliver Williamson (1986) writes:

"As generic demand grows and the number of supply sources increases, exchange that was once transaction-specific loses this characteristic and greater reliance on market-mediated governance is feasible. Thus vertical integration may give way to obligational market contracting, which in turn may give way to markets. (p. 123)"

In today's international B2B world, vertical integration is likely to be absent in many markets. Small and medium enterprises (SMEs) are often not able to afford permanent physical presence in distant markets, with all the cultural and language differences. Bilateral relational arrangements would then tend to yield to trilateral arrangements where possible, and eventually into market governance modes. In this scenario, marketing would have come full circle back to market governance albeit with higher technological and informational efficiency afforded by the new economy tools. Contractual agreement is essentially a trilateral governance mode.

In order to set the context of the research we will examine a recent case from our field research in international distribution of a software product.

□ AN EXAMPLE: SOFTWARE LAUNCH

Typical issues in cross-border distribution in the new economy are set in context by this example. An established US based company in the CAD/CAM sector formed a strategic alliance with a European company that had devised a break-through software application product. The new product had significant enhancements, new functionality, and vastly improved user interface. In accordance with market prospects for this next generation nature of the CAD/CAM application, a new company was floated with the product, with development facilities in the European country, and marketing offices in USA's Silicon Valley overseeing worldwide distribution. The Asian region had a variety of arrangements. For instance, the India market was handled by a subsidiary, and a local software development center was also established, whereas the Asia-Pacific market was to be penetrated through alliances with carefully selected local distributors. The software company established a worldwide web site, developed CD-ROM based training materials, and even devised interactive training games for popularizing base level familiarity with the software. The company sought host country distributors for customization, training and after sales support services, as well as market development.

Negotiations with the primary distributor in one Asia-Pacific country were initially promising. After the initial correspondence and discussions, however, disagreements rapidly surfaced. Issues of exclusivity were particularly important. The software company refused to grant exclusivity to the Asian distributor. Some concerns affecting both parties were (a) the distributor would not make adequate market development effort; (b) stalling by the distributor led to company fears that the distributor was attempting to develop a rival product; (c) the distributor in turn feared the software company was attempting to develop rival channels and that market development efforts would be reaped by others; and (d) alternative channels would lead to an erosion of bargaining power when new versions of the software were introduced .

Negotiations on the contractual agreements began to follow a pattern. All negotiations were held locally in the Asian country with the software company's VP Marketing (USA), and VP Operations (Europe) in attendance. The VP of the distribution firm would agree to various stipulations in the contractual agreement drafted by the software company. The CEO of the distribution firm would arrive independently the next day and revise all commitments previously agreed upon. An additional difficulty was the senior executives were speakers of three different native languages. The distributor hired the local translation agency, and the software company began to question the translation agency's vested interest in prolonging negotiations. Soon negotiations became interminable and the issues turned to personalities and "honor." Finally, the individuals originally involved quit when the chances of satisfactory contractual agreement seem remote and receding. Market development activities have completely stalled. The simplified example reveals some key issues in "new economy" cross-border B2B marketing, that we develop in the next sections. The paper proceeds with the model and hypotheses in section 3. The methodology and data for the empirical study is described in section 4; and the results of the data analysis and discussion follow in 5. We conclude with some issues for further research and managerial implications.

❏ MODEL AND HYPOTHESES

We now develop a simple conceptual model grounded in the TCE framework, employing the key constructs on behaviors and perceptions in cross-border B2B distribution channels. Exhibit 1 (a) depicts the model schematically.

Exibit 1(a) *Market-behavioral-perceptual model of contract agreements. A conceptual model for path analysis*

X Variable	Label	Y Variable	Label
Ses	Share of exports of overall firm's sales	PICA	Perceived Importance of Contract Agreement
Rpd	Reputation of distributor	SERV	Service support
Sdm	Firm's share of all domestic sales in product class	NEGN	Negotiation
Asr	Annual sales revenues of firm	ITDP	Interdependence
Sem	Firm's share of all exports sales		

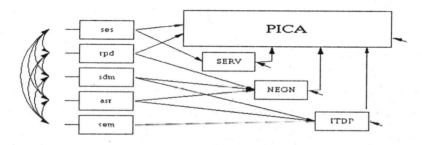

Exhibit 1(b) *Results of Path Analysis*

Goodness of Fit Statistics

Degrees of Freedom = 14
Minimum Fit Function Chi-Square = 13.25 (P = 0.51)
Root Mean Square Error of Approximation (RMSEA) = 0.0

Normed Fit Index (NFI) = 0.94
Non-Normed Fit Index (NNFI) = 1.01
Standardized RMR = 0.060
Goodness of Fit Index (GFI) = 0.97
Adjusted Goodness of Fit Index (AGFI) = 0.92
Squared Multiple Correlation for Structural Equations

SERV	NEGN	ITDP	PICA
0.07	0.13	0.19	0.48

Standardized Total and Indirect Effects

Standardized Total Effects of X on Y

	ses	rpd	sdm	asr	sem
SERV	0.26	- -	- -	- -	- -
NEGN	- -	−0.09	0.23	0.24	- -

(Contd.)

Exhibit 1(b) (*Contd.*)

ITDP	--	--	-0.32	0.21	0.50
PICA	0.17	-0.25	0.11	0.16	0.04

Standardized Indirect Effects of X on Y

	ses	**rpd**	**sdm**	**asr**	**sem**
PICA	0.01	-0.05	0.11	0.16	0.04

Standardized Total Effects of Y on Y

	SERV	**NEGN**	**ITDP**	**PICA**
PICA	0.04	0.59	0.08	--

Hypothesis	Path	Standardized Coefficient	T value	Supported at .05 level
H1a	ses, PICA	0.16	2.21	Yes
H1b	rpd, PICA	-0.20	-2.86	Yes
H2	SERV, PICA	0.04	.59	No
H3	ses, SERV	0.26	2.79	Yes
H4	NEGN, PICA	0.59	8.44	Yes
H5a	rpd, NEGN	-.09	-.94	No
H5b	sdm, NEGN	0.23	2.50	Yes
H5c	asr, NEGN	0.24	2.62	Yes
H6	ITDP, PICA	0.08	1.14	No
H7a	sdm, ITDP	-.32	-2.99	Yes
H7b	asr, ITDP	.21	2.39	Yes
H7c	sem, ITDP	0.50	4.65	Yes

Perceived importance of contractual agreements (PICA). Contractual agreements are of a variety of kinds. The literature has identified the use and role of contractual agreements in mitigating the effects of transaction costs in situations of uncertainty and information asymmetries. Quantity discounts agreements are a way of implementing discriminatory pricing, but also serve to coordinate uncertainties on retail demand. Fixed fees are necessary to compensate the distributor for participation in the channel. Royalties are negotiated in order to ensure the right level of forward pricing and provide the right incentives in double-sided information asymmetries. Agreements on marketing and advertising expenses are necessary when the costs may not be observed or when local advertising is necessary. Profit sharing is probably the most difficult agreement, with future revenues and cost predictions and market development issues at stake. With greater uncertainty in revenue models new economy firms will face potential information inefficiencies.

The perception of importance is a key concern since it determines how quickly the parties reach contractual agreement, and the amount of relevance such agreement has to future of the relationship. Time scales are highly foreshortened in the new economy. The purpose in our model is to determine the degree to which PICA can be explained by the channel behaviors that actually occur. To begin with, we consider some control variables that directly impact the importance of contractual agreement.

Hypothesis 1a: Greater share of exports in total sales (ses) results in higher perceived importance of contractual agreement (PICA).

Hypothesis 1b: Greater reputation of distributor (rpd) results in lower perceived importance of contractual agreement (PICA).

Service Support (SERV). The support provided in the channel for customer service is an important relational characteristic. Distributors often offer maintenance contracts, extended warranties, toll-free customer service lines, local web sites and call centers, and other customer care methods as support. The costs of providing such efforts are often not observable and may not be directly compensated. Is the distributor doing all he can for market development? Inefficiencies are inherent even when instant communication is the norm. Monitoring of support services may then be necessary. The ability of contractual agreements to cater to moral hazard problems in support services will increase their importance when such service, monitored or otherwise, is necessary. Hence,

Hypothesis 2: Higher service support (SERV) results in higher perceived importance of contractual agreements (PICA).

Hypothesis 3: Greater share of exports in total sales (ses) results in higher service support (SERV).

Negotiation intensity (NEGN). In any ongoing relationship, conflicts will arise. It is not the absence of conflict that companies seek, but the efficient resolution of conflict situations through positive negotiations. The ability of the companies to employ successful negotiation strategies in an ongoing relationship has been noted by several authors (Walter & Gemunden 2000; Narus & Anderson 1995). Shared goals that are recognized as such, become necessary for smooth negotiation. Contractual agreement is one way of formalizing shared goals in a mutually visible way. Contract on predictable contingencies will further enable the parties to negotiate the difficult situations when contingencies cannot be anticipated. The greater the negotiations intensity, the higher importance will be perceived for prior contractual agreements. Hence,

Hypothesis 4: Higher negotiation intensity (NEGN) results in higher perceived importance of contractual agreements (PICA).

Hypothesis 5a: Greater reputation of the distributor (rpd) results in lower negotiation intensity (NEGN).

Hypothesis 5b: Greater share of domestic market (sdm) results in higher negotiation intensity (NEGN).

Hypothesis 5c: Greater share of annual sales revenue (asr) results in higher negotiation intensity (NEGN).

Interdependence intensity (ITDP). The exclusivity and "sole distributor" status in cross-border distribution is a much sought after privilege. In addition, the firm often seeks assurance for its part that other brands will not be presented by the distributor. Mutual interdependence owes its origin to these bilateral exclusivity arrangements. Opportunism problems in transaction put pressure on the parties to formalize these arrangements in contractual agreements. Then the need to monitor and enforce exclusivity is reduced. Hence,

Hypothesis 6: Higher interdependence (ITDP) results in higher perceived importance of contractual agreements (PICA).

Hypothesis 7a:Higher share of domestic market (sdm) results in lower interdependence (ITDP).

Hypothesis 7b: Greater annual sales revenue (asr) results in higher interdependence (ITDP).

Hypothesis 7c: Greater share of export market (sem) results in higher interdependence (ITDP).

Several of the above hypotheses received conceptual support from our field research on new economy B2B firms engaged in cross-border marketing. The data set for the empirical tests of these hypotheses comes from survey research on old economy B2B firms in cross border marketing. We next examine the empirical methodology and data set.

◻ METHODOLOLOGY AND DATA

The model was estimated with data from a survey on exporters from the US, predating the growth of the world wide web. The data was collected in 1993, from a national survey supported by CIBER at the University of Maryland at College Park. Some descriptive details follow.

Sample profile: The data set is from a national sample survey of US based exporters *prior* to the advent of international "click and brick" business marketing. The respondent profile summarized below matches the SME firm that will likely have strong incentives to use the internet extensively when B2B exchanges become available in their industry verticals. In the data set, the median age of the firm was 38 years, with the median number of years exporting 19 years. Median number of employees was 57, and median annual sales was $6 million. The median volume of sales through their primary product-channel was $0.25 million; and the median country share of the world wide market of the product was 0.10. Finally, the economic regions where independent distributors or representatives were used broke down as Canada 71.7%, Mexico 63.6%, Western Europe 58.4%, South East Asia (excluding China) 52.6%, South America 52.0%, Central America 49.1%, Australia/New Zealand 48.6%, Africa (excluding Middle East) 31.8%, China 30 %, Eastern Europe 24.3%, Pacific Rim 13.3%. Further details are available from the author.

Measurement Scales: Using the data set profiled above, a variety of contractual agreements are investigated for their degree of perceived importance. We next develop and validate a perceived importance scale for contractual agreements, and we operationalize the intensity of negotiation and interdependence. The descending order of perceived importance of contract agreement is on quantity discounts, on marketing/advertising, on fixed fees, on royalties, and on post-sales profit sharing. A single scale was constructed by averaging the items, and this scale had a coefficient alpha of 0.73. While this passes the level suggested by Nunnally (1978) for construct reliability in field research, we intend to interpret the scale as an index. Hence, confirmatory factor analysis is not attempted. The scale is distributed between 1= Not at all important and 7 = very important, and has a mean of 2.61, and a standard deviation of 1.32. On the whole, perceived importance of contractual agreement, PICA, varies quite a lot around the neutral position. We attempted a similar scale development effort for the behavioral items. Each of these scales should be interpreted as an index, and a formative measure, where a higher score between 1 and 7 indicated a higher level of the variable. Therefore, we formed one index SERV by averaging two items of service support and monitoring; these were to do with whether service support was provided (Always – Never) and whether the distributor was monitored (Intensively – Not at all). NEGN averaged two items on negotiation intensity; these were on wholesale price and on profit margin (A great deal – None). The third index ITDP averaged three items on interdependence; these were brand exclusivity (Only brand – One of many), distributor exclusivity (Sole/exclusive – Many), and distributor dependency (A great deal – None). The resulting variables were all directly observed, and since only formative scales were used, we do not assume any latent variables in the subsequent analysis. We now turn to the results of the model estimation.

☐ RESULTS AND DISCUSSION

We employed path analysis to test the hypotheses. Several reasons justify the methodology of path analysis. First, simultaneous multiple regression equations characterize the model. Second, there are no latent variables for a confirmatory factor analytical model. All measures were formative rather than reflective scales. Lastly, we wished to identify the many direct and indirect effects of control variables, through the structural paths, and determine their relative effects in a standardized model. LISREL 8.30 (Joreskog & Sorbom 1999) was used. Exhibit 1(b) presents the main results and the standardized estimates are shown on the model path diagram of Exhibit 1(a). The fit indices are all excellent. All coefficients were in the right direction, and all but three of the twelve hypotheses were supported at the .05 level of significance. These results are discussed next in the context of new and old economy cross-border B2B.

Old and New: Negotiation intensity was hypothesized to increase PICA in the new; it shows very significant evidence of doing so in the old. We hypothesized that SERV and ITDP would both increase PICA in the new; both however fail to show convincing evidence of doing so in the old. Of the three, NEGN appears to have far greater effect than either SERV or ITDP, since the standardized coefficient is .59 versus .04 and .08. Overall, negotiation intensity has a significant direct effect on perceived importance of contractual agreement, accounting for 83 percent of the structural effect from the behavioral variables. Our model explains a total of 48 percent of the variation in PICA, as is evident from the squared multiple correlation in Exhibit 1(b). The control variables in our model explain 13 percent of the variation in NEGN.

The hypothesis that service support behaviors tend to increase the perceived importance of contract agreements was not supported. Old economy businesses could differ from new economy businesses in this count. In the brick and mortar world service does not often require the rapid response times from the firm, and may be independently arranged, outside of the exporting relationship. In the new economy, firms would have to provide services on-line and in real time. Our model's single control variables for SERV explains only 7 percent of its variation (see the squared multiple correlation in Exhibit 1(b)).

The hypothesis that interdependence will increase the perceived importance of contract agreement was not supported. Here again, the old may differ from the new economy firms. Difficulties due to information asymmetries may reduce the importance of contractual agreement in brick and mortar markets. The increased availability of information and reduced transaction costs associated with costless information allows new economy firms to learn of contract violations earlier. Our control variables explain 19 percent of the variation in ITDP (see Exhibit 1(b)).

The empirical tests therefore are indicative of the degree of support our hypotheses receive from the old economy data set. The extrapolations to the new economy firms are exploratory in nature. The next section summarizes the main findings of the paper and notes its contributions to theory and practice.

□ CONCLUSIONS

The hypothesized effects that found support were indications of bridges between the new (theory) and the old (practice); the effects that failed to find support would be interpreted as areas where gaps in the new and the old had yet to be bridged. With some caveats we can offer some recommendations to managers based on our findings. We found that nine hypothesized effects found support from the data and three did not. This is interesting since it implies that B2B marketing distribution practices developed over the years for essentially old economy firms need not necessarily be irrelevant to the new economy.

Most importantly, the intensity of negotiation is associated with increased perceived importance of contract agreement in the old. Managers ought to budget time and effort for protracted cross-border negotiation when comprehensive contractual agreements are needed, both in old and new marketing. A greater share of domestic market is likely to increase the negotiation intensity, as is greater annual sales revenue. A manufacturer in the old economy is likely to be similar to a software company in the new economy in this effect, since the bigger more important players domestically will tend to have greater staying power in cross-border negotiation. Contractual agreements are perceived as more important when the firm is dependent on exports to a larger extent. Reputation of distributors will lower the perceived importance of contracts. Service activities are higher when the exports are a bigger share of sales.

Share of domestic market and annual sales revenues will increase the interdependence of channel partners. A greater share of the export market from the exporting country is likely to lead to more interdependence in the channel relationship. Whether the old or new, a firm with greater international presence could demand more of its distributors and would likely establish more dependent relationships. In all of these effects, managers should not expect changes when they adopt new economy marketing approaches. However, some differences did arise. Service provision does not affect the perception of contract importance. Reputation of the distributor does not impact negotiation intensity. Interdependence appears not to significantly influence perceived importance of contract agreements. Since interdependence is more closely related to contracts in the new economy than in the old, managers should break with older habits and seek cross-border partners that are dependent on their business.

A more general conclusion is that governance modes that require contractual agreements are likely to offer continued advantages. From the institutional context of transaction costs, this is significant. New economy activities show growth of market alternatives with B2B exchanges on the one hand, and of bilateral approaches to international B2B markets with strategic alliances and mergers on the other. The intermediated relationship with contractual agreements has higher importance when negotiations are ongoing features of the relationships. Formal contract management services for B2B exchanges help channel partners who expect future negotiations. The services will be activated at the initiation of relationships and will be revisited from time to time. Intermediaries will continue to playa role here. Some cross border B2B relationship marketing theory may not find justifications from old economy practices; however, a great deal of the theory does find support in older practices.

REFERENCES

Joreskog, Karl and Dag Sorbom (1999), '*LISREL 8.30,*' Scientific Software International, Inc.

Klein, Saul, Gary L. Frazier, and Victor J. Roth (1990), 'A Transaction Cost Analysis Model of Channel Integration in International Markets,' *Journal of Marketing Research,* Vol. XXVII, May.

Narus, James A. and John C. Anderson (1995), 'Using teams to manage collaborative relationships in business markets,' *Journal of Business-to-Business Marketing,* Vol 2, 3, pp. 17-46.

Nunnally, J.C. (1978), '*Psychometric Theory,*' McGraw Hill, New York, London.

Walter, Achim and Hans Georg Gemunden (2000), 'Bridging the gap between suppliers and customers through relationship promoters: theoretical considerations and empirical results,' *Journal of Business & Industrial Marketing,* Vol 15, 2/3, pp. 86-105.

Williamson, Oliver E. (1986), '*Economic Organization: Firms, Markets and Policy Control,*' New York University Press, NY.

Chapter 33

Relationship Marketing for Creating Value in Business Markets

■ **G A Anand**

Abstract

Marketing to Industrial/Business customers in India has slowly evolved from a purely Cost-Quality-Delivery (CQD) model to a Key Account Management model. In the CQD model customer relationship largely tended to be one-on-one mainly between the seller and buyer. However, marketers selling to large organizations have realized the competitive advantage that customer intimacy brings and the importance of formalizing the process of managing customer relationships. Key Account Management largely involves mapping the suppliers strengths, business goals and culture and identifying the customers that can be best served profitably. Once Key Accounts are identified it becomes imperative to manage the Relationship at various levels in the customers organization. This is also necessitated by the fact, that organizational requirements are not easily articulated, and requires multi level contacts by the vendor to fully understand the needs. The model entailed is descriptive for the first two stages and is prescriptive in the next two. However, all the four stages are shown in a single flow and represented as a "Relationship Chain." The chain is a four stage evolutionary model of the supplier/ Customer relationship. The inroads into the customer begins from a single level relationship focusing purely on tangible delivery, finally evolving into a multi level contact matrix working together to enhance value to both organizations. Customer Relationships provide the key to understanding and anticipating customer's needs. As the supplier interacts more at various levels with the customer they develop a "Lock-in" which the competitors find difficult to break. The Customers in turn find it difficult to switch suppliers since the costs of developing a relationship afresh is high.

Key Words: *CQD model, Key Account Management, Relationship Chain, Contact Matrix, Value. Lock-in*

□ INTRODUCTION

Most Business-to-Business marketing companies have been managing relationships, earlier on a one to one level and lately as a multi level contact matrix. The very nature of business markets makes it imperative for vendors to develop and manage customer intimacy so as to give them insights into customers needs. These insights are used in tailoring Product/ Service offerings to best satisfy the customer and also in pricing, to deliver optimal profitability to the vendor. However, one-to-one relationships suffer from two key problems:

(a) An excessive dependency on individual salespersons. This often leads to loss of the account when the salesperson leaves or retires from the vendor's organization.

(b) When the relationship is limited to the single individual level both at the vendor and customer end, the understanding of customer needs may be fraught with hidden agendas of individuals, judgmental errors and communication problems.

A dedicated Key Account team solves the problem by forming a contact matrix wherein different members from the team develop and maintain contacts at various levels in the customer's organization. This ensures continuity of relationship at the organizational level and allows for filtering of judgmental errors and ensuring a common agenda for both. Thus not only better insights are gained, but the vendor is able to anticipate needs and utilize the insights to customize Product/ Service offerings. It also allows him to manage customer perceptions, which is as important as managing reality.

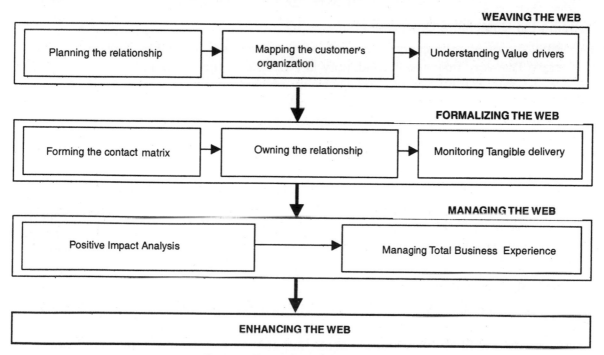

Fig. 1 *The Relationship Chain*

The paper does not go into the aspects of Key Account Management involving Internal Analysis, deciding on the Core Value Proposition, Team formation and Customer Selection. The model below concentrates on the relationship building activities after a Key Account (Customer) has been identified with whom the vendor wishes to conduct business profitably on a long-term basis.

The formation of a relationship is akin to a web that needs to be Woven, Instituted, Managed and continually Enhanced.

□ WEAVING THE WEB

The first stage involves laying the foundation for the relationship and involves three sets of activities:

Planning the Relationship

The physical delivery of Services/Goods/Solutions is the basic requirement that has to be met. Unless the basic need is fulfilled competitively, the next layer cannot be built. The vendor has to understand the customer's requirement in physical terms-Specifications, Performance, Quality, Reliability, Support, etc. He has to benchmark himself against current competitive offerings and prepare to fulfill them. The "value proposition" i.e. the sum total of all the tangible and intangible offerings that will differentiate the vendor from the competition is decided. Finally, a plan for short term, medium term and long term goals is framed in terms of market-share, profitability and relationship.

Mapping the Customers Organization

The initial stages of contact with the customer may be either through a single sales person or a team. The very first step is to identify key people in the customer's organization and the power structure. Key people are Decision makers for the particular Product/Service, Influencers in the decision-making process and Sponsors - people who are highly experienced and knowledgeable about the organization and/ or about the product/ service offered. Sponsors are especially important when it comes to selling complex technical products or services.

Examples:

Decision Makers: Project Manager, Purchase Manager, Managing Director etc.

Influencers: End Users, Production Managers, Finance Managers, R&D Managers etc.

Sponsors: People who have spent many years in the organization and have been in User/ Decision making roles in the past. By dint of their expertise are respected in the organization.

Understanding the Value Drivers

Once an understanding in gained about the customer's organization and the key people it is important to understand the value drivers for each of the key people. Value driver is defined as the tangible/intangible elements that arise out of an offer and interaction that are perceived as important by the concerned people.

Examples would be Price, Cost in Use, Technology, Know How, Response time, etc. Value drivers are different for different people. For example, the Purchase manager driven by need to show reduction in purchase cost, may value price as the key driver whereas the project manager may perceive Technology and Cost in use as the value driver. The value driver for a sponsor may be cutting edge technology.

□ FORMALISING THE WEB

At the end of the first stage there is some business that is being transacted. Customer Satisfaction is monitored through contacts with the key people in the customer's organization. It is now time to formalize the relationship, which involves three sets of activities:

Forming the contact matrix

The Key Account Manager is formally decided at this stage. The Key Account Manager orchestrates the relationships between the organizations. He is responsible for the health and direction of the relationship. The understanding gained about the customer's organization and the key people are now used to develop the contact matrix. A cross-functional Key Account team is formed to interact with the key people identified at the customer. Members of the team are then "matched" with the key people in the customer's organization based on the understanding gained on the individual value drivers. For example the R&D person in the team may be matched with the end user in the customer's organization since the interaction can lead to better understanding of use of the product and helping in optimal design of the product/service offering.

Owning the Relationship

A road map is then designed including a timetable of visits and meetings so as to ensure regular contact between people in the contact matrix and development of relationships. Two elements are important while designing the contact matrix: Hierarchy and personal chemistry. Hierarchy is a key factor in Industrial marketing. Most successful Business-to-Business relationships have a very strong contact at senior levels of both organizations. Hence, the Key Account team must involve members with appropriate seniority to interact with senior people in the customer's organization. Personal Chemistry is an important aspect that cannot be ignored. Sometimes, it can have considerable impact deciding on the nature of the relationship. It is the Key Account Manager's responsibility to recognize bad chemistry and appropriately counsel and if necessary re-organize the contacts. At all points of time the vendor takes responsibility for the relationship. He has to ensure that despite the multiple contacts there is a consistency in meetings and no disputes arise due to contradictory promises or commitments. The team must present a single 'face' to the customer.

Monitoring Tangible Delivery

This is the most fragile time of the relationship. The strong customer contacts held by few people have been replaced by a cross functional team. While, the contact matrix is being managed by the Key Account manager delivery of promises is extremely important. This stage decides the future of the relationship. Due to the introduction of a new network of contacts there is some uneasiness in the customer. A serious failure in delivery of promises, either tangible or intangible can lead to a reduction in confidence on the customer's part and can be perceived as a breach of trust. All efforts made so far may be shattered pulling the relationship back to stage one.

□ MANAGING THE WEB

With the passage of time the "Web" of relationship is instituted. There is a multiple point of contact and the relationship is no more dependent on individuals. The customer by now is beginning to develop a certain level of trust and the occasional failure on delivery is forgiven. The vendor on his part has begun to gain a deeper understanding not only of the customer's explicit needs but also of his tacit needs. He has a window into the customer's organization and is often privy to "inside information" i.e. the customer's grapevine. The Key Account Manager who is often the Sales manager is now reoriented from a pure sales role to that of an orchestrator. However, the relationship has to be now managed to deliver greater "value" i.e. profitability for the vendor and enhanced solutions to the customer. This is done in two steps:

Positive Impact Analysis

The institutionalized contacts open many doors to the customer's organization. It allows the vendor to observe processes, which were earlier unknown. Using this increased exposure the vendor first sets out to list all the activities of the customer and interfaces involved in buying, usage and obsoletion of the product or service bought. The interfaces are classified into three groups:

Necessary: These are basic—they have to be fulfilled without which there is no business.
E.g.: Quotations, On-time delivery etc.

High Impact: These involve activities where customer involvement is high and creative execution lessening customer involvement will have considerable impact.
E.g.: Preparation of proper tax forms in the required formats and ensuring reliable delivery.
Having a toll free number available at all times to ensure ready contact anytime.

Low Impact: These are activities in which any improvements made will not be noticeable by the customer.
E.g.: Improving the presentation quality on packaging?

High Impact activities may or may not fall in the "Necessary" activities group. These activities are studied and processes designed/ modified in such a manner as to have a Positive Impact on the customer.

Managing Total Business Experience

As critical and important activities and processes are designed to suit customer requirements, the vendor's organization is aligned to the customer. All points of interaction are monitored and quality of interaction specified internally. All interactions ranging from receiving telephone calls to involved technical discussions enhance the customer's positive experience of conducting business with the vendor.

❑ ENHANCING THE WEB

At a stage when all contacts of the customer are managed, the relationship is now under control. The customer has placed a considerable amount of trust in the vendor and has rewarded the vendor by making him the lead supplier and the supplier of choice. The vendor's increased understanding has helped in optimizing products, processes and solutions to improve profitability. However, the vendor must always remember that it is a business relationship. The customer always has the prerogative of breaking the relationship when he perceives his interests are not best served.

At this stage most of the tangible delivery items such as product and processes are in place. Value perceived by the customer is now increasingly in the form of know-how. In individual interactions various contacts in the customer's organization will constantly seek additional information on technology and latest trends involved in the product/ service he uses. He now seeks the partnership of the vendor to serve the end customer.

Hence, the vendor has to create systems and structure within that constantly updates the knowledge and skills of the Key Account Team. This know-how development is not only in the Product/Service concerned but also with respect to the customer's business.

To do so, the vendor identifies Knowledge areas concerned. For example a vendor to an automotive manufacturer may identify 3 knowledge areas:

1. The Technology concerned
2. Manufacturing processes which employ the product/service of the vendor
3. The automotive end market

Having done so, he ensures a regular up-gradation of knowledge and skills of the team members through:

1. Databases
2. Seminars
3. Training programs

The team members are therefore in a position to continuously add "value" to the relationship with their individual contacts. Hence, the relationship is continuously enhanced.

The vendor at this stage is gains a "lock-in" on the customer at various levels, which become difficult and costly for competitors to imitate.

□ CASE STUDY

Background

The case studied here concerns a paint supplier and an MNC car manufacturer. Paint supply to a car manufacturer is an involved selling. As is the case with most Industrial supplies, the vendor has to first understand the specifications prepare samples, get approval and quote competitively. However, he also has to make it run on the paint shop and in the process modify the product if need be to suit application conditions on line and factor in painter expertise. To add to this paint is not any exact science but is an empirical science. Variations in environment and application conditions often result in defects in the painting line and the supplier needs to keep ready at hand, a technical service team. Therefore, the paint supplier's involvement starts from the supply of paint and continues into solving "field" problems if any that may crop up after sale of the vehicle.

Situation

The vendor was transacting business and leveraging an international collaboration had managed to become the "sole supplier" to the manufacturer for all his paint requirements. A competent team of paint technologists was also stationed full time at the manufacturer's site. The paint specification was well understood, all supplies met with the manufacturer's requirement. However, the relationship was troubled, characterized by poor production in the paint shop. The purchase department who had recently gained in importance and with whom the vendor had no contacts was gunning for a price reduction. The threat of loss of business was looming large over the vendor. To add to the local problems, the vendor's relationship with the international collaborator was also strained. When the customer began talking to competitors, the vendor decided to institute a Key Account Manager to control the situation.

Analysis: (Weaving the Web)

The KA manager formed a team including mainly the paint technologists on site and "mapped the organization" and the "Value Drivers" and came up with the following:

(a) Wherever contacts currently existed, the relationships were "hot and cold" as there was no formal mechanism of maintaining contacts and ensuring delivery of promise.

(b) The value driver for the paint shop which was the primary agency involved was "production throughput" whereas the vendor's team was primarily involved in trouble shooting paint defects which often degenerated into a blame fixing game between the vendor's team and the paint shop.

(c) The international collaborator was the second important agency since they wielded considerable influence with the manufacturer. Their value driver was "smooth paint shop operation and control."

(d) The Purchase department, the third agency with whom no efforts were made to develop relationships earlier wanted to establish their power. Hence, their value driver was Control over vendors and Price.

Action: (Formalizing the Web)

Based on the analysis (Weaving the Web), a roadmap was defined and executed to get the relationship back on track:

1. A *contact matrix* was drawn linking key people in all the three departments with relevant people from the vendor's side. The Technical team was matched with the paint shop, the Key Account Manager with the international collaborator and the Marketing Manager with the VP, Purchasing.

2. The team *owned the relationship* and formal meetings were designed ensuring regular contacts with the concerned people. Weekly reports were sent to the international collaborators giving them status updates. Production throughput was monitored and analyzed on a daily basis with paint shop. Purchase was kept updated on new activities in the paint shop. A tour of the paint shop was given to key people in the Purchasing department.

3. Most importantly, *delivery was monitored to match value drivers*. Production throughput delivery and paint shop operational control was instituted and monitored.

◻ SUMMARY

With focus on "production" instead of trouble-shooting, the production throughput improved substantially in the paint shop. The controls and regular reporting in place the operation of the paint shop was smooth. The team was focused on the value drivers. The relationship was back on track. The Purchase department who had obtained a price reduction from all the vendors was happy with a token price reduction from the vendor.

The threat of competitive entry was stalled and trust was largely re-instituted in the relationship. The stage was set to move up to the next level on the relationship chain.

REFERENCES

Cheverton, Peter (1999), 'Key Account Management—The Route to Profitable Key Supplier Status', London: Kogan page.

Chapter 34

Value and Stability of Cooperative Buyer-Seller Relationships in Industrial Markets: An Empirical Study

■ **T Werani**

Abstract

Relationship value is one of the most important topics within the scope of relationship management. Therefore, this paper on the one hand aims at defining and measuring the value of cooperative buyer-seller relationships. On the other hand measurement results are integrated in a theory-based model of relationship stability. Research results for a sample of 309 Austrian managers holding marketing and procurement positions, respectively, show that the value of cooperative business relationships is mainly determined by benefit and less by cost aspects. Furthermore, it turns out that value-based management of cooperative business relationships can be considered as an important determinant of relationship stability.

Key Words: *Cooperative Buyer-Seller Relationships, Relationship Value, Value Concept, Value Measurement, Relationship Stability*

☐ INTRODUCTION

Cooperative buyer-seller relationships in industrial markets have become increasingly important during the last years, although they are by no means new management concepts. This rise in importance particularly seems to be due to the fact that cooperation became instruments of strategy (Wilson and Möller, 1995). It follows from the strategic role of cooperation that both buyer and seller should be interested in an enduring interaction. This leads us to the question for the determinants of the stability of cooperative buyer-seller relationships. Thus, it is the aim of this paper to develop and empirically test a model of relationship stability. Since we expect relationship value to be of crucial importance for the management and, finally, the stability of cooperative buyer-seller relationships (Wilson, 1995; Anderson, 1995), value is measured from both buyer and seller perspective and measurement results are integrated in the proposed model of relationship stability.

□ THEORETICAL BACKGROUND AND HYPOTHESES

Cooperative Business Relationships

Business relationships between buyers and sellers play a key role within the intensive discussion on relationship management both in academic theory and business practice. However, in many cases a biased understanding of business relationships can be stated that may be characterized as follows: Business relationships are of importance where buyer and seller have a very closed relation, adapt their behavior to each other, negotiate about relatively high value volumes, have to deal cooperatively with complex transaction situations, or where similar conditions apply (Engelhardt and Freiling, 1995). While such situations often may occur in industrial markets, they do not justify the general identification of business relationships with cooperative business relationships since disregarding the manifold spectrum of buyer-seller relations (Campbell, 1985) leads to a problematic understanding of relationship management. To our mind, a cooperative business relationship differs from the general understanding of a business relationship by the specific quality of the interaction process. To describe this quality, the following five hypotheses are formulated:

H_1: Cooperative as compared with non-cooperative business relationships are characterized by a higher degree of long-term orientation.

H_2: Cooperative as opposed to non-cooparative business relationships involve higher relationship-specific investments.

H_3: In cooperative business relationships contractual safeguarding plays a minor role than in non-cooperative relationships.

H_4: Cooperative business relationships are characterized by a higher frequency of interaction than non-cooperative business relationships.

H_5: In cooperative business relationships contact persons change less frequently than in non-cooperative relationships.

Decision Theoretic Value Concept and Definition of the Concept of Relationship Value

While dealing with the value of (cooperative) business relationships is still in its early stages, in the fifties and sixties of the last century an intensive discussion of the value concept from the perspective of the firm took place in the German-language literature on business administration. In this context, four general views about the nature of value can be identified (Wittmann, 1956; Engels, 1962): value objectivism, identification of value with price, value as subject-object relation, and a value concept based on decision theory. The latter is a further development of the notion of value as subject-object relation, originating from the work of Engels (1962), and is discussed in more detail below.

The decision theoretic value concept (Engels, 1962; Stützel, 1976; Wöhe, 1986; Roeb, 1994) starts out from the notion that the value of economic goods is always the result of a rational calculation of the valuing person against the background of given goals, alternatives and environmental variables and, therefore, is a measure of preferability. Since alternatives and environmental variables have to be considered to be given, the goals, which are to be reached by the respective economic goods, remain as variable determinants of value. These goals are subjectively determined and axioms in the sense that they are not particularly scrutinized. While the decision theoretic value thus in this respect has subjective nature, it is diametrically opposed to purely subjective value on the other hand: it represents objective value in so far as it can be examined intersubjectively, i.e. can be calculated by everyone, provided that the respective goal function, alternatives and environmental variables are known.

To sum up, the decision theoretic value is a measure of the preferability of a particular alternative in a specific decision situation. This raises the question how to operationalize this measure adequately. Since from the perspective of a firm acting on the basis of the economic principle any alternative that comes into consideration in a decision situation has to be judged with regard to resources employed and resulting benefits (Löffelholz, 1967), the decision theoretic value can be defined as follows (Mühleder, 1996, p. 27):

$$\text{Value} = \frac{\text{Benefits}}{\text{Sacrifice}} \tag{1}$$

Thus, out of a set of alternatives the one will be preferable that results in the relatively largest ratio of benefits and sacrifice. It has to be mentioned that several authors (e.g. Mellerowicz, 1952; Löffelholz, 1967) consider benefits and sacrifice to be constituent for a firm's value creation without reasoning on the basis of the decision theoretic approach. Therefore, this approach needs not necessarily to be present, if value is defined according to formula (1). On the other hand, it becomes apparent that defining value as ratio or difference between benefits and sacrifice[1] is an appropriate, but not the only possible proceeding.

With reference to the decision theoretic approach, we define the value of a cooperative business relationship as follows:

The value of a cooperative business relationship is a measure of its preferability in a specific decision situation. It has its origin in cooperative buyer-seller interaction and results from the difference between estimated relationship benefits and sacrifice.

The difference between our understanding of relationship value and a number of alternative approaches focused on industrial markets (Wilson and Jantrania, 1994; Biong, Parvatiyar, and Wathne, 1996; Ford and McDowell, 1997) especially is that the latter disregard relationship sacrifice. Thus, these approaches only conceptualize relationship benefits, but not relationship value.

Determinants of the Stability of Cooperative Business Relationships

Interaction processes between buyers and sellers in industrial markets comprise not only economic exchange but social exchange in general. Therefore, theories from social psychology, which deal with stay/leave decisions of interaction partners, form an appropriate basis for a model that integrates various determinants of the stability of cooperative business relationships and in particular enables the empirical assessment of the effects of relationship value on relationship stability.

In their version of social exchange theory Thibaut and Kelley (1959) suggest two standards for the evaluation of relationship outcome and, therefore, relationship value: the comparison level (CL) and the comparison level for alternatives (CL_{alt}). The CL arises out of the sum of own experiences in relationships and knowledge concerning other relationships which one has observed or read about. It reflects the expectations of a relationship partner and for this reason is the standard against which the satisfaction with the relationship is evaluated: Relationship outcomes above CL are experienced as relatively satisfying, and those below CL are perceived to be unsatisfactory. On the other hand, the CL_{alt} is defined as the best currently available alternative to the present relationship. The less the probable outcome in the current relationship exceeds CL_{alt}, the more the partners will be tempted to leave the relationship. Hence, the difference between present relationship outcome and CL_{alt} defines the level of dependence on the relationship. In the end, relationship stability is determined by the interplay of satisfaction and dependence: A partner who is satisfied with the relationship is usually dependent on it.

More recently, Thibaut and Kelley's theory has been extended by Rusbult (1980, 1983). Her "Investment Model" basically suggests that commitment to a relationship (which equals dependence in Thibaut and Kelley's framework) is not only determined by relationship satisfaction and available alternatives but also by the investments put into a relationship. The more heavily invested a person is in a relationship, the higher this person's commitment will be. Investments in a relationship may either be extrinsic (e.g. shared possessions) or intrinsic (e.g. emotional energy), and will be lost, if the relationship terminates. Therefore, if there are such investments, the partners concerned will hesitate to leave the relationship, since this would mean losing the resources invested. With regard to commitment one has to distinguish two aspects. While the personal commitment is determined by relationship satisfaction, available alternatives together with investments control the structural commitment (Söllner, 1993).

Both social exchange theory and Rusbult's model focus on past relationships and alternatives to present relationships. However, it also seems possible to compare what one partner receives from a relationship with what the other partner gets out of it. This point is taken up especially by equity theory (Walster, Walster, and Berscheid 1978). The theory states that an equitable relationship exists if all participants, in terms of inputs into and outcomes from the exchange, are receiving equal relative gains. Since it is maintained that any deviation from this ideal leads to lower relationship satisfaction, it becomes clear that relationship equity via the development of satisfaction is a further determinant of personal commitment and, therefore, finally relationship stability.

The foregoing discussion provides the theoretical basis for the following hypotheses that underlie our model of relationship stability:

H_1: The more the present relationship value exceeds the comparison level (CL), the higher will be the degree of relationship satisfaction.

H_2: The more the present relationship value exceeds the comparison level for alternatives (CL_{alt}), the higher will be the commitment towards the relationship.

H_3: The higher the degree of relationship satisfaction, the higher will be the commitment towards the relationship.

H_4: The higher the commitment towards the relationship, the more stable the relationship will be.

H_5: The more extrinsic nonretrievable investments are tied in a relationship, the higher will be the commitment towards the relationship.

H_6: The more intrinsic nonretrievable investments are tied in a relationship, the higher will be the commitment towards the relationship.

H_7: The more equitable a relationship, the higher will be the degree of relationship satisfaction.

Since according to Michaels, Acock and Edwards (1986) relationship duration may also be considered as a determinant of commitment, the last hypothesis is:

H_8: The longer the duration of a relationship, the higher will be the commitment towards the relationship.

❑ DATA COLLECTION

Data collection was done by a completely standardized mail survey and restricted to Austrian companies acting predominantly as manufacturers in industrial markets. On the basis of the *Hoppenstedt Company-Database Austria* 312 managers holding marketing positions ("seller survey") and 176 managers holding procurement positions ("buyer survey") were contacted, who acted as key informants for the cooperative business relationships under consideration. In this context, we abstracted from specific types of cooperative relationships and did not focus on particular industries. Respondents were asked to select a cooperative relationship for judgement in which the respective buyer or seller is predominantly acting as manufacturer, too. Furthermore, to avoid that every respondent chose his or her favorite business partner, respondents were randomly assigned to one of three groups. The groups were asked to assess a business relationship with which they are highly, on average, and less satisfied, respectively. An effective sample of 309 usable questionnaires was obtained, with the seller survey resulting in 208 and the buyer survey in 101 responses. This equals an adjusted response rate of 67.1% for the seller survey and 58.4% for the buyer survey[2].

❑ TESTS OF HYPOTHESES ON COOPERATIVE BUSINESS RELATIONSHIPS

Hypotheses testing was carried out via paired t-tests and the results[3] are summarized in Table 1. Since for each hypothesis the means, that are based on a 7-point rating scale, differ significantly in the expected direction, all formulated hypotheses are confirmed. Thus, both from buyer and seller perspective cooperative as compared with non-cooperative business relationships are characterized by a higher degree of long-term orien-

Table 1 *Characteristics of Cooperative Business Relationships*

Characteristic (Hypothesis)		Mean Cooperative vs. Non-cooperative Business Relationship		t-Value	One-sided Significance
Long-term orientation (H₁)	(B)	5.42	2.53	16.99	**
	(S)	5.68	2.58	30.34	**
Relationship-specific investments (H₂)	(B)	4.27	3.21	5.73	**
	(S)	4.80	3.08	13.14	**
Contractual safeguarding (H₃)	(B)	4.46	4.93	-2.39	**
	(S)	4.17	4.84	-4.47	**
Frequency of interaction (H₄)	(B)	4.47	3.74	4.46	**
	(S)	4.94	3.42	12.61	**
Change of contact persons (H₅)	(B)	2.36	5.64	-22.87	**
	(S)	2.71	5.34	-23.59	**

(B) = Buyer survey; (S) = Seller survey; ** = $p < .01$

tation, higher relationship-specific investments, lower importance of contractual safeguarding, higher frequency of interaction, and less frequently changing contact persons.

☐ MEASUREMENT OF RELATIONSHIP VALUE: BUYER PERSPECTIVE

Conjoint analysis was used to measure the value of cooperative business relationships on a non-monetary basis. For the buyer survey the required relationship scenarios that reflect different constellations of cooperative business relationships with sellers were based on the relationship value concept from buyer perspective, which was developed in a preceding base study (Werani, 1998) and comprises one sacrifice and four benefit dimensions. Our proceeding was to work out relevant relationship attributes on the basis of these dimensions and to define adequate attribute levels afterwards. Using the Orthoplan module in SPSS®, twenty-five relationship scenarios were generated. Group results of conjoint analysis for the buyer sample, which are based on the respondents' preferences for the relationship scenarios, are summarized in Table 2.

The utilities in Table 2 indicate that from buyer perspective the value of a cooperative business relationship reaches its maximum if the relationship is characterized by strong increase of competitiveness of the own company, technology and know-how transfer that happens relatively often, strong economic effects, increased mutual trust, and medium coordination costs. In this context it has to be pointed out that the relation between attribute levels and relationship value does not always follow a linear pattern.

Relative importance shows that the extent of coordination costs has the smallest influence on relationship value, which corresponds to the results of an expert-opinion survey in the preceding base study (Werani, 1998)[4].

Table 2 *Results of Relationship Value Measurement — Buyer Sample*

Relationship Attribute/Attribute Level	Utility	Relative Importance
Increase of Competitiveness of Own Company		32.96%
no increase	−4.06	
small increase	−1.11	
medium increase	1.57	
strong increase	3.60	
Transfer of Technology and Know-how Through Joint		10.40%
Product Development		
happens never	−1.54	
happens from time to time	.10	
happens relatively often	.88	
happens permanently	.56	
Economic Effects (Like Increase in Productivity, etc.)		20.29%
for Own Company		
no effects	−2.53	
weak effects	−.59	
medium effects	.93	
strong effects	2.19	
Relations With Seller		26.20%
no mutual trust	−3.62	
little mutual trust	−1.06	
increased mutual trust	2.47	
very strong mutual trust	2.21	
Coordination Costs Within Own Company and Between		10.15%
Own Company and the Partner		
small costs	.71	
medium costs	.82	
high costs	−1.53	

Kendall's tau = .95 (p = .00)

▢ MEASUREMENT OF RELATIONSHIP VALUE: SELLER PERSPECTIVE

For the seller survey the development of relationship scenarios, which reflect different constellations of cooperative business relationships with buyers, was done analogously to the proceeding for the buyer sample. Starting out from the relationship value concept from seller perspective (Werani, 1998), which comprises one sacrifice and three benefit dimensions, sixteen relationship scenarios were generated that had to be ranked by the respondents. Table 3 presents group results of conjoint analysis for the seller sample.

The utilities in Table 3 show that from seller perspective the value of a cooperative business relationship is maximized if it is characterized by strong strengthening of the strategic position in the industry through trusting relations, strong economic effects, joint development of ideas and products that happens relatively often, and small coordination costs. Again, the relation between attribute levels and relationship value does not always follow a linear pattern. Just as in the buyer survey relative importance indicates that relationship value is least influenced by the extent of coordination costs.

Table 3 *Results of Relationship Value Measurement — Seller Sample*

Relationship Attribute/Attribute Level	Utility	Relative Importance
Strengthening of Strategic Position in the Industry		
Through Trusting Relations		35.75%
no strengthening	−3.15	
small strengthening	−.90	
medium strengthening	1.27	
strong strengthening	2.78	
Economic Effects (Like Increase in Productivity, etc.)		
for Own Company		23.63%
no effects	−2.02	
weak effects	−.91	
medium effects	1.03	
strong effects	1.90	
Joint Development of Ideas and Products		22.12%
happens never	−2.57	
happens from time to time	.43	
happens relatively often	1.10	
happens permanently	1.04	
Coordination Costs Within Own Company and Between		
Own Company and the Partner		18.50%
small costs	1.30	
medium costs	.46	
high costs	−1.76	

Kendall's tau = .98 (p = .00)

☐ TEST OF THE MODEL OF RELATIONSHIP STABILITY

The hypotheses underlying the proposed model of relationship stability were tested using LISREL®. Results are presented for the seller survey since the buyer sample was too small for testing all hypotheses.

As a first step, reliability and validity of the measurement model were analyzed through confirmatory factor analysis[5]. Results (composite reliability > .67, AVE > .52; c^2/df = 1.43, RMSEA = .05, CFI = .99, GFI = .97, AGFI = .96) point to an adequate measurement model, which on the basis of the chi-square difference test also fulfills the requirements for discriminant validity. With regard to the assessment of relationship value effects within the model of relationship stability it has to be mentioned that for each of the two constructs "present relationship value given CL" and "present relationship value given CL_{alt}" one indicator was computed on the basis of the disaggregated conjoint analysis results for the seller sample. This ensures a direct connection between value measurement and the model of relationship stability.

Since the measurement model turned out to be consistent with the data, subsequently the structural model could be tested. All criteria (χ^2/df = 1.37, RMSEA = .04, CFI = .99, GFI = .97, AGFI = .96) point to a satisfying model fit.

On the basis of the standardized path coefficients in Figure 1 the hypotheses H_1 through H_4 can be confirmed. In particular it becomes apparent that the judgement of relationship value against the two standards CL and CL_{alt} determines the commitment towards a cooperative relationship both indirectly (effect size = .37) and directly (effect size = .32). Commitment in turn can be considered as effective predictor of relationship stability (R^2 = 62.1%).

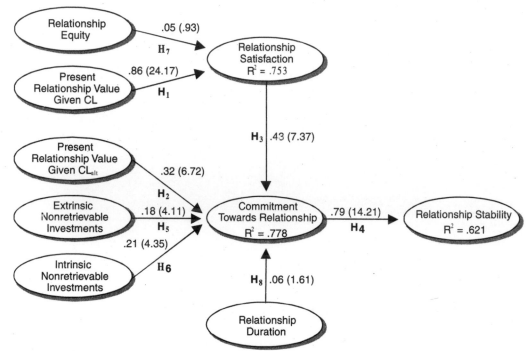

.xx (y.yy) = standardized path coefficient (*t*-value); R^2 = variance explained

Fig. 1 *Results of Testing the Model of Relationship Stability*

Testing the hypotheses H_7 and H_8 shows that both relationship equity and relationship duration influence their target constructs (relationship satisfaction and commitment, respectively) in the expected direction but not significantly ($t < 1.96$). On the other hand the hypotheses H_5 and H_6 can be confirmed since both extrinsic and intrinsic nonretrievable investments exercise a significant positive influence on the commitment towards a relationship.

To sum up, for the seller sample the proposed model of relationship stability can be completely confirmed on the basis of the direction of the expected effects. Moreover, all path coefficients with the exception of hypotheses H_7 and H_8 are significant. Not least, the adequacy of the model becomes apparent in the high degree of variance explained for the three target constructs relationship satisfaction, commitment towards relationship, and relationship stability.

□ MANAGERIAL IMPLICATIONS

The empirical results lead to the following conclusions for management practice:

1. Relationship value measurement through conjoint analysis has demonstrated that the value of cooperative business relationships is mainly determined by benefit and less by cost aspects. While the minor importance of relationship costs may be explained by the fact that the realization of relationship management concepts, at least in Austria, is still in its early and "euphoric" stages, attention should be drawn to the notion of relationships as investments: Within the scope of relationship controlling any (cooperative) business relationship should be evaluated on the basis of its benefit-cost ratio.

2. Value-based relationship management finally leads to stable cooperative business relationships. In order to be able to judge the adequacy of relationship value for the partner it is necessary to know about his alternatives to the present relationship and his minimum expectations regarding relationship value. This requires an intensive and open communication of the relationship partners and refers to the fact that value-based management of cooperative business relationships may necessitate a revision of current management practice.

3. Since both relationship satisfaction, which determines personal commitment, and all constructs controlling structural commitment (present relationship value given CL_{alt}, extrinsic and intrinsic nonretrievable investments) show significant effects, it becomes apparent that personal as well as structural commitment exercise a strong influence on relationship stability. Therefore, if a partner acts in an opportunistic way and takes advantage of structural bonds, such a strategy can only be temporarily "successful" since the relationship inevitably is destabilized by a decrease in personal commitment.

4. From the seller perspective, extrinsic and intrinsic nonretrievable investments are important determinants of structural commitment and, consequently, relationship stability. Therefore, a buyer who is interested in a stable cooperative business relationship should aim at motivating his supplier to invest in the relationship, e.g. by means of an initial investment which builds trust.

□ NOTES

As compared to formula (1), the value quantity changes mathematically but not in substance by looking at the difference between benefits and sacrifice.

The high response rates are explained by the fact that we contacted those persons who agreed in a preceding base study (Werani, 1998) to participate in the second research step discussed here.

The results also refer to respondents who participated only in the base study (Werani, 1998) preceding the second research step presented here.

Because of the correspondence of qualitative and quantitative research results it is unlikely that the low importance of the cost factor is caused by the difference in the number of attribute levels (e.g. Wittink, Krishnamurthi, and Reibstein, 1989) in our conjoint design.

Because of the specific data basis (Werani, 1998, p. 204) the ULS method was used for parameter estimation.

REFERENCES

Anderson, J. C. (1995), 'Relationships in Business Markets: Exchange Episodes, Value Creation, and Their Empirical Assessment,' *Journal of the Academy of Marketing Science*, Vol. 23, No. 4, pp. 346-350.

Biong, H., Parvatiyar, A., and Wathne, K. (1996), 'Why Do Some Companies not Engage in Partnering Relationships?' in *Proceedings of the 12th International Conference on Industrial Marketing and* H. G. Gemünden, T. Ritter, and A. Walter, *Purchasing: Interaction, Relationships and Networks*, Vol. 2, eds., Karlsruhe: University of Karlsruhe, pp. 733-753.

Campbell, N. C. G. (1985), 'An Interaction Approach to Organizational Buying Behavior,' *Journal of Business Research*, Vol. 13, pp. 35-48.

Engelhardt, W. H. and Freiling, J. (1995), 'Integrativität als Brücke zwischen Einzeltransaktion und Geschäftsbeziehung', *Marketing - Zeitschrift für Forschung und Praxis*, Vol. 17, No. 1, pp. 37-43.

Engels, W. (1962), *Betriebswirtschaftliche Bewertungslehre im Licht der Entscheidungstheorie*, Köln/Opladen: Westdeutscher Verlag.

Ford, D. and McDowell, R. (1997), 'Why Do They Do That?: The Ideas which Underlie Relationship Value,' *Work-in-Progress Paper presented at 13th IMP Conference*, Lyon.

Löffelholz, J. (1967), *Repetitiorium der Betriebswirtschaftslehre*, 2nd ed., Wiesbaden: Gabler.

Mellerowicz, K. (1952), *Wert und Wertung im Betrieb*, Essen: Girardet.

Michaels, J. W., Acock, A. C., and Edwards, J. N. (1986), 'Social Exchange and Equity Determinants of Relationship Commitment,' *Journal of Social and Personal Relationships*, Vol. 3, pp. 161-175.

Mühleder, K. (1996), 'Wertgestaltung - Ein Beitrag zur Gestaltung von Produktinnovationen,' *Journal für Betriebswirtschaft*, Vol. 46, No. 1, pp. 23-35.

Roeb, T. (1994), *Markenwert: Begriff, Berechnung, Bestimmungsfaktoren*, Aachen: Mainz.

Rusbult, C. E. (1980), 'Commitment and Satisfaction in Romantic Associations: A Test of the Investment Model,' *Journal of Experimental Social Psychology*, Vol. 16, pp. 172-186.

Rusbult, C. E. (1983), 'A Longitudinal Test of the Investment Model: The Development (and Deterioration) of Satisfaction and Commitment in Heterosexual Involvements,' *Journal of Personality and Social Psychology*, Vol. 45, No. 1, pp. 101-117.

Söllner, A. (1993), *Commitment in Geschäftsbeziehungen – Das Beispiel Lean Production*, Wiesbaden: Gabler.

Stützel, W. (1976), 'Wert und Preis,' in *Handwörterbuch der Betriebswirtschaft*, 4th ed., E. Grochla and W. Wittmann, eds., Stuttgart: C. E. Poeschel, pp. 4404-4425.

Thibaut, J. W. and Kelley, H. H. (1959), *The Social Psychology of Groups*, New York: Wiley.

Walster, E., Walster, G. W., and Berscheid, E. (1978), *Equity: Theory and Research*, Boston et al.: Allyn and Bacon.

Werani, T. (1998), *Der Wert von kooperativen Geschäftsbeziehungen in industriellen Märkten – Bedeutung, Messung und Wirkungen*, Linz: Trauner.

Wilson, D. T. (1995), 'An Integrated Model of Buyer-Seller Relationships,' *Journal of the Academy of Marketing Science*, Vol. 23, No. 4, pp. 335-345.

Wilson, D. T. and Jantrania, S. (1994), 'Understanding the Value of a Relationship,' *Asia-Australia Marketing Journal*, Vol. 2, No. 1, pp. 55-66.

Wilson, D. T. and Möller, K. (1995), 'Dynamics of Relationship Development,' in *Business Marketing: An* K. Möller and D. T. Wilson, *Interaction and Network Perspective*, eds., Boston: Kluwer Academic Publishers, pp. 53-69.

Wittink, D. R., Krishnamurthi, L., and Reibstein, D. J. (1989), 'The Effect of Differences in the Number of Attribute Levels on Conjoint Results,' *Marketing Letters*, Vol. 1, No. 2, pp. 113-123.

Wittmann, W. (1956), *Der Wertbegriff in der Betriebswirtschaftslehre*, Köln/Opladen: Westdeutscher Verlag.

Wöhe, G. (1986), *Einführung in die Allgemeine Betriebswirtschaftslehre*, 16th ed., München: Vahlen.

Chapter 35

The Global Account Manager as Political-Entrepreneur

■ **Kevin Wilson and Tony Millman**

Abstract

Our early work in Key Account Management (KAM) led to the development of a Relationship Development Model that provided the basis for much of the work of other researchers in the field of KAM. More recently we have turned our attention to the emerging management task of Global Account Management (GAM).

*A major concern of our GAM studies has been the nature of the role of the global account manager and we have developed a number of models that explore the notion of the global account manager as **Political Entrepreneur.***

The aim of this paper is to introduce a Contextual Model of Political-Entrepreneurial Behaviour and to integrate this with our previously published work on the Political Entrepreneur, the Model of Global Account Manager Boundary Spanning Behaviour and the Relationship Development Model.

Key Words: *Global Account Management, Relationship, Political Entrepreneur*

□ INTRODUCTION

A recurring question emerging from our research, consultancy, and management training workshops on global account management (GAM), is: What is the nature of the role performed by global account managers?

Global account managers are normally recruited/promoted from *within* multinational selling companies, typically from the pool of national account/sales managers, on the assumption that thorough knowledge and experience of the company's organisation and products/services is an essential prerequisite. They perform a boundary-spanning role across two important organisational interfaces: first, the *internal* interface between global and national account management, which is often embedded in a headquarters/subsidiary relationship; and second, the *external* interface between the selling company and the dispersed activities of its global accounts. Were the role only concerned with boundary spanning, then it would be little different, although with added degrees of complexity, from the role performed by general line sales people. Its obvious complexity and developing strategic importance suggests that we may be witnessing the emergence of a fundamentally new managerial position. In recognition of the need to navigate sensitive commercial/political aspects of these interface relationships, we have dubbed the global account manager as performing the role of *political entrepreneur*.

In an earlier paper (Millman and Wilson 2000) we have explored the boundary-spanning roles that may be played by the global account manager in terms of the degree of identification they might display towards their own organisation and that of the global account. In this paper we will build upon that discussion and introduce a model that explores the degree to which the application of political and entrepreneurial skills may be impacted upon by contextual factors, and how the application of these skills may be related to stages of relational development.

The nature of the global account manager role and how it is performed has significant implications for companies seeking to recruit, develop and retain global account managers. Further, an understanding of the contextual factors that impact upon the role will influence the way they are deployed and how effectively they perform the role to enhance the quality and profitability of relational interaction.

Our paper commences with a critical review of the literature on boundary-spanning roles and goes on to explore recent thinking around the relationship skills that are required for strategic account management in a global context (Wilson et al 2000). Our recent exploratory research on GAM interface relationships is then interpreted using two conceptual models. The first revisits our previous work (Millman and Wilson 2000) and emphasises global account manager dilemmas and transitions at the external interface and the second examines the application of political and entrepreneurial skills within the context of developing relationships. These capture the essence of the global account manager as political entrepreneur, giving due consideration to contextual factors such as organisational complexity, cultural diversity and industrial setting.

□ AN OVERVIEW OF THE LITERATURE

Boundary–spanning roles

The notion of "boundary-spanning" has its origins in *open systems* approaches to strategic management and marketing, typically centring on the process of internal organisational adaptation to external environmental change. People occupying the role of boundary-spanner have been variously described as "linking pins", "information brokers", "gate keepers" providing "human bridges", and the organisation's "antenna in the external business environment".

Our current focus is the boundary-spanning role performed by global account managers, though we recognise that there are many other people whose primary role involves face-to-face interaction with customers (e.g. senior marketing/sales executives, project managers, sales staff, customer service/support staff, applications development engineers, public relations officers). There are also internally-based staff who, perhaps, have less face-to-face contact, but occupy an important relationship-building role nevertheless (e.g. in sales administration, distribution, credit control). Most of the early literature, however, resides within sales management and explores the well-worn track of role conflict and ambiguity (see Belasco, 1966; Blake and Mouton, 1970; Walker et al, 1995; Aldrich and Herker, 1977; Singh and Rhoads, 1991; Singh, 1993). These writers raise a number of pertinent issues which may be translated to the role of global account managers:

"...one reason why the sales person is susceptible to high levels of role conflict and ambiguity is that he occupies a boundary position in his firm and, therefore, has a large and diverse role set, i.e. people in related positions, both within and outside his company, who depend on his performance in some fashion... and are rewarded by it or require it to perform their own tasks" (Walker et al, 1975, p33).

"Boundary roles involved with maintaining or improving the political legitimacy or hegemony of the organization not only represent the organization but also mediate between it and important outside organizations" (Aldrich and Herker, 1997, p 220).

"...in comparison with role conflict, role ambiguity is more amenable to managerial intervention" (Singh and Rhoades, 1991, p 329).

"...whether boundary spanners can discriminate *empirically* among what researchers see as *conceptually* distinct facets of role ambiguity is unknown" (Singh and Rhoads, 1991, p 329).

"Because of the nature and complexity of boundary-spanning roles it is probably futile and perhaps counterproductive to expend resources on programs that eliminate role ambiguity ... managers may find it rewarding to put their efforts behind programs that reduce and/or help boundary spanners to cope with ambiguity in *specific facets of their role*", e.g. targeting boss and company-related ambiguities or designing jobs with greater autonomy (Singh, 1993, p 27).

The potential for role ambiguity and conflict is increased in the boundary-spanning role performed by global account managers because of the complexity of the co-ordinating function they perform. Not only are they expected to co-ordinate the activities of their own organisation in delivering the *global promise*, but very often those of their customer and with little direct authority over those charged with the local implementation of global strategy.

Role of the Global Account Manager

"A Global Account is one that is of strategic importance to the achievement of the supplier's corporate objectives, pursues integrated and co-ordinated strategies on a world wide basis and demands a globally integrated product/service offering". Wilson et al (2000).

The role and competencies required of the global account manager have received our increasing attention in recent years (see Millman, 1996, 1999; Millman and Wilson, 1996,

1998, 1999; Wilson et al, 2000). While we can claim to have achieved modest success in teasing out and prioritising lists of desirable personal attributes/traits and skills/competencies, we have also been drawn irresistibly towards some of the softer, higher order *meta-skills/competencies* that separate out the few highly effective global account managers from the mediocre. As the title of our paper suggests, this has led us to those particular meta-skills/competencies that underpin the role of the global account manager as *political entrepreneur*.

The following extracts capture our earlier thoughts on what this role entails:

Millman and Wilson (1999) suggest that global account managers require "... finely tuned political instincts that enable them to navigate the corridors of power, to reconcile conflicting interests, and to enlist the support of people at all levels".

Millman (2000) alludes to the "... political/cultural milieu" at the buyer/seller interface and coping with the unrelenting pressures of different time zones".

Wilson, Croom, Millman and Weilbaker (2000) envisage the global account manager as "... knowing the people to speak to, the buttons to press and the strings to pull, both in their own organisation and that of the customer".

As we, and our fellow researchers, proceeded with qualitative research, a tentative typology of global account managers began to emerge which enabled us to present a clearer picture of what we mean by political entrepreneur (Croom et al, 1999). These three manager types were labelled *Analyst, Politician,* and *Entrepreneurial Strategist.* The skill sets associated with these types were seen as being both hierarchical and cumulative. Hierarchical in the sense that Analysts tend to be relatively new to GAM and are primarily sales oriented, while Politicians and Entrepreneurial Strategists tend to possess broader business experience, together with higher levels of managerial/commercial know-how and sophistication. The cumulative component is important in that the Entrepreneurial Strategist must also develop analytical and political skills.

Analysts tend to be team-orientated trouble-shooters typically possessing outstanding knowledge of products/services, technologies, and customer industries. Many Analysts perceive themselves primarily as international sales managers focusing on global sales targets, sales from regional/national territories, share of customer spend, rather than upon opportunities for enhancing levels of value creation and customer profitability.

Politicians combine diplomatic and linguistic skills with cultural empathy and knowledge of global business trends/opportunities. They engage their senior managers in the GAM process where appropriate and are adept at achieving objectives via influence/persuasion.

Entrepreneurial Strategists operate with a fair degree of autonomy. They display high levels of business acumen and look beyond the confines of exchange relationships for business opportunities. They seek out synergistic potential through combining core competencies of their own organisation with those of their global account, even if this requires the formation of new ways of working and organisational entities

To these three typographies we would add the function of ***global co-ordinator***. At a basic level, where business/account objectives may be concerned with increasing global sales volume, the global account managers' role is concerned with co-ordinating the operational capabilities (manufacturing, logistics, billing, packaging etc.) of the supplier organisation to ensure that the customer receives a global offering that also conforms to local demand within a uniform pricing structure.

As the complexity and strategic importance of the role develops, co-ordination encompasses the realisation of synergies between individual, team and organisational competencies. Synergistic value and leverage is created through the co-ordination of these competencies to address operational and strategic orders of problem resolution that create cost savings, innovative ways of managing the value creation process, and the realisation of entrepreneurial opportunity. The main elements of this model and its contextual complexity are represented in Exhibit 1 below.

The role of the political entrepreneur in this typology is clearly a boundary-spanning role, performed at both the *internal* interface between global and local account management (embedded in the headquarters/subsidiary relationship) and at the *external* interface between the selling company and the dispersed activities of its global account. Our concern in this paper is to explore this role at both these interfaces. The internal interface is where much of the global account managers' ability to manage potential conflict/ambiguity depends on positive or negative perceptions of his/her mediating role and thus where political skills may be of primary importance. The external interface provides the forum within which both political and entrepreneurial skills may be applied.

Exhibit 1 identifies some of the diverse elements that the global account manager must deal with in order to manage the evolution of the relationship with the global customer. In achieving the level of integration and co-ordination necessary to realise the relationship's

Exhibit 1   *The Political Entrepreneur*

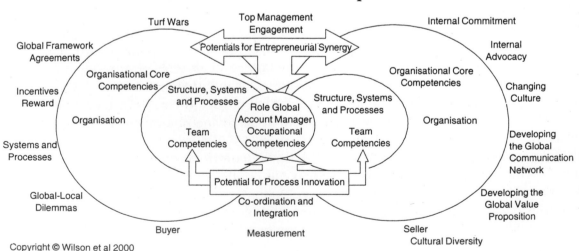

Copyright © Wilson et al 2000

value potential the global account manager must exhibit high levels of both political and entrepreneurial skill. The degree to which these skills are, or can be applied, will depend upon a number of factors:

The global capability of both buyer and supplier.

The willingness of buyer and seller to collaborate in some form of partnership.

The degree of organisational complexity and cultural diversity which surrounds the relationship.

The state of relational interdependence and entanglement (relational stage).

The boundary spanning behaviour adopted by the global account manager.

The interplay of the last three factors will provide the focus for discussion in this paper. Two conceptual models will be presented in an attempt to extend our understanding of the global account manager role and these will be linked to the Relational Development Model (Millman and Wilson 1995). The first is a summary of our previous work on boundary spanning roles (Millman and Wilson 2000), the second is our model of political-entrepreneurial behaviour, which explores the behavioural constraints imposed by the extent of relational intensity and organisational/cultural complexity.

☐ THE GLOBAL ACCOUNT MANAGER AS "POLITICAL ENTREPRENEUR"

A Model of Boundary-Spanning Behaviour

The boundary-spanning role of the global account manager is not merely concerned with the creation of interactive networks, but with identifying the potentials that exist for problem resolution and the creation of synergistic value. The performance of global account managers is firmly rooted in how well he/she is prepared for, adapts to, and performs the boundary-spinning role and how effectively they apply political and entrepreneurial skills.

In a recent paper (Millman and Wilson 2000) we proposed a conceptual model of role behaviour which incorporates career aspects of the employer/employee relationship yet allows us to elaborate on the political/entrepreneurial aspects of performing the global account manager's role in a multicultural environment. Our model—which we term an "Identification Space"—is represented graphically in Exhibit 2.

Exhibit 2 *A Model of Boundary-Spanning Behaviour*

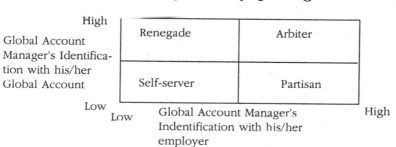

We identified four boundary-spanning behaviours that we classified as ***self-server; renegade; partisan*** and ***arbiter:***

The Self-server (Low/Low) feels closer affiliation to their personal career interests than to the interests of either their employer or their global account.

The Renegade (Low/High) displays strong affinity towards his/her account which may reflect close personal relationships and the attractiveness of the account, or its national home culture.

The Partisan (High/Low) shows a strong orientation towards their employer that may be linked to a perception that long term career prospects are tied to political developments at headquarters.

The Arbiter (High/High) role represents a well balanced global/local approach that effectively reconciles the tensions that exist between self interest and that of both the client and the employer.

The space occupied by the global account manager impacts strongly upon the role they perform and the way in which they perform it. The Self-server is likely to focus on analytical, political, and entrepreneurial capabilities largely for personal advantage. Renegades and Partisans are unlikely to realise the full potential of the buyer/seller relationship because their actions may undermine the interests of one or other of the parties. Both may be accomplished analysts and highly political in their activities; both may be adept at recognising and seizing entrepreneurial opportunity, and realising strategic intent; but neither may be able to exploit the synergistic potentials inherent in the balanced integration of buyer and seller competencies and interests.

We observe that analytical, political, entrepreneurial, and co-ordinating skills are best employed to create synergistic value for both buyer and seller when employed by the global account manager occupying the Arbiter space.

Many of the factors affecting identification, however, are outside the control of the global account manager, resources are limited, and access to individuals across dispersed sites varies considerably. At the individual level, changes in just a handful of key staff on both sides can dramatically alter the network of personal relationships. Indeed, one major source of anxiety among global account managers is the fear that many years of relationship building and commercial arrangements can be undone by dislocations related to mergers/acquisitions, strategic alliances, downsizing, de-layering etc. Operating in the role of Arbiter in the top right hand corner of the space, therefore, demands exceptional managerial/leadership skills to navigate a way through the political/cultural milieu and to identify/exploit opportunities to create superior customer value. Exhibit 3 summarises these issues.

Exhibit 3 *Political and Entrepreneurial Boundary–spanning Behaviour of Global Account Managers*

	Political Role	*Entrepreneurial Role*
Self-server	Acts to manipulate both buyer and seller for personal advantage and protection.	Seeks business opportunities to achieve personal Career aspirations and objectives.
Renegade	Manipulates supplier for the customer's with the customer's consideration of the corporate and/or national culture.	Identifies commercial advantage for the advantage. Identifies customer with little strategic/operational impact upon the seller.
Partisan	Attempts to increase personal standing with the seller. Identifies with the seller's corporate and/or national culture.	Identifies commercial advantage for the seller with little consideration of the strategic/ Operational impact upon the customer.
Arbiter	Facilitates achievement of relational and financial goals that benefit buyer, seller, *and* self. Builds multicultural Relationships and promotes meritocracy	Seeks business opportunities and perceives synergistic potentials of value to buyer, seller, *and* self. Geocentric approach to identifying/ transferring expertise and exploiting opportunities.

The degree to which the global account manager exercises political and entrepreneurial skills, whatever boundary-spanning behaviour they exhibit, will to a large degree be dependent upon contextual factors.

A Model of Global Account Manager Political and Entrepreneurial Behaviour

Exhibit 4 presents a model of global account manager behaviour that explores the impact of *context* upon the exercise of political and entrepreneurial capabilities. Two sets of factors are identified that prescribe the context in which the political entrepreneur operates. The first is the degree of organisational complexity and cultural diversity that surrounds the global relationship. Complexity and diversity depend upon two factors: Firstly, upon the span of the relationship (the geographical spread of organisational touch points that exist throughout the world). The second is the level of organisational penetration (the levels at which the global account manager operates both within their own and their client organisation).

Exhibit 4 *The Impact of Context on the Role of the Political Entrepreneur*

Levels of Organisational complexity and cultural diversity

High

Pe   **PE**

Low   **pe**   **pE**

High

Low   Degree of organisational interdependence and integration

Where the customer operates in many different countries and where those operations include multiple functions; where the global account manager is required to have many multifunctional relationships, at different levels within the client organisation, then the organisational context may be perceived as highly complex. Conversely, where there are few touch points and penetration is low, the organisational context is low in complexity.

We have observed that where the organisational context is complex, there tends to be higher levels of political activity with divergent views, competing factional interests and different cultural perspectives influencing the global buyer-seller relationship. In order to operate effectively within this context the global account manager must be capable of applying high levels of diplomacy, cultural sensitivity, networking and political skill. Thus in Exhibit 2 political behaviour is classified as *P*, denoting that high levels of political behaviour are required, or *p*, denoting a low requirement for political behaviour.

If the global account manager is to be able to identify entrepreneurial opportunity they must have a detailed knowledge of both their own organisation and that of their customer. They must have a detailed knowledge of organisational, team and individual competencies, the resources of both organisations and a clear understanding of the strategic imperatives facing the client. Such knowledge, which allows the identification of the potentials for problem resolution, process innovation and the creation of entrepreneurial value, grows as relationships evolve in terms of entanglement and interdependence.

Exhibit 4 shows the varying degrees of opportunity for exercising entrepreneurial capabilities depending upon the closeness of the buyer-seller relationship. Where the relationship is well developed the entrepreneurial opportunities are high, denoted by *E*, where new or underdeveloped, then those opportunities are low, denoted by *e*.

This provides four contrasting political-entrepreneurial behaviours identified as *pe, pE, Pe, and PE*. These have been linked to levels of organisational complexity and inter-organisational interdependence and the way in which these activities are manifested will also be effected by the nature of the boundary spanning role occupied by the global account manager.

◻ DISCUSSION AND INTEGRATION

The role of global account manager is an emerging one. The difficulties and complexities, as well as the strategic potential of the role are as yet poorly understood. A number of tentative observations may be drawn from the models we have presented here when they are related to the Millman-Wilson Relational Development Model that offer some insights into the nature of the role.

The Millman-Wilson (1995) model was based on exploratory research and concepts drawn from the sales strategy (Wotruba, 1991), supply chain management (Lamming, 1993) and interaction literature (Ford 1980 and Dwyer et al 1987). The model identified six stages in the development of key account relationships which may equally well be applied in the global context, as shown here:

- pre-GAM
- early-GAM
- mid-GAM
- partnership-GAM
- synergistic-GAM
- uncoupling-GAM

Each of these stages is characterised by varying degrees of dyadic complexity and closeness and each stage holds implications for relational strategists.

Consideration of the Relational Development Model may provide insights into the ways in which political and entrepreneurial skills may be applied and when the differing roles of arbiter, renegade, partisan and self server may legitimately be applied. Whilst these roles are a reflection of organisational commitment, and will impact upon the way in which political and entrepreneurial skills are applied within the relationship (Exhibit 3), they may also be adopted consciously by the global account manager to achieve particular goals.

The global account manager's role is more than that of boundary spanner. They are essentially concerned with identifying and exploiting entrepreneurial opportunity within the buyer-seller relationship. In order to achieve this they must develop a deep understanding of the core competencies of their own and their client organisations, be able to marshal those competencies through the application of both political and entrepreneurial capabilities.

At *pre-GAM* to *early-GAM* stages in the development of global relationships there is a need to develop networks of contacts, to gain knowledge about the customer's operations and to begin to assess the potential for relational development. It is unlikely that concepts of value potential can go much beyond assessing the global client's need for the basic product-service offering of the supplier. At this stage we suggest that the organisational-cultural context may be relatively simple and by definition the relationship is poorly developed. The demand for the application of political skills and the opportunity to apply entrepreneurial skills are both low *pe.* At this stage also the global account manager may occupy the renegade identification space in order to win the early trust of the account or be partisan until he is convinced of the potential for relational development.

From *early to mid-GAM* there is an increasing need for political skills to be applied as the potential of the account is identified and the global account manager is called upon to ensure that the resources of the supplier configure to best serve the needs of the customer. Detailed knowledge of the global customer and their core competencies, the depth of the relationship, and the potential for creating relationship specific entrepreneurial value, are all limited at this stage. The application of political and entrepreneurial skills is therefore rated as *Pe*. It is also suggested that at these stages the global account manager may play the *renegade* or the *partisan* depending upon whether he/she needs to develop trust within the account or guard against opportunistic behaviour. Depending upon the degree of trust that has been developed he/she may also begin to exhibit *arbiter* behaviour.

Mid to partnership-GAM may be characterised by the global account manager having developed a strong vertical and horizontal network of relationships within the client organisation. As the relationship has developed in closeness so the need to promote the client's interests within the selling company also recedes and political activity becomes less necessary in order to gain access to resources and support.

As the relationship has developed so has the knowledge about the account and in order to consolidate or grow the relationship further opportunities for joint value creation must be identified that go beyond the effective delivery of the global product/service offering. It is at this stage that entrepreneurial skill, in terms of being able to recognise the potential for creating new opportunities for value creation that address both the core competencies and the strategic interests of both buyer and seller, come into play. The importance of political-entrepreneurial skill application at this stage may be represented by *pE*.

The boundary-spanning role of the global account manager at this stage, and in the next, must be that of the *arbiter*. Whilst it is acknowledged that for a number of reasons we have explored previously, the account manager may act in other ways, in order to perform effectively within the context of the relationship he/she does best by adopting the arbiter role.

As the relationship develops through *partnership* into *synergistic-GAM* so the demand for political skill and the opportunity to apply entrepreneurial skill increases to be reflected in *PE*. The closer the relationship, the greater the knowledge about the customer and the greater the potential for creating entrepreneurial·value. At the same time, however, the realisation of entrepreneurial opportunity will involve fundamental changes in the way each organisation operates and the need for the application of political skill in driving those changes increases.

At any stage in the relationship it may become necessary to disengage and *uncoupling-GAM* occurs. It is suggested that when this stage is reached the global account manager may need high levels of political expertise *(Pe)* and will need to act in a partisan fashion in order to extricate his company from the relationship with the minimum of disruption and loss.

One final point. The Relational Development model is not intended to suggest that all relationships should, or can develop through all stages. Some will never develop beyond the pre-GAM stage, others will rest in the early stages of mid or partnership GAM and by their nature, very few will develop to synergistic GAM. What this suggests is that different relationship may allow for the employment of global account managers with different levels of political and entrepreneurial skill and with varying abilities to exhibit different boundary-spanning behaviours.

☐ CONCLUSION

In this paper we have explored the nature of the role performed by the global account manager as *Political-Entrepreneur*. Using a number of conceptual models we have identified dominant managerial role behaviours at the buyer-seller interface and provided insights into the kind of political and entrepreneurial meta-skills/competencies required in performing the boundary-spanning role. The occupation of these identification spaces and the application of political entrepreneurial skills have further been linked to the stage of development reached in the GAM relationship.

We are aware that in this newly emerging field we have merely scratched the surface of the role of the global account manager and hope that our work will serve to stimulate others to explore what we believe to be an important area of interest.

REFERENCES

Aldrich, H. and Herker, D (1977), 'Boundary-Spanning Roles and Organization Structure', *Academy of Management Review*, April, pp 217-230.

Belasco, J.A. (1966), 'The Salesman's Role Revisited'; *Journal of Marketing*, Vol 30 (April), pp. 6-8.

Blake, R.B. and Mouton, J.S. (1970),' *The Grid for Sales Excellence: Benchmarks for Effective Salesmanship'*, New York: McGraw-Hill.

Croom, S., Wilson, KJ., Millman, AF., Senn, C and Weilbaker, DC (1999),'How to Meet the Challenge of Managing Global Customers', *Velocity, Journal of the Strategic Account Management Association*, Vol. 1, No. 4, pp. 36-46.

Millman, A.F. (1996),'Global Account Management and Systems Selling', *International Business Review*, Vol. 5, No. 6, pp. 631-645.

Millman, A.F. (1999),'From National Account Management to Global Account Management in Business-to business Markets', *Fachzeitschrift fur Marketing*

THEXIS, Vol. 16, No. 4, pp. 2-9.

Millman, A.F. (2000),'How Well Does the Concept of Global Account Management Travel Across Cultures?', *Journal of Selling and Major Account Management,*

Vol. 2, No. 2 (Winter), pp. 31-46.

Millman, A.F. and Wilson, K.J. (1995),'From Key Account Selling to Key Account Management', *Journal of Marketing Science Issue 1*

Millman, A.F. and Wilson, K.J. (1996),'Developing Key Account Management Competencies', *Journal of Marketing Practice*,Vol. 2, No. 2, pp. 7-22.

Millman, A.F. and Wilson, K.J. (1998),'Global Account Management: Reconciling Organisational Complexity and Cultural Diversity', proceedings of the Fourteenth *Industrial Marketing and Purchasing (IMP)* Conference, Turku School of Economics and Business Administration, Finland, September.

Millman, A.F. and Wilson, K.J. (1999),'Developing Global Account Management Competencies"',proceedings of the Fifteenth *Industrial Marketing and Purchasing (IMP)* Conference, University College Dublin, Republic of Ireland, September.

Millman, A.F. and Wilson, K.J. (2000),'Career Development of Global Account Managers: The Dilemma of the Political Entrepreneur',Paper presented at the Sixteenth Annual Industrial Marketing and Purchasing (IMP) Conference, University of Bath, United Kingdom, September 2000.

Singh, J. (1993),'Boundary Role Ambiguity: Facets, Determinants, and Impacts', *Journal of Marketing*, Vol.57 (April), pp. 11-31.

Singh, J. and Rhoads, G.K. (1991),'Boundary Role Ambiguity in Marketing-Oriented Positions: A Multidimensional, Multifaceted Operationalization', *Journal of Marketing Research*, Vol. 28 (August), pp. 328-338.

Walker, O.C.., Churchill, G.A. and Ford, N.M. (1975),'Organizational Determinants of the Industrial Salesman's Role Conflict and Ambiguity', *Journal of Marketing*, Vol. 39 (January), pp. 32-39.

Wilson, K.J.., Croom, S., Millman, A.F. and Weilbaker, D.C. (2000),'The SRT-SAMA Global Account Management Study', *Journal of Selling and Major Account Management*, Vol. 2, No. 3 (Spring) 2000, pp. 63-93.

Chapter 36

Valuing Information in Transportation Logistics

■ **V Prem Kumar and Manabendra N. Pal**

Abstract

There has been a lot of debate on the importance of information and the expenditure incurred thereby for setting up an information system for a firm. We have attempted to determine the operational value of information in the transportation logistical scenario. We have transformed the conventional Vehicle Routing Problem (VRP) to a problem with associated penalties and found out a solution methodology for the same. We have utilised this problem to find the marginal difference in expenditure incurred by the firm because of the absence of information and otherwise. This accumulated difference of expenditure should be more than the cost of setting up the information system and, thus, provide a benchmark for the decision-makers. The implementation work is on progress, but this approach is intuitively favourable.

Key Words: _Vehicle Routing, Penalty Cost, Optimisation, Information Valuation, Heuristic, Scheduling._

□ INTRODUCTION

Information is one of the most important parameter in any logistical situation. Information sharing is commonly observed between the supplier, manufacturer and retailer setup and it assumes importance when dealing with customised products. It is absolutely true that information sharing is always beneficial, but it still remains to be seen when the benefits derived are massive and when they are marginal. We are attempting to study the quantification of benefits arising as a result of Electronic Data Interchange (EDI) in the transportation of finished goods. This can help the decision-makers to justify the investments for Electronic Data Processing (EDP) and communication systems for the supply chain.

There has been little previous research in the area of information valuation in logistical situations. But incidentally, a lot of work has been done in the area of incorporation of information flow into inventory control and production planning circumstances.

We study the differences in costs, relating to situations where the manufacturer has complete information about the demands at the different retailers vis-à-vis where he makes intelligent surmises about the demands at different retailer locations based on previous patterns and statistical distributions. A certain penalty cost would be associated with any demand that cannot to be fulfilled. The penalty cost can be both tangible as well as intangible. Since the deliverable are considered to be Fast Moving Consumer Goods (FMCG), the tangible penalty cost would assumed to be the same as the cost of lost sales. The intangible penalty would arise from the inability to satisfy customer's aspirations. We have developed an efficient algorithm to optimise transportation routing with tangible penalty costs. Once the transportation is optimised for both the deterministic and stochastic cases, the difference in the costs between the cases of complete information and little or no information would give us an estimate of the value of information.

The routing and scheduling of vehicles is an important component of the costs in many logistical situations. The Vehicle Routing Problem (VRP) considers a set of customers along with their demands (supplies) and a depot in which a certain number of vehicles are stationed. The distance between the customers and depot is known. The objective of the problem is to minimise the total distance travelled such that each customer is visited exactly once. Further, the sum of the demands (supplies) on a vehicle's route may not exceed its capacity and the total length of the route should not exceed a given upper limit L.

The graph theoretic formulation of the VRP assumes the customer-depot setup as a graph, G = (V, A) with every customer location and the depot as a vertex, ie. set V and the corresponding connection between these vertices as undirected arcs, ie. set A. A = (i, j) where i, j ∈ V.

Each customer location node for the VRP can be a demand node or a supply node, wherein the vehicle is expected to either distribute or collect the material. Similarly, the depot can act as a sink or source depending on the nature of transportation. However, we would assume the depot to be the source node and all the customer location as demand points for the sake of consistency.

□ MATHEMATICAL FORMULATION AND LITERATURE SURVEY

There is an abundance of literature on the approximation and exact techniques for transportation optimisation by the use of Vehicle Routing. It should be noted that there has been seldom any techniques developed for Transportation Optimization under penal conditions. All the earlier literature focuses on complete demand satisfaction and incorporates the same in the constraints of the problem. We have introduced the idea of incomplete demand satisfaction with suitable penalty for unsatisfied demands. We present the mathematical formulation (ILP) for the VRP with penalties. Some of the key ideas in this formulation have been adapted from the classic ILP formulation suggested by Fisher and Jaikumar [1981] for the General VRP without the concept of penalties.

$$\text{Min} \sum_{i} \sum_{j} \sum_{k} c_{ij} x_{ijk} + \sum_{i} A_{i} p_{i} \tag{1}$$

Such that

$$\sum_{i} A_{i} \cdot y_{ik} \leq Q_{k}, \qquad k = 1, \ldots, K \tag{2a}$$

$$\sum_{ij} c_{ij} \cdot x_{ijk} \leq d_{k}, \qquad k = 1, \ldots, K \tag{2b}$$

$$\sum_{k} y_{0k} = K \tag{3a}$$

$$\sum_{k} y_{ik} = 1, \qquad i = 1, \ldots, n \tag{3b}$$

$$y_{ik} = \{0, 1\}, \qquad i = 0, \ldots, n \text{ and } k = 1, \ldots, K \tag{4}$$

$$\sum_{i} x_{ijk} = y_{jk}, \qquad j = 0, \ldots, n \text{ and } k = 1, \ldots, K \tag{5}$$

$$\sum_{j} x_{ijk} = y_{ik}, \qquad i = 0, \ldots, n \text{ and } k = 1, \ldots, K \tag{6}$$

$$\sum_{ij \in S \times S} x_{ijk} \leq |S| - 1, \qquad S \subseteq \{1, \ldots, n\}; \ 2 \leq |S| \leq n - 1 \text{ and } k = 1, \ldots, K \tag{7}$$

$$x_{ijk} = \{0, 1\}, \qquad i = 0, \ldots, n; \ j = 0, \ldots, n \text{ and } k = 1, \ldots, K \tag{8}$$

$$(A_{i} - q_{i}) = 0 \qquad \text{for all } i \tag{9}$$

$$A_{i} = 0 \qquad \text{for all } i \tag{10}$$

where x_{ijk} = 1 if the vehicle k travels from customer i to customer j directly,

= 0 otherwise

y_{ik} = 1 if the vehicle k caters to customer location i,

= 0 otherwise

c_{ij} = Cost/distance of travelling directly from customer i to customer j

q_{i} = Quantity demanded at customer i

p_{i} = Penalty cost of not fulfilling the demand at customer location i

A_{i} = Actual demand that is not satisfied at the location i

Q_{k} = Capacity of vehicle k

d_{k} = Cost/distance bound for vehicle k

Two well-known combinatorial optimization problems are embedded within this formulation. Constraints (2) – (4) represent the generalised assignment problem and ensure that each route begins and ends at the depot (customer 0), that every customer is serviced by some vehicle, and that the load and distance assigned to a vehicle is within its capacity. If the y_{ik} are fixed to satisfy (2) – (4), then for a given k, constraints (5) – (8) define a TSP over the customers assigned to vehicle k. All the literature for the VRP assumes total demand satisfaction at the various customer locations and may not be really useful for our studies. Nevertheless, we have outlined some of the classic exact and approximate techniques for VRP solution.

Christofides and Eilon [1969] extended the concept of a 3-optimal tour to an r-optimal tour. The minimal tour through n points has the property that it is an n-optimal tour. The complexity of the solution increases exponentially with r. For any given tour, there are C(n, r) ways in which r links can be chosen and removed, leaving r disconnected chains, some of which consist of single points. Foster and Ryan [1976] described an approximate method that over-constrains the definition of a feasible route to a "small" initial feasible region and thus provide a faster rate of convergence to the solution of an over-constrained model. The over constraints are progressively relaxed to expand the set of feasible routes. The feasible region is restricted by the imposition of additional implicit constraints:

- Routes serve a sector of the region with center at the depot. Deliveries within the sector are seldom bypassed.
- Adjacent routes seldom cross.
- For any given subset of deliveries, the optimal route is just the "travelling salesman" solution for that subset of deliveries.

By restricting the composition of feasible routes, the method effectively solves an over-constrained VRP with an imposed structure. The set of feasible routes defined by this method is referred to as the "petal set" since the routes produced radiate from the depot like the petals of a flower.

Fisher [1994] modelled the VRP as the problem of finding a minimum cost K-tree with two K edges incident on the depot and subject to the operational constraints. The side constraints are dualized to obtain a Lagrangean problem that provides lower bounds for branch-and-bound search algorithm. Achuthan et al [1996] proposed an exact algorithm based on a new sub-tour elimination constraint. Achuthan et al [1998] proposed some new cutting planes that provide an improved picture of the solution space. These cutting planes are instrumental in enhancing the solutions for the VRP using Branch and Cut methods.

Tallon et al [2000] has presented an empirical approach to quantify the business value of the Information Technology in a firm. Their approach has a strong bias of the chief of the organisation and his advisers as the authors have completely relied on chiefs' views. Raju and Roy [2000] developed a game-theoretic model to understand how firm and industry characteristics moderate the effect of market information on firm profits. Their results suggest that information is more valuable when product substitutability is higher, suggesting that information is of greater value in more competitive industries.

□ ALGORITHM

Having gone through the literature, we find that some heuristics like the variants of sweep method are very powerful, but somewhat time extensive, because of the need to solve a large number TSPs. On the other hand, heuristics based on savings method are less time consuming, but less accurate too at the same time. In our study, we have left the decision of the selection of the suitable VRP algorithm to the user and we have, rather, concentrated on devising a good technique for dealing with the problem under penalty conditions.

The key feature of this algorithm is that it utilises the Lagrangean approximation techniques from the mathematical formulation discussed earlier. Similarly, to insert the locations in the route, this algorithm uses the concepts of savings method (introduced by Clarke and Wright [1962]), thereby avoiding the need to solve a large number of TSPs. Hence, the proposed algorithm is expected to be faster as well as fairly accurate, both simultaneously.

Here is a description of some terminologies that may be used in the proposed algorithm:

- C : Total cost of routing the vehicle without penalties.
- Q and d : Permissible Load and distance for the vehicles.
- p : Penalty cost for not satisfying one unit of demand load (assumed to be the same for all the locations).
- C[dist(k)] : Cost corresponding to the distance covered in route k.
- load(k) : Total load in route k.
- LOAD and DIST : Peak load and distance for a route.
- dist(k) : Total distance corresponding to the route k.

Here is a brief description of the different steps of the proposed algorithm. The flow-chart for the same is given in the appendix.

1. Solve the problem without the penalty costs by any classical method for VRP. Compute the total cost C.
2. Find route k such that Max {C[dist(k)] − p.load(k)} = 0. If there are no such routes then go to step 7.
3. Dismember the route and add the locations of route k by insertion such that the capacity constraints are ignored but distance constraints are maintained. For inserting the locations of route i, add location j (? route i) to route k (k ? i) such that the savings achieved is the maximum and distance constraints are not violated. If it is not possible to fit all the locations with some route or the other, go to step 6.
4. Compute the total cost C_1 for the new route structure such that the cost for all the routes i, exceeding capacity constraints, ie. load(i) = LOAD, is given as:

$$C[dist(i)] - \{LOAD - load(i)\} \cdot p$$

5. If $C_1 < C$, replace the new route structure else continue.
6. Go to step 2 and find a new route.
7. Stop and the current route structure is the final solution.

This algorithm for the optimization of transportation routing under penalty conditions that is presented above is an approximate heuristic and does not guarantee optimality. The heuristic is inherently intuitive in nature and it can be seen in the step 2 of the algorithm wherein non-pliability of the condition given in the step leads to the final solution under penalty conditions same as the solution without penalty.

The obvious question that arises is how do we value the information with this algorithm. We would assume two cases here—one, wherein we just have a predicted demand or a distribution (with known mean) and two, where we are able to find the exact demand because of the fact that the information system is in place. We apply the given algorithm for the second case and find out the costs incurred for the distribution of the item. We, then, apply the same algorithm for the predicted value (in case of absence of information) and determine the costs. Once the actual distribution is carried out, we may incur additional costs on account of unsatisfied demands at certain customer locations. The total costs in this case would be usually higher than the case with complete information, or

Flow-chart for the algorithm

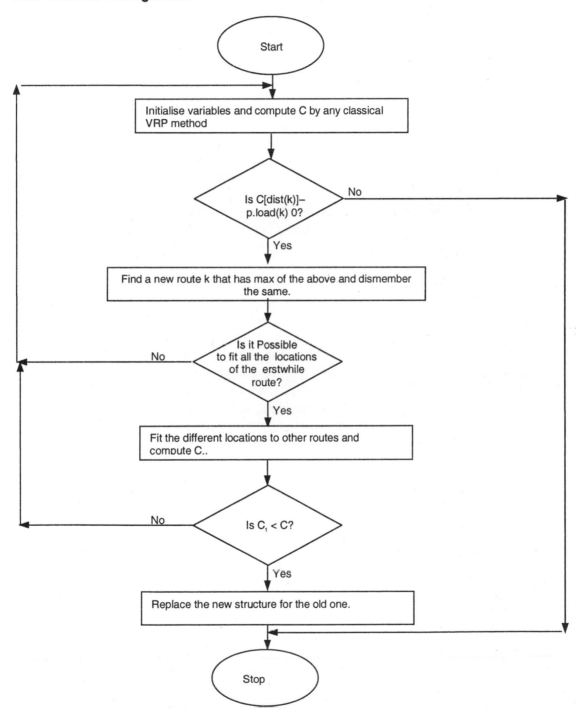

completely known demands. The difference in costs over an extended period of time is an indicator of the value of information in the distribution activity for the firm.

◻ CONCLUSION

Information can be put to best use only in a vertically as well as horizontally integrated organisation. The complete information in supply chains has a number of advantages. Apart from reducing the total (penalty and logistics) cost to the manufacturer, it also helps in streamlining the inventory and logistics of the higher and lower echelons in the chain, viz. suppliers and retailers. This would result in the further reduction of the costs to the customer. Lower cost of the product may entail the manufacturer to improve the service quality and hence would result in better CRM.

When valuing the information for transport logistics in our paper, we have taken only the operational aspects of the leverage gained from information. Apart from the operational gains, an improved information system can be of strategic importance too. It can play a significant role in building the brand image, improving the customer satisfaction levels, streamlining inventory management and securing competitive advantage for the firm. These benefits of the information are extremely difficult to be quantified and hence we have not considered them in our valuation. Even on the operational side, the information can be used beyond demand determination. It can be used for procurement logistics, facilities location, among a host of other activities.

It is not absolutely impossible to determine the intangible parameters of the benefits of information. We strongly believe that future research can be carried out in determining the total value, ie., and both operational and strategic value of information with the help of certain classical techniques like DEA or the balanced scorecard.

REFERENCES

N. R. Achuthan, L. Caccetta and S. P. Hill (1996) 'A New Subtour Elimination Constraint for the Vehicle Routing Problem', *European Journal of Operational Research*, Vol. 91, No. 3, pp. 573.

N. R. Achuthan, L. Caccetta and S. P. Hill (1998) 'Capacitated Vehicle Routing Problem: Some New Cutting Planes', *Asia-Pacific Journal of Operational Research*, Vol. 15, No. 1, pp. 109.

R. H. Ballou and Y. K. Agarwal (1988) ' A Performance Comparison of Several Popular Algorithms for Vehicle Routing and Scheduling', *Journal of Business Logistics*, Vol. 9, No. 1, pp. 51.

R. H. Ballou (1990) ' A Continued Comparison of Several Popular Algorithms for Vehicle Routing and Scheduling', *Journal of Business Logistics*, Vol. 11, No. 1, pp. 111.

G. P. Cachon and M. L. Fisher (2000) 'Supply Chain Inventory Management and the Value of Shared Information', *Management Science*, Vol. 46, No. 8, pp. 1032.

N. Christofides and S. Eilon (1969) 'An Algorithm for the Vehicle-Dispatching Problem', *Operations Research Quarterly* Vol. 20, No. 3, pp. 309.

G. Clarke and J. Wright (1964) 'Scheduling of Vehicles From a Central Depot to a Number of Delivery Points', *Operations Research*, Vol. 12, No. 3, pp. 568.

M. L. Fisher and R. Jaikumar (1981) 'A Generalised Assignment Heuristic for Vehicle Routing', *Networks* Vol. 11, No. 2, pp. 109.

M. L. Fisher (1994) 'Optimal Solution of Vehicle Routing Problems Using Minimum K-Trees', *Operations Research* Vol. 42, No. 4, pp. 626.

B. A. Foster and D. M. Ryan (1976) 'An Integer Programming Approach to the Vehicle Scheduling Problem', *Operations Research Quarterly*, Vol. 27, No. 2, pp. 367.

J. S. Raju and A. Roy (2000) 'Market Information And Firm Performance', *Management Science*, Vol. 46, No. 8, pp. 1075.

P. P. Tallon, K. L. Kraemer and V. Gurbaxani (2000) 'Executives' Perception of the Business Value of Information Technology: A Process Oriented Approach', *Journal of Management Information Systems*, Spring, Vol. 16, No. 4, pp. 145.

Chapter 37

Managing Relationships in Supply Chains of the 21st Century

■ **Subrata Mitra and A K Chatterjee**

Abstract

In the last decade, Customer Relationship Management (CRM) and Supply Chain Management (SCM) have assumed importance as tools for creating and sustaining competitive advantage for the corporates. In this paper, the gradual evolution of CRM and SCM is traced, and the role of CRM in the context of SCM is discussed. A case study is presented, where problems on relationship management are pointed out, and possible remedies are suggested in order to sustain the relationship in the long run. Finally, the evolving role of CRM in the context of emerging issues in supply chains, namely advances in IT, e-commerce and globalization, is discussed.

Key Words: *Customer Relationship Management, Supply Chain Management, Competitive Advantage, E-commerce, Globalization*

□ INTRODUCTION

Since the last decade, Customer Relationship Management (CRM) and Supply Chain Management (SCM) have assumed importance as tools for creating and sustaining competitive advantage for the corporates. The objective of CRM is to build long-term relationships with the potential customers. SCM, on the other hand, tries to improve the efficiency of the production and distribution process by taking a holistic view right from the procurement of raw materials to the consumption of finished goods. The ultimate aim of both CRM and SCM is to create "customer value", so that the customers are not easily weaned away by the competitors. For SCM to be effective, it is imperative to have coordination, cooperation, transparency and sharing of information among the supply chain partners. The operational aspects of SCM will fall short of achieving the desired objectives, unless the behavioural aspects are taken care of by CRM.

This paper discusses the evolving relationships among the supply chain partners as we march through the 21st century. The following section briefly discusses the evolution of SCM and CRM. The role of CRM in the context of SCM is discussed in the next section. A case study of a food products company is presented illustrating the problems faced by the company in managing relationships with its distributors. Finally, the emerging issues in supply chains, namely advances in IT, e-commerce and globalization, and the role of CRM in this context are discussed.

□ EVOLUTION OF SCM AND CRM

The evolution of SCM can be traced back to "distribution management" in the 1970's where there was no coordination among the various functions of an organization, and each was committed to attain its own goal. This myopic approach transformed into "integrated logistics management" in the 1980's that called for the integration of various functions to achieve a system-wide objective (Vrat, 1999; Seturam, 1999). SCM, which evolved in the 1990's due to increased competition and globalization (Thomas and Griffin, 1996), further widens this scope by including the suppliers and customers into the organizational fold, and coordinating the flow of materials and information from the procurement of raw materials to the consumption of finished goods. The objectives of SCM are to eliminate redundancies, and reduce cycle time and inventory so as to provide better customer service at lower cost. The focus has shifted from the "share of the market" paradigm to the "share of the customer" paradigm, wherein the goal is to create "customer value" leading to increased corporate profitability, shareholder value, and sustained competitive advantage in the long run (Evans and Danks, 1998). The successive stages of evolution of SCM, the central characteristics of each stage, and the drivers of change are shown in Fig. 1.

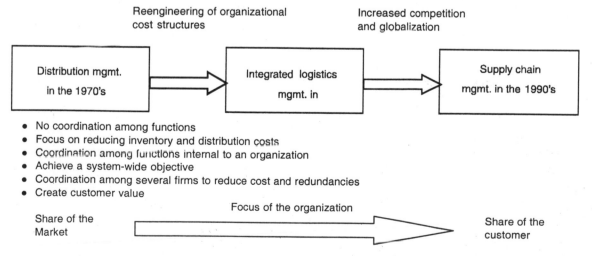

Fig. 1 *Evolution of Supply Chain Management*

CRM, on the other hand, had its roots in the "relationship marketing" concepts that emerged in the 1980's (Berry, 1983; Levitt, 1983; Jackson, 1985; Christopher, Payne and Ballantyne, 1991). CRM requires organizations to lay more emphasis on retaining existing customers rather than on creating new ones (Clark and Payne, 1997). Initially perceived to be a marketing function, it has gradually turned out to be a cross-functional responsibility with the definition of customer including internal members besides final consumers. The evolution of relationship marketing from the functionally based transaction marketing is shown in Fig. 2.

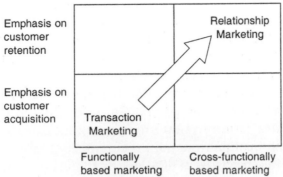

Source: Payne, 1997

Fig. 2 *Transition to Relationship Marketing*

Seth (1998) defined relationship marketing as the ongoing collaborative business activities between a supplier and a customer on a one-to-one basis for the purpose of growing the total market by creating better end user value at reduced cost. The emphasis is on the words "ongoing" and "collaborative". Research shows that there is a direct relation between the customer retention rate and corporate profitability. A 5% increase in the customer retention rate results in 20-125% increase in profitability, in NPV terms (Payne, 2000).

☐ ROLE OF CRM IN THE CONTEXT OF SCM

In the context of SCM, where alliances and partnerships are the keys to success, CRM plays an important role in building long-term relationships. Apart from the end users, it involves internal employees, channel members and other external entities such as advertising agencies and consulting organizations (Srivastava et al., 1999). The success of relationships depends on sharing of savings from the supply chain, which may be reinvested to further enhance its efficiency, and sustain the competitive advantage (Chen, 1997).

The supply chain of tomorrow will look like a virtual organization, seamlessly integrated through sharing of data and savings as well. The bonding between the partners will be closely held by the relationship management practices, as diagrammatically shown in Fig. 3.

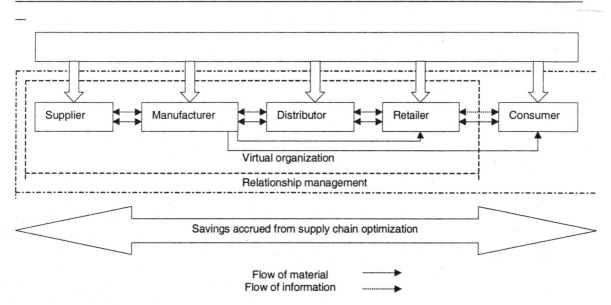

Fig. 3 *Future Supply Chain Network*

In the earlier days, manufacturers used to wield power and dictate relationships in supply chains. But over the last few years, the dynamics of relationships are changing as the power is gradually shifting from manufacturers to intermediaries and customers. Japanese auto makers have drastically cut down the number of suppliers, who are required to meet stringent quality norms in return of assured large volumes of business. A study by A. T. Kearney reveals that 20% of the current in-suppliers will be delisted by 2003 (Buttle, 2000). Wal-Mart and Kmart are forcing their suppliers to install EDI links to monitor and manage inventories at the stores (Poirier and Reiter, 1996). Freight carriers like UPS and FedEx, who played a passive role in supply chains till recently, are now acting as powerful links for direct-selling manufacturers to deliver quality service at the customer's doorstep (Stern et al., 1996).

It may appear that relationship marketing is more applicable to the Service sector than the FMCG sector. As Fig. 4 shows, there is a transition from transaction marketing to relationship marketing as we move from the FMCG sector to the Service sector.

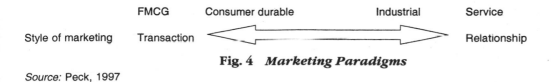

Fig. 4 *Marketing Paradigms*

Source: Peck, 1997

But as far as relationship management in the context of SCM is concerned, it is equally important for all the sectors since it not only concerns the end consumers, but also involves internal and external channel partners as well.

☐ CASE STUDY OF A FOOD PRODUCTS COMPANY[*]

A study of the distribution system of the dairy division of a major food products company was carried out to examine the relationship between the company and its distributors. The study was confined to Calcutta and its adjoining areas. It reveals that though the company is going steady with its sales programmes, it is paying less attention to the distributors' problems. The distributors feel that their grievances are not properly addressed, and the dissatisfaction is manifested in terms of high attrition rates in the recent years. The frequent change of distributors is expected to adversely affect the sales volumes in the long run, unless corrective measures for sustaining long-term relationships are taken by the company.

Background of the Company

The company, with an annual turnover of Rs. 1169 crore and a net profit of Rs. 51 crore for the year 1999-2000, is a major player in the bakery business. It is mainly known for its biscuits division. Currently around 90% of its turnover are due to its biscuits business. However, the company is in the process of transformation from being primarily a manufacturer of bakery products to a comprehensive food and beverages company. It initiated this process in 1997 by the launch of its dairy products, namely dairy whitener and cheese. Later on, butter and ghee were also introduced; the sales volumes for which are yet to pick up. The current market share of the company is around 10% for dairy whitener and 35% for cheese. Last year, the dairy business accounted for a little over Rs. 100 crore of the total turnover. The company expects it to go up to one-third of its projected turnover in the coming years.

Distribution System of the Dairy Division

Currently the company does not have a production facility for its dairy whitener and cheese products; instead it procures its requirements from a factory in Maharashtra, and sells them through conventional distribution channels. The factory has a contract with the company, and has excess production capacity to meet the company's current requirements within a short span of time. The various Stock Keeping Units (SKUs) are shipped from the factory to the Carrying and Forwarding Agents (C&FAs), and from the C&FAs to the Authorised Wholesalers (A/Ws), which constitutes the primary sales of the company. The Authorised Wholesalers (also known as distributors) in turn sell to retailers, independent wholesalers and institutions such as hotels and restaurants, which constitutes the secondary sales. The company takes care of the primary freight between the factory and the

---

[*] The authors are grateful to Prof. Sudas Roy of IIM Calcutta for helping us to carry out the case study.

C&FAs as well as the secondary freight between the C&FAs and the A/Ws. Fig. 5 shows the distribution system for the dairy products.

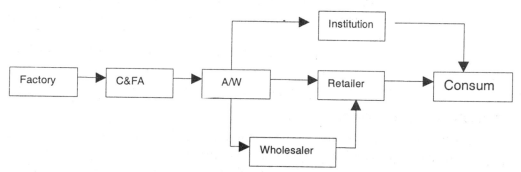

Fig. 5 *Distribution System for the Dairy Products*

The distribution network is divided into four regions. The eastern region consists of West Bengal, Bihar, Orissa and the North Eastern states, the headquarters of the region being located at Calcutta. There are 8 C&FAs and around 185 distributors in this region. 3 C&FAs are located in West Bengal, including one in Calcutta. The average turnover of the eastern region is about Rs. 2.5 crore per month. West Bengal is the largest market with 35% and 70% of the sales volumes for dairy whitener and cheese respectively in this region. Out of the 3 C&FAs in West Bengal, Calcutta is the biggest one handling about 35-40% of total sales volume in the state.

Problems Faced by the Distributors

While interacting with the concerned persons of the company and a few of its distributors, it was found that the distributors were facing the following major problems in doing business with the company.

- The foremost problem is that the distributors are made to carry one month's stock in excess. The company's policy is to push stock to expedite secondary sales under inventory pressure. Two distributors confirmed that they were made to invest in 5-6 weeks' of inventory by the company, though the sales volumes were not enough to justify the investment.
- No credit facility is currently being extended by the company to the distributors, and payment for the primary sales has to be made immediately. On the other hand, the distributors have to extend credit facilities to the retailers for doing business. So, they are losing on account of investment in market credit when they themselves do not get the same facility, as well as investment in inventory when the small margins due to low sales volumes do not justify its economics.
- The outstanding claims to the company against damaged SKUs, SKUs whose shelf lives have been over, and promotional items that the distributors have to provide from their own stock, are also high. The company often takes more than the necessary time for settlement of claims.

- The distributors are required to invest in refrigerators/coolers, which are not subsidized by the company. For small distributors with inadequate sales volumes, investment in coolers becomes an additional financial burden. On the other hand, the company provides coolers worth Rs. 10000 to the retailers, whose sales volumes are only Rs. 2000 per month.
- The company has neither any incentive scheme, nor a formal mechanism to help the distributors reduce their losses.
- The company does not have any training programme for the distributors' salesmen.

Recommendations for the Company

The above problems have generated dissatisfaction among the distributors, and this is manifested in terms of frequent change of distributors in the last two years. As far as the long-term strategy of the company is concerned, it cannot afford to appoint a distributor who remains with it for a short period. There has to be a sustained relationship for long-term business prospects, quite similar to its biscuits division, which enjoys a lasting and satisfactory relationship with its distributors.

The following steps are recommended for the company.

- The distributors are made to carry one month's excess stock pumped in by the company. They find it uneconomical to have their money blocked in this way in the light of current sales volumes, which are yet to pick up. It was observed that the distributors' business would have been viable had they carried maximum 7-15 days' stock. The company might meet its primary sales targets by pushing stock to the distributors, but it should also ensure that there is no build-up of excess stock at the latter's place, more so because the products are perishable in nature.
- The company can think of extending credit facilities to the distributors for at least one week, as it itself gets credit from the factory and the transporter for 45 days.
- Claims of the distributors against damaged SKUs, SKUs for which shelf lives are over and promotional items that the distributors provide from their own stock, should be promptly settled by the company.
- The company has several incentive schemes for the retailers. But they have none for the distributors. The margins are also lower for the distributors. The company should think of some incentive schemes and higher margins for them at least for the initial period when the sales volumes are not high.
- The company should have a training programme for the distributors' salesmen to motivate them, and an incentive scheme in recognition of their performance.

☐ EMERGING ISSUES IN SUPPLY CHAINS AND THE ROLE OF CRM

In this section, the emerging issues in supply chains, namely advances in IT, e-commerce, and globalization, and the role of CRM in this context are discussed.

IT-Enabled Supply Chain and E-Commerce

Advances in IT have made it possible for supply chains to quickly adapt and respond to the changing market scenario, and reduce redundancies by better coordination. New technology, such as bar coding and scanning, can be used to track the shelf movement of items at the retail outlets, and the information can be instantaneously transmitted up the supply chain through EDI, so that the suppliers, manufacturers and distributors can align their activities according to the changing demand patterns. A seamless flow of information across the supply chain also enables to reduce inventory redundancies, paperwork and delay in responding. Lack of information often results in uncontrolled variations in inventory positions and order quantities as one moves up the supply chain, which is known as the "bullwhip effect" (Lee et al., 1997).

IT, and now the Internet, has also made it possible for organizations to do business efficiently electronically, as it is evident from the growing trends of business-to-business (B2B) and business-to-consumer (B2C) e-commerce. In 1997, e-commerce accounted for $1 billion. According to Forrester Research, that number is expected to reach $1.3 trillion by 2003 (Caldwell, 2000). Apart from expanding the geographic scope, e-commerce improves the supply chain efficiency by making the entire process of order placing, raising invoices and payment transactions online, thus avoiding unnecessary delays and costs associated with the erstwhile paper transactions. B2C e-commerce (for example, Amazon.com) allows customers to shop at their convenience and get the ordered items delivered at their doorsteps. The shopping convenience is going to get a further boost with the evolution of mobile commerce or m-commerce that will allow customers to place orders from WAP (Wireless Application Protocol)-enabled mobile phones.

On the relationship management front, the adoption of IT and e-commerce activities requires cooperation, coordination and transparency among the channel partners. There should be a high degree of mutual trust and willingness to share information. Wal-Mart and Kmart are sharing the data on shelf movement of items with their suppliers through dedicated EDI links, who themselves monitor and manage inventories at the stores. Companies selling their products through the Internet also have to take an initiative for developing customized and interactive web sites to attract and retain customers. Dell Computer Corp. is a classic example that revolutionized the supply chain with its assemble-to-order concept. Now Dell is applying the same principle to its customer service and support business by leveraging supplier relationships (Saccomano, 1999). Amazon.com is another classic case to e-market a commodity product (i.e., books and music CDs) backed by highly personalized service (Caldwell, 2000).

☐ GLOBAL SUPPLY CHAIN

With the liberalization of trade and opening up of economies in most of the countries, multinational corporations are setting up shops of their own or going into some kind of joint ventures with their domestic counterparts to form global supply chains. With the developments in IT and the Internet, the opportunity is immense. But to compete successfully in this borderless world, organizations have to adopt new strategies moving from a local and regional approach to a truly global operation. Managing global supply chains might be quite complex, but on the other hand it facilitates leveraging the core competencies of supply chain partners. Whirlpool borrowed expertise from different countries to design new refrigerator technology; similarly Texas Instruments' engineers in the US and India collaborate for new product development to speed products to market (Anderson et al., 1998).

Forming global supply chains requires, apart from maintaining close alliances with the freight carriers and domestic partners, a detailed understanding of factors such as tariff/non-tariff barriers, volatility of currency exchange rates, tax laws, government rules and regulations, cultural differences, infrastructures, economic condition and political stability in the concerned countries. A good relationship with the law makers and regulators in the government goes a long way in developing a trouble-free supply chain. It is also necessary to train personnel with foreign language, negotiation, and problem-solving skills, who are willing to take the challenge of developing key relationships with new supply chain members (Handfield and Nichols Jr., 1999).

◻ CONCLUSION

CRM and SCM have assumed importance as tools for creating and sustaining competitive advantage. The evolution of CRM and SCM is discussed in this paper. The role of CRM in the context of SCM is examined, and a case study is presented to identify the current problems on relationship management and the possible measures that should be taken to sustain the relationship in the long run. The emerging issues in supply chains, namely advances in IT, e-commerce and globalization, and the role of CRM in this context are also discussed.

REFERENCES

Anderson, D., Dhillon, Y. and Remnant, J. (1998), 'Global Supply Management: Satisfying the global customer', In: Gattorna, J. (ed.), *Strategic Supply Chain Alignment*, Gower, pp. 325-337.

Berry, L. L. (1983), 'Relationship Marketing', In: Berry, L. L., Shostack, G. L. and Upah, G D. (eds.), *Emerging Perspectives on Services Marketing*, American Marketing Association, Chicago, pp. 25-28.

Buttle, F. (2000), 'The CRM Value Chain', Source: *http://www.crm-forum.com/academy/cvc/ppr.htm*.

Caldwell, J. (2000), 'Building a Sustainable e-business CRM Strategy', *Agency Sales*, Vol. 30, No. 5, pp. 23-27.

Chen, J. (1997), 'Achieving Maximum Supply Chain Efficiency', *IIE Solutions*, Vol. 29, No. 6, pp. 30-35.

Christopher, M., Payne, A. F. T. and Ballantyne, D. (1991), *Relationship Marketing: Bringing Quality, Customer Service and Marketing Together*, Butterworth-Heinemann: Oxford.

Clark, M. and Payne, A. (1997), 'Customer Retention: Does employee retention hold a key to success?', In: Payne, A. (ed.), *Advances in Relationship Marketing*, Kogan Page, London, pp. 41-52.

Evans, R. and Danks, A. (1998), 'Strategic Supply Chain Management: Creating shareholder value by aligning supplying chain strategy with business strategy', In: Gattorna, J. (ed.), *Strategic Supply Chain Alignment*, Gower, pp. 18-37.

Handfield, R. B. and Nichols Jr., E. L. (1999), *Introduction to Supply Chain Management*, Prentice-Hall: New Jersey.

Jackson, B. B. (1985), 'Build customer relationships that last', *Harvard Business Review*, November-December, pp. 120-128.

Lee, H., Padmanabhan, P. and Whang, S. (1997), 'Information Distortion in a Supply Chain: The Bullwhip Effect', *Management Science* Vol. 43 No. 4, pp. 546-558.

Levitt, T. (1983), 'After the sale is over...', *Harvard Business Review*, Vol. 6, No. 1, pp. 87-93.

Payne, A. (1997), 'Relationship Marketing: A Broadened View of Marketing', In: Payne, A. (ed.), *Advances in Relationship Marketing*, Kogan Page, London, pp. 29-40.

Payne, A. (2000), 'Customer Relationship Management', Key Note address to the inaugural meeting of the Customer Management Foundation, London, Source: *http://www.crm-forum.com/academy/apcrm/ppr.htm*.

Peck, H. (1997), 'Building Customer Relationships through Internal Marketing: A Review of an Emerging Field', In: Payne, A. (ed.), *Advances in Relationship Marketing*, Kogan Page, London, pp. 83-111.

Poirier, C. C. and Reiter, S. E. (1996), *Supply Chain Optimization*, Berrett-Koehler: San Francisco.

Saccomano, A. (1999), 'Dell Computer Builds Service', *Traffic World*, Vol. 259, No. 4, pp. 26-27.

Seth, J. (1998), 'Creating Value through Relationship Marketing: New Experiences, New Insights', Source: Shainesh, G. (1999), 'Enhancing Customer Relationships through Effective Supply Chain – Putting the Act Together', In: Sahay, B. S. (ed.), *Supply Chain Management for Global Competitiveness*, Macmillan, pp. 1115-1127.

Seturam, S. (1999), 'Corporate Profitability and Supply Chain', In: Sahay, B. S. (ed.), *Supply Chain Management for Global Competitiveness*, Macmillan, pp. 77-93.

Srivastava, R. K., Shervani, T. A. and Fahey, L. (1999), 'Marketing, Business Processes, and Shareholder Value: An Organizationally Embedded View of Marketing Activities and the Discipline of Marketing', *Journal of Marketing*, Vol. 63, pp. 168-179.

Stern, L. W., El-Ansary, A. I. and Coughlan, A. T. (1996), *Marketing Channels*, 5th ed., Prentice-Hall: New Delhi.

Thomas, D. J. and Griffin, P. M. (1996), 'Coordinated Supply Chain Management', *European Journal of Operations Research*, Vol. 94, pp. 1-15.

Vrat, P. (1999), 'Supply Chain Management in India: Problems and Challenges', In: Sahay, B. S. (ed.), *Supply Chain Management for Global Competitiveness*, Macmillan, pp. 10-24.

Section V

CRM in Services

Status of Customer Relationship Management in India
A Survey of Service Firms

■ **G Shainesh and Ramneesh Mohan**

Abstract

Worldwide, service firms have been the pioneers in adopting the practice of customer relationship management practices. In India too, the service firms took some of the early initiatives in CRM, specially in financial services. The survey was conducted among managers belonging to hospitality, IT, telecom, and financial services to understand the relationship management practices and programs adopted by them. It addresses issues such as quality and customer centric processes, employee empowerment, technology selection, customer knowledge strategies and individualisation of market programs.

Key Words: *Customer Centric Processes, Customer Knowledge Strategies, Technology Selection, Empowerment*

□ INTRODUCTION

Relationship management is emerging as the core marketing activity for businesses operating in fiercely competitive environments. On average, businesses spend six times more to acquire customers than they do to keep them (Gruen, 1997). Therefore, many firms are now paying more attention to their relationships with existing customers to retain them and increase their share of customer's purchases.

Worldwide service organisations have been pioneers in developing customer retention strategies. Banks have relationship managers for select customers, airlines have frequent flyer programs to reward loyal customers, credit cards offer redeemable bonus points for increased card usage, telecom service operators provide customized services to their heavy users, and hotels have personalized services for their regular guests.

Literature Review

Till recently, most marketers focussed on attracting customers from its target segments using the tools and techniques developed for mass marketing in the industrial era. In the information era, this is proving to be highly ineffective in most competitive markets.

Slowing growth rates, intensifying competition and technological developments made businesses look for ways to reduce costs and improve their effectiveness. Business process re-engineering, automation and downsizing reduced the manpower costs. Financial re-structuring and efficient fund management reduced the financial costs. Production and operation costs have been reduced through Total Quality Management (TQM), Just in Time (JIT) inventory, Flexible Manufacturing Systems (FMS), and efficient supply chain management. Studies have shown that while manufacturing costs declined from 55% to 30% and management costs declined from 25% to 15%, the marketing costs have increased from 20% to 55% (Sheth, 1998). The practice of relationship marketing has the potential to improve marketing productivity through improved marketing efficiencies and effectiveness (Sheth and Parvatiyar, 1995).

Still relationship marketing appears to be an expensive alternative to firms practicing mass marketing due to the relatively high initial investments. Firms would adopt relation-ship marketing only if it has the potential to benefit them. The benefits come through lower costs of retention and increased profits due to lower defection rates (Reichheld and Sasser, 1990). When customers enter into a relationship with a firm, they are willingly foregoing other options and limiting their choice. Some of the personal motivations to do so result from greater efficiency in decision making, reduction in information processing, achieving more cognitive consistency in decisions and reduction of perceived risks with future decisions (Sheth & Parvatiyar, 1995).

In the context of service, relationship marketing has been defined as attracting, main-taining and in multi-service organisations enhancing customer relationships (Berry 1983). Here attracting customers is considered to be an intermediary step in the relationship building process with the ultimate objective of increasing loyalty of profitable customers. This is because of the applicability of the 80-20 rule. According to Market Line Associates, the top 20% of typical bank customers produce as much as 150% of overall profit, while the bottom 20% of customers drain about 50% from the bank's bottom line and the revenues from the rest just meeting their expenses.

Berry (1983) recommended the following five strategies for practicing relationship mar-keting:

(i) developing a core service around which to build a customer relationship,
(ii) customizing the relationship to the individual customer,
(iii) augmenting the core service with extra benefits,
(iv) pricing services to encourage customer loyalty, and
(v) marketing to employees so that they will perform well for customers.

Developments in information technology, data warehousing and datamining have made it possible for firms to maintain a 1 to 1 relationship with their customers. Firms can now manage every single contact with the customer from account management personnel, call centers, interactive voice response systems, on-line dial-up applications, and websites to build lasting relationships. These interactions can be used to glean information and insights about customer needs and their buying behavior to design and develop services which help create value for the customers as well as the firms. Although customised as well as off the shelf technological solutions are available in the marketplace, businesses need to do a lot more than just adopt these solutions to implement customer relationship management (CRM) practices.

Successful implementation of CRM requires a strategic approach, which encompasses developing customer centric processes, selecting and implementing technology solutions, employee empowerment, customer information and knowledge generation capabilities to differentiate them, and the ability to learn from best practices.

Research Objectives

The current research was aimed at determining the approach being adopted by businesses in India for relationship marketing. The research focussed on the following major issues –
- Do managers in service firms believe that their processes are customer centric?
- Do they select technology on the basis of an understanding of customer needs?
- Have they empowered their employees to deliver superior service?
- Do they have a customer knowledge strategy? How well do they manage their customer relationships?

It adopted the framework recommended by Peppers, Rogers and Dorf (1999) for the survey to understand the status of relationship marketing across service businesses in India.

Methodology

The research was exploratory in nature and adopted a two-stage process. During the first stage, 77 managers of service firms operating in India were surveyed through respondent administered questionnaires. These managers belonged to the following three categories –

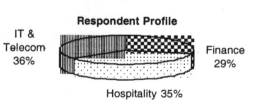

Respondent Profile

IT & Telecom 36%

Finance 29%

Hospitality 35%

(a) Hospitality industry encompassing hotels and restaurants
(b) IT and Telecom industry which included software firms and telecom service providers
(c) Financial services included commercial banks and mutual funds

The survey focussed on the quality and customer centric processes, technology selection, employee empowerment, and customer knowledge strategy to gauge the status of CRM practices in these firms.

In the second stage, managers of select firms in each category of services were interviewed to understand the relationship marketing practices adopted by them. These interviews explored the following issues –

1. What are the various CRM initiatives undertaken by the firm?
2. How do they develop these programs?
3. How do they measure the effectiveness of these programs?
4. How successful are these programs in retaining customers?

Analysis of Findings

Processes

The managers reported a wide divergence with respect to the adoption of quality assurance across the three sectors. The IT and telecom sector is at the forefront of adopting a formal quality management organisation. Most of the players in the finance and hospitality sector report having some methods in place to ensure quality management initiatives. About 8% of the overall sample have indicated the absence of any quality initiatives in their organisations.

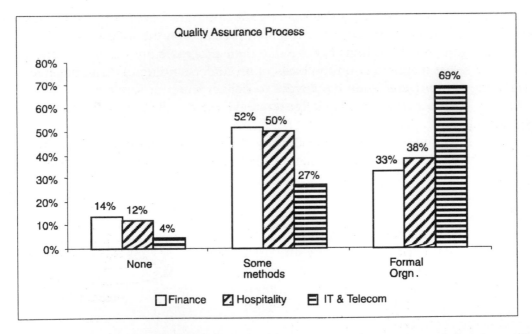

At a broad level, most managers believe that they understand most of the interactions between customers and their business processes. About 50% of them have indicated that they have a full understanding of all possible interactions between customers and their business processes. Customer-centric marketing emphasizes understanding and satisfying the needs, wants, and resources of individual consumers and customers rather than those of mass markets or market segments (Sheth, Sisodia and Sharma 2000). In customer-centric marketing, marketers assess each customer individually to determine whether to serve that customer directly or via a third party. Also, customer-centric marketers determine whether to create an offering that customizes the product and/or some other element(s) of the

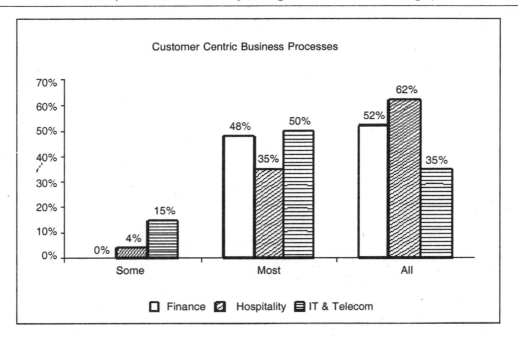

marketing mix or standardize the offering. Therefore it is very important to have an understanding of all the linkages between the customers and the business processes which help fulfill the customer needs.

Technology Selection

Information technology (IT) is a major facilitator for CRM implementation. In response to the question on whether they take consider customers' needs when selecting and imple-

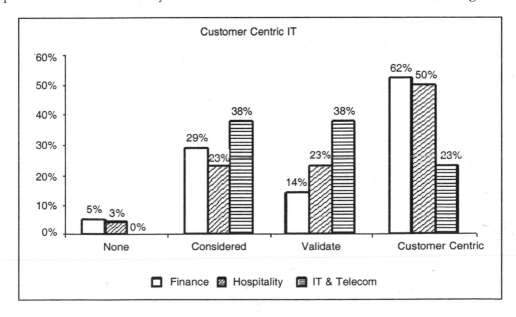

menting IT, about 30% of managers have indicated that they consider customer needs. Only 14% managers in financial services do customer validation when selecting technology. While only 23% the managers in IT & telecom firms believe that their technology selections are customer centric whereas this was over 50% in the other two sectors.

Employee Empowerment

When asked whether their employees are empowered to make decisions in favor of the customers, less than a quarter of the managers across the three sectors indicated that every employee is empowered to take actions to ensure the ultimate satisfaction of the customer. Most of them feel that their employees have been empowered to take independent decisions within the guidelines. This aspect of limited empowerment gets reinforced when one looks at the linkage between the employee's rewards with customer centric behavior. Over 18% of the respondents across the sectors have reported no linkages or use of ad hoc methods to reward customer centric behavior.

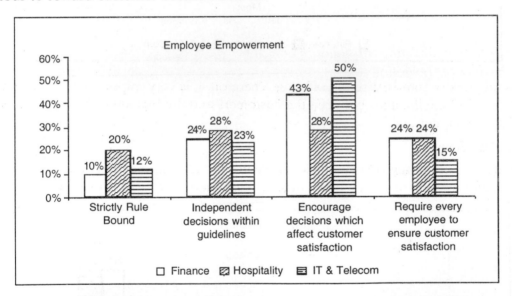

Facilitation of employees for their role fulfillment through IT is another aspect of employee empowerment. IT helps employees respond to customer queries and provide support in a fast and timely manner. It helps them access information which is normally spread across the organisation. Over 54% of IT and telecom firms have provided the most effective technology to all employees who interact with customers. This reduces to 42% for the hospitality and 19% for the financial services sector.

Customer Knowledge Strategy

Customer knowledge gets built when information is collected systematically over a period of time. This can be done through regular surveys and also during customer interactions. But importantly this information has to be combined with the organisation's experiences

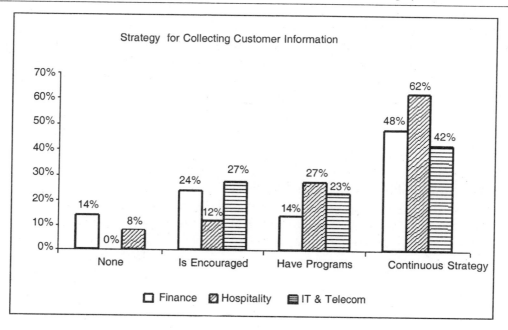

with customers to build rich customer profiles, buying behavior, preferences and usage patterns.

Over 60% managers in the hospitality industry have indicated that they have a continuous strategy for collecting customer information. In most of the services, opportunities to come in direct contact with their customers are high in comparison to other businesses

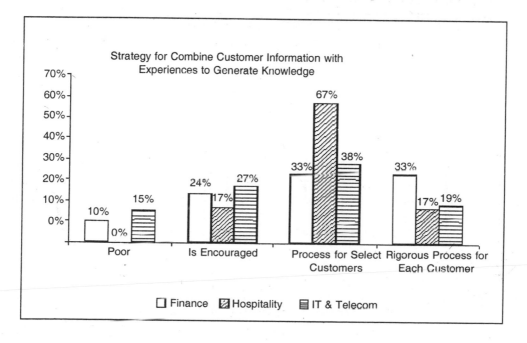

who have intermediaries and hence have a arms length relationship with their customers. Therefore it is natural for service firms to collect customer information on a regular basis. But information collection is just the first step in generating customer knowledge. This information has to be combined with experiences to develop consumer insights which help them serve their customers better.

When it comes to combining customer information with experiences, service firms seem to be economizing. Most of them seem to be doing it for select customers. Hotels do it for their regular guests specially those who have enrolled for their membership schemes. Financial service providers selectively do it for their high net worth individuals who typically use multiple offerings of the service provider.

Most service firms rely on periodic surveys to understand their customers' expectations and also understand and anticipate their behaviors. Over 40% of managers in the financial services have indicated that they work with customers as a team to ensure that their expectations are met or exceeded. It is very important to work with customers to understand their expectations as research has consistently indicated that one of the major reasons for poor service quality is the gap between managers perceptions about customers expectations and actual customer expectations (Parasuraman, Zeithaml and Berry 1985).

The purpose of collecting customer information and developing knowledge is to be able to differentiate customers and meet their specific requirements. Peppers, Rogers and Dorf (1999) have recommended a four stage process of Identification, Differentiation, Interaction, and Customization for implementing one to one relationships with customers. Over 50% managers in financial services have indicated that they have critical business information about their relationships with individual customers. This falls to about 40% in the hospitality and IT services.

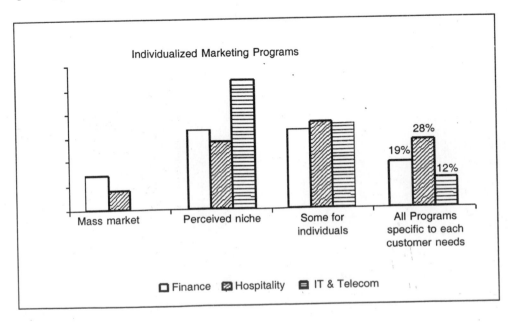

Customer knowledge can be used to initiate customization of the service for customers based on their needs. By tailoring the elements of services marketing mix, firms can customize their offerings to all or select customers.

A majority of the marketing programs are targeted for smaller segments of the markets. But there is a growing trend towards individualizing these programs. With the emergence of e-commerce, this trend is going to further intensify.

Some of the important findings of the depth interviews with managers of these services are:

(a) The relationship initiatives undertaken by firms have been directed towards customer retention. The initiatives were mostly membership /privilege schemes with gradations based on frequency and value of usage / purchase.

(b) Most of them also indicated that these schemes were table stakes i.e. they cannot survive in the business without these schemes if everyone else offers them. But the race is always to differentiate on the basis of convenience for customers.

(c) The source and reasons for adopting these programs were found to be diverse - frontline initiatives, adaptation of successful programs in parent organisations abroad especially for the multinational firms, or copying competitor's offerings. Pioneers in the industry like one of the multinational bank, which introduced the concept of relationship manager, adopted the practices of their parent organisation.

(d) A common finding, across sectors, was the absence of measures for determining the effectiveness of these programs. Managers were convinced that these retention programs had long term benefits but they were still grappling with metrics which would indicate that the investments were paying off.

(e) In several cases, there was a lack of coordination across functional departments. Although managers admitted that cooperation and coordination were crucial, they accepted that many a times, only marketing and customer service ended up as the 'program champions'. This had impact on the success of the overall program.

(f) The managers of firms who have been successful in relationship management reported strong top management support for their initiatives as well as complete employee involvement cutting across departmental boundaries.

❑ CONCLUSIONS

Relationship marketing is emerging as a new area of focus for service firms in India. But these are mainly based on some loyalty programs and investments in technology for enhancing the capability of databases. Managers should ensure that while investing in databases, technology, human resources and relationship marketing programs, attempts should also be made to develop milestones, which help them sustain these initiatives. These milestones become benchmarks against which future programs get evaluated. Measurement metrices get developed over a period of time when one starts collecting information about customers, their buying patterns, usage behavior, referrals, etc. and start linking them to the marketing programs.

Successful firms take a long term strategic view of customer relationship management. It cannot be solely managed through periodic programs. To be successful, firms need to be marketing oriented before initiating relationship marketing initiatives. A holistic approach which leads firms to develop customer centric process, integrate technology through customer oriented approaches, motivate employees to perform to their full potential through empowerment are prerequisites for firms to successfully utilise their customer knowledge for customized or even 1to1 marketing.

REFERENCES

Gruen, T. W. (1997), 'Relationship Marketing : The Route to Marketing Efficiency and Effectiveness', *Business Horizons*, November – December, pp. 32-38.

Berry, L. L. (1983), 'Relationship Marketing of Services : Growing Interest, Emerging Perspectives', *Journal of the Academy of Marketing Science*, Vol. 23, No. 4, pp. 236-245.

Parasuraman, A., Zeithaml, V. A., and Berry, L. (1985), "A Conceptual Model of Service Quality and its Implications for Future Research," *Journal of Marketing,* Fall, pp. 41-50.

Payne, A. (2000), 'Relationship Marketing : The UK Perspective', in Sheth, J. N. and Parvatiyar, A. (eds.) *Handbook on Relationship Marketing*, Sage Publications, Inc.: New Delhi, pp. 39-68.

Reichheld, F. F. and Sasser, W. E. (1990), 'Zero Defections : Quality Comes to Services', *Harvard Business Review*, September – October, pp. 105-111.

Sheth, J. N. and Parvatiyar, A. (1995) 'Relationship Marketing in Consumer Markets: Antecedents and Consequences', *Journal of the Academy of Marketing Science*, Vol. 23, No. 4, pp. 255-271.

Sheth, J. N. (1998, June), 'Creating Value through Relationship Marketing: A New Business Model', Paper presented at the *1998 Conference on Relationship Marketing : Creating Partnerships that Enrich Customer Value and Boost Marketing Productivity*, Atlanta, GA.

Sheth, J. N., Sisodia, R. S., and Sharma, A., (2000) 'The Antecedents and Consequences of Customer Centric Marketing', *Journal of the Academy of Marketing Science*, Winter, Vol. 28, Issue 1, pp. 55-66.

Impact of the Service Supply-Demand Mismatches on Relationship Intention and Integrity
A Preliminary Model and Findings

■ **M L Agrawal and Joby John**

Abstract

Relationship marketing as a new marketing template is now well recognized around the world. All marketing actions need to justify themselves in the light of their contribution to the overall relationship with the target customers. Building enduring relationships is more challenging in service industries due to the perishable nature of most services. Service marketers cannot inventory a finished service ahead of the demand. It causes frequent mismatches between supply and demand—forcing the firm to employ actions that are potentially harmful to customer relationships.

This paper links the impact of these supply-demand mismatches to relationship marketing and particularly to relationship intention and integrity. Anchored in the R4 model of relationship marketing deliverables, the paper hypothesizes the impact of the service supply mismatches on the R4 variables of relationship marketing.

Key Words: *Service vs. Goods, Perishability, Supply-Demand Mismatches; Relationship Marketing; Relationship Intention, Relationship Integrity; R4 Framework.*

□ INTRODUCTION

Perishability of services is viewed as one of the most fundamental characteristics that distinguish services from goods (Sasser, Olsen and Wyckoff, 1978). While manufacturing firms can inventory supplies of their finished products as a hedge against fluctuation of demand, services businesses can not since the service product is *time, place and person bound* (Lovelock, 1996). This leads to frequent supply-demand mismatches in services where either the service supply falls short of or exceeds its demand with potentially serious consequences to customer relationships.

It is now well established that firms need to remodel themselves along the lines of relationship marketing. Their marketing strategies and activities must establish, develop and maintain successful 'relational exchanges' (Morgan and Hunt, 1994, P. 22). Thus, any situation that forces the firm to employ actions that endanger customer relationships require careful thought and analysis.

Service supply and demand mismatches are situations that require careful thought and analysis, since the firm's actions to manage such situations could be inconsistent with the goals of the relationship marketing. Loyal customers are forced to look out for an alternative if their regular service supplier faced supply glitches. Many of these customers may eventually like the alternative service provider enough not to ever return to the service supplier (Shemwell and Cronin, 1994). Similarly, when service supply exceeds demand, it causes a serious financial loss to service providers. It is like having a 'running tap without a stopper' (Lovelock, 1996. P 220). Thus, service supply and demand mismatches negatively impact service firms in two significant ways:

1. They lower profitability of the firms, and
2. They hurt relationships with the customers.

This research paper examines these concerns and empirically tests the following questions:

- Do service supply demand mismatches impact relationship marketing in services?
- If so, how do they impact the relationship marketing deliverables?
- Which services are more prone to these impacts?
- What needs to be done to minimize these stresses and repair the damage to relationship marketing?

The Issue of Service Supply-Demand Mismatch

A service mismatch is conceptualized here to refer to 'situations pertaining to specific time, location, personnel or equipment etc. where service firms are momentarily unable to meet demand for their services, or conversely, when their service capacity remains momentarily underutilized'.

Most service mismatches occur due to the unique demand cycles of services, which could be natural, culturally driven, or behaviorally induced. For example, the family vacation has to be in a particular period of the year and services consumed during family vacations cannot be produced and stored for use when the demand for such services is plentiful. This is because services are perishable. Most services exist only during the time they are performed. While service supply falling short of its demand is a common occurrence in the developing countries owing to their poor infrastructure, it is in fact a global phenomenon. Be that as it may, the scenario represents what Kotler had described as - 'irregular demand' (Kotler, 1973). Thus, a theater owner can not roll back supply of the already installed yet unsold seats for a Thursday night showing of a movie. It also can not install more seats—over its maximum capacity, for the Friday opening of a major Hindi movie. Similarly, a hotel owner can not inventory a room unoccupied in slack season and add it to its inventory for the forthcoming busy season. Thus, the "non-storability" or the perishability of services forces inevitably unprofitable consequences of a supply-demand mismatch and presents the firm with one of the biggest managerial challenges. Fundamentally, three dyadic situations emerge between service demand and supply:

- Supply < demand
- Supply > demand
- Supply = demand

The service supply-demand mismatches manifest as a result of *overfull demand or slack supply or slack demand*. Ineffective management of demand-supply imbalances has varied implications. The inability to match supply with the demand hits the profitability of service marketers in several ways. First, it is a lost business opportunity because the service firm is unable to cater to all the demand. Second, it irks the loyal customers. Third, if the installed capacity is under-utilized, fixed cost per unit remains as high as ever. Such problems have widely been noted in sectors like hospitals, hospitality, tax accounting firms etc. Table 1 summarizes implications of the service supply mismatches to both marketers and customers.

Table 1   *Implications of Service Supply-Demand Mismatch to Marketers and Customers*

Supply < Demand		Supply > Demand		Supply = Demand	
Marketer	Customer	Marketer	Customer	Marketer	Customer
Services not readily available (staff does not turn up on time)	Non-fulfillment of desired service	Services available as and when required.	Customers are delighted	Services available as and when required.	Customers are confident about the services
Services are available only at a higher cost. Performance is uncertain.	Trust of customer in the service gets lower. Satisfaction level of the customers reduces.	Better solutions are offered to customers. Much better value is given by services.	Customer re-purchase services willingly.	Solutions come as soon as the problem is noted. Service staff is ready to provide solutions at optimum cost.	Customers are sought to be satisfied. Customers might repurchase.
Quality is poor and no effort is made to improve it either. The challenge is how to: Maintain service quality, customer satisfaction and customer trust?	Reluctance to re-purchase Buying more is apparently ruled out. The challenge is how to: Meet the desired level of services. Develop alternatives for the existing service provider? Locate a provider who has better reputation.	Supplier tries to excel in quality and customizes services. The challenge is how to. Improve the quality of service? Enhance additional demand? Communicate offerings to the customer without appearing greedy or desperate? Maintain reputation?	The challenge is how to: Keep on getting an augmented service?	Quality is just right. Performance is guaranteed The challenge is how to: Induce additional variants/ facilities? Delight the customer? Use effectively the slack resources? maintain customer expectations	He might use more from the existing supplier. The challenge is how to: Get desired services at lowest cost? Get intangibles like respect, recognition, etc.

The Charm of Relationship Marketing

Patterson and Ward (2000) define relationship marketing as the 'establishment of a long-term relationship between the service supplier and customer to their mutual benefit (Swartz and Iacobucci, 2000). They listed five conditions for a long-term relationship to occur in relational exchanges. They are individual need, value, customer satisfaction, effective communication and, mutuality. The benefits of relationship marketing to the marketers include opportunities to cross-sell; higher customer retention; reduced operation costs, higher buying among the long-term customers and, a higher probability of positive word of mouth (Patterson and Ward 2000). According to Gwinner, Gremler and Bitner, (1998), the benefits of relationship marketing helps customers too. These include 'Confidence benefits' (such psychological benefits as the feeling that they can trust the service provider); Social benefits (e.g. recognition by the service providers) and Special treatment benefits (e.g. receiving priority or special deals etc.)

A variety of antecedents of relationship marketing have been recently identified (Paterson and ward, 2000). Crosby and Taylor (1983) for instance, proffered customer commitment as an antecedent of relationship marketing. They maintained that all of us display a "tendency to resist changing preference". It has two antecedent processes. The first process conceptualized as the 'informational process' deals with the cognitive structure (how we manage information) about the preference. They argued that the need to maintain a consistent informational structure (e.g., beliefs, reasons for purchase /repurchase) helps maximize one's resistance to change. The second process- the identification process, deals with personal attachment (how we identify and link important values and self – images to a preference). The stronger the link, the greater is the resistance to change.

Our study places relationship marketing in the context of demand and supply in services and identifies two aspects of relationship marketing for testing the impact of the service supply and demand mismatches:

- Relationship Intention
- Relationship Integrity

Relationship Intention is conceptualized here as the 'degree of interest, enthusiasm and excitement among customers in wanting to continue a relationship in future with their current suppliers'. Relationship integrity on the other hand, is conceptualized as 'the degree of commitment among customers in wanting to continue relationship in future with their current suppliers'. For relationship marketing to flourish, both intentions and integrity need to be high. Services marketers especially look for these two as indicators of relationship marketing commitment.

Another issue of importance to service marketers is regarding the deliverables of relationship marketers. The most common relationship deliverable of relationship marketing is 'business growth' (Patterson and Ward, 2000). Agrawal (2000) proposed the '4R' logic of relationship marketing. These 4Rs are conceptualized as follows:

R1 Resell: It refers to the potential of selling the same product more or again to the current customers. More appropriate to fast moving consumer goods (FMCG) and services, it is also referred to as brand loyalty.

R2 Retain: It refers to the potential selling of other products as well to the current customers. Equally important to the FMCG or a durable company, the deliverable is also known as cross selling of products and reflects brand equity.

R3 Refer: It refers to the potential of provoking a positive word of mouth from current customers to potential customers. Perceived to be equally important to the FMCG or durable marketers, the deliverable is most helpful to service marketing.

R4 Repute: It refers to the potential of earning reputation among the customers, competitors and collaborators. Equally important to the FMCG or durable marketers, the deliverable facilitates charging a price premium and protects the firm against competitive threats or consumer actions. It reflects corporate image.

The Hypothesized Model

Demand and supply mismatches affect positively and negatively the relationship intention and integrity among the service buyers. Each deliverable of the R4 framework of relationship marketing is affected by the service mismatch. Table 2 presents these consequences:

Table 2 *The Hypothesized Impacts of the Service Supply –Demand Mismatches on the R4 Deliverables*

Relationship deliverables / Service Supply-Demand Dis equilibriums	Supply < Demand	Supply > Demand	Supply = Demand
Reselling	Not immediately	Higher	Unchanged or higher
Retention	Lower Increased risk of losing customer forever.	Higher	Unchanged or higher
Referrals	Low High for negative word of mouth.	Higher	Unchanged or higher
Reputation	Little	Higher	Unchanged or higher

The Research Framework

The core issue—the impact of service demand and supply mismatch, was researched in three different ways. The first was to conceptually model the consequences (See Table 1). Second, we collected from a sample of ten respondents what is known in the marketing research literature, the 'third person account' of how service buyers might react in the event of service supply mismatches in a select service situation. These were hospitals, hotels, airlines, public, power supply and retail banking. contact the first author for details). Their responses are shown in Table 3.

Table 3 *Impacts of the Service Supply-Demand Mismatch in Healthcare*

Relationship	Demand > Supply	Demand < Supply	Demand = Supply
Retention	In case the high demand is on account of seasonal problems the retention rate would fall to a lesser extent than if the high demand were on account of the popularity of the doctor & not seasonal. A patient not getting an appointment may be lost forever.	Retention would be high because of reasons as above. Retention would also depend on other factors like the consistency (or enhancement) of quality of service vis-à-vis perceived value (which reinforces the level of satisfaction of the patient.)	Retention would various factors say on the consistency (or enhancement) of quality of service vis-a vis perceived value for the service which reinforces the level of satisfaction of the patient.
Referral	Possibility of loss of revenue from prospective patients due to the word of mouth of a dissatisfied (because of not getting an appointment) patient.	Referral would depend on various "other factors" similar to those stated above. Loss of revenue by way of overhead expenditure.	Retention would depend on various factors say on the consistency (or enhancement) of quality of service vis-a, vis perceived value for the service, which reinforces the level of satisfaction of the patient.
Reputation	Reputation would be affected to a lesser extent if the basis of repute of the medical practitioner were the perceived quality of service. However it is possible that a dissatisfied patient may by word of mouth spread an image of "arrogance" which would be detrimental to the practitioner's repute.	In case the situation of a low demand is because of the poor quality of service, then the reputation would further deteriorate. If the situation of low demand were because of seasonal factors, the harm to reputation would be to a lesser degree.	Retention would various factors say on the consistency (or enhancement) of quality of service vis-a, vis perceived value for the service that reinforces the level of satisfaction of the patient.

Finally, we administered a field questionnaire pertaining to the following questions:
- Recent usage of service products
- Recollection of a stock out situation.
- Momentary feelings and reaction in those situations
- Intention to return to such service suppliers
- Commitment to such suppliers
- Mentioning the same among their friends and neighbors
- Overall, an impression of such service firms.

The sample consisted of 68 valid respondents at a major management school in the eastern part of India. 27% of the respondents were women. The respondents belonged to all parts of the country, hailing from the high to middle income families. They were regular users of most services where supply-demand mismatches occur. Each respondent took 10 12 minutes to complete the questionnaire.

The Findings and Preliminary Model

The field investigation brought the following findings:

1. All respondents were irritated by frequent supply shortages of the services they used in public utilities (e.g. domestic power) and in private services (e.g. telecom and restaurants).
2. Unexplained and apparently mismanaged supplies irked them more.
3. Their immediate reaction was not to return to the service supplier.
4. However, it did not last long.
5. Quality of service mitigated their initial bitterness.
6. They tended to trade off service quality with the temporary insufficiency of service supplies.
7. They attributed supply mismatches to the generally poor environment of India. Still, the respondents blamed the supply deficiencies to an uncaring attitude of the service suppliers.
8. Most respondents delayed their return to service suppliers (particularly to hotel and doctors) for quite a while as they remembered supply shortage.
9. Reverse was the behavior for restaurants, however. The greater the supply shortage of a restaurant, the stronger was their desire to return to such establishments. They deemed it a mark of its superior quality.
10. Leisurely served customers spent more by as much as 25% than what they had intended.
11. Unhurriedly served respondent claimed to have bought at least one item on impulse (more that they had planned earlier).
12. They mentioned their mismatch experience (inadequate supply) to an average eight others. The experience of a positive mismatch (lower demand) was shared with an average three others.

Dealing with the Mismatch

Given the negative impact of the service supply-demand mismatches on relationship marketing deliverables in services, naturally service marketers may want to minimize those gaps and manage the lack of synchronization of service supply and demand. In the service supply demand mismatch, service supply is a more controllable variable from the marketer's perspective. Thus, service suppliers can manage service mismatch by managing their supply function more effectively. They may consider the following guidelines:

1. Learn what constitutes the backbone of the service supply. Is it the physical facility in which the service is performed, or is the service personnel whose labor and skills create service supply? It could as well be the equipment that produces service supply. Recognize them more closely (Fisk, Grove and John, 2000).

Table 4 *Presents a model of how the consequences of supply-demand mismatches affect the 4R's of relationship marketing*

Relationship deliverables	Supply < Demand	Supply > Demand	Supply = Demand
Reselling			
Not immediately Risk of	losing the customer if the service supply shortage is perceived to be because of mis-marketing. Unchanged if the service supply shortage is infrequent and service recovery better. Higher if the service under reference is 'he or in'.	Generally higher Risk of losing the customer if the service supply excess is perceived to be because of poor quality or service. Unchanged if the service supply excess is attributed to the natural or seasonal factors. Higher if supply excess is perceived to be out of a marketing design'.	Set to rise Unchanged at worst
Retention	Definitely lower if the service supply shortage is perceived to be because of mis-administration of marketing.	Generally higher	Set to rise since buyers expect a similar experience or demonstration of marketing competence.
	On-hold even if the service supply shortage is non-recurring and service recovery better. Largely unaffected if the previous supply shortages was fairly explained. Unchanged for those services that deemed 'in vogue, hep, in or monopolistic'.	Unchanged if the piggyback services are not perceived to be as good as the first service. Reinforces brand loyalty.	Unchanged at worst Reinforces brand loyalty
	Increased risk of losing customer forever rises.	Mild suspicions if everything is ok.	
Referrals	Lower Reluctant or conditional Higher negative word of mouth.	Higher Hesitant if the supply excess is recurring. Tend to go down if the supply excess is unexplained.	Definitely higher Unchanged at worst A note of caution may be appended while giving a positive word of mouth.
Reputation	Generally Dented	Generally Enhanced Unchanged at worst	Generally Enhanced Unchanged at worst. Improves confidence among the buyers.

2. Estimate the optimum capacity—the number of customers who can be effectively served under ideal conditions. The optimum capacity is different from the maximum capacity. A service performance deteriorates if it were stretched to the maximum capacity. It also deteriorates when the capacity falls below the minimum.
3. Educate service customers to curtail usage during peak periods.
4. Encourage customers to plan service demand by appointments.
5. Charge a premium for service use during periods of short supply.
6. Reinforce the need and reasons to wait during supply mismatches.
7. Conduct regular quality audits as an essential bulwark against a possible criticism. Since customers traded service quality with service the pains of service mismatch, it will be particularly helpful.
8. Create lifestyle aura around services since it helps relationship marketing even in case of mismatches.

The Discussion

The preliminary model and findings have several implications. Academically, the horizon of relationship marketing is pushed to a new dimension of demand and supplies mismatch. The area has not been explored so far. As Patterson and Ward (2000) recommended, 'relationship marketing is a powerful marketing tool and that we have yet to learn about relationships and how to successfully integrate marketing relationship techniques in the marketing plans' (pp. 340). The paper follows the advice and expands our understanding of relationship marketing.

Indian service practitioners stand to learn most from these findings since demand supply mismatches of services are regular and inevitable in some of services here. The first and foremost message to them is that they remain more vigilant since each mismatch means revenue lost. Secondly, they need to realize more seriously that if they lost customers even temporarily to their competitors, their risk of losing the customers permanently rises significantly, particularly in the present era of privatization, liberalization and globalization in the Indian service sector. Service disequilibriums dent their reputation to serve customers in a consistent manner. Finally, it helps them understand how to cement relationship intention and integrity among their customers even while their services remain fundamentally perishable and mismatches unavoidable.

REFERENCES

Agrawal, M.L (2000) 'World Class Marketing' *Management and Labor Studies*, XLRI Jamshedpur, July 2000.

Barnes, J.B. (1995) 'The Quality and Depth of Customer Relationships', in Proceeding of the 24th European Marketing Academy Congress, Paris, 1393-1402.

Berry L (1995) 'Relationship Marketing of Services: Growing Interest, Emerging Perspectives', *Journal of Academy of Marketing Sciences,* Vol. 23 No. 4 pp. 236-45.

Fisk R.P, S.J.Grove and Joby John (2000) '*Interactive Service Marketing',* Houghton Mifflin Company, Boston.

Gwinner, Kevin, Dwayne and Mary Jo Bitner (1998) 'Relational Benefits in Service Industries: The Customers' Perspective', *Journal of the Academy of Marketing Science*, Vol. 26 No. 2, pp. 101-14.

Keavenchy, Susan M (1995) 'Customer Switching in Service Industries: An Exploratory study', *Journal of Marketing,* Vol. 59 pp. 71-82.

Kotler, P. (1973) 'The Majors Tasks of Marketing Management', *Journal of Marketing,* Vol. 37, October, pp. 42-49.

Lovelock C.H. (1988) 'Strategies for Managing Capacity Constrained Service Organizations' in C.H. Lovelock (ed.) *'Managing Service: Marketing. Operations and Human Resources'*, Prentice hall. Englewood Cliffs, NJ pp. 163-75

Lovelock, C.H. (1998) *' Services Marketing'*, third edition, Prentice Hall, NJ.

Morgon R. and S.D. Hunt (1994) 'The Commitment Trust Theory of Relationship Marketing', *Journal of Marketing,* Vol. 58 (July) pp. 20-38.

Patterson Paul G and Tony Ward (2000) 'Relationship Marketing and Management', in Swartz, T.A. and Dawn Iacobucci (2000): *'Handbook of services marketing and Management'*, Sage Publications

Radas Sonja and S.M.Shugan (1998) 'Managing Service Demand: Shifting and bundling', *Journal of Services Research*, Vol. 1 No. 1, pp. 47-64.

Sasser W.E (1976) 'Match Supply and Demand in Service Industries', *Harvard Business Review*, Vol. 54, Nov-Dec. pp. 133-40.

Sasser, W. Earl, R. Paul Olsen, and D. Daryl Wyckoff (1978) *'Management of Service Operations Text, Cases and Readings'*, Boston, Allyn & Bacon.

Shemwell, D.J Jr. and J. Joseph Cronin Jr. (1999) 'Services Marketing Strategies for Coping Demand Supply Imbalances', *Journal of Services Marketing*, MCB University press, pp.14-24.

Swartz, T.A. and Dawn Iacobucci (2000), *'Handbook of Services Marketing and Management'*, Sage Publications.

Zeithaml, V., A. Parasuraman, and Berry. L (1985) 'Problems and Strategies in Services Marketing', *Journal of Marketing*, Vol. 49, No. 2, pp. 33-46

Chapter 40

Relevance of CRM for Hospital Services

■ **K M Mita**

Abstract

Patient needs are driver for efficient hospital services. Personal contact and relationships are very important in health care environment. In this paper, apart from reviewing significance of CRM practices for hospital services it has been attempted to study relevance and significance of CRM for hospitals keeping three broad groups of outpatient, inpatient and emergency services in view. All other services such as diagnostic services, nursing services, dietary services, pharmaceutical services, sterlization supply management services, linen services, laundry services, etc.; are suggested to be viewed as part of these three broad groups, and CRM practices more or less apply to all in the same fashion. In particular, it has been discussed at length how certain industrial engineering or management science techniques like queuing theory can be utilized for estimation of very vital resources such as medical staff size (outpatient services), hospital bed numbers (inpatient services), and ambulance fleet size (emergency services), that affect planning of all other hospital resources and ultimately lead to improved patient satisfaction. It is emphasized that apart from directly improving relationship aspects with patients and their relatives, availability of such vital resources in hospitals in adequate numbers, among others, can go a long way in improving CRM practices in hospitals.

Key Words: *Hospital Service, Patient Satisfaction, Management Science*

□ INTRODUCTION

Customer Relationship Management (CRM) which has overriding significance for any business is no less significant for hospital services (Salam, 2000). Hospitals are most important element in any health care delivery system. A hospital plays a major role in maintaining and restoring the health of the people. Care of the sick and injured, preventive health care, health-related research, and training of medical and paramedical staff are general broad functions of a hospital. It involves both outpatient and inpatient hospital services and on many occasions emergency medical services. An important resource in a hospital is a human resource. This should be particularly emphasized in the context of a hospital since relationship of medical staff plays important role in treating patients – the hospital customers. Following growing trends towards corporatization and privatization of health services, patients and society at large have multiple choices. Hospitals should maintain high degree of transparency and accountability in their services, as only then patients will develop durable relationships with them. In fact, effective CRM practices should become one of the key strategies for efficient hospital services. In health care, CRM practices are essentially patient—focussed strategies that involve effective management of hospital interface and interaction with patients. Hospitals that are more internally focussed and do not believe in maintaining durable relationship with them may eventually end up losing them. Patients may stay longer with a hospital or a private practitioner, if they feel it cares for them.

Effective CRM practices in a hospital may mean providing service related information to a patient very quickly, responding to the patient appointment and an admission requests promptly, dealing with patient queries and complaints expeditiously, exercising all kinds of flexibilities in serving patients, and extending best of care and courtesies to the patients. One possible way through which a patient can be kept satisfied and informed is that such individuals in hospitals with whom the patient is having frequent interface should be made well aware to answer general queries. For example, if a patient makes queries about an unsettled bill or requests for a fresh appointment, such staff should be quick to arrange requisite assistance. This type of helpful attitude aided by computer networking can go a long way in keeping existing and future patients satisfied and score a competitive advantage over other hospitals.

According to the Encarta World English Dictionary (Darling and Russ, 2000), a 'relationship is the connection between two or more people or groups and their involvement with each other, especially as regards how they behave and feel towards each other and communicate or cooperate'. CRM practices for hospital services can be described as organized endeavours to establish and improve relationship between the hospital and the patient and his/her relatives, with the twin objective of assisting the patient; and the hospital to enjoy a good reputation in the community. CRM practices also have a major implication for the vision, mission, values, culture, processes and services structure of a hospital. CRM practices not merely relate to just being nice to the patient, these are concerned with providing service of the highest degree with uncompromising sincerity (Sims, 2000). Normally, more cordial relationships may exist where patients may have more frequent and personal contact. CRM strategies may help hospitals to enhance many of their relationships with patients and their relatives and stakeholders like hospital administrators, medical and paramedical staff, and community at large. The CRM in hospitals should be seen as strategy to serve, satisfy, retain and attract patients. The CRM could be viewed as hospital-wide growth strategy aimed at knowing and serving patients using the latest technology to create a personal, caring and service-oriented interface.

Hospital's customers include not only individuals but also the organizations which engage them on periodic health check up/maintenance of their employees. Instances are not uncommon when organizations keep changing hospitals for their employees when they find that there are some relationship issues which hospitals do not properly address to. It is thus important that hospitals should pay due attention to the CRM practices to retain individuals as also the organizations they serve.

Delivering value is building block of relationships. Value is not just the price of the service delivered or discounts offered. In fact, patient perceptions of value are based on a number of factors that include quality-of-service, ease-of-delivery-without-hassles, speed, responsiveness, flexibility and service excellence. Hospital administration should endeavor to improve hospital productivity, service quality and cost. It is always possible to improve hospital productivity and reduce cost while improving or maintaining service quality at the same level. CRM strategies should be one of the key issues in hospital management. CRM solution should include broad array of systems, software and professional services that should help hospitals in making on time deliveries to hospitals.

□ LEVERAGING MANAGEMENT SCIENCE FOR PATIENT SATISFACTION

The major concern in CRM practices in hospitals is the quality of outpatient, inpatient and emergency services. Entire hospital staff, should be proficient in CRM practices, and should be a friend, philosopher and guide to the patients, whose welfare, comfort and satisfaction should be their prime concern. It is important to have cordial doctor-patient interface and a durable hospital-patient relationship (Das, 2000). Hospitals deal with human beings under stress and strain, and hence it is important that there is no gap between supply and demand of facilities either. Medical and paramedical staff should not be merely expert in their profession but they should be available in optimum size. Certain other very vital hospital resources like beds in wards for inpatient services and ambulance fleet for emergency services should be provided in adequate strength which along with adequate medical and paramedical staff size help in building a deep and abiding hospital-patient relationship.

For computing very vital hospital resources like medical staff size, number of hospital beds, and ambulance fleet size a set of important queuing characteristics have been computed for varying server size. These include average waiting; probability of waiting more than specified waiting or average waiting as desired; probability of absolutely no waiting; and probability of all servers being busy. (Mital, 1981, 1982, 1983, 1988). In the present analysis, a set of multi-channel queuing models have been used which, among others, include specific model for probability of waiting more than a specified time; and a model that measures probability of all servers being busy (Erlang Loss Model). Resource estimates based on average waiting (E_t) may lead to somewhat lower estimates as average arrival and service rates based on past one year statistics may not reflect critical stress situations during the year when actual waiting at certain moments may be much more than the average waiting. Hence, for achieving higher patient satisfaction and consequent improved CRM practice, it is proposed that resource estimates be based on such queuing characteristics like probability of waiting higher than the average waiting P_w (> t) or probability that all servers are busy (P_s). Description of different variables and characteristics in these cases are as follows (Mital, 1975, 1978, 1979):

λ = the arrival rate (outpatient or inpatient arrival rate, ambulance call rate)

μ = the service rate

S = the number of servers (doctors, beds or ambulances)

n = the number of patients in system awaiting service or being served

In a multi-channel queuing model, the probability of zero units in the system at time t, $P_o(t)$ is given by,

$$P_o(t) = \left[\sum_{n=0}^{S-1} \frac{1}{n!} \left(\frac{\lambda}{\mu} \right)^n + \frac{1}{S!} \left(\frac{\lambda}{\mu} \right)^S \left(\frac{S\mu^{-1}}{S\mu - 1} \right) \right]$$

The average time a patient has to wait before being served is,

$$E_t = \frac{\mu \left(\frac{\lambda}{\mu} \right)^S}{(S-1)! \, (S\mu - \lambda)^2} \cdot P_o(t)$$

The probability that a patient shall have to wait for some time, P_w (> 0), is

$$P_w(>0) = \frac{\left(\frac{\lambda}{\mu} \right)^S}{S! \left(1 - \frac{\lambda}{S\mu} \right)}$$

The probability that a patient shall have to wait more than time period 't' following non-availability of servers, P_w (> t), is given by,

$$P_w(>t) = \exp\left[-S\mu t \left(1 - \frac{\lambda}{S\mu} \right) \right] P_w(>0)$$

$$= \exp\left[-S\mu t \left(\frac{\lambda}{S\mu} \right) \right] \cdot \frac{\left(\frac{\lambda}{\mu} \right)^S}{S! \left(\frac{\lambda}{S\mu} \right)}$$

The probability that patient shall not have to wait at all is given by,

$$= [1 - P_w(>0)]$$

The probability that all servers are busy, P_s is given by,

$$P_s = \frac{\frac{1}{S!}\left(\frac{\lambda}{\mu}\right)^S}{\left[1 + \sum_{n=1}^{S}\frac{1}{n!}\left(\frac{\lambda}{\mu}\right)^S\right]}$$

The expected number of patients waiting for service is given by E_n,

$$E_n = \frac{\left(\frac{\lambda}{\mu}\right)^{S+1}}{\left(S-\frac{\lambda}{\mu}\right)\sum_{n=0}^{S}\left(\frac{S!}{n}\right)\left(1-\frac{n}{S!}\right)\left(\frac{\lambda}{\mu}\right)^N}$$

All queuing characteristics hold true under steady state conditions only i.e. when $\frac{\lambda}{S\mu} < 1$

□ OUTPATIENT SERVICES AND CRM

Outpatient services are one of the most important areas of a hospital which provide diagnostic, curative, preventive and rehabilitative services. It is not uncommon that OPDs are overcrowded and that patients have to spend considerable part of their time waiting at different places. Hospital clinics generally function for about 5-6 hours a day (3 to 4 hours in the morning and 1 to 2 hours in the afternoon). In some hospitals, a doctor in charge of a clinic examines about 25-40 patients per hour. This is considered to be excessive, as a doctor should not be expected to attend to more than about 10 patients (new and old) per hour. However, in practice a doctor is constrained to see more patients. Normally, a doctor should not be expected to attend more than 20 patients (old and new) per hour in any case (Das, 2000).

First interface of patient or his/her relatives with hospital is the hospital reception/ enquiry counter which is also involved with registration and admission formalities. The relationship founded at this point will go a long way in building overall positive image of the hospital (Das, 2000). The CRM practice up to this stage involves that the patient is properly received and courteously guided about the investigations that are being contemplated.

This case history relates to queuing analysis of a moderate sized public hospital which involved data for outpatient visits for one complete year (Table 1). It involved patient arrival and service rate analysis for physician, opthalmologist, dentist, paediatrician, radiologist, pathologist and surgeon (Mital, 1978, 1988). This type of queuing analysis helps in selecting medical staff size corresponding to prescribed service level in terms of specified combination of different queuing characteristics which leads to improved patient satisfaction.

Table 1 *Variation in Queuing Characteristics P_s, E_t, P_w (>0), [1-P_w (>0)], P_w (>t), P_s and E_n with Increasing Medical Staff Size (S) in Different Specialities (Outpatient Services)*

Category	S	P_o	E_t (Min.)	P_w (>0)	[1-P_w(>0)]	P_w (>t)	P_s	E_n
Physicians	10	0.000197	4.717	0.472	0.527	0.294	0.134	2.262
s	11	0.000230	1.852	0.289	0.710	0.216	0.091	0.876
691.53(λ)	12	0.000244	0.780	0.168	0.831	0.142	0.059	0.374
83.53 (Φ)	13	0.000251	0.342	0.941	0.905	0.085	0.036	0.164
	14	0.000253	0.150	0.499	0.959	0.047	0.021	0.072
	15	0.000254	0.064	0.252	0.974	0.024	0.011	0.031
Opthalmo	1	0.350778	7.773	0.649	0.350	0.339	0.393	1.201
-logist	2	0.509987	7.494	0.237	0.762	0.135	0.113	1.764
51.01 (λ)	3	0.521330	7.054	0.055	0.944	0.029	0.023	1.008
78.57(Φ)								
Dentist	1	0.047550	180.95	0.952	1.047	0.367	0.487	19.077
32.97(λ)	2	0.354480	2.79	0.464	0.535	0.225	0.188	0.279
39.61(Φ)	3	0.382114	0.37	0.174	0.825	0.074	0.056	0.037
Paediatri-	1	0.507132	3.40	0.492	0.507	0.301	0.330	0.479
Cian	2	0.604578	0.22	0.138	0.861	0.088	0.075	0.031
46.47(λ)	3	0.610420	0.02	0.023	0.976	0.014	0.012	0.002
94.28(Φ)								
Radio-	1	0.072302	257.91	0.927	0.927	0.366	0.481	11.903
Logist	2	0.366261	5.51	0.445	0.445	0.219	0.182	0.254
15.23(λ)	3	0.392058	0.73	0.161	0.161	0.070	0.053	0.033
16.41(Φ)								
Patho-	1	0.074614	46.136	0.925	0.074	0.366	0.480	11.476
Logist	2	0.367341	1.013	0.443	0.556	0.218	0.181	0.252
82.09(λ)	3	0.392998	0.134	0.160	0.839	0.069	0.053	0.033
88.70(Φ)								
Surgeon	1	0.107846	2.963	0.892	0.107	0.365	0.471	7.380
2.49(λ)	2	0.383052	0.089	0.418	0.581	0.208	0.173	0.221
2.79(F)	3	0.406741	0.011	0.144	0.855	0.063	0.049	0.028

☐ INPATIENT SERVICES AND CRM

Inpatient services are an important element in health care delivery which are provided in hospital wards which can be of general type like male, female wards or speciality wards. Speciality wards may include maternity wards, isolation wards, or wards for patients who need hospitalization in particular specialities such as orthopedics, paediatrics, psychiatry, etc. Intensive Care Units are essentially the wards for critically-ill patients.

During patient hospitalization, medical and nursing staff should extend utmost personalized care to the patients undergoing treatment. In maintaining CRM practices at this stage, support services like dietary, linen, housekeeping, pharmaceutical services, etc. should be kept up to the mark which can go a long way in enhancing patient satisfaction (Das, 2000). Medical staff should also provide all relevant and possible information to patients for their adequate understanding of treatment options, risks involved in various procedures, duration and the likely expenditure for treatment. All possible queries, doubts, apprehensions, and precautions to be followed, prior to, during, and after any procedure or surgery, should be explained and clarified in simple layman's language to the patient. In addition, some of these explanations may be given in the form of leaflets or brochures (Das, 2000).

Patients fears need to be allayed by the attending doctors. Non-verbal communication such as facial expressions, eye contact, pleasing gestures, and a comforting touch helps in building up this relationship which may help in providing anxiety-free stay for the patient in hospital. Nursing services are vital aspect of CRM practices, which should be properly maintained. In inpatient services, nurses play major role in building strong relationships with patients. A cordial behaviour and congenial relationship are some of the main aspects CRM practices in nursing care.

The housekeeping staff help in keeping the hospital clean and tidy. Many of them come in direct contact with the patients. Their services are important aspects of CRM practices as their activities contribute directly to the patient's comfort and peace of mind. During the patients stay in the hospital, his physical comfort contributes greatly to his progress. Hence, maintenance services assume considerable significance in hospital CRM practices. The maintenance crew is expected to attend to the complaint as early as possible, diagnose the fault, and rectify it.

Hospital security apart from security responsibilities also have role in affecting welfare and happiness of the patients in many ways (Das, 2000). They should be somewhat more flexible than the traditional security in other organizations as they often need to allow entry of relatives when they find them in overriding distress.

Bed is a very important resource for any inpatient services on which planning of all other resources depend. This queuing analysis relates to inpatient services of a female ward in a moderately sized public hospital (Table 2). This helps in estimating the number of beds in consonance with the service level desired by the hospital administration (Mital, 1975, 1981) which also leads to higher degree of patient satisfaction for customer services.

Table 2 *Variation in Queuing Characteristics P_o, E_t and P_s with Increasing Number of Beds(S) in Female Ward (Inpatient Services)*

Beds(S)	P_o	E_t			P_s
		Days	Hours	Minutes	
24	2.8459×10^{-11}	5.0092	120	13	0.07987
25	4.5209×10^{-11}	1.7170	41	12	0.07393
26	5.6121×10^{-11}	0.8461	20	18	0.06580
27	6.4189×10^{-11}	0.4765	11	26	0.05639
28	7.0485×10^{-11}	0.2838	6	49	0.04661
29	7.5472×10^{-11}	0.1731	4	9	0.03719
30	7.9375×10^{-11}	0.1062	2	33	0.02868
31	8.2337×10^{-11}	0.0650	1	34	0.02141
32	8.3846×10^{-11}	0.0452	1	5	0.01548

Average paitients arriving per day (λ)　　　　　= 23.14/6.6 = 3.50
Number of patients served on each bed per day (Φ) = 1/6.6 = 0.1515
$$\lambda/\Phi = 23.14$$

❏ EMERGENCY MEDICAL SERVICES AND CRM

The word emergency is derived from Latin word 'urgens' which means urgent. Medical emergency (casualty) is a situation in which a patient needs urgent and high quality medical care. It works 365 days a year and 24 hours a day. The foremost requirement of emergency services is that it should be done without delay. The CRM practice in emergency services implies that patients should be brought to the casualty from the patient home/site with minimum possible response time and attended with minimum delay. Patients of cardiac problems, strokes, fires in high-rise buildings, accidents, building collapse, natural calamities, or any critical health conditions are dealt with in emergency medical services. In most hospitals, ambulance service operates under direct charge of the Emergency Department. It is thus vulnerable for poor CRM practices if the standards of service fall below public expectation. After an ambulance brings a patient to the hospital, the Emergency Department provides round-the-clock service and prescribed treatment (Mital, 1990). When the patient is brought to the examination room, he is examined by a doctor on duty on emergency basis. Later, specialists advice may also be sought depending upon the nature and severity of the patient's condition. Patients not requiring any admission are treated here and following recovery discharged from here only. Patients needing further treatment are sent to the concerned emergency ward, and those needing observation are sent to the observation ward/ICU (Mital, 2000). Nurses/ambulance personnel assigned to receive calls in Emergency Department for dispatching ambulances should be experienced enough as a desirable CRM practice to distinguish between a symptom that can wait for a doctor's appointment the next day or one for which the ambulance needs to be promptly dispatched for immediate treatment. Ambulance alarm and communication system is thus an important CRM feature of ambulance service which helps to minimize the delay.

Two standards of CRM effectiveness for ambulance services are response time and service time. Response time is the time elapsed from the dispatch of an ambulance until its arrival at the emergency scene. Service time starts from the moment of dispatch of the ambulance till the arrival of the patient at the hospital. Whereas the first measure indicates quick response of the ambulance in reaching the site, the second measure reflects rapid transport of the patient from the site to the hospital where he is to be treated. A queuing analysis for a moderately sized hospital for estimating optimum ambulance fleet size in keeping with the prescribed service level by the hospital administration is included herein (Table 3). As an effective CRM practice the focus of ambulance service has undergone change in recent years with growing emphasis on the need to deliver timely and effective pre-hospital care (Mital, 1990, 2000). Efficient ambulance service with adequate fleet size is also one of the important factors for patient satisfaction at initial stages. Ambulance crew is now more commonly known as Emergency Medical Technicians who within the framework of CRM are viewed as key members of the patient care team. Dispatch of medical records in advance from the ambulance to the doctors for serving better can reduce the diagnosis time and regular treatment can start either during journey or immediately upon arrival in hospital. The paramedic using a common wireless network sends the patients details to the hospital in advance while accompanying the person to the hospital.

Table 3 *Variation in Queuing Characteristics P_o, E_t and P_w (>0), P_w (>t) and P_s with Increasing Ambulance Fleet Size (S) (Emergency Medical Services)*

Ambulances	P_o	E_t (Min.)	P_w (>0)	P_w (>10)	P_w (>20)	P_w (>30)	P_s
2	0.1166	168.00	0.6980	0.5910	0.5010	0.4240	0.3260
3	0.1916	19.00	0.2666	0.1510	0.0857	0.0487	0.1466
4	0.2034	4.00	0.0874	0.0333	0.0127	0.0048	0.0547
5	0.2056	0.07	0.0247	0.0063	0.0012	0.0004	0.0170
6	0.2058	0.04	0.0060	0.0010	0.0001	0.0000	0.0046
7	0.2059	0.02	0.0001	0.0001	0.0000	0.0000	0.0010

Average call rate = 1.26 calls/half hour
Average call rate during peak period (I) = 1.90 calls/half hour
Service rate (F) = 30/24.85 = 1.21 calls/half hour

□ CONCLUSIONS

In the future, hospitals should move from service-centric to patient-centric strategies. The future of a hospital rests in the ability to provide service levels that far exceed beyond patient expectations. Patients don't want multiple choices but simply expect that their demands be filled up to their full satisfaction. The strength of a hospital largely depends on strength of its relationship with patients. It is the relationship which can sustain a corporate hospital's profitability when it is losing business on account of introduction of new medical technology or price-cutting by other corporate hospitals. Hospitals should benchmark their service levels vis-à-vis other hospitals by undertaking benchmarking exercises or comparing with service level databases maintained by several hospital productivity and cost consultants. Learning to effectively interact with patients and develop dependable relationship with them should be the hallmark of healthy CRM practices for hospitals.

REFERENCES

Darling, J. and Russ, D. (2000), 'Relationship Capital', *Executive Excellence,* July, pp. 14.

Das, U.V.N.(2000), 'Patient Relations in Hospitals', in 'Srinivasan, A.V. (ed.), *Managing Modern Hospital,* Response Books (Sage Publications), New Delhi,' pp. 328-343.

Mital, K.M., *et al.* (1975), 'Bed Allocation Problem: A Case Study', *Opsearch,* Vol. 12, No. 30,.

Mital, K.M. (1978), 'Congestion Analysis in Hospital Clinics : A Case Study', *Indus. Engg. Jour. (India),* Vol. 7, No. 5, pp. 3-6.

Mital, K.M.(1978), 'Estimation of Hospital Bed Requirements : *A* Case Study', ORSA/TIMS 'Joint National Meeting', Los Angles, November 13-15. Also published in *Industrial Engineering Journal (India),* 1981.

Mital, K.M., *et al* (1979), 'Methodology for Estimating Bed Requirements', *Health and Population (NIHFW Jour.),* Vol. 2, No. 4, pp. 281-288.

Mital, K.M. (1981), 'Application of Erlang Loss Model in Selection of Ambulance Fleet Size: A Case Study', *Indus. Engg. Jour.,* Vol. 10, No. 12, pp. 3-9.

Mital, K.M. (1982), 'A Methodology for Estimating Ambulance Requirements', *Health and Population (NIHFW Jour.),* Vol. 5, No.1, pp. 11-22.

Mital, K.M.; Saxena, S. ; Datta, S. and Deshpande, P.M. (1983), *Estimation of Medical Staff Size,* A Working Report, New Delhi.

Mital, K.M. (1988), *Modelling and Analysis of Corporate Manpower Planning Process for Time-Dependent Career Growth Policy,* Ph. D thesis, IIT, Delhi, October., pp. 253-272.

Mital, K.M. (1990), 'A Priority Dispatching Rule for Ambulance Service', *Udyog Pragati,* March, pp. 33-42.

Mital, K.M. (2000), 'Analysis of Ambulance Service', in 'Raghavachari, M. and Ramani, K.V. (ed.), *Delivering Service Quality : Managerial Challenges for the 21st Century* (December 28-29, 1999), Macmillan India Ltd, New Delhi 110002,' pp. 322-3290.

Salam, S. and Kumar, S. (2000), 'Integrated Call Centres in Health Care Organizations', *Express Computers,* August 21, pp. 10.

Sims, D. (2000), 'CRM: Six Unavoidable Truths'. *CRM Community.* Accessed on August 5.

Building Customer Relationships
The Taj Air Caterers Experience

■ **Ajit Mathur**

Abstract

There is a lot of research supporting the profitable impact of long term customer relationships. Practicing managers always intuitively prided themselves on strong relationships with their customers. This paper shares the actual experience of Taj Air Caterers, the leading airline catering company in India. Author has described Customer Relationships and its dynamics based on his own experience. Three brief cases, namely, relationships with Singapore Airlines, Virgin Atlantic and GE Capital have been used to illustrate the approach. Paper ends with key learnings and insights, for both practicing managers and those wishing to pursue further enquiry.

Key Words: *Relationship, Relationship Potential, Relationship Boosters, Long Term Profitability*

□ INTRODUCTION

Broadly, the shift in emphasis from customer acquisition to customer retention has been at the heart of Relationship Marketing. Payne (1995) provides three basic frameworks:

- Transition from 'Transaction' to 'Relationship' in the marketing world.
- **Six markets** model, wherein besides Customer markets, five more are advocated, namely, Internal markets, Referral Markets, Influence Markets, Recruitment Markets and Supplier Markets, which need to be considered if the customer is to be served satisfactorily.
- Concept of a **Relationship Marketing Ladder**, where from the lower rung to the highest, the prospect is turned into a customer and then into a client; the next higher rungs being the supporter, advocate and finally the partner.

Above frameworks describe the concept of relationship in a systematic manner, and author has found them useful in a variety of situations. Storbacka et. al (1994) have contributed the Relationship Profitability Model, wherein service quality, customer satisfaction and customer relationship profitability linkages have been explored. This model has been one of the finest understandings of the underlying dynamics of the relationships.

This article focuses on author's own view of relationship, a framework to categorize customers in order to get maximum mileage, strategies to deal with various categories, and some conceptual learnings based on his own experience in the industry. It is focused on business-to-business marketing.

□ RELATIONSHIP VIEW OF BUSINESS

Relationship is the fundamental characteristic of any 'living' set of entities. Organizations are no different and therefore we see relationships as the binding force, which lend growth, vibrancy, energy and joy to both, those who supply a product or service, and those who receive it. In today's complex world, every organization works in a network of such relationships.

From an organizational perspective, relationships provide perpetual stream of revenues and profits, often increasing over a period of time, resulting in positive referrals, new business opportunities and quite often, a challenge to remain focused and efficient. Therefore, whichever way we look at it, it is beneficial to build strong, positive and mutually beneficial bonds.

Author's own view is that an organization has limited amount of energy, at any given point of time, physical and emotional put together. You can certainly expand it but at that time, management's task is to make best use of what it has. It is far more desirable to focus on building long-term profitable relationships with chosen fewer customers than to drain away this crucial energy in several short term, unstable relationships or haphazard customer acquisitions. Since, all existing and potential customers may not offer the same 'relationship potential', it is necessary to take a careful strategic view periodically of the mix that an organization has, and 'push-in' certain cases, 'pull-out' in certain other cases. A few may be kept on 'hold' till one could decide. This view is shown in Figure 1.

It must, however, be understood that any organization will have to carry a mix of 'Loyal', 'Not so loyal' and 'others' type of customers, simply because the latter two constantly get sieved out to add to the first category. It's almost like retrieving gold from the sand. Constant sifting is necessary and once you have the right 'prospect', you gotta put in energy to make good value out of it.

Author also holds the view that relationship is a two way street but service provider will have to take the initiative of hand holding in initial years, and even afterwards. If the customer is unwilling but your goal is to put him on the relationship bridge, then initial push has to come from you. In many cases, we have seen, organizations losing potentially good customers because either the relationship was taken for granted or customer was dubbed as 'unwilling'.

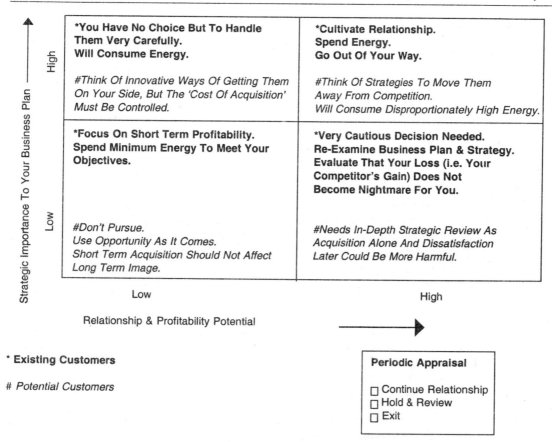

Fig. 1 *Categorizing Customers*

□   ABOUT TAJ AIR CATERERS

Taj Air Caterers is the Airline Catering Division of the Taj Group of Hotels. It has annual revenues of approx. US$ 23 million and caters to over 25 leading international and domestic airlines. Its three major facilities at Delhi, Mumbai and Chennai produce approximately 31,000 meals daily and employ 2400 staff. This paper describes Taj's efforts to build long term profitable relationships with its select customers. Three typical cases illustrate different aspects of relationship building. Experience with Singapore Airlines is spread over two decades and the relationship has not only stood the test of time but has matured. The relationship potential with Virgin Atlantic provided the winning edge in a fiercely competed bid and is built into the system in several unique ways. The relationship with GE (where Taj Air Caterers provides catering services for its employees) is still evolving in a new business setting. This experience is followed up by practical learnings, which can be applied in a variety of situations.

□ EXPERIENCES

Case 1: Singapore Airlines

Singapore Airlines (1999-00 revenues S $ 8.2 billion) has an enviable track record of growth and profits. It has been creating industry benchmarks and is known for its inflight services. As a matter of fact, besides technology, its differentiation strategy is mainly built around its inflight product. Taj Air Caterers is proud to have almost two decades of association with Singapore Airlines. It has been a privilege to work with such a forward-looking organization. What started as supply of inflight food & beverages has over a period of time evolved into a strong mutually beneficial relationship.

Taj now actively participates in product design and influences service design, wherever necessary. This has evolved after getting an insight into Singapore Airlines' customer profile and their needs. The product is designed to reflect their passengers' preferences, which are quite different in Delhi and Mumbai, and on different sectors ex-Mumbai. Since a lot of Indians travel back to India from Singapore, next logical step was product redesign ex-Singapore. And as we both realized popularity of Indian meals globally, Taj Chefs now conduct an annual workshop on Indian cuisine for Singapore Airlines' caterers worldwide. When it created World Gourmet Panel of known celebrity chefs to create Signature dishes for its First and Business Class passengers, Taj's Chef joined the roll of honor amongst eight best known worldwide. Today, we are glad to work with Singapore Airlines in whichever way passenger satisfaction can be enhanced. In turn, Taj has benefited from volume and revenue growth of Singapore Airlines in the Indian market. Our staff gets trained at their catering subsidiary, SATS. We share a lot of information and can access technology issues, for instance. In 1999, Taj and Singapore Airlines became Joint Venture partners in Chennai catering facility of Taj, a fine testimony to our relationship.

Case 2: Virgin Atlantic

Virgin Atlantic airlines, founded in 1984, is known for its heady mix of fun, innovation and professionalism. It is also known for its unique inflight product complete with massage onboard! Taj Air Caterers is proud to have won the contract to supply inflight food & beverages to Virgin.

In this case, the basic approach was to build a relationship than just somehow get the contract. Taj offered a one-stop quality solution to Virgin's needs ranging from catering and cabin cleaning to Lounge, Limos and hotels. We also promised them a marketing push out of India and promote Virgin brand. In turn, they would promote Taj hotels. We urged them to look at long term value creation and seamless service. We also reduced the number of contact points (persons) to just three for any needs across Taj Group, and in Delhi or in London. There was yet another unique point worth mentioning that we built the relationship on total transparency of relevant information. We anticipate Virgin's rapid growth in Indian market and hope to take this relationship to much higher level. In a short period of less than six months, we are already involved in helping them redesign menus out of London.

As each important event gets concluded, we take one more step towards winning customer's confidence. 'Self audits', for example, is a unique step to build long term trust. Like in many other cases, we have a dedicated team to serve Virgin – the idea is to understand all the nitty-gritty details and create a smooth service delivery system, which completely meets their needs on a continuous basis.

Other Airlines

Taj Air Caterers has a very strong relationship orientation, which comes naturally in dealing with all its clients. There are so many other fascinating experiences. For instance, when United Airlines was operating out of Delhi (now planning to come back to India next year), our mutuality and trust was of the highest order. It was built around highly motivated team, cutting across functions, which delivered an exceptional product and service. We call these teams as PPS Teams (Plan – Produce – Serve Teams). When they needed a quick turnaround, for example, during fog, Taj stood by them and achieved a hundred percent success. I can't remember any United program where Taj was not involved. All United marketing programs had a Taj representative, which ensured that customers voice was heard first hand.

With all our other clients, we keep a very close contact so that we **anticipate** customers' needs and deliver a highly customized product. This coupled with our flexible attitude produces the winning edge.

Case 3: GE Capital International Services

GE Capital International Services (GECIS) is a subsidiary of GE Capital. It started its operations in India, in Gurgaon (near Delhi) a few years back and has grown rapidly. Taj first came in contact with GECIS in end 1998, when it decided to diversify into Institutional Catering. Institutional Catering until then was limited to small players, whose focus was on supply of food (the physical product).

Taj defined its business as 'Enhancing the well-being of customers' employees' than mere provider of food. The journey with GECIS started in July 1999, and without doubt, has been one of the most exciting and challenging one. The first step was to make menu and service design interactive. Today, based on employees' feedback and preferences, menus are constantly adjusted on a weekly basis. Besides the Operations Team, there is a full time Customer Relations Executive assigned to GE. She handles all feedback, queries, suggestions and works closely with GE Administration on one hand and our operations on the other hand. An e-mail connectivity is underway, wherein Taj Customer Relations will respond within a stipulated time frame directly to GE employees and analyze satisfaction. Also on cards is a 'Fitness Program' where Taj's experts will share information of food nutrition, exercise etc. with GE employees. Similarly, a Loyalty Program is being designed wherein for purchases of snacks and confectionary, GE employees can obtain attractive discounts at Taj outlets/hotels. With another company, Taj is even involved in cafeteria design and selection of equipments.

As relationship is building up, Taj is benefiting by way of increasing volumes and positive referral. GE has a reliable partner who can provide variety of services at short notice. In one instance, heating ovens were installed overnight when employees were not happy with 'cold' food. For their very special catering needs, they know Taj would deliver.

With expectations running high and the employee profile that GE has (young, computer literate, vocal, ambitious), Taj is still learning to cope up with this high-pressure situation. In long run, we want to be a part of their growth and hope that relationship enters into a more stable and mature phase. It is also necessary to keep doing things which keeps relationship alive and kicking. For example, special menus are provided practically on all festivals, keeping in view the sentiment attached with each of them, and these colorful initiatives do not go unappreciated.

◻ INSTITUTIONAL CATERING: OTHER CUSTOMERS

We are trying to understand the market and its dynamics. We already have five prestigious clients. Relationship building is high on our agenda. It's too early to predict but we are on the right track, going by the feedback we have. Our desire is to go much beyond provisioning of food. We should be the reliable partners for any kind of food/beverage services that an organization might need, whenever they think of their employees' welfare, a meeting, a get-together or an outing. Thus we become one-stop shop, and keep excitement on.

Since, our platform is 'well-being', we are already talking long term care and concern. We wish to be known for providing such a care, than just food. We believe, this is the only way to build long term relationships in this kind of business, where 'vendors' edge out each-other on commercial terms frequently. From customer's angle, it has long term reliability and assurance in place, considering employees are the most valuable asset, and their satisfaction and productivity are key issues.

◻ LEARNINGS

As a practicing manager and out of our experience, I have summarized few key lessons:
   i) Long term, profitable relationships can be built when both, the service provider and the customer, rise above the 'transaction' approach, and work in an atmosphere of mutuality and trust.
   ii) Generally speaking, in the initial years of relationship, it is the service provider who has to work very hard, as customer gets to know all the facets of the relationship and has a chance to get onto 'relationship–bridge', even if it was not thought of being important initially.
   iii) Relationship, like real life, goes through ups and downs, and it takes a great amount of maturity and courage to handle the 'lows'. If one rises to the occasion when the other needs him, the relationship gets a booster.

iv) Relationships provide 'security'. Greater the number of linkages between the service provider and the customer, greater is the bonding and the 'security'. Strategic bundling of services is a useful methodology in this context.

v) Top management must be committed to the relationship, as their example is followed throughout the organization.

vi) Both the Marketing and the Operating strategy must be geared to meet the Relationship goals, especially where quick responses are required. Cross-functional Teams are a wonderful solution.

vii) An issue worth exploring is also to ask whether the customer is willing to give relationship a chance or not? It might be difficult or too expensive to push an unwilling partner, and in such cases, either the whole dynamics must change or else relationship goals must be revisited.

viii) Author's own concept of relationship is shown in Fig 2. As a new customer is won, it rapidly moves on the 'needs' continuum and if the Service Provider cannot respond adequately and quickly, it can endanger the whole relationship. As one can see, this kind of thinking pushes the Service Provider harder on one hand, and the customer has a chance to evaluate the 'net value' in dealing with a specific Service Company over others.

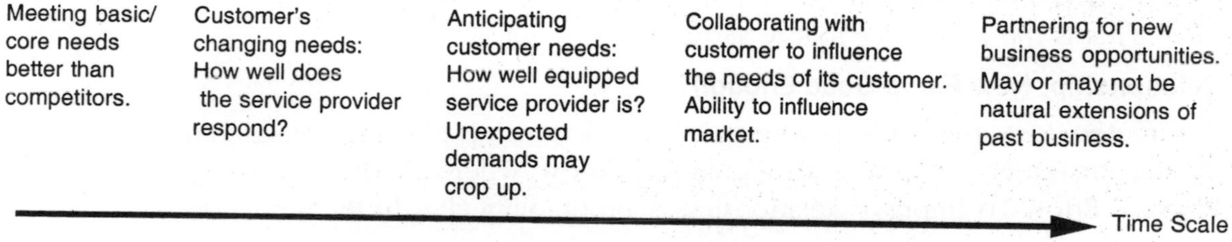

Meeting basic/ core needs better than competitors.	Customer's changing needs: How well does the service provider respond?	Anticipating customer needs: How well equipped service provider is? Unexpected demands may crop up.	Collaborating with customer to influence the needs of its customer. Ability to influence market.	Partnering for new business opportunities. May or may not be natural extensions of past business.

→ Time Scale

Fig. 2 *What Happens to Customer Needs, as Relationship grows?*

ix) The effort required in the initial years of relationship is quite large (Accountants can prove in many cases that it is not worth it!) but as time progresses, both relationship and profitability start looking up. See Fig. 3, when the relationship is mature, effort plateaus out as understanding deepens to a great extent and good, intelligent effort can keep it going. It must be noted that customer also is obliged to put effort to take the relationship forward, and this fact must be appreciated by both the partners.

□ SOME MORE INSIGHTS

Relationship Boosters

Whenever relationship curve is plateauing or drooping, one needs to take pro-active steps, what author wishes to call as 'Relationship Boosters'. These are imaginative steps to give a 'new look' to the whole relationship, much like we see rejuvenated consumer products with the 'New' or 'Extra' label trying to woo the customers. Lets put it this way: Customers need constant reassurance that you have not forgotten them. Relationship Boosters can come in variety of ways. It can range from providing new or additional benefits at no or little cost to doing something which is a 'pleasant surprise' to doing something which is not even directly connected with your business but helps the customer. In our case, we have been using opportunities to train airline crew, host their meetings or get-togethers or guiding them on issues other than catering, finding vendors, or even referring customers to them.

How to Treat Customers Who do not Have Great Relationship Potential?

Everybody knows how to treat customers those who have large relationship potential. My view is that in real world, one has to exercise extreme caution and politeness in dealing with those customers who do not hold great promise. The basic premise is simple: You cannot ignore the fact that they are your customers as of now or that who knows one day they might become attractive or they might bring negative referrals to you etc., if treated shabbily. It is utterly important to handle such relationships in a sensitive manner. One of the best ways is to be polite, fact-driven and transparent and never offensive, personality – driven or shrouded in mystery. Customers like clean, honest answers anyday. Also, some minimum relationship must be kept even if you have exited out a customer relationship or vice-versa. This is business and who knows you need each other at some future point of time. This is the policy we follow at Taj Air Caterers.

Relationship: How Far is Good Enough?

Yet another sensitive issue is whether your relationship is being considered as 'Intrusion' by the customer. In that case, we should know where to draw the line Emotional & Physical Effort To Improve Relationship & Profitability (Put In By Service Provider)

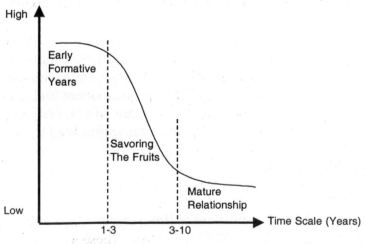

Fig. 3 *Effort on the Part of Service Provider to Build and Sustain Relationship*

My experience is that every individual and every organization has such an invisible boundary, which if you cross, may yield negative feelings and results. That's a major reason as to why free Internet accounts remain unsubscribed. You'd rather pay than to disclose your passport and credit card number! It is entirely unnecessary to dabble into the internal happenings of your customers' organizations. Similarly, excessive mailers, phone calls or e-mails, no matter how good the intention is, tends to put off prospects. We are extremely careful about this aspect and good marketers know it intuitively.

Each Organization's Perspective is Unique

Just as your gain is somebody's loss, your loss will be somebody's gain. You don't have to get disturbed because your perspective of profitability, long-term and what constitutes relationship may be quite different from your competitor. Well, that's how market gets segmented. However, when new prospects are brought into the market or a 'mild' user is targeted to become 'heavy' user, it will take a while before you know where to focus. So, initially relationship net will have to be thrown open and wide. Later, using intelligent analysis, one can estimate how much and how far to go. Readers Digest has done a good job using these rudimentary insights. We constantly look for successful relationship strategies pursued by successful businesses and don't mind adapting the chosen ones for our business.

□ CONCLUSION

Relationship, as we discussed earlier, is a natural corollary to any interaction. The challenge before practicing managers is to **balance between long-term goals and short-term gains**. Top management must define its policy in this regard. It is useful to project customer revenues and costs on a time scale and carefully plan customer acquisition program. An organization must judiciously allocate its energy towards various categories of existing and potential customers. Marketers must get into relationship dynamics within each category, and give it appropriate treatment so that it stays healthy and vibrant.

REFERENCES

Payne, Adrian (1995), *Advances in Relationship Marketing*, London: Kogan Page Limited, pp. 29 – 38
Storbacka, Kaj, Strandvik, Tore and Grönroos, Christian (1994) 'Managing Customer Relationships for Profit', *International Journal of Service Industry Management*, Vol. 5, No. 5, pp 21–28.

Chapter 42

Relationship Management Practices in Hospitality Industry

A Study of Hotels and Restaurants in Calcutta

■ **Sipra Mukhopadhyay**

Abstract

The study explores strategies adopted by hospitality industry to maintain customer relationship. There are various facets, namely, satisfaction, loyalty, retention measures, complaint management-failure and recovery. These get reflected in strategies such as segmentation and targeting with appropriate product offer, product innovation, demand and quality management, complaint management—redressal /feedback system. The study finds out how these have been used by industry to maintain relationship. It does not attempt to identify linkages among these facets.

Based on a survey of purposive sample comprising of hotels and restaurants (existing and new) in the city of Calcutta the study focused on the service providers' perspective. A convenience sample was used to obtain feedback from users of restaurants.

Analysis based on qualitative and quantitative techniques indicated that segmentation and targeting with appropriate product and pricing (more so for the restaurants) along with product innovation were the major strategy thrust in the industry. There seemed to be a lack of rigid control system despite growing competition. Feedback analysis indicated that a balanced mix of tangibles and intangibles would achieve the desired result.

Key Words: _Customer Relationship, Satisfaction, Loyalty, Retention Measures, Compliant Management, Rigid Control System._

❑ INTRODUCTION

Hospitality product, is largely people based, consumed and experienced in close encounter with the service provider, lasting more than one interaction. This is punctuated by "Moments of Truth" leading to dis/satisfaction. Hence People, Physical Environment (Ambience), and Process have significant role to play. The intangibles (service, ambience) along with the tangibles (food, lodging etc.) are equally important. Getting the right blend makes hospitality service fairly complex and challenging.

Though hotels and restaurants belong to the same Industry, these satisfy very specific needs depending on service characteristics and the targets catered to. While hotels serve to provide 'home away from home',restaurants offer an ambience expected to be different from that of home. Hence the emphasis on various aspects of servicing are not the same.

The interaction with customers in hotels is often of a longer duration, where the concept of EAI (extended affective interaction, see Price et al., 1995) holds. This in turn raises certain expectations, namely, Responsiveness, Empathy, and Assurance, essential components of total offer. For restaurants. ' Responsiveness' maybe the single most important factor.

The entry and exit barriers are higher in hotel business.

Both face product as well as brand competition. While hotels compete with similar 5-star services available in the city, they have corporate guest houses to keep in mind. Restaurants lose business to other food joints having location advantage. They are also under pressure from various clubs patronized by corporate members. It may be noted that such clubs offer variety of facilities (games, swimming) than a food outlet . There is significant difference in the ambience or environment. The clubs are homely, informal whereas restaurants are formal and impersonal. Besides, there are clubs catering to specific needs, sports, swimming, gyms. The competition however is indirect, generic in nature.

The business thrives mostly on prosperity of a region. Indeed for hotels,,business mostly accrue from transient population . In the case of restaurants, affluence,age composition of local population, and active support of business houses are decisive factors These in turn depend on the state of economy of the region. In this context, the city of Calcutta is not an ideal choice . It has neither a vibrant economy nor does it host major cultural or sports events.

In view of the above, attracting and retaining customers become crucial.

□ OBJECTIVE

There are many facets for maintaining customer relationship. These are satisfaction, loyalty, complaint management and related retention measures. These get manifested in various decision areas, viz, Proper Segmentation and Targeting, Quality and Demand Management., Product innovation, Customer Handling-feedback and redressal. These all have tangible and intangible elements which need to be offered in the right blend to achieve desired experience.

The study explores these very aspects in the framework of Planning, Implementation and Control. As in any marketing situation this consists of

(a) setting objectives and desirable future 'Want',

(b) collecting resources 'Can',

(c) Managing firms environment 'Should',

(d) Defining ethical standing 'Allowed'{Long Range Planning, Vol. 30, p. 934, extracted from Services Management, Looy et al, 1998}. It may be noted that 'a' above, relates to opportunity scanning ; 'b' to analysis of strengths and weakness ; 'c' and 'd' to managing threats and constraints.

Specifically the study responds to the following research questions.

How is relationship built on:

RO1—Segmenting and targeting – matching the offer with segment and helping demand management.

RO2—Quality management- and related issues of costs etc.

RO3—Demand management-loss due to lost and disappointed customers during peak, as also lost hours during lean business.

RO4—Product Innovation to gain differentiation and matching customer needs.

RO5—Overall experience to customers in relation to mix of tangibles and intangibles, synergy and trade-off, which may finally contribute to image and positioning.

RO6—Customer Handling -Feedback and redressal

The scope is limited to 5-star hotels and up market restaurants in the city of Calcutta.

☐ OVERVIEW

Amongst the major studies on hospitality industry, two relevant ones are discussed. The thrust in the first study (Buttle, 1986) is on the overall marketing strategy, detailing the functional areas, covering research and consumer behavior . The other (Kotler et al., 1998) adopting the same approach also examines retention and the levels of relationship. Both the studies appear to apply framework of "planning–implementation-control." In the process, specific characteristics of the industry, i.e., exception to rules, do not get highlighted.

The focus of this study is much more narrow, that of 'managing relationship' .

Various reasons have been identified as to why customer switch and the need for retention. (Keaveney et al., 1995) . Firms gain much more by retaining a core loyal customer than by continually attracting new business/clients .Ample evidence, which need not be enumerated separately, exists in service literature .

Relationship is value addition, it goes beyond the product. In manufacturing industry, value addition is through after sales service, intangible component being the interaction of service personnel with customer (Gureja 1997). It is a progression from simple transaction to relational bonds embracing social or/and business partnership.[1] This depends on the level of interaction between server and receiver .This could be casual or occasional to a regular encounter of short or longer duration A salesman on one day tour in a city stops over for lunch or dinner, whereas another stays for some days taking food from the same restaurant or hotel. Expectations of the two individuals may not be the same. The former

---

[1] Today it an extensively researched subject. The term "commercial friendships" draws from concept of relationship marketing. (Price et al 1999).

may look for "overall satisfaction", the latter "trust and commitment". (Garbarino et al., 1999). Thus for a regular client `trust and commitment could be—pay later, my kind of food

Aim of the provider in either situation is to get repeat buy, convert an irregular to a regular buyer. In order to identify needs/expectations, proper segmentation becomes crucial.

This not only helps to match the segment needs, but also even out demand fluctuation, through multi period pricing with product to match. (Desiraju et al., 1999). Since differentiation rather than standardisation drives the industry, the costs involved need to be assessed. Extent of customisation and for whom are critical decisions. The measure CRA, (customer return on asseets) could act as control (Rust et al., 1999). Some of these aspects have been examined in **RO1**.

Again loyalty is much more complex and not necessarily linked to satisfaction (Oliver, 1997, 1999). Hence a service provider needs to examine other issues, such as ' the nature of trade- off that a consumer adopts resulting in absence or presence of loyalty. In other words, it is imperative to explore what contributes to retention. These could be demand and quality management. This study examines related issues, such as cost to the consumer in accessing services (location) and compensation offered in case of complaint (Smith et al., 1999). The firm too must commit costs to enhance quality of service. These could be inspection, prevention, internal and external costs. (Armistead et al., 1994). There are ways and means to reduce failure costs. To measure gain due to quality enhancement, ROQ (Rust et al., 1999) was used . Probing was done to understand familiarity with the concept and its usage. The relevant issues have been addressed in **RO2** and **RO3**.

Relationship is sustained on a balanced mix of tangibles and intangibles. Food or cuisine forms significant saleable feature, whereas ambience along with service add to the overall effect. The typical issues are trade-off, synergy, enhancing value of intangibles and tangibles. (Heene et al., 1998). These have been examined in **RO4** and **RO5**.

Retention strategy as spelt out in various studies (Lowenstein,1997; Armisted et al.,1994, Osel et al., 1998, Lovelock, 1996, Zeithaml et al., 1996), need to be planned, and supported by Grievance cell, Complaint Handling system reflecting customer orientation . There are ways to assess effectiveness (Ossel et al, 1998, Looy and others 1998). These have been probed in **RO6** and discussed in the next section.

□ METHODOLOGY

Sample: The city has five 5-star hotels, [2]four of these were contacted . Of the 50 restaurants catering to up market segment, 15 were contacted. Selection was purposive based on the popularity of the units. This was in keeping with the objective of the study. Care was taken to represent different areas of the city.[3]

---

[2] One of these located at air port has not been considered. The sixth one, running under losses has been excluded.

[3] Most of the frequently visited restaurants are clustered around the same area.

It was easier to get the profile of the customer for restaurants,since they were local and often regular visitors. They also lent an identity and an image to the restaurant. The customers of hotels were much more heterogeneous, though some of them were repeat buyers.

The information was collected from the sales/ marketing manager through structured interviews.

RO1-

Segmentation not only helped to specify needs and match the offer given a consumer or a segment but also even out the demand fluctuations, more so, for restaurants. It was expected that profile of visitors to food joints, pubs or disco would change over the week as also over the day. Such sharp segmentation was not possible in the case of hotels. Seasonalty was virtually absent.

Probing was done on whether i. any planning was done as to the kind segments to cater to, and the planning of total offer; ii. What resources were used and iii. if some details / record of the patrons or segment(s) were maintained. iv.Whether the concept of CRA was understood or used.

RO2-

Quality management : The components are both intangibles and tangibles. The emphasis here was on tangibles,viz food and lodging facilities . The basic issues related to costs involved in planning resources, inducting skills, training; maintenance and control. And this involved managing inspection, prevention, internal and external costs . Finally whether costs were controlled through appraisal, prevention and minimization of failure. And if ROQ (See Rust et al., 1999) was used as control measure.

RO3-

Demand management : Examined how lean or peak periods were dealt with. If ARGE (asset revenue generating efficiency, see Lovelock, 1996) was used to assess effectiveness.

RO4-

Product Innovation: Since 'Tangibles ' contribute significantly to Hospitality industry, the respondents were probed on what they considered their ' specialty ' in cuisine, beverages or others.

RO5-

Overall experience: Blend of intangibles with tangibles lending uniqueness to a service product . Related issues were examined, viz,

What and how values could be added to tangible and intangible components .

What synergy and trade -off were possible between the two elements

RO6-

Feedback and redressal : The focus was on Control exploring whether complaint handling system existed, if so, support, its place in the organisation structure, and compensation.

Success of Retention (Ossel et al 1998) was measured on the basis of:
- Ratio of complaints to compliments
- Speed of handling complaints
- Customer response to complaint handling
- Number of projects /changes resulting from complaint analysis.

Finally it was important to know what was achieved after the various measures.

An index of success was developed to which service provider responded adding his own views. (see Findings).

Since it was possible to get a sample of service users of restaurants, a feedback from them on Perception, Image (word association), was obtained . Ratings on relevant attributes as also Repeat Buy were recorded. The sample numbering 30, was drawn from students of management institutes .

Measures and Analysis

For the service provider responses were against presence or absence of given practices. Since the variables were dichotomous in nature, simple cross breaks could be used. Major mentions were noted on the basis of frequency. For positioning and image, word association was applied (see Appx - Exbt 1). This was supported by MDS and Clustering. Only units with more than ten entries were considered. These ranged from two to more than ten.

☐ FINDINGS

Restaurants

These could be categorized according to the core need satisfied as indicated below.
- Simple entertainment, recreation - providing live music
- Fun, pleasure- nightclub disco, pub disco. *
- Excitement- celebrity days, facility for games*
- Relaxation- traditional, soft recorded music.

All the new units (5-10) years claimed variety in cuisine, a mix of international favorites.
* At least four of the six 5-star hotels, have opened up separate discos. As of now only one restaurant has this facility.

Consumer profile: While most of them were local drawn from affluent families, a good number came from other cities, as tourists and on business. Interestingly for at least one unit, outstation visitors were through referrals. Weekend visitors were families, the bias generally being toward younger group through out the week. Quite a few units drew patrons locally. Centrally located joints attracted highly mobile upper income category.

Consumer expectation: According to a survey (Das et al., 1999), considerations in selecting a restaurant were-

Quality of music, Quality and range of food and beverages, Ambience and recreation - special events, live music, Convenience- location, service hours, booking facility, Dance floor, Quality of service.

Emphasis or importance would tend to vary over individuals or groups. Clearly 'dance floor' should receive priority over others from young or teenage couples. This was supported from the feedback (Exhibit 1), MDS (Figure 1), cluster analysis (Figure 2).

The joints A7 and A13 leading in frequency over others (also likely repeat buy) were close to each other in clustering and positioning (Figures 1 & 2). Given the feedback as above, the two major dimensions appeared to be 'value for money' and 'ambience/ overall experience'. Convenience or location was embedded in 'ambience', as most of the food joints were in and around the same place (Park Street). Hence 'cost' of the consumer in terms of convenience could not be isolated and highlighted. In this particular case, 'location' also contributed to 'ambience'. Both A7 and A13, close to educational complex (schools and colleges) attracted teenage crowd. More than the interior décor,the environment around the place evoked a sense of belonging,'my kind of people'.

Word association along with frequency and positioning clearly indicated that a good balance of tangibles and intangibles may lead to repeat buy or retention.

Both A7 and A13 with average rating, seemed to be popular. Given the profile of the segment, comprising occasional users, 'overall experience/ satisfaction 'seemed to work. Though based on a limited sample, these supported earlier findings (Garbarino and Oliver 1999).

The Tables below provide the findings on relationship management .

Stated Objective(s): maximize capacity utilization or turnover, control cost to earn profit.

Table 1 *Relationship Management—Restaurants*

Facets	Observation
Segmentation and targeting	Broadly, by week days and week end guests, by hours of the day,lunch, dinner, and snack groups. No formal planning, based on industry norms. One unit in the process developing consumer data bank CRA- no such concept, though repeat buyers and guests on referrals were noted..
Demand management	Options to manage peak time were either to invest for expansion or lose business, tendency to opt for latter. Lean - go for office catering, club and home delivery else forego. At least one of these exhibited ingenuity in managing demand through multi period pricing and segmentation (see Exht 2)Occupancy measured in terms of turnover (see below). No concept of ARGE.
Quality management	Nearly all invested in recruiting skills and training ; high turnover of employees mentioned. Supervision and inspection by a few top units. These were mostly privately owned, family run businesses. ROQ- measured in terms of trend in guests turn over. Benchmarking- no evidence.
Product Innovation,	Nearly all, though strategy appeared to be 'imitation'. There were a few exceptions. Some claimed specialty in coffee, international cuisine. (exht 3). The practice was to take feedback on new items introduced in the menu.
Others: Ambience, Infrastructure	Some had invested heavily - to give them distinctive feature- One of them had also unique feature of combining ambience of restaurant with that of disco. No bench marking or feedback.
Customer handling Consumer feedback, Recovery	There was no formal cell in the organization structure. A specimen structure given (Exbt 4) . The approach was reactive. Informal, verbal feedback taken Recovery: Mainly in compensation, free replacement for rejected food; verbal apology. Complaints were monitored. No follow up.

Success Index : (Rev - expenditure)/ asset: found difficult to operationalise

Percentage of repeat buy – noted, but not recorded

Image - no feedback taken

Referred guests or guest on referral - noted, but not recorded

Stated objectives: measured in terms of load factor or turn over . This was based on the number of batches over capacity . A turnover of 2.5 times during weekdays and 4.0 times on weekends indicated satisfactory performance for a successful unit.

Cost of wastage/leftovers was being controlled by preparing limited menu.

The findings reflect the service providers perspective as it was not possible to contact users.

Stated objectives: Sending back a happy customer, match up to international standard.

Table 2 *Relationship Management-Hotels*

Facets	Observation/Comments
Segmentation and targeting	Basically on price and services (benefits) . A typical segmentation of a leading hotel was as given below.[4] Efforts were on to target local younger generation inclined toward western culture. CRA- no evidence, may be informal.
Quality management	Effort to close the expectation perception gap through initial research apparently not present. Post analysis and follow up seemed to be the practice. Dictated by industry norms. Staff at different levels were being recruited from management institutes. (hotels and general). Process : SOP- standard operation procedure, these were rules provided to staff to carry out various operations and were monitored. Blueprinting- little evidence, may not be revealed. Apparently planning was 'top down'. Directions from top management. ROQ- may be used, details not given. Bench marking – little evidence, except one unit which did regularly to be at par with international standard. Feedback from room guests.
Demand management	As most of them never experienced over - demand, the challenge was in managing lean business. Planning: conference, discount offers. Hosting events. The usual practice was to use RPD, ie, room per day. ARGE- may be informal, not revealed.
Product Innovation	Appeared to be the major thrust. With services oriented toward local consumers, competition was in offering excitement, entertainment to the local rich. Each of the them had separate pub/disco within the premises.
Over all experience ambience infrastructure	Ambience; more through various events. No major changes in infrastructure except in adding supplementary services to cater to local segment. There was little evidence of experimentation with cuisine as found in restaurants . Clearly there was a trade off - in investing between tangible and intangibles.
Customer Handling	Complaint handling cell examined complaints, approach seemed to be reactive. Very little on relation management. Though selectively concession were extended to certain corporate houses. Recovery – apology, free replacement. Concept of valued customer seemed to be present, as some kept in touch with customers selectively .CRA-may be used informally Benchmarking : reported by two units. Data on complaints recorded., Analysis or measures (ratio, speed of handling etc) if any, not disclosed.

[4] The segments were- I, corporate groups, ii, domestic free individual traveler, iii, foreign free individual, iv, conferences, v, crews, vi, group incentive traveller.

Success Index: Image - feedback taken. Satisfaction- internal feedback Data on repeat buy, referred guests were available. Whether these were analysed for decision taking not clear. Profit through occupancy rate appeared to be underlying objective .

Cost due to wastage- disposal of wastage could be costly as this had be within given norms.

◻ DISCUSSION AND CONCLUSION

Though the coverage for hotels was adequate, it was extremely difficult to obtain information more so from those attached to well known corporate names. In absence of consumer feedback, it was difficult to differentiate hotels except by the corporate names attached to them. As a result richness of the data suffered. It was not possible to get measure of success index as used by hotels. Restaurants were much more cooperative . Most of them were run by entrepreneurs, individuals, husband wife team or families .

Faced with stagnant economy and sluggish business, major thrust in the hotels industry seemed to be on product innovation . This was reflected either in the form of range of tangibles, such as, food and prices ranges; or in intangible in the form of ambience and entertainment . Providing technology backed infrastructure to facilitate internal and external communication and personalisation of services were other areas of investment.

At\present hotels have expanded services to the rich local segment. (adding supplementary services). Those located in the city have opened up pub discos, night club discos. These cater largely to young people inclined towards western culture from affluent families. Besides additional revenue, these tend to achieve visibility (image ?) amongst the local population and generate fair amount of WOM, influencing visitors and tourists through social/formal ties. The hotels also compete with one another in hosting various events such as fashion shows, diamond exhibition, or celebrity nights

The feedback on restaurants was obtained from a sample of students aged below 25 years. A sizable section came to stay for short duration, not more than 3 years. Hence 'loyalty' or 'repeat buy ' were difficult to assess as most of them could be described as at trial or experimenting stage. The feedback thus suffered from sample bias. Yet it could be realised that both tangible as also intangible contribute to repeat buy

Restaurants competed locally where location advantage gave competitive edge. Some of the centrally located old restaurants were losing business to those in the residential areas. It may be added, that, in this case, location contributed to ambience and convenience. A family may look for convenience, opting for local outlet . An interesting finding was people enjoying dinner at a food joint (providing relatively less costly food than hotels) but enjoying rest of the evening in the discos and pubs attached to hotels. Hence consumers who were highly mobile picked up their place to eat and to enjoy and relax. Thus both competitive as also a supplementary relation existed between the two. It may be noted that restaurants are not allowed by law to have discos.

The overall strategy of the industry in this city could be summed up as 'imitation', where the thrust is on product innovation either in tangibles or intangibles. The objective appears to be to keep the numbers coming rather than retaining. There is little effort to control attrition. This may explain RPD (room per day) as measure of demand management in hotels.

What then helps to build relationship?

A limited sample (only one city) and absence of feedback from consumers of hotels, no firm conclusion can be derived. It can only be surmised on the basis of popularity of hotels, that initially corporate name helps to attract, thereafter, 'location' and 'responsiveness' take over. It may be emphasized that 'responsiveness' reflect on culture fostered through internal marketing. In the case of restaurants, " overall satisfaction" seems to work..

. Consideration will however vary with segments. Any generalization would be risky on the basis of this study.

It would seem that Internal Marketing would assume significance in this industry marked by high turn over of employees at different levels . It is likely to be a major investment area along with product innovation as a competitive tool.

REFERENCES

Aramistead, Coling G. and Clark,G. (1994), Customer Service and Support, London : Pitman Publishing

Bains, Mandeep and others(1999), Positioning Strategy: A Project Report On Services Marketing, National Institute of Management, Calcutta,

Buttle, Francis., (1995), Hotel and Food Services Marketing, London: Holt, Rinehart and Winston

Das, Rohit and others (1999), 'Do We Go to Someplace Else', A Project Report on Services Marketing, National Institute of Management, Calcutta

Desiraju, Ramarao and Steven M. S. (1999), 'Strategic Service Pricing and Yield Managemen' *Journal of Marketing*, Vol. 63, pp. 44-56.

Garbarino, Ellen and Mark S. J.(1999), 'The Different Roles of Satisfaction, Trust, and Commitment in Customer Relationships', *Journal of Marketing*, Vol. 63, pp. 70-87.

Gureja, Gopal, K., (1997), Creating Customer Value, New Delhi: Tata McGraw Hill Publishing

Heene, Aime, B., L.ooy,V. and Dierdonck, R. V. (1998), Defining A Service Strategy In Services Management, eds Looy and others, London: Pitman Publishing.

Keaveney, Susan M., (1995), 'Customer Switching Behavior in Service Industries: An Exploratory Study', *Journal of Marketing*, Vol. 59, pp. 71-82.

Kotler, Philip.,Bowen,J. and Makens,J.(1996), Marketing for Hospitality & Tourism, U.S.A.: Prentice Hall International.

Looy, B. Van., Roland V. Dierdonck and P. Gemmel, (1998), Services Management –An Integrated Approach, London: Pitman Publishing

Lovelock, Christopher H., (1996), Services, Marketing, New Delhi: Prentice Hall International.

Lowenstein Mchael W. (1997), Customer Retention, Calcutta: Oxford University Press.

Oliver, Richard L., (1997), Satisfaction-A Behavioral Perspective On The Consumer, Singapore: McGraw-Hill International.

Oliver, Richard L., (1999), 'Whence Consumer Loyalty?', *Journal of Marketing*, Vol. 63, pp. 33-44.

Ossel, G. Van and Stremersch, S. (1998), Complaint Management in Services Management; eds Looy and others, London, Pitman Publishing.

Price, Linda L., Eric J. Arnould, and Patrick Tierney (1995), 'Going to Extremes: Managing Service Encounters and Assessing Provider Performance', *Journal of Marketing*, Vol. 59, pp. 83-97.

Price, Linda L., and Eric J. Arnould (1999),'Commercial Friendships: Service Provider – Client Relationships in Context', *Journal of Marketing*, Vol. 63, pp. 38–56.

Rust, Ronald,T., Zahorote, A. J. and Keiningham, T.L.(1999), *Service Marketing, Bangalore,* AWL International Student Edition.

Smith, Amy K., Ruth N. Bolton, and Janet Wagner,(1999), 'A Model of Customer Satisfaction with Service Encounters Involving Failure and Recovery', *Journal of Marketing Research*, Vol. 36, pp. 356-72

Zeithaml, Valarie, A. and M. Jo Bitner, (1996), *Services Marketing,* Singapore: McGraw Hill International.

Chapter 43

Customer Relationship Management
Lessons from the Hospitality Industry

■ **Christopher C Doyle**

Abstract

Until recent years, relationship management has been largely ignored by most industries outside the service sector. Classical marketing theory and practice has focused on customer acquisition rather than customer retention. However, due to the intrinsic nature of the service industry, customer relationships are critical to ensure customer loyalty. This is especially true of the hospitality industry, where relationships create more value for the customer than factors like price and product features, and therefore enhance the lifetime value of the customer to the organisation. The leading hotel brands have always made the effort to go beyond customer satisfaction and ensure value through relationships rather than transactions, resulting in high levels of customer delight and subsequently, loyalty. Recent studies have vindicated this approach, showing that customer satisfaction is not sufficient to build loyalty. Moreover, there has been a convergence in recent years, between the service and manufacturing industries and the latter can adapt the customer retention strategies of the former to build greater loyalty.

Key Words: _Retention, relationships, lifetime value, loyalty, delight, convergence._

☐ INTRODUCTION

Traditionally, strategies for growth in revenue, branding, positioning and profitability have all been developed with the primary objective of increasing market share through a focus on customer acquisition rather than the consolidation of existing customer relationships. There has also been a belief among most organisations that since their organisations are not in direct contact with the eventual consumer, the customer relationship is not directly relevant to increasing market share; the equity and positioning of the brand will lead to greater market share.

While this approach has its merits, there is a realisation today that customer retention is more profitable than customer acquisition. Frederick Reichheld (1996) states that on average, U.S. corporations lose half of their customers in 5 years; a typical company has a defection rate of 10-30% per year and raising the customer retention rate by 5% can increase the value of an average customer (lifetime profits) by 25 to 100%. Much of this profit gain is due to the fact that roughly 70% of all sales come from repeat purchases of loyal customers.

It is also being increasingly recognised that loyal customers buy more often and more per transaction, pay premiums more willingly and are more likely to recommend the product or service to others (Barsky, 1998).

These findings recognise the philosophy of the service industry, in particular, the hospitality industry, which has traditionally followed the principles of customer relationship management.

□ THE HOSPITALITY INDUSTRY

Traditionally, the hospitality (and service) industry has been perceived to be different from other industries for the following reasons:
  (a) perishability : a hotel room, if not sold today, cannot be carried as inventory
  (b) intangibility : a hotel stay is an experience; it is intangible
  (c) inseparability : simultaneous production and consumption of all hotel services
  (d) variability : of service delivery

Moreover, the service delivery process becomes part of the marketing process for a hotel. Simply put, the marketing department communicates a promise to the customer: this creates awareness, expectations, and influences the ultimate purchase decision. However, in order to deliver this promise, it is essential for the organisation to build an internal process and systems that encourage employees to give their best in terms of service to customers. And finally, the delivery of the promise is effected by the operational employees who become an integral part of the marketing process, through their interaction with the customer while delivering the promise.

The marketing process as described above thus has a fundamental impact on the moment of truth, which is basically every moment when the customer interacts with the hotel or an employee of the hotel during the marketing process.

In the hospitality industry, expectations are created by the promise. Expectations may also be influenced by prior experience, opinions of friends and associates or on the image of the hotel. Every guest walks into a moment of truth with an expectation. So it is really the moment of truth that defines value for a guest.

For a hotel, therefore, service quality is of utmost importance, especially in view of the fact that a lot of employee-guest interactions are carried out in the absence of direct supervision. Weinstein and Johnson (1999) have defined three levels of the service offering, which I have adapted to reflect the three levels at which hotels operate in order to provide value:

(a) Core benefits : the basic need satisfied by the hotel in response to what the customer is actually seeking. This reflects the basic product the guest wants to purchase e.g. a room, a meal, status etc.

(b) Hygiene factors: these are the minimum acceptable level of service attributes that customers would expect in a hotel e.g. direct dial telephone services, wake up calls, laundry services, air conditioning, restaurants, in-room television etc. If these services are not delivered or delivered poorly, customers experience dissatisfaction. However, simply offering them or performing them adequately does not lead to customer delight, since customers take them for granted as part of the service package

(c) Satisfiers: these attributes differentiate the hotel from its competitors while simultaneously exceeding customer expectations. They have the potential to create high customer satisfaction levels once expectations regarding hygiene factors have been met. These are value-added services that go beyond what the customer expects and these create value.

□ THE HOSPITALITY INDUSTRY AND CRM

There are numerous definitions of Customer Relationship Management (CRM) by various experts on the subject. I will attempt to define CRM from the point of view of the hospitality industry.

The CRM process in hotels is governed by the basic principle that good service does not guarantee customer satisfaction. And satisfaction does not guarantee loyalty. There is therefore, a need for strong customer relationships to build loyalty. For the hospitality product, the customer relationship is governed by the moment of truth. This fundamental truth, combined with the unique characteristics of the service industry has traditionally focussed the complete attention of the service provider on the customer. Even a market share oriented approach would necessarily need to take care of the customer.

Let us take a look at implications the unique characteristics of the hospitality industry have on building customer relationships:

(i) perishability: the hospitality product cannot be stored. Hotels normally do not face a constant pattern of demand throughout the year. Demand could vary on a daily basis, or with seasons and even business cycles. While pricing and promotions are normally utilised as strategies to manage variation, they may not be sufficient to ensure efficient management of demand. However, combined with loyalty built through relationships, these strategies can result in better demand management, thus minimising variation and optimising occupancy and yield. The same logic applies to peak periods, since there could be congestion and turning away guests with confirmed reservations and thereby considerable damage to customer relationships, if demand and inventory are not efficiently managed.

(ii) Intangibility: while the physical structure and certain components of the hospitality product are tangible, a hotel stay is primarily an experience and is consummated by the service elements of the product. Since the management of the moments of truth essentially depends on the intangible factors, these are critical for building successful customer relationships.

(iii) Inseparability: consumption of a hospitality product is inseparable from its production; the product is consumed while it is being produced, which necessarily means that the producer and consumer interact at the point of consumption. This means that unlike manufactured goods, there is no scope for quality checks prior to consumption. Any change in delivery methods can affect the quality and value of the service. Since inseparability defines the moment of truth, it is critical to manage the moments of truth in order to provide value and build successful customer relationships

(iv) Variability : according to Palmer (1998), there are two dimensions to variability :

    (a) the extent to which production standards vary from a norm, both in terms of outcomes and of production processes

    (b) the extent to which a service can be deliberately varied to meet the specific needs of individual customers.

Due to the high involvement of customers in the service delivery process in hotels, variability in production standards is a major concern. This is especially true of the many hotel services where employees and customers interact in the absence of supervision. Extensive and intensive training of employees is required, in order to ensure successful service delivery, and constant attention to motivation and morale is needed in order to ensure successful management of the interaction and therefore customer relationships.

Where the service can be deliberately varied to meet the specific needs of individual customers, an opportunity arises for the hotel to utilise the variation to build customer relationships based on the unique preferences and requirements of individual customers. This may take the form of mass customisation for key segments or individual customisation for key guests.

It is obvious from the above analysis, that since the hospitality industry is dependent for repeat purchase on the experience the customer has during her stay, brand equity and positioning are built more through the customer experience and moments of truth than through traditional strategies followed by tangible products.

The key to CRM in the hospitality industry is the presence of satisfiers as defined earlier. The tangible elements of the hospitality product are manifested in the core benefits and hygiene factors, which are necessary conditions in order to eliminate customer dissatisfaction. But it is really the satisfiers that create value for the customer. Satisfiers are often intangible in nature and can be critical in building relationships and loyalty. The tangible elements can often be duplicated by competition, and do not sustain competitive advantage over other hotel brands. But satisfiers, if focussed on and developed, have the potential to become unique to a hotel and can build a definitive competitive advantage.

A small case study will serve to illustrate the nature of CRM in the hospitality industry. At Hilton Singapore, we recently had a fairly large meeting with around 330 participants, from an American MNC. Their requirements were quite challenging with several last minute requests and changes. In the words of our client, "we had many complicated require-ments, including quick turnover for room set-ups, multiple changes (some last minute) quick response to audio-visual support...even support to organise evening activities".

The entire ballroom was occupied. We had to turnover the entire ballroom in less than an hour during lunch into 3 separate rooms. As it was an e-biz event, all participants had to use a laptop, thereby requiring over 100 power points.

We also went the extra mile in the arrangements and co-ordination for their evening programmes (dinner at the famous Seafood Centre and a night out at Boat Quay). At times, we even helped out at the reception.

We were told just one week before the event that they also required a cocktail for 330 on one evening, but the poolside was already confirmed by another client for a dinner of 40. We had to suggest and arrange alternative arrangement for the client who had con-firmed the space. We convinced the earlier client to dine on Sentosa Island instead - with transfers and any cost difference taken cared of. As a result, we had two very happy clients.

Although we had some minor hiccups (audio-visual didn't work the way our client wanted on the first day), the situation turned out positively for us. The management team; chief engineer, assistant engineer, F&B manager, asst banquet director, banquet operations manager, senior sales manager and several other operations and engineering staff were involved in solving the problem. Our attention and immediate action taken gave our clients assurance of our dedication and strengthen our working relationship. We received a glowing thank you letter wherein the client attributed part of the success of the meeting to the effort of our Hilton Singapore team.

I will now attempt to summarise the discussion above in a definition:

> *Customer relationship management in hospitality is the continuous process of man-aging the moments of truth and a search for opportunities to create value for the customer with the ultimate objective of generating customer loyalty based on the con-stant interaction of the customer with the product and employees of the hotel.*

☐ PRINCIPLES OF CUSTOMER RELATIONSHIP MANAGEMENT IN THE HOSPITALITY INDUSTRY

Let us now take a look at the basic principles underlying the CRM strategies of the hospi-tality industry.

1. The basic objective of CRM is fulfilled only when the customer has a relationship with the hotel, and not just with a few customer contact employees. Effective CRM goes beyond service; it involves implementing systems and processes to ensure that the marketing process promises, builds an environment for effective delivery, and finally delivers the promise in a manner that exceeds the customer's expectation, thus add-ing value and building the relationship.

2. All employees are involved in initiating and building relationships with customers: relationship building is not restricted to sales and marketing personnel. Sometimes the relationship may be initiated by customer contact employees.

3. The relationship goes beyond databases and customer preferences: It involves the use of this information to not only target customers with appropriate products, but also to create value for the customer through customisation.

4. It is important to be consistent in both the service offering as well as the service delivery in order to build the relationship. If there is too much employee-dependent variability, then the relationship could end up as one between the guest and the employee, which is not the objective of CRM.

5. Difference between promotions and relationships: promotions do not build loyalty, they can only grow market share for short periods. Relationships are long term and take time to build. A lot of effort needs to be put in consistently in order to build and sustain a relationship.

6. Understand the customer's perspective and what the customer actually wants, and put in systems to deliver services accordingly, so that the customer knows that the hotel understands her needs accurately.

7. There should be a sense of reliability on the hotel and its services. If the customer knows that the hotel can be relied on to consistently provide the same service, the relationship will be stronger and longer lasting. Reliability builds trust, which is critical to any relationship.

8. The hotel should ensure that the customer gets complete information on all services and products. Not only should the information be complete, but it should also be accurate.

9. Loyal customers should be rewarded. It is important to distinguish between regular guests and others. It is also important to build strong relationships with regular guests since It is much more cost effective to reward loyal customers than it is to acquire new customers.

All CRM strategies are based on the recognition and practice of these principles.

☐ CUSTOMER RELATIONSHIP STRATEGIES AND PRACTICES IN THE HOSPITALITY INDUSTRY

1. Hotels maintain guest profiles or guest histories of all guests visiting their hotels. Guest profiles capture information on guest details such as contact details, organisation, designation and also preferences such as type of room, food etc. In addition, guest histories capture information on past stays of the guest and are invaluable as leads to guest preferences that may not be expressed by the guest.

2. Guest feedback forms: invite comments from guests on the quality of their experience and the services offered, and any suggestions for improvement.

3. There is also constant interaction between the guest and customer contact employees like the front desk (reception), and front office (lobby). Guest relation executives are specifically employed to interact with guests and define profiles and preferences as also to obtain information on the guest's stay and any problems that she may be facing or any comments that she may have. A very small percentage of guests actually fill in the feedback form and these employees, therefore, have an important role to play in understanding guest needs.

4. Human resources: it is easy for the focus on customer orientation to be so strong that the organisation does not focus sufficiently on the people who will deliver the service. The hospitality industry is a people intensive industry. Moreover, as discussed earlier, most services are delivered by customer contact employees without any direct supervision of senior mangers or supervisors. It is essential therefore, to ensure that the human resource is not only of a high quality, but also remains motivated to perform the critical tasks they are assigned.

It is important to recruit employees who have the necessary temperament and attitude to interact and manage guests especially under pressure. It is possible to instil mechanical skills, but interpersonal skills are more difficult to inculcate. Moreover, customer contact employees undergo rigorous training in the various aspects of customer interaction and customer management including crisis management. It is also important to define the exact role and responsibility the employee plays in interacting with and building guest satisfaction. Finally, customer contact employees need to be empowered to perform their functions efficiently. It is difficult to deliver services efficiently if constant approval is required from supervisors or senior managers for even basic service delivery.

5. Constant interaction with guests and client organisations, including entertainment of key clients, in order to understand guest needs and to obtain feedback on their satisfaction levels with the hotel

6. Warranties or guarantees: to reinforce the reliability and consistency factors as well as provide assurance of quality. For example, Embassy Suites, an all suite chain owned by Hilton Hotels Corporation, offers a 100 % satisfaction guarantee which offers the customer total satisfaction or no payment.

7. Guest loyalty programmes: It is essential that a guest reward programme provide value to a guest through appropriate rewards. It is important for the programme to be different in order to attract the guests who carry other loyalty cards, as well as identify and retain the best customers. The HHonors™ programme, for example has 2000 participating hotels in 53 countries, more than 7 million members enrolled in 223 countries and 40 partners (airlines/car rentals/cruises). It is the only hotel loyalty programme to allow Double Dipping™, which entitles the member to earn both hotel points and free airline miles for the same stay. The programme has four VIP levels reflecting the usage of different guests and also providing greater value for each level

based on usage. For the hotel, the programme profiles users, tracks past stays, and identifies sources markets. For the guest, the programme provides bonus hotel points, bonus airmiles, room upgrades, and other such offers to create value for loyal customers and differentiate the brand from other loyalty programmes.

8. Service recovery: service failure is inherent in the service delivery process, subject as it is to so many factors including the human element of variability. Service recovery is essentially the process of recovering from the failure of a moment of truth and rebuilding relationships with guests. It is very important for customer contact employees to find out as soon as possible when the service has failed to meet guest expectations. This is extremely important since many guests do not report their dissatisfaction to the hotel, but never come back and may even tell their friends about the bad experience. The other important thing about recovery is the speed with which action is taken, since most relationships can be successfully salvaged and rebuilt if the action taken is speedy and appropriate. In fact, if the service recovery is managed well, it is possible that the relationship may be stronger than it would have been without the service failure. Service recovery can also be performed during the production process itself, rather than wait for long after the service failure, since if expectations have not been met during the early stages of the service process there is often the possibility that it may be recovered by significantly exceeding expectations at a later stage. (Palmer, 1998) Sometimes, service recovery can also be pre-emptive in nature, if the service failure can be anticipated and appropriate action taken prior to the actual service failure. This is particularly the case when failure is dependent on circumstances that may not be possible to control.

☐ HOW OTHER INDUSTRIES CAN PROFIT FROM THE CRM EXPERIENCE OF THE HOSPITALITY INDUSTRY

Today, there is a fair amount of convergence between the service and manufacturing industries. The relationship between the customer and the brand is becoming key to brand success and brand loyalty even for manufactured products, as much as any other brand building exercise. The importance of maintaining a customer over the life of the brand and encouraging repeat purchase and brand loyalty through CRM is gaining ground.

With technology making rapid advances, many brands today need intangibles to differentiate themselves from competition. When many products are purchased, there is normally an element of service attached. And many manufacturers can actually differentiate or create value for their product by offering a service or bundle of services at the point of purchase. A good example is car finance being offered by the automobile manufacturer while purchasing a car.

Products can also benefit by increasing the level of involvement of the customer in the purchase. This can be done by increasing the interaction of the customer with the employee of the manufacturer or the dealer of the product and building relationships with the customer for future repeat purchases, even after the product has been purchased.

It is also possible for products to use the principle of variability as discussed above to open new opportunities for relationships. For example Levi's now offers Personal Pants which are custom made to fit the individual measurements of women (Weinstein & Johnson, 1999).

The importance of satisfiers can also be utilised effectively to build loyalty for products. All products satisfy a core need for the customer, and, as in the case of hospitality services, all products also have certain hygiene factors, which are essential to the performance of the product as per customer expectations. The addition of satisfiers, whether in the form of additional features and benefits, or services adding value to the product and going beyond customer expectations can greatly enhance brand loyalty and relationships.

Where services are offered, attention to individual customers, a focus on service quality and customer delight are important, for example in the case of products which require after sales service. Especially where a company has a wide product range, it is important to build brand loyalty so that the customer does not need to look at other brands for future products purchased. Service recovery is also critical for such products and is often the determining factor for brand loyalty and future purchases. If the after sales service for one product does not meet customer expectations, it is possible that the customer may never purchase any other products with the same brand name, thus destroying lifetime value for that brand. And of course, it is extremely important that, when a warranty is extended, it should be honoured so that the customer has a sense of reliability and trust with the brand.

For frequently purchased products, frequency-marketing incentives can also be used. For products not purchased very often, marketing exercises to create relationships through value added is possible for example, automobile clubs offering special services and facilities for members.

The key to successful CRM is to identify key customers both on the basis of current purchase and future potential, and ensure that there is a continuous search for opportunities to add value for them, customise wherever possible and continuously monitor the relationship.

Finally it is extremely important to note that while customer orientation is critical, no relationship can be successfully initiated and managed without satisfied, motivated and empowered employees.

REFERENCES

Barsky J (1998), *Finding The Profits In Customer Satisfaction: Translating Best Practices into Bottom-Line Results,* San Francisco, CA: Contemporary Books.

Palmer A (1998), *Principles of Services Marketing,* Berkshire, England: McGraw Hill.

Reichheld F.F. (1996), *The Loyalty Effect: The Hidden Force Behind Growth, Profits and Lasting Value,* Boston, MA: Harvard Business School Press.

Weinstein A and Johnson C (1999), *Designing And Delivering Superior Customer Value: Concepts, Cases, and Applications,* Fort Lauderdale, FL: CRC Press LLC.

Relationship Management Programme

The Titan Experience

■ **Manoj Chakravarti**

Abstract

*Customer Relationship Management is the crucial differentiator in today's retailing scenario. It is therefore in the best interests of the organisation to focus on a lifetime customer with a view to retain and increase their custom over a period of time. The advances in computer and information management technology have made it possible to build such one-to-one relationships with their customers. Focussing on **information-driven marketing**, a strategy which builds customer loyalty through customer bonding, Titan took up the CRM initiative by introducing The Titan Signet. An exclusive Loyalty programme, it is based on the creation of a database of loyal customers, rewarding their loyalty, and interacting with these valued customers through ways and means of receiving feedback , suggestions and responding to them. While currently the use of Direct media is high, the future is in the effective use of the Internet to advance and customize this relationship to each individual.*

Key Words: *Customer Bonding, Loyalty, Create Database, Retain through Reward, Maximise Through Dialogue, Value Enhancement, e-CRM.*

❑ IMPORTANCE OF CUSTOMER RELATIONSHIP MANAGEMENT IN TODAY'S SCENARIO :

"There is only one boss; the customer. And he can fire everybody in the company, from the chairman on down, simply by spending his money somewhere else."

> *Sam Walton – Founder Wal-Mart stores*

Customer Relationship Management is the crucial differentiator in today's retailing scenario. Around the world, market leaders have been increasingly moving towards relationship marketing programmes. No longer is there talk of a mass approach; instead a 'one-to-one' marketing with the main focus on customer satisfaction, is the marketing mantra.

❏ IS CUSTOMER SATISFACTION ENOUGH?

Customer satisfaction is a necessary but not a sufficient condition for market leadership. A satisfied customer is one whose expectations have been met. A happy customer on the other hand is one whose loyalty is guaranteed, which ultimately leads to market leadership. Thus, **loyalty** is the fundamental engine of profit and growth in a competitive marketing scenario.

Loyal customers are die-hard ones. As advocates of the brand, they spread a positive image of the brand/organisation which is most convincing to the potential customer since it is based on a first hand experience.

❏ CREATING CUSTOMER LOYALTY

It is therefore in the best interests of the organisation to focus on the lifetime customer with a view to retain and increase their custom over a period of time. The focus should be no longer limited to ensuring that prospective customers who have bought a competitor's brand switch to theirs; *but to ensure that their customers remain loyal and return not only to buy more - but to buy more often.*

❏ IS A CRM PROGRAMME COST-WORTHY?

A strong relationship will encourage the customer to return to you time and again. He will have a vested interest in maintaining communication with the company. He may even come to regard competitive communication with disdain.

Achieving such loyalty is not without its cost. It takes both an up front and an ongoing commitment and may be fairly expensive, but with great value enhancement.

Research has proved that it is more economical for a brand to retain a loyal customer as against nurturing a potential one. It is now an accepted fact that it is five times more expensive to get a new customer as it is to retain an existing one. That is why every major airline runs frequent flyer programmes, and hotels offer special rates and special services to repeat clientele.

❏ TECHNOLOGY TAKES MATTERS FORWARD

What is different today, is that the advances in computer and information management technology along with the effective use of the Internet, have made it possible for large companies with hundreds of thousands customers to attempt to build such one-to-one relationships with their customers.

It is a big step forward from "image based " marketing because it recognizes the importance of other goals besides image creation, support and global advertising .

It also recognises that these goals can be achieved through means other than general advertising which are more personal, and on an individual, one-to-one basis.

Today, the focus is on *information-driven marketing*, a strategy which builds customer loyalty through customer bonding.

A clear strategic plan for improved customer bonding should include –

- development of a database with plans for collecting , storing and analyzing information collected from your customer
- use of direct media to reach and address your customers on a one-to-one
- means for carrying on a dialogue with your customer

Therefore, the crucial need for a CRM initiative that can identify, differentiate, interact and provide a listening ear to the customers' feedback, complaints and suggestions.

❑ THE TITAN EXPERIENCE

The Indian watch market and consumer in 1985, were timekeeping with the very basic mechanical watch—simple, plain and utilitarian. With its entry into the watch market in 1986-87 with watches of international quality and styling, Titan created a paradigm shift from mechanical to quartz. . It changed watches from a mere time keeping device to an 'objet d'art' and today to a fashion accessory.

Titan was born of a dream to offer the Indian consumer the most basic of products – time, with the promise of precision, quality, style and wide choice on par with international brands. Titan with its international collection of over 1000 quartz models, is the undisputed leader in the Indian quartz market, with a 40 % share of this segment. With the introduction of aesthetically designed clocks and jewellery into its brand portfolio, Titan has offered the consumer 'time' with designer appeal.

Moreover, Titan bridged the gap that existed in the product and retailing standards in the watch industry in India. It was Titan who pioneered the retail revolution in India, setting up the chain of high profile outlets.

Exclusive Titan showrooms, 'The World of Titan', promises world class experience along with world class products. With 117 showrooms across 71 cities, The World of Titan showrooms have helped to bring about a revolution in the standards of watch retailing in India. Comparable to some of the best stores in the world, the Titan Showrooms are conveniently located, pleasurable to shop in, and provide courteous and efficient services, both while selling a watch or while offering after sales service – making it the most preferred place to buy the most preferred watch from.

❑ WHY CRM?

As customer awareness increases with every passing year, the watch buyer also has a variety of choices from Indian and foreign watch brands to choose from. An opportunity was sought to ensure that the World of Titan customer received not only a satisfactory experience in terms of product, price and quality but a noticeably 'happy' one as well – inducing him therefore, to be loyal to the brand.

As mentioned earlier, the bonding with the customer or the development of a lasting relationship with him is not just through one relationship program but through the very essence of the company reflected in its attitude and approach to its customer. Therefore the need for a Relationship Management Programme at the World of Titan showroom chain, which extends beyond the normal loyalty programs, and is built into our retailing strategy, our marketing plans and into our service philosophy.

☐ WHAT DID TITAN DO?

The Titan Signet was one such CRM initiative undertaken at TITAN in May 1995 to provide that 'extra' touch to its special customers at the exclusive World of Titan stores.

Its mission was to create a sense of belonging of the customer to the store and vice versa by:
- Building a special relationship with high life time value Titan customers
- Recognising and rewarding his/her loyalty to Titan.
- Providing a platform for direct feedback from these valued customers to the company

☐ WHERE?

It initially started in 6 showrooms in Bangalore. Today the Titan Signet has been extended to 102 World of Titan showrooms across 59 cities all over India.

☐ HOW ?

First and foremost the Company firmly believed that building customer loyalty and building a customer information base was a key component of its marketing strategy.
- The strongest customer bonds require what is called The Three D's – Database, Dialogue , and Direct Media – these 3 elements are the heart and soul of deep & lasting customer bonds.

To create a relationship means one has to
- know the customers likes and dislikes – his psyche (database)
- keep up a continuous learning process about the customer (dialogue)
- have some way of communicating directly with them (direct media)

The Titan Signet Model ☛ Critical Success factors : Recognition , Reward, Response

☐ CREATE YOUR CUSTOMER BASE

It is not possible to have a relationship with someone you cannot **identify**, so it is absolutely critical to 'know' **your customers**.

Membership to the Titan Signet club is through value based enrolment, which also captures and stores the profile of the member through a data management system.

This database is a repository for the information needed to have a mutually rewarding relationship with customers. For purposes of *building* such a relationship, it includes these 3 categories of information:

- Basic information such as customer name and address
- Relevant information about that individual such as age and income level, family status and buying intention. This is dynamic and subject to change.
- Data captured whenever the customer makes a transaction.
  Every customer purchase presents you with an invaluable opportunity to enhance your understanding of how your customers like to do business.

❑ RETAIN YOUR LOYAL CUSTOMERS

All customers are valuable. However much valuable these customers are, the frequency of purchases from these customers should determine the differentiation in rewarding them. The Titan Signet differentiates its customers.

Loyal customers, therefore, with the potential to return time and again with their custom as well as theirs, are infinitely more valuable. This **differentiation** is **by rewarding loyalty**. Through its Rewards programme, based on awarding points for every purchase made, The Titan Signet is thus an inducement to the customer to not only enrol but return to purchase more ... and more often.

Bonus points awarded during special offers and schemes offer that additional pull to the customer to return to the showroom time and again.

The customer may benefit through recognition and rewards. The company benefits from every interaction with the customer by not only increasing sales but by gathering more information that can be used to guide future marketing choices.

❑ MAXIMISE THE RELATIONSHIP WITH YOUR CUSTOMER

Interaction with the customers induces a more 'personal' feeling and touch to the customer relationship programme.

Dialogue is the process of interacting directly with prospects and customers. To foster dialogue, ways and means will have to be provided for this individual to react directly to whatever communication is sent to them. Dialogue continually refreshes the database of marketing information, which is being built, enabling an alert watch on what customers want.

The most advanced relationship programme/ database marketing will send communication geared to the customers' specific interests and they measure his response to every offer sent through various interactive techniques. The offerings made are a desirable part of the customers' every day life.

As part of The Titan Signet programme, the members are kept informed on various new products being offered by Titan. Contests, offers and promotions from brands are constant through the membership period ensuring that Titan is always in the subconscious of our valued customers. Offers from other lifestyle brands also keep the customers' interest alive.

Listening to our customers. The Titan Signet provides a ready platform for the members to talk about their experiences at the World of Titan showrooms, their suggestions and their views. We listen, learn and apply them to continuously increase our Company's sensitivity to the customers needs.

□ WHAT IS THE RESULT?

A successful "loyalty Programme"!

Success of any customer relationship programme depends on the support of a database, use of direct media, such as customized direct mail, newsletters, monthly statements, and a solid reward system that builds continuously. We could define this as – making each purchase a customer makes, increase the value of the next purchase to that customer. In return the company profits by increased sales to such customers who also act as brand ambassadors.

30% of the membership base returned to buy from The World of Titan Showrooms alone. Customer relationship - bonding - loyalty. Success .

□ BEHIND THE SCENES

While the Signet programme has taken customer bonding one step further in Titan, there are many behind-the-scene activities which ensure that the programme is run efficiently, effectively and with the a level of enthusiastic participation from our World of Titan showrooms.

- Showroom personnel are trained not only in the operations of the programme at the showroom but also in the finer details of customer relationship management.
- Enrolments in the programme are tracked on a monthly basis for each showroom, along with the data on purchases made by Signet members who have returned to the showroom to buy again.
- Signet operations form a part of the quarterly appraisal for our showrooms, thereby ensuring that they earn more marks on their effective and efficient performance.
- A grievance redressal system is in place to ensure that our valued customers are responded to within a stipulated time frame.

The collaterals for Titan Signet programme include

- an enrolment-cum-scheme leaflet and form
- an embossed and tipped personalised card
- a rewards catalogue depicting the various items redeemable on accumulation of points
- posters, take-ones etc.

These form part of the programme which continuously highlight the status of a Titan Signet member.

☐ CARE FOR THE PEOPLE WHO CARE FOR YOUR CUSTOMERS

While the entire focus here has been on the relationship built between Titan and its end-customers, mention should also be made of Titan's continuous relationship with its primary customers, The World of Titan showrooms.

The very 'face' of the company, The World of Titan showroom is an integral part of the Titan family and every care is taken to ensure that similar "customer bonding" takes place with these valuable primary customers. From fun filled annual business meets to a rewards system for target achievement, this relationship although different also comprises the creation of a long-term mutually profitable association. Every aspect of this relationship is reviewed and appraised in a systematic manner through processes designed for only that purpose:

- Franchisee Feedback Forms [they appraise our performance as a Company]
- Quarterly Performance Appraisal [we review their operations]

Excitement is also built in through the Rewards Khazana programme, where high level of performance and target achievements are suitably lauded with rewards ranging from consumer durable products to Tanishq, to even pleasure trips abroad !

Thus a relationship that grows stronger in time; with the people who matter who directly interact with the customers that matter most.

☐ THE FUTURE?

No matter how well an organisation is doing there is always room for improvement . And continuously assessing the strategic vision enables the Company to stay ahead of changes in that corner of the world & in the competitive landscape.

The Internet is playing a key role in the management of a CRM strategy, as the above activities move from the written word to the 'web'.

We look forward to spreading warmth through **the Web** to our exclusive members of The Titan Signet. The contact opportunities are undeniably infinite, invigorating, inexpensive and international. The ideal platform for The Titan Signet, it provides the optimum benefits of a one-to-one customer relation programme, the effective use of which will result in value enhancement for the customer, the Brand, the Company.

Advantage Titan.

REFERENCES

Cross Richard, Smith Janet, *Customer Bonding*.
Sewell Carl, *Customers For Life*.
Tasca Bob, *You Will Be Satisfied*.
The Quest For Loyalty – Creating Value through Partnership.

Chapter 45

Customer Relationship Management at APTECH

■ Pradip H Sadarangani, Sanjaya S Gaur and Nilesh S Vani

Abstract

The Case of APTECH Ltd. deals with an organization in the intensely competitive information technology education and software services industry. In such markets where technology is changing by the minute, organizations take initiatives to obtain even the slightest competitive edge. The company described in the case is in the process of implementing a Customer Response System across its fifteen hundred odd centres. The impact of such a move is being felt on customer satisfaction ratings and the critical word of mouth that attracts new inquiries. There are, of course certain implementation issues to be tackled. In order to evaluate the system implementation at test centers, and to work through the implementation in the remaining one thousand five hundred centers; APTECH is considering some cultural and organizational issues within the organization. Also, besides its relationships with customers, it is working on its relationships with business partners and employees.

Key Words: *Customer Response System (CRS), Customer Automation System (CAS), Implementation, and Relationships*

□ INTRODUCTION

Today, computers are not restricted to computer software field only; in fact they have become a necessary part of every business industry. This has led to a tremendous rise in the demand for trained computer professionals. With the increasing focus on computer software development by Indian government and NASSCOM along with many software export houses, this demand is bound to increase even further in the near future and in the years to come. The Indian computer software industry itself has grown from a mere Rs. 0.3 billion ten years back to Rs. 70 billion today. The rapid growth of this industry has lead to the high growth in the computer education and training business. Private institutes today produce about 65% of the software professionals and remaining by Government affiliated universities. It is projected that this gap will reach approximately 2,00,000 (Source: NASSCOM) by the end of the century. The growth in demand in future is expected to be spurred by the growth in the IT sector both domestic and international, which is growing at the rate of 30-40%. The demand for trained computer professionals has shown an increasing trend over the years. As a result of this many entrepreneurs took to this opportunity and opened computer-training institutes. Over the years these institutes have developed rapidly to become huge in terms of their spread and the number of students churned out. Notably among them are companies like NIIT, APTECH, SSI, TULEC, BITS, IEC, LCC, SQL-STAR etc.

☐ STRUCTURE OF IT EDUCATION INDUSTRY

The IT education industry in India is estimated to be around 625crores. Although there are many players, it is mainly dominated by NIIT and APTECH in the organised sector. This sector is growing at the rate of 20%. The market shares are as shown below:

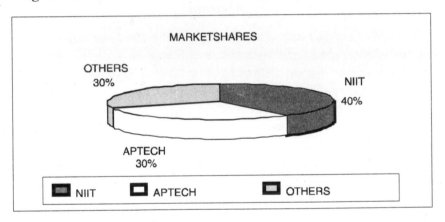

☐ ABOUT APTECH

APTECH is a Rs. 366 crores information technology education and software services company with its headquarters in Mumbai. Starting operations in 1986 with one training centre in Mumbai, APTECH today is a global technology corporation with over fifteen hundred training centres in over twenty countries. The company also has significant interests in software and assists corporations the world over with innovative technology solutions. The organisation is structured in the form of nine global Strategic Business Units (SBUs) as follows:
- Mainline Education
- ARENA Multimedia
- Asset International—Training for software professionals
- International Education

- Online Varsity
- Global Software Solutions
- e-commerce
- Knowledge Management / Technology based Training
- B connect B—Application Services Provider

These SBUs function as independent business entities and have their main research and development activities headquartered in India. Marketing offices and training centres are spread all over the world and the company operates wholly owned subsidiaries and Joint Ventures in different parts of the world to provide APTECH products and services. APTECH enrolled approximately two lakh students in its training centres, in the year ending December 1999, represented by the first four SBUs. In February 2000, APTECH has started an online varsity. It hopes that within the next two years there will be over five lakh online students. This is over and above students in their training centres.

In APTECH's organisation structure, there are six divisional offices that report to the head office. Each brand has a separate office. Regional offices, in turn, report to the divisional offices. The number of regional offices that report to divisional offices range from four to twelve. A number of centres report to each regional office. The number of centres reporting to a regional office is sought to be limited to fifty, but it can be as high as two hundred and twenty. APTECH has designed its management structure in response to the needs of quick decision-making and operational flexibility. Even though hierarchies and designations do exist, APTECH is a highly informal organisation where communication moves in all directions; decision-making has to a large extent been delegated. The three basic tenets of APTECH's vision are:

- To be an Education and Information Technology Megacorp
- To be the preferred choice of customers world-wide
- To be the best place to work in

APTECH's goal is to achieve a turnover of 1000 crores by the year 2002. APTECH, is concerned about the customer satisfaction ratings. It is convinced that there is a strong correlation between customer satisfaction ratings and the critical word of mouth that attracts new enquiries and is also convinced of a need for a solution to plug the problem. APTECH aspires to build repeat business through industry focus and product / template strategy. In the words of APTECH's Chairman, Atul Nishar, "Our focus on customer delight means an emphasis on creating enduring client relationships and developing solutions for them through the intensive use of technology." It is in this context that we examine the CRM approach by APTECH for it's training division. The CEO, Mr. Ganesh Natarajan, has this to say about it.

☐ CRM AT APTECH

"There are two sides to APTECH's business: student education, and corporate consultancy, training, software etc. Eighty percent of the students enrol at APTECH because of word of mouth. There is qualitative and quantitative research. However, what experience was shared is not documented. Therefore, now we have a system known as Customer Response System (CRS) that captures any suggestion, complaint or query made by a student. As far as reusable templates are concerned, they are widely used in e-commerce and ERP solutions. For an ERP solution we have an e-link template that reduces development time by sixty percent. We also have a service portal where plug and play solutions can be downloaded. As far as students are concerned CRM is providing unlimited access to anyone in the organisation."

☐ HOW DID APTECH GET INTO CUSTOMER CARE?

Firstly, APTECH was in the Knowledge Management business. There was a need to be able to practice what one preached. Secondly, there was the business imperative. The need to be at the vanguard of quality initiatives was recognised. There were already manual systems in place, both formal and informal. Formal mechanisms included feedback forms, while informal channels included faculty interaction and open houses. However, these contained an element of subjectivity. If a student had a good rapport with centre staff his/her feedback, complaints, suggestions, and queries were paid cognisance. A need was felt for a more quantifiable metric. Students, being young, are wary of expressing their concerns. An element of monotony had crept into the manual systems - students said what they were expected to say. In the feedback forms emphasis was placed on the contents of the courses.

☐ CRM ROADMAP AT APTECH

There are two units of CRM - CRS and CAS. Using CRS, a student gives feedback on Centre, Product, People, and Specific issues. R.O., Product Design, and General Management for Monitoring Centre performance, Improving or revamping the product, Making Policy decisions, and for Overall improvement in delivery process use this feedback. Where policy decisions are taken, they affect CAS (Centre Automation System) and RAS (Regional Automation System) and changes are incorporated as necessary.

The Second Unit CAS (Centre Automation System) is the database of students. Currently this database is used by Centre Personnel for student tracking and by the R.O for monitoring Centre Performance in terms of product delivery. The plan is to have a Web Interface, so that students can access their information on a limited basis. This will help the student to judge his/her current status and accordingly plan if any corrective action is required. E-mail facility is already available for APTECH members, so that student can consult the respective Faculty/Centre personnel in case any assistance is required for planning. It is also planned to use the available information and extend the concept to a Call centre, so those enquiries can be directed to the nearest point, as convenient to them. Company also plans to use the database being built up for alumni, so that students placed by them, can be given value added inputs on a time to time basis, depending on their requirements and current job profile.

❏ CUSTOMER RESPONSE SYSTEM (CRS)

CRS is a customer service solution and not a data crunching operation. It covers three locations: centre, regional office, and head office. In the centres and regional offices CRS consists of the Client Server module, while in the head office it consists of the Client Server as well as the Knowledge Management modules. There are multiple objectives of CRS:

- Provide sufficient information, through an easy to access interface, to the Customer for judging their current status and make a plan for the future based on the same.
- Provide an interface for the Customer to communicate his/her views on the service received by them.
- Have a mechanism in place to capture warning signals at an early stage to enable proactive preventive action.

❏ TECHNOLOGY BEHIND CRS

The Client Server module has a back end developed in Oracle, and a front end developed in Powerbuilder. The Knowledge Management module is developed in Lotus Notes. In each centre CRS are linked to the Centre Automation System. In the regional office it is linked to the regional automation system. The Client-Server module has various screens like review categories/notifications - Exception, Today's feedback, Awaiting Ratification, Ratified, and Pending Closure. A flow chart, indicating the mechanics of how the Client-Server module functions, is shown in Exhibit 1.

Exhibit 1 *Flow Diagram of Client Server Module*

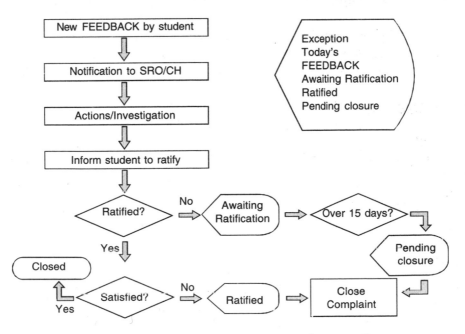

◻ CRS INTERFACE

At the centre level, students, student relationship officer (SRO) and administrators interface with the system. Whereas, at the regional office level the regional head, regional SRO, and the administrator interface with the system. While, at the head office the administrator and the knowledge integrator interface with the system.

Features at the centre level—There is a complaint registering facility for students. The system provides accessibility to all students. It enables ease of complaint retrieval by centre management. Analysis reports on complaints can be generated. Also, exception reports can be produced. There is a complaint closure facility. The student ratifies all complaints. The student receives a complaint acknowledgement. A facility to send reminders/repeat a complaint has been provided. The student receives intimation for ratification of complaint redressed. The SRO/Centre Head is notified of all complaints. There is a facility to request for immediate regional office/head office intervention by SRO/Centre Head. Dynamic querying on complaint data can be done. A facility to query on complaint status and for forced closure of feedback has been provided.

Features at Regional office level—Complaint entry by regional office personnel is possible. The feature of automatic escalation of complaints has been provided. Analysis reports across centres and exception reports can be generated. The regional office has access to complaint information form all centres, updated weekly. There is a facility to find out details of complaints logged earlier by a student while receiving a complaint. Dynamic querying on complaint data and query on complaint status are possible. Personnel at the regional office can participate in discussions to resolve complaints and be informed about action taken at head office. They also have access to knowledge repositories at head office.

CRS Reports—The different reports generated by CRS are: Complaint category wise frequency analysis, Cycle time for redressal analysis, Status report, Status statistics, Complaint details, Exception report, Complaint recurrence analysis, and Root cause analysis.

◻ KNOWLEDGE MANAGEMENT MODULE

The Knowledge Management module can be viewed from two perspectives - User and knowledge administrator/integrator. The architecture of the Knowledge Management module is shown in Exhibit 3. Mr. Jahangir Kazimi, Solution Architect of the Knowledge Management module says that from the users' perspective it consists of six links:
- Discussion Group
- Knowledge Repository
- Latest Updates
- Best Practices
- FAQs

Exhibit 2 *Architecture*

Complaint Management System—KM Functional Architecture

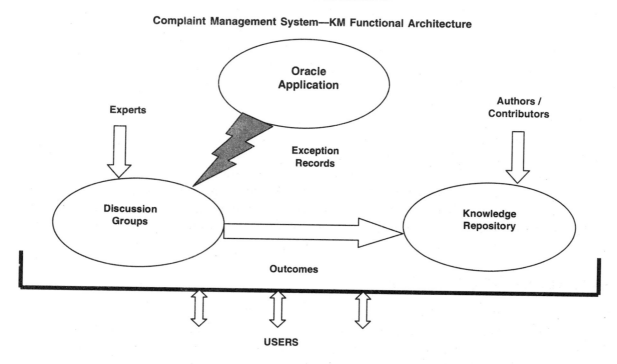

Discussion Group—feedback is grouped by category, by centre, region, or author. It is possible to trace the thread of a complaint. Where it originated, who responded first, next and so on? The status of a feedback can be discerned. One of the options under discussion group is Priority Issues - This contains complaints that are not resolved for a certain number of days. Once a discussion is concluded more responses are not required.

Knowledge Repository—Once a feedback is closed in may or may not be knowledge enriching. If it is generally applicable it undergoes a process of cleansing and filtering and is then stored in the Knowledge Repository. The default view is my view. This consists of the tasks allotted to the user by the knowledge integrator. There is a blank format that the user can fill in. The user can also initiate a request to author. All documents go through a two-stage validation process. Each document has to have an approver. The approved document is then forwarded to the knowledge integrator for incorporation in the Knowledge Repository.

Latest Updates—Contains complaints by category e.g. by author. There are various ways of presenting information.

Best Practices—There are various document forms such as best practice, root-cause, and problem-solution.

FAQs—Here the answers to frequently asked questions are stored.

Besides these five options there are search mechanisms. There are different search features. One way is to search for a keyword in the entire document. Another way is to search for keywords assigned by the author.

The knowledge integrator validates the structure and content of the Best Practice, Root Cause, and Problem Solution documents. The knowledge integrator acts as a link between the Knowledge Management and client Server modules. The functions of the knowledge integrator are twofold. First, he / she acts as a facilitator, ensuring that the right people interact to find the correct solution. He / she acts as a moderator - closing, declaring, and concluding discussions. The knowledge integrator can notify employees, with a date by which to contribute, if they are not participating on a particular issue. Second, the knowledge integrator drives what is happening in the forums. Whether a feedback is knowledge enriching or not is not a black and white issue. Therefore, there is the concept of a brewing tank. Knowledge is created, captured, and stored. No immediate decision is taken on putting it in the Knowledge Repository. It is possible that after a review of the expired discussions, some knowledge item is placed in the Knowledge Repository.

☐ IMPLEMENTATION PROCESS

There are Faculty, Counsellor, Administrative Staff and other Category of members in a centre. It was imperative that all members of the Centre were convinced about this system. To achieve this an exhaustive session was conducted to all members of the Centre covering the various aspects of the system and the advantages of the system. The main challenge was to remove the phobia of COMPLAINT and replace this as a suggestion for improvement. This cannot be achieved in one round of training, so at least 2 to 3 rounds of training were conducted, which was reinforced by the top management, whenever a communication took place. Once the Centre Staff was convinced, and then the second step of introducing the system to students was undertaken. This was 2-step procedure:
   (a) Publicise the existence of the system for usage of students. This was done
      (i) By putting up posters in the centre.
      (ii) Announcing in the classes by the faculty.
      (iii) Informing them during informal meetings by Counsellors, Centre Head etc.
   (b) Encourage the students to use the system, by promptly attending to the feedback's received.
   Since the CRS was coupled with CAS no additional infrastructural requirement was there to implement CRS in the Centre. The whole process of implementation in a centre took roughly one calendar month time.

☐ CONCLUSIONS

The primary requirement for any system to get implemented successfully is the buy – in process of the end user. The complete success depends on how much the user is convinced about the benefits of the system to be implemented. For CRS there are 3 Users namely: Student, Centre Head and Student Relation Officer.

Through word of mouth amongst the students the usage of CRS as a platform for communicating the feedback to the centre is increasing on day-to-day basis. Since APTECH is in the early stages of implementing CRS, the only two parameters currently that they are looking at is the response time and resolution time on a feedback. As the system matures, two of the major metrics that will be looked at is product delivery and time for delivery.

The Customer's Viewpoint—Few Students of APTECH franchised centre where CRS had not yet been installed and few students from a centre run directly by APTECH where CRS went online in February 2000 were interviewed to understand its immediate impact. Students from the first type of centres were highly dissatisfied because there basic expectations in terms of service and facilities were not met, they didn't know anything about CRS or any system by which they can give the feedback on which some meaningful action can be taken. They were also not at all sure if franchised centre would act on the feedback. While students from APTECH run centres were highly satisfied with the facilities, and services as they exceeded their expectations. They started using the system in the fourth week of April 2000 and have found it very useful. They have seen the actions being taken very fast on the issues raised by them using CRS.

The benefits of CRS were predicted to be manifold. First, APTECH's business is a people oriented service. Some of the employees are brilliant, and possess domain specific expertise. There existed informal networks within the organisation, e. g. a particular employee was considered to be the "boss" in Java programming, and would be consulted on this particular subject. Second, the aim was to go beyond customer service. The endeavour was creating a virtuous cycle, a spiral process, of a learning organisation. Third, was to measure the performance of employees. Fourth, was to create a tighter and well-knit network among employees. Lastly, it was to improve the quality of response to feedback. CRS has helped APTECH in reaping these benefits.

Chapter 46

Benefits of Implementing a CRM System in Cellular Telecom Services

■ **M Dadlani, R Shanker and P Chopra**

ABSTRACT

CRM is a discipline as well as a set of discrete software technologies which focuses on automating and improving the business processes associated with managing customer relationships with in the areas of sales, marketing, customer care and support. CRM applications not only facilitate the coordination of multiple business functions but also coordinate multiple channels of communication with customer – face to face, call centre and the web – so that organizations can accommodate their customers preferred channel of interaction. A rich customer relationship fuels effective acquisition, nurturing and retention of customers. CRM aims to provide organizational effectiveness by reducing sales cycles and selling costs, identifying markets and channels for expansion, and improving customer value, satisfaction, profitability and retention. In the present era, the customers want to drive all the interactions. Service Industry is trying to drive their commerce through web to help reduce their operating overheads besides providing a better customer service.

Key Words: *Churn rate, customer loyalty, service level, customer satisfaction, front end, middle ware, back end, customer interaction points.*

❑ INTRODUCTION

Customer Relationship Management – the ability to provide a meaningful sales and service experience—promises to be a means of differentiation; of providing customers with a reason to frequent your business rather than that of your competitors. CRM promises *competitive differentiation in a parity environment*. More and more organisations are realising that a customer-centric operation is no longer an optional differentiator but it is a key to remain in business. Technology enabled relationship management is a framework for developing both the culture and the infrastructure for a customer-centric operation.

Alternatively, CRM is defined as a continuous process of identifying, attracting and retaining profitable customers.

ERP applications have helped the companies to automate and optimise business processes in areas such as finance, manufacturing, inventory management and human resources etc. Like ERP, CRM solutions focus on automating and improving business processes, albeit in front-office areas such as marketing, sales, customer service, and customer support. Whereas *ERP* implementation can result in improved organisational *efficiency*, *CRM* aims to provide organisational *effectiveness* by reducing sales cycle and selling cost, identifying markets and channels for expansion, and improving customer value, satisfaction, profitability, and retention. While CRM applications provide the framework for embodying, promoting and executing best practices in customer-facing activities, ERP provides the backbone, resources and operational applications to make organisations more efficient in achieving these goals. CRM also acts an enabler for e-business by developing a web-based collaboration between the company and its suppliers, partners and customers. It can extend the traditional channels of interaction such as direct sales force or telebusiness to the web by providing a framework for managing the interactions and transactions.

CRM applications, often used in combination with data-warehousing, E-commerce applications, and call centres, allows companies to gather and access information about customers' buying histories, preferences, complaints, and other data so that they can better anticipate what customer will want. The goal is to ***instil greater customer loyalty***

☐ CRM BUSINESS CYCLE

A typical CRM business cycle has the following stages:
- Understand and Differentiate
- Develop and Customise
- Interact and Deliver
- Acquire and Retain
- Prioritising and Changes
- Creating an Action Plan
- Measuring Success

These stages are interdependent and continuous.

☐ UNDERSTAND AND DIFFERENTIATE

CRM Business Cycle starts with understanding the customer-what they value, what types of services are important to them, how and when they like to interact and when they want to buy. The activities involved in understanding the customers are:
- Profiling of customers based on demographics, purchase patterns and channel preference.

- Segmentation to identify logical unique groups of customers
- Customer valuations to understand profitability

DEVELOP AND CUSTOMISE

Products, services, channels and media are customised based on the needs of quantitative customer segments. The extent of customisation is based on the potential value and delivered by the customer segment.

INTERACT AND DELIVER

Customers interact in many different ways with many different areas of organisations, including call centres, customer service and online services. Organisations must ensure:
- All areas of the organisation have easy access to relevant, actionable customer information
- All areas are trained how to use customer information to tailor interactions

ACQUIRE AND RETAIN

A company will want to clone in its prospecting and acquisition efforts for the customers that produce greatest value for the organisation. Customer retention is based on an organisations ability to deliver on customer's definition of value.

PRIORITISING AND CHANGES

Due to the dynamic nature of any business the requirements of the customer and the ability of the organisation of the extent to which it can satisfy those requirements keep on changing. An organisation needs to continuously monitor, and prioritise its customers depending on their value deliverability and accordingly make suitable changes in its deliverables.

CREATING AN ACTION PLAN

The organisation needs to develop an action plan so that the deliverables reach the prioritised customer.

MEASURING SUCCESS

As implementing CRM is time consuming and requires a significant commitment across the organisation, it is crucial that action plan
- Establishes the means of measuring progress on CRM initiative (the barometers of measuring performance improvements are within the organisation MIS. e.g.: number

of complaints, churn percentage, number of transactions per customer, cost of servicing a customer, employee to subscriber ratio, etc.)

- Establishes enterprise-wide measures of success, and metrics that can be applied to all CRM initiatives
- Applies these metrics on an ongoing basis to ensure continued funding of CRM initiatives

Each of potential initiatives should be tied to projected improvements in customer dynamics—acquisition, retention, penetration and reactivation. The next step is to determine how improvements in these dynamics impact revenue, cost, and competitive differentiation.

CRM involves knowing your customers individually and having some mechanism for interacting with them and customising business for them. This is an inherently **integrative operation**. One of the benefits of CRM is that it would make a company's customers more loyal. Every time a company interacts with a customer, the company customises its service more closely suited to the customer's needs. The company is getting a little higher up on the **customer's learning curve**. Moreover, the company is making the product increasingly valuable to the customer. The relationship with customer is developing in its own context. This is called **learning relationship** because the relationship is getting smarter with time. To create this kind of learning relationship, there are three criteria. First, it is necessary to have a good design interface .It is has to be easier for a customer to give a company its information and for the company to capture that information. Second, is to have good memory. The company has to remember what the customer told them. An organisation needs to have standard parameters hard coded into CRM to capture critical customer details at every customer interaction. Thirdly, the company has to have the ability to integrate the information into the way it handles the customer.

CRM is more than just technology. With CRM, one is operating in a different dimension of competition—finding products and services for customers, as opposed to finding customers for the products and services the company sells. The technology is crucial, but it's also important to have managers with the vision to imagine what this technology the enterprise to accomplish

☐ CRM IN HMTL

Hutchison Max Telecom Limited (HMTL) is the leading cellular operator in India. It has a subscriber base of 200,000 in Mumbai, 205,000 in Delhi, 120,000 in Gujarat and 40,000 in Calcutta. In Mumbai, there are around 14000 customer interactions in a day, i.e. on an average a single customer interacts at once in 14 days. Therefore, one can appreciate the need for having an effective customer relation.

The customer interactions can be segmented into various categories

Email: 2%
Direct Walk-In: 5%

Fax/Letter: 8%
Calls: 85%

The peak load hours are from 10.00 AM to 11.00 PM. In a Retail Telecom Industry the cost of handling a customer can be calculated by assigning the various cost factors such as cost of operation of call office, cost of mailers, staffing cost, etc. It is not possible to effectively find out quantitatively the benefits of having a CRM. Instead of the Cost-Benefit Analysis, it is recommended to study the cost of not effectively serving the customer (i.e. when CRM is not in place). A typical commercial CRM package to be installed at HMTL would cost around Rs.5 Crore (Assuming one would go for a top of the line CRM package like a Siebel, Vantive, Clarify, Oracle). Though the internationally accepted payback period is around 28 months, in the Indian context one cannot apply the same yardstick as the profile of the customers as well as the manpower costs differ. The complete transition from the internally developed CRM to a commercial CRM package would take 6 to 12 months. The customer dynamics of the cellular telecom industry include:

- 20% of the customers contribute to 80% of the revenue
- 20% of the customers contribute to 90% of the profits
- 68% of the customers walk-away because of the poor service
- A new sale is approximately 5 times more costly than a sale to an existing customer

□ PARAMETERS FOR MEASURING THE EFFECTIVENESS OF CRM IMPLEMENTATION

The benefits of implementation of CRM in Retail Telecom can be achieved in the following areas.

- Staffing Cost: In call centre at HMTL, the staff requirement is around 100, which can be reduced to around 80 after the complete implementation of the CRM package. This value is arrived based on the expert opinion and heuristics, as sufficient historical data is not available.
- Total activation turnaround time: This is the time taken to activate a new account. Presently it is around 70 minutes and with effective implementation, it can be perceived to decrease by 90%.
- Churn Prevention: In Mumbai presently there are two Cellular operators – HMTL and BPL. There is a continuous shifting of dissatisfied customer from one operator to another. The operators strive to increase their customer base while making the customer transition to its competitor minimal. Assuming ceterus paribus and full-scale successful implementation of CRM it can be reduced up to 90%. However, churn is dependant on a number of parameters outside the scope of an organisations control e.g. the regulatory environment, competition activity, the value added services, the quality of service.
- Easier handling of peak loads
- Customer Service can be Improved

- Customer History records
- Accurate MIS on productivity monitoring and turnaround times for issue resolutions
- Reduction in the number of process steps
- Improved working capital management.

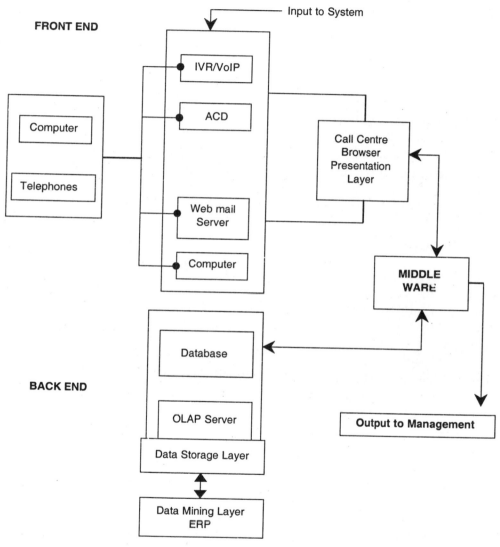

Fig. 1 *CRM Scheme*

☐ FRONT END

Front end is the interaction point for all the customers with the company. Front end is provided for two reasons:

1. To provide services

2. To handle complaints
3. View customer history

The customer calls/complaints can be routed through and solved through various channels. Some of the complains can be solved automatically (i.e. through VoIP and IVR) while others require human interaction.

In case of telephone call, the call is first received buy the IVR (interactive voice response)/VoIP (voice over internet protocol), and complaints, if possible, are resolved there itself. Otherwise, the call escalates to ACD (automatic call distributor), which intelligently distributes the calls to various hotline executives. It becomes necessary to have an intelligent ACD because of diversity in the types of calls handled (complains, new sales, corporate complaints and sales, billing etc). VoIP makes it possible to resolve complaint without human intervention and convey the same to the customer.

A customer interaction happens through computer (internet), telephone, or in person. In case of complaint being mailed, it will go to web mail server that can be handled either by staff or by automated system.

Executives can have live chat with customer on Internet using computer.

□ PRESENTATION LAYER

The hotline executive has access to all information available from back end and front end about the particular customer in the presentation layer. At presentation layer the executive uses his sense of judgement to clear complaints and updates the back end information.

□ BACK END

It contains all relevant customer related historical data that is automatically or manually captured through all above mentioned customer interaction points. Data mining and OLAP tools are used for effectively utilising the raw information. Back end also includes Integration with all satellite systems within an organisation.

□ MIDDLE WARE

It contains statistical tools for analysing the customer information and making it available to hotline executive as well as to top management through reports.

The authors recommend the Benefits and Cost to be analysed under the following heads:

Cost Parameters: The cost parameters are directly available in the monetary terms:
- Cost of product acquisition (CRM package) including opportunity cost and training cost is approximately Rs.5 Crore
- Staffing cost
- Telephone outcall cost

Table 1 *Benefits of CRM*

FRAMEWORK FOR EVALUATION OF CRM BENEFITS

Marketing	Customer Support	Sales
Identify and target customers based on Recency, Frequency, and Monetary (RFM)	Strengthen shared relationships with individualised customer care based on specific customer history and preference	Improve field sales and sales management through real time information sharing
Manage marketing campaigns with clear goals and quantifiable objectives.	Improve call centre efficiency and help desk support through automated scripting based on non solutions	Increase sales efficiency through wireless and internet based order entry
Create and manage solid sales leads for field representatives Increase in marketing and cross selling opportunities	Increase call centre efficiency through automated call routing, call tracking, and entitlement processing, work flow, problem resolution	Improved territory management with up to date real time account information updates
Increase returns on marketing investments through accurate targeting and one-to-one marketing	Decrease support and service costs while increasing customer satisfaction by extending web based support functionality directly to customer	Improve the entire sales force by capturing, distributing and leveraging the success and expertise of highest performers
Improved product development process with knowledge gained directly from customer interaction	Centralise all customer contact – from sales, support, field service and marketing – to deliver excellent customer service Provide option of self service to customer over the company's website	Increase revenue per visit by focussing on growing the best accounts

- Delay Cost
- Transition cost

In India, the pertinent question skewing this decision is the fact that at any given point in time, manual processes seem more cost effective due to cheaper manpower costs.

Benefit Parameters: The benefits are attributed in the following ways:

- Improvement in Customer Service
- Reduced Staffing
- Minimising Churn
- Improved control of peak loads
- Fewer mistakes in billing
- Reduction in number of process steps
- Improved speed of communication
- Reduction in redundant activities
- Improved working capital management

Calculation of Benefits: The benefits can be assigned to the various Customer interaction Points and correspondingly benefits in that area can be found out.

1. Call centres
   - Reduction in Staff Cost
   - Enhanced productivity (subscriber to agent ratio)
   - Quicker turnaround times
   - Saving due to call handling by alternate channels
2. Customer Centre
   - Staff Cost reduction
3. Corporate Relation
   - Staff Cost reduction
   - Call Reduction
4. Credit
   - Elimination of P/V required for DA customers
5. Customer Relation
   - Staff Cost Reduction
   - Call escalation benefit
6. Marketing
   - Churn Prevention
   - Segmented promotions
   - Customer behaviour on network

The conversion of these benefits to the monetary terms enables one to gauge the applicability of the effectiveness of the implementation of CRM in the organisation.

REFERENCES

Bhandari, B. (2000), 'Agent Orange Comes Calling', *Business Standard Weekend*, May 20 / May 21. pp. I.

Brown, S. (1997), *'Breakthrough Customer Service—Best Practices of Leaders in Customer Support'*, John Wiley & Sons, Canada.

Brown, S. (1999), *'Strategic Customer Care—An Evolutionary Approach to Increasing Customer Value and Profitability'*, John Wiley & Sons, Canada.

Curry, J. and Curry, A. (2000), *'The Customer Marketing Method – How to Implement and Profit from CRM'*, Free Press, New York.

www.crm-forum.com

www.crmassist.com

www.ncr.com/publications

www.vantive.com

www.siebel.com

Customer Relationship Management in Customer Service
The Titan Experience

■ H G Raghunath

Abstract

The big thing that's happening in the market place is the change in customer's expectation about every thing that we offer, be it the buying experience, product usage experience or the after sales service experience. Listening, understanding and responding to the customer therefore, is critical to be in business. Excellent customer service is now a requirement for survival in our fragmenting, fast changing, quality conscious and highly competitive market.

The operating principle is

"Listening to customers must become everyone's business. With most competitors moving ever faster, the race will go to those who listen and respond most intently".

— Tom Peters, Thriving on Chaos

To know what exactly customers want, we need to build relationship with customers and tailor our organisation to nurture this relationship. Market ownership is the key hence, the ownership stems from a relationship. Therefore, we need to keep our customers forever.. forever satisfied.

Key Words : Customer Expectation, Loyalty, Listening, Responding, Market ownership, Buying, Product usage and Service experience.

☐ TITAN CUSTOMER SERVICE—THE MISSION

- To provide superior values to the customer on a sustained basis
- Cement a relationship

- Increase trust
- Build enduring brand values

The Service philosophy which has evolved during the years in Titan (including the change of name from After Sales Service to Customer Service) is a *'3 R'* one:

- Repair the hurt feelings of the customer
- Repair the watch
- Repair the damage caused to Titan's reputation by repairing the above two.

Repair the Hurt Feelings of the Customer

It is critical that the customer's complaint is handled with utmost care and through high quality interaction, in order that, the customer feels comfortable and his hurt feelings are addressed.

This involves:

- recruiting the right frontline service personnel and training them to ensure high qual-ity customer interaction.

    The front line staff go through a dedicated training program called Front Line Performance Improvement Program (FPIP). The training is followed up with effectiveness measurement at individual sites to ensure continuity and actual performance. Gaps if any, are identified and plugged through a separate process.

- Providing a showroom like (similar to buying experience) ambience for service called Watch Care Centers. The chain has 53 Watch Care Centers.

It is proper that the customer expects a similar ambience at the time of addressing his complaints as did he experience while buying a Titan product at the showrooms. Realising this, the Watch Care Center is created on these lines. Facilities such as decent seating, air conditioning, clean drinking water, magazines to browse during the waiting time, pleasing music, education posters to enhance his understanding on watch maintenance, see-through repair shop to enhance his confidence, are some of the features created.

- **Personal capabilities**
    Grooming
    Personality
    Responsiveness
    Product Knowledge
- **Customer interaction process**
    Welcome/Greeting, Attention given to customer
    Problem understanding, Relationship Building
    Resolving queries/doubts
    Value addition (Standby watches/Home delivery)

Pro-active selling (Accessories)

Feedback generation (Feedback mailer)

Post-service follow-up

- **Operational Parameters**

TAT–Repairs : Trend of KRA performance achievement

TAT–Delivery : Trend of KRA performance achievement

Service revenue : Track the performance trend (+ ve/–ve)

Feedback mailers received : % Response trend

Revenue per customer : Trend

Overall rating–Trend based on customer feedback mailers

- **Interiors (Tangibles)**

Wall décor—Wall paintings on product/Accessories

Furniture—Condition/maintenance

Product (Accessory) display–In Mood Windows/Cuboids

Magazines/take away's

Commitment diary

Clean filtered drinking water

Proper Lighting

Credit card acceptability

Plant/flower arrangement

Air-conditioning

Product brochures

Channel music

Repair the Watch

A fully equipped service center manned by Factory trained and experienced service engineers ensures quality repair.

Every service engineer goes through a training program at the Service HQ which includes technical skills, product knowledge and complaint handling techniques.

Titan service is ISO 9001 certified, thereby ensuring that all repair activities follow a strict, systematic process which is controlled and measured through ISO audit system.

Post training effectiveness measurement and the service efficiency is carried out through an extensive biannual audit program called SERQUAL This evaluation is used to categorise service centers as Best, Better, Good and Bad performers. The matrix used is very effective and helps move the low ranked performers go up the ladder through monitoring.

Key performance measures

Speed of repair – measured as Repair Time taken

60% in < 20 mnts, 95% in < 4 days, 99% in < 7 days, 100% in < 15 days

2. Repeat returns - < 0.2%

In case the repair time is estimated to be more than 7 days, a stand-by watch is offered to the customer so that he is not inconvenienced without a watch.

Repair the damage caused to Titan's reputation by handling the first two repairs to customer's satisfaction.

Network expansion – Approach followed

The key to provide quick and efficient service is by providing service access to all Titan customers. The process of service network expansion is to identify Titan watch population locations and set up service facility there. The Titan service network comprises of 512 service outlets providing Total service access to 85% of the watch population.

The next step is to ensure service access and spread to all Titan customers. This is done by :

- By providing training to Dealers
- Parts supply at Dealer's door steps
- High quality tools & equipment supply to ensure repair quality
- Providing updates of technical information
- Monitor & measure their performance

Measure every thing !

The only true and reliable measurement of service quality is the assessment of customer's recent service experience, and the customer's assessment is final.

"Quality is not measured by me. It is not even measured by you. Quality is in the eyes of customers. If they are not happy with you, you are not happy with us".

— *John Guerra, AT&T*

Customer's satisfaction on service is measured through a feedback process at service centers. The customer fills up a mailer questionnaire to provide his feedback on his service experience. On a scale of 10 he evaluates us on 10 key parameters. The feedback is reviewed, appropriate corrective actions taken and the process goes on.

In order to motivate the customer to give the feedback, a system to reward the best suggestion is in place. The award winning suggestions are displayed across the service network.

Based on customer's feedback, some of the improvements implemented include, enhancing the service working hours, correcting the service charges, questionnaire in local languages, enhanced speed of repair, to name the few. This process has led us to implement service standards based on customer's expectations.

As a continuous improvement initiative, even the content of the questionnaire was reviewed and changed to suit changing customer's expectations.

A nation wide customer satisfaction survey is conducted covering both end consumers and Dealers using an external market research agency. The findings of this survey are analyzed to work out action plans to further enhance the level of service provided to them.

Dealer meets across India are conducted periodically. During these meets, their feedback on service levels and suggestions are received. Corrective actions are implemented.

Dealer's satisfaction in regard to parts availability (parts indented Vs parts supplied) is measured continuously as a percentage of unprocessed value of parts against indents.

Every function in Customer Service Department has a KRA and performance measures. For Eg., despatches within 3 days is a KRA target for Parts Stores. Response within 48 hrs is the target for Customer Service Cell.

Teach your customers to get the best service

It is found from research that most customers don't read the operating manual or the guarantee terms and conditions. It is important therefore, to educate the customers so that they maintain the product well. This ensures that the product lasts long and provides trouble free performance.

Colorful education posters and leaflets are displayed and are available at all service centers for customers to pick up. In addition, an illustrative brief is provided in the operating manual/guarantee card. Service charges for each type of repair and details of repair are displayed at all service centers so as to be transparent.

Service timing is not 9 to 5 P.M.!

Realising the need to keep the service center open even during lunch breaks and after office hours, which is the time convenient for customers to come. Titan service centers are kept open till 7. P.M without lunch break. Voice recording facility is available at service centers for after hour use.

There are plans to keep service centers open even on Sundays & other holidays in specific locations.

The learning : Customers call us only when they need us.

Say thank you to the complaining customer !

The customer actually does a favour by complaining. Hence, we realised that the customer should actually be thanked for complaining since, he is providing us an opportunity to learn and improve.

Every service customer is given a thank you card at all watch care centers thanking the customer to have given us an opportunity to serve him. Greeting cards during festive occasions get added.

On completion of the post service follow up, the customer is thanked again. The customer who buys a strap is thanked, a customer who gives a suggestion is thanked. At every opportunity we say *'Thank You"* to the customer.

Dealer's time is precious

Dealers in Metro locations find it very difficult to return the defectives and pickup the serviced ones during business hours. He needs to spend a significant amount of his valuable business time if he were to visit the service center.

Realising how valuable his business time is, a courier facility has been implemented to pick up and deliver service watches at his door step.

The benefits!

Dealer's confidence on Titan's service is multiplied.
Customers get their service watches in time and their loyalty for the brand and the dealer goes up.

End customer's time is not less precious !

Keeping in view of the speed of complaint and query handling requirement, the service activity is computerised. Large data base is available for use either by the customer or by us when needed. In metro locations, multi-terminal complaint handling facility is provided in order to ensure quick redressal and minimised customer waiting time.

Customer's time is very valuable, especially, in cities where a lot time is spent on travel. Realising this, we offer home delivery of serviced watches from all Watch Care Centers at a nominal cost.

A Titan customer seeking assistance in regard to either service, product or any information on Titan could log in and register his query through Planetcustomer.com, a service portal. The response is guaranteed within 72 hrs.

For Institutional customers and Canteen Stores Department, who buy large quantities of watches, service camps are conducted in their premises periodically to ensure "provide service at customer's door step" keeping in view the difficulty, such a customer has to face if he were to visit a service center.

Keep in touch with the customers regularly

10% of the total customers serviced, are contacted one month after their service experience in order to check and understand the performance of the watch and customer's satisfaction on service. In addition, his/her suggestions if any for improvement are recorded. Also, checked and evaluated is his repurchase intention/referral intention.

This process allows us to be in touch with the customer again and allows customer in turn to provide his valuable feedback. The loop gets closed, the relationship continues.

Free Watch care weeks are conducted regularly to provide special service access, build customer awareness on Titan service and to be in touch with customers.

Corporate Customer Service Cell

This cell addresses the complaint of the customer who encounters problem in getting proper service or has a problem with the product. Normally, this customer writes to us seeking redress.

The response/acknowledgement is assured within 48 hrs. The complaint is considered resolved only after the customer/concerned service staff confirms the resolution of the issue. Every customer letter is attached with a "Customer activity slip" to confirm issue closure for our records.

Empowerment

The customers expect quick solutions and spot decisions by the frontline service staff & their expectations keep changing.

Our frontline service personnel are EMPOWERED to take decisions to suit customer's needs. The service organisation is 7 years old in the empowerment journey.

The effect of empowerment is so positive but the cost of empowerment is a fraction of the total service revenue. The empowerment system has resulted in the frontline staff developing the ownership of the complaint handling process.

Motivation of Frontline Staff is the Key to Provide Excellent Service

Service with a smile, day in and day out is a difficult task but a must. To measure the "smile" parameter across the service network is almost an impossible task but, it is a promise to our customer. Motivation of the frontline therefore, is the key. Competition amongst the service staff is the route to achieve excellence.

The service center teams including the frontline staff compete with each other for the "Best Service Center Award" held annually at the National level. The top three service teams are honoured in the annual National Service Convention with the rewards and prizes galore in the presence of Top management. The celebration and the high spirits are worth seeing to be believed.

The basis of selection is largely dependent on customer's rating on service experience through the mailer questionnaire and their performance in KRAs achievement.

Competition has helped in developing *"To be the Best"* attitude amongst the Service personnel.

Let the Customer be With You for Ever

A large customer data base that we have is a Golden mine of opportunities, the opportunities to have customers for life ! Every year around 1.6 million customers use Titan service, be it a simple battery or strap replacement or any other service. We intend to pool this customer base into a Service Club or a Customer Contact Club. We intend to seek customer's suggestion on service delivery, evaluate our service against best practices, implement the suggestions, reward the customer, improve.. improve…improve.

Customer is Your Advocate

Treating customer service as an on going and continuous opportunity for value addition to the customer value chain, creates a solid loyal customer base. From here, relationship improves from one level of intrinsic quality to another. This is a route to creating frequent buyers. The emphasis of customer service function is therefore that of developing a long term relationship with the customer.

To summarise, we believe

Our relationship doesn't end with the sale of the watch, but begins
What we sell is not just a product or service

We sell - Benefits

Our commitment

Service Plus: A Comparative Study of Indian and US Hotels

■ **Mukesh Chaturvedi**

Abstract

The hospitality industry, comprising of mainly hotels, is still in the development stage in India. This paper presents the current scenario in Indian hospitality industry which shows that, with globalization of business and markets, the concept of service has taken a new meaning and acquired new dimensions. Indian hotels too have world class technology facilities and compare well with the best in the world in pampering their guests.

Key Words: *Hi-tech Hospitality, Relationship Marketing, CRM Strategy*

□ INTRODUCTION

Share of services as a proportion of GDP has been on the rise the world over (World Development Indicators 1995). Of course, compared to 83 per cent of Hong Kong and 72 per cent of the USA, India's services' share is only 46.6 per cent. It is, rather, one of the lowest for even sub-Saharan Africa has 48 per cent. But, the good news is that it has been rising per se – in 1980, it was 36 per cent, and, in 1995, it was 41 per cent.

Which all services have been growing and what does it show? Hospitality & travel, banking & finance, entertainment & communication, and a host of other services like beauty care, education & training, health care, courier, placement, repairs & maintenance, etc. And, they all indicate that the life style of people is changing. People are becoming more health conscious; people are taking more time out for leisure; and people are more concerned about their future and are planning their lives better. And, people are willing to pay for it. Our approach to life is changing. We want to live it fully and enjoy it rather than complete it as formality and duty.

At the same time, it also means more and more dependence on "others".

A service, basically, is an activity. "Others" perform these activities and we buy / hire these activities for benefits and satisfaction. The very nature of the service makes it largely 'provider' oriented. Therefore, the expertise and the courtesies of service providers become most critical to the overall satisfaction of the client.

There is another aspect of every service. At the core of every service lies the basic reason why some one would buy a service. The next level provides that benefit and satisfaction. And, the third level is the extension of the satisfaction – Service Plus. Most of the service marketers are able to take care of only the first two levels; only few have been able to realize the real value of, and evolve upto, the "Plus" level.

The process of liberalization and globalization paved way for the entry of multinationals into India and moving of Indian business abroad. This resulted in an increase in business travel substantially. Thus, coupled with the increase in personal travel, in the last one decade, the travel boom has been up and the tourism industry has emerged as the largest and the fastest growing industry. Asia has experienced the fastest growth. In other words, Indian hospitality industry has had an opportunity for a major growth in the recent past.

The hospitality industry, comprising of mainly hotels, is still in the development stage in India. There are, basically, three well – organized five-star hotel chains, viz., Oberoi, Taj and ITC, operating in the metros and important centres of tourism. In terms of service and professional standards, they are comparable with the best in the world. But, in terms of size and operations, they are still small.

Hospitality is paying attention to a guest's needs. It is seen in terms of food and comfort offered by the host. It is a matter of behaviour, and it depends largely on the attitude of the host. Therefore, the host has to be courteous and has to serve for satisfaction through his/her verbal/non-verbal interaction. Every guest is to be made to feel that he/she is the most important person.

In a hotel, service comprises the ambience - architecture, interiors and the mood; physical comfort; the food; the people and the warmth. Hospitality is an experience. To be different, it has to have a unique style.

Unfortunately, in many hotels, both here and abroad, the author has experienced that the host try to impress the guest with their dress, accent, mannerism, etc., whereas the crux of Service Plus lies somewhere else.

This paper presents the current scenario in Indian hospitality industry which shows that with the globalization of business and markets the concept of service has taken a new meaning and acquired new dimensions. Indian hotels too have worldclass technology facilities and compare well with the best in the world in "pampering" their guests.

☐ GROWTH AND THE FUTURE

According to Pannell Kerr Forster's City Survey 2000 (PKF Research, August 2000), international business at hotels in India does not show any significant gains. Still, rooms are bring added at a ferentic pace: Mumbai – 3,256 by 2003 (10 players including Radisson, Le

Meridien, Intercontinental and Hyatt Regency); Delhi – 891; Chennai – 350 (Magunta Oberoi); Bangalore 423 by 2001 (Krishna Continental and Leela Palace).

According to the leading players in the industry, Delhi is fast emerging as the latest destination of the international business traveller. Sanjiv Tyagi, Vice-President & General Manager, Radisson Hotel says that, with a relatively stable government in the country and the opening up of sectors such as insurance and telecom, the market is bullish. More business travellers are coming to the capital, and they have had a 70 per cent occupancy during April 1999 – March 2000. He would know better for Radisson is right next to the International Airport at New Delhi.

Grand Hyatt, which had a 'soft launch' recently, also believes that, with Delhi moving towards becoming an all season destination for business travellers, there will be need for more facilities to take them away from the stress of boardrooms.

The Forte Hotel Group, which owns the Meridien chain of hotels will soon have eight hotels in India by 2001. With this, Meridian will have as many hotels in India as in the UK and become the largest international operator in India.

Currently, the Group has four hotels in India – Delhi, Bangalore, Pune and Chennai. Two more are to open by the end of 2000 in Mumbai and Cochin, and, then, two more in Goa and Mumbai. With all these properties, the Group hopes to have nearly 4,000 rooms in India by 2004.

But, why India? Why such a big expansion plan? According to Michel Noblet, Regional Managing Director of the Forte Hotel Group, with more than one billion people, they recognize the tremendous opportunity that the Indian market and neighbouring countries bring. Actually, Bernard Lambert, President and Managing Director, Le Meridien Hotels and Resorts, seems to have been encouraged by the first quarter results of their flagship hotels which have shown a 14 per cent increase in 2000. That indicates the potential for both corporate business and tourism in the country.

□ HI-TECH HOSPITALITY

To be able to provide good quality service, hotels in India too are acquiring state-of-the-art technology. The new consciousness seems to be that it is not the lobby but the basement that is the heart of a hotel. The Oberoi Group is one of such believers.

Its newly-established Trident brand of hotels in Agra, Chennai, Cochin, Udaipur and Jaipur are equipped with the latest, user-friendly devices. For example, instead of washing machines, there is a computerised 'washer extractor' which automatically selects from a range of detergent combinations according to the fabric being washed. The marking machine uses a thermal adhesive process for identification to avoid (ugly) stains. And there are flat work irons for crisply pressed linen within minutes.

On the other side, they have a large number of vapour absorption chillers instead of vapour compression chillers. The former do not require any gas for refrigeration. For air-conditioning, they use the eco-friendly gas Hydro Chloro Fluoro Carbon (IICFC) in place of Chloro Fluoro Carbon (CFC). The former has much lower ozone depleting potential. Even the Italian dry cleaning machine is eco-friendly, for it recycles the perchhloro ethylene being used in this process.

However, the most sophisticated pieces of equipment are the enormous heat pumps used for air-conditioning (cooling and healing) the rooms. With a computerized control room, these pumps are on auto mode switching on and off according to load requirements. The heat generated as a bi-product of the compression of heat pump is used to heat water through the plate heat exchanger. Even the latest, ultraheat storage tank is an out-and-out energy saver. When fitted with cooling systems it reduces air-conditioning and refrigeration costs and also levels off peak loads.

The Trident in Udaipur has recently won the 'Green Consciousness' award from the Green Globe in the UK for its efforts towards environmental preservation. Exhaust scrubbers installed in the boilers and diesel engine rooms to improve the quality of air omission; the reverse osmosis system to ensure purification of all the water supplied in the hotel; and the equipment installed to ensure that all waste material is properly reutilised are the reasons for this recognition. They have achieved such break throughs in almost all aspects of hoteliering. A sewage treatment plant designed by the German specialist Dr Scholz, which works on the principle of purification through rotating biological disks, first makes bacteria eat into the sludge and then disinfects the treated water through chlorination for use in gardening. To retard the deterioration of waste material; a huge walk-in refrigeration is used to store wet garbage.

Investing in such expensive technology and equipment – the dishwasher capable of cleaning 18 plates per minute at a consistent water temperature of 90 degrees C to the hugely popular Cimbali coffee machine – is unusual for, mostly, the hotels spend all of their money, effort and time on 'external' detailing. But, Ms. Ragini Chopra, Vice-President, Business Development, Oberoi Group opines that, in hospitality industry, it has to be a conscious decision to acquire the latest technology and devices and focus on 'behind-the-scenes' detailing to be able to provide the best service.

□ STRATEGIES FOR EFFECTIVE CUSTOMER RELATIONSHIPS

The Forte (Meridien chain of hotels) Group's expansion plan is accompanied with relationship marketing techniques to increase consumer interest and satisfaction. Recently, it launched a client loyalty program called moments.com. Open to travellers all over the world, this is a multi-million pound reward and customer recognition program. Every time a member spends £2 on food, drink or accommodation, he/she gets one "moments" point. These points can be exchanged for packages available at the Forte Group of Hotels. Le Meridien has established another first for an international hotel group in India by opening a local market reservations centre for domestic and international reservations.

Earlier, the "packages" were seasonal only – summer, winter, holiday. Now, they are personal as well. For example, a leading hotel group, Taj, is introducing exclusive holiday packages for single women travellers – action-packed with activities. The group is also developing "reunion packages" – reunion with a long lost friend.

If single women should no longer be weary of holidaying alone, so should the senior citizens be. The Ashok Group of Hotels has introduced special packages for those above 65. By producing their age certificates, they can avail a 50 per cent discount on most of the facilities offered by the hotel.

Some hotel groups, like ITC, have introduced "personalized cards". By paying a stipulated amount of money, the card holder is entitled to free entry into key facilities, great discounts and special offers.

Another time-tested tool used by hotels for effective customer relationships is the "magazine" – ITC's 'Namaste', Oberoi's 'The Chronicle', Hyatt Regency's 'Events', Le Meridien's 'Bon Appetit' and 'The Park Magazine'. The pioneer as well as the leader is Namaste.

Namaste is a 20-year old quarterly with an objective of show casing India, the Indian culture. Each issue is theme based and specially designed for more than just flipping through.

If The Chronicle has the distinction of having the largest collection of lithographs and reflects the Group's concern for art and culture, Events boasts of "ethnic" touch with a contemporary look, pertinent pictures and earthy fonts; and, Bon Appetit depends on good reading material for their guests' reading pleasure.

The Pak Magazine is the latest entrant. Designed by a graphic designer from a leading advertising agency, it focuses on how hotels can be eco-friendly. An attempt is being made to pack quality information with inputs from other three centers in India.

It can be seen that hotels are taking care to ensure that their magazines reflect their brand positioning. Once merely a PR exercise, the hotel magazine has grown into a creative enterprise with big budgets – e.g., Rs. 3 lakh for 6,500 copies of Events – and striking looks for brand building and effective customer relationships.

HOSPITALITY: The Maurya Sheraton Way

ITC Maurya Sheraton at New Delhi can easily be distinguished for the worldclass quality of service. In the year 2000, it was patronized by the Presidents of the USA and Russia, Prime Minister of Japan, and the Captains of industry like Bill Gates and Michael Dell. Each one of these guests, especially the first three, was a challenge for Maurya to prove itself and a most coveted opportunity for everlasting goodwill. But, it was easier said than done.

If the Hotel had to largely focus on the Russian Presidents' liking for color "pink" and import flowers and Russian dolls for the lobby, for Bill Gates, the Hotel had to be more proactive.

Microsoft chief and the world's richest man, Bill Gates has a penchant for time management for he is a firm believer of the dictum "Time is Money". This is reflected even in his food and dining habits. He is known to stay away from alcohol because of his thrust on saving time and expects to be served food within four minutes of placing an order.

So, what does the Hotel do? Stock up his favourite drink, Cherry Coke, and retains the same kitchen staff team that served him during his earlier visit in 1997. The team would be able to serve him his favourite Indian dishes, like murg pasanda, jack fruit kebab, seekh kabab, jhinga kari, khatee aloo, vegetable biryani, jira pulao, kesari phirni, pudina rumali, and tandoori roti. Bill Gates had shown a tremendous liking for these dishes last time.

To pamper him, the Hotel not only stocked his favourite snacks, like potato chips, nuts, candies and muffins, in his room, but also kept chocolates by his bedside as he loves byting into them at night. And, when it comes to having a byte, according to his associates, the Microsoft boss enjoys "macro" bytes and "soft" breads, especially burgers.

However, easily, to date, the best example of "service plus" and "effective customer relationship management" is the flawless arrangements at the time of the US President, Bill Clinton's stay at the Hotel, which is also evident from Bill Clinton's two-line note in the Visitor's Book: " Thank You for the beautiful suite, fine food and marvelous hospitality. Bill Clinton, March 24, 2000." This is not just a noting, it is rather, a "certificate of appreciation" and an international benchmark for the Indian hospitality industry.

In fact, the President is reported to have personally met the staff in various departments, like house-keeping, room-service and the Bukhara restaurant, and appreciated their efforts. These departments have also been individually given appreciation notes by various members of the White House team. For the technical support provided by the Hotel, it received a certificate of appreciation from the White House Communication Agency.

According to the Hotel officials, the President was particularly impressed by the Hotel staff for converting one of the rooms in the Chandragupta Suite into a dressing room and providing a "Stepper" for exercising every morning. Even to handle the Presidents' clothes, special stands had to be made. After the departure of the President and his (White House) staff, the Hotel was flooded with requests from guests, visitors and public to have a glimpse of the suite.

Preparations for the Presidents' stay started months in advance. Details were obtained from the White House not only on the "likes" and "dislikes" of Mr Clinton, but even those of his personal staff. The Hotel had specially imported skimmed milk, juices, fruits, alcohol and flowers for the guests. A White House staff member was pleasantly surprised to see a copy of USA Today with a tag on his favourite sports pages in his room everyday. Two of the White House valets had their own special valets given to them by the Hotel to facilitate their requirements.

Special checklists were prepared for other important guests too, like Madeline Albright, Strobe Talbott and Sandy Berger. For example, Ms Albright is allergic to fish but enjoys a particular brand of wine, which was placed in her room. Similarly, Mr. Clinton's favourite brand of gin was kept in his suite. Even the ice had to be made from a special brand of mineral water.

ITC Maurya might have had and handled 100 per cent occupancy several times before, but the scene was very much different on this occasion for the schedule of, virtually, every occupant of the 500 rooms was linked to the President's movements. For instance, on the day when President was to go to Rajghat, the Room Service simultaneously received orders for 100 breakfasts and all of them had to be delivered in 10 minutes since the media wanted to reach the venue before the President.

With the entire White House practically operating from the Hotel, the housekeeping staff was kept on his toes,. As many as 40 rooms were converted into offices. The technical staff was instructed to have contingency plans ready for any eventuality. Even the elevators had to be synchronized since the Secret Service would inform the Hotel authorities at the last minute which elevator was required for the President on 16th floor.

And, perhaps, the most daunting task for the Hotel was to ensure smooth check-in and check-out for the White House staff and the media. More than 150 guests were checked-in in less than 20 minutes on their arrival at the Hotel.

The work was not really over once the President left the Hotel. One, it had to arrange for the "wheels-up party" for the White House staff and US Secret Service at the Ghungroo discotheque. As a tradition, the wheels-up party is celebrated once the US President completes his visit and takes off on Air Force One. Two, it had to get all the 40 rooms functioning as White House from the Hotel back in shape. It took one full day to remove just the high-tech gadgets installed at the President's Suite. One more day was spent on removing from all over the Hotel tonnes of equipment that had been specially flown in from Washington, D.C. Then, there were special dish antennas, modulators and receivers provided for uplinking live from the Hotel. Also, one of the rooms which was converted into a "gift room" to receive gifts for the President. All the gifts and bouquets were cleared by the security in this room before being forwarded. And, three, above all, having bid goodbye to the most valuable guest, the Hotel executives had to catch up on their sleep. For, over five days, they had not got more than three hours of sleep.

◻ CONCLUSION

In conclusion, it can be said that effective customer relationship is not just the function of infrastructure & facilities, technology & information, comfort & food, and people & warmth. It is a process; the process of planning, organizing, staffing, coordinating, controlling and budgeting. And, this process needs to be managed most efficiently for the best of results.

Section VI

CRM in Financial Services

Chapter 49

Relationship Marketing Strategies and Customer Perceived Service Quality
A Study of Indian Banks

■ **Koushiki Choudhury, Avinandan Mukherjee and Ashish Banerjee**

Abstract

Relationship marketing implies attracting, maintaining and enhancing customer relationships. It is beneficial because acquiring new customers is more costly than retaining existing ones, long-time customers tend to be less price sensitive and provide free word-of-mouth advertising. One of the determinants of the success of the relationship marketing strategies of a firm is how the customers perceive the resulting service quality. In India, with the onset of financial deregulation, banks are functioning increasingly under competitive pressures. In this era, in order to prosper, it will be imperative for banks to focus on developing long-term relationships with their customers. This paper explores as to what kind of relationship marketing strategies Indian banks are pursuing in today's highly competitive environment, and what is the effect of these strategies on service quality as perceived by the customer. The paper develops a conceptual model of the impact of relationship marketing on customer perceived service quality.

Key Words: *Relationship Marketing, Service Quality*

❏ INTRODUCTION

Relationship marketing implies attracting, maintaining and enhancing customer relationships. Servicing and selling to existing customers is viewed to be just as important to long-term marketing success as acquiring new customers (Berry, 1983). Some of the benefits of pursuing relationship marketing that accrue to the firm stem from the fact that acquiring new customers is more costly than retaining existing ones, that long-time customers tend to be less price sensitive, and that long-time satisfied customers usually provide free word-of-mouth advertising and referrals. One of the determinants of the success of the relationship marketing strategies of a firm is how the customers perceive the resulting service quality. This is because it is the perceived service quality that is the key driver of perceived value. It is this perceived value which determines the strength of the company-customer relationship (Berry, 1991).

The forces of deregulation, globalization and advancing technology have greatly increased the competitive pressures in the banking industry. The Indian banking industry too is going through turbulent times. Since the financial reforms started, banks have been given a great degree of freedom in determining their rate structure for deposits and advances, as well as their product range. The freedom of choice which bank customers did not have earlier because of standardised products and regimented interest rates has now been given to the customers. Banks are functioning increasingly under competitive pressures emanating from within the banking system, from non-banking institutions as well as from the domestic and international capital markets (Subramanian et al., 1997). Thus, in this era of increased competition, in order to prosper, it will be imperative for banks to focus on developing long-term relationships with their customers. The focus of banks should be to shift their orientation from transaction marketing to the cultivation of relationship marketing.

This paper explores the kind of relationship marketing strategies that Indian banks are pursuing in today's rapidly changing and highly competitive environment, and what is the effect of these strategies on service quality as perceived by the customer.

□ METHODOLOGY

For studying the relationship marketing strategies being followed by the banks, individual in-depth interviews were conducted with the managers of two public and two private sector banks. The open structure of the questions ensured that unexpected facts or attitudes as well as underlying motivations could be pursued. The key facets of relationship marketing that were explored were the management of demand and supply, customer complaint management, monitoring of customer retention, products and services, relationship pricing, and customizing of the relationship. The customers (224 in total) of two public and two private sector banks were questioned on the service quality of their bank using a 7-point, 15 item service quality scale, adapted from the SERVQUAL scale (Zeithaml et al., 1990). A description of the 15 service quality items are presented in Table 1.

Table 1 *Items of Service Quality Scale. V Stands For Variable*

Variable description

V1. YOUR Bank's physical facilities are visually appealing
V2. Materials associated with the service (such as pamphlets and statements) are informative at YOUR BANK.
V3. YOUR BANK has guidance signs indicating as to which counters are offering which services.
V4. When YOUR BANK promises to do something by a certain time, it does so.
V5. When you have a problem, YOUR BANK shows a sincere interest in solving it.

(Contd.)

Table 1 (*Contd.*)

V6. YOUR BANK performs the service right the first time.

V7. YOUR BANK insists on error-free records

V8. Employees of YOUR BANK tell you exactly when services will be performed.

V9. Employees of YOUR BANK give you prompt service.

V10. You feel safe in your transactions with YOUR BANK.

V11. Employees of YOUR BANK are consistently courteous with you

V12. Employees of YOUR BANK have the knowledge to answer your questions.

V13. YOUR BANK has operating hours convenient to all its customers

V14. YOUR BANK has employees who give you personal attention.

V15. Employees of YOUR BANK understand your specific needs.

Factor analysis of the items was conducted, and was followed by a varimax rotation to examine the dimensionality of the items. A subsequent analysis of the relationship marketing strategies of these banks and their customer perceived service quality levels was carried out.

❑ RESULTS

The relationship marketing strategies being pursued by the four banks are given below in the form of caselets.

❑ THE NATIONAL BANK

The National Bank is one of the largest banks in India in terms of profits, assets, deposits, branches and employees.

Management of Demand and Supply

The National Bank does not have specific policies to smoothen the random fluctuations in demand so as to shift demand from peak periods and increase demand in slack periods. The bank leaves it to its customers to learn when the facilities are crowded and when they are not. Since demand cannot be perfectly controlled, it is necessary that National Bank considers the efficient management of its resources by altering capacity by increasing it to meet high demand and contracting it in slack periods. Branch manager, sometimes, requests employees with comparatively lesser work on a particular day to help any overburdened employee dealing directly with the customer. However this is difficult, since there is usually one set of ledgers having all the entries or a single PC.

Managing Customer Complaints

In National bank, complaints are usually not solicited by any means. Customers, when they have a problem, usually complain to the branch manager and the branch manager is supposed to resolve the problem then and there. In case the problem is taking some time in getting resolved, the branch manager is supposed to let the customer know the status of the complaint. However there is no monitoring of whether the branch manager actually does so.

Customer Retention

According to the bank management, "the employees have no time to ask customers as to why they are closing their accounts", in case of account closures.

Products and Services

The National bank does not have any segmentation strategy. Only recently has it started opening personal banking branches to cater to the needs of high profile retail customers. Targeted mainly at high net-worth individuals, these one-stop shops are aimed at offering a wide range of consumer finance schemes.

Relationship Pricing

The National Bank has no relationship pricing strategies.

Customizing the Relationship

The bank does not have any database on customers where the lifestyle information and specific preferences and characteristics about individual customers are kept so that services can be personalized.

□ THE PRUDENTIAL BANK

The Prudential Company was one of the first in India to receive an 'in principle' approval from the Reserve Bank of India (RBI) to set up a bank in the private sector.

Management of Demand and Supply

The Prudential bank provides certain services, which can help to shift customers away from the branch so as to avoid crowding. The ATMs of the bank are networked all across the country and give customers the power to access their accounts 24 hours a day from anywhere in India. The bank also has phonebanking and Internet banking services wherein a customer can carry out various financial transactions. Prudential bank verbally encourages its customers to avail of these facilities to the extent of even giving certain financial inducements in order to avoid a rush in the bank's branch. Prudential Bank also contracts direct sales agents who can come over to the customer's house to open an account.

Management of Customer Complaints

When a customer complains and if the complaint cannot be resolved quickly, feedback is given to the customer regarding the status of his complaint. In fact, if a customer complains, the bank has to reply within 24 hours to the customer's complaint, informing the customer about the status of his complaint. This activity of the bank is audited twice a year. Gold customers are sometimes called to find out if they are content with the way their problems have been solved. Certain branches of the bank insist that when a problem is solved, the customer has to send a letter indicating that the problem has been solved to his satisfaction. There is also a branch meeting held every week where employees discuss the problems they have faced as well as problems that customers are facing. Again, every quarter when senior officials visit the branches, there are meetings when each branch gives presentations on their business operations and relate the various expectations and problems that customers have with the bank's services. The regional managers and the managing directors of the bank make surprise visits to the branches from time to time and interacts with the customers and employees so as to unearth customer's problems if any or to find out about the trend in customer needs.

Customer Retention

Everyday the bank keeps track of how many accounts are closing and in which accounts heavy withdrawals are taking place. In case of heavy withdrawals the employees are supposed to ask the customers so as to learn the reasons for the withdrawal and also to try to retrieve the situation. In fact, his superiors question the branch manager in case he fails to stop the heavy withdrawals on accounts and in case of customers not renewing their fixed deposits.

Products and Services

The Prudential Bank has segmented its product-market into two broad divisions: Prudential Regular and Prudential Gold. The Gold scheme is for customers over 21 years old and whose accumulated balance across all accounts in his name exceeds Rs. 5 lakhs. The Gold customer is given certain privileges such as personalised services, fee waivers, free demat accounts, enhanced ATM withdrawal limit, priority locker allotment, subsidised interest rates, free debit cards, waiver of charges on standing instructions within a certain limit and cheques payable at par. The Gold customers are assigned to Relationship Managers who provide a one-stop solution for the clients.

Relationship Pricing

Relationship pricing strategies encourage customers to have multiple accounts and services with the bank. The bank has several relationship pricing programs, such as Prudential Gold, access to a no minimum balance savings account if one has a fixed deposit account of a minimum of Rs.25000, to name a few.

Customizing the Relationship

In the case of Gold customers, the bank is trying to get information such as the dates of the customers' anniversary and their children's birthdays. In fact, the bank does send out greeting cards to its Gold customers on such occasions. The bank also tries to glean additional information from these Gold customers such as their education level, their investment preferences, whether they possess vehicles and credit cards, so as to come up with new products.

□ THE CENTURY BANK

The Century Bank, a public sector bank, was set up in the year 1865 by a group of Europeans in Kanpur, with a subscribed capital of Rs. 3 lakhs.

Managing Demand and Supply

The Century Bank does not have specific policies to smooth the random fluctuations in demand so as to shift demand from peak periods and increase demand in slack periods. It has not forayed as yet into the world of home banking, internet banking or phone banking and has only recently started putting up its ATM network. Branch managers, sometimes, on their own initiative, requests people with comparatively lesser work on a particular day to help overworked people dealing directly with the customers. However, this is difficult, since there is usually one set of ledgers having all the entries or a single PC.

Managing Customer Complaints

In the case of complaints filed by the customers with the branch manager, the branches file the customer complaints in registers and there are instructions to the branch managers to let the customers know about the status of their complaint, if the problem is taking some time to get solved. However, there is no monitoring of whether the customer is being kept informed as to the status of his complaint. The bank however nowadays insists that the customers tell in writing that the complaint has been solved. Carrying out customer satisfaction surveys on their own initiative is not a usual feature of this bank. However, in view of the increasingly competitive market, the bank has now decided to do quarterly customer satisfaction surveys.

Customer Retention

In Century Bank, the frequency of use of an account is tracked, but only for operational reasons and not in order to find out as to why customers are defecting. However, the bank has in the last few months started a bi-monthly newsletter for its employees and the importance of customer satisfaction and retention is being discussed in this newsletter.

Products and Services

The segmentation strategy of this bank is ad-hoc and it has not segmented its customers according to their demographics, behavioural characteristics or other features.

Relationship Pricing

The bank is pursuing relationship pricing. For account holders, the bank's credit card comes with a waiver of the Rs.100 admission fee and a lower annual fee for the first two years.

Customizing the Relationship

Century Bank does not have any database on customers where the lifestyle information and specific preferences about individual customers are kept so that services can be personalized. However, the bank is trying to provide somewhat differentiated services for certain groups of customers. The bank has identified savings bank accounts with more that Rs 25000 deposit and is providing a special counter and faster and better services in certain branches for such accounts.

□ THE MILLENNIUM BANK

The Millennium Bank is a private bank set up by the Millennium Group.

Managing Demand and Supply

The Millennium Bank provides efficient services, which can help to shift customers away from the branch so as to avoid crowding. The Millennium bank provides free ATM services to its customers. The ATMs of the bank are networked across the country and gives customers the power to access their accounts 24 hours a day from anywhere in India. The bank also has phonebanking services 24 hours a day as well as Internet banking services. It has agents for opening accounts at the customers' premises. The retail branches of the Millennium Bank do provide for diversions to the customers by way of reading materials like newspapers and magazines. This serves to reduce the perception of waiting time.

Managing Customer Complaints

Usually customers go to the branch manager to complain and there is a suggestion box in the branch manager's room. If a customer complains and the complaint cannot be resolved quickly, the status of the complaint is made known to the customer. When the problem is solved, in the case of serious problems, the regional officer sends an apology to the customer and asks him if the problem has been solved to his satisfaction. There is also a monthly branch meeting which all employees attend and where the latest guidelines, circulars, changes in procedures, as well as the problems that customers are facing are discussed. Sometimes, when the regional managers comes to the branches for inspection, he talks to the frontliners about customer needs and problems. On every branch anniversary, customers are invited to the branch and their suggestions are solicited. On this occasion, the regional managers of the bank visit their branches and interact with the customers and employees and in these sessions, customer service issues are discussed.

Customer Retention

The bank keeps track of all account closures and withdrawals in the Fixed Deposit accounts on a continuous basis. In case of closures and/or heavy withdrawals the customers are questioned, so as to learn the reasons for their withdrawal and so as to try to retrieve the situation.

Products and Services

The bank has segmented its customers into two broad segments- regular and HNW (high net worth). HNW customers are required to maintain at least Rs.1 lakh in their savings account. They are assigned to relationship managers and the latter are supposed to attend to all his needs. The HNW customers are also given other free financial services. In the case of credit cards too, the Millennium Bank has segmented its customers on a price-quality platform.

Relationship Pricing

The bank has several relationship pricing programs. For instance, for its high net worth customers, do not have to processing fees for car loans and housing loans. Again, for both the HNW and Powerpay customers, demand drafts, fund transfers and pay orders are all free.

Customizing the Relationship

The bank has come up with a scheme where it is asking customers to give certain information during the opening of their accounts so as to glean the customers' lifestyle information. The bank plans to use the database to send personalised messages, for instance, say birthday cards as well as to design financial products and cross-sell other financial products. In the case of its HNW customers, the bank does send out greeting cards on certain occasions.

☐ THE PERFORMANCE OF THE BANKS WITH REGARD TO SERVICE QUALITY

With the factor analysis, the 15 service quality items could be reconfigured into four dimensions, namely-"customer-orientedness", "competence", "tangibles" and "convenience". The factor "customer-orientedness" comprised variables like extent of prompt service, consistent courtesy, and knowledge to answer customer's questions, convenient operating hours, personal attention and understanding of specific customer needs. Variables like extent of interest in problem solving, right service, error-free records, service-time guarantee and safety of transactions combined to define "competence". The "tangibles" factor consisted of variables like extent of visual appeal of physical facilities and information conveyed by published materials. Variables like guidance signs and timeliness combined to define "convenience". The factors and their variables are presented in Table 2.

Table 2 *Results of the factor analysis*

	Rotated Component Matrix[a]			
	Component			
	1	*2*	*3*	*4*
V1	.228	.281	.822	.120
V10	4.896.E-02	.661	.187	-4.22E-02
V11	614	.391	.250	8.357E-02
V12	.514	.421	.174	.332
V13	.809	-5.82E-02	.211	6.121E-02
V14	.836	.246	.1977	.707E-02
V15	.763	.295	.148	.222
V2	.306	.209	.790	.194
V3	.125	.108	.183	.917
V4	.465	.464	.145	.495
V5	.535	.593	.116	301
V6	.473	.654	.140	.109
V7	8.78 2E-02	.757	.193	.201
V8	.447	.635	.136	.255
V9	.523	.483	.298	.294

Extraction Method: Principal Component Analysis. Rotation Method: Varimax with Kaiser Normalization.
a.Rotation converged in 7 iterations.

For each bank, factor scores for the 4 different factors were averaged. The ranks obtained by the banks on each factor are shown in Table 3:

Table 3 *Rankings the Four Banks on the Four Factors*

Factors→ Banks↓	Customer oriented	Competence	Tangibles	Convenience
Prudential	1	2	2	1
Millennium	2	1	1	4
Century	3	3	4	2
National	4	4	3	3

Rank 1 = best; Rank 4 = worst

☐ THE EFFECT OF RELATIONSHIP MARKETING ON CUSTOMER-PERCEIVED SERVICE QUALITY

Service Quality Factor-competence

In the case of the service quality factor competence, it can be seen from Table 1 that Prudential Bank and Millennium Bank have done well compared to the Century and the National banks. As has been evinced in the cases of the relationship marketing strategies of the banks, both the Prudential and the Millennium bank take care to ensure a certain degree of service efficiency. Both these banks are more responsive to complaint management than are the public sector banks National and Century. In both these banks when a customer complaints and if the complaint cannot be resolved quickly, feedback is given to the customer regarding the status of his complain. In fact, in the case of the Prudential Bank, certain branches of the bank insist that when a problem is solved, the customer has to send a letter indicating that the problem has been solved to his satisfaction. The regional managers and the managing directors of the Prudential Bank make surprise visits to the branches from time to time and interact with the customers and employees so as to unearth customer's problems if any. In the case of the Millennium Bank, on every branch anniversary, customers are invited to the branch and their suggestions are solicited.

The reasons as to why the public sector banks especially the National Bank fared poorly when it came to "competence" are manifold. In the case of both these banks, if the problem is taking some time in getting resolved, the branch manager is supposed to let the customer know the status of the compliant. However there is no monitoring of whether the branch manager actually does so. Neither do the senior managers of the bank interact with the customers to see whether customer needs are being satisfied. The Century bank however nowadays tries to ensure that customers give in writing that they are satisfied with the problem resolution, so as to keep a check on errant branch managers.

Service Quality Factor-tangibles

In case of the service quality factor "tangibles", it can be seen from Table-3 that Prudential Bank and Millennium Bank have done well compared to Century and National banks.

Both Prudential and Millennium banks maintain neat and aesthetically decorated branches. In case of Millennium bank, the branches are also quite spacious with ample seating arrangements and reading materials for the customers. The Prudential and Millennium banks provide certain services, which can help to shift customers away from the branch so as to avoid branch crowding. These services are:

- The banks provide free ATM services to its customers. The ATMs of the bank are networked all across the country and gives customers the power to access their accounts 24 hours a day from anywhere in India.
- The banks have phonebanking and Internet banking services, wherein the customer can carry out a host of financial transactions.
- The branches of both the banks send books of cheque deposit slips to customers and also have cheque deposit boxes where the customers can drop the cheques that need to be deposited, thus obviating the need for customers to spend a longer time than is necessary in the branch premises, thus reducing branch traffic.
- The bank also contracts sales agents who come over to the customer's house and helps him in completing all the formalities of opening an account.

Prudential bank verbally encourages its customers to avail of these facilities to the extent of even giving certain financial inducements in order to avoid a rush in the bank's branch. The retail branches of the Millennium Bank also provide for diversions to the customers by way of reading materials like newspapers and magazines.

The Century and National Bank on the other hand do not have specific policies to smoothen the random fluctuations in demand so as to shift demand from peak periods and increase demand in slack periods. To a large extent, these banks leave it to its customers to learn when the facilities are crowded and when they are not. National Bank and Century Bank, however, have just forayed into the world of ATMs and till now do not provide alternative services to the customers so as to reduce branch crowding. Neither do the National Bank and the Century Bank so as to conduct certain transactions outside the branch premises and prevent branch crowding contract any flexible workforce. The retail branches of these banks also do not provide for any diversions to the customers by way of reading materials and the like.

Service Quality Factor-customer-orientedness

In case of the service quality factor customer orientedness, from Table 1 it can be seen that Prudential Bank and Millennium Bank have done well compared to the Century and the National banks. Both these banks practice several relationship marketing strategies which serve to enhance the service quality of the banks. The banks have taken steps to monitor the satisfaction of their customers, segment their customers and come up with customized services. The Prudential bank tries to ensure that its high networth (HNW) clients do not have to stand in queue. For instance, if the relationship manager is dealing with one HNW client and if another HNW client comes along, even the branch manager comes forward to takeover. As far as customer retention is concerned, in case of heavy withdrawals the employees are supposed to ask the customers so as to learn the reasons for the withdrawal and also to try to retrieve the situation. Again, the Prudential and the Millennium Bank have segmented their customers into two broad divisions: regular and high net-worth. The latter is given certain financial privileges and personalised services. Relationship pricing strategies encourage customers to have multiple accounts and services with the bank. Both the Prudential and the Millennium banks have several relationship pricing programs. For instance, the Prudential bank has several relationship pricing programs, including Prudential Gold, in the sense of a comprehensive package of priority banking and investment services which are available to privileged customers completely free. In case of the Millennium Bank, for instance, its high net worth customers, do not have to processing fees for car loans and housing loans. The capability to organize, analyze and segment is essential to make relationship marketing work. An excellent database containing not only customer's purchase histories but also other relevant information like lifestyle information is needed, so that banks can anticipate a customer's present and future needs and come up with customized products. In the case of Gold customers, the Prudential bank is trying to get information such as the dates of the customers' anniversary and their children's birthdays. The bank also tries to glean additional information from these Gold customers such as their education level, their investment preferences, whether they possess vehicles and credit cards. The Millennium bank has come up with a scheme where it is asking customers to give certain information during the opening of their accounts so as to glean the customers' lifestyle information. The bank plans to use the database to personalize its services and to design financial products.

The Century Bank and the National Bank on the other hand have hardly taken steps to monitor the satisfaction of their customers, segment their customers or come up with personalised services. The National Bank for instance hardly does any customer satisfaction surveys on its own initiative unless directed by the RBI or the IBA. As far as monitoring their customer retention rate, the bank management say that, "the employees have no time to ask customers as to why they are closing their accounts", in case of account closures. The Century bank is somewhat ahead of the National Bank in this regard. In view of the increasingly competitive market, the bank has now decided to do quarterly customer satisfaction surveys and in the last few months started a newsletter for its employees where the importance of customer satisfaction and retention is being discussed. The Century bank unlike National bank is also pursuing relationship pricing, in the case of its credit cards. The Century bank however like the National bank does not have any provision for personalising its service for some or all of its customers. It is trying to provide somewhat differentiated services though for customers who have deposit of more that Rs. 25,000.

Service Quality Factor-convenience

The most important item in this factor is the presence of guidance signs in the bank. On "convenience", Prudential bank has done well, together with the Century bank, whereas the National bank and the Millennium bank have fared poorly. The Prudential bank has very detailed guidance signs within its branches depicting as to which counters are offering which services and what are the transactions that can be carried out at any specific counter. The Century and the National banks have few guidance signs, without any details. For instance, these banks have guidance signs at counters depicting the types of accounts and the account numbers that those counters handle. Millennium bank on the other hand has no guidance signs at all.

REFERENCES

Berry Leonard L., Parasuraman A., (1991), *Marketing Services: Competing through Quality*, New York:The Free press, A Division of Macmillan, Inc.

Berry L.L., (1983), 'Relationship marketing', in Berry L.L., Shostack G.L. and Upah G.D. (Eds), *Emerging Perspectives on Services Marketing*, American Marketing Association, Chicago, pp. 25-28.

Subramanian K, Velayudham TK (1997), *'Banking reforms in India: Managing change'*, New Delhi:Tata McGraw Hill Publishing Co.Ltd.

Zeithaml Valerie A., Parasuraman A., Berry Leonard L., (1990), *'Delivering Quality Service'*, New York: The Free press, a division of Macmillan, Inc.

Chapter 50

Building Customer Relationships Through Call Centers in Banking and Financial Services

■ **Vinod Dumblekar**

Abstract

CRM is a philosophy that directs the organisation to build its processes around its customers' needs. The Call Center (CC) is a CRM-embedded automation that builds long term, strategic relationships with its customers. It assures high volume performance for organisations, and fast, consistent services for their customers. Banks and other financial services providers can benefit more than other industries because they deal in information and funds that are electronically transacted. The CC is a technology-cum-attitude driven alternative to existing channels of the providers. American providers have put up a sterling performance in CC for their Indian counterparts. Indian organisations have just made an entry, but awareness and interest in the gains in its business application are steadily increasing. The CC is a strategic investment, and therefore must be driven by top management. However, process changes, technology integration and absorption, and regular cultural training are vital for success of the investment.

Key Words: *Customer Service Representative, IVR, CTI, ACD, Screen Pop-ups.*

❑ INTRODUCTION

In an economy of converging technologies, morphing markets and web-paced communications, customers get ready access to an unprecedented amount of information from anywhere in the globe and at any time of day or night. In response, a host of new financial products and services emerges to serve these customers. In a competitive environment, the one idea that is likely to succeed will be the customer centric model, where the organisation builds long term strategic relationships with its customers.

It is Customer Relationship Management (CRM) that encapsulates this view better than other concepts and technologies like BPR, TQM, SCM and ERP. The customer is king, and his loyalty is fickle. Organisations must therefore equip themselves, technologically and culturally, to meet the challenges of customer search, retention and satisfaction. CRM is a business approach and a strategy that establishes a single link between back office and front office, uniting them into a single entity for benefit of the customer. Different functions share a common database. Disparate and unrelated functions like sales force automation, inventory, customer services, sales and after-sales support come together for a common cause: the customer. The CRM gains are staggering: Kumar (2000) quotes an Andersen Consulting study in the US which concluded that the typical US$ 1 billion high-tech company could gain as much as US$ 130 million in profits by merely improving their customer relationships.

CRM is the philosophy that has been driving fundamental change in leading progressive organisations. CRM first seeks to understand the needs and values of their prospects and customers, by profiling their demographics and interactions with the organisation. Next, it helps to align the organisation's capabilities and resources in order to deliver better value to its prospects and customers. The organisation benefits in many ways: increased customer retention, more loyalty, expanded referrals, more revenue and therefore, higher profits per sale. Direct costs are lower because distribution channels are optimised, and marketing costs are lower because of improved targeting of the customer (Dumblekar, 2000).

□ DEFINING THE CALL CENTER

CRM is embedded into every Call Center (CC). A CC is an arrangement where the division of an organisation or its intermediary acts as a link with their customers. The typical CC is an area where several specially trained employees (called Customer Services Representatives or CSR) man a bank of telephones to handle queries on products and services. Traditionally, the CC is a single-function unit limited to customer support and sometimes, sales.

The Contact Center is an upgraded form of the CC. Harris (2000) says that a Contact Center is a CC unit that is integrated from two perspectives, media (email, Internet, fax and data) and functional (linkage to a central database, and working in concert with other sales and service channels, such as direct sales). The CC has great potential for improving expense ratios, standardising services and improving service quality to customers. The integrated CC can be approached through various 'touchpoints' such as phone, email, touchscreen kiosk, fax and Internet chat.

The CSR of the Contact Center is an active salesman, not a passive middleman routing queries. He uses a bank of telephones that is supplemented by computer terminals and high-end CRM software. The most basic customer interactions like enquiries are automated, and the CSR gets more time for sales or customer services with personalised care.

Typical CC software would link telecom hardware to IT databases at the back end, and communicate automated information to the callers in the form of interactive voice response (IVR), and screen pop-ups layers through the CSR. New CC systems incorporate internet technologies and be web-enabled, allowing more interactivity for their callers, while keeping the basic model for customer interaction unchanged (Haines, 2000).

Customer service applications at the CC include help desks, technical support, product information, service calls, scheduling, catalogue services, reservations, and other one-time needs (ITSpace, 2000). CC telemarketing has been mostly used for sales prospecting, solicitations for donations, surveys, and opinion polls. Most Indian applications are in the nature of reminders for credit card and loan outstandings, credit card telemarketing and telesurveys.

According to Shapiro (2000), an organisation has three major channels of interaction with the customer: the phone, the web and face-to-face contact. These mean different forms of complexity for the CC. The resultant technology ranges from and covers sophisticated Automated Call Distributor (ACD) and telephony equipment, routing schemes, databases and pop-ups, predictive dialing apparatus and access to a huge database at the back end. The ACD is a computerized phone system that responds to the caller with a voice menu and connects the call to next available CSR. The e-CRM CC incorporates email, chat, Computer Telephone Integration (CTI) to cover customers over a larger territory, and laptops and palmtops (for virtual and offsite CC).

Components of the Call Center

The CC system has three entities: the caller, the CC and the Bank or financial services provider. Figure 1 is a brief depiction of the key activities of a CC serving a Bank. The Caller communicates with the PBX linked to the IVR, where he selects an option that relates to his need. The trigger in the CTI for the screen pop-up could be either the caller's telephone number or his account number, although this may be supported by a unique Customer Identification Number. The Caller may either seek a demand draft or his account statement, or if in doubt, seek the CSR's intervention. This model can be extended to other financial products and services, too, and show different forms of telecommunication links, call centre infrastructure and the requisite CRM software.

The typical CC organisation is built around its Chief Customer Officer, to whom report Supervisors in charge of 10-12 CSR, each. The Supervisors manage self-directed teams, where intervention is limited to abnormally long calls received by the CSR. The central idea is to maximise the number of callers attended, with the correct information.

The focus of the CC should be threefold: get new customers, keep existing customers and grow profitable customers (Anton, 2000). This is possible when its effectiveness and efficiency is measured and monitored, regularly. The first critical measure of effectiveness of the CC is caller satisfaction (and complaints, if any), which may be determined through customer interviews). A second is the proportion of calls handled without further transfers or clarifications through a second call, which may be measured through electronic tracking

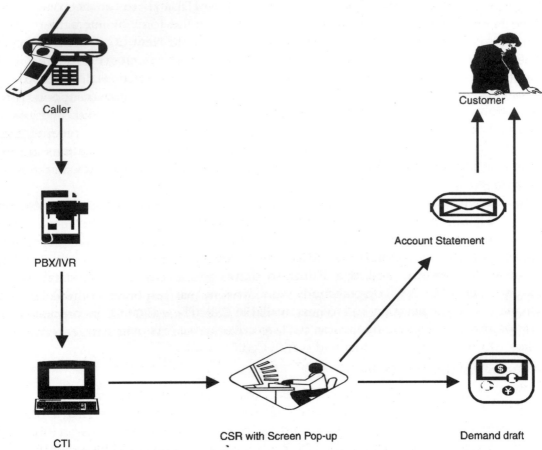

Caller

PBX/IVR

CTI

CSR with Screen Pop-up

Demand draft

Account Statement

Customer

Fig. 1 *Flowchart of Activities in the Call Center Serving a Bank*

within the CC. The efficiency of the CC may be measured in terms of cost per call, calls per shift, the average time taken to handle and complete a call, and calls abandoned and converted, and revenues per seat or call.

□ CALL CENTERS FOR BANKS AND FINANCIAL SERVICES-OVERSEAS

In the US, deregulation and competition has prompted Banks to rely on CC for their marketing programmes (Callcentermagazine, 1998). Customers seek more financial products to buy at their convenience. Consequently, the CC is used to maintain accounts and customers, to cross-sell and up-sell products and services such as insurance, generate and qualify leads, process accounts, and provide retail support and collections. Call blending technologies are used to collect data from advertisement responses for sales promotions. Telebanking facilitates customers in larger cities, because fewer people have the time to visit their banks, increasing the need for more CC.

The gains and experiences of overseas banks and financial services firms abroad in their CC have been widely reported, mostly on the Web, and are enlightening. Fleet Bank, Boston, MA handles over 100,000 inbound calls per month and makes 150,000 outbound calls per month at its CC (Callcentermagazine, 1998). Over a hundred CSR engaged in cross-selling and up-selling financial products such as loans, insurance and investments. Dime Savings Bank, NY receives over 6,000,000 calls per year, while its 200-seat CSR attended to over 50,000 hours of outbound calls, using software that consolidated customer and product information from all databases and provide the CSR a comprehensive portfolio of each customer. Household Credit Services, Salinas, CA, one of the country's top three credit card issuers with 15 million cardholders and 200 credit card products has three CC that logs 2.7 million calls per month. Bank of America, San Francisco has 3,200 CSR at its two CC, both supported by video conferencing, and linked them with a third, all offering home equity credit, car and other loans by phone.

Callcentermagazine (1997) reports of Hibernia National Bank that was ranked as one of the top five banks by US Banker. The Bank used 30 CSR and 78 phone lines to make 18,000 calls a week to market services such as loans, CDs and checking accounts to retail and business organisations. Their software enabled them to manage both inbound and outbound calls, capture and process customer data, and focus their operations. In their first year of operations, they spoke to 316,593 people and sold 35,000 bank products and services.

Hollman (2000) reports of Merrill Lynch, Manhattan, NY, who received 50 million calls per year in 1998 at its 3 CC for its banking, money lending, securities and brokerage products. Their speech recognition and IVR software handled over 80% of the inbound calls. They regularly monitored the performance of their CSR, through third party vendors, mail surveys to customers and random calls, wherein the CSR report card was based on technical competency, service skills, communication ability, demeanor and call control. Prudential, Newark, NJ established a network of 20 CC with more than 4,000 CSR to handle more than 20 million calls in 1999. More than 80% of their investment calls and 60% of their securities calls were implemented through their IVR system. PNC Bank's CC at the National Financial Service Center at Pittsburgh, PA handles 130,000 calls per day from its customers and from other banks and organisations. The CSR are grouped into teams that handle inbound sales, outbound telemarketing campaigns and inbound services. PNC Bank's subsidiary, PFPC at Wilmington, DE is a mutual funds services firm that handles 12,000 calls per day at its 250-CSR CC. For telemarketing campaigns, they use a predictive dialer, covering 20,000 calls per day. The CC of Central Carolina Bank and Trust Company, Durham, NC uses 64 CSR to handle 25,000 calls per day, 90% of which were handled by the IVR system, alone. Constant performance reviews supported by incentives and career advancements have helped reduced CSR turnover.

☐ CALL CENTERS FOR BANKS AND FINANCIAL SERVICES - INDIA

The Indian Banking sector claimed a total deposits of Rs 972,947 crore and total credit of Rs 466,826 crore across a network of 65,521 branches (18,501 or over 28% in urban and metro areas) in 297 commercial banks (RBI). On 31 March 2000, the 100 top city centers (a fifth of the total network) contributed 59%, and used 74.7% of those funds as credit, presenting much potential for the focussed promotion and delivery of services. Accounting reforms coupled with sharper disclosure standards, competition, rising operational costs and narrower spreads have adversely affected industry profits (Rangarajan, 1996). The industry is also under pressure from the ongoing liberalisation and privatisation measures. In the other financial products and services sectors such as mutual funds, insurance, equity and debt investments, and credit cards, the markets are similarly turbulent. These challenging times call for innovative alternatives, but despite the vast opportunities, the CC industry for these sectors is yet to take off.

For all sectors, the fledgling Indian CC industry claimed about 60 CC, and estimated revenues of Rs 1,500 crore and a total of 80,000 CSR by March 2001 (Duttagupta, 2000). Her report finds three models of CC in India. One could be the MNC who shifts its overseas CC operations to take advantage of our low-cost labour English speaking population. Singh (2000) reported that entry level salary for CSR in Britain was GBP 15,000 per annum (about Rs 100,000 per month) but the Indian rate was barely Rs 7,000 per month). Another could be the Indian entrepreneur who sets up the CC to address overseas markets. The third is the Indian CC that serves only its Indian customers. For the bank and financial services sector, actual performance has been limited, so far.

The **first** model is seen in media reports (Mehta, 2000) of **GE Capital International Services (GECIS)**. It is the largest in the field, and manages a 2,000-seat CC at Gurgaon and Hyderabad offering many other IT-enabled services, too, reported revenues of Rs 2,650 million in 1998-99.

The **second** model in practice is the Joint Venture (JV) between **HDFC** and **Tata Consultancy Services** (TCS) to set up CC at Navi Mumbai, Chennai, Bangalore and Pune with a total of 1,700 seats and 6,000 employees within 2-3 years (Mehta, 2000). The JV would engage in insurance claims processing, revenue accounting and medical transcription services from leading banks, insurance and financial services firms in USA and UK, with whom the two promoters have strong strategic relationships.

The **third** application of the model is **HDFC Bank**'s 19-seat CC at Mumbai, which incorporates both CTI and IVR, with technology from Servion[t] and iFlex (Source: Servion[t]). The system was integrated with their host computer and software (Finware and Microware) and their EPABX, and provides seamless information on a round-the-clock basis to callers. This CC provides a range of telebanking facilities for their customers such as:

Account balance enquiry, and Statements of specific account transactions between specified dates, by fax

Cheque stop payment instruction, and issue of additional Cheque book

Demand draft purchase facility

Authorise money transfer between accounts, including payment of utility bills (courier, power and telephone) against account balance

Information on Interest rates for different types of accounts, and exchange rates for different foreign currencies against the Rupee

Credit card payment information, and activation and de-activation facility

Their 12-seat unit at Gurgaon is younger and is about 2 years old, and offers identical services. It handles about 4,500 calls a day in a 8.30 am – 8.30 pm operation, throughout the year. 80% of the calls are handled by the IVR-CTI automation, with the rest being attended by the CSR. Neither unit is web-enabled, offer toll free facilities, operate a common countrywide database, or are in telecommunication link with one another. They run two partially overlapping shifts, cater only to their local customers, and are limited in their scope.

□ COST/BENEFIT ANALYSIS

The fixed costs of a new CC are typically dictated by the choice of site, technology and infrastructure used. The choice of location has been guided by real estate costs and the availability of English speaking people. Indian CC have been established in metro 'suburbs' like Navi Mumbai and Gurgaon. Technological options depend upon the level of adoption of existing infrastructure, such as the Internet, by the Bank. There may be other requirements in the form of PC monitors and LAN system, EPABX, Internet connectivity, telecom infrastructure, data warehousing and mining software, and ACD, IVR and CTI complements.

According to Nasscom, a CC facility with seating capacity of 100 persons could cost between Rs.4 to 4.5 crore including premises, leased circuits, hardware and software. According to Hollman (2000), the typical startup costs for Bank CC was estimated at US$ 2 million for a 12-seater by a US-based IT research and advisory firm. Hollman reports of Datamonitor who assesses that labour costs comprise 64% of all operations, whereas the remaining 36% cover overheads and replacement of equipment. Such examples may vary on account of size and country of operations, and technology levels of CC. Attrition rates may exceed 25% (Braunthal and Amuso, 2000), and this adds to the cost of training and retraining the CSR. In countries experiencing high growth rates of the CC phenomenon, such as USA (Mehta, 2000), UK (Singh, 2000) and India (Duttagupta, 2000), the shortage of qualified labour will be a major problem. Labour costs may also rise, correspondingly. However, recent developments in IT and related technologies such as telecommunications have been rapid, and investment costs have been constantly dropping for some time.

With such a wide of critical inputs available, a quick analysis is not easy. Any fresh investment must be justified in terms of incremental and expected growth in business and revenues that can be accurately linked to operations in that CC. This must be a top management driven initiative and be accompanied by strategic changes such as BPR and cultural training within the banks. Those banks who already have a strong IT systems, customer databases, and e-Commerce systems in place would win the race (Web Scribes, 2000). The Bank or financial services provider must begin with a strategic perspective with CRM as a core philosophy. A customer centered culture and responsive attitudes, a tradition of adopting and adapting IT automation swiftly and painlessly, competent product development personnel, strong growth plans in its business segments, and commitment to constant training and development of its people are some of the key requirements of this philosophy.

◻ DISCUSSIONS

Due to the economic liberalisation in India, banks and financial services like insurance, derivatives, mutual funds and other securities have already been exposed to difficult conditions. There is heightened competition, and new players have entered with new technology, new products and services. Regulations have been tightened. NPA (non-performing assets) in the banking sector has grown. Profitability has been affected. On the other hand, customers have come to demand more, with quicker deliveries. They have failed to stay with one provider for long. Financial sectors also await growth opportunities in their respective markets. Clearly, CRM automation is the need of the hour.

The US market in outsourced CC services in 1998 was worth US$ 17 billion (Mehta, 2000). With 100,000 CC in 2000, it had a growth rate of 20% annually, whereas the UK with barely 5,000 CC was slated to grow faster at over 40% (Singh, 2000). Consistent innovation, commitment to the cause of the customer and supportive technology ensured a high level of customer satisfaction. The history and success of CC in US and UK are encouraging for the financial sector in India, and must be emulated.

CC delivers gains for any industry that needs a customer interface and where the success of transactions is based entirely on information availability. CC can drive focussed direct marketing campaigns using captive data supported by technology such as predictive dialers. CC cuts effort, time and costs for their customers, for more value to them. Quick and consistent services delivered whenever desired by the customers can help to retain existing customers. Promotion campaigns stand a better chance of success. CC can increase customer satisfaction, and allow financial products and services providers to operate on a 24x7x365 global scale. CC builds relationships with prospective and current customers by managing information, and delivers products and services at speeds that facilitate customer retention and creation.

REFERENCES

(1997), How Banks rake in profits, www.callcentermagazine.com, February.
(1998), Banking on Sophisticated Call Centers, www.callcentermagazine.com, February.
(2000), Call Centers are a-calling, www.itspace.com/itspacealpha/features/jobs/articles/callcenters.asp
(2000), Call Centres, www.nasscom.org

(2000), Weekly Statistical Supplement, RBI, www.rbi.org, 22 September.

Anton, Jon (2000) Customer Service Call Centers: 'The New Corporate Battleground', drjonanton@aol.com.

Braunthal, Peter and Amuso, Colleen (2000), *'Customer Service Management/Strategy: Key Issues in 2000'*, www.ciol.com/gartnerchannel/callcenters.

Coelho, Sonya (2000), Customer is King always, *Economic Times,* 31 July.

Dumblekar, Vinod (2000), 'Call Center: Opening New Vistas', **PCWorld,** August.

Duttagupta, Ishani (2000), 'Hello, It's You I'm Looking For', *Economic Times*, 16 July.

Haines, Steven (2000), 'Webbed Call Centres', *Economic Times*, 21 September.

Harris, Kimberly (2000), 'Internet integration: Aid to online customers', www.ciol.com

Hollman, Lee (2000), 'Dial "M" for Money: Banking and Financial Institutions profit from Call Centers', www.callcentermagazine.com.

Kumar, Deepak (2000), 'Relationship is Capital', *DataQuest*, 31 July.

Mehta, Anil (2000), 'HDFC and TCS float JV', *Economic Times*, 9 October.

Rangarajan, C (1996), 'Competition in the Financial System: Issues and Implications', *Inaugural Address at the 19th Bank Economists' Conference*, Mahabaleshwar, 16 December.

Shapiro, Jeffrey (2000), 'CRM: Tying The Knot With Your Customers', www.callcentermagazine.com.

Singh, Shalini (2000), 'Call Centre Colleges Knock At The Door', *Economic Times*, 26 August.

Web Scribes (2000), 'CRM: Case For Increasing Adoption Pace', www.ciol.com.

Chapter 51

User Satisfaction of Banking Software Products

Importance-Performance Mapping

■ **R Srinivasan and Mrunalini S Rao**

Abstract

This study investigates the key factors of Banking software products that leads to user satisfaction. We make use of a structured questionnaire as research instrument to survey the bank employees of various banks using banking software. The sample frame of the study encompasses the Computer Planning and Policy Division personnel and clerks, officers and managers of the banks. Factor analysis was used to arrive at the key factors leading to user satisfaction. Seven factors were Output, Vendors Marketing skills, Implementation, Maintainability, Performance, User friendliness and Security have a significant effect on User Satisfaction. The importance–performance map plotted helps in identifying the opportunities and threats for each of these products and shows that Products B has more number of threats followed by Product A.

Key Words: _User Satisfaction factors, Opportunities and threats._

☐ INTRODUCTION

Businesses today are continually looking for ways to achieve a competitive advantage. Margins are shrinking, competition is increasing. Customers are the most important asset of any Business. Consequently, applying some management resources to improve the customer's experience—and maximize the profit potential of that asset—is important. Many companies in the country are now adopted various such concepts like QFD, CRM etc, where the customer occupies the pivotal point.

Many software companies in India have adopted these methods in order to develop good software products. A few of them have already developed web-based products and also financial products catering to banks and other financial institutions. Banking software product is one such and is implemented in almost all the nationalized and private banks, to automate their transactions. Some of the reputed IT companies in the country have developed banking software to achieve this objective.

Banking software development has the following phases. First phase consists of developing the modules for the transactions using a software language, at the vendor's site, which forms 60% of the task. Second phase involves customizing the product as per their requirements and is done at the customer site.

Some of the modules that have been automated by the software product, are core modules which consists of Customer Information and services, Transaction Processing, General Ledger and security, Fund and Non-Fund based modules like loans, OD and Guarantees respectively, Demand Liability Modules like SB/CA and other modules like remittances, safe deposit and safe custody etc.

◻ LITERATURE REVIEW

The success or effectiveness of any software product or information system depends on the satisfaction derived by the users (Gatian, 1994, pp. 119-131). The concept of user satisfaction occupies a central position in marketing thought and practice. The centrality of this concept is that the profits are generated by satisfying the needs and wants of the users or customers.

This field of research emerged in the early 1970s and has accelerated in the recent years. It is hypothesized that consumer satisfaction is positively related to the product performance, dimensions of which were categorized qualitatively into Instrumental i.e. natural attributes of the product like capability, usability etc. and Expressive i.e. psychological or determinant attributes like color, style etc (Swan and Combs ,1976, pp. 25-33).

It was later identified that the distribution channel plays a unique role in satisfying the needs of the retailer than the manufacturer by proposing a non-traditional multiphase satisfaction program based on major components of satisfaction process, (Oliver L, Richard, 1981, pp. 25-48).

The customer/user satisfaction concept was applied in the area of information systems in the early 1980s. Bailey and Pearson (1983) developed a measuring instrument was to analyze computer user satisfaction. This instrument is widely adopted by researchers and practitioners for its high validity and reliability and also statistical rigor. They identified 39 factors affecting user satisfaction and developed a questionnaire using 7 point semantic differential scale of adjective pairs.

Ives et. Al. (1983) critically examined measures of user information satisfaction developed by other researchers like Gallagher, Jenkins and Ricketts, Lacker and Lessig and compared these with Pearson's instrument. From their analysis they selected Pearson's instrument based on Derivation, Empirical support, Level of coverage and No. of indicators. Pearson's instrument was again used to validate user satisfaction for office automation success (Wan and Wah, 1990, pp. 203-208). Many of the variables for our study are taken from the Bailey and Pearson's study to analyze banking software.

Bridging the gap between the system developers and the users will have a positive effect on the user satisfaction hypothesis was established which lead to the acceleration of research studies on user involvement and conflict resolution etc (Christensen, 1991, pp. 73-75). Many researchers have researched upon various dimensions of user satisfaction in isolation. A contingency model to relate user involvement with user satisfaction by framing hypotheses on system plan, attitude of the project team towards users, perception of managers and evaluation of MIS team was developed which lead to user involvement (Kwasi Amoaka Gympah and Kathy B. White ,1993, pp. 1-10).

Amoli et.al (1996) developed an instrument to measure End User Computing Satisfaction to a specific scenario became inevitable. It was identified that the outcome-oriented variables related with user performance of Information systems. A deep felt need to investigate the validity of usage and user satisfaction lead to certain other extended studies (Gelderman, 1998, pp. 11-18). It was identified that User satisfaction and organizational performance are significantly related and user satisfaction is a better measure than usage.

There are studies done considering all the dimensions of user satisfaction like, A comprehensive model and instrument to measure the small business user satisfaction with Information Technology was developed. It was tested for its reliability and validity of the instrument developed which was an offshoot of Bailey and Pearson's instrument (Palvia 1996, pp. 127-137). A study was also conducted to understand the perceived importance o Information systems success factors on both system and human aspects in which vendo related variables were included into the instrument along with the system elated items (Li 1997, pp. 15-28).

From this brief literature review few dimensions were identified and few other were added to suit our study. They are Implementation, Maintainability, Security, Reliability Output, User Friendliness, Vendor's ability to meet the needs and Marketing skills product User Involvement, User's Performance, Training and Support given to the Users and Service Capability.

□ METHODOLOGY

The study makes an attempt to measure the dimensions identified through the literature review and also those identified with the interaction held with software professionals, to basket all the relevant dimensions of banking software products. It also makes an attempt to compare these products by using Importance-Performance map, which is similar to Quadrant or SWOT analysis. It uses a structured questionnaire to measure the perceptions of the users of the software.

□ QUESTIONNAIRE

A questionnaire using a five-point likert scale was developed including all the dimensions mentioned above. The questionnaire measures the importance of a variable leading to satisfaction, scale ranging from extremely unimportant to extremely important and also measures the performance of the software w.r.t each of the attributes using a satisfaction scale, ranging from extremely satisfied to extremely dissatisfied. The questionnaire was checked for its reliability and validity in the Pilot study.

☐ PILOT STUDY
VALIDITY OF THE QUESTIONNAIRE

Content Validity

The content validity of the questionnaire was checked qualitatively by evaluating all the dimensions with the software professionals like product managers and also bank employees like the computer section personnel and the managers. Few questions were dropped because of its irrelevancy and few others were rephrased. This was again checked with the software professionals and bank employees for its face and content validity.

Reliability

The reliability of the instrument as well as each variable was assessed. During this process few items were dropped and only relevant items which had high correlation were considered. The table below shows the Cronbach's alpha for each of the dimensions. The reliability of the instrument was estimated by calculating the Cronbach's alpha for the whole instrument, which was 0.82 for important scale and 0.78 for satisfaction scale. From the above values we find that the instrument was reliable. The alpha values ranges between 0.56 to 0.93.

Table 1 (a) *Cronbach's Alpha value for each Variable [importance scale]*

Variables	Cronbach's alpha
Implementation	0.96
Maintainability	0.90
Reliability	0.59
Ease of Use	0.80
Security	0.82
Performance	0.91
Output	0.86
Vendor's	0.93
Vendor's Marketing skills	0.79
User Involvement	0.85
Training/Support	0.75
Service	0.81

Table 1 (b)   *Cronbach's Alpha value for each variable [Satisfaction scale]*

Variables	Cronbach's alpha
Implementation	0.61
Maintainability	0.69
Reliability	0.62
Ease of Use	0.80
Security	0.62
Performance	0.78
Output	0.66
Vendor's	0.54
Vendor's Marketing skills	0.65
User Involvement	0.69
Training/Support	0.67
Service	0.65

Construct Validity

The construct validity of the instrument was tested by subjecting it to factor analysis. The results show that dimensions having Eigen value more than 1 explained 83.9% of the variance. This shows high construct validity. Factor analysis was conducted using Principle Components analysis as the extraction technique and Varimax as the method of rotation. Eight factors emerged with Eigen values greater than 1. The table below gives the details of the total variance explained and the 8 factors. Examining the rotated component matrix in the horizontal direction identified items with in each factor and factors were labelled by grouping these items.

Table 2   *Construct Validity shown by factor analysis*

Total Variance Explained

Component	Initial Eigen values		
	Total	% of Variance	Cumulative %
1	6.861	22.871	22.871
2	5.630	18.765	41.636
3	3.512	11.708	53.344
4	2.6502	8.835	62.178
5	2.498	8.328	70.506
6	1.620	5.400	75.907
7	1.316	4.388	80.295
8	1.105	3.683	83.978

Extraction Method: Principal Component Analysis.

□ MAIN STUDY

The modified questionnaire was administered on a sample of bank employees in various fully computerized branches of randomly selected banks. Out of the 200 questionnaires distributed, 141 were usable. Others had many missing data and hence dropped.

☐ ANALYSIS

The data collected was subjected to Factor analysis again to arrive at the key factors of user satisfaction using Principal Component method of analysis and Varimax rotation. This gave seven factors having Eigen value more than 1. By examining the rotated component matrix, the items were grouped under the given seven factors and later depending on their correlation they were libelled. The key factors for user satisfaction identified through the analysis are Implementation, Maintainability, Performance, Security, Ease of Use, Output and Vendors Marketing skills.

Although the above analysis has given us the key factors of user satisfaction, all the other variables used in the study were important enough for the product to be effective. Hence we computed the mean of each of these variables for both importance and satisfaction dimensions. IT was then plotted on a four-quadrant map, where the X-axis is Importance and the Y-axis is Performance, for the products considered in the study. Different shapes on the graph represent these products.

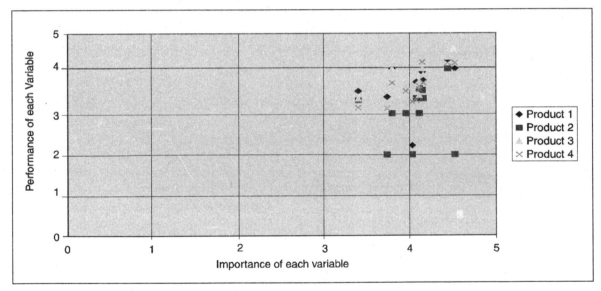

Fig. 1 *Importance-Performance Map for the Products*

☐ CONCLUSIONS

The analysis suggests that
1. Factors that are related to the product like Accuracy of the output, Implementation, Maintenance, Ease of use, and Security should be considered as key factors in satisfying the users.

2. Vendor's marketing ability of the software are very important factor, related to vendors, in satisfying the users of banking software, as they can make a better buying decisions.

3. Importance-Performance Map plotted for the products clearly shows that Product B has more number of threats followed by Product A. Users are dissatisfied with attributes like Service, Training and Support given to the user and Output. Output is also one of the key factors of user satisfaction, which implies that it is a serious threat.

4. The vendor of Product B should try and improve report generation format and make it more flexible compared to the existing standards. He should allow the user to specify the format of the reports. User manuals should be provided having clear explanations about the usage of the software in the language understood by a layman coupled with a brief training session. Providing updated versions of the software with better functionality and fast delivery.

5. Product A on the other hand has one threat, which is the training and support given to the users. They also should provide the users with good user manuals and give them a practical training on the usage of the software and its behavior.

6. The remaining Products do not have any major threats but there are few variables on which the performance of these products are on the border line. Product B again has three variables like user involvement, Performance of the individual and also Maintainability, which are key factors again, on which the performance scores neutral. This could any moment become a threat if not given due consideration. They should make their product more flexible to accommodate any changes in the modules so that maintenance becomes easy.

7. Although the products are performing well on other factors, due consideration should be given to those factors that are close to the border line of threat and opportunity. Very few factors fall above the satisfaction line i.e. 4 on the Y-axis, which clearly shows that there is a need to understand users expectations and wants and satisfy them, and this region poses lot of opportunities for the vendors to revise the existing products.

REFERENCES

Amoli and Farhoomand, (1996), 'A Structural Model of End User Computing Satisfaction and User Performance', *Information and Management*, V30(2), pp: 65-73.

Bailey and Pearson, (1983), 'Development of a Tool for Measuring and Analyzing Computer User Satisfaction', *Management Science*, V29(5), pp: 530-545.

Christensen, M. Dawn, (1991), 'The Gap Between System Developers and Users', *Information Systems Management fall*, pp: 73-75.

Churchill, JR., and Suprenant, (1982), 'An Investigation into the Determinants of Customer Satisfaction', *Journal of Marketing Research*, V19(4), pp: 491-504.

Gatian, W. Amy, (1994) 'Is User Satisfaction a Valid Measure of System Effectiveness', *Information and Management*, V26(3), pp: 119-131.

Gemoets and Adam Mahmood, (1990), 'Effect of the Quality of User Documentation on User Satisfaction with Information Systems', *Information and Management*, V18(1), pp: 47-54.

Gelderman, (1998), 'The Relation between User Satisfaction, Usage of Information System and Performance', Information and Management, V34(1), pp: 11-18.

Ives, Olson and Baroudi, (1983), 'The Measurement of User Information Satisfaction', Communications of *The ACM*, V26(10), pp: 785-793.

Kwasi Amoaka Gyampah and Kathy B. White, (1993),'User Involvement and User Satisfaction - An Exploratory Contingency Model', *Information and Management*, V25(1), pp: 1-10.

Kekre Sunder, Krishnan and Kannan Srinivasan, (1995), 'Drirs of Customer Satisfaction for Software Products: Implications for Design And Service Support', *Management Science*, V41(9), pp: 1456-1470.

Li Y. Eldon,(1997), 'Perceived Importance of Information Success Factors: A Meta Analysis Of Group Differences', *Information and Management*, V32(1), pp: 15-28.

Oliver, (1981), 'Measurement and Evaluation of Satisfaction Processes in Retail Settings', *Journal of Retailing*, V57(3), pp: 25-48.

Plewa and Lyman, (1992), 'Keeping the Customer Satisfied. The New CIO Mandate', *Information Systems Management, winter*, pp: 54-61.

Palvia, C. Prashanth, (1996), 'A Model and Instrument for Measuring Small Business User Satisfaction with Information Technology', *Information and Management*, V31(3), pp: 127-137.

Swan and Combs, (1976), 'Product Performance and Consumer Satisfaction : A New Concept', *Journal of Marketing*, V40(2), pp: 25-33.

Woodruff, Cadotte and Jenkins, (1983), 'Modeling Consumer Satisfaction Processes Using Experience Based Norms', *Journal of Marketing Research*, V20(3), pp: 296-304.

Wan and Wah, (1990), 'Validation of a User Satisfaction Instrument for Office Automation Success', *Information and Management*, V18(4), pp: 203-208.

Organizing for Relationship Management
The Case of Banking Industry

■ **Sami Bacha**

Abstract

The aim of this paper is to emphasize the part of competencies in direct relationship, using information technologies, with customers and partners. Built on the results of three case studies in the banking industry we propose a relationship management methodology based on competencies.

Key Words: *Relationship Management, Competencies, Externalization, Information Technologies, Banking.*

❑ INTRODUCTION

The firm capacity to establish, to maintain and to manage privileged relationships with external actors is considered as a competitive advantage (Day, 1997 ; Anderson and Weitz, 1989). The literature in management insists on both the relational aspect and on the transactional logic of the relational exchange (Dwyer, Schurr and Sejo, 1987; Macneil 1980). The rapid progress of information technologies facilitated the structuring of these relationships. In the last few years, firms have implemented technological solutions which allow them to establish direct relationships with external actors by eliminating most intermediaries between members of the organization and outside targets.

Built on the result of three case studies in the banking industry, this paper tries to demonstrate that the attraction and the development of these relationship are expected to mobilize specific capacities (Altman, Irwin and Dalmas, 1983; Scanzoni, 1979), and to manage relational competence (Boutal, 1997). We propose a relationship management methodology based on the organization of competencies.

□ RELATIONAL MANAGEMENT VERSUS THE TRANSACTIONAL MANAGEMENT

Theoretical Concepts

Cooperation, strategic alliances and relationship management have become a phenomena characterizing the globalization of businesses and increasing markets interdependence (Rechenmann, 1999). To face the increasingly competition, organizations try to develop some strategic advantages by establishing durable relationships (Day, 1997; Ganesan, 1994; Dwyer, Schurr and Sejo, 1987). Within this context, a better understanding of the relational exchange must facilitate the development and the efficiency of the buyer-seller relationships. Sheth and Parvatiyar (1995) qualify relationship management as a variable association state in the time and constituted of a large range of connections between animated or inert objects. An association based on the continuity and the stability of relationships rather than on the repetition of the same behavior over time.

Hence, firms try more and more to maintain the dialogue with their customers, to collect more information and to propose them specific products and services. The relational marketing seeks to develop close interactions with customers and supplier to enhance value shares for both parties (Peppers, Rogers and Dorf, 1999; Sheth and Parvatiyar 1994). Henceforth, tangible and physical characteristics of the transaction (discrete exchange) are added to its intangible, social and symbolic aspects (continuous exchange) to reconsider the commercial exchanges. This dichotomy constitutes the antecedent of the fundamental distinction between transactional marketing and relational marketing.

At the same time, firms focus their activities on their know-how and their available competence and try to reduce activities which do not add value (Howells, 1999). The development of subcontracting and consulting activities, the multiplication of services and the progress of communication and logistics tools encouraged this externalization phenomenon (Boscheck, 1988; Hunt and Morgan, 1994). Thus firms tie a set of vertical relationship with upstream actors (suppliers, subcontractors and providers).

Development of Information Technologies: A New Determinant of Relationship Management

The shift from transactional exchange to a relational one not only modified the nature of the buyer-seller dyad but also changed the habits and behaviors of actors (Rechenmann, 1999; Nueno and Oosterveld, 1988). Firstly, relations with subcontractors and suppliers are often reinforced by bringing together their information systems permitting a bigger reciprocity of reports (Berry and Linoff, 1997). However, the implementation of inter-organizational information system usually took a long time due to the fact that protocols and software used by the parties were often not standardized and also setting up costs were relatively high. Therefore, the standardization operated around protocol networks, then around visualization software and finally around the components of treatment applications, facilitates the setting up of inter-organizational relations as well as the development of supple applications. The development of extranet came later.

Secondly, relationships with customers is completely denatured (Boscheck, 1998). Indeed, habitual communication channels (press, radio, TV, etc.) are no longer able to create and maintain privileged relationship with customers. Consumers today seek communication tools, which allow them free access and a real interaction with firms (Monge and Eisenberg, 1987).

To the extent that the new information and communication technologies offer new possibilities to establish an exchange and dialogue with actual and potential customers, they can consolidate their loyalty and allow managers to operate a refined and efficient selection. Indeed, technology investments offer an information infrastructure that permit not only to reduce transaction and communication costs but also to elaborate a rich and efficient data basis (Stump and Sriram, 1997). For this reason, managers consider new information technologies not only like a new distribution method of their products but also as a new advertisement and communication channel, offering them proximity with customers (Lavigne, 1999; Hunt, Shelby and Morgan, 1994).

The Case of the Banking Industry

The banking industry is especially concerned by this double relational phenomenon. Firstly, externalization projects grow regularly, notably concerning data process subcontracting (Maulde, 1997), accounting treatments and realization of a set of non-strategic activities. The research for permanent means to reduce operating costs and the confrontation to two data processing challenges (Euro conversion and Year 2000) encouraged the externalization of information systems.

Secondly, in an industry where innovation and differentiation notions provide limited advantages, banks are obliged to compensate the margin erosion by mass production and by an improvement of their customers' relationship. They look for a balance between two somewhat conflicting tendencies: the automated mass treatment to reduce costs and the development of the relational marketing in order to satisfy customers subjected to numerous solicitations from the competition. Several tendencies can be observed: the development of the home banking concept, the direct bank, the evolution of the agency function (consulting, insurance, etc.). However developments in Internet will attract most banks' attention. Indeed, an investigation in 2000[1] revealed that reduction of the physical network will start once the Internet trade volume reaches a level of 20% to 25% of total transactions. By the year 2001, the development of new information and communication systems should attract more than 20% of the actual customers.

☐ DETERMINANTS OF A RATIONAL BUYER-SELLER DYAD

The Relational Competence Concept

Developments of management and relational marketing permit firms to coordinate their relationships with customers. They must learn to know about the customer needs in order

---

[1] Cf. to the survey realised by J.P. Morgan, Standard & Poors and Merril Lynch published in the magazine « la tribune » of 2000, 13 june.

to conquer and develop their loyalties (Ganesan, 1994). The control of these relationships, although they are computerized or no, upstream or downstream, require thus some specific knew-how and competencies. According to P. X. Meschi (1996), the competence is the consequence of a coordinated and valorizing combination of a set of individual professional capacities. So we can advance that relational competencies appropriate to firms depend on the formation of synergism between the various competencies associated to every actors (Kim, 1993; Fiol, 1994). Whereas a review of the literature concerning the relational marketing and the partnership management show us that firms leading partnership projects with their customers are confronted to a double challenge: on the one hand, maintaining a constant links between the firms and consumers, when using new information and communication technologies ; on the other hand, making possible a personalization of the relationship without neglecting its interpersonal and interactive aspect (Altman, Irwin and Dalmas, 1983).

In this optics of relational network, a firm should develop sharp competencies in order to maintain the coherence of its offer, to control the quality of services and products proposed by suppliers and providers, to accelerate the information transmission. That's why they are increasingly incited not only to concentrate their efforts in the domain of the internal and external logistics (Fabbe-Coste, 1999; Paché, 1991), but also in the domain of the communication (Mohr, Fisher and Nevin, 1999). These efforts are of as much more necessary than the exchanged information, with upstream and downstream are, are very numerous and various. These information may be impersonal or personal (i.e. a particular demand emanating from a customer). In this last case actors concerned by the relationship are obliged to work together and thus some personal links can be knotted. This process allows relatively spontaneous information exchanges (Scanzoni, 1979) and escaping to hierarchy control (monge, 1987). Consequently, we note that partnerships are not only piloted by formal systems but kept up also by the existence of a set of interpersonal connection (Altman, Irwin and Dalmas, 1983).

Concerning upstream relationships, these moments of spontaneity are numerous and some privileged relations can appear between two or several actors. These will not only exchange views on their professions and their firms, but also on their private lives. Thanks to that, relationships between organizations are reinforced, since they are based on friendship links. Thus, the success of inter-organizational relationships depends on the human aspect of the management and it is the nature of exchanges between the key actors that determines the efficiency of cooperation relationships (Jutter and Hans, 1995; Larson, 1992).

Within the banking industry, the physical contacts with each customer are less numerous than with suppliers and providers. This report can be explained by the plurality of customers, among whom only a few person generate a high margin, making very expensive the mobilization of a large number of commercial counsellors. However, relationships with customers can also include an interpersonal aspect. Several customers converse regularly with their bank counsellor by telephone or when they visit agencies.

The Concept of Trust and the Relational Management

All commercial exchange systems cannot exist without a trust that acts as strength that seals the seller-buyer relationships and influence the long-term orientation of this relationship (Geyskens, Steenkamp and Kumar, 1998). Firms are directly concerned by this establishment process of the trust between sellers and their customer, because trust generated by the seller is transferred as well to suppliers as to customers and influences the future interaction anticipation. Thus, firms having for declared strategy to establish a long-term relationships must not only win the upstream and downstream partner 's trust but also they have to do everything possible to institutionalize this generated trust (Geyskens, Steenkamp and Kumar, 1998).

Several arguments have been advanced to justify the trust role in the consolidation of relationships. According to the theory of the organization, the concept of trust is analyzed like a means to reduce the uncertainty and risks in buyer-seller relationships, it permits to decrease transactional costs and make the exchange more flexible (Walter and Ritter, 2000; Graf et al, 1999). On the other hand, the literature in psychology and in marketing (Doney and Connon, 1997) define trust like the credibility perception and the partner's kindliness.

In spite of the unavoidable problems of measure and divergences of opinion, a consensus emerges from this literature: trust is seen like an personal expectation carrying on the reliability of words and promises of another individual. Consequently, trust results from the appraisal of the partnership expertise, of its reliability and its previous behaviors (Morgan and Hunt, 1994). Thus, it is qualified as both antecedent and consequence of the upstream and downstream partnership relation.

Within the banking industry, the trust notion is doubly important. First, besides of its capacity to limit risks it allows customers to commit themselves towards only one bank that previous behaviors were satisfactory. Given that money constitutes the exchange support, the trust between seller and buyer is essential to the establishment but also to the reinforcing of the relationship. Second, the trust functions like a mechanism control decreasing the opportunist behaviors within a exchange context characterized by the uncertainty and dependence (Walchholfer & al, 1998 ; Raiffa, 1982).

◻ THE METHODOLOGY

Through a study, we try to identify and to characterize competencies used in the two following relational processes:
- Upstream relationship : the externalization of the check treatment;
- Downstream relationship: the creation of direct relationship with the individual customers categories.

This study has been led within three banking houses belonging to a big banking group. We will first of all explain reasons that drove us to choose the banking industry and more especially the banking group, object of studies. We will explain why we kept the two processes of externalization of the check treatment and the one of creation of direct relations between the bank and its individual customers. Finally, we will present the collection and analysis methods data used to underscore some results.

The Choice of the Banking Industry and the Bank Group

The choice of a study carrying on banking houses has been motivated by the importance of relational activities and the increasingly development of information and communication technologies in this sector. The main part of bank activities can be analyzed as the research of efficiency by the adjustment of different types of information, notably the macro-economic information (the bank environment) and more detailed information about customers. The place occupied by information and the necessity to manage it incite the banking responsibles to invest heavily in the new information and communication technologies (Lavigne, 1999). Currently, it seems that the major stake of banks resides in the improvement of the relation with its customers and in the diversification of interconnection means with them (Rechenmann, (1999). Within this context, the study of relationship in the banking industry appears very important.

As for the bank group, the choice is justified by a methodological consistency and external validity reasons (Thiétart, 1999; Strauss and Corbin J., 1990). Because of its particular structure, composed of a set of independent regional bank but federated by a common organism, we could achieve comparisons between different processes in several banks while ascertaining a certain consistency at the strategic and politic character levels. The choice of each of banks is founded on the criteria of expertise level of new technologies and notably the Internet technologies. Thus we chose a bank possessing a website permitting interactivity with the customer, a bank possessing a website describing only the bank structure and product, and finally, a bank not having a website.

The Choice of Relational Process

To illustrate the upstream relationship between a bank and service provider, we chose the process of externalization of the check treatment. The transverse character of this process, implying providers and customer, oriented our choice.

As for the choice of the strategic segment "individual customers", we privileged this category because of the volume of customers that it includes and of the costs that it misleads. Concerning costs, a uniform rules management of this segment is little profitable in terms of commissions. That's why it's important to study it in depth, thanks to the technological tools, in order to propose targeted offers improving the global profitability of the segment. Indeed, the setting up of relationships between the bank and its customers based on new information and communication technologies is an objective that shares the majority of bank houses (Boscheck, 1988).

The following table specifies the different character in relation with our study in the three banks that we visited:

Table 1 *Characters of the three studied banks*

Site	Externalization checks and direct relationships via «Internet»
A	• Externalisation of the check treatment achieved in 1992 : results judged satisfactory; • Project at very short term of an Internet site describing the bank and its products • Project at very short term of a customer access to their account via the Web, allowing the customer to do basic operations, but no offer of specific products • Externalisation of data process
B	• Externalization of the check treatment achieved in 1995; • Existence of an Internet site permitting to describe the bank and its products; • Existence of a complete bank site at distance; • Numerous projects of marketing one to one; • Data process is not externalized
C	• Externalization of the check treatment ongoing, • No project of bank at distance in short-term • Internet site permitting to describe the bank and its products • Externalized data process

The Research Methodology

To study the role of competencies in the establishment of social relationship, we adopt a qualitative approach and collect qualitative data (R. K. Yin, 1989). By another way, we released a set of individual interviews (Edwards, 1998) with a certain number of managers[2] in the three retained banks. The ranks and functions of people interviewees are specified in Table 2.

Table 2 *Rank and function of interviewed person*

Site	Rank and function of interviewed person
A	• President of the director board • Executive chief • Assistant executive chief and responsible of the internal organization and of the financial department • Responsible individual customers
B	• President of the director board • Assistant executive chief responsible of the internal organization • Director of the individual market • Actual responsible of checks • Old responsible of checks • Responsible of the internal organization
C	• Executive chief

During these interviews, we explained clearly the object of the study without indicating our personal approach in order to not influence the interviewed person. We used a the-

---

[2]A total of 17 hours of discussion was required.

matic approach to analyze the content of the interviews (Blanchet et Gotman, 1994). This thematic analysis permitted to clear a set of results that we are going to describe now.

☐ THE RESULTS FORMULATION

The study led within the banking houses resulted in the formulation of three main results concerning the management of relational competencies. We can first of all note that departments concerned by the establishment of relationships are similar in all cases. Second, it is important to notice that the externalization of data process activity provokes a rarefaction of technological competence. Finally, we will insist on the mean role occupied by the organization department in the establishment of relational process.

Relational Process and Departments Concerned

The three studied cases permitted to note that four departments contribute generally in the establishment of relationships with suppliers and with customers : the department of organisation, production, exploitation and, more rarely, the data process department.

The organisation department has for main function to assure the cross-process link and to ensure the efficiency of the internal organisation. Besides, it assures the co-ordination with some institutional actors.

The production department has in charge the processes aiming the development of bank products and services. For that, it is in permanent relationships with services providers and suppliers in order to search for the more adapted resources to their offer.

The exploitation department has for function to assure the distribution of products and services to customers. It represents a commercial department being at the interface of the bank and its customers.

Differently from the three previous departments, the data process one doesn't have the same importance in all studied banks. Indeed, the data process department of banks knew these last time important distress. The major role of the new information and communication technologies in this sector, as well as the high level of requisite competence to master them dragged a strong increase of allocated resources. Because of the decentralised structure of the group, the adopted technological solutions began to present a big heterogeneity. In order to reduce the computer expenses, numerous banks confide their data processing to subcontractors. They kept only an embryonic data process department assuring the tool using. So, it is the organisation department that takes in charge the monitoring of technological development as well as the study of the technical feasibility of an externalisation project.

The Rarefaction of Technological Competence

The externalization of the data process generates, within two banking houses, a rarefaction of available competencies. This defaulting has dual consequences: on the one hand it limits the technological coordination, on the other hand; it affects the direct relationships with the customers without restricting those with partners.

First of all, the lack of coordination is illustrated in these cases by the fact that persons hired in upstream project and possessing some technological competencies are not the same that those implied in another downstream project. This situation risks to generate incoherence as well at the level of the heterogeneity of protocols, materials and applications within a same network, as at the level of the data storage.

Then, we only observed two cases of successful direct relationships with customers among the four studied cases. Persons interrogated justify the absence of direct relationships in their banks by the externalization of the data process activity. We propose here a more precise explanation based on the various kind of competence required:

- During the phase of establishment or the phase of consolidation of the relationship
- Concerning an upstream or downstream relationship.

Upstream relationships (with a service supplier) require interpersonal competencies permitting the establishment of the links. During the attraction phase, actors seek to estimate the reliability of the suppliers through visits, discussions with some of its customers, etc. Therefore, an interpersonal and trustworthy links will be knotted and could be lasted in the time. On the other hand, the technological competence is going to be used during the definition of specification. In this situation, technological competencies constitute a support permitting the consolidation of the relationship but not its establishment. Besides, it is even possible that these competencies will be provided by the service providers himself, through the junction of its system of information then with the one of the bank.

Concerning relations with the downstream, the situation is completely different. The main characteristic of the individual customers segment is its volume: we are in presence of a multitude of customer. Consequently, it seems too expensive (human and financial resources) to strike up interpersonal relationships with them. Technological competencies must be used during the attraction phase to refine the segmentation and to encourage the customer's responsible to entry in contact with them. The consolidation of the relationship will require however a strong interpersonal competencies since it will be necessary, notably on behalf of the customer's responsible, to determinate the basis of a durable relation. So technological competencies appear to constitute the key factor permitting the establishment of the bank-customer relationships.

Regard to these observations, we recognize the existence of variations in the use of the necessary competencies during the establishment then during the consolidation of relationships. The table here illustrates our reasoning:

Table 3 *Requisite Key Competencies in the Development of Relationship*

Type of relation Phase of the relation	Upstream	Downstream
Establishment	Interpersonal competencies	Technological competencies
Consolidation	Technological competencies	Interpersonal competencies

This necessity of many technological competencies for the establishment of relations with the downstream, could explain the weak number of projects of this type in the studied banks. Thus, the externalization of the data process activity operated by numerous banks would drive to make more difficult the establishment of relationships with customers, whereas it doesn't necessarily constitute an obstacle to relationships with suppliers.

The Structuring and the Organization of the Relational Exchange

During our study, we noted that the organization department constitutes the core of the relational management. Indeed, at least one member of this department participated in every relational project, as well with upstream actors as downstream:

Table 4 *The Transverse Character Of Bank Relational Process*

Intersection of relational process

The processing department doesn't appear in this diagram, because the externalisation of the data process drove to the bursting of its missions and its expertise to the profit of the providers and different internal services. Thus, it exists a risk to see appear technological incoherence between the different projects, as well as a defaulting of relational competencies. It seems therefore necessary make a rigorous management of the technological and relational competence.

☐ DISCUSSIONS AND PERSPECTIVES

We propose here a method permitting to manage simultaneously two projects making upstream and downstream relationships. We noted that every project was composed by many actors having identified competencies. During the progress of the project, these actors can vary: someone can leave to another project, other actors can arrive. In these conditions, our objective is to put in adequacy the required competencies with the available one. We first of all suggest that every project includes actors belonging to borders of the organization (person working with suppliers or providers and person working with customers) in order to assure the transversally in the resolution of problems. The objective here is to limit incoherence between process.

Because of the rarefaction of available competence, we propose then an exchange of actors between the two projects at the end of the establishment phase of the relationship. Let's add that this swinging will encourage the transversally in the relational process organization. Table 5. illustrates this notion of exchange:

Table 5 *Example of Competencies Management*

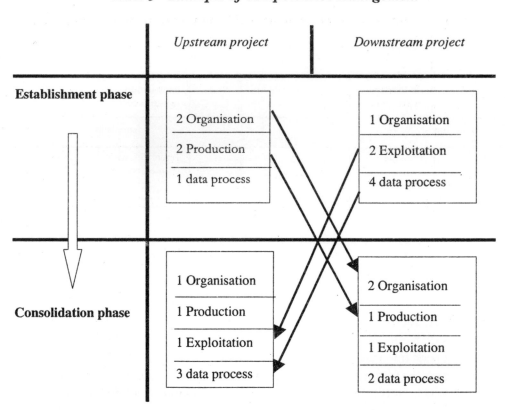

	Upstream project	Downstream project
Establishment phase	2 Organisation 2 Production 1 data process	1 Organisation 2 Exploitation 4 data process
Consolidation phase	1 Organisation 1 Production 1 Exploitation 3 data process	2 Organisation 1 Production 1 Exploitation 2 data process

In this table, we indicate four exchanges of actors occurring at the end of the phase of the relationships establishment. Let's retail them by indicating their reasons:

1. Passage of a member of the organization department toward the downstream project: the objective is to assure the coordination of processes at the level of the internal organization.
2. Passage of a member of the production department toward the downstream project: the objective is to assure the technical coordination between processes.

3. Passage of a member of the exploitation department toward the upstream project: it permits to assure the coordination at the level of the customer's needs. Indeed, the staff of the exploitation is theoretically the best one who knows the customer's needs. The attention carried to this level permits to increase and to control the quality of supplied service.

4. Passage of two members of the data process department toward the upstream project: it permits to make solutions to the requisite competencies evolution, projects of suppliers externalization requiring more technological competencies in the phase of consolidation. Once again, it contributes to the technological coordination.

To complete this rotating management of the relational projects, we propose the use of GroupWare tools. These tools could drive to the development of real bases of knowledge containing:

- A documentary basis regrouping testimonies actors of project already realized and technical documents (guide of procedure);
- Names and roles of these actors to contact them;
- A forum of discussion between actors of a project ongoing.

☐ CONCLUSION

The case studies conducted in three different banking houses allowed us to formulate several results. The most important concerns the absence of technological competencies as a limitation in establishing direct relationships between suppliers and customers. To solve this problem we propose a method of dynamic management of the project team based on establishing adequacy between existing and required competencies. More precisely, this method is based on a sequential distribution of competencies along the phases of establishment and consolidation of the upstream and downstream relationships in order to highlight knowledge and know-how of the different actors.

This model proposition needs to be reviewed and verified empirically through future interviews with bank managers. However, whereas the externalisation strategies constantly evolve, we emphasise the importance of the supplier/customer relationship management as well as the competencies required.

REFERENCES

Altman, I. and Dalmas, A. (1983), *The Development of Interpersonal Relationship*, NY : Holt.

Anderson, E. and Weitz, B. (1989), 'Determinants of Continuity in Conventional Industrial Channel Dyads', *Marketing Science*, Vol. 8, No. 4, pp. 310-323.

Berry, J. A. and Linoff, G. (1997), *Datamining - Techniques Appliquées au Marketing, à la vente et aux Services Clients,* Paris : Masson.

Blanchet, A. and Gotman, A. (1994), *L'enquête et ses méthodes: l'entretien ,* Paris : Nathan Université.

Boscheck, R. (1998), 'New Media Economics are Transforming Consumer Relations', *Long Range Planning,* Vol. 32, No. 6, pp. 873-878.

Boutall, T. (1997), *Compétences Managériales : le guide*, Paris : Demos.

Brulhart, F. and Fabbe-Costes, N. (1999), 'Réseaux de partenaires : Concepts et mise en actes, 2 ème colloque', *La métamorphose des organisations : quelles compétences pour développer et contrôler l'entreprise relationnelle*, pp. 21-23.

Day, G. (1997), 'Maintaining the Competitive Edge: Creating and Sustaining Advantage in Dynamic Competitive Environments', *Wharton on Dynamic Competitive Strategies*, pp. 48-75.

Doney, P. M. and Connon, J. P. (1997), 'An Examination of the Nature of Trust in Buyer-Seller Relationships', *Journal of marketing*, Vol. 61, No. 2, pp. 35-51.

Dwyer, F. R., Schurr, P. H. and Oh, S. (1987), 'Developing Buyer-Seller Relationships', *Journal of Marketing*, Vol. 51, No. 4, pp. 11-27.

Edwards, D. (1998), 'Types of Case Study Work: A Conceptual Framework for Case Based Research', *The Journal of Humanistic Psychology*, Beverly Hills, Summer, pp. 36-70.

Fiol, C. M. (1994), 'Consensus, Diversity and Learning in Organization', Organization *Science, Vol.* 5, No. 3, pp. 403-420.

Ganesan, S. (1994), 'Determinants of Long-term Orientation in Buyer-Seller Relationships', *Journal of Marketing,* Vol. 58, No. 2, pp. 1-19.

Geyskens, I., Steenkamp, J. B. and Kumar, N. (1998), 'Generalization about Trust in Marketing Channel Relationships using Meta-Analysis', *International Journal of Research in Marketing*, Vol. 15, pp. 223-248.

Graf, R. et al (1999), La confiance : son statut et sa valeur normative, A.F.M, 15 éme Congrès International, Strasbourg, mai.

Howells, J. (1999), 'Research and Technology Outsourcing', *Technology Analysis & Strategic Management,* Vol. ll, No. l, pp. 7-29.

Jutter, U. and Hans, P. (1995), 'Interactive System's value creation through Relationship Marketing', *American Marketing Association*, pp.16-23.

Larson, A. (1992), 'Network Dyads in Entrepreneurial Setting: A Study of the Governance of Exchange Relationships', *Administrative Science Quarterly*, No. 37, pp. 76-104.

Lavigne, L. (1999), 'L'évolution des systèmes d'information à l'horizon 2005', *Revue Banque,*No. 599, pp. 31-33.

Levinger, G. and Snoek, J. D. (1972), *Attraction in relationship : A new look at Interpersonal Attraction,* Morristown, New Jersey.

Macneil, I. R. (1980), *The New Social Contract, An Inquiry into Modern Contractual Relations*, New Haven:Yale University Press.

Maulde de, E. (1997), 'SSII et sous-traitance bancaire', *Revue Banque*, No. 578, pp. 75-77.

Meschi, P. X. (1996), Le concept de compétences en stratégie: perspectives et méthodes, *Colloque de l'A.I.M.S,* Lille

Mohr, J., Fisher, R. and Nevin, J. (1999), 'Communicating for Better Channel Relationships', *Marketing Management*, Summer, pp. 39-45.

Monge, P. R. and Eisenberg, E. M. (1987), Emergent Communication Networks, in F. M.

Morgan, R.M and Hunt, S.D. (1994), 'The Commitment-Trust Theory of Relationship Marketing', *Journal of Marketing*, Vol.58, July, pp. 20-38.

Parvatiyar A. and J. Sheth, (1994), Paradigms Shift in Marketing Theory and Approach :. The Emergence of Relationship Marketing, *Relationship Marketing : Theory, Methods and Applications*, Atlanta, Center for Relationship Marketing, Emory University.

Parvatiyar,V. and Sheth, J. (1995), 'Relationship Marketing in Consumer Markets : Antecedents and Consequences', *Acedemy of Marketing Science Journal*, Vol. 23, pp. 255-272.

Peppers, Rogers, K.M. and Dorf, B. (1999), ' Is your Company ready for one-to-one Marketing ?', *Harvard Business Review,* Vol. 77, No. l, pp. 151-160.

Raiffa, H. (1982), *The Art and Science of Negotiation*, Cambridge : Harvard University Press.

Rechenmann, J. J. (1999), L'internet et le Marketing, Edition d'Organisation.

Scanzoni, J. (1979), 'Social Exchange in Developing Relationships', *Social Exchange and Behavioral Interdependence*, R. L. Burgess and T. L. Huston, eds, NY : Academic Press.

Strauss, A. and Corbin, J. (1990), *Basics of Qualitative Research : Grounded Theory Procedures and Techniques,* Sage Publications : Newbury Park.

Stump, R.L and Sriram, V. (1997), 'Employing Information Technology in Purchasing: Buyer-Supplier Relationships and Size of Supplier Base', *Industrial Marketing Management,* Vol. 26, pp. 127-136.

Thiétart, R.A. (1999), *Méthodes de Recherche en Management,* Paris : Dunod.

Walter, A. and Ritter, T. (2000), Value-creation in Customer-Supplier Relationship : The role of Adaptation, Trust and Commitment, *29 th EMAC Conference* in Rotterdam.

Yin, R. K. (1991), *Case Study Research : Design and Methods,* New York : Sage.

Introduction of e-CRM in the Indian Insurance Sector

Customer and Intermediary Preferences

■ **S Ragunath and Joseph Shields**

Abstract

The onset of e-commerce has led to the traditional insurance firms resorting to online transactions. Such a transition however has not been as smooth as was expected in many countries in the West. After the recent deregulation of the Indian insurance industry, new opportunities have opened up for online insurance transactions in the Indian market. Apart from the resistance due to the channel conflicts from the agents, the end user response has also not been that encouraging in certain sectors of the industry, owing to an anticipated lack of personal interaction from the seller. The present work proposes that the roadmap for online insurance could be smoothened by the introduction of e-CRM techniques in the online insurance business, by making the present agents and middlemen as network partners for information gathering, transfer, servicing and processing. The findings are based on field data from 7 Indian cities among customers and agents. The study has found that the implementability of e-CRM is high in the stages of 'Routine Post-sale Transactions' and 'Nonroutine Post-sale Transactions' while it can be used in tandem with human interaction in the 'Pre-sale Interaction' and 'Sale Transaction' stages. Human action alone can help in stage 1 viz., 'Customer Research'. The perceptions have been found to be significantly different in both the life and general insurance segments, with the willingness of agents for participation in data mining being very low in the general insurance segment.

Key Words: *CRM, e-CRM, Life, General, Agents, Customers, India, Insurance*

☐ OBJECTIVES OF THE STUDY

Companies worldwide are realizing the increasing importance of technology in the insurance industry and the trend is catching up in India also with the opening up of the Insurance sector. Technology has been found to be a key determinant to the insurance industry's success around the world over the next five years (Forbes, 1998). The onset of e-commerce has led to the traditional insurance firms resorting to online transactions. Such a transition however has not been as smooth as was expected in many countries in the West. The major hurdle such online transactors have faced is from the traditional agents and middlemen, who felt threatened that their commissions and brokerage charges would be effected by such transactions. While in Europe, the introduction of online transactions had been easy in the non-life segments like property, car and travel, the life sector had been ridden by 'channel conflicts (Economist, 2000b). As a result companies like Allstate have invested more into non-life related insurance transactions on the web, compared to life insurance transactions (Economist, 2000a). Apart from the resistance due to the channel conflicts from the agents, the end user response has also not been that encouraging in the life sector, owing to a lack of personal interaction, as a buyer expects to talk to a human about human insurance (Economist, 2000b).

The present work proposes that the roadmap for online insurance could be smoothened and enabled by the introduction of e-CRM (Electronic Customer Relationship Management) techniques in the online insurance business, by making the present agents and middlemen as network partners for the activities relating to information gathering, transfer and servicing. From the market attractiveness perspective (Abell and Hammond, 1979), the market appears to be attractive from the Market, Economic & Technical and Competitive factors (Pant, 2000, UN, 2000). Worldwide, it is felt that there is a need to educate the prospective buyers about the benefits of life insurance and also a need for hard selling the products (Woods and Mitchel, 1999) and India does not seem to be any better. Many insurance professionals have shifted their practices from selling death benefits to selling living benefits in the West (Brenner, 2000). However careful consideration needs to be given to the environmental factors relating to the regulatory climate, social acceptance and human resource factors (Abell and Hammod, 1979; Aaker, 1998). With the regulatory environment already changing favorably, it would be interesting to understand the readiness and attractiveness of the market from the perspective of the social acceptance (customers and users) and the human resource acceptance (agents and middlemen).

The following questions would be addressed as part of the study:

- Is the Indian insurance market ready for CRM enabled online transactions?
- Can online transactions be introduced in the life insurance sector with the help of the agents?

The implementability of e-CRM is studied from the market acceptance perspective. The research has been restricted to the urban market and the computer users and professionals.

☐ APPLICATION OF CRM IN INSURANCE

Distribution channels and cost control were found to be critical factors for success in the insurance industry (Davidson, 2000). The direct delivery channels, especially the Internet, are replacing the captive sales force (Friedman, 2000). These delivery channel strategies are driven by the desire to reduce expenses and increase productivity (Davidson, 2000). Computing is used to reduce costs and to compete. Technology is not only more efficient than manual methods, but it is more accurate and complete, protecting both the interests of the insurer and the insured/claimant (Fox, 2000). With the help of data mining, patterns, links and discrepancies can be discovered without an outlay of substantial time and effort (Smith, Willis and Brooks, 2000). The CRM movement dates at least to the early 1990s, when insurers began constructing client databases to track relationships at the customer and agent levels, and to help cross-sell products.

An insurance CRM strategy can be implemented through data warehousing and mining, interactive Web sites, call centers, hand-held devices and other business intelligence systems that enable a company to better know and service its customers, and in turn win their long-term loyalty (Sodano, 2000). The main technology components include:

(a) data warehouse with customer, contract, transaction and channel data
(b) analysis tools to examine the database and identify customer behavior patterns
(c) campaign management tools to allow the insurer's marketing department to define communications and facilitate automatic generation of those communications; and
(d) interfaces to the operational environment to maintain the marketing database and communications channels to deliver the messages (Insurance & Technology, 1999).

However, human intervention appears to be inevitable in the insurance industry, owing to the expectations of the customers. A study conducted by IVANS has found that consumers are most likely to shop for autocoverage (42 percent) and least likely to shop for health coverage (13 percent) online (Insurance & Technology, 2000b). A study conducted in Singapore to understand the relative importance of listening, speaking and writing, it was found that listening is a key factor in the insurance industry (Goby and Lewis, 2000). These re-emphasize the need for a human element in the transactions, more so in the life and health insurance areas, where insurance of humans is concerned. While the human touch in CRM can be achieved through Internet Telephone and Videophone technologies (Windows Business Series, 1999), the idea seems to be far fetched at least for the present.

CRM can be introduced in various stages of the insurance value chain. After the repeal of the 1933 Glass-Steagall Act eliminating the boundaries between banks, brokerage houses and insurers in the late nineties, EDS went live with a pilot CRM solution for one of its largest insurance clients. The solution not only allows policy holders and customer service representatives to make changes to existing policies and quote new policies, but also, when fully functional, it will allow the company to perform sophisticated data mining and database marketing (Long, 1999). Insweb Corp, a provider of online insurance services, has introduced a business model which changes from referring leads to traditional brokers to selling insurance policies directly. The new e-commerce and CRM solution for the life insurance industry announced by Sybase, Inc. and Data Executives International includes a web-based application environment, electronic ordering and interpretation of results, underwriting case management and data warehousing to support CRM (Trembly,

2000a, b). In India however, the insurance web sites like 123bima.com, insurance-india.net are not yet catering to the online transaction needs of the customers.

CRM in the insurance sector is of four levels:

1. Full-service suite-of-product vendors
2. Vendors that provide some but not all CRM applications – sales, marketing, call center software provider
3. ERP
4. e-CRM (call centers and Internet products).

Insurance needs applications from more than one level of vendor culminating in the last level of e-CRM (Insurance & Technology, 2000a). CRM cannot however exist independent of ERM - Employee Relationship Management and VRM – Vendor Relationship Management (Tehrani, 1999). The attitude of the quasi-employees i.e., the agents towards automation at their expense needs to be taken into consideration (ERM). The value chain of customer interaction citing the possible role CRM can play in each of the links is shown in Fig 1. The present work focuses on the perceptions of agents and buyers on the introduction of e-CRM viz., call centers and internet products in the insurance sector.

STAGES

Customer Research	Pre-sale Interactions	Sale Transaction	Routine Post-sale Interaction	Non-routine Post-sale Interaction	
Consumer Buying Behavior Payment Patterns Consumer Profile	Comparison of Insurance Products Customization of Products Clarification of FAQs and specific queries	Order placing Payment Order Processing Payment processing	Routine information sharing (new products/services, advisory services etc) Investment specific information sharing Short-term payments /redemptions	Ontime/Endtime settlement Claims processing in times of eventualities	Activities
• Accuracy • Compreh-ensiveness	• Decision making • Customiz-ation • Scrutiny	• Speed • Accuracy • Delivery	• Speed • Transparency	• Accuracy • Fairness • Speed • Transparency	

Expected benefits from e-CRM

Fig. 1 *Value Chain of Customer Interaction in Insurance and Possible Benefits of e-CRM*

☐ METHODOLOGY

A questionnaire based survey was carried out for customers and agents. Owing to the technology relatedness of the study, the research was limited to urban areas only. The questionnaires for customers were administered to over 500 respondents across three major cities of India – Calcutta, Bangalore and Madras and from four upcoming cities – Bhubaneswar, Vishakapatnam, Rajahmundry and Vijaywada. Of the 500 responses, only 423 were found to be useful. Questionnaires were administered to two types of agents viz., life and general. Of the 400 responses received from the agents, only 138 agents dealing with life insurance alone and 184 dealt with life as well as general insurance were useful.

The customers were asked questions relating to their motives behind insurance purchases, perception on the information needs, perception on the services provided, expectations on product customization and versatility of service, internet usage patterns and expectations on the interaction from the insurance companies

The agents were asked questions relating to their willingness to work full-time for the insurance company, areas of interest in customer relationship management, level of satisfaction with the company, perceptions on different modes of interaction with customers and perception on the information needs.

☐ FINDINGS

Perceptions of the intermediaries: Separate factor analyses were carried out for both general and life insurance agents. The results of the factor analysis for life insurance agents are shown in Table 1. The factor analyses were carried out on the following variables:

FT1: Willingness to sell policies
FT2: Willingness to sell other financial products of the insurance agency
FT3: Willingness for customer relationship through telephone
FT4: Willingness for customer relationship through e-mail / internet
FT5: Willingness for customer relationship with direct personal interface
FT6: Willingness to provide research assistance on customer behavior
FT7: Willingness to provide research assistance on customer background

Table 1 *Factor Analysis Output for Life Insurance Agents*

	Factor	
	1	2
FT1	.548	8.554E-02
FT2	.560	−9.025E-02
FT3	.416	.203
FT4	.278	.528
FT5	.554	−1.364E-02
FT6	.849	−.210
FT7	.788	−5.260E-02

Extraction Method: Unweighted Least Squares   a.2 Factors extracted.   7 Iterations required

The variables for the general insurance agents were not found to be significantly correlated. However, among the variables for the life insurance agents, FT6 and FT7 have a high degree of correlation (0.792) and they are also loaded in a single factor (Factor 1). Hence the propensity of the life insurance agents to work full-time for sharing information relating to the customer behavior and also relating to the customer background emerges to be high.

A factor analysis was also run on the 13 variables for customers. The variables related to level of awareness about the where the funds are invested, eagerness to know where the funds are invested, readiness to purchase other products offered by insurance companies apart from insurance policies, importance of transaction time during purchase of insurance policies, satisfaction relating to the range of offerings of insurance companies, satisfaction relating to the degree of customization of insurance offerings, expected frequency of interaction from the agents, expected frequency of interaction by the insurance company on phone, expected frequency of interaction by the insurance company through the net, satisfaction relating to the quality of information shared by insurance companies, expected degree of customization of insurance products, perception on the qualification of the agents for a better information intensive interaction and perception on the trustworthiness of agents for sharing more details about oneself. It emerged from the factor analysis that none of the variables are significantly correlated. Also, it was surprising to note that none of the variables could be reduced to any significant factors. This could probably be a result of the lack of awareness about the CRM techniques and also about the relatedness of various operations involved in CRM. It could be possible that the respondents perceived each of the issues as unrelated ones. This is quite possible in service sectors like insurance where there existed a high governmental control and also a very low understanding of the benefits that could accrue out of the investments made.

Keeping in view the results from factor analysis, further analysis was carried out with rank sums and weight sums on the Likert scales independently for various variables. Analysis was also carried out based on the relatedness of the various issues addressed in the questionnaire as far as traditional CRM techniques go. The results are presented below.

Table 2 *Agent Preferences on Full-time Activities (Percentages of the Sample)*

Activity	Life (% of the sample)	Gen (% of the sample)
Selling of policies	82.6	55.4
Selling of other financial products of the insurance agency	63.7	73.9
Customer relationship through telephone	44.2	38.0
Customer relationship through e-mail / internet	18.8	37.5
Customer relationship with direct personal interface	76.0	39.6
Providing research assistance on customer behavior	66.7	40.2
Providing research assistance on customer background	64.4	40.2

Table 3 *Preferences on Sale Mode and Subscription (Rank Sums)*

Parameter	Customer	Life Agent	Gen. Agent
Mode of Sale			
Direct	658	148	188
Telephonic	1163	299	393
E-mail	1113	417	561
Internet	1296	515	698
Direct Sale			
Face to face int.	594	146	186
Easy to compel	927	281	389
Less costly	1017	400	529
Subscription			
Tax benefits	903	177	222
Security – ill health	1123	456	600
Security – spouse	981	343	483
Investment	1483	390	535

Agent Satisfaction: In general the satisfaction scores on the commission paid to the agents was very low for the general insurance agents, with the life insurance agents scoring 108 and the general insurance agents scoring –15.

Agent Association Preference: Of the total responses received, 89% of the life insurance agents and 96 per cent of the general insurance agents showed an inclination to work full-time with the companies. However, there were glaring differences in their preferences in relation to the activities of work. While the general insurance agents preferred telephone and e-mail interaction over personal interaction, the life insurance agents however preferred personal interaction over telephone and e-mail, with e-mail interaction being the least preferred. However, comparatively the life insurance agents expressed more willingness to be part of the network for building a database on customer behavior and customer background (Table 2). Only 13.7% of the life insurance agents owned a computer compared to their general insurance counterparts, where the percentage is 56.5%. The corresponding figures for telephone ownership is as high as 90% in both the cases (Table 7). The agents appear to be overall satisfied with the transparency, dependability and trustworthiness of their companies (Table 6), but feel that the company can pay more commissions.

Preferences of the Customers: The most widely held view about the motivation for insurance cover is tax saving (Table 7). While the eagerness to know more about fund management is very high among customers, the level of awareness regarding the same is dismally low (Table 5). While the weightage associated with the ease of replacing a personal direct sales transaction by web-based transaction was low (100), the weightage for preferring the same was medium (189) among customers (Table 7). This could be due to the fact that the customers attached a high weightage for human interaction during the sale process, a view echoed by the agents (Table 3). The customers seek a greater degree of customization,

Table 4 *Perceptions on Telephone and Internet Transactions (Rank Sums)*

Parameter	Telephone			Internet		
	Cust.	*L.Agent*	*G.Agent*	*Cust.*	*L.Agent*	*G.Agent*
Saves Time	961	222	297	801	263	294
Less Costly	1368	309	373	1242	343	588
Easy to argue	1385	517	649	1713	609	825
Very impersonal	1475			1717		
Search is time-consuming	1756			2002		
India is not yet ready	1938	454	784	1404	324	517
Leads to false identity		693	758		681	788
Prone to pranks		701	1003		661	867

Table 5 *Perceptions on Information Processing Needs*

Parameter	Customer	Life Agent	Gen. Agent
Importance of Transaction Time	V.High (614)		
Customers referring friends to agents	V.Low (-209)	Low (84)	Med (154)
Customers sharing personal details	V.Low (-592)	V.Low (-25)	Med (89)
Customers calling agents	V.Low (-206)	V.Low (-17)	Med (109)
Importance of Information in Life Sector	High (509)	High (131)	High (189)
Importance of Information in Gen. Sector	Med (219)		High (209)
Adequacy of Information in Life Sector		Low (76)	Med (155)
Adequacy of Information in Gen. Sector			Low (92)
Adequacy of Information in Health Sector			Low (96)
Ease of Getting Relevant Information		Low (20)	Med (161)
Willingness to be an Information Channel		98% *	88% *
Expected Frequency of Interaction from Agent	High (261)		
Expected Frequency of Phone Interaction from Company	High (227)		
Expected Frequency of E-Mail Interaction from Company	Very High (542)		
Awareness About Fund Management	V. Low (-321)		
Eagerness to Know About Fund Management	V. High (429)		

Numbers within brackets indicate the sum of weights on a Likert scale of –2 to +2
* Percentages of the Sample

wider product range and better quality of information. They also feel that the agents are neither equipped for such information processing needs and nor trustworthy for the customers to share their personal information (Table 6).

Ease of e-CRM Introduction: Across the board, there was an agreement that telephone and internet interactions save time and are less costly (Table 2). The same view was echoed by the agents and customers. However, there was a feeling that India is not yet ready for Internet based transactions across the board (Table 4). While the customers preferred telephonic transactions, the life insurance agents felt that India was not yet ready for the same (Table 4), a view not shared by their general insurance counterparts. There is a

Table 6   *Perceptions on Interactions*

PARAMETER	Customer	Life Agent	Gen. Agent
Trustworthiness of the Company		High (154)	High (152)
Dependability of the Company		High (161)	Low (242)
Transparency of the Company		High (147)	High (125)
Paying Power of the Company for more Commission		Very High (112)	High (160)
Satisfaction on the Range of Offerings	V. Low (-258)		
Satisfaction on the Customization of Offerings	V. Low (-346)		
Satisfaction on the Quality of Information Shared by Insurance Companies	V. Low (-307)		
Expected Customization of Information	V. High (654)		
Perceived Qualifications of the Agents for Information Processing	V. Low (-553)		
Perceived Trustworthiness of Agents for Information Processing	V. Low (-264)		
Interim Returns as a Preferred Option	V. High (70.21%)		
Insurance as a Preferred Investment	High (Rank 1)*		

Numbers within brackets indicate the sum of weights on a likert scale of −2 to +2
* Rank

Table 7   *Enablers of Web-based Transactions in Insurance*

Parameter	Customer	Life Agent	Gen. Agent
Ownership of Computer		13.7% *	56.5% *
Ownership of Telephone		95.6% *	90.2% *
Perception on Ease of Replacement of Direct Sales by Web-based Sales for Insurance	Low (100)		
Web as Preferred Sales Medium for Insurance	Med (189)		
Average Number of Hours Spent on Internet per Day per Respondent	1.97		

Numbers within brackets indicate the sum of weights on a likert scale of −2 to +2
* Percentages of the Sample

preference among the customers to get information inflows through e-mail rather than from interrupting phone calls or personal interaction (Table 5).

☐ THE PROPOSED MODEL

Unlike the traditional insurance model where agents act as intermediaries between the company and the end buyer, the model presented in this study proposes that the agent can be used as an enabler for building an effective CRM system and be part of an information management network operated by the insurance companies. Figure 2 maps the ease of introduction of e-CRM in each of the elements in the value chain of insurance transactions.

STAGES				
Customer Research	**Pre-sale Interactions**	**Sale Transactions**	**Routine Post-Sale Interactions**	**Post-Sale Interactions**
Mode Suitability				
HUMAN	HUMAN / e-CRM	HUMAN / e-CRM	e-CRM	e-CRM
Role of Agents – General Insurance				
X Agents not Willing	Human Interaction	e-CRM Human Interaction	e-mail/web based interaction	e-mail/web based interaction
Role of Agents – Life Insurance				
Human Interaction	Human Interaction	e-CRM Human Interaction	Telephonic Interaction suitable presently Need to move to e-mail/web based interaction	e-mail/web based interaction
Role of Customers & Benefits Expected				
Human Interaction	Human Interaction e-CRM for Customization	Human Interaction Preferred currently e-CRM the ultimate choice	e-mail/web-based interaction most preferred Benefit of speed and avoidance of nuisance while on job	e-mail/web based interaction Benefit of speed and accuracy of transactions

Fig. 2 *The Introduction of e-CRM in Insurance*

The study has found that the implementability of e-CRM is high in 'Routine Post-sale Transactions' and 'Non-routine Post-sale Transactions'. e-CRM can be used in tandem with human interaction in the 'Pre-sale Interaction' and 'Sale Transaction' stages. While it appears to be easy to involve the life insurance agents for data mining, such an option does not seem conducive for general insurance. The 'Sale Transaction' stage could be either e-CRM driven or human enabled. A major concern in the last two stages is the mismatch between the expectations of the customers and what the life agents can deliver. While the customers prefer e-mail inputs on the latest information, the life agents are not prepared even for telephonic interactions, whereas the general insurance agents are prepared for e-mail interactions. The companies could either involve the life agents only till stage 3 and employ others for e-CRM interactions in stage 4 and 5 or train the agents for e-mail interactions also and educate them on its importance, while encouraging telephonic interactions in the meantime. This could also involve investments for IT as a very low percentage of life insurance agents own computers.

☐ KEY ISSUES TO BE ADDRESSED

The following issues need to be addressed specifically while dealing with e-CRM introduction:

- Need to educate Life Insurance Agents on the importance of telephone and e-mail interactions (The General Insurance Agents appear to be aware of the benefits)
- Need to improve the information flow to customers about a) Products and Services b) Fund Management
- Need to enable better customization of products and services as most of the users expressed willingness to enjoy interim benefits rather than one-time financial returns.

REFERENCES

Aaker, D.A., *Strategic Market Management,* John Wiley & Sons.

Abell, D.T., and Hammond, J.S., (1979), *Strategic Market Planning: Problems and Analytical Approaches* Englewood Cliffs, N.J.: Prentice Hall.

Brenner, G.D. (2000), 'Why Life Insurance is Still Important', *Journal of Financial Service Professionals,* May 2000, pp. 54-58.

Davidson, S. (2000), 'Looking at the Life Insurance Industry', *Community Banker,* March 2000, pp. 40-41.

Economist (2000a), 'European Insurance, Run for E-cover', *Economist,* June 10-16, 2000, pp. 90.

Economist (2000b), 'The State of Allstate', *Economist,* July 22-28, 2000, pp. 80.

Forbes, S.W., (1998), 'A Global Survey of the Life Insurance Industry', *Journal of the American Society of CLU & ChFC,* May 1998, pp. 60-64.

Fox, B.R., (2000), 'Technology:The New Weapon in the War on Insurance Fraud', *Defense Counsel Journal,* April 2000, pp. 237-244

Francalanci, C. and Galal, H. (1998), 'Information Technology and Worker Composition: Determinants of Productivity in the Life Insurance Industry', *MIS Quarterly,* June 1998, pp. 227-241.

Friedman, A.S. (2000), 'The E-ing of Insurance', *Advisor Today,* June 2000, pp. 83-90.

Goby, V.P., and Lewis, J.H., (2000), 'The Key Role of Listening in Business: A Study of the Singapore Insurance Industry', *Business Communication Quarterly,* Vol. 63(2), pp. 41-51.

Insurance & Technology (1999), 'Profiting from the Relationship', *Insurance & Technology,* March 1999, pp. 34-35.

Insurance & Technology (2000a), 'Hitting the CRM Bullseye', *Insurance & Technology,* March 2000, pp. 28-29.

Insurance & Technology (2000b), 'More Consumers Turning to Net for Insurance', *Insurance & Technology,* July 2000, pp. 10.

LIMRA International (1998), 'Individual Life Insurance Sales in the United States', March 1998.

Long,T., (1999), 'Deregulation Drives Insurers to Mine Data', *Enterprise Partner,* December 13, 1999, pp. 17.

Pant, N., (2000), 'Development Role for Insurance Regulator', *Business Line,* May 8, 2000.

Smith, K.A., Willis, R.J., and Brooks, M. (2000), 'An Analysis of Customer Retention and Insurance Claim Patterns Using Data Mining: A Case Study', *The Journal of Operational Research Society,* Vol. 52 (5), pp. 532-541.

Sodano, A., (2000), 'Leveraging CRM to Build Better Products', *National Underwriter,* June 26, 2000, pp. 23-27.

Tehrani, N., (1999), 'CRM Cannot Exist Without ERM and VRM', *Call Center Solutions,* September, pp. 4-8.

Trembly, A.C., (2000), 'CRM Products Debut at LOMA Forum', *National Underwriter,* April 3, 2000, pp. 43.

Trembly, A.C., (2000), 'CRM is King at Systems Forum', *National Underwriter,* April 10, 2000, pp. 17.

UN (2000), United Nations Social Indicators Web page ("child bearing" section), Site Address: www.un.org/Depts/unsd/social/childbr.htm

Windows Business Series (1999), 'Benefits of E-CRM', *Windows Business Series,* August, pp. 2a-6a.

Woods , D.F., and Mitchel, J.O., (1999), 'Is There Still a Market for Individual Life Insurance?', *Journal of Financial Service Professionals,* January 1999, pp. 74-81.

Strengthening Customer Relationships That Lead Toward Increased Business for CPA Firms

□ **Joseph Ben-ur and David Satava**

Abstract

One of the most important ways for CPAs to develop more business is to create and increase the personal relationship with both new and existing clients. Many CPAs are not fully aware, nor do they completely understand, how mutually beneficial business relationships are initiated, developed, and strengthened over time. This paper will apply the Sheth, Mittal, and Newman (1999) Model of Relationship-Based Buying to help CPAs develop and understand the practical strategies that lead toward increased and strengthened relationships with clients. CPAs applying this model should experience increasing new business. The model includes factors to increase trust and commitment such as cost-benefit factors from the CPA's client perspective: perceived risk, switching costs, and perceived value of the services provided by the public accounting firm. This paper will help CPAs to establish and enhance the marketable value of the relationship for new and existing clients.

Key Words *: Marketing, CPA, Customer Relationship*

□ INTRODUCTION

CPA firms, along with most businesses, want to develop long-term relationships with their clients. Public accounting firms try to establish a mutual trust relationship that hopefully leads to providing all of the accounting needs for their client. If a business can determine what motivates customers to stay loyal to them for the long-term, then from a business perspective that should lead to higher profits (Reichheld and Sasser, 1990). The purpose of this paper is to provide practical and realistic suggestions for developing and maintaining long-term profitable relationships with clients.

☐ THE MODEL

Sheth, Mittal, and Newman (1999), developed a model of relationship buying that identifies the factors that affect trust and commitment of the buyer and therefore increases loyalty, buying, willingness to pay more for quality services, higher level of positive word-of-mouth and goodwill among customers. The model breaks these factors into two groups; one involves cost-benefit factors and the other involves social-cultural factors. We will apply this model to the CPA and client relationship.

☐ COST-BENEFIT FACTORS

In the case of accounting services, the cost-benefit factors that affect loyalty of the client would be: the cost of searching for another public accounting firm, the risk involved when changing to another CPA firm, the cost of terminating the contractual relationship with the CPA firm, the cost of building a new relationship with the new accounting firm, and finally, the loss or gain of benefits that the new accounting firm may or may not provide.

☐ SEARCH COSTS

Changing CPA firms takes a client time, money, and emotional stress. Clients once they developed a long-term relationship with a professional accounting firm would generally want to avoid the time, monetary, and emotional costs involved with searching for a new CPA. This is especially true since the main sources of information available on accounting services providers are word-of-mouth and print media such as the yellow pages. The best evaluation that can be achieved before signing a contract is personal face-to-face contact, and reliable knowledge of the value of the service is reached only after years of service and significant accumulation of experience.

☐ RISK OF CHANGING CPA FIRMS

Any alternative that the client chooses that is different from the current CPA firm will be risky because of the lack of knowledge and experience with the new public accounting firm. As we all know, there is no guarantee that the new CPA firm will be better or even equally as good as the current professional accounting firm. Thus, there are three kinds of risk associated with changing CPA firms (1) *Performance risk* is the risk that the new CPA firm may not be able to meet the expectations of their new client. These expectations could be in terms of: a) timely service, b) frequent contact with the client, c) personal and friendly relationship, d) complete knowledge of client's firm financial situation, market, and accounting needs, e) the application of the most recent knowledge to the client benefit, and f.) relationship beyond professional interest. (2) *Financial risk* represents the cost associated with poor or inferior service by the new accounting firm that may require paying for additional unexpected services including legal services, or any additional cost that is beyond what was expected or planned. (3) *Social risk* occurs when mistakes made by the new accounting firm somehow damages the reputation of the client. All of these risks are avoided if the client stays with the current public accounting firm.

☐ TERMINATION COSTS

With respect to the CPA firm, there are costs that are directly related to the act of changing service providers, such as the costs of bringing the new CPA firm up to speed concerning important accounting, tax, and software issues. If the previous CPA firm has installed an accounting package that the new CPA firm is not familiar with, the new CPA firm may have to put in a number of hours into learning the new software. It is unlikely that the new firm will do this for free. The new CPA firm may have incentive to introduce a new accounting package that they are familiar with. This will cost the client more time and money to learn the new accounting package. Thus, there are costs involved with creating and learning to maintain the new relationship from both the client and the new CPA firm's perspective, which the client is responsible for financially.

☐ BUILDING THE NEW RELATIONSHIP

CPAs are not only responsible to the client; they are responsible to the public to be accurate and trustworthy when they present the company's financial picture. Clients worry about public image, the keys to which are held by the CPA. Building a new business relationship like any personal relationship takes time. Time is needed to build trust between the client and the CPA firm. In the beginning, both client and CPA firm spend significant amounts of time evaluating and re-evaluating each other. Both spend time evaluating the relationship because they are unsure of the other's commitment and trustworthiness. Each engages in frequent communication to establish the perception of commitment and trustworthiness on the other side. Gradually this effort diminishes as trust is established. Trust is very important in this professional relationship.

☐ BENEFITS GAINED AND LOST

When a client leaves a CPA firm, they hope to gain more than they lose. Yet, it will be some time before they will be able to calculate whether the benefits outweigh the losses. Benefits would include better service and more professionalism. By service, we mean timely service, frequent contact with the client, a personal and friendly relationship, and a relationship beyond professional interest. By professionalism, we mean complete knowledge of client firm's financial situation, market, and accounting needs, and the application of the most recent knowledge to the client's benefit.

☐ SOCIAL CULTURAL FACTORS

The second factor of the Sheth, Mittal, and Newman (1999) model is one that involves social-cultural factors. These socio-cultural factors include: early socialization, reciprocity, networks, and friendship. Let us start explaining these factors in more detail.

☐ EARLY SOCIALIZATION

Socialization-based choice and loyalty is a way the client reduces perceived risk. A client may have had early exposure or contact with or reference to a certain CPA company as a result of social contact, all dependent on the social-cultural environment they were raised in. Parents, relatives and friends are always ready to provide word-of-mouth regarding CPA firms they have used or are using. In addition, many accounting firms have high reputations and are well known in the community. A choice made in favor of such a professional CPA firm is a measure for risk reduction. Therefore, a company needs to build its reputation and encourage positive word-of-mouth and referrals.

☐ RECIPROCITY

Reciprocity is described as buying products or services from the client (Sheth et. al., 1999), such as a CPA firm that uses the airline they audit for business and personal air travel. We will also want to think that reciprocity could mean actions taken by both client and CPA firm to improve business and personal relationships in order to strengthen the relationship and increase loyalty. This could be applied to elements of the business transaction and terms of exchange such improving financial terms or payment schedule in exchange for additional services. It could also be applied to the personal relation such invitation to golf club in exchange for invitation to yacht club.

☐ NETWORKS

CPA's can belong to a network of companies that provide service to each other on preferential basis to assure the success of all its members. The network will provide clients with high commitment, solidarity and loyalty. Relationship buying is a regular practice in such networks.

☐ BUYING BASED ON FRIENDSHIP

A CPA may have many friends who can become his/her clients. Membership in a national association could be one source of friendship. In addition, friendship can be developed to help keep clients more satisfied, loyal, and wanting to continue the business relationship.

☐ THE ESSENCE OF THE RELATIONSHIP—TRUST AND COMMITMENT

In every human relationship, there is a perceived risk. That is true in business relation as well. This perceived risk is a result of our assumption that every business transaction can create dissatisfaction between the parties involved. This is especially true when the relation is built on intense human interaction such as in CPA relations with clients. Each side has different expectations and each side judge the other against these expectations. Either the CPA or the client, intentionally or unintentionally, may act in a way to harm the other party. There are two main variables, which can reduce the perceived risk in any relation between buyer and seller; these two variables are trust in each other and commitment to each other (Morgan and Hunt, 1994.)

☐ TRUST

Sheth et al (1999) suggested the following definition for trust - "Trust is the willingness to rely on the ability, integrity, and motivation of the other party to act to serve my need and interest as agreed upon implicitly or explicitly." That is, trust is the belief that the other party will use his or her professional talents on my behalf. Some would say that relying upon others is a sign of weakness. But, is it really? How many people would know how to repair a computer or an automobile? In this modern advanced technological world, we must rely on others to assist us with our personal and professional needs. Not only must these other people be knowledgeable, skillful, and credible, they must have our best interests in mind, and if they do, we will consider them to be trustworthy and depend on their services.

☐ COMMITMENT

Not only is trust important in developing a successful relationship, so is commitment. We want the other person committed to using their talents on our behalf. If the other party is self-serving or more interested in what they have to gain from a financial situation, then they are not committed to helping the other person and therefore we have a problem that will eventually lead to one of the parties to the relationship leaving. Thus, commitment is very important for an enduring and successful relationship as it helps during good times as well as bad times. True commitment goes beyond the financial benefits of the relationship. As a reward for true commitment, clients stay with their CPAs longer.

☐ OUTCOMES OF RELATIONSHIP-BASED BUYING

The importance of relationship-based buying is in establishing long-terms relationships that lead to a gradual increase in loyalty. This should lead to more business with the client. Such possibilities exist in a CPA firm's environment when the client first asks for advice and finds that advice valuable. In time, the client will increase the amount of work they give the accounting firm. The accountant has numerous ways to generate revenues. They include auditing, tax, management advisory services, computer and software installation, forensic accounting, consulting, being an expert witness, etc. (Rittenberg and Schwieger, 1997).

Thus, under the right conditions, the CPA can use one successful service engagement to obtain other business from the client. Such cross selling is very profitable because it eliminates the need to find the client and build a new relationship. As time passes, the relationship should develop and lead to higher perceived value and increase in satisfaction and loyalty to the extent that he/she is willing to pay more for the services. In such a relation, the client is usually happy to spread the word about his good CPA firm. Word-of-mouth advertising is one of the most important consequences of relationship buying.

To conclude, the outcome of relationship buying is the increase in value to the client. Clients in such a relationship believe they are receiving value, whether tangible or intangible. Client goodwill can be used to gain more cooperation, willingness to accept temporary problems, and willingness to pay more for perceived quality.

Other Considerations—Maintaining Relationship/After-Marketing

After-marketing is the process of providing continued satisfaction and reinforcement to individuals or organizations that are part or current customers (Vevra, 1996). This requires maintaining a customer information file that contains a history of previous interactions and transactions. This information is needed to initiate contact and to respond to future calls from clients. The CPA also needs to collect any information created by informal contact with the client. For the most part, informal surveys can be obtained through casual conversation with the client. Thus, instead of a formal survey, the CPA could take the client to lunch to talk about the relationship. The CPA could verify if the client is satisfied with the firms work and ask about what direction the client plans to be going in the next few years to see if their might be some services the CPA firm could assist with.

☐ CONCLUSION

The Importance of Relationship Buying is the CPA and Client's Exchange

As Sheth et al (1999) suggested, when both switching cost and perceived risk of alternatives are low, the buyer will prefer transactional exchange rather than relationsnip buying. In a CPA exchange with a client, there is a high level of perceived risk in alternatives and high switching cost, and the customer will prefer relational buying to manage and control risk. Therefore, the CPA needs to (1) strengthen the relation by maintaining competitive, quality service so that every other alternative will look more risky, and make sure that the client has higher investment in the relation and (2) since there is a learning curve in every relationship, on the seller side as well as the buy side, trust and commitment that develop in time are precious to both sides and the switching is usually less likely to happen. As much as the client is willing to pay more, the seller has the power to give the buyer incentive to stay by sharing with the customer some of the profit gained as a result of lowering the cost of serving a loyal customers. This creates a long lasting bond.

REFERENCES

Morgan, M. R. and Hunt, D. S. (1994) 'The Commitment-Trust Theory of Relationship Marketing', *Journal of Marketing*, Vol. 58, July, pp. 20-38.

Reichheld, F. F., and Sasser, E. Jr., (1990) 'Zero Defection: Quality Comes to Service', *Harvard Business Review*, September-October, pp. 105-11.

Rittenberg, E. L., and Schwieger, J. B. (1997), *Auditing Concepts for a Changing Environment*, Fort Worth: The Dryden Press.

Sheth, N. J., Mittal, B., and Newman, I. B. (1999), *Customer Behavior – Consumer Behavior and Beyond*, New York: The Dryden Press, pp. 734-48.

Vavra T. (1996) *After Marketing; How to Keep Customers for Life Through Relationship Marketing*, 2nd ed., Chicago: Irwin Professional Publications.

Winning Strategies and Processes for Effective CRM in Banking and Financial Services

■ Anjana Grewal

Abstract

The author of the paper has presented a case study on relationship management practices developed in a leading foreign bank in India in the early nineties. It is a practical paper providing insights on what makes it happen. A model has been developed thereafter. The model outlines ten stages for effective customer relationship practices in financial services. These span across defining the customer relationship, understanding transaction behaviour and business volumes for different customers. Developing a customer profitability model, creating the organisation structure to support relationship management practices, developing training programmes, relationship pricing ,continuously evaluating the role of relationship managers. With emerging technologies the new trends expected of the relationship role.

Key Words: *Customer Relationship, Transaction Behavior, Customer Profitability, Organisation Structure, Training, Pricing.*

☐ BACKGROUND

There has been a focus on customer relationship management as a specialised practice in the recent years. The author of this paper, in the early nineties, focused and streamlined the customer relationship management practices in a leading foreign bank in India in the area of retail. While the bank had some of these practices in place, they were effectively channelled as a strategy to create high paced growth and sustainable competitive advantage for the bank.

☐ CASE STUDY

The leading foreign bank had a major presence in India. It had a representation through 56 branches in fourteen cities. Its retail customer accounts exceeded a base of over six lakh customers. From the late eighties, the bank had been maintaining a growth rate in deposits within a range of 15- 20 % per annum upto the early nineties. It undertook a restructuring exercise in 1988, wherein it moved from geographical areas of control, to business areas. The key business areas into which the bank was divided was personal banking, corporate banking, investment banking which included treasury and merchant banking, supported by human resources, technology, property services, finance and taxation, legal, etc. By 1988, all the branches were completely computerised.

The personal banking business division further transformed itself into the RETAIL BANK in 1990. It was headed by the General Manager - Retail Bank The Branch Network of 56 branches were classified as retail and reported to the Business Unit Head through Area Chiefs. The business profile was essentially liabilities - deposits. The deposits were broadly divided into domestic deposits and non- resident deposits. Sixty five percent of the deposits were domestic rupee deposits and thirty five per cent of the deposits were foreign currency non-resident deposits.

Between 1991-1993, the bank introduced several innovative retail products and services. It was the first institution to launch a real credit card in the country. ATMs were introduced. Discretionary investment advisory, lending against shares as per RBI directives packaged to give the customer greater convenience were amongst the introductions in the early nineties.

A focus was given to the NRI business strategy. This resulted in the opening of several overseas markets and the business grew at a phenomenal pace of over 40%. The Retail Bank Segment maintained very healthy growth rates in business, in customer retention and acquisition. The bank provided ongoing training in the areas of new products and services and service excellence to all its staff. Customer Service at branches was always a key focus area.

However in 1993 there was a major money market/ stock market scam, in which several foreign banks were involved indirectly due to their relationships with key brokers in the market. The leading foreign bank's investment arm which had large value relationships with several brokers found itself in the midst of a controversy. This involvement affected the entire bank's perception in the market place.

☐ STRATEGY REVIEW

A major strategy review was undertaken by the Retail Bank .Existing strategies were evaluated in the context of the market position. The Retail Marketing Team led by Country Manager Marketing developed defensive and growth strategies based on strengthening its key customer relationships.

□ CRITICAL RELATIONSHIP MANAGEMENT STRATEGIES

Internal brainstorming led to a conclusion. The key strength of front-line staff across branches was the " people touch ". This manifested itself in different ways across the branch network .For customers with long-standing relationships, staff members always went that extra mile to service with care and concern. It sometimes involved calling up a customer and informing him that a particular cheque had come through clearing. In other cases it meant getting the customer a good exchange rate from its treasury division, in some other instances it meant that care was shown through the extra time spent with the customer during his branch visit talking about the family. The personal touch was common across branches , whether it was a branch in Amritsar or a branch in Calcutta or Bombay. These effective customer relationships needed recognition and institutionalisation. Customer Research further indicated that customers were looking for a relationship manager at the Branch.

□ CUSTOMER STRUCTURE AND BRANCH STRUCTURE

A customer base analysis was undertaken at every branch. The customer accounts were classified by the overall business contribution whether in deposits, lending or other fee income. A customer relationship sometimes extended across family members. This led to the definition of the base nuclear family which would constitute the customer. Very often a customer's relationship extended across branches. Once again, a primary branch and a satellite branch was defined for a customer relationship.

Designated officers were named **Relationship Managers.** Primary responsibilities of relationship managers were defined. They had to focus and build the key relationships which accounted for 80% of the branch business. This redesignation led to a greater focus and consciousness of the role amongst the staff. Relationship Managers started playing a pivotal role in getting their customers the best pricing and servicing experience across the bank.

□ CUSTOMER PROFITABILITY MODEL

A customer profitability model was developed. The profitability model examined the nature of deposits- what percentage of the composition were time or demand deposits, the lending relationships, other fee income generated across the accounts, transactions across accounts. The cost structure was examined and bench marks were established. The model was developed on a spreadsheet. Branches initially did a snapshot exercise for their customer base. This was later converted into a rigorous exercise which was conducted every quarter.

□ TRAINING PROGRAMME

A training programme was developed for the relationship managers. The objective of the training programme was to enable relationship managers to understand their role more effectively. They were educated on the economic environment, the available financial instruments, tax incentives and tax structures. The softer side of developing and maintaining relationships was discussed at these workshops so that skills could be honed.

Exchange of ideas and practices amongst relationship managers at the training programmes led to a strengthening of the concept. The transformation was evident in the business consolidation which resulted at a very critical time in the organisation's history.

□ POSITIONING AND ADVERTISING

An advertising campaign was conceived focusing on customer relationships and the relationship manager. The campaign was developed regionally - North/ South / East /West. It was a testimonial campaign depicting strong relationships of the bank at the retail level.

The copy focused on the relationship and the relationship manager. The execution was in black & white but the company house colour was used very effectively to give the layout a distinction. The sign off which the bank used for several years thereafter was…For You, Since 1854….The Relationship Bank.

The external communication verbalised the internal metamorphosis. Customer Reassurance was apparent. The weakened market position of the bank as a result of the scam was very effectively countered. The impact was positive and long term. The bank to this day is known as the **Relationship Bank.**

□ HIGH NETWORTH PRODUCT/ SERVICE

This product /service concept was developed to bring into perspective the customer base that contributed highly to branch profits. Based on the customer profitability model, and branch customer base analysis the top customers contributing to profitability were preselected as priority bank customers. These customers were designated as CGC customers.

The priority service included the following benefits -
The benefits were broadly divided into banking and non- banking benefits.
1. In the area of banking, a relationship manager was assigned customerwise. A special service lounge was developed in some of the branches. While interest rate flexibility did not exist because it was the regime of interest controls by the central bank, relationship pricing by way of fee waivers was developed.

The non- banking benefits were:
1. A special recognition card was forwarded in a leather pack which contained personalised stationery for the customer's use.

2. The customers were accorded a free gold credit card with very high pre-set limits,
3. Through the gold card, a special tie -up was developed with the ITC hotel chain by way of key benefits. These included special room tariffs, early check-in and late check-out facilities at ITC hotels.
4. On the gold card, the customer could opt for at least two free add-on cards.
5. Higher accident insurance covers were provided on the CGC gold cards.
6. Alliances with airlines with special benefits were arranged.
7. A special newsletter providing details a financial update of the market was sent to CGC customers every month.
8. Special events were arranged for the priority club customers.

Relationship Strategy

What had been initiated as a defensive strategy in a difficult period, became a growth engine for the retail bank segment bank in the years 1994-96.

In the processes that were developed a winning relationship strategy had been embedded and implemented.

Process Model for Effective Relationship Management in Financial Services

A successful process model can consist of the following ten steps.
1. Define the customer relationship - This definition must be borne out of discussion with staff who deal with customers. The primary relationship and the primary channel need to be part of the definition.
2. What are the products, services and channels used by the customers must be exhaustively researched? Categorisation of customers by transaction volumes and business volumes must be done.
3. Exhaustive MIS tracking for product and channel usage must be set up and analysed for costs. Customer Information Systems must be effective and recent.
4. Create the organisation structure to support Relationship Management. Bring clarity into the ownership with regular reviews.
5. Processes should support relationship management providing adequate authority delegation.
6. Train for Relationship Management.
7. Develop Customer Profitability tools.
8. Relationship Pricing needs to be evaluated across all segments of the business, and appropriate policies need to be developed.
9. Customer contact programmes must be implemented and reviewed. Decide how close a contact you wish to maintain with your customers.
10. Add value to the relationship by encouraging customers to be loyal to the institution.

◻ THE CHANNEL EVOLUTION

The technology in banking is leading to a further evolution in relationship management. Call Centres , ATMs, and now the Internet is leading to reduced transaction costs, greater customer convenience, less face to face interactions and more technology interface. The relationship manager now needs to understand which channels his customers use and for what transactions. He has to lead them in this wired world to understand and use technology effectively. Customer Education needs to be focused on. The communication channels are also undergoing a change, its e-mails , banking using the mobile phone.....

So how does the personal touch continue........**through specialised knowledge.**

The customer offering would also change .....do you now offer customers pages on the web?....

◻ THE FINANCIAL ADVISOR

The product array for customers is ever growing. The relationship manager of the future will have to don the role of a financial guide for his customers. Therefore his strength and relationship will be based on knowledge. This will lead to customers seeking out their financial guide, their financial planner.....the new challenge for winning strategies in financial services. Continue to question how close your customers would like you to be...

Section VII

Abstracts

Chapter 56

Building R&D Lab/Industry Relationships
The Case of CSIR, India

■ **Ashok K Gupta, H R Bhojwani, Rajindar Koshal and Manjulika Kosha**

□ INTRODUCTION

In India a vast and diversified publicly funded R&D structure has been set-up, including 40 national laboratories employing about 10,000 highly qualified scientific and technical personnel under the Council of Scientific and Industrial Research (CSIR). With the liberalisation of the Indian economy in 1991, CSIR was faced with a challenge to become more market responsive and customer oriented. One of the key ingredients to become *Market oriented* is to collect, disseminate and use customer information to quickly respond to market opportunities or changing customer needs (Kohli and Jawaroski 1990). In the context of CSIR labs with dominant mission to conduct applied research, their level of market-orientation could be assessed in terms of the importance and frequency of labs' interaction with industry in the areas of working on industry sponsored R&D projects, providing consultancy services to industry, licensing labs' technology to industry, providing training to industry personnel in new technologies, sharing research findings with industry, jointly working on R&D projects with industry, disseminating research findings and learning more about industry needs by organising seminars and workshops, and working and visiting each other's facilities and labs.

□ RESEARCH OBJECTIVE

A research study was designed to gain insights into the perceptions of senior scientists and lab directors about the practices and protocols adopted by the management of CSIR to realise its objectives of becoming market-oriented and customer-focused. Specifically, the study was designed to understand:
- Importance of labs' interaction with industry
- Frequency of labs' interaction with industry

- Barriers to interaction with industry
- Initiatives taken to improve labs interaction with industry
- What do labs that are more successful in transferring their technologies to industry do differently from their less successful counterparts?

☐ RESEARCH METHODOLOGY

Based on a comprehensive literature search (Roessner and Bean 1990, 1991; Baron 1990; Hughes 1993; Nordwall 1993; Thayer 1994), a questionnaire was developed to understand the perceptions of senior scientists and lab directors regarding the management of labs and their interaction with industry. Personalised letters along with the questionnaire were mailed to 35 CSIR laboratory directors and 60 senior-most scientists. The sample covered almost the entire population directly responsible and accountable for the market orientation of the laboratories. In this paper, the data from scientists and directors working in labs that consider their primary mission to be one or more of the following:

- to conduct applied research focused on specific application
- to conduct contract R&D aimed at developing/modifying designs or products or processes
- to generate resources by providing scientific/technical services

were analysed to learn about the success and barriers faced in achieving market-orientation. Accordingly, the responses from 49 scientists and 11 lab directors from these "Applied Mission Labs" are included in the analysis reported in this article. These "applied labs" are the ones that could benefit most from their interaction with industry by becoming market oriented and customer-focused.

☐ RESULTS

Detailed results are published in the authors' forthcoming article, "Managing the process of market orientation by publicly funded laboratories: the case of CSIR, India," R&D Management, Vol. 30, No. 4, pp. 289-296, 2000.

☐ CONCLUSIONS

About 58% of the respondents indicated that their laboratories have succeeded in becoming market oriented. However, their perception is that the economic impact on customers who have availed of the laboratory's output or services has not yet been realised. While it would have been useful as well as desirable to calibrate these internal perceptions with that from potential users/ customers of CSIR, in this exploratory study we limited ourselves to only the perceptions of lab personnel. Future studies could be conducted to include customers' perceptions of usefulness of labs' technologies. Based on the analysis of available data and a comparison of 'successful and 'not-so-successful' laboratories in CSIR some useful lessons can be learnt namely:

☐ MAKE CUSTOMER/INDUSTRY INTERACTION A PRIORITY

In general, we found that there is a significant difference between the importance that labs' scientists (and directors) attribute to industry interaction and the level of frequency of interaction actually achieved. Both 'successful' and 'not-so-successful' groups of laboratories assign a great deal of importance to industry interaction. However, this sense of importance has not been translated into effective action agenda, especially, in 'not-so-successful' labs. A major barrier to industry interaction that scientists perceive is lack of programs to make industry aware of what labs can offer to industry. As a result industry perceives little gain from interaction and has no incentive to work with labs. Business development/ marketing of the laboratory knowledge-base has not been considered an important and directed activity. This needs to be made more visible in the publicly funded R&D labs. It appears that 'successful' labs have developed some cost-effective programs by allocating funds to promote labs and designating a specific person or a group for facilitating industry interaction. Successful labs have also set some budget requirements to be met from external sources; creating extra pressure to market labs' technologies. We also observed some significant differences between the perceptions of directors and senior scientists with respect to the initiatives undertaken to improve interaction, indicating that intra-laboratory communication needs to be encouraged and strengthened. Market orientation has to be a shared vision with ownership at all levels.

☐ PERFORMANCE EVALUATION AND REWARD SYSTEM FOR LABS AND SCIENTISTS TO INCLUDE MARKET FOCUSSED CRITERIA

The data indicates that 70% of respondents feel that the pressure on scientists to produce R&D that will result in gains to the economy has increased in the last three years. However, only 41% respondents feel that the career advancement of scientists depends on the market-usefulness of their R&D efforts. There is thus a need to introduce market-focused performance measures for the laboratories and for scientists. This perhaps also applies to publicly funded R&D organisations in other countries too where scientific excellence/ recognition and not R&D that is of value to economy/ society is assigned a major weight in career advancement and appointments. Some of these criteria for performance evaluation of lab and scientists could include: number of technologies transferred to industry, revenue generated from royalties, R&D contracts or technical services, meeting of targets set for marketing of labs' technologies. Scientists could share in the royalties generated by the lab.

☐ INVEST IN HUMAN RESOURCE DEVELOPMENT

When asked to give their wish list where additional funds could be invested in the labs, scientists gave top priority to upgrade lab facilities and computers, better libraries, and funds for travel. Lack of systematic planning for training and skills development was indicated to be a major weakness of the CSIR. Investment in infrastructure and human resource development is necessary for rapid advancements in science & technology. The half-life of knowledge and skills of scientists and engineers, is continuously plummeting necessitating investment in upgrading skills of human resources . Also to be market oriented besides S&T knowledge there is a need to help scientists and technical personnel to understand & acquire skills in business processes which are generally considered to be of low value in publicly funded R&D. Modernising the science and technology (S&T) knowledge-base and business skills of its ageing S&T population (average age ~ 50 years) still remains to be the greatest challenge for CSIR in becoming market oriented.

REFERENCES

Baron, Seymour, 'Overcoming Barriers to Technology Transfer,' *Research-Technology Management*, January-February 1990, p. 38-43.

Hughes, David, "Industry Seeks Expertise in Federal Lab Interaction,' *Aviation Week & Space Technology*, November 8, 1993, p. 51-52.

Kohli, Ajay and Bernard Jawaroski, 'Market Orientation: The Construct, Research Propositions, and Managerial Implications,' *Journal of Marketing*, 54 (April) 1990.

Nordwall, Bruce D, 'Many Civil Uses For Defence Technology,' *Aviation Week & Space Technology*, November 8, 1993, p. 44-45.

Roessner, J. David and Alden S. Bean, 'How Industry Interacts With Federal Laboratories,' *Research-Technology Management*, July-August 1991, p. 22-25

Roessner, J. David and Alden S. Bean, 'Industry Interactions with Federal Laboratories,' *Technology Transfer*, Fall 1990, p. 5-14

Thayer, Ann M, 'Companies Find Benefits and Barriers in Co-operative R&D with Federal Labs,' *C&EN*, August 29, 1994, p. 17-19.

Chapter 57

Why Web Site Hits don't Translate into Web Sales

Implications for Building Relationships Versus Selling on the Web

■ **Mita Sujan, Harish Sujan and Alan D. J. Cooke, Barton Weitz**

Abstract

Often, web site hits don't translate into web sales. Our research begins to address this issue. The mental operations used to make these two judgments—judgments about the site and judgments about specific purchase items differ. Thus, web strategies that facilitate the building of site equity, and liking for the agent at the site might, if not constructed with care, hurt sales.

Key Words: *Internet Agents, Electronic Site Equity, Web Relationships*

☐ THE ROLE OF INTERNET AGENT

The Internet offers consumers access to a many alternatives with relatively low search costs. Electronic agents will play an important role in helping consumer process information about this wide array of alternatives. Electronic agents perform a variety of tasks including defining needs, forming consideration sets, making recommendations, and negotiating purchases. The purpose of our research is to investigate the effects of agent recommendations on consumers' judgments of unfamiliar alternatives. The research suggests how agent recommendation sets should be constructed to build consumer demand for unique and unfamiliar products.

Many web sites incorporate agents to provide recommendations to consumers. For example, a consumer might enlist the services of an agent at a web site selling books. The agent provides a set of recommendations based on information about the consumer's preferences and/or preferences of similar consumers. Suppose that the set of recommended books are all positively evaluated by the consumer, but are also well known to the consumer. In this case, the consumer will find limited benefit from the recommendations, but will feel that the recommendations are consistent with his/her preferences. On the other hand, if the consumer is unfamiliar with all of the recommended books, the recommendations can provide the benefit of new information to the consumer, but the consumer may find it difficult to assess the quality of the recommendations. Thus, an agent's recommendation set both identifies potentially desirable items and provides a signal of the quality of the recommendations. A recommendation set with a mix of familiar and unfamiliar items provides both new information and a context for evaluating the quality of the unfamiliar recommendations.

☐ THE IMPORTANCE OF CONTEXT IN INTERNET AGENT RECOMMENDATIONS

The importance of context in judgment and choice has been well-established, as has its role in interpreting unfamiliar stimuli. Context is likely to be especially important on the Internet for two reasons. First, since consumers lack familiarity with electronic agents and the sites that host them, context is likely to play an enhanced role. Second, and more important, the Internet is an ideal medium to exploit the effects of context on judgments. Web page designs can be changed dynamically and individualized for the consumer. It is easy to embed specific recommendations in a recommendation set. It is also possible to present1 or hide particular information about the alternatives as the situation warrants. In addition to context, the interactivity of the Internet can be exploited to provide experiential information to consumers about new and unfamiliar items, especially on attributes that can be conveyed through the electronic medium such as audio and visual attributes or reviews by other consumers. To return to the previous example, consumers might choose to base their evaluations on reviews posted by other consumers, rather than infer quality of a new book based on the recommendation set provided by the electronic agent. Thus, it becomes important to understand the role of context when such information is available.

☐ MARKETING THE UNFAMILIAR ON THE INTERNET

Thus, the goal of this research is to develop a better understanding of how electronic agents can most effectively recommend items that are unfamiliar to consumers.
Internet works for familiar items in one of two ways. The Internet may be almost a commodity market where you shop for the know branded good at the lowest price, or as a highly specialized niche market where you try and find the item you truly value through extensive search and no importance to price. But, if the Internet is to become a medium of the future, it is important to try and market the unfamiliar.

Several streams of research, including work on risk aversion and the research on mere exposure effects and repetition suggest that unfamiliarity is a disadvantage in preference assessments; unfamiliar alternatives are typically liked less than familiar alternatives.

P1: In the absence of contrary information, unfamiliar recommendations from electronic agents are judged negatively.

□ THE ROLE OF CONSUMER GOALS ON THE INTERNET

Though, in general consumers are unlikely to value unfamiliar choices, many studies suggest that consumers' perception of information is strongly influenced by their goals. Several goals have been identified for consumers' behaviors on the Internet (Alba, et al., 1997). One goal that is specifically related to Internet search is building an information bank. In this paper, we distinguish between the specific types of information consumer's search for on the Internet. Specifically, consumers might be interested in acquiring information related to the *product category*. Under such a search goal, when new and useful information about the domain is being sought, unfamiliar recommendations might be valued. Conversely, consumers might wish to build an information bank related to the *efficacy of sites and agents*. Because unfamiliar alternatives are difficult to evaluate, they may receive less attention under the latter goal.

P2: Unfamiliar recommendations are judged less negatively when consumers are concerned with evaluating the usefulness of the recommendations made by the electronic agent than when they are concerned with evaluating the quality of the recommendations made by the electronic agent.

□ THE IMPACT OF SIZE AND QUALITY OF THE RECOMMENDATION SET

Besides consumer goals, one cue that may mitigate the negative effects of unfamiliarity is the number of familiar items that are included in the recommendation set. We know of no studies that have examined recommendation set size as a signal of quality of a specific option included in the set. However, related results suggest that the focal unfamiliar recommendations (together with the overall recommendation set) will be judged more favorably as the number of familiar items in the recommendation set increases.

Another cue that may mitigate the effects of unfamiliar recommendations is the quality of the familiar recommendations in the recommendation set. Consumers may infer that the unfamiliar recommendations are similar to the familiar recommendations, either in overall attractiveness or along specific dimensions. This suggests that unfamiliar alternatives may appear more attractive when mixed with other attractive alternatives (an assimilation effect). Thus, individuals may be more likely to buy an unfamiliar product from an agent that recommends better alternatives, even though individuals may already own those contextual alternatives. This result suggests that sales sites can use, for example, individualized purchase history, such that when a consumer subsequently visits the site for new product recommendations, the new items can be nested within a context of "recommendations" that the consumer is already known to own and like.

We believe that recommendation context plays a role for all agents; both electronic agents and human salespeople use context to their advantage. However, a number of factors that are unique to the Internet suggest that these effects may be especially pronounced for electronic agents. Thus, we forward the following propositions about the impact of the size (P3) and quality (P4) of the recommendation set on judgments of unfamiliar options recommended by electronic agents.

P3: Unfamiliar recommendations are judged less negatively as the number of familiar items in the recommendation set increases.

P4: Unfamiliar items are judged less negatively as the preference for the familiar items in the recommendation set increases.

❑ EXPERIENTIAL INFORMATION ON THE INTERNET

One important aspect of the Internet is that search can result in experiential information. For example, Internet sites and electronic agents can provide audio information on new CD releases or another consumer's direct account of a new book or movie. One conjecture is that given the uniqueness and novelty of this kind of experiential information—a defining characteristic of the Internet—experiential information about a new and unfamiliar recommendation will be overwhelming positive. This reasoning is consistent with previous research, which has generally predicted that providing direct experience is the most effective way to communicate.

P5: Unfamiliar items are judged less negatively as more experiential information is provided.

❑ COMBINING CONTEXT AND EXPERIENTIAL INFORMATION ON THE INTERNET: NEGATIVE EFFECTS FOR THE ITEM.

One more subtle issue, is how do various pieces of positive information on the Internet combine. Information has two roles—an evaluative role. Positive information about options is better than not so positive information and one would imagine it would enhance evaluations of the new item. But information has a second role—that of describing and labelling and categorizing the new item as similar to or separate from the contextual recommendations. Experiential information can be individuating. Our contention her is that on the net two positive sources of information—a positive recommendation context through design of the web page and positive experiential information about the new alternative— can together produce a contrast between old and new items so that the new alternative is judged less favorably than if it were presented in isolation. When this experiential information serves to distinguish unfamiliar recommendations from familiar recommendations, consumers tend to contrast the familiar and unfamiliar recommendations. This implies that when contextual suggestions are well liked, providing distinguishing information will tend to reduce the attractiveness of the unfamiliar recommendations. Thus, it is important to understand information processing on the net. Because of the interaction of the information variables, and the possibility of counter-intuitive results, information processing on the web has to be carefully understood and managed. Despite the properties of the Internet and its inherent ability to provide a great deal of information, purchase likelihoods on the Internet might be enhanced by the information principle "less is more."

P6: Unfamiliar items may be judged more negatively as more information is provided, i.e., both contextual and experiential information as the potential for information contrast exists.

☐ COMBINING CONTEXT AND EXPERIENTIAL INFORMATION ON THE INTERNET: POSITIVE EFFECTS FOR THE AGENT.

Much of the current thinking on "more is better" in providing information on the Internet may come from strategies aimed at enhancing liking for the agent and building site equity. It appears that agents and sites that provide a great deal of information are appealing. The disassociation between agent and item evaluation may arise from the following thought processes. Recommendation sets of familiar items may provide consumers the basis for judging agents and unfamiliar items, but can also serve as a basis against which to compare unfamiliar items. Thus, judgments of the unfamiliar items themselves may be contrasted with, rather than assimilated to, the judgments of the familiar items, when distinctive information causes the familiar and the unfamiliar items to be seen as separate from one other. Since the comparison process is necessarily at the item level, agent judgments should not exhibit such contrast judgments, even when information that distinguishes familiar and unfamiliar items is available. Thus, evaluations of electronic agents, and the judgments of the specific unfamiliar items they recommend might show a disassociation.

P7: Internet agents may be judged more positively as more information is provided, i.e., both contextual and experiential information.

☐ CONCLUSION

Our research offers designers of electronic agents both an opportunity and a caution. They are encouraging because they suggest that it may be possible to overcome consumers' general negativity towards unfamiliar recommendations by recommending alternatives that the consumer is known to like. This information is often available in the form of sales records or on-line survey results. However, these results suggest that applying this method blindly may hurt rather than help sales. Information about the unfamiliar items must be perceived as similar to that about the familiar items, or consumers may contrast the two sets, resulting in lower evaluations for the unfamiliar recommendations than if no context had been provided. Thus experiential information that can be individuating for the new item needs to be carefully constructed and provided. If the agent has access to experiential information about the product that is thought to be attractive, it may be wise to minimize the effects of recommendation context. This can be achieved by presenting few familiar alternatives, or by separating the familiar and unfamiliar alternatives spatially or temporally.

Finally, it is important to note that our research suggests that in the electronic commerce medium, factors that might aid agent and site evaluation (a strong, salient context incorporating many well-liked familiar recommendations) might in fact have deleterious effects on purchase probabilities of new items, depending on the information presented. Thus, while strategies may result in consumers trusting the site, those strategies may also reduce sales. This notion is provocative, and though much more research is warranted, it might begin to explain the popularity of the Internet, but its inability to produce profit.

Seller Influence Tactics (SITs) and Their Impact on Customer Relationships

■ **Richard McFarland, Goutam Challagalla and Naresh Malhotra**

Abstract

The shift from product-focused transactional selling to customer-focused relationship selling has been discussed in detail in the marketing and sales literature. Because the dynamics of relationship selling are quite distinct from that of transactional selling, several scholars note that salespeople have to adopt a different set of influence tactics when engaged in relationship selling. Indeed, influence tactics that are effective in transactional selling may be counterproductive in relationship selling. It is therefore surprising that no academic study has investigated what seller influence tactics or SITs are effective in relationship selling.

Another reason for the interest in SITs has to do with enormous cost of face-to-face sales calls. The average sales call costs firms more than $250 (Hite and Johnston 1998) and in some industries it is substantially more (close to $500). Under these circumstances it is not surprising that organizations are particularly concerned with better understanding how different SITs impact customer relationships (or trust) and salesperson performance. To the best of our knowledge, we are the first to examine the use of influence tactics on trust of the salesperson.

◻ SITs

Selling at its core is a form of influence (Bass 1997; Spiro and Perreault 1979); hence we study what actually occurs on a sales call in terms of salesperson influence behaviors. We call these behaviors *Seller Influence Tactics* (SITs). These are behaviors that are used by industrial sellers to influence buyers in purchase situations. Our focus is on behaviors that are used by an individual salesperson with an individual customer to generate purchases. The theoretical foundation for SITs can be found in the interpersonal influence literature (e.g., Marwell and Schmitt 1967).

Influence tactics in the marketing literature are classified into two categories. The first category is coercive tactics, which includes threats and promises. The second is rational tactics and it also includes two tactics—information exchange and recommendations. While these two categories of influence tactics are used in the personal selling domain, there is one important class of influence tactics that is missing from this literature.

Past research (cf. Evans 1963; Webster 1968; Whitmore 1972) indicates that *emotional influence tactics* are both prevalent and critical in personal selling. Evans (1963) views the interaction between salesperson and customer as a *social interaction.* In any social interaction, emotions can play an important roll. For instance, whether the customer likes the salesperson or not can have a critical impact on his success (O'Shaughnessy 1971-72); hence, emotional influence tactics such as the use of ingratiation become crucial. We build and extend upon the marketing literature by introducing emotional influence tactics to the personal selling context.

☐ DATA COLLECTION AND MEASUREMENT TESTING

We gained the cooperation of a Fortune 500 company who agreed to participate in our study. They manufacture and selling farm equipment (harvesters, tractors, etc.) both domestically and internationally. The sample frame consisted of their entire North America division, which consists of 100 territories blanketing the U.S. and Canada. 1260 questionnaire where mailed to customers across all territories. 72 where eliminated due to incorrect addresses, customers who no longer did business with the dealership, or where deceased. 459 responses where received, for a response rate of 39%. 22 questionnaires where thrown out because of large amounts of missing data. Thus the final sample size was 437.

The three broad SIT categories represent 6 influence tactics. More specifically, they are: Emotional SITs (ingratiation and inspirational appeals), Rational SITs (information exchange and recommendations), and Coercive SITs (threats and promises). A confirmatory factor analysis was conducted. It was found that, consistent with the literature, ingratiation and inspirational appeals were reflective of a higher order factor (Emotional), information exchange and recommendations were reflective of a higher order factor (Rational), and threats and promises were first order factors. The measurement model was tested in LISREL 8.30, and results indicate an excellent model fit.

☐ HYPOTHESES TESTING AND RESULTS

Emotional and Rational SITs are hypothesized to have a positive impact on both trust and performance, while Coercive SITs are hypothesized to have a negative impact on Trust, and a non-significant impact on performance. Hypotheses are tested using structural equations modeling (LISREL 8.30). Seven of nine hypotheses are supported, and importantly it is shown that emotional SITs (introduced in our study) have a significant positive influence on both trust and performance. The structural model fit well, with a chi-square of 827 with 414 degrees of freedom, RMSEA = 0.06, and CFI = 0.93.

Contributors

Adam Stewart is a Senior Lecturer at the School of Marketing, Faculty of Business, RMIT University, Melbourne, Australia.

Agrawal Arvind is Vice President of Solutions Integrated Marketing Services.

Agrawal M. L. is a Professor of Marketing and Co-ordinator of Center for Services Management and Management Development Programs at XLRI, Jamshedpur.

Ahooja Vijay is a B-Tech from IIT Delhi and an MBA from IIM Calcutta. He has close to 19 years of rich experience in consulting and international marketing roles with organizations such as TATA UNISYS, DCM DataSystems, Crompton Greaves and PricewaterhouseCoopers. At present, he is working as a Principal with PricewaterhouseCoopers and looking at the E-commerce, CRM and ERP segments. He has been instrumental in revamping the CRM system with Crompton Greaves that was involved in EPABX manufacture as well as setting up of software exports in DCM DataSystems so as to be able to meet the fast changing needs of overseas clients.

Anand G A is a Mechanical Engineer from NIE, Mysore University and a PGDM from IIM, Bangalore. He has a rich industry experience of close to ten years and is currently working as a Relationship Manager with Clarient (MCS Software Solutions Ltd.). He was instrumental in setting up the Key Account Management system in ICI – OEM Paints Division.

Angur Madhukar G. is a Professor of Marketing at the University of Michigan-Flint, USA.

Bacha Sami is a teacher-cum-researcher in management at the University of Nice Sophia Antipolis, France. He has presented papers in several conferences across the globe and has published in several journals. His research interests include Banking, Bank Management, Risk Management and Relationship Management.

Bajaj Chetan has a Masters in Commerce from the Delhi School of Economics and is a Fellow of the Indian Institute of Management, Bangalore. He has over 15 years of experience in reputed consulting and industrial firms including PriceWaterhouse, ABC Consultants and Apollo Tyres. He has taught at Xavier Institute of Management, Bhubaneswar, IMT Ghaziabad, Asia Pacific Institute of Management, and Antwerp University, Belgium. His areas of interest include International Business Strategy, Customer Relationship Management and Supply Chain Management. He has handled consultancy projects for several companies in India and abroad.

Banerjee Ashish is Professor and Group Coordinator of Marketing at the Indian Institute of Management, Calcutta. He has a PGDM from Indian Institute of Management Calcutta and a Ph.D. from Calcutta University. He spent several years in management positions in well-known Indian companies before moving to an academic career. His research interests include Strategic Marketing and International Marketing.

Bansal Harvir S. is an Assistant Professor of Marketing in School of Business and Economics at Wilfrid Laurier University, Waterloo, Canada. He did his Ph.D. in Management from Queen's University, Canada in 1997. His research interests are focused on the areas of Consumer Switching in Services, Internationalization of Services, Tourism, as well as analysis of interactions with structural equation modeling techniques. His work has been published in the Journal of Service Research. He has presented papers and published in proceedings of various international conferences.

Bansal Sharat is the national head of the Performance Improvement practice of PricewaterhouseCoopers in India. He is a B.Tech from IIT-Kanpur and an MBA from IIM-Bangalore. With some earlier experience in industry, Sharat moved to consulting and has for the last 20 years advised a large numbers of MNCs, Indian Corporates, PSUs and government organisations on a range of issues including business strategy and restructuring, business process re-engineering, performance improvement and change management. He has directed, managed and participated in over 200 consulting engagements in these areas.

Ben-Ur Joseph is an Assistant Professor of Marketing at the University of Houston-Victoria, teaching in the MBA and BBA programs. A graduate of the University of Illinois, he has published in Management Science and Energy Economics and presented papers in conferences on the topics of perceived Internet Security, Electronic Business, and Electronic Distance Education. His main interests today are Relationship Marketing and the effect of new technologies on Marketing Education, Practices, and Offerings.

Bhatia Anil B. is a Civil Engineer from Sardar Patel College of Engineering, Mumbai and a PG Diploma in Industrial Management from National Institute of Industrial Engineering (NITIE) Mumbai, He also has a CPIM (Certification in Production And Inventory Management) from APICS. He worked with Technical Consultants Humphrey and Glasgow for three years and is presently working as a Senior Business Analyst with the Enterprise Solutions Division of Infosys, Bangalore. He is a member of the Implementation team of Infosys, which is implementing Oracle 11I at the Travel Corporation UK. He has also published several papers on CRM Tools at the website "CRMASSIST.COM". The areas of his research interest include Technological Tools in CRM and eCRM , System Integration and Data Warehousing.

Bhojwani H R is presently working as Head, R&D Planning and Business Development at Council of Scientific & Industrial Research, India.

Bose Kallol is an MBA graduate from the University of New Brunswick, Fredericton, Canada. He holds a BA from Pune University in India.

Chakravarti Manoj studied Economics at St.Stephen's College, Delhi and completed his post-graduation from the Delhi School of Economics. He started his career with India Foils Limited, where he worked for 13 years. He then worked for the Bahawan Group, one of the largest trading organizations in the Middle East for thirteen years, in various capacities including heading the Seiko and Casio divisions. He is currently General Manager (Retailing) at Titan Industries Ltd., Bangalore.

Challagalla Goutam is Associate Professor of Marketing at Georgia Tech. He received his Ph.D. in Marketing from the University of Texas at Austin. Goutam has published several papers in top marketing and psychology journals and also serves on the editorial board of the *Journal of the Academy of Marketing Science* and *Journal of Personal Selling and Sales Management*. His primary research interest is in Sales Management. He teaches Sales Management and Marketing & E-Commerce and is a recipient of the *E. Roe Stamps Excellence in Teaching Award*.

Chatterjee A. K. is a Professor of Operations Management at the Indian Institute of Management Calcutta. He is a Mechanical Engineer from Jadavpur University and Fellow of the Indian Institute of Management Ahmedabad. He has over twenty years of professional and teaching experience. His research interests lie in Scheduling, Production and Inventory Management.

Chaturvedi Mukesh is Professor in the Marketing Area at Management Development Institute (MDI), Gurgaon, India. He is, perhaps, the only academic to have worked in the field of Direct Marketing in India. Professor Chaturvedi has an M.M.S. and a Ph.D. from BITS, Pilani. Prior to joining MDI, he taught at XLRI, Jamshedpur and BITS, Pilani. His teaching, consulting, training and research interests include direct marketing, personal selling, advertising, corporate image building, etc. He has rendered consultancy services to banks, insurance and other public & private sector companies. A prolific writer, his publications include Welcome Back!? Coca-Cola (Eureka), New Product Development (Wheelers), Buying Research (Wheelers) and Direct Marketing; Concepts and Cases (Excel). He is, currently, working on Effective Direct Marketing Practices. He has published many papers in reputed journals, and presented papers at various national/international conferences and seminars. He is also an alumnus of the prestigious International Visitor Program of USIA, Washington, D.C., USA.

Chaturvedi Kapil is an Electrical Engineer from Regional Institute of Technology Jamshedpur and is currently pursuing his PG Diploma in Industrial Management from NITIE, Mumbai. He is a Microsoft Certified Professional (MCP). He has worked for two years in the areas of Sales & Marketing , Order Handling, Business Development and SAP Implementation with Swiss Swedish Multinational ABB and was part of the implementation team of SAP R/3 at ABB Nashik. His research interests include technological tools in CRM and eCRM, System Integration, and Data warehousing.

Choudhury Avijit works with the Business Intelligence Unit at ICICI Limited. The BIU is the Business Lead for all CRM related initiatives for the entire retail group of ICICI. He has completed his PGDBM from XLRI Jamshedpur and is a graduate engineer from the Jadavpur University, Calcutta. His research interests include Web-centric marketing and International Technology Transfer.

Chopra Pawan, a university gold medallist, is a BE in Electrical Engineering from Punjab Engineering College, Chandigarh. He worked with Larsen and Toubro in Quality Control and Reliability Department for a year. Thereafter he joined CEDTI (Centre for Electronics Design and Technology of India) as Engineer/Scientist and worked there for two years. Presently, he is studying for a Post Graduate Diploma in Industrial Management (PGDIM), NITIE, Mumbai.

Choudhury Koushiki is enrolled in the Fellow Programme in Marketing area at the Indian Institute of Management Calcutta. She has an MS degree in Biology from Pennsylvania State University, USA. Her areas of research include Services Marketing and Relationship Marketing.

Cooke Alan D J is an Assistant Professor of Marketing at the University of Florida, Gainesville, Florida, USA.

Coldwell John is the Managing Director at InfoQuest Customer Relationship Management Ltd, UK.

Dadlani Mahesh is a Hotel Management Graduate from the Sophia's Polytech Bombay. He has subsequently done his B.A in Economics and an M.B.A in Marketing. He has a total work experience of about 10 years—the last five years being in Hutchison Max Telecom, which operates its cellular service in Mumbai under international brand name of Orange. He is the Customer Relations Manager at Orange, Mumbai. He oversees Corporate Relationships, Retention and Loyalty and Premium Customer Management.

Darragh Don M is the Director, Sales and Marketing, of ASCC Inc. Pennsylvania, USA,

Deans Kenneth R is a Senior Lecturer at the Department of Marketing, University of Otago, New Zealand.

Doyle Christopher C. is an Economics graduate from St. Stephen's College, Delhi University and a PGDM from Indian Institute of Management Calcutta. He has a rich industry experience in several companies and is currently working as Director of International Sales—India, Hilton International. He has to his credit several successful brand launches in the consumer products industry (1993, 1994), successful turnaround of the New Delhi Hilton (1997), pre opening of the Hilton Hanoi Opera, Hanoi, Vietnam (1998) and start up of Hilton's India office (1998).

Dumblekar Vinod is a graduate in Science and has a postgraduate degree in Business Administration from Faculty of Management Studies, University of Delhi. He is an Associate Professor at All India Management Association (AIMA) and handles subjects in Finance, Strategic Management and Quality. He is fully engaged in the entire range of academic functions and has also initiated the adoption and customisation of indigenous software and scenarios in AIMA's computer simulated management games. As the Games Administrator for the prestigious National and Student Management Games, he oversaw 5 National championships involving over 1,400 participants in 350 teams, and adapted the Games for training over 200 trainees in Corporates. His research interests are in the areas of Finance, Distance Education, Information Technology and Leadership.

Eagle Lynne teaches at the Department of Commerce, Massey University, New Zealand and is interested in researching Advertising Effectiveness, Marketing Communications, Brand Equity and Electronic Commerce.

Emerson Michael is the Senior Vice President of Global Marketing for Recognition Systems where he is responsible for worldwide marketing functions. He joined the company in 1999. Prior to joining Recognition Systems, he was Senior Manager of the Datawarehouse Group at Ernst & Young. He also worked at BI Performance Services as Director of Database Marketing and at Donnelley Marketing as Director of Technology. He was awarded a patent in 1999 for the Database Link Campaign Management software. He is also a member of the Direct Marketing Association. He graduated summa cum laude from Bethel College in 1979 and is currently a Ph.D. candidate in Industrial Psychology at the University of Minnesota.

Gaur Sanjaya S. is a doctorate in Management. He did his graduation in Engineering and post graduation in Management with specialization in Marketing Management. He is Assistant Professor of Marketing and Coordinator of Management Development Programmes at SJM School of Management in IIT Bombay. He has been the Area coordinator of Marketing at S.P. Jain Institute of Management and Research, Mumbai and has also been the Core Marketing Faculty at Indian School of Mines, Dhanbad and Birla Institute of Technology & Science, Pilani. His areas of interest include Customer Relationship Management, Relationship Marketing, Strategic Marketing, and Development of Marketing Attitude and Orientation.

Ghodeshwar B. M is an Associate Professor of Marketing at National Institute of Industrial Engineering. He has done his MBA and PhD. in Marketing from Osmania University, Hyderabad. He has a total of 18 years of experience in conducting Executive Development Programs in the areas of Marketing Strategy, International Marketing and Customer Service Management. He has published many research papers in the area of Marketing and has research interests in Marketing Strategy, Brand Management, and Customer Service.

Grewal Anjana is a Chemical Engineer from BUDCT (Bombay University, Department of Chemical Technology). She did her Masters in Management Studies from Jamnalal Bajaj Institute of Management Studies and is also registered for a Doctoral Programme at JBIMS. She has over twenty years of work experience, spanning the FMCG and Financial Services Sector. The companies she has been associated with include Geoffrey Manners (American Home Products), Colgate Palmolive, ANZ Grindlays Bank and Global Trust Bank. She is at present working as Associate Director—Business Development at Birla SunLife Insurance. She has pioneered the use of innovative strategies in Consumer Banking and is also the author of a Book on "Bank Marketing" which is used for the CAIIB exams by the Indian Institute of Banking. Her research interests include Quantitative Methods in Customer Relationship Management.

Gupta Ashok K is the Charles G. O'Bleness Professor of Marketing at College of Business, Ohio University, USA.

Gupta Gagan is a Senior Consultant with the Performance Improvement Practice of PricewaterhouseCoopers in India. He is a Telecom Engineer, and an MBA from Jamnalal Bajaj Institute of Management Studies, Mumbai. He moved to Consulting with a work experience of about four years in Financial Services. For the last three years, he has worked on a number of consulting assignments in areas of Customer

Relationship Management, Supply Chain Management and E-commerce. He has consulted a number of companies operating in the B2B domain, including a division of a Fortune 500 company and a large multinational with world leadership in its markets.

Hopewell Rosalind has been in the computer industry for 14 years, starting as an Account manager with the software provider Cognos and moving onward to Director of Customer Development for The Interchange Group and specialising in the expertise of understanding Customer Service and Support via. such companies as the Help Desk User Group (now CSM) , IBM (Corepoint) and now holding the role of Head of Customer Management Solutions in iDESK plc. She has presented papers on the value of 'knowing your customer' at various seminars/conferences around the world.

Hoskins Graham is the Director of Aura Consulting Ltd, London.

Jauhari Vinnie has a Master's degree in Electronics and a PhD in Corporate Entrepreneurship from IIT, Delhi. She has also done her MBA, where she was awarded a gold medal. She is currently working as Associate Professor and Associate Dean at Institute for International Management & Technology (collaboration with Oxford Brookes University, U.K.). She has over two dozen publications to her credit and is in the process of completing two books. Her areas of interest include Strategic Management, Entrepreneurship and Marketing.

John Joby is Professor and Chair, Department of Marketing at Bentley College, Waltham, MA, USA.

Kitchen Philip is the Martin Naughton Chair in Business Strategy at the Queen's University, Northern Ireland. His research interests lie in the areas of Corporate Communications, Brand Communications and Promotion Management.

Koshal Manjulika is a Professor at the College of Business, Ohio University, USA.

Koshal Rajinder is a Professor at the College of Business, Ohio University, USA.

Kumar Alok is a graduate from IIT Kharagpur. He is currently working as Chief General Manager-Customer Care at Escotel Mobile Communication. He has a rich experience of 21 years in Sales/Branch Management, Total Quality & ISO 9000 system implementation in Service, He has set up the Customer Care operations for Escotel Mobile Communications. He is also a Founding Member & Director of CRM Foundation and Member of CII National Committee on Customer Focus & Marketing. He has also established 'Escotel' Chair at IIM –Lucknow on Customer Relationship Management.

Lal Sameer is post graduate in Chemical Technology from U.D.C.T., Mumbai University and Masters in Management Sciences, with specialization in Marketing from N.M.I.M.S. He has worked as a Product Manager and was responsible for managing the CRM activities for all divisions of Glaxo. His additional responsibilities included looking after three brands, one of them being a new launch. He is currently working with Ranbaxy Labs as Manager—Direct Marketing, and is responsible for the setting up of the CRM function at it's largest division.

Lindgreen Adam has a Masters in Food Science Technology and in Business Administration as well as a Doctorate in Marketing. At present he is working as an Assistant

Professor at Université Catholique de Louvain, Belgium. He has published several papers in various journals and presented in conferences across the globe. His research interests include Relationship Marketing, Relationship Management, Relationship Quality, Industrial Marketing and Purchasing, Network Relationships, Supply Chain Management, Customer Retention, Customer Loyalty, Marketing Strategy, Agribusiness, Consumers' Attitude Toward Genetically Modified Food Products, Customer Satisfaction, Customer Delight in Cross-Cultural Settings and Emotions, such as Surprise.

Malhotra Naresh teaches at the DuPree College of Management, Georgia Institute of Technology Atlanta, Georgia, USA.

Mansur Sangeeta is an MBA and a JRF of the University Grants Commission, pursuing Ph.D. in Marketing at the Department of Management Studies, Indian Institute of Science, Bangalore. Her interests include consumer behaviour, marketing research, social marketing, and developmental (NPO) sector.

Mathur Ajit is a graduate in Mechanical Engineering from NITIE and a Doctorate in Management from Mumbai University. He has a rich experience of about 19 years in the industry. He is currently working as General Manager—Taj Air Caterers. He is also a visiting guest faculty at IIM Ahmedabad and IIM Indore. He has travelled widely, having gone to the US as a Rotary scholar and having represented India in a Management Symposium held at Tapei. His case entitled 'Skyline Catering' won a prize in a global competition held at Singapore Institute of Management. His research interests include Strategy in Services, Service Quality, Services Marketing and Relationship Marketing.

McFarlane Richard teaches at the DuPree College of Management, Georgia Institute of Technology Atlanta, Georgia, USA.

Millman Tony is a member of the faculty at the University of Buckingham School of Business, United Kingdom.

Mishra Randhir did his graduation in Engineer and worked for Larsen and Toubro. Thereafter he joined IIM Bangalore for the doctoral program. He is a recipient of the P D Agarwal – TCI Award for Doctoral Research and is currently working with Clarient Inc. USA.

Mital K M is a Mechanical Engineer from University of Roorkee. He has also done his Masters in Production Engineering from University of Roorkee and Ph.D. in Industrial Engineering from IIT Delhi. He has authored four books and contributed over 100 research papers in diverse fields of Management/Energy. He has had a rich experience of over twenty years in organizations such as BHEL and ONGC. At present he is working as Deputy General Manager, Engineers India Limited.

Mitra Subrata is a Doctoral candidate in Operations Management at the Indian Institute of Management Calcutta. He has done B.E. in Electronics and Telecommunication and M.E. in Production Management from Jadavpur University. He has over four years of work experience in IT hardware industry. His research interests lie in Multi-echelon inventory, Logistics and Supply Chain Management.

Mohan Ramneesh is an MBA from Management Development Institute, Gurgaon with specialisation in Operations Management and Information Management. A gold medallist during his MBA program, his areas of interest include Supply Chain Management, e-business, Customer Relationship Management, ERP and Consumer Behaviour. He has published/presented over a dozen papers in both international and national journals and conferences. He completed his graduation in Mechanical Engineering, as a Special Class Railway Apprentice, from the Indian Railway Institute of Mechanical and Electrical Engineering, Jamalpur. He has served the Indian Railways first as an Assistant Mechanical Engineer, handling maintenance of diesel locomotives, and then as Divisional Mechanical Engineer, involved with the operations of locomotives, over the Moradabad Division of Northern Railway. Currently, he is working with the IT Application Team of Electrolux India and is the Project Co-ordinator of a customised SCM module—development and implementation—with the organisation.

Mukherjee Avinandan is an Assistant Professor of Marketing and Chairman of Computer Services at the Indian Institute of Management Calcutta. He is an Engineer and a Fellow in Management with specialization in Marketing from the Indian Institute of Management, Ahmedabad, India. He has visited and taught at well-known business schools in France, UK and USA. His research interests include Internet Marketing, Marketing Research and the interface between Marketing and Information Technology.

Mukhopadhyay Sandeep is a doctoral candidate at IIM Calcutta.

Mukhopadhyay Sipra is a Professor of Marketing at the National Institute of Management, Calcutta.

Mulye Rajendra is a Lecturer at the School of Marketing, Faculty of Business, RMIT University, Melbourne, Australia.

Nargundkar R. has a Bachelor's degree in Electrical Engineering from Osmania University, Hyderabad, a Post Graduate Diploma in Management from Indian Institute of Management, Bangalore, and a Ph.D. in Management from Clemson University, U.S.A. He has worked in the Advertising and Marketing Research industries in India. He has over 14 years of teaching experience in India and the U.S.A. He has published several research papers and articles in various conference proceedings and journals, including a publication in the Academy of Management Journal, U.S.A. His current areas of research and consulting include Services Marketing, Business Process Reengineering and World Class Marketing.

Natarajan Rajesh is doing his Fellow Programme in Management, QMIS Area, at IIM Bangalore. He is an Electronics Engineer from University of Mumbai. His research interests include Data Mining: Theory and Applications, DBMS, Soft Computing and Intelligent Systems.

Nath Prithwiraj is a doctoral candidate at the Indian Institute of Management Calcutta.

Pal Manabendra N. is a Professor of Operations Management at IIM Calcutta. His research interests include Fuzzy Logic and Group Decision-Making, Meta Heuristic Techniques,

Combinatorial Optimisation, Supply Chain Management, Heuristic and Algorithm building and Scheduling.

Paliwal Pramod is an Assistant Professor at the Pacific Institute of Management, Udaipur.

Parvatiyar Atul is President, iCRM and Adjunct Associate Professor of Marketing at Goizueta Business School, Emory University. He received his MBA and PhD from Banaras Hindu University, India. He has authored a number of articles in the areas of international marketing, business alliances, and environmental marketing. His previous research has been published in the Journal of the Academy of Marketing Science, International Business Review, Research in Marketing and Journal of Business Research. He is co-editor of Research in Marketing and serves on the editorial review board of International Marketing Review and the International Journal of Customer Relationship Management.

Prem Kumar V. is a Doctoral Student in OR and Systems Analysis at IIM Calcutta. His research interests include Fuzzy Logic and Group Decision-Making, Meta Heuristic Techniques, Combinatorial Optimisation, Supply Chain Management, Heuristic and Algorithm building and Scheduling.

Raghunath H G is a graduate in Science as well as in Electronics & Communication Engineering from Bangalore University. After having served at HMT Electronic Watch Division in the areas of Manufacturing and Assembly for 7 years between 1979-86, he joined Titan Industries Limited. At present he is the Head of Customer Service – Worldwide on the Consultative Committee of Watch and Clock Technology, Government of Karnataka. He has delivered lecturers on Customer Relationship Management in a number of organisations. He is also a member of the Apex Group for the TBEM Quality Model in line with Malcolm Balridge Quality Award Model.

Raghunath S. is a Professor in Corporate Strategy and Policy at Indian Institute of Management, Bangalore. He was a visiting scholar at the Graduate School of Business, Stanford University, where he engaged in research on strategy making in IT companies. His consulting work has focused on how business leaders can create value for customers in a hyper competitive market and how to develop a cohesive organization to champion and sustain growth. He has published several papers. His research interests include strategic networks, business alliances and joint ventures, changing nature of customer and supplier relationships in the new information economy and use of IT in managerial decision making and control.

Raman Kalyan is an Associate Professor of Marketing at the University of Michigan, USA.

Ranjan Rajiv is a Civil Engineer and a PGDMIT from Indian Institute of Information Technology & Management–Gwalior. Presently he is working as Executive Manager Marketing, in Vedica Software Private Limited. His area of interest in research is E-CRM.

Rao Mrunalini S is a Research student in the Department of Management Studies at the Indian Institute of Science, Bangalore.

Sadarangani Pradip H is a Research Scholar in the Marketing Area at the SJM School of Management, Indian Institute of Technology, Mumbai.

Satava David is an Assistant Professor of Accounting at the University of Houston-Victoria, where he teaches accounting to both undergraduates and graduates. He received his doctorate from Mississippi State University. He has presented in conferences around the United States and has also published in a number of accounting journals. He is a licensed CPA and previously owned a public accounting practice in the San Francisco Bay Area.

Shainesh G. is an Assistant Professor of Marketing at the Management Development Institute, Gurgaon. He is Fellow of the Indian Institute of Management, Bangalore. A recipient of the PD Agarwal—TCI Award for Doctoral Research in Management and the Citibank Special Research Award, his research interests are in the areas of relationship management, service management, and service quality. He has held managerial positions at Western Coalfields Ltd., Nagpur and Sterling Holiday Resorts International Ltd., Chennai before switching to academics.

Shanker Ravi did his BE in Electrical Engineering from Delhi College of Engineering (DCE), Delhi. He has worked at the Indian Rayon and Industries Limited for four years in Project Commissioning and Operations Management. He is currently studying for a Post Graduate Diploma in Industrial Management at the National Institute of Industrial Engineering (NITIE), Mumbai.

Shanthakumar Daniel K., is currently a Visiting Senior Professor with Academy for Management Excellence, Chennai. He received his Masters and Doctorate in Organizational Behavior from Brigham Young University, Utah, U.S.A. He has been a consultant, teacher, and trainer for over 20 years. He has taught at Brigham Young University and National University of Singapore.

Sharma Bhuvan is an Electrical Engineer. Presently he is doing PGDMIT from the Indian Institute of Information Technology & Management-Gwalior. He worked with Ingersoll-Rand (India) Limited for three years as member of Product Engineering and Marketing team. His research interests include IT enabled Marketing & E-business strategies.

Shekar B. is a Ph.D. in Computer Science from IISc Bangalore. He is currently teaching in the QMIS area at the Indian Institute of Management, Bangalore. His research interests include Classification, Knowledge-based Systems and Problem Solving Mechanisms.

Shergill Gurvinder teaches at the Department of Commerce, Massey University, New Zealand. His research interests lie in the areas of Marketing Research, Marketing Strategy, Diversification Strategy and Financial Performance.

Sheshadri Sudhi is Professor and Coordinator of the Marketing Area at the Indian Institute of Management, Bangalore.

Sheth Jagdish N is the Charles H. Kelistadt Professor of Marketing at Emory University. He has published more than 200 books and research papers in different areas of marketing. His book 'The Theory of Buyer Behavior' (1969), with John A. Howard, is a classic in the field. He has recently published two scholarly books: 'Marketing Theory:

Evolution and Evaluation', with D. M. Gardner and D. E. Garrett (1988); and 'Consumption Values and Market Choices', with B. I. Newman and B. L. Gross (1991). He is on the editorial board of atleast a dozen scholarly journals in marketing, international business and quantitative methods; he is also series editor of Research in Marketing. In 1989, he received the Outstanding Educator Award from the Academy of Marketing science, and in 1992 he received the P. D. Converse Award from the American Marketing Association. He is also a Fellow of the American Psychological Association and Past President of the Association for Consumer Research.

Shields Joseph is a Mechanical Engineer, presently pursuing his Doctoral Program in Corporate Strategy & Policy Area at Indian Institute of Management, Bangalore, after having worked for 6 years in Oil & Natural Gas Corporation Ltd., at Bombay. He is a recipient of the PD Agarwal -TCI Research Fellowship for the year 2000. His research interests include strategic alliances and collaborative strategy, strategy formulation in high technology industries and strategy formulation in the service sector.

Singh Deepali is a Marketing faculty at the Indian Institute of Information Technology & Management, Gwalior. Her research interests lie in E-Marketing.

Singh Rakesh is an Assistant Professor of Business Economics and Environment at the Narsee Monjee Institute of Management Studies.

Srinivasan R., Fellow from IIM-B, currently Associate Professor in Marketing at the Department of Management Studies, Indian Institute of Science, Bangalore. He is a recipient of international Statistical Institute Award (1983) and the Colombo Plan Award (1989). He has a post doctorate from the University of Leeds, UK. He has 65 publications to his credit and apart from academia, has the distinction of serving in some of the reputed organisations like TCE, ASCI and NITIE. His current interests are strategic policy initiatives and strategic marketing.

Sujan Harish is a Associate Professor of Marketing at the Pennsylvania State University.

Sujan Mita is Charles and Lilien Binder Faculty Fellow and Professor of Marketing at Pennsylvania State University, USA.

Vani Nilesh S. is the Head—Customer Care Cell at Aptech Ltd., Mumbai.

Verma Saket is a Mechanical Engineer by training and holds a PGDBM (Manufacturing) from S.P. Jain Institute of Management and Research, Mumbai. He has a wide range of industry experience ranging from white goods to pulp and paper. He has been associated with project planning/execution and facilities management prior to joining consulting. As a consultant his areas of interest and contribution include Business Transformation through Technology, Supply Chain Management and Enterprise Performance Improvement. At present he is associated with the IBM Consulting Group in India.

Weitz Barton A is the J C Penny Eminent Scholar and Professor of Marketing at University of Florida, USA.

Werani Thomas is an Assistant Professor of Marketing at Johannes Kepler University, Linz (Austria). His research interests focus on Relationship Marketing, Marketing Research and Product Management.

Wilson Kevin is the Chief Executive Officer of the Sales Research Trust, UK and a member of faculty at the Southamton Business School, UK.

Xavier M. J. obtained his Doctorate in Management (1984) from the Indian Institute of Management, Calcutta. He has been a teacher, trainer and consultant for over 17 years. He has authored three books and published more than 50 articles in Journals and Magazines in India and Abroad. His book 'Marketing in the New Millennium' has won the DMA-Escorts Award for the Best Management Book of the Year 1999. He has served as Visiting Faculty at a number of business schools in India and abroad including The University of Buckingham, U.K., Post Graduate Institute of Management, Sri Lanka and The Texas Christian University, U.S.A. He is currently the Dean of the Academy for Management Excellence at Chennai, India.